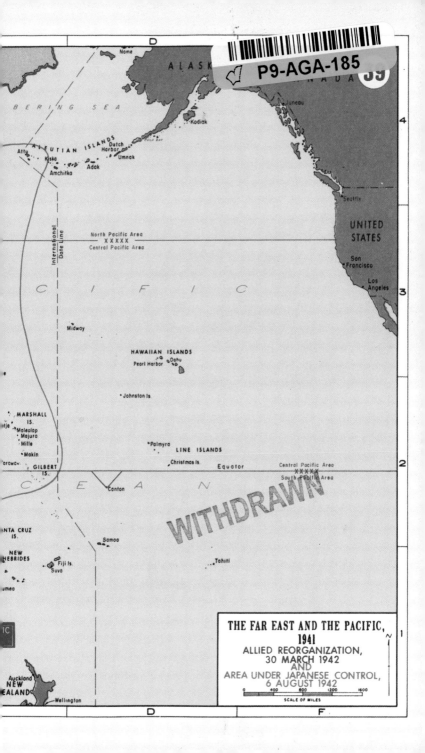

ALASKA

CANADA

39

P9-AGA-185

BERING SEA

Nome

Juneau

Kodiak

COLD BAY

ALEUTIAN ISLANDS

Dutch
Harbor

Attu

Kiska

Umnak

Amchitka

Adak

Seattle

UNITED
STATES

International Date Line

North Pacific Area
X X X X X
Central Pacific Area

San
Francisco

Los
Angeles

P   A   C   I   F   I   C

Midway

HAWAIIAN ISLANDS

Pearl Harbor   Oahu

Johnston Is.

MARSHALL
IS.

Maloelap
Majuro
Mille

Makin

Palmyra   LINE ISLANDS

Christmas Is.   Equator

Central Pacific Area
X X X X X
South Pacific Area

Tarawa

GILBERT
IS.

O   C   E   A   N

Canton

WITHDRAWN

ANTA CRUZ
IS.

Samoa

NEW
HEBRIDES

Fiji Is.

Suva

Tahiti

umea

IC

Auckland

NEW
ZEALAND

Wellington

THE FAR EAST AND THE PACIFIC, 1941

ALLIED REORGANIZATION,
30 MARCH 1942
AND
AREA UNDER JAPANESE CONTROL,
6 AUGUST 1942

0   400   800   1200   1600

SCALE OF MILES

Library of America, a nonprofit organization,
champions our nation's cultural heritage
by publishing America's greatest writing in
authoritative new editions and providing resources
for readers to explore this rich, living legacy.

WORLD WAR II MEMOIRS
THE PACIFIC THEATER

WORLD WAR II MEMOIRS

THE PACIFIC THEATER

With the Old Breed at Peleliu and Okinawa
E. B. Sledge

Flights of Passage
Samuel Hynes

Crossing the Line
Alvin Kernan

Elizabeth D. Samet, *editor*

THE LIBRARY OF AMERICA

Contents

List of Maps

Introduction

BY ELIZABETH D. SAMET

In 1945, a bored U.S. naval staff officer stationed on Guam in the Western Pacific, and anticipating the invasion of Japan, read all the way through Virgil's *Aeneid* for the first time in the Latin of his Oxford Classical Text. "The next landings would be on Honshu, and I would be there," Robert Fitzgerald recalled decades later in the postscript to his splendid translation of the epic poem: "More than literary interest, I think, kept me reading Virgil's descriptions of desperate battle, funeral pyres, failed hopes of truce or peace." As the three memoirs in this volume—E. B. Sledge's *With the Old Breed at Peleliu and Okinawa*, Samuel Hynes's *Flights of Passage*, and Alvin Kernan's *Crossing the Line*—eloquently testify, desperate battles, funeral pyres, failed hopes, and a constellation of related terrors dominated World War II as thoroughly as they had the wars of antiquity.

Human beings have been reading and writing about battles almost as long as they have been fighting them. A chain links the twenty-first-century infantry soldier poring over the Akkadian epic *Gilgamesh* in Afghanistan or the helicopter pilot reading Joseph Heller's novel *Catch-22* in Iraq all the way back to Alexander the Great, who reputedly considered a copy of Homer's *Iliad* essential equipment on his campaign to conquer the world. It was Alexander's way of keeping the example of Achilles always before him. Plutarch records that Julius Caesar once amazed his friends by weeping over a history of Alexander. "Do you not think," Caesar demanded, "it is matter for sorrow that while Alexander, at my age, was already king of so many peoples, I have as yet achieved no brilliant success?" Napoleon's extensive traveling library included Homer in addition to a generous selection of military historians. The publisher James Redpath's series of inexpensive paperbound editions marketed to Civil War soldiers, *Books for the Camp Fires*, featured *The Battle of Waterloo* (an excerpt from Victor Hugo's *Les Misérables*). The British poet and memoirist Edmund Blunden soldiered in the trenches of

World War I with a copy of Caesar's *Commentaries on the Gallic War*.

Practical instruction, distraction, solace, inspiration, communion—reading fulfills any number of ends for soldiers. While a soldier's selections naturally range well beyond the subject of war, tales of military life inevitably have a special intensity for readers in a combat theater. Fitzgerald found in Virgil not merely an antidote to the tedium that rules the periods between action during wartime but a literary mirror that reflected across almost two millennia his own anxieties about how his war would end. Sailors whose taste did not run to Latin poetry still had a variety of war stories available to them, several in the form of Armed Services Editions, oblong pocket-sized paperbacks designed to fit in a cargo pocket and distributed to millions of military personnel around the world. There were old sagas renewed (T. E. Lawrence's translation of Homer's *Odyssey*), recent tales of historic events (C. S. Forester's Hornblower novels of Napoleonic-era naval warfare), as well as fresh stories about the latest war: Ernie Pyle's *Brave Men*, for example, or *An American Guerrilla in the Philippines*, Ira Wolfert's account of a stranded navy lieutenant, Iliff David Richardson, who aided the Philippine resistance.

When Fitzgerald later came to translate Virgil, he was also indirectly translating his war into a comprehensible experience. Turning one's war into words gives imaginative shape to what is by definition a destructive, elusive activity—an event that resists attempts to give it narrative shape. The World War II correspondent A. J. Liebling suggested the challenges of such work by refusing to write an epilogue to a collection of his war writings published in 1964: "I have been advised to write an epilogue to this book to 'give it unity' and 'put it in perspective,' but I find this difficult, because war, unlike drama, has no unities, classical or otherwise. It is discursive, centrifugal, both repetitive and disparate. Also, I have never got it into perspective myself."* To a certain extent, writing war demands rewriting it. A writer takes possession of an experience that once possessed him or her. Yet ownership—putting it into perspective, to borrow Liebling's phrase—comes at a

---

*From *Mollie and Other War Pieces*, printed by Library of America in *A. J. Liebling: World War II Writings* (2008).

price. Reassembling memories invites omission, revision, distortion: an inconvenient detail forgotten, a shameful occurrence suppressed, a traumatic episode erased or recovered only fragmentarily and at great cost. Owing to self-preservation or simple forgetfulness, every narrative of remembrance works some violence on the actual facts for the sake of coherence; every memoir is a careful negotiation between past and present, between the actor embroiled in war and the narrator who somehow survived it.

Communities also crave such coherence, and the way nations remember war owes a great deal to artistic expression, be it in the form of writing, music, film, or monument. This cultural history is often itself a battleground on which competing stories vie for control. This was certainly the case for the war on which the World War II generation grew up. One of the most influential modes of remembering World War I belongs to the trench-poets, the claustrophobic intensity of whose lyrics encapsulates the plight of the modern soldier: puny, anonymous, imprisoned within a landscape disfigured by mechanized warfare. Memoirs like Robert Graves's *Good-bye to All That* and Edmund Blunden's *Undertones of War* complemented the disillusioned poetry of Wilfred Owen, Siegfried Sassoon, and Isaac Rosenberg.

Among the most definitive statements on the British poetry of the First World War is that of an American veteran of the Second, Paul Fussell, who fought with the 103rd Infantry Division in France. In his landmark study *The Great War and Modern Memory*, Fussell argued that the trench-poets ushered in a new, modern way of looking at war. Fundamentally ironic, their perspective ostensibly superseded both the heroic model of the ancient epic and the realistic vision of the nineteenth-century novel. Fussell believed World War II presented "even more preposterous ironies" than did its predecessor, and he waged a lifelong campaign as a critic to expose them. "Every war is ironic," he wrote, "because every war is worse than expected. Every war constitutes an irony of situation because its means are so melodramatically disproportionate to its presumed ends."

It may have taken World War I to popularize this view among a sizeable audience, but soldiers, in marked contrast to home-front jingoists and saber-rattlers, have always known the irony of war. Even Achilles knew it and said so: "Do not make light of Death before me," he told the yet-living Odysseus, who envied him his preeminence among the Underworld heroes in Homer's *Odyssey* (here in T. E. Lawrence's translation). "Would that I were on earth a menial, bound to some insubstantial man who must pinch and scrape to keep alive! Life so were better than King of Kings among these dead men."

Electric as the trench-poets' ironic vision proved to be, theirs was a necessarily incomplete account molded by the grinding stalemate of the Western Front in contrast to the expanses of Eastern Europe or the Middle East; by the infantryman's earthbound perspective as opposed to the aviator's bird's eye view or the sailor's floating isolation. At least in some respects, T. E. Lawrence's narrative of his campaigns in the Arab Revolt in *Seven Pillars of Wisdom* might have come from a different conflict altogether. It is also the case, as the historian Jay Winter has shown in *Sites of Memory, Sites of Mourning: The Great War In European Cultural History*, that public memorials to the war, often deeply conservative and traditional, presented a sharp contrast to the radical disaffection of the trench-poets. In other words, several different ways of remembering World War I were in fact available to those who would fight the next war.

Samuel Hynes notes that as a boy he read Robert J. Hogan's pulp fiction series *G-8 and His Battle Aces* "like everybody else," yet his generation's idea of war would not be simplistically heroic. "The war-in-their-heads, when war came," he notes to his contemporaries in *The Soldiers' Tale: Bearing Witness to Modern War*, "would not be the romantic fancies of nineteenth-century writers but the antiwar myth of the Western Front" found in poetry as well as in Erich Maria Remarque's hugely popular novel *All Quiet on the Western Front*. Nevertheless, while this myth may have turned a few readers into conscientious objectors, Hynes claims, "the myth had not dispelled the excitement we felt at the prospect of actually being in a war of our own." Even the "terrible particulars" of the Western Front, as depicted in books and on film, "became somehow part of the excitement." Hynes explained why those that grew up on irony went to war anyway: "Every new generation will respond anew to war's great seduction . . . to the chance to be where danger is," he wrote in *A Soldier's Tale*. He went on to suggest that it was a finely calibrated sense of irony that effectively "inoculated Americans against . . . disillusionment" in World War II.

Hynes differentiates World War I, which "began in idealism but lost its moral certainty as the fighting wore on," from World War II, which "began with a clearer sense of moral necessity and never lost it." The "Good War," as it would come to be known, waged as it was against the unambiguous evils of fascism, remade the country and the world. This collection is being published in the midst of the eightieth anniversary of the American entry into that war, which gave Americans a version of ourselves we far prefer to that, say, offered by Vietnam. This heroic model might be described as an amalgamation of Humphrey Bogart's reluctant hero Rick Blaine in *Casablanca*; John Wayne's Sergeant Stryker in *The Sands of Iwo Jima*; and Tom Hanks's schoolteacher turned infantry officer, the quintessential citizen-soldier, in *Saving Private Ryan*. What Winter called "nostalgic history" satisfies a deep desire for the moral certainty to which Hynes calls attention. The unprecedented devastation of aerial bombardment, the uncomfortable alliance with the totalitarian regime of the Soviet Union, and the race-hatred that helped to brutalize the war in the Pacific melt before the power of the image: Rick Blaine marching off to join the Free French garrison at Brazzaville; the dead Stryker surrounded by his squad, who have finally understood that his toughness concealed his love; the American flag flying over the military cemetery in Normandy.

As Hynes and Fussell recognized, the romance of war rises Phoenix-like from the ashes of destruction to wash away contradictions. Fiction offers a more diverse range of stories than do the cinematic flag-wavers, and the veteran-novelists arguably most familiar to many readers today refused to salvage much from the wreckage: Kurt Vonnegut's excoriating *Slaughterhouse-Five* plunges readers into a firebombed Dresden while the cynicism of Heller's *Catch-22* punctures illusions of honor and patriotism. These novels, together with Norman Mailer's *The Naked and the Dead* and James Jones's war trilogy —*From Here to Eternity*, *The Thin Red Line*, and *Whistle*— offer up the soldier as a victim of cataclysmic forces. The poetry of many World War II veterans like Harvey Shapiro, Lincoln

Kirstein, and Louis Simpson, has been largely neglected, but it can be found in the Library of America's *Poets of World War II* (2003), edited by Shapiro, who called this body of work "neither pious nor patriotic," but "often bawdy, bitchy, irreverent."

And what of the memoirists? The best of them are deeply reflective and rarely facile. No genre deals more explicitly with the treacheries of recollection than the *memoir*, its very name deriving from the French word for memory. Memoirs are a type of autobiography, a genre central to the American literary tradition, the most celebrated example being *The Autobiography of Benjamin Franklin*. Throughout the colonial and early national periods spiritual autobiographies, travel memoirs, and captivity narratives, such as Mary Rowlandson's account of her capture and ultimate release by Native Americans during King Philip's War, held the stage. These gave way during the antebellum period to another kind of captivity narrative: the slave narrative, which is indispensable to understanding the American experience. The war memoir has a special place within the national tradition of life writing. The genre's first heyday occurred in the latter decades of the nineteenth century, when a flood of Civil War memoirs, diaries, and journals appeared. From volunteers to professional soldiers trained at West Point, from Ohio Yankees to Mississippi Rebels, the survivors of two highly literate armies rehearsed their war stories. Southern memoirs formed no small part of a regional literary tradition that rewrote and revised the conflict. Artfully crafted and assiduously tended, it proved influential and damaging in its tendency to sentimentalize the war and to obfuscate its politics by denying that slavery at the root of the conflict.

The most celebrated (and bestselling) of all these memoirs, however, was written from an emphatically Union perspective. *Personal Memoirs of U. S. Grant* is generally regarded as one of the finest examples of the military memoir. Grant's publisher, Mark Twain, reaching back to the beginnings of the genre, likened the book to Caesar's *Commentaries*. From memoirs such as these we derive some of the most indelible images of war across time and space. It is difficult, for example, to forget Grant's description of the evening of the first day's fighting at Shiloh: "Some time after midnight, growing restive under the storm and the continuous pain [after a fall from his horse], I moved back to the log-house under the bank. This had been taken as a hospital, and all night wounded men were being brought in, their wounds dressed, a leg or an arm amputated as the case might require, and everything being done to save life or alleviate suffering. The sight was more unendurable than encountering the enemy's fire, and I returned to my tree in the rain."

The moments of suffering and hardship that fill military memoirs are matched only by those of the joy of survival. One of the first military memoirs in the Western world, Xenophon's *Anabasis*, chronicles the experience of a detachment of Greek mercenaries, the "Ten Thousand," forced to retreat after a disastrous expedition under the command of the Persian prince Cyrus. After a harrowing thousand-mile march across the Mesopotamian desert, the troops at last reach the coast, and the exuberant cry of "The sea! The sea!" reverberates through the ranks. Several centuries later, Caesar's two *Commentaries* (written in the third person), set a standard for the genre in matters of design, narrative momentum, and psychological insight. The cumulative force of Caesar's accounts of the war in Gaul and the Civil War against Pompey are matched by the acuity of detail: the depiction of rumor spreading quickly through a military camp; the portrait of the soldiers of opposing armies lamenting across the lines "because they had fought against men who were their friends and kinsmen"; the extended portrait of Critognatus, an influential member of the Arvernian tribe in Gaul, who in a rousing speech advocated resorting to cannibalism during a siege in preference to surrendering to the Romans. It was "a fine policy to establish," he declared, "for the sake of liberty."

The long arc of American military autobiography stretches from the colonial period and the Civil War forward to our twenty-first-century conflicts: Joseph Plumb Martin's diary, subsequently published as *Memoir of a Revolutionary Soldier*; the memoirs of Grant and of William T. Sherman; the novelist Hervey Allen's powerful personal history *Toward the Flame*, which begins with the disclaimer, "I have tried to reproduce in words my experience in France during the Great War. There is no plot, no climax, no happy ending to this book." Some of the finest American war memoirs, Philip Caputo's *A Rumor of War*, Tim O'Brien's *If I Die in a Combat Zone, Box Me Up and Ship Me Home*, and Tobias Wolff's *In Pharaoh's Army*, emerged from the protracted and unsuccessful war in Vietnam. Most recently, incisive autobiographical writing has emerged from the wars in Afghanistan and Iraq: Elliot Ackerman's *Places and Names*, Brian Castner's *The Long Walk*, Matt Gallagher's *Kaboom*, Nathaniel Fick's *One Bullet Away*, and Kayla Williams's *Love My Rifle More Than You*, to name just a few.

The three books in this volume must stand in for the hundreds of memoirs from the Pacific published after World War II. The literary abilities of Sledge, Hynes, and Kernan set them apart from many of their contemporaries. In *A Sketch of the Past*, an autobiographical work begun in the spring of 1939 and carried on throughout the first year of the war, Virginia Woolf claimed that most memoirists fail: "They leave out the person to whom things happened," she explained. "The reason is that it is so difficult to describe any human being. So they say: 'This is what happened'; but they do not say what the person was like to whom it happened. And the events mean very little unless we know first to whom they happened." In each of these memoirs the person to whom things happen is never lost amid the welter of events; the difficult work of introspection animates their pages.

Extraordinary as they are, however, these books also have a more representative value as social history, providing as they do insight into American society in the 1940s, especially with regard to regional differences, race, class, and sexual mores. In admirable and deplorable ways, the armed forces of World War II reflected the times. A much greater proportion of the population served in uniform than does today in the all-volunteer force, yet that service was segregated by race and gender. Owing to the prejudices of the era, the roles of African Americans and women was severely constrained. Most Black soldiers, for example, were limited to combat-support functions, and only the emergency of the Battle of the Bulge led the American army briefly, and partially, to integrate some combat units.

A collection such as this one can offer only a limited perspective on a complex global conflict. Readers whose curiosity is whetted by the memoirs in this volume can explore various aspects of the Pacific Theater in Robert Leckie's fine account of his participation with the 1st Marine Division in the Guadalcanal Campaign in *Helmet for My Pillow*; the diaries—published as *Between Tedium and Terror*—of Sy M. Kahn, who served in the Southwest Pacific with a port battalion of the Army Transportation Corps; and Charlton Ogburn's *The Marauders*, an account of service with Merrill's Marauders in the jungles of Burma.

A reader who wishes to follow the American campaigns in the Mediterranean and European Theaters would do well to begin with Franklyn Johnson's *One More Hill*, an account of his service in North Africa, moving on to Italy with Harold L. Bond's *Return to Cassino*, before proceeding to France with Charles R. Cawthon's *Other Clay*, which follows an infantry battalion from the D-Day landing on Omaha Beach across France to the German border. In *Before Their Time* Robert Kotlowitz recounts his experiences with the Third Army, most searingly, the massacre of his platoon in France. Fussell's *Doing Battle* chronicles its author's loss of innocence in combat. Finally, a very different kind of memoir, Victor Brombert's *Trains of Thought*, tells the story of its author's youth in France, his family's escape to the United States, and his subsequent enlistment in the U.S. Army, with which he made his way, in an exquisite example of Fussell's irony, back to France by way of Omaha Beach.

Aviators who flew in the war against Germany and Italy are especially well represented among war memoirists. Bert Stiles's *Serenade to the Big Bird*, a raw contemporaneous account by a pilot who did not survive the war, has become something of a cult classic. Philip Ardery's *Bomber Pilot* is a thoughtful meditation on the demoralizing and all-too-often deadly experience of flying bombers from North Africa and England, while John Muirhead's *Those Who Fall* chronicles the experiences of a bomber pilot who became a prisoner of war. No picture of the European war in the air would be complete without a discussion of the contributions of African Americans. Charles W. Dryden's *A-Train: Memoirs of a Tuskegee Airman* documents not only his combat experience but also his career-long battle with the military's institutionalized racism.

Aerial bombardment, long-range shelling, and other technological innovations redefined the meaning of "combatant" for American men and women serving overseas in World War II. There are invaluable memoirs by front-line nurses, including

GI Nightingale, Theresa Archard's account of her experiences in North Africa. In *The Intrepid Woman* Betty Ann Lussier recounts her experience first as an Air Transport Auxiliary pilot and later in the counterintelligence branch of the OSS.

The three memoirs in this volume—E. B. Sledge's *With the Old Breed at Peleliu and Okinawa,* Samuel Hynes's *Flights of Passage,* and Alvin Kernan's *Crossing the Line*—recollect the war in the Pacific from the markedly different perspectives of land, air, and sea. Sledge, a Marine infantryman, fought a "totally savage" war deep in the coral dust of Peleliu and the mud of Okinawa. Hynes, by contrast, fought a "flying war," the dangerous days of his naval aviator's life, surviving "all the ways that airplanes can kill you," punctuated by drunken nights in makeshift officers' clubs on a series of Pacific islands. Kernan also spent part of his war in the air as a gunner in a torpedo bomber, but flying from an aircraft carrier, his home was the sea and that small floating world within it. Taken together, these books provide a rich sense of some of war's universals— fear, courage, skill, brutality, regret, boredom, and exhilaration —while also reminding us that no one's war ever looks quite like anyone else's.

Three memoirs, three combatants, three professors: Sledge became a biologist, while Hynes and Kernan both specialized in literature during an era in which the educational provisions of the GI Bill helped shape the lives of so many veterans. Why is this important? Because their books, all three written de- cades after the war, are so clearly the creations of men as com- mitted to the life of the mind as they once had been to the life of action. In other words, these writers have the gifts of patient reflection and precise expression required to make vis- ceral experience legible to those who did not share it as well as to the writers themselves. These memoirs are the antithesis of the "you-had-to-be-there" kind of war story that imagines a potential enemy in every reader who was not. Instead, like the best teachers, Sledge, Hynes, and Kernan generously open up the distant unfamiliar spaces of their war experience to the rest of us. Each is alive to nuance, contradiction, and the power of detail. All understand that war is a grim and destructive busi- ness, remembering it a creative art.

WITH THE OLD BREED AT PELELIU AND OKINAWA

E. B. Sledge

In memory of Capt. Andrew A. Haldane,
beloved company commander of K/3/5,
and to the Old Breed.

*The deaths ye died I have watched beside,
and the lives that ye led were mine.*
Kipling

Rifles were high and holy things to them, and they knew five-inch broadside guns. They talked patronizingly of the war, and were concerned about rations. They were the Leathernecks, the Old Timers. . . . They were the old breed of American regular, regarding the service as home and war as an occupation; and they transmitted their temper and character and viewpoint to the high-hearted volunteer mass which filled the ranks of the Marine Brigade. . . .

"The Leathernecks" in *Fix Bayonets!*
by John W. Thomason, Jr., Charles Scribner's
Sons, Cornwall, N.Y. 1926. pp. x–xiii

CONTENTS

FOREWORD

It was my privilege to assume command of the 3d Battalion, 5th Marines, 1st Marine Division (Reinforced) on 10 April 1944 during the final phase of the New Britain campaign. New Britain was its second combat operation.

Although we didn't know it at the time, two more campaigns lay before the battalion, Peleliu and Okinawa. Each of them would be of greater intensity and extract a greater cost than did the first two. And when the division departed New Britain for a "rest camp" on Pavuvu in the Russell Islands, we began comprehensive training for what was to become Operation Stalemate on Peleliu Island in the Palau Islands. That operation was to receive little publicity or recognition, but it was certainly to be one of the bloodiest and hardest fought in the Pacific war.

Among the replacements who joined us during this period was a young Marine known as "Sledgehammer," more properly listed as Pfc. E. B. Sledge. He was assigned to Company K, under the command of Capt. Andrew Haldane, one of the finest company commanders in the entire Corps.

Sledgehammer has a Ph.D. now and is a professor of biology at the University of Montevallo, Montevallo, Alabama. But he has never forgotten his experiences with Company K during the fights for Peleliu and Okinawa.

Although I commanded the 3d Battalion during its training period for Peleliu, it was my fate—through the vicissitudes of seniority, or the lack thereof—to be transferred to the regimental staff before we sailed for Peleliu. That was a source of deep regret on my part.

It's customary for historical accounts to be written about military campaigns. It's not unusual for officers to write their personal narratives of such operations. But it's all too rare for an ordinary Marine infantryman to set down in print his own impressions of war. This is the man who actually closes with the enemy, who endures a plethora of privations along with pain and all too often death, who is the lowest common denominator when battle is joined.

Sledgehammer Sledge was such a Marine. In this book we see the war as he himself saw it. Anyone who has served in the ranks will find many situations analogous to his own experiences recounted accurately in the recital of fears, frustrations, and small triumphs. It's fascinating and instructive reading.

Brig. Gen. Walter S. McIlhenny
U.S. Marine Corps Reserve (Ret.)

Avery Island, Louisiana

PREFACE

THIS BOOK is an account of my World War II experiences in training and in combat with Company K, 3d Battalion, 5th Marine Regiment, 1st Marine Division during the Peleliu and Okinawa campaigns. It is not a history, and it is not my story alone. I have attempted, rather, to be the spokesman for my comrades, who were swept with me into the abyss of war. I hope they will approve my efforts.

I began writing this account immediately after Peleliu while we were in rest camp on Pavuvu Island. I outlined the entire story with detailed notes as soon as I returned to civilian life, and I have written down certain episodes during the years since then. Mentally, I have gone over and over the details of these events, but I haven't been able to draw them all together and write them down until now.

I have done extensive research with published and unpublished histories and documents pertaining to my division's role in the Peleliu and Okinawa campaigns. I have been amazed at the vast difference in the perception of events recounted in these narratives as contrasted to my experience on the front line.

My Pacific war experiences have haunted me, and it has been a burden to retain this story. But time heals, and the nightmares no longer wake me in a cold sweat with pounding heart and racing pulse. Now I can write this story, painful though it is to do so. In writing it I'm fulfilling an obligation I have long felt to my comrades in the 1st Marine Division, all of whom suffered so much for our country. None came out unscathed. Many gave their lives, many their health, and some their sanity. All who survived will long remember the horror they would rather forget. But they suffered and they did their duty so a sheltered homeland can enjoy the peace that was purchased at such a high cost. We owe those Marines a profound debt of gratitude.

E.B.S.

ACKNOWLEDGMENTS

Although this is a personal account, which was originally written for my family, there have been numerous people who have helped shape it into book form for the general reader.

First I want to thank Jeanne, my wonderful wife. She typed the Peleliu portion of the manuscript from stacks of my handwritten pages, and was the first to suggest that this narrative might be of interest to others than our family. She has encouraged and aided me with ideas, advice, editing, and typing. That the lengthy original manuscript was completed after years of spare-time writing and research during graduate school and child rearing is due as much to her assistance as to my efforts.

Deepest appreciation is extended to my editor, Lt. Col. Robert W. Smith, USMC (Ret.). During his last year as editor of the *Marine Corps Gazette*, he became interested in seeing this complete account in book form during our work on extracts which appeared as a three-part article, "Peleliu: A Neglected Battle." His interest has been my good fortune. In addition to his vast editing skill, Bob has been an inexhaustible source of good ideas and advice. On more than one occasion he has bolstered my sagging morale when I've become weary with what is not a happy subject. His objectivity has guided me through the forest when I couldn't see the trees, and when it was painful to both of us to omit parts of the original. I am grateful for his sensitivity and impeccable professionalism.

I want to thank my publisher, Col. Robert V. Kane, USA (Ret.), and Adele Horwitz, Editor in Chief of Presidio Press, who saw in my verbose original manuscript a story that should be told.

This book could not have been written without the benefit of Marine Corps historical material. My requests for help were rapidly and efficiently granted in every instance. For this I want to thank Brig. Gen. Edwin H. Simmons, USMC (Ret.), Director of Marine Corps History and Museums, Benis Frank, Ralph Donnelly, and Henry I. Shaw.

For their help and encouragement I express my gratitude

to Brig. Gen. Walter McIlhenny, USMC (Ret.), Lt. Col. John A. Crown, USMC (Ret.), Brig. Gen. Austin Shofner, USMC (Ret.), Capt. John A. Moran, USMC (Ret.), and Maj. Allan Bevilacqua, USMC (Ret.).

M. Sgt. Robert F. Fleischauer, USMC (Ret.), is due recognition and thanks for his fine work on the maps and sketches.

I thank Mrs. Hilda Van Landingham for typing the first draft of the Okinawa portion. Mary Francis Tipton, Reference Librarian at the University of Montevallo, merits my deepest appreciation for her help. Dr. Lucille Griffith, Professor Emeritus of History, University of Montevallo, was one of the first people to suggest this account be published. Her faith in it is redeemed, and I thank her.

My heartiest thanks to my old K/3/5 buddies who have assisted so much in verifying company casualty figures, countless other details, and photograph identification: Ted (Tex) Barrow, Henry A. Boyes, Valton Burgin, Jessie Crumbacker, Art Dimick, John Hedge, T. L. Hudson, William Leyden, Sterling Mace, Tom Matheny, Jim McEney, Vincent Santos, George Sarrett, Thomas (Stumpy) Stanley. If I have omitted any names, I apologize. Any errors in the manuscript are solely mine.

I appreciate the cooperation and understanding of my sons John and Henry and their patience with a father who was often preoccupied with past events.

A grant from the University of Montevallo Faculty Research Committee aided in the preparation of the manuscript.

E.B.S.

PART I

PELELIU: A NEGLECTED BATTLE

FOREWORD TO PART I

THE 1st Marine Division's assault on the Central Pacific island of Peleliu thirty-seven years ago was, in the overall
perspective of World War II, a relatively minor engagement.
After a war is over, it's deceptively easy to determine which
battles were essential and which could have gone unfought.
Thus, in hindsight, Peleliu's contribution to total victory was
dubious. Moreover, World War II itself has faded into the
mists with the more immediate combat in Korea and Vietnam.

To the men of the 1st Marine Division who made the assault on Peleliu (the youngest of whom are in their fifties today), there was nothing minor about it. For those who were
there, it was a bloody, wearying, painful, and interminable
engagement. For a single-division operation, the losses were
extraordinarily heavy.

Eugene B. Sledge served in Company K, 3d Battalion, 5th
Marines throughout the battle. I had the privilege of commanding Company I of the same battalion in the same period.
His account awoke vivid memories which had lain dormant
for years.

Don't read this personal narrative seeking the significance
of the battle or of grand strategy. Rather read it for what it is,
intense combat as seen by an individual Marine rifleman. For
those who have experienced battle elsewhere, the similarities
will be obvious.

John A. Crown
Lieutenant Colonel
U.S. Marine Corps

Atlanta, Georgia

CHAPTER ONE

Making of a Marine

I ENLISTED IN the Marine Corps on 3 December 1942 at Marion, Alabama. At the time I was a freshman at Marion Military Institute. My parents and brother Edward had urged me to stay in college as long as possible in order to qualify for a commission in some technical branch of the U.S. Army. But, prompted by a deep feeling of uneasiness that the war might end before I could get overseas into combat, I wanted to enlist in the Marine Corps as soon as possible. Ed, a Citadel graduate and a second lieutenant in the army, suggested life would be more beautiful for me as an officer. Mother and Father were mildly distraught at the thought of me in the Marines as an enlisted man—that is, "cannon fodder." So when a Marine recruiting team came to Marion Institute, I compromised and signed up for one of the Corps' new officer training programs. It was called V-12.

The recruiting sergeant wore dress blue trousers, a khaki shirt, necktie, and white barracks hat. His shoes had a shine the likes of which I'd never seen. He asked me lots of questions and filled out numerous official papers. When he asked, "Any scars, birthmarks, or other unusual features?" I described an inch-long scar on my right knee. I asked why such a question. He replied, "So they can identify you on some Pacific beach after the Japs blast off your dog tags." This was my introduction to the stark realism that characterized the Marine Corps I later came to know.

The college year ended the last week of May 1943. I had the month of June at home in Mobile before I had to report 1 July for duty at Georgia Tech in Atlanta.

I enjoyed the train trip from Mobile to Atlanta because the train had a steam engine. The smoke smelled good, and the whistle added a plaintive note reminiscent of an unhurried life. The porters were impressed and most solicitous when I told them, with no little pride, that I was on my way to becoming a Marine. My official Marine Corps meal ticket got me a large, delicious shrimp salad in the dining car and the admiring glances of the steward in attendance.

On my arrival in Atlanta, a taxi deposited me at Georgia Tech, where the 180-man Marine detachment lived in Harrison Dormitory. Recruits were scheduled to attend classes year round (in my case, about two years), graduate, and then go to the Marine base at Quantico, Virginia, for officers' training.

A Marine regular, Capt. Donald Payzant, was in charge. He had served with the 1st Marine Division on Guadalcanal. Seeming to glory in his duty and his job as our commander, he loved the Corps and was salty and full of swagger. Looking back, I realize now that he had survived the meat grinder of combat and was simply glad to be in one piece with the good fortune of being stationed at a peaceful college campus.

Life at Georgia Tech was easy and comfortable. In short, we didn't know there was a war going on. Most of the college courses were dull and uninspiring. Many of the professors openly resented our presence. It was all but impossible to concentrate on academics. Most of us felt we had joined the Marines to fight, but here we were college boys again. The situation was more than many of us could stand. At the end of the first semester, ninety of us—half of the detachment—flunked out of school so we could go into the Corps as enlisted men.

When the navy officer in charge of academic affairs called me in to question me about my poor academic performance, I told him I hadn't joined the Marine Corps to sit out the war in college. He was sympathetic to the point of being fatherly and said he would feel the same way if he were in my place.

Captain Payzant gave the ninety of us a pep talk in front of the dormitory the morning we were to board the train for boot camp at the Marine Corps Recruit Depot, San Diego, California. He told us we were the best men and the best Marines in the detachment. He said he admired our spirit for wanting to get into the war. I think he was sincere.

After the pep talk, buses took us to the railway station. We sang and cheered the whole way. We were on our way to war at last. If we had only known what lay ahead of us!

Approximately two and a half years later, I came back through the Atlanta railway station on my way home. Shortly after I stepped off the car for a stroll, a young army infantry-man walked up to me and shook hands. He said he had noticed my 1st Marine Division patch and the campaign ribbons on my chest and wondered if I had fought at Peleliu. When I said I had, he told me he just wanted to express his undying admiration for men of the 1st Marine Division.

He had fought with the 81st Infantry Division (Wildcats) which had come in to help us at Peleliu.* He was a machine gunner, had been hit by Japanese fire on Bloody Nose Ridge, and was abandoned by his army comrades. He knew he would either die of his wounds or be cut up by the Japanese when darkness fell. Risking their lives, some Marines had moved in and carried him to safety. The soldier said he was so impressed by the bravery, efficiency, and esprit of the Marines he saw on Peleliu that he swore to thank every veteran of the 1st Marine Division he ever ran across.

The "Dago people"—as those of us bound for San Diego were called—boarded a troop train in a big railroad terminal in Atlanta. Everyone was in high spirits, as though we were headed for a picnic instead of boot camp—and a war. The trip across the country took several days and was uneventful but interesting. Most of us had never been west, and we enjoyed the scenery. The monotony of the trip was broken with card games, playing jokes on each other, and waving, yelling, and whistling at any and all women visible. We ate some meals in dining cars on the train; but at certain places the train pulled onto a siding, and we ate in the restaurant in the railroad terminal.

Nearly all of the rail traffic we passed was military. We saw long trains composed almost entirely of flatcars loaded with tanks, halftracks, artillery pieces, trucks, and other military equipment. Many troop trains passed us going both ways. Most of them carried army troops. This rail traffic impressed on us the enormousness of the nation's war effort.

*Together with the 1st Marine Division, the U.S. Army's 81st Infantry Division comprised the III Amphibious Corps commanded by Maj. Gen. Roy S. Geiger, USMC. For the Palau operation, the 1st Marine Division assaulted Peleliu on 15 September 1944 while the 81st Division took Angaur Island and provided a regiment as corps reserve. The 81st Division relieved the 1st Marine Division on Peleliu on 20 October and secured the island on 27 November.

We arrived in San Diego early one morning. Collecting our gear, we fell into ranks outside our cars as a first sergeant came along and told the NCOs on our train which buses to get us aboard. This first sergeant looked old to us teenagers. Like ourselves, he was dressed in a green wool Marine uniform, but he had campaign ribbons on his chest. He also wore the green French *fourragère* on his left shoulder. (Later, as a member of the 5th Marine Regiment, I would wear the braided cord around my left arm with pride.) But this man sported, in addition, two single loops outside his arm. That meant he had served with a regiment (either the 5th or 6th Marines) that had received the award from France for distinguished combat service in World War I.

The sergeant made a few brief remarks to us about the tough training we faced. He seemed friendly and compassionate, almost fatherly. His manner threw us into a false sense of well-being and left us totally unprepared for the shock that awaited us when we got off those buses.

"Fall out, and board your assigned buses!" ordered the first sergeant.

"All right, you people. Get aboard them buses!" the NCOs yelled. They seemed to have become more authoritarian as we approached San Diego.

After a ride of only a few miles, the buses rolled to a stop in the big Marine Corps Recruit Depot—boot camp. As I looked anxiously out the window, I saw many platoons of recruits marching along the streets. Each drill instructor (DI) bellowed his highly individual cadence. The recruits looked as rigid as sardines in a can. I grew nervous at seeing how serious—or rather, scared—they seemed.

"All right, you people, off them damned buses!"

We scrambled out, lined up with men from the other buses, and were counted off into groups of about sixty. Several trucks rolled by carrying work parties of men still in boot camp or who had finished recently. All looked at us with knowing grins and jeered, "You'll be sorreee." This was the standard, unofficial greeting extended to all recruits.

Shortly after we debused, a corporal walked over to my group. He yelled, "Patoon, teehut. Right hace, forwart huah. Double time, huah."

He ran us up and down the streets for what seemed hours and finally to a double line of huts that would house us for a time. We were breathless. He didn't even seem to be breathing hard.

"Patoon halt, right hace!" He put his hands on his hips and looked us over contemptuously. "You people are stupid," he bellowed. From then on he tried to prove it every moment of every day. "My name is Corporal Doherty. I'm your drill instructor. This is Platoon 984. If any of you idiots think you don't need to follow my orders, just step right out here and I'll beat your ass right now. Your soul may belong to Jesus, but your ass belongs to the Marines. You people are *recruits.* You're *not* Marines. You may not have what it takes to be Marines."

No one dared move, hardly even to breathe. We were all humbled, because there was no doubt the DI meant exactly what he said.

Corporal Doherty wasn't a large man by any standard. He stood about five feet ten inches, probably weighed around 160 pounds, and was muscular with a protruding chest and flat stomach. He had thin lips, a ruddy complexion, and was probably as Irish as his name. From his accent I judged him to be a New Englander, maybe from Boston. His eyes were the coldest, meanest green I ever saw. He glared at us like a wolf whose first and foremost desire was to tear us limb from limb. He gave me the impression that the only reason he didn't do so was that the Marine Corps wanted to use us for cannon fodder to absorb Japanese bullets and shrapnel so genuine Marines could be spared to capture Japanese positions.

That Corporal Doherty was tough and hard as nails none of us ever doubted. Most Marines recall how loudly their DIs yelled at them, but Doherty didn't yell very loudly. Instead he shouted in an icy, menacing manner that sent cold chills through us. We believed that if he didn't scare us to death, the Japs couldn't kill us. He was always immaculate, and his uniform fitted him as if the finest tailor had made it for him. His posture was erect, and his bearing reflected military precision.

The public pictures a DI wearing sergeant stripes. Doherty commanded our respect and put such fear into us that he couldn't have been more effective if he had had the six stripes of a first sergeant instead of the two of a corporal. One fact emerged immediately with stark clarity: this man would be the master of our fates in the weeks to come.

Doherty rarely drilled us on the main parade ground, but marched or double-timed us to an area near the beach of San Diego Bay. There the deep, soft sand made walking exhausting, just what he wanted. For hours on end, for days on end, we drilled back and forth across the soft sand. My legs ached terribly for the first few days, as did those of everyone else in the platoon. I found that when I concentrated on a fold of the collar or cap of the man in front of me or tried to count the ships in the bay, my muscles didn't ache as badly. To drop out of ranks because of tired legs was unthinkable. The standard remedy for such shirking was to "double time in place to get the legs in shape"—before being humiliated and berated in front of the whole platoon by the DI. I preferred the pain to the remedy.

Before heading back to the hut area at the end of each drill session, Doherty would halt us, ask a man for his rifle, and tell us he would demonstrate the proper technique for holding the rifle while creeping and crawling. First, though, he would place the butt of the rifle on the sand, release the weapon, and let it drop, saying that anyone who did that would have a miserable day of it. With so many men in the platoon, it was uncanny how often he asked to use my rifle in this demonstration. Then, after demonstrating how to cradle the rifle, he ordered us to creep and crawl. Naturally, the men in front kicked sand onto the rifle of the one behind him. With this and several other techniques, the DI made it necessary for us to clean our rifles several times each day. But we learned quickly and well an old Marine Corps truism, "The rifle is a Marine's best friend." We always treated it as just that.

During the first few days, Doherty once asked one of the recruits a question about his rifle. In answering, the hapless recruit referred to his rifle as "my gun." The DI muttered some instructions to him, and the recruit blushed. He began trotting up and down in front of the huts holding his rifle in one hand and his penis in the other, chanting, "This is my rifle," as he held up his M1, "and this is my gun," as he moved his other arm. "This is for Japs," he again held aloft his M1; "and this is for fun," he held up his other arm. Needless to say, none of us ever again used the word "gun" unless referring to a shotgun, mortar, artillery piece, or naval gun.

A typical day in boot camp began with reveille at 0400 hours. We tumbled out of our sacks in the chilly dark and hurried through shaves, dressing, and chow. The grueling day ended with taps at 2200. At any time between taps and reveille, however, the DI might break us out for rifle inspection, close-order drill, or for a run around the parade ground or over the sand by the bay. This seemingly cruel and senseless harassment stood me in good stead later when I found that war allowed sleep to no man, particularly the infantryman. Combat guaranteed sleep of the permanent type only.

We moved to two or three different hut areas during the first few weeks, each time on a moment's notice. The order was, "Platoon 984, fall out on the double with rifles, full individual equipment, and seabags with all gear properly stowed, and prepare to move out in ten minutes." A mad scramble would follow as men gathered up and packed their equipment. Each man had one or two close buddies who pitched in to help each other don packs and hoist heavy seabags onto sagging shoulders. Several men from each hut would stay behind to clean up the huts and surrounding area as the other men of the platoon struggled under their heavy loads to the new hut area.

Upon arrival at the new area, the platoon halted, received hut assignments, fell out, and stowed gear. Just as we got into the huts we would get orders to fall in for drill with rifles, cartridge belts, and bayonets. The sense of urgency and hurry never abated. Our DI was ingenious in finding ways to harass us.

One of the hut areas we were in was across a high fence from an aircraft factory where big B-24 Liberator bombers were made. There was an airstrip, too, and the big four-engine planes came and went low over the tops of the huts. Once one belly-landed, going through the fence near our huts. No one was hurt, but several of us ran down to see the crash. When we got back to our area, Corporal Doherty delivered one of his finest orations on the subject of recruits never leaving their assigned area without the permission of their DI. We were all impressed, particularly with the tremendous number of push-ups and other exercises we performed instead of going to noon chow.

During close-order drill, the short men had the toughest time staying in step. Every platoon had its "feather merchants" —short men struggling along with giant strides at the tail end of the formation. At five feet nine inches, I was about two-thirds of the way back from the front guide of Platoon 984. One day while returning from the bayonet course, I got out of step and couldn't pick up the cadence. Corporal Doherty marched along beside me. In his icy tone, he said, "Boy, if you don't get in step and stay in step, I'm gonna kick you so hard in the behind that they're gonna have to take both of us to sick bay. It'll take a major operation to get my foot outa your ass." With those inspiring words ringing in my ears, I picked up the cadence and never ever lost it again.

The weather became quite chilly, particularly at night. I had to cover up with blankets and overcoat. Many of us slept in dungaree trousers and sweat shirts in addition to our skivvies. When reveille sounded well before daylight, we only had to pull on our boondockers [field shoes] before falling in for roll call.

Each morning after roll call, we ran in the foggy darkness to a large asphalt parade ground for rifle calisthenics. Atop a wooden platform, a muscular physical training instructor led several platoons in a long series of tiring exercises. A public address system played a scratchy recording of "Three O'Clock in the Morning." We were supposed to keep time with the music. The monotony was broken only by frequent whispered curses and insults directed at our enthusiastic instructor, and by the too frequent appearance of various DIs who stalked the extended ranks making sure all hands exercised vigorously. Not only did the exercises harden our bodies, but our hearing became superkeen from listening for the DIs as we skipped a beat or two for a moment of rest in the inky darkness.

At the time, we didn't realize or appreciate the fact that the discipline we were learning in responding to orders under stress often would mean the difference later in combat—between success or failure, even living or dying. The ear training also proved to be an unscheduled dividend when Japanese infiltrators slipped around at night.

Shortly we received word that we were going to move out to the rifle range. We greeted the announcement enthusiastically. Rumor had it that we would receive the traditional broad-brimmed campaign hats. But the supply ran out when our turn came. We felt envious and cheated every time we saw those salty-looking "Smokey Bear" hats on the range.

Early on the first morning at the rifle range, we began what was probably the most thorough and the most effective rifle marksmanship training given to any troops of any nation during World War II. We were divided into two-man teams the first week for dry firing, or "snapping-in." We concentrated on proper sight setting, trigger squeeze, calling of shots, use of the leather sling as a shooting aid, and other fundamentals.

It soon became obvious why we all received thick pads to be sewn onto the elbows and right shoulders of our dungaree jackets: during this snapping-in, each man and his buddy practiced together, one in the proper position (standing, kneeling, sitting, or prone) and squeezing the trigger, and the other pushing back the rifle bolt lever with the heel of his hand, padded by an empty cloth bandolier wrapped around the palm. This procedure cocked the rifle and simulated recoil.

The DIs and rifle coaches checked every man continuously. Everything had to be just so. Our arms became sore from being contorted into various positions and having the leather sling straining our joints and biting into our muscles. Most of us had problems perfecting the sitting position (which I never saw used in combat). But the coach helped everyone the way he did me—simply by plopping his weight on my shoulders until I was able to "assume the correct position." Those familiar with firearms quickly forgot what they knew and learned the Marine Corps' way.

Second only to accuracy was safety. Its principles were pounded into us mercilessly. "*Keep* the piece pointed toward the target. *Never* point a rifle at anything you don't intend to shoot. *Check* your rifle *each* time you pick it up to be sure it isn't loaded. Many *accidents* have occurred with 'unloaded' rifles."

We went onto the firing line and received live ammunition the next week. At first, the sound of rifles firing was disconcerting. But not for long. Our snapping-in had been so thorough, we went through our paces automatically. We fired at round black bull's-eye targets from 100, 300, and 500 yards. Other platoons worked the "butts."* When the range officer ordered, "Ready on the right, ready on the left, all ready on the firing line, commence firing," I felt as though the rifle was part of me and vice versa. My concentration was complete.

Discipline was ever present, but the harassment that had been our daily diet gave way to deadly serious, businesslike instruction in marksmanship. Punishment for infractions of the rules came swiftly and severely, however. One man next to me turned around slightly to speak to a buddy after "cease firing" was given; the action caused his rifle muzzle to angle away from the targets. The sharp-eyed captain in charge of the range rushed up from behind and booted the man in the rear so hard that he fell flat on his face. The captain then jerked him up off the deck and bawled him out loudly and thoroughly. We got his message.

Platoon 984 took its turn in the butts. As we sat safely in the dugouts and waited for each series of firing to be completed, I had somber thoughts about the crack and snap of bullets passing overhead.

Qualification day dawned clearly and brightly. We were apprehensive, having been told that anyone who didn't shoot high enough to qualify as "marksman" wouldn't go overseas. When the final scores were totaled, I was disappointed. I fell short of "expert rifleman" by only two points. However, I proudly wore the Maltese Cross–shaped sharpshooter's badge. And I didn't neglect to point out to my Yankee buddies that most of the high shooters in our platoon were Southern boys.

Feeling like old salts, we returned to the recruit depot for the final phases of recruit training. The DIs didn't treat us as

---

*"Butts" refers to the impact area on a rifle range. It consists of the targets mounted on a vertical track system above a sheltered dugout, usually made of concrete, in which other shooters operate, mark, and score the targets for those on the firing line.

veterans, though; harassment picked up quickly to its previous intensity.

By the end of eight grueling weeks, it had become apparent that Corporal Doherty and the other DIs had done their jobs well. We were hard physically, had developed endurance, and had learned our lessons. Perhaps more importantly, we were tough mentally. One of our assistant drill instructors even allowed himself to mumble that we might become Marines after all.

Finally, late in the afternoon of 24 December 1943, we fell in without rifles and cartridge belts. Dressed in service greens, each man received three bronze Marine Corps globe-and-anchor emblems, which we put into our pockets. We marched to an amphitheater where we sat with several other platoons.

This was our graduation from boot camp. A short, affable-looking major standing on the stage said, "Men, you have successfully completed your recruit training and are now United States Marines. Put on your Marine Corps emblems and wear them with pride. You have a great and proud tradition to uphold. You are members of the world's finest fighting outfit, so be worthy of it." We took out our emblems and put one on each lapel of our green wool coats and one on the left side of the overseas caps. The major told several dirty jokes. Everyone laughed and whistled. Then he said, "Good luck, men." That was the first time we had been addressed as men during our entire time in boot camp.

Before dawn the next day, Platoon 984 assembled in front of the huts for the last time. We shouldered our seabags, slung our rifles, and struggled down to a warehouse where a line of trucks was parked. Corporal Doherty told us that each man was to report to the designated truck as his name and destination was called out. The few men selected to train as specialists (radar technicians, aircraft mechanics, etc.) were to turn in their rifles, bayonets, and cartridge belts.

As the men moved out of ranks, there were quiet remarks of, "So long, see you, take it easy." We knew that many friendships were ending right there. Doherty called out, "Eugene B. Sledge, 534559, full individual equipment and MI rifle, infantry, Camp Elliott."

Most of us were designated for infantry, and we went to Camp Elliott or to Camp Pendleton.* As we helped each other aboard the trucks, it never occurred to us why so many were being assigned to infantry. We were destined to take the places of the ever mounting numbers of casualties in the rifle or line companies in the Pacific. We were fated to fight the war first hand. We were cannon fodder.

After all assignments had been made, the trucks rolled out, and I looked at Doherty watching us leave. I disliked him, but I respected him. He had made us Marines, and I wondered what he thought as we rolled by.

*Camp Elliott was a small installation located on the northern outskirts of San Diego. It has been used rarely since World War II. Thirty-five miles north of San Diego lies Camp Joseph H. Pendleton. Home today of the 1st Marine Division, it is the Marine Corps' major west coast amphibious base.

CHAPTER TWO

Preparation for Combat

MOST OF the buildings at Camp Elliott were neat wooden barracks painted cream with dark roofs. The typical two-story barracks was shaped like an H, with the squad bays in the upright parts of the letter. The many-windowed squad bays held about twenty-five double-decker metal bunks. The room was big, roomy, and well lighted. The ensuing two months were the only period during my entire service in World War II that I lived in a barracks. The remaining time I slept under canvas or the open sky.

No one yelled at us or screamed orders to hurry up. The NCOs seemed relaxed to the point of being lethargic. We had the free run of the camp except for certain restricted areas. Taps and lights out were at 2200. We were like birds out of a cage after the confinement and harassment of boot camp. With several boys who bunked near me, I sampled the draught beer at the slop chute (enlisted men's club), bought candy and ice cream at the PX (post exchange), and explored the area. Our newly found freedom was heady stuff.

We spent the first few days at Camp Elliott at lectures and demonstrations dealing with the various weapons in a Marine infantry regiment. We received an introduction to the 37mm antitank gun, 81mm mortar, 60mm mortar, .50 caliber machine gun, .30 caliber heavy and light machine guns, and the Browning Automatic Rifle (BAR). We also ran through combat tactics for the rifle squad. Most of our conversation around the barracks concerned the various weapons and whether or not it would be "good duty" to be on a 37mm gun crew, light machine gun or 81mm mortar. There was always one man, frequently—in fact, usually—a New Englander who knew it all and claimed to have the latest hot dope on everything.

"I talked to a guy over at the PX who had been through 81mm mortar school, and he said them damn mortars are so heavy he wished to hell he had gotten into 37mm guns so he could ride in a jeep while it pulled the gun."

"I talked to a guy over at Camp Pendleton, and he said a mortar shell blew up over there just as it was fired and killed the instructor and all the crew. I'm getting into light machine guns; they say that's a good deal."

"Like hell. My uncle was in France in World War I, and he said the average life of a machine gunner was about two minutes. I'm gonna be a rifleman, so I won't have to tote all that weight around."

So it went. None of us had the slightest idea what he was talking about.

One day we fell in and were told to separate into groups according to which weapon we wanted to train with. If our first choice was filled, we made a second selection. The mere fact that we had a choice amazed me. Apparently the idea was that a man would be more effective on a weapon he had picked rather than one to which he had been assigned. I chose 60mm mortars.

The first morning, those in 60mm mortars marched behind a warehouse where several light tanks were parked. Our mortar instructor, a sergeant, told us to sit down and listen to what he had to say. He was a clean-cut, handsome blond man wearing neat khakis faded to just that right shade that indicated a "salty" uniform. His bearing oozed calm self-confidence. There was no arrogance or bluster about him, yet he was obviously a man who knew himself and his job and would put up with no nonsense from anybody. He had an intangible air of subdued, quiet detachment, a quality possessed by so many of the combat veterans of the Pacific campaigns whom I met at that time. Sometimes his mind seemed a million miles away, as though lost in some sort of melancholy reverie. It was a genuine attribute, unrehearsed and spontaneous. In short, it couldn't be imitated consciously. I noted this carefully in my early days in the Marine Corps but never understood it until I observed the same thing in my buddies after Peleliu.

One man raised his hand, and the sergeant said, "OK, what's your question?"

The man began with, "Sir." The sergeant laughed and said, "Address me as sergeant, not sir."

"Yes, sir."

"Look, you guys are U.S. Marines now. You are not in boot camp anymore. Just relax, work hard, and do your job right, and you won't have any trouble. You'll have a better chance of getting through the war." He won our respect and admiration instantly.

"My job is to train you people to be 60mm mortarmen. The 60mm mortar is an effective and important infantry weapon. You can break up enemy attacks on your company's front with this weapon, and you can soften enemy defenses with it. You will be firing over the heads of your own buddies at the enemy a short distance away, so you've got to know exactly what you're doing. Otherwise there'll be short rounds and you'll kill and wound your own men. I was a 60mm mortarman on Guadalcanal and saw how effective this weapon was against the Japs there. Any questions?"

On the chilly January morning of our first lesson in mortars, we sat on the deck under a bright sky and listened attentively to our instructor.

"The 60mm mortar is a smoothbore, muzzle-loaded, high-angle-fire weapon. The assembled gun weighs approximately forty-five pounds and consists of the tube—or barrel—bipod, and base plate. Two or sometimes three 60mm mortars are in each rifle company. Mortars have a high angle of fire and are particularly effective against enemy troops taking cover in defilades or behind ridges where they are protected from our artillery. The Japs have mortars and know how to use 'em, too. They will be particularly anxious to knock out our mortars and machine guns because of the damage these weapons can inflict on their troops."

The sergeant then went over the nomenclature of the gun. He demonstrated the movements of gun drill, during which the bipod was unstrapped and unfolded from carrying position, the base plate set firmly on the deck, the bipod leg spikes pressed into the deck, and the sight snapped into place on the gun. We were divided into five-man squads and practiced these evolutions until each man could perform them smoothly. During subsequent lessons he instructed us in the intricacies of the sight with its cross-level and longitudinal-level bubbles and on how to lay the gun and sight it on an aiming stake lined up with a target. We spent hours learning how to take a compass reading on a target area, then place a stake in front of the gun to correspond to that reading.

Each squad competed fiercely to be the fastest and most precise in gun drill. When my turn came to act as number one gunner, I would race to the position, unsling the mortar from my right shoulder, set it up, sight in on the base stake, remove my hands from it and yell, "Ready." The sergeant would check his stopwatch and give the time. Many shouts of encouragement came from a gunner's squad urging each man on. Each of us rotated as number one gunner, as number two gunner (who dropped the shells into the tube at number one's command), and as ammo carriers.

We were drilled thoroughly but were quite nervous about handling live ammunition for the first time. We fired at empty oil drums set on a dry hillside. There were no mishaps. When I saw the first shell burst with a dull *bang* about two hundred yards out on the range, I suddenly realized what a deadly weapon we were dealing with. A cloud of black smoke appeared at the point of impact. Flying steel fragments kicked up little puffs of dust all around an area about nine by eighteen yards. When three shells were fired from one weapon, the bursts covered an area about thirty-five by thirty-five yards with flying fragments.

"Boy, I'd pity any Jap that had all that shrapnel flying around him," murmured one of my more thoughtful buddies.

"Yeah, it'll tear their asses up all right. But don't forget they're gonna be throwing stuff at you just as fast as they can," said the mortar sergeant.

This, I realized, was the difference between war and hunting. When I survived the former, I gave up the latter.

We also received training in hand-to-hand combat. This consisted mostly of judo and knife fighting. To impress us with the effectiveness of his subject, the judo instructor methodically slammed each of us to the ground as we tried to rush him.

"What good is this kind of fighting gonna do us if the Japs can pick us off with machine guns and artillery at five hundred yards?" someone asked.

"When dark comes in the Pacific," the instructor replied, "the Japs always send men into our positions to try to infiltrate the lines or just to see how many American throats they can slit. They are tough and they like close-in fighting. You can handle them, but you've got to know how." Needless to say, we paid close attention from then on.

"Don't hesitate to fight the Japs dirty. Most Americans, from the time they are kids, are taught not to hit below the belt. It's not sportsmanlike. Well, nobody has taught the Japs that, and war ain't sport. Kick him in the balls before he kicks you in yours," growled our instructor.

We were introduced to the Marine's foxhole companion, the Ka-Bar knife. This deadly piece of cutlery was manufactured by the company bearing its name. The knife was a foot long with a seven-inch-long by one-and-a-half-inch-wide blade. The five-inch handle was made of leather washers packed together and had "USMC" stamped on the blade side of the upper hand guard. Light for its size, the knife was beautifully balanced.

"Everybody has heard a lot about all those kinds of fancy fighting knives that are, or should be, carried by infantry troops: throwing knives, stilettos, daggers, and all that stuff. Most of it is nothing but bull. Sure, you'll probably open more cans of C rations than Japs with this knife, but if a Jap ever jumps in your hole, you're better off with a Ka-Bar than any other knife. It's the very best and it's rugged, too. If you guys were gonna fight Germans, I'd guess you'd never need a fighting knife, but with the Japs it's different. I guarantee that you or the man in the next foxhole will use a Ka-Bar on a Jap infiltrator before the war is over." He was right.*

All of our instructors at Camp Elliott did a professional job. They presented us with the material and made it clear that our chances of surviving the war depended to a great extent on how well we learned. As teachers they had no problem with student motivation.

But I don't recall that anyone really comprehended what was happening outside our own training routine. Maybe it was the naive optimism of youth, but the awesome reality that we were training to be cannon fodder in a global war that had already

---

*The U.S. Marine Corps still uses Ka-Bar's fine fighting knife. The manufacturer's name now has become to Marines a noun (*kabar*) meaning their fighting knife.

snuffed out millions of lives never seemed to occur to us. The fact that our lives might end violently or that we might be crippled while we were still boys didn't seem to register. The only thing that we seemed to be truly concerned about was that we might be too afraid to do our jobs under fire. An apprehension nagged at each of us that he might appear to be "yellow" if he were afraid.

One afternoon two veterans of the Bougainville campaign dropped into my barracks to chat with some of us. They had been members of the Marine raider battalion that had fought so well along with the 3d Marine Division on Bougainville. They were the first veterans we had met other than our instructors. We swamped them with questions.

"Were you scared?" asked one of my buddies.

"Scared! Are you kiddin? I was so goddamn scared the first time I heard slugs coming at me I could hardly hold onto my rifle," came the reply.

The other veteran said, "Listen, mate, everybody gets scared, and anybody says he don't is a damn liar." We felt better.

The mortar school continued during my entire stay at Camp Elliott. Swimming tests were the last phase of special training we received before embarking for the Pacific. Mercifully, in January 1944 we couldn't foresee the events of autumn. We trained with enthusiasm and the faith that the battles we were destined to fight would be necessary to win the war.

Earlier, on 20–23 November 1943, the 2d Marine Division carried out its memorable assault on the coral atoll of Tarawa in the Gilbert Islands. Many military historians and others consider the battle for Tarawa as the first modern head-on amphibious assault.

A coral reef extended out about five hundred yards and surrounded the atoll. Tarawa was subject to unpredictable dodging tides that sometimes lowered water levels and caused Higgins boats (LCVP: Landing Craft, Vehicle and Personnel) to strand on the reef.

Plans called for the use of amphibian tractors (LVTs: Landing Vehicles, Tracked; now called assault amphibians) to carry the troops across the reef. But only enough amtracs existed to take in the first three waves. After the first three assault waves got

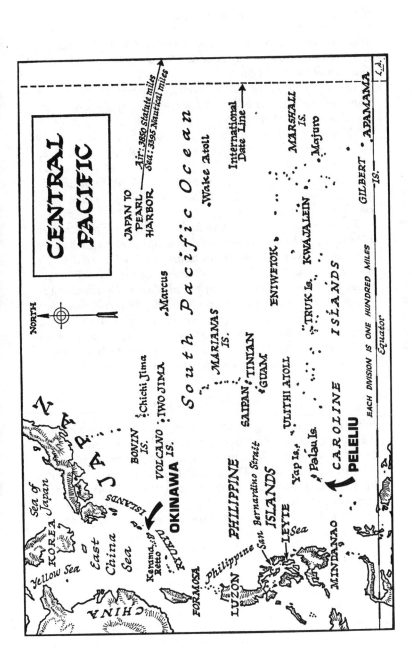

ashore in amtracs, the supporting waves had to wade across the reef through murderous Japanese fire, because their Higgins boats hung up at the reef's edge.

The 2d Division suffered terrible losses—3,381 dead and wounded. Its Marines killed all but seventeen of the 4,836 Japanese defenders of the tiny atoll.

There was loud and severe criticism of the Marine Corps by the American public and some military leaders because of the number of casualties. Tarawa became a household word in the United States. It took its rightful place with Valley Forge, the Alamo, Belleau Wood, and Guadalcanal as a symbol of American courage and sacrifice.

The young Marines at Camp Elliott didn't have the remotest idea that in about nine months they would participate as part of the 1st Marine Division in the assault on Peleliu. That battle would prove to be so vicious and costly that the division's losses would just about double those of the 2d Marine Division at Tarawa. To add tragedy to its horror, hindsight would show that the seizure of Peleliu was of questionable necessity. As more than one Marine historian has said, it's unfortunate to the memory of the men who fought and died on Peleliu that it remains one of the lesser known and poorly understood battles of World War II.

OVERSEAS AT LAST

Early on the morning of 28 February 1944, the men of the 46th Replacement Battalion got off trucks at dockside in San Diego Harbor and lined up to board a troopship that would take us to the Pacific. The *President Polk* had been a luxury liner of the President Line during peacetime. Painted battleship gray, the ship now looked gloomy and ominous with its antiaircraft guns and life rafts. I had the uneasy feeling that this was going to be a one-way trip for some of us.

Loaded down with full transport pack, bed roll (mattress with canvas cover), M1 carbine, and helmet, I struggled up a steep gangplank. Once on deck we went into our troop compartment one deck below. A blast of hot, foul air hit me as I entered the hatch and started down the ladder. About halfway down, the man in front of me slipped and clattered to the bottom. We were all concerned about his fall and helped him up and into his gear again. Later such an incident would elicit almost nothing but a casual glance and a quick helping hand.

We stood crowded in the compartment and waited for what seemed like hours for an officer to check the muster roll and assign each of us to a sack or rack (bunk). Each sack consisted of canvas laced onto a pipe frame hinged to metal uprights, head and foot, extending from deck to the overhead. Chains held each rack onto the ones above and below.

When I crawled onto mine, I realized the rack above was only about two feet away. With mattress unrolled and gear laid out, a man barely had room to stretch out. I had to climb up about four racks to get to mine, which was almost at the highest level.

Dim electric bulbs overhead gave us barely enough light to see. As soon as I could, I went topside searching for relief from the foul, crowded compartment. The deck was jammed, too, but the air was fresh.

Many of us were too excited to sleep, so we explored the ship for hours, talked to the crewmen, or watched the completion of loading. Finally, around midnight, I went below and climbed into my rack. Several hours later I awoke to the vibration of the ship's engine. I pulled on my boondockers and dungaree pants and jacket and raced topside, filled with apprehension and excitement. It was about 0500. The deck was crowded with other Marines subdued by the realization that each turn of the ship's screws would take us farther from home and closer to the unknown.

Harsh questions raced through my mind. Would I ever see my family again? Would I do my duty or be a coward? Could I kill? Fantasy captivated me in the brief period. Maybe I'd be put into a rear-echelon outfit and never see a Japanese. Maybe I'd be an infantryman and disgrace my outfit by running away from the enemy. Or, maybe I'd kill dozens of Japanese and win a Navy Cross or Silver Star and be a national hero.

The tension finally broke as we watched the sailors rushing about casting off hawsers and lines, preparing the ship for the open sea.

The *President Polk* moved on a zigzag course toward a destination unknown to those of us sweltering in her bowels. Our daily routine was dull, even for those like myself who rather enjoyed being aboard a ship. We rolled out of our racks each morning about sunrise. Brushing my teeth and shaving with nonlathering shaving cream was my morning toilet. Each day an officer or NCO led us through an exercise period of calisthenics. And we could always count on a rifle inspection. Other than that, we had practically no duties.

Every few days we had abandon-ship drills, which helped offset the boredom. And the ship's crew conducted gun drills frequently. The first time they held target practice with live ammunition was exciting to watch. Yellow balloons were released from the bridge. As they were caught by the wind, the gunners opened fire upon order from the fire control officer. The rapid-fire 20mm and 40mm antiaircraft guns seemed to do an effective job. But to some of us Marines, the 3-inch and 5-inch cannons didn't accomplish much other than hurt our ears. Considering the number of balloons that escaped, we felt the gun crews should have practiced more. This was probably because none of us had ever had any experience with antiaircraft guns and didn't realize what a difficult type of gunnery was involved.

Beyond some letter writing and a lot of conversation—so-called bull sessions—we spent much of our time waiting in chow lines strung along gangways and passages leading to the ship's galley. Chow was an unforgettable experience. After the inevitable wait in line, I entered the hatch leading to the galley and was met with a blast of hot air laden with a new set of odors differing only slightly from the typical troop compartment aroma. To the same basic ingredients (paint, grease, tobacco, and sweat) were added the smells of rancid cooking and something of a bakery. It was enough to turn a civilian's stomach inside out, but we rapidly and necessarily adjusted.

We moved along the cafeteria-style line and indicated to sweating navy messmen what foods we wanted served onto shining compartmentalized steel trays. The messmen wore skivvy shirts and were tattooed profusely on their arms. They all mopped the sweat from their faces constantly. Amid the roar of ventilators, we ate standing at long folding tables. Everything was hot to the touch but quite clean. A sailor told me that the tables had been used as operating tables for Marine casualties that the ship took on during one of the earlier Pacific campaigns. That gave me a strange feeling in the pit of my stomach every time I went to chow on the *President Polk*.

The heat was intense—at least 100 degrees—but I gulped down a cup of hot "joe" (black coffee), the stuff that replaced bread as the staff of life for Marines and sailors. I grimaced as the dehydrated potatoes battered my taste buds with an unsavory aftertaste characteristic of all World War II–vintage dehydrated foods. The bread was a shock—heavy, and with a flavor that was a combination of bitterness, sweetness, and uncooked flour. No wonder hot joe had replaced it as the staff of life!

After chow in the steaming galley, we went topside to cool off. Everyone was soaked with sweat. It would have been a relief to eat on deck, but we were forbidden to take chow out of the galley.

One day, as we moved along some nameless companionway in a chow line, I passed a porthole that gave me a view into the officers' mess. There I saw Navy and Marine officers clad neatly in starched khakis sitting at tables in a well-ventilated room. White-coated waiters served them pie and ice cream. As we inched along the hot companionway to our steaming joe and dehydrated fare, I wondered if my haste to leave the V-12 college life hadn't been a mistake. After all, it would have been nice to have been declared a gentleman by Congress and to have lived like a human being aboard ship. To my immense satisfaction, however, I discovered later that such niceties and privileges of rank were few on the front lines.

During the morning of 17 March we looked out across the bow and saw a line of white breakers on the horizon. The Great Barrier Reef extends for thousands of miles, and we were to pass through it to New Caledonia. As we neared the reef, we saw several hulks of wooden ships stranded high and dry, apparently blown there years ago by some storm.

As we closed on the harbor of Noumea, we saw a small motor launch head our way. The *Polk* signaled with flags and blinker lights to this pilot boat, which soon pulled alongside. The pilot climbed a ladder and boarded the ship. All sorts of nautical protocol and mutual greetings between him and the ship's officers ensued as he went to the bridge to guide us in. This man was a middle-aged, pleasant-looking civilian dressed in a neat white Panama suit, straw hat, and black tie. Surrounded by sailors in blue denim and ship's officers in khaki, he looked like a fictional character out of some long-forgotten era.

The blue water of the Pacific turned to green as we passed into the channel leading into the harbor of Noumea. There was a pretty white lighthouse near the harbor. White houses with tile roofs nestled around it and up the base of slopes of high mountains. The scene reminded me of a photo of some picturesque little Mediterranean seaport.

The *President Polk* moved slowly through the harbor as the speaker system ordered a special sea detail to stand by. We tied up to a dock with long warehouses where United States military personnel were moving crates and equipment. Most of the shipping I saw was U.S. Navy, but there also were some American and foreign merchant freighters along with a few quaint-looking civilian fishing boats.

The first Pacific native I saw wasn't dressed in a hula skirt or waving a spear but nonchalantly driving a freight-moving tractor on the dock. He was a short muscular man—black as ink —clad only in a loin cloth with a bone in his nose and a bushy head of kinky hair like a Fuzzy Wuzzy out of a Kipling story. The incredible thing about this hair was its color, beautiful amber. A sailor explained that the natives were fond of bleaching their hair with blueing they got from Americans in exchange for seashells. Bone in the nose notwithstanding, the man was an admirable tractor driver.

NEW CALEDONIA

After weeks at sea, cramped into a troopship, we were relieved to move onto land again. We piled into Marine Corps trucks and drove through the main section of Noumea. I was delighted to see the old French architecture, which reminded me of the older sections of Mobile and New Orleans.

The trucks sped along a winding road with mountains on each side. We saw small farms and a large nickel mine in the valley. Some of the land was cleared, but thick jungle covered much of the low areas. Although the weather was pleasant and cool, the palms and other growth attested to the tropical climate. After several miles we turned into Camp Saint Louis, where we would undergo further training before being sent "up north" to the combat zone as replacements.

Camp Saint Louis was a tent camp comprised of rows of tents and dirt streets. We were assigned to tents, stowed our gear, and fell in for chow. The galley rested on a hill just past the camp's brig. In full view were two wire cages about the size of phone booths. We were told that those who caused trouble were locked in there, and a high-pressure fire hose was turned on them periodically. The strictness of discipline at Camp Saint Louis caused me to assume the explanation of the cages was true. In any event, I resolved to stay out of trouble.

Our training consisted of lectures and field exercises. Combat veteran officers and NCOs lectured on Japanese weapons, tactics, and combat methods. Most of the training was thorough and emphasized individual attention. We worked in groups of ten or twelve.

I usually was placed in a squad instructed by a big redheaded corporal who had been in a Marine raider battalion during the fighting in the Solomon Islands. Big Red was good-natured but tough as nails. He worked us hard. One day he took us to a small rifle range and taught us how to fire a Japanese pistol, rifle, and heavy and light machine guns. After firing a few rounds from each, Red put about five of us into a pit about five feet deep with a one-foot embankment in front and the steep slope of a ridge behind as a backstop.

"One important thing you must learn fast to survive is exactly what enemy fire sounds like coming at you and what kind of weapon it is. Now when I blow this whistle, get down and stay down until you hear the whistle again. If you get up before the signal, you'll get your head blowed off, and the folks back home will get your insurance."

Red blew the whistle and we got down. He announced each type of Japanese weapon and fired several rounds from it over our hole into the bank. Then he and his assistants fired them all together for about fifteen seconds. It seemed a lot longer. The bullets popped and snapped as they went over. Several machine-gun tracers didn't embed in the bank but bounced off and rolled—white-hot, sizzling, and sputtering—into the hole. We cringed and shifted about, but no one got burned.

This was one of the most valuable training exercises we underwent. There were instances later on Peleliu and Okinawa which it prepared me to come through unscathed.

A salty sergeant conducted bayonet training. He had been written about in a national magazine because he was so outstanding. On the cinder-covered street of an old raider camp, I witnessed some amazing feats by him. He instructed us in how to defend ourselves barehanded against an opponent's bayonet thrust.

"Here's how it's done," he said.

He picked me out of the squad and told me to charge him and thrust the point of my bayonet at his chest when I thought I could stick him. I got a mental image of myself behind bars at Mare Island Naval Prison for bayoneting an instructor, so I veered off just before making my thrust.

"What the hell's the matter with you? Don't you know how to use a bayonet?"

"But, Sarge, if I stick you, they'll put me in Mare Island."

"There's less chance of you bayoneting me than of me whipping your ass for not following my orders."

"OK," I thought to myself, "if that's the way you feel about it, we have witnesses."

So I headed for him on the double and thrust at his chest. He sidestepped neatly, grabbed my rifle behind the front sight, and jerked it in the direction I was running. I held onto the rifle and tumbled onto the cinders. The squad roared with laughter. Someone yelled, "Did you bayonet him, Sledgehammer?" I got up looking sheepish.

"Knock it off, wise guy," said the instructor. "You step up here, and let's see what you can do, big mouth."

My buddy lifted his rifle confidently, charged, and ended up on the cinders, too. The instructor made each man charge him in turn. He threw them all.

He then took up a Japanese Arisaka rifle with fixed bayonet and showed us how the Japanese soldiers used the hooked hand guard to lock onto the U.S. blade. Then, with a slight twist of his wrist, he could wrench the MI rifle out of the opponent's hands and disarm him. He coached us carefully to hold the M1 on its side with the left side of the blade toward the deck instead of the cutting edge, as we had been taught in the States. This way, as we parried a Japanese's blade, he couldn't lock ours.

We went on long hikes and forced marches through the jungles, swamps, and over endless steep hills. We made countless practice landings from Higgins boats on small islets off the coast. Each morning after chow we marched out of camp equipped with rifles, cartridge belts, two canteens of water, combat pack, helmet, and K rations. Our usual pace was a rapid route step for fifty minutes with a ten-minute rest. But the officers and NCOs always hurried us and frequently deleted the ten-minute rest.

When trucks drove along the road, we moved onto the sides, as columns of infantry have done since early times. The trucks frequently carried army troops, and we barked and yapped like dogs and kidded them about being dogfaces. During one of these encounters, a soldier hanging out of a truck just ahead of me shouted, "Hey, soldier. You look tired and hot, soldier. Why don't you make the army issue you a truck like me?"

I grinned and yelled, "Go to hell."

His buddy grabbed him by the shoulder and yelled, "Stop calling that guy soldier. He's a Marine. Can't you see his emblem? He's not in the army. Don't insult him."

"Thanks," I yelled. That was my first encounter with men who had no esprit. We might grumble to each other about our officers or the chow or the Marine Corps in general, but it was rather like grumbling about one's own family—always with another member. If an outsider tried to get into the discussion, a fight resulted.

One night during exercises in defense against enemy infiltration, some of the boys located the bivouac of Big Red and the other instructors who were supposed to be the infiltrators and stole their boondockers. When the time came for their offense to commence, they threw a few concussion grenades around and yelled like Japanese but didn't slip out and capture any of us. When the officers realized what had happened, they reamed out the instructors for being too sure of themselves.

The instructors had a big fire built in a ravine. We sat around it, drank coffee, ate K rations, and sang some songs. It didn't seem like such a bad war so far.

All of our training was in rifle tactics. We spent no time on heavy weapons (mortars and machine guns), because when we went "up north" our unit commander would assign us where needed. That might not be in our specialties. As a result of the field exercises and obstacle course work, we reached a high level of physical fitness and endurance.

During the last week of May we learned that the 46th Replacement Battalion would go north in a few days. We packed our gear and boarded the USS *General Howze* on 28 May 1944. This ship was quite different from the *President Polk*. It was much newer and apparently had been constructed as a troopship. It was freshly painted throughout and spic and span. With only about a dozen other men, I was assigned to a small, well-ventilated compartment on the main deck, a far cry from the cavernous, stinking hole I bunked in on the *Polk*. The *General Howze* had a library from which troop passengers could get books and magazines. We also received our first atabrine tablets. These small, bitter, bright yellow pills prevented malaria. We took one a day.

On 2 June the *General Howze* approached the Russell Islands and moved into an inlet bordered by large groves of coconut palms. The symmetrical groves and clear water were beautiful. From the ship we could see coral-covered roadways and groups of pyramidal tents among the coconut palms. This was Pavuvu, home of the 1st Marine Division.

We learned we would debark the next morning, so we spent our time hanging over the rail, talking to a few Marines on the pier. Their friendliness and unassuming manner struck me. Although clad neatly in khakis or dungarees, they appeared hollow-eyed and tired. They made no attempt to impress us green replacements, yet they were members of an elite division known to nearly everybody back home because of its conquest of Guadalcanal and more recent campaign at Cape Gloucester on New Britain. They had left Gloucester about 1 May. Thus, they had been on Pavuvu about a month.

Many of us slept little during the night. We checked and rechecked our gear, making sure everything was squared away.

The weather was hot, much more so than at New Caledonia. I went out on deck and slept in the open air. With a mandolin and an old violin, two of our Marines struck up some of the finest mountain music I'd ever heard. They played and sang folk songs and ballads most of the night. We thought it was mighty wonderful music.

WITH THE OLD BREED

About 0900 the morning of 3 June 1944, carrying the usual mountain of gear, I trudged down the gangplank of the *General Howze*. As we moved to waiting trucks, we passed a line of veterans waiting to go aboard for the voyage home. They carried only packs and personal gear, no weapons. Some said they were glad to see us, because we were their replacements. They looked tanned and tired but relieved to be headed home. For them the war was over. For us, it was just beginning.

In a large parking area paved with crushed coral, a lieutenant called out our names and counted us off into groups. To my group of a hundred or more he said, "Third Battalion, Fifth Marines."

If I had had an option—and there was none, of course—as to which of the five Marine divisions I served with, it would have been the 1st Marine Division. Ultimately, the Marine Corps had six divisions that fought with distinction in the Pacific. But the 1st Marine Division was, in many ways, unique. It had participated in the opening American offensive against the Japanese at Guadalcanal and already had fought a second major battle at Cape Gloucester, north of the Solomon Islands. Now its troops were resting, preparing for a third campaign in the Palau Islands.

Of regiments, I would have chosen the 5th Marines. I knew about its impressive history as a part of the 1st Marine Division, but I also knew that its record went back to France in World War I. Other Marines I knew in other divisions were proud of their units and of being Marines, as well they should have been. But the 5th Marines and the 1st Marine Division carried not only the traditions of the Corps but had traditions and a heritage of their own, a link through time with the "Old Corps."

The fact that I was assigned to the very regiment and division I would have chosen was a matter of pure chance. I felt as though I had rolled the dice and won.*

The trucks drove along winding coral roads by the bay and through coconut groves. We stopped and unloaded our gear near a sign that said "3rd Bn., 5th Marines." An NCO assigned me to Company K. Soon a lieutenant came along and took aside the fifteen or so men who had received crew-served weapons training (mortars and machine guns) in the States. He asked each of us which weapon he wanted to be assigned to in the company. I asked for 60mm mortars and tried to look too small to carry a seventy-pound flamethrower. He assigned me to mortars, and I moved my gear into a tent that housed the second squad of the 60mm mortar section.

For the next several weeks I spent most of my time during the day on work parties building up the camp. The top sergeant of Company K, 1st Sergeant Malone, would come down the company street shouting, "All new men outside for a work party, on the double." Most of the time the company's veterans weren't included. Pavuvu was supposed to be a rest camp for them after the long, wet, debilitating jungle campaign on Cape Gloucester. When Malone needed a large work party he would call out, "I need every available man." So we referred to him as "Available" Malone.

None of us, old hands or replacements, could fathom why the division command chose Pavuvu. Only after the war did I find out that the leaders were trying to avoid the kind of situation the 3d Marine Division endured when it went into

---

*The history of the 5th Marines continued after World War II. The regiment fought in the Korean War and again in Vietnam. Thus it is the only Marine regiment to have fought in all of the nation's major wars in this century.

No Marine division fought in World War I. [The 5th and 6th Marine Regiments fought in France as part of the 2d Division (Regular) American Expeditionary Force (AEF), a mixed unit of Marine and Army brigades.] But the 1st Marine Division was the only Marine division to fight in Korea. Along with the 3d Marine Division, it also fought in Vietnam. It is, therefore, the sole Marine division to have fought in all of our major wars during the past sixty years.

Today the 5th Marines still forms a part of the 1st Marine Division. Stationed on the west coast, the division can deploy units for duty in the western Pacific.

camp on Guadalcanal after its campaign on Bougainville. Facilities on Guadalcanal, by then a large rear-area base, were reasonably good, but the high command ordered the 3d Division to furnish about a thousand men each day for working parties all over the island. Not only did the Bougainville veterans get little or no rest, but when replacements came, the division had difficulty carrying out its training schedule in preparation for the next campaign, Guam.

If Pavuvu seemed something less than a tropical paradise to us replacements fresh from the States and New Caledonia, it was a bitter shock to the Gloucester veterans.* When ships entered Macquitti Bay, as the *General Howze* had, Pavuvu looked picturesque. But once ashore, one found the extensive coconut groves choked with rotting coconuts. The apparently solid ground was soft and turned quickly to mud when subjected to foot or vehicular traffic.

Pavuvu was the classical embodiment of the Marine term "boondocks." It was impossible to explain after the war what life on Pavuvu was like. Most of the griping about being "rock happy" and bored in the Pacific came from men stationed at the big rear-echelon bases like Hawaii or New Caledonia. Among their main complaints were that the ice cream wasn't good, the beer not cold enough, or the USO shows too infrequent. But on Pavuvu, simply living was difficult.

For example, most of the work parties I went on in June and July were pick-and-shovel details to improve drainage or pave walkways with crushed coral, just to get us out of the water. Regulations called for wooden decks in all tents, but I never saw one on Pavuvu.

Of all the work parties, the one we hated most was collecting rotten coconuts. We loaded them onto trucks to be dumped into a swamp. If we were lucky, the coconut sprout served as a handle. But more often, the thing fell apart, spilling stinking coconut milk over us.

---

*After Guadalcanal, the 1st Marine Division went to Melbourne, Australia, for rest and refitting for the New Britain campaign. When Cape Gloucester ended, the men assumed they were headed back to Australia. Instead they were dumped on a deserted island in the Russell Islands group, sixty miles from Guadalcanal.

We made sardonic, absurd jokes about the vital, essential, classified work we were doing for the war effort and about the profundity and wisdom of the orders we received. In short, we were becoming "Asiatic," a Marine Corps term denoting a singular type of eccentric behavior characteristic of men who had served too long in the Far East. I had done a good deal of complaining about Pavuvu's chow and general conditions during my first week there; one of the veterans in our company, who later became a close friend, told me in a restrained but matter-of-fact way that, until I had been in combat, there was really nothing to complain about. Things could be a good deal worse, he said, and advised me to shut up and quit whining. He shamed me thoroughly. But for the first weeks on Pavuvu, the stench of rotting coconuts permeated the air. We could even taste it in the drinking water. I'm still repulsed even today by the smell of fresh coconut.

The most loathsome vermin on Pavuvu were the land crabs. Their blue-black bodies were about the size of the palm of a man's hand, and bristles and spines covered their legs. These ugly creatures hid by day and roamed at night. Before putting on his boondockers each morning, every man in the 1st Marine Division shook his shoes to roust the land crabs. Many mornings I had one in each shoe and sometimes two. Periodically we reached the point of rage over these filthy things and chased them out from under boxes, seabags, and cots. We killed them with sticks, bayonets, and entrenching tools. After the action was over, we had to shovel them up and bury them, or a nauseating stench developed rapidly in the hot, humid air.

Each battalion had its own galley, but chow on Pavuvu consisted mainly of heated C rations: dehydrated eggs, dehydrated potatoes, and that detestable canned meat called Spam. The synthetic lemonade, so-called battery acid, that remained after chow was poured on the concrete slab deck of the galley to clean and bleach it. It did a nice job. As if hot C rations didn't get tedious week in and week out, we experienced a period of about four days when we were served oatmeal morning, noon, and night. Scuttlebutt was that the ship carrying our supplies had been sunk. Whatever the cause, our only relief from monotonous chow was tidbits in packages from home. The bread made by our bakers was so heavy that when you held a slice by one side, the rest of the slice broke away of its own weight. The flour was so massively infested with weevils that each slice of bread had more of the little beetles than there are seeds in a slice of rye bread. We became so inured to this sort of thing, however, that we ate the bread anyway; the wits said, "It's a good deal. Them beetles give you more meat in your diet."

We had no bathing facilities at first. Shaving each morning with a helmet full of water was simple enough, but a bath was another matter. Each afternoon when the inevitable tropical downpour commenced, we stripped and dashed into the company street, soap in hand. The trick was to lather, scrub, and rinse before the rain stopped. The weather was so capricious that the duration of a shower was impossible to estimate. Each downpour ended as abruptly as it had begun and never failed to leave at least one or more fully lathered, cursing Marines with no rinse water.

Morning sick call was another bizarre sight during the early days on Pavuvu. The Gloucester veterans were in poor physical condition after the wettest campaign in World War II, during which men endured soakings for weeks on end. When I first joined the company, I was appalled at their condition: most were thin, some emaciated, with jungle rot in their armpits and on their ankles and wrists. At sick call they paired off with a bottle of gentian violet and cotton swabs, stood naked in the grove, and painted each other's sores. So many of them needed attention that they had to treat each other under a doctor's supervision. Some had to cut their boondockers into sandals, because their feet were so infected with rot they could hardly walk. Needless to say, Pavuvu's hot, humid climate prolonged the healing process.

"I think the Marine Corps has forgotten where Pavuvu is," one man said.

"I think God has forgotten where Pavuvu is," came a reply.

"God couldn't forget because he made everything."

"Then I bet he wishes he could forget he made Pavuvu."

This exchange indicates the feeling of remoteness and desolation we felt on Pavuvu. On the big island bases, men had the feeling of activity around their units and contact through air and sea traffic with other bases and with the States. On Pavuvu

we felt as though we were a million miles from not only home
but from anything else that bespoke of civilization.

I believe we took in stride all of Pavuvu's discomforts and
frustrations for two reasons. First, the division was an elite
combat unit. Discipline was stern. Our esprit de corps ran
high. Each man knew what to do and what was expected of
him. All did their duty well, even while grumbling.

NCOs answered our complaining with, "Beat your gums.
It's healthy." Or, "Whatta ya griping for? You volunteered for
the Marine Corps, didn't ya? You're just gettin' what ya asked
for."

No matter how irritating or uncomfortable things were on
Pavuvu, things could always be worse. After all, there were no
Japanese, no bursting shells, no snapping and whining bullets.
And we slept on cots. Second, make-up of the division was
young: about 80 percent were between the ages of eighteen
and twenty-five; about half were under twenty-one when they
came overseas. Well-disciplined young men can put up with
a lot even though they don't like it; and we were a bunch of
high-spirited boys proud of our unit.

But we had another motivating factor, as well: a passionate
hatred for the Japanese burned through all Marines I knew.
The fate of the Goettge patrol was the sort of thing that
spawned such hatred.* One day as we piled stinking coconuts,
a veteran Marine walked past and exchanged greetings with
a couple of our "old men." One of our group asked us if we
knew who he was.

"No, I never saw him," someone said.

"He's one of the three guys who escaped when the Goettge
patrol got wiped out on Guadalcanal. He was lucky as hell."

"Why did the Japs ambush that patrol?" I asked naively.

---

*During the first week of the Guadalcanal campaign, the Marines captured
a Japanese soldier who claimed some of his starving comrades west of the
Matanikau River would surrender if the Marines would "liberate" them.
With twenty-five picked men (scouts, intelligence specialists, a surgeon, and
a linguist) from the division's headquarters and the 5th Marines, Col. Frank
Goettge—the division's intelligence officer—went on a mission more human-
itarian than military. The Japanese ambushed the patrol as it debarked from
landing craft in the darkness. Only three Marines escaped.

A veteran looked at me with unbelief and said slowly and emphatically, "Because they're the meanest sonsabitches that ever lived."

The Goettge patrol incident plus such Japanese tactics as playing dead and then throwing a grenade—or playing wounded, calling for a corpsman, and then knifing the medic when he came —plus the sneak attack on Pearl Harbor, caused Marines to hate the Japanese intensely and to be reluctant to take prisoners.

The attitudes held toward the Japanese by noncombatants or even sailors or airmen often did not reflect the deep personal resentment felt by Marine infantrymen. Official histories and memoirs of Marine infantrymen written after the war rarely reflect that hatred. But at the time of battle, Marines felt it deeply, bitterly, and as certainly as danger itself. To deny this hatred or make light of it would be as much a lie as to deny or make light of the esprit de corps or the intense patriotism felt by the Marines with whom I served in the Pacific.

My experiences on Peleliu and Okinawa made me believe that the Japanese held mutual feelings for us. They were a fanatical enemy; that is to say, they believed in their cause with an intensity little understood by many postwar Americans—and possibly many Japanese, as well.

This collective attitude, Marine and Japanese, resulted in savage, ferocious fighting with no holds barred. This was not the dispassionate killing seen on other fronts or in other wars. This was a brutish, primitive hatred, as characteristic of the horror of war in the Pacific as the palm trees and the islands. To comprehend what the troops endured then and there, one must take into full account this aspect of the nature of the Marines' war.

Probably the biggest boost to our morale about this time on Pavuvu was the announcement that Bob Hope would come over from Banika and put on a show for us. Most of the men in the division crowded a big open area and cheered as a Piper Cub circled over us. The pilot switched off the engine briefly, while Jerry Colonna poked his head out of the plane and gave his famous yell, "Ye ow ow ow ow ow." We went wild with applause.

Bob Hope, Colonna, Frances Langford, and Patti Thomas put on a show on a little stage by the pier. Bob asked Jerry how he liked the trip over from Banika, and Jerry answered that it was "tough sledding." When asked why, he replied, "No snow." We thought it was the funniest thing we had ever heard. Patti gave several boys from the audience dancing lessons amid much grinning, cheering, and applause. Bob told many jokes and really boosted our spirits. It was the finest entertainment I ever saw overseas.*

Bob Hope's show remained the main topic of conversation as we got down to training in earnest for the coming campaign. Pavuvu was so small that most of our field exercises were of company size rather than battalion or regimental. Even so, we frequently got in the way of other units involved in their training exercises. It was funny to see a company move forward in combat formation through the groves and become intermingled with the rigid ranks of another company standing weapons inspection, the officers shouting orders to straighten things out.

We held numerous landing exercises—several times a week, it seemed—on the beaches and inlets around the island away from camp. We usually practiced from amtracs. The newest model had a tailgate that dropped as soon as the tractor was on the beach, allowing us to run out and deploy.

"Get off the beach fast. Get off the damned beach as fast as you can and move inland. The Nips are going to plaster it with everything they've got, so your chances are better the sooner you move inland," shouted our officers and NCOs. We heard this over and over day after day. During each landing exercise, we would scramble out of our tractors, move inland

---

*I renewed my acquaintance with Bob Hope last spring when he played in a charity golf tournament in Birmingham, Alabama. Earlier I had sent him copies of the *Marine Corps Gazette* (November and December 1979 and January 1980) that had serialized portions of my Peleliu story. He was enthusiastic about the account and remembered well the young Marines of the 1st Marine Division on Pavuvu. Despite a clamoring public on a hectic day in Birmingham, this most gracious man took the time to reminisce with me about the old breed.

about twenty-five yards, and then await orders to deploy and push forward.

The first wave of tractors landed rifle squads. The second wave landed more riflemen, machine gunners, bazooka gunners, flamethrowers, and 60mm mortar squads. Our second wave typically trailed about twenty-five yards behind the first as the machines churned through the water toward the beach. As soon as the first wave unloaded, its amtracs backed off, turned around, and headed past us out to sea to pick up supporting waves of infantry from Higgins boats circling offshore. It all worked nicely on Pavuvu. But there were no Japanese there.

In addition to landing exercises and field problems before Peleliu, we received refresher instructions and practice firing all small arms assigned to the company: M1 rifle, BAR, carbine, .45 caliber pistol, and Thompson submachine gun. We also learned how to operate a flamethrower.

During instruction with the flamethrower, we used a palm stump for a target. When my turn came, I shouldered the heavy tanks, held the nozzle in both hands, pointed at the stump about twenty-five yards away, and pressed the trigger. With a whoosh, a stream of red flame squirted out, and the nozzle bucked. The napalm hit the stump with a loud splattering noise. I felt the heat on my face. A cloud of black smoke rushed upward. The thought of turning loose hellfire from a hose nozzle as easily as I'd water a lawn back home sobered me. To shoot the enemy with bullets or kill him with shrapnel was one of the grim necessities of war, but to fry him to death was too gruesome to contemplate. I was to learn soon, however, that the Japanese couldn't be routed from their island defenses without it.

About this time I began to feel a deeper appreciation for the influence of the old breed on us newer Marines. Gunnery Sergeant Haney* provided a vivid example of their impact.

---

*Gunnery Sgt. Elmo M. Haney served with Company K, 3d Battalion, 5th Marines in France during World War I. Between the two world wars, he taught school in Arkansas for about four years, then rejoined the Marine Corps where he was assigned to his old unit. He fought on Guadalcanal and at Cape

I had seen Haney around the company area but first noticed him in the shower one day because of the way he bathed.
About a dozen naked, soapy replacements, including myself,
stared in wide-eyed amazement and shuddered as Haney held
his genitals in his left hand while scrubbing them with a GI
brush the way one buffs a shoe. When you consider that the
GI brush had stiff, tough, split-fiber bristles embedded in a
stout wooden handle and was designed to scrub heavy canvas
782 (web) gear, dungarees, and even floors, Haney's method
of bathing becomes truly impressive.

I first saw him exert his authority one day on a pistol range
where he was in charge of safety. A new second lieutenant, a
replacement like myself, was firing from the position I was to
assume. As he fired his last round, another new officer behind
me called to him. The lieutenant turned to answer with his
pistol in his hand. Haney was sitting next to me on a coconut-
log bench and hadn't uttered a word except for the usual firing range commands. When the lieutenant turned the pistol's
muzzle away from the target, Haney reacted like a cat leaping
on its prey. He scooped up a large handful of coral gravel and
flung it squarely into the lieutenant's face. He shook his fist at
the bewildered officer and gave him the worst bawling out I
ever heard. Everyone along the firing line froze, officers as well
as enlisted men. The offending officer, with his gold bars shining brightly on his collar, cleared his weapon, holstered it, and
took off rubbing his eyes and blushing visibly. Haney returned
to his seat as though nothing had happened. Along the firing
line, we thawed. Thereafter we were much more conscious of
safety regulations.

Haney was about my size, at 135 pounds, with sandy crew-
cut hair and a deep tan. He was lean, hard, and muscular.

Gloucester with Company K. In the latter action he won a Silver Star for heroism when he "took care of some Japs by himself with a few hand grenades,"
as one Marine described the scene.

Haney was more than fifty years old when the 1st Marine Division assaulted
Peleliu. Although a gunnery sergeant by rank, he held no official position in
Company K's chain of command. In the field he seemed to be everywhere
at once, correcting mistakes and helping out. He withdrew himself from the
front lines on the second day of Peleliu, admitting sadly that he could no longer take the heat and the battle.

Although not broad-shouldered or well-proportioned, his torso reminded me of some anatomy sketch by Michelangelo: every muscle stood out in stark definition. He was slightly barrel-chested with muscles heaped up on the back of his shoulders so that he almost had a hump. Neither his arms nor his legs were large, but the muscles in them reminded me of steel bands. His face was small-featured with squinting eyes and looked as though it was covered with deeply tanned, wrinkled leather.

Haney was the only man I ever knew in the outfit who didn't seem to have a buddy. He wasn't a loner in the sense that he was sullen or unfriendly. He simply lived in a world all his own. I often felt that he didn't even see his surroundings; all he seemed to be aware of was his rifle, his bayonet, and his leggings. He was absolutely obsessed with wanting to bayonet the enemy.

We all cleaned our weapons daily, but Haney cleaned his MI before muster, at noon chow, and after dismissal in the afternoon. It was a ritual. He would sit by himself, light a cigarette, field strip his rifle, and meticulously clean every inch of it. Then he cleaned his bayonet. All the while he talked to himself quietly, grinned frequently, and puffed his cigarette down to a stump. When his rifle was cleaned he reassembled it, fixed his bayonet, and went through a few minutes of thrust, parry, and butt-stroke movements at thin air. Then Haney would light up another cigarette and sit quietly, talking to himself and grinning while awaiting orders. He carried out these proceedings as though totally unaware of the presence of the other 235 men of the company. He was like Robinson Crusoe on an island by himself.

To say that he was "Asiatic" would be to miss the point entirely. Haney transcended that condition. The company had many rugged individualists, characters, old salts, and men who were "Asiatic," but Haney was in a category by himself. I felt that he was not a man born of woman, but that God had issued him to the Marine Corps.

Despite his personal idiosyncrasies, Haney inspired us youngsters in Company K. He provided us with a direct link to the "Old Corps." To us he *was* the old breed. We admired him —and we loved him.

Then there was Company K's commanding officer, Capt. "Ack Ack" Haldane.* Late one afternoon as we left the rifle range, a heavy rain set in. As we plodded along Pavuvu's muddy roads, slipping and sliding under the downpour, we began to feel that whoever was leading the column had taken a wrong turn and that we were lost. At dusk in the heavy rain, every road looked alike: a flooded trail cut deeply with ruts, bordered by towering palms, winding aimlessly through the gloom. As I struggled along feeling chilled and forlorn and trying to keep my balance in the mud, a big man came striding from the rear of the column. He walked with the ease of a pedestrian on a city sidewalk. As he pulled abreast of me, the man looked at me and said, "Lovely weather, isn't it, son?"

I grinned at Haldane and said, "Not exactly, sir." He recognized me as a replacement and asked how I liked the company. I told him I thought it was a fine outfit.

"You're a Southerner, aren't you?" he asked. I told him I was from Alabama. He wanted to know all about my family, home, and education. As we talked the gloom seemed to disappear, and I felt warm inside. Finally he told me it wouldn't rain forever, and we could get dry soon. He moved along the column talking to other men as he had to me. His sincere interest in each of us as a human being helped to dispel the feeling that we were just animals training to fight.

Acclaimed by superiors and subordinates alike for his

*Capt. Andrew Allison Haldane, USMCR, was born 22 August 1917 in Lawrence, Massachusetts. He graduated from Bowdoin College, Brunswick, Maine, in 1941.

Captain Haldane served with the 1st Marine Division on Guadalcanal and was commanding officer of Company K at Cape Gloucester, where he won the Silver Star. During a five-day battle, he and his Marines repulsed five Japanese bayonet charges within one hour in the predawn darkness. He led Company K through most of the fight for Peleliu. On 12 October 1944, three days before the Marines came off the lines, he died in action. The Marines of Company K, and the rest of the division who knew him, suffered no greater loss during the entire war.

Bowdoin College annually honors the memory of Captain Haldane by presenting the Haldane Cup to the graduating senior who has displayed outstanding qualities of leadership and character. The cup was a gift from officers who had served with Captain Haldane in the Pacific. Among them was the late senator from Illinois, Paul Douglas, himself a member of the 5th Marines on Peleliu and Okinawa.

leadership abilities, Captain Haldane was the finest and most popular officer I ever knew. All of the Marines in Company K shared my feelings. Called the "skipper," he had a strong face full of character, a large, prominent jaw, and the kindest eyes I ever saw. No matter how often he shaved or how hard he tried, he always had a five o'clock shadow. He was so large that the combat pack on his back reminded me of the bulge of his wallet, while mine covered me from neck to waist.

Although he insisted on strict discipline, the captain was a quiet man who gave orders without shouting. He had a rare combination of intelligence, courage, self-confidence, and compassion that commanded our respect and admiration. We were thankful that Ack Ack was our skipper, felt more secure in it, and felt sorry for other companies not so fortunate. While some officers on Pavuvu thought it necessary to strut or order us around to impress us with their status, Haldane quietly told us what to do. We loved him for it and did the best job we knew how.

Our level of training rose in August and so did the intensity of "chicken" discipline. We suffered through an increasing number of weapons and equipment inspections, work parties, and petty clean-up details around the camp. The step-up in harassment, coupled with the constant discomforts and harsh living conditions of Pavuvu, drove us all into a state of intense exasperation and disgust with our existence before we embarked for Peleliu.

"I used to think the lieutenant was a pretty good joe, but damned if I ain't about decided he ain't nothin' but a hosse's ass," grumbled one Marine.

"You said that right, ole buddy," came back another.

"Hell, he ain't the only one that's gone crazy over insisting that everything be just so, and then bawlin' us out if it ain't. The gunny's mean as hell, and nothin' suits him anymore," responded yet another man.

"Don't let it get you down, boys. It's just part of the USMC plan for keeping the troops in fighting shape," calmly remarked a philosophical old salt of prewar service.

"What the hell you talking about?" snapped an irritated listener.

"Well, it's this way," answered the philosopher. "If they get us mad enough, they figure we'll take it out on the Nips when we hit this beach coming up. I saw it happen before Guadalcanal and Gloucester. They don't pull this kind of stuff on rear-echelon boys. They want us to be mean, mad, and malicious. That's straight dope, I'm telling you. I've seen it happen every time before we go on a campaign."

"Sounds logical. You may be right. But what's malicious?" someone said.

"Forget it, you nitwit," the philosopher growled.

"Right or not, I'm sure tired of Pavuvu," I said.

"That's the plan, Sledgehammer. Get you fed up with Pavuvu, or wherever the hell you happen to be, and you'll be hot to go anywhere else even if the Nips are there waiting for you," the philosopher said.

We fell silent, thinking about that and finally concluded he was right. Many of the more thoughtful men I knew shared his view.

I griped as loudly as anyone about our living conditions and discipline. In retrospect, however, I doubt seriously whether I could have coped with the psychological and physical shock and stress encountered on Peleliu and Okinawa had it been otherwise. The Japanese fought to win. It was a savage, brutal, inhumane, exhausting, and dirty business. Our commanders knew that if we were to win and survive, we must be trained realistically for it whether we liked it or not.*

---

*In the postwar years, the Marine Corps came in for a great deal of undeserved criticism, in my opinion, from well-meaning persons who did not comprehend the magnitude of stress and horror that combat can be. The technology that developed the rifled barrel, the machine gun, and high-explosive shells has turned war into prolonged, subhuman slaughter. Men must be trained realistically if they are to survive it without breaking mentally and physically.

CHAPTER THREE

On to Peleliu

I N LATE August we completed our training. About the 26th, Company K boarded LST (landing ship, tank) 661* for a voyage that would end three weeks later on the beach at Peleliu.

Each rifle company assigned to the assault waves against Peleliu made the trip in an LST carrying the amtracs that would take the men ashore. Our LST lacked sufficient troop compartment space to accommodate all of the men of the company, so the platoon leaders drew straws for the available space. The mortar section got lucky. We were assigned to a troop compartment in the forecastle with an entrance on the main deck. Some of the other platoons had to make themselves as comfortable as possible on the main deck under and around landing boats and gear secured there.

Once loaded, we weighed anchor and headed straight for Guadalcanal, where the division held maneuvers in the Tassafaronga area. This area bore little resemblance to the beaches we would have to hit on Peleliu, but we spent several days in large- and small-unit amphibious landing exercises.

Some of our Guadalcanal veterans wanted to visit the island's cemetery to pay their respects to buddies killed during the division's first campaign. The veterans I knew were not allowed to make the trip to the cemetery, and there was a great deal of understandable bitterness and resentment on their part because of this.

Between training exercises, some of us explored the beach area and looked over the stranded wrecks of Japanese landing barges, the troopship *Yamazuki Maru*, and a two-man

---

*LSTs were a class of shallow-draft amphibious ships developed just before World War II. An LST could drive its front end directly onto a beach and then unload its cargo of vehicles through the large clamshell doors that formed the ship's bow when closed. Or as in the case at Peleliu, LSTs could debark troop-carrying assault amphibians (amtracs) at sea. Advanced models of the LST serve the American fleet today.

submarine. One of the Guadalcanal veterans told us what a helpless feeling it had been to sit back in the hills and watch Japanese reinforcements come ashore unopposed during the dark days of the campaign when the Japanese navy was so powerful in the Solomon Islands. Evidence of earlier fighting remained in the goodly number of shattered trees and several human skeletons we found in the jungle growth.

We also had our lighter moments. When the amtracs returned us to the LST each afternoon, we hurried to our quarters, stowed our gear, stripped, and went below to the tank deck. After all the amtracs were aboard, the ship's CO (commanding officer) obligingly left the bow doors open and the ramp down so we could swim in the blue waters of Sealark Channel (called more appropriately Iron Bottom Bay because of all the ships that had been sunk there during the Guadalcanal campaign). We dove, swam, and splashed in the beautiful water like a bunch of little boys, and for a few fleeting hours forgot why we were there.

The thirty LSTs carrying the 1st Marine Division's assault companies finally weighed anchor early on the morning of 4 September to make the approximately 2,100-mile voyage to Peleliu. The trip proved to be uneventful. The sea was smooth, and we ran into rain squalls only once or twice.

After chow each morning, several of us went aft to the ship's fantail to watch Gunnery Sergeant Haney's show. Dressed in khaki shorts, boondockers, and leggings, Haney went through his ritual of bayonet drill and rifle cleaning. He kept the scabbard on his bayonet and used a canvas-covered stanchion running down from the ship's superstructure as his target. It was a poor substitute for a moving parry stick, but Haney didn't let that stop him. For about an hour he went through his routine, complete with monologue, while dozens of Company K men lounged around on coils of rope and other gear, smoking and talking. Sometimes a spirited game of pinochle went on almost under his feet. He was as oblivious of the players as they were of him. Occasionally a sailor would come by and stare in disbelief at Haney. Several asked me if he were Asiatic. Not being able to overcome the temptation to kid them a bit, I told them no, he was just typical of our outfit. Then they would stare at me as they had at Haney.

I always had the feeling that sailors looked on Marine

infantrymen as though we were a bit crazy, wild, or reckless. Maybe we were. But maybe we had to develop a don't-give-a-damn attitude to keep our sanity in the face of what we were about to endure.

In the ranks, we knew little about the nature of the island that was our objective. During a training lecture on Pavuvu we learned that Peleliu must be taken to secure Gen. Douglas MacArthur's right flank for his invasion of the Philippines, and that it had a good airfield that could support MacArthur. I don't recall when we heard the name of the island, although we viewed relief maps and models during lectures. (It had a nice sounding name, Pel' e loo.) Although our letters from Pavuvu were carefully censored, our officers apparently feared taking a chance on some character writing in code to someone back home that we were to hit an island named Peleliu. As a buddy said to me later, however, no one back home would have known where to look for it on a map anyway.

The Palaus, the westernmost part of the Caroline Islands chain, consist of several large islands and more than a hundred smaller ones. Except for Angaur in the south and a couple of small atolls in the north, the whole group lies within an encircling coral reef. About five hundred miles to the west lie the southern Philippines. To the south at about the same distance is New Guinea.

Peleliu, just inside the Palau reef, is shaped like a lobster's claw, extending two arms of land. The southern arm reaches northeastward from flat ground to form a jumble of coral islets and tidal flats overgrown thickly with mangroves. The longer northern arm is dominated by the parallel coral ridges of Umurbrogol Mountain.

North to south, the island is about six miles long, with a width of approximately two miles. On the wide, largely flat southern section, the Japanese had constructed an airfield shaped roughly like the numeral 4. The ridges and most of the island outside the airfield were thickly wooded; there were only occasional patches of wild palms and open grass areas. The thick scrub so completely masked the true nature of the terrain that aerial photographs and pre–D day photos taken by United States submarines gave intelligence officers no hint of its ruggedness.

The treacherous reef along the landing beaches and the heavily defended coral ridges inland made the invasion of Peleliu a

*combination of the problems of Tarawa and of Saipan. The reef,
over six hundred yards long, was the most formidable natural
obstacle. Because of it, troops and equipment making the assault
had to be transported in amtracs; Higgins boats could not negotiate across the rough coral and the varying depths of water.*

Before leaving Pavuvu, we had been told that the 1st Marine
Division would be reinforced to about 28,000 men for the
assault on Peleliu. As every man in the ranks knew, however, a
lot of those people included in the term *reinforced* were neither
trained nor equipped as combat troops. They were specialists
attached to the division to implement the landing and supply
by working on ships and later on the beaches. They would not
be doing the fighting.

Upon sailing for Peleliu, the 1st Marine Division numbered
16,459 officers and men. A rear echelon of 1,771 remained on
Pavuvu. Of these, only about 9,000 were infantrymen in the
three infantry regiments. Intelligence sources estimated that
we would face more than 10,000 Japanese defenders on Peleliu. The big topic of conversation among us troops had to do
with those comparative strengths.

"Hey, you guys, the lieutenant just told me that the 1st Division is gonna be the biggest Marine division to ever make a
landing. He says we got reinforcements we never had before."

A veteran looked up from cleaning his .45 automatic and
said, "Boy, has that shavetail lieutenant been smoke-stacking
you!"

"Why?"

"Use your head, buddy. Sure we got the 1st Marines, the
5th Marines, and the 7th Marines; them's infantry. The 11th
Marines is our division artillery. Where the hell's all them people who is supposed to 'reinforce' the division? Have you seen
'em? Who the hell are they, and where the hell are they?"

"I don't know, I'm just telling you what the lieutenant said."

"Well, I'll tell you who them 'reinforcements' is. They's all
what they call specialists, and they ain't line company Marines.
Remember this, buster. When the stuff hits the fan, and you
and me are trying to live through that shootin' and the shellin',
them damned specialists'll be settin' on they cans back at division CP [command post] on the beach, writin' home about
how war is hell. And who is gonna have all the casualties and

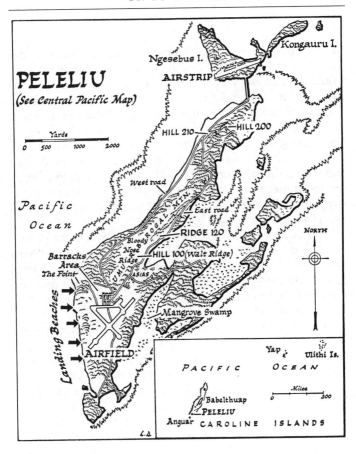

lose all the men fightin' the Nips? The 1st Marines, the 5th
Marines, and the 7th Marines'll all catch hell, and the 11th Marines'll lose some men too. Wake up, boy, them shavetail lieutenants is as useless as tits on a boar hog. The NCOs run things
when the shootin' starts."*

---

*During World War II, amphibious planners considered the safe ratio of at-
tackers to defenders in an amphibious assault to be three to one. To the leaders
at Peleliu, the total Marine force of 30,000 provided a safe margin over the
Japanese. Although at least one regimental commander—the redoubtable Col.
Lewis B. ("Chesty") Puller—pointed out the disparity in actual combat forces,
the division's commander, Maj. Gen. William H. Rupertus, and his staff believed his fears were groundless.

D MINUS I

After evening chow on 14 September 1944, a buddy and I leaned against the rail of LST 661 and talked about what we would do after the war. I tried to appear unconcerned about the next day, and he did too. We may have fooled each other and ourselves a little, but not much. As the sun disappeared below the horizon and its glare no longer reflected off a glassy sea, I thought of how beautiful the sunsets always were in the Pacific. They were even more beautiful than over Mobile Bay. Suddenly a thought hit me like a thunderbolt. Would I live to see the sunset tomorrow? My knees nearly buckled as panic swept over me. I squeezed the railing and tried to appear interested in our conversation.

The ships in the convoy turned into dark hulks gliding along as the squawk box interrupted our conversation, "Now hear this. Now hear this." Talking quietly in pairs and small groups, the men around us seemed to pay more than the usual attention to the command. "All troops lay below to quarters. All troops lay below to quarters."

My buddy and I went to our forecastle compartment. One of our NCOs sent a work party to another compartment to draw rations and ammunition. After it returned, our lieutenant came in, gave us "at ease," and said he had some things to say. His brow was knit, his face drawn, and he looked worried.

"Men, as you probably know, tomorrow is D day. General Rupertus says the fighting will be extremely tough but short. It will be over in four days, maybe three. A fight like Tarawa. It's going to be rough but fast. Then we can return to a rest area.

"Remember what you've been taught. Keep your heads down going in on the amtrac. A lot of unnecessary casualties at Saipan were the result of men looking over the side to see what was happening. As soon as the amtrac stops on the beach, get out on the double, and get off the beach fast. Keep out of the way of amtracs on their way back out to pick up more troops from the supporting waves. Our tanks will be coming in behind us, too. The drivers have their hands full and can't dodge around the infantry, so you keep out of their way. Get off the beach fast! The Japs will plaster it with everything they've got, and if we get pinned down on the beach, artillery and mortars will ruin us.

"Have your weapons ready because the Japs always try to stop us at the beach line. They may meet us at the beach with bayonets as soon as our naval gunfire barrage lifts and moves inland. So come out of the amtracs ready for anything. Have a round in the chamber of your small arms and lock your pieces [snap on the safety]. Have the canister containers of your high-explosive mortar rounds untaped and stowed in your ammo bags ready for immediate use as soon as we are called on to deliver fire on the company front. Fill your canteens, draw rations and salt tablets, and clean your weapons. Reveille will be before daylight, and H hour will be at 0830. Hit the sack early. You will need the rest. Good luck and carry on."

He left the compartment and the NCOs issued us ammo, K rations, and salt tablets.

"Well," said one man, "that scuttlebutt we heard during maneuvers on Guadalcanal about how this blitz gonna be rough but fast must be true if the division CG says so."

"San Antone," muttered a Texan. "Imagine, only four, maybe three days for a battle star. Hell, I can put up with anything for no longer than that."

He reflected the feelings of most of us, and we were encouraged by the commanding general's announcement confirming the oft-repeated "rough but fast" rumors we had been hearing.* We kept trying to convince ourselves that the CG knew what he was talking about. We all dreaded a long, protracted campaign that would drag on beyond endurance like Guadalcanal and Cape Gloucester. Our morale was excellent, and we were trained for anything no matter how rough. But we prayed that we could get it over with in a hurry.

We sat on our sacks, cleaned our weapons, packed our combat packs, and squared away our gear. Throughout history,

---

*In a sealed letter opened D day minus 1 by civilian news correspondents assigned to cover the battle, Maj. Gen. William H. Rupertus predicted that Peleliu would fall in four days after a short, tough fight. His forecast colored the tactical thinking ashore for much of the next month. Because of his optimism, many of the thirty-six newsmen never went ashore; of those who did, only six stayed through the critical early stages of the battle. Thus, the medium's eyes saw little of what actually happened.

combat troops of various armies have carried packs weighing many pounds into action; but we traveled light, carrying only absolute necessities—the way fast-moving Confederate infantry did during the Civil War.

My combat pack contained a folded poncho, one pair of socks, a couple of boxes of K rations, salt tablets, extra carbine ammo (twenty rounds), two hand grenades, a fountain pen, a small bottle of ink, writing paper in a waterproof wrapper, a toothbrush, a small tube of toothpaste, some photos of my folks along with some letters (in a waterproof wrapper), and a dungaree cap.

My other equipment and clothing were a steel helmet covered with camouflaged-cloth covering, heavy green dungaree jacket with a Marine emblem and *USMC* dyed above it on the left breast pocket, trousers of the same material, an old toothbrush for cleaning my carbine, thin cotton socks, ankle-high boondockers, and light tan canvas leggings (into which I tucked my trouser legs). Because of the heat, I wore no skivvy drawers or shirt. Like many men, I fastened a bronze Marine emblem to one collar for good luck.

Attached to my web pistol belt, I carried a pouch containing a combat dressing, two canteens, a pouch with two fifteen-round carbine magazines—clips, we called them, and a fine brass compass in a waterproof case. My kabar hung in its leather sheath on my right side. Hooked over the belt by its spoon (handle), I carried a grenade. I also had a heavy-bladed knife similar to a meat cleaver that my dad had sent me; I used this to chop through the wire braces wrapped around the stout crates of 60mm mortar shells.

On the stock of my carbine I fastened an ammo pouch with two extra clips. I carried no bayonet, because the model carbine I had lacked a bayonet lug. Onto the outside of my pack, I hooked my entrenching tool in its canvas cover. (The tool proved useless on Peleliu, because of the hard coral.)

All officers and men dressed much the same. The main differences among us were in the type of web belt worn and the individual weapon carried.

We tried to appear unconcerned and talked about anything but the war. Some wrote last letters.

"What are you going to do after the war, Sledgehammer?" asked a buddy sitting across from me. He was an extremely intelligent and intellectually active young man.

"I don't know, Oswalt. What are you planning to do?"

"I want to be a brain surgeon. The human brain is an incredible thing; it fascinates me," he replied.

But he didn't survive Peleliu to realize his ambition.

Slowly the conversations trailed off, and the men hit the sack. It was hard to sleep that night. I thought of home, my parents, my friends—and whether I would do my duty, be wounded and disabled, or be killed. I concluded that it was impossible for me to be killed, because God loved me. Then I told myself that God loved us all and that many would die or be ruined physically or mentally or both by the next morning and in the days following. My heart pounded, and I broke out in a cold sweat. Finally, I called myself a damned coward and eventually fell asleep saying the Lord's Prayer to myself.

D DAY, 15 SEPTEMBER 1944

I seemed to have slept only a short time when an NCO came into the compartment saying, "OK, you guys, hit the deck." I felt the ship had slowed and almost stopped. If only I could hold back the hands of the clock, I thought. It was pitch dark with no lights topside. We tumbled out, dressed and shaved, and got ready for chow—steak and eggs, a 1st Marine Division tradition honoring a culinary combination learned from the Australians. Neither the steak nor the eggs was very palatable, though; my stomach was tied in knots.

Back in my compartment, a peculiar problem had developed. Haney, who had been one of the first to return from chow about forty-five minutes earlier, had ensconced himself on the seat of one of the two toilets in the small head on our side of the compartment. There he sat, dungaree trousers down to his knees, his beloved leggings laced neatly over his boondockers, grinning and talking calmly to himself while smoking a cigarette. Nervous Marines lined up using the other toilet one after another. Some men had been to the head on the other side of the compartment while others, in desperation, dashed off to the heads in other troop compartments. The facilities in our compartment normally were adequate, but D day morning found us all nervous, tense, and afraid. The veterans already knew what I was to find out: during periods of intense fighting, a man might not have the opportunity to eat or sleep, much less move his bowels. All the men grumbled and scowled at Haney, but because he was a gunnery sergeant, no one dared suggest he hurry. With his characteristic detachment, Haney ignored us, remained unhurried, and left when he pleased.

The first light of dawn was just appearing as I left my gear on my bunk, all squared away and ready to put on, and went out onto the main deck. All the men were talking quietly, smoking, and looking toward the island. I found Snafu* and stayed close by him; he was the gunner on our mortar, so we stuck together. He was also a Gloucester veteran, and I felt more secure around veterans. They knew what to expect.

He pulled out a pack of cigarettes and drawled, "Have a smoke, Sledgehammer."

"No thanks, Snafu. I've told you a million times I don't smoke."

"I'll bet you two bits, Sledgehammer, that before this day is over you'll be smokin' the hell outa every cigarette you can get your hands on."

I just gave him a sickly grin, and we looked toward the island. The sun was just coming up, and there wasn't a cloud in the sky. The sea was calm. A gentle breeze blew.

A ship's bell rang, and over the squawk box came, "Get your gear on and stand by." Snafu and I hurried to our bunks, nodding and speaking to other grim-faced buddies who were rushing to get their gear. In the crowded compartment we helped each other with packs, straightened shoulder straps, and buckled on cartridge belts. Generals and admirals might worry about maps and tons of supplies, but my main concern at the moment was how my pack straps felt and whether my boondockers were comfortable.

The next bell rang. Snafu picked up the forty-five pounds of mortar and slung the carrying strap over his shoulder. I slung

---

*Cpl. Merriell A. ("Snafu") Shelton came from Louisiana.

my carbine over one shoulder and the heavy ammo bag over the other. We filed down a ladder to the tank deck where an NCO directed us to climb aboard an amtrac. My knees got weak when I saw that it wasn't the newer model with the tailgate ramp for troop exit in which we had practiced. This meant that once the amtrac was on the beach, we'd have to jump over the high sides, exposed much more to enemy fire. I was too scared and excited to say much, but some of the guys grumbled about it.

The ship's bow doors opened and the ramp went down. All the tractors' engines roared and spewed out fumes. Exhaust fans whirred above us. Glaring daylight streamed into the tank deck through the opened bow of the ship as the first amtrac started out and clattered down the sloping ramp.

Our machine started with a jerk, and we held on to the sides and to each other. The amtrac's treads ground and scraped against the iron ridges on the ramp, then it floated freely and settled onto the water like a big duck. Around us roared the voices of the ships' guns engaged in the preassault bombardment of Peleliu's beaches and defensive positions.

The Marine Corps had trained us new men until we were welded with the veterans into a thoroughly disciplined combat division. Now the force of events unleashed on that two-mile by six-mile piece of unfriendly coral rock would carry us forward unrelentingly, each to his individual fate.

Everything my life had been before and has been after pales in the light of that awesome moment when my amtrac started in amid a thunderous bombardment toward the flaming, smoke-shrouded beach for the assault on Peleliu.

Since the end of World War II, historians and military analysts have argued inconclusively about the necessity of the Palau Islands campaign. Many believed after the battle—and still believe today—that the United States didn't need to fight it as a prerequisite to General MacArthur's return to the Philippines.

Adm. William F. ("Bull") Halsey suggested calling off the Palau operation after high-level planners learned that Japanese air power in the Philippines wasn't as strong as intelligence originally had presumed it to be. But MacArthur believed the operation should proceed, and Adm. Chester W. Nimitz said it was too late to cancel the operation, because the convoy was already underway.

Because of important events in Europe at the time and the lack of immediate, apparent benefits from the seizure of Peleliu, the battle remains one of the lesser known or understood of the Pacific war. Nonetheless, for many it ranks as the roughest fight the Marines had in World War II.

Maj. Gen. (later Lt. Gen.) Roy S. Geiger, the rugged commander of the III Amphibious Corps, said repeatedly that Peleliu was the toughest battle of the entire Pacific war. A former commandant of the Marine Corps, Gen. Clifton B. Cates, said Peleliu was one of the most vicious and stubbornly contested battles of the war, and that nowhere was the fighting efficiency of the U.S. Marine demonstrated more convincingly.

Peleliu also was important to the remainder of the Marines' war in the Pacific because of the changes in Japanese tactics encountered there. The Japanese abandoned their conventional all-out effort at defending the beach in favor of a complex defense based upon mutually supporting, fortified positions in caves and pillboxes extending deeply into the interior of the island, particularly in the ridges of Umurbrogol Mountain.

In earlier battles, the Japanese had exhausted their forces in banzai *charges against the Marines once the latter had firmly established a beachhead. The Marines slaughtered the wildly charging Japanese by the thousands. Not a single* banzai *charge had been successful for the Japanese in previous campaigns.*

But on Peleliu the Japanese commander, Col. Kunio Nakagawa, let the Marines come to him and the approximately 10,000 troops of his proud 14th Infantry Division. From mutually supporting positions, the Japanese covered nearly every yard of Peleliu from the beach inland to the center of Nakagawa's command post, deep beneath the coral rock in the center of the ridge system. Some positions were large enough to hold only one man. Some caves held hundreds. Thus the Marines encountered no one main defense line. The Japanese had constructed the perfect defense-in-depth with the whole island as a front line. They fought until the last position was knocked out.

Aided by the incredibly rugged terrain, the new Japanese tactics proved so successful that the 1st Marine Division suffered more than twice as many casualties on Peleliu as the 2d Marine

Division had on Tarawa. Proportionately, United States casu-
alties on Peleliu closely approximated those suffered later on Iwo
Jima where the Japanese again employed an intricate defense-in-
depth, conserved forces, and fought a battle of attrition. On an
even greater scale, the skillful, tenacious defense of the southern
portion of Okinawa used the same sophisticated, in-depth defen-
sive system first tested on Peleliu.

CHAPTER FOUR

Assault into Hell

H-HOUR, 0800. Long jets of red flame mixed with thick black smoke rushed out of the muzzles of the huge battleships' 16-inch guns with a noise like a thunderclap. The giant shells tore through the air toward the island, roaring like locomotives.

"Boy, it must cost a fortune to fire them 16-inch babies," said a buddy near me.

"Screw the expense," growled another.

Only less impressive were the cruisers firing 8-inch salvos and the host of smaller ships firing rapid fire. The usually clean salty air was strong with the odors of explosives and diesel fuel. While the assault waves formed up and my amphibious tractor lay still in the water with engines idling, the tempo of the bombardment increased to such intensity that I couldn't distinguish the reports of the various types of weapons through the thunderous noise. We had to shout at each other to be heard. The big ships increased their fire and moved off to the flanks of the amtrac formations when we started in so as not to fire over us at the risk of short rounds.

We waited a seeming eternity for the signal to start toward the beach. The suspense was almost more than I could bear. Waiting is a major part of war, but I never experienced any more supremely agonizing suspense than the excruciating torture of those moments before we received the signal to begin the assault on Peleliu. I broke out in a cold sweat as the tension mounted with the intensity of the bombardment. My stomach was tied in knots. I had a lump in my throat and swallowed only with great difficulty. My knees nearly buckled, so I clung weakly to the side of the tractor. I felt nauseated and feared that my bladder would surely empty itself and reveal me to be the coward I was. But the men around me looked just about the way I felt. Finally, with a sense of fatalistic relief mixed with a flash of anger at the navy officer who was our wave commander, I saw him wave his flag toward the beach. Our driver revved the engine. The treads churned up the water, and we started in—the second wave ashore.

We moved ahead, watching the frightful spectacle. Huge geysers of water rose around the amtracs ahead of us as they approached the reef. The beach was now marked along its length by a continuous sheet of flame backed by a thick wall of smoke. It seemed as though a huge volcano had erupted from the sea, and rather than heading for an island, we were being drawn into the vortex of a flaming abyss. For many it was to be oblivion.

The lieutenant braced himself and pulled out a half-pint whiskey bottle.

"This is it, boys," he yelled.

Just like they do in the movies! It seemed unreal.

He held the bottle out to me, but I refused. Just sniffing the cork under those conditions might have made me pass out. He took a long pull on the bottle, and a couple of the men did the same. Suddenly a large shell exploded with a terrific concussion, and a huge geyser rose up just to our right front. It barely missed us. The engine stalled. The front of the tractor lurched to the left and bumped hard against the rear of another amtrac that was either stalled or hit. I never knew which.

We sat stalled, floating in the water for some terrifying moments. We were sitting ducks for the enemy gunners. I looked forward through the hatch behind the driver. He was wrestling frantically with the control levers. Japanese shells were screaming into the area and exploding all around us. Sgt. Johnny Marmet leaned toward the driver and yelled something. Whatever it was, it seemed to calm the driver, because he got the engine started. We moved forward again amid the geysers of exploding shells.

Our bombardment began to lift off the beach and move inland. Our dive bombers also moved inland with their strafing and bombing. The Japanese increased the volume of their fire against the waves of amtracs. Above the din I could hear the ominous sound of shell fragments humming and growling through the air.

"Stand by," someone yelled.

I picked up my mortar ammo bag and slung it over my left shoulder, buckled my helmet chin strap, adjusted my carbine sling over my right shoulder, and tried to keep my balance. My heart pounded. Our amtrac came out of the water and moved a few yards up the gently sloping sand.

"Hit the beach!" yelled an NCO moments before the machine lurched to a stop.

The men piled over the sides as fast as they could. I followed Snafu, climbed up, and planted both feet firmly on the left side so as to leap as far away from it as possible. At that instant a burst of machine-gun fire with white-hot tracers snapped through the air at eye level, almost grazing my face. I pulled my head back like a turtle, lost my balance, and fell awkwardly forward down onto the sand in a tangle of ammo bag, pack, helmet, carbine, gas mask, cartridge belt, and flopping canteens. "Get off the beach! Get off the beach!" raced through my mind.

Once I felt land under my feet, I wasn't as scared as I had been coming across the reef. My legs dug up the sand as I tried to rise. A firm hand gripped my shoulder. "Oh god, I thought, it's a Nip who's come out of a pillbox!" I couldn't reach my kabar—fortunately, because as I got my face out of the sand and looked up, there was the worried face of a Marine bending over me. He thought the machine-gun burst had hit me, and he had crawled over to help. When he saw I was unhurt, he spun around and started crawling rapidly off the beach. I scuttled after him.

Shells crashed all around. Fragments tore and whirred, slapping on the sand and splashing into the water a few yards behind us. The Japanese were recovering from the shock of our prelanding bombardment. Their machine gun and rifle fire got thicker, snapping viciously overhead in increasing volume.

Our amtrac spun around and headed back out as I reached the edge of the beach and flattened on the deck. The world was a nightmare of flashes, violent explosions, and snapping bullets. Most of what I saw blurred. My mind was benumbed by the shock of it.

I glanced back across the beach and saw a DUKW (rubber-tired amphibious truck) roll up on the sand at a point near where we had just landed. The instant the DUKW stopped, it was engulfed in thick, dirty black smoke as a shell scored a direct hit on it. Bits of debris flew into the air. I watched with that odd, detached fascination peculiar to men under fire, as a flat metal panel about two feet square spun high into the air then splashed into shallow water like a big pancake. I didn't see any men get out of the DUKW.

Up and down the beach and out on the reef, a number of amtracs and DUKWs were burning. Japanese machine-gun bursts made long splashes on the water as though flaying it with some giant whip. The geysers belched up relentlessly where the mortar and artillery shells hit. I caught a fleeting glimpse of a group of Marines leaving a smoking amtrac on the reef. Some fell as bullets and fragments splashed among them. Their buddies tried to help them as they struggled in the knee-deep water.

I shuddered and choked. A wild desperate feeling of anger, frustration, and pity gripped me. It was an emotion that always would torture my mind when I saw men trapped and was unable to do anything but watch as they were hit. My own plight forgotten momentarily, I felt sickened to the depths of my soul. I asked God, "Why, why, why?" I turned my face away and wished that I were imagining it all. I had tasted the bitterest essence of war, the sight of helpless comrades being slaughtered, and it filled me with disgust.

I got up. Crouching low, I raced up the sloping beach into a defilade. Reaching the inland edge of the sand just beyond the high-water mark, I glanced down and saw the nose of a huge black and yellow bomb protruding from the sand. A metal plate attached to the top served as a pressure trigger. My foot had missed it by only inches.

I hit the deck again just inside the defilade. On the sand immediately in front of me was a dead snake about eighteen inches long. It was colorful, somewhat like American species I had kept as pets when a boy. It was the only snake I saw on Peleliu.

Momentarily I was out of the heavy fire hitting on the beach. A strong smell of chemicals and exploding shells filled the air. Patches of coral and sand around me were yellowed from the powder from shell blasts. A large white post about four feet high stood at the edge of the defilade. Japanese writing was painted on the side facing the beach. To me, it appeared as though a chicken with muddy feet had walked up and down the post. I felt a sense of pride that this was enemy territory and that we were capturing it for our country to help win the war.

One of our NCOs signaled us to move to our right, out of the shallow defilade. I was glad, because the Japanese probably would pour mortar fire into it to prevent it being used for shelter. At the moment, however, the gunners seemed to be concentrating on the beach and the incoming waves of Marines.

I ran over to where one of our veterans stood looking to our front and flopped down at his feet. "You'd better get down," I yelled as bullets snapped and cracked all around.

"Them slugs are high, they're hittin' in the leaves, Sledgehammer," he said nonchalantly without looking at me.

"Leaves, hell! Where are the trees?" I yelled back at him.

Startled, he looked right and left. Down the beach, barely visible, was a shattered palm. Nothing near us stood over knee high. He hit the deck.

"I must be crackin' up, Sledgehammer. Them slugs sound just like they did in the jungle at Gloucester, and I figured they were hittin' leaves," he said with chagrin.

"Somebody gimme a cigarette," I yelled to my squad mates nearby.

Snafu was jubilant. "I toldja you'd start smokin', didn't I, Sledgehammer?"

A buddy handed me a smoke, and with trembling hands we got it lit. They really kidded me about going back on all my previous refusals to smoke.

I kept looking to our right, expecting to see men from the 3d Battalion, 7th Marines (3/7), which was supposed to be there. But I saw only the familiar faces of Marines from my own company as we moved off the beach. Marines began to come in behind us in increasing numbers, but none were visible on our right flank.

Unfamiliar officers and NCOs yelled and shouted orders, "K Company, first platoon, move over here," or "K Company, mortar section, over here." Considerable confusion prevailed for about fifteen minutes as our officers and the leaders from our namesake company in the 7th Marines straightened out the two units.

*

From left to right along the 2,200-yard beach front, the 1st Marines, the 5th Marines, and the 7th Marines landed abreast. The 1st Marines landed one battalion on each of the two northern White beaches. In the division's center, the 5th Marines landed its 1st Battalion (1/5) over Orange Beach One and its 3d Battalion (3/5) over Orange Beach Two. Forming the right flank of the division, the 7th Marines was to land one battalion (3/7) in the assault over Orange Beach Three, the southernmost of five designated beaches.

In the confusion of the landing's first few minutes, K/3/5 actually got in ahead of the assault companies of 3/7 and slightly farther to the right than intended. As luck would have it, the two companies got mixed together as the right flank of the division. For about fifteen minutes we were the exposed right flank of the entire beachhead.

We started to move inland. We had gone only a few yards when an enemy machine gun opened up from a scrub thicket to our right. Japanese 81mm and 90mm mortars then opened up on us. Everyone hit the deck; I dove into a shallow crater. The company was completely pinned down. All movement ceased. The shells fell faster, until I couldn't make out individual explosions, just continuous, crashing rumbles with an occasional ripping sound of shrapnel tearing low through the air overhead amid the roar. The air was murky with smoke and dust. Every muscle in my body was as tight as a piano wire. I shuddered and shook as though I were having a mild convulsion. Sweat flowed profusely. I prayed, clenched my teeth, squeezed my carbine stock, and cursed the Japanese. Our lieutenant, a Cape Gloucester veteran who was nearby, seemed to be in about the same shape. From the meager protection of my shallow crater I pitied him, or anyone, out on that flat coral.

The heavy mortar barrage went on without slackening. I thought it would never stop. I was terrified by the big shells arching down all around us. One was bound to fall directly into my hole, I thought.

If any orders were passed along, or if anyone yelled for a corpsman, I never heard it in all the noise. It was as though I was out there on the battlefield all by myself, utterly forlorn and helpless in a tempest of violent explosions. All any man could do was sweat it out and pray for survival. It would have been sure suicide to stand up in that fire storm.

Under my first barrage since the fast-moving events of hitting the beach, I learned a new sensation: utter and absolute helplessness. The shelling lifted in about half an hour, although it seemed to me to have crashed on for hours. Time had no meaning to me. (This was particularly true when under a heavy shelling. I never could judge how long it lasted.) Orders then came to move out and I got up, covered by a layer of coral dust. I felt like jelly and couldn't believe any of us had survived that barrage.

The walking wounded began coming past us on their way to the beach where they would board amtracs to be taken out to one of the ships. An NCO who was a particular friend of mine hurried by, holding a bloody battle dressing over his upper left arm.

"Hit bad?" I yelled.

His face lit up in a broad grin, and he said jauntily, "Don't feel sorry for me, Sledgehammer. I got the million-dollar wound. It's all over for me."

We waved as he hurried on out of the war.

We had to be alert constantly as we moved through the thick sniper-infested scrub. We received orders to halt in an open area as I came upon the first enemy dead I had ever seen, a dead Japanese medical corpsman and two riflemen. The medic apparently had been trying to administer aid when he was killed by one of our shells. His medical chest lay open beside him, and the various bandages and medicines were arranged neatly in compartments. The corpsman was on his back, his abdominal cavity laid bare. I stared in horror, shocked at the glistening viscera bespecked with fine coral dust. This can't have been a human being, I agonized. It looked more like the guts of one of the many rabbits or squirrels I had cleaned on hunting trips as a boy. I felt sick as I stared at the corpses.

A sweating, dusty Company K veteran came up, looked first at the dead, and then at me. He slung his M1 rifle over his shoulder and leaned over the bodies. With the thumb and forefinger of one hand, he deftly plucked a pair of hornrimmed glasses from the face of the corpsman. This was done as casually as a guest plucking an hors d'oeuvre from a tray at a cocktail party.

"Sledgehammer," he said reproachfully, "don't stand there with your mouth open when there's all these good souvenirs laying around." He held the glasses for me to see and added, "Look how thick that glass is. These sonsabitches must be half blind, but it don't seem to mess up their marksmanship any."

He then removed a Nambu pistol, slipped the belt off the corpse, and took the leather holster. He pulled off the steel helmet, reached inside, and took out a neatly folded Japanese flag covered with writing. The veteran pitched the helmet on the coral where it clanked and rattled, rolled the corpse over, and started pawing through the combat pack.

The veteran's buddy came up and started stripping the other Japanese corpses. His take was a flag and other items. He then removed the bolts from the Japanese rifles and broke the stocks against the coral to render them useless to infiltrators. The first veteran said, "See you, Sledgehammer. Don't take any wooden nickels." He and his buddy moved on.

I hadn't budged an inch or said a word, just stood glued to the spot almost in a trance. The corpses were sprawled where the veterans had dragged them around to get into their packs and pockets. Would I become this casual and calloused about enemy dead? I wondered. Would the war dehumanize me so that I, too, could "field strip" enemy dead with such nonchalance? The time soon came when it didn't bother me a bit.

Within a few yards of this scene, one of our hospital corpsmen worked in a small, shallow defile treating Marine wounded. I went over and sat on the hot coral by him. The corpsman was on his knees bending over a young Marine who had just died on a stretcher. A blood-soaked battle dressing was on the side of the dead man's neck. His fine, handsome, boyish face was ashen. "What a pitiful waste," I thought. "He can't be a day over seventeen years old." I thanked God his mother couldn't see him. The corpsman held the dead Marine's chin tenderly between the thumb and fingers of his left hand and made the sign of the cross with his right hand. Tears streamed down his dusty, tanned, grief-contorted face while he sobbed quietly.

The wounded who had received morphine sat or lay around like zombies and patiently awaited the "doc's" attention. Shells roared overhead in both directions, an occasional one falling nearby, and machine guns rattled incessantly like chattering demons.

We moved inland. The scrub may have slowed the company, but it concealed us from the heavy enemy shelling that was holding up other companies facing the open airfield. I could hear the deep rumble of the shelling and dreaded that we might move into it.

That our battalion executive officer had been killed a few moments after hitting the beach and that the amtrac carrying most of our battalion's field telephone equipment and operators had been destroyed on the reef made control difficult. The companies of 3/5 lost contact with each other and with 3/7 on our right flank.*

As I passed the different units and exchanged greetings with friends, I was astonished at their faces. When I tried to smile at a comment a buddy made, my face felt as tight as a drumhead. My facial muscles were so tensed from the strain that I actually felt it was impossible to smile. With a shock I realized that the faces of my squad mates and everyone around me looked masklike and unfamiliar.

As we pushed eastward, we halted briefly along a North-South trail. Word was passed that we had to move forward faster to a trail where we would come up abreast of 3/7.

We continued through the thick scrub and heavy sniper fire until we came out into a clearing overlooking the ocean. Company K had reached the eastern shore. We had reached our objective. To our front was a shallow bay with barbed wire entanglements, iron tetrahedrons and other obstacles against landing craft. I was glad we hadn't tried to invade this coast.

About a dozen Company K riflemen commenced firing at Japanese soldiers wading along the reef several hundred yards away at the mouth of the bay. Other Marines joined us. The

---

*Historical accounts of battles often leave a reader with the impression that the individual participants had a panoramic view of events. Such is not the case, however. Even the historians have never been able to piece together completely what happened to 3/5 on D day at Peleliu.

enemy were moving out from a narrow extension of the mangrove swamp on the left toward the southeastern promontory on our right. About a dozen enemy soldiers were alternately swimming and running along the reef. Some of the time only their heads were above the water as my buddies sent rifle fire into their midst. Most of the running enemy went down with a splash.

We were elated over reaching the eastern shore, and at being able to fire on the enemy in the open. A few Japanese escaped and scrambled among the rocks on the promontory.

"OK, you guys, line 'em up and squeeze 'em off," said a sergeant. "You don't kill 'em with the noise. It's the slugs that do it. You guys couldn't hit a bull in the ass with a bass fiddle," he roared.

Several more Japanese ran out from the cover of the mangroves. A burst of rifle fire sent every one of them splashing. "That's better," growled the sergeant.

The mortarmen put down our loads and stood by to set up the guns. We didn't fire at the enemy with our carbines. Rifles were more effective than carbines at that range. So we just watched.

Firing increased from our rear. We had no contact with Marine units on our right or left. But the veterans weren't concerned with anything but the enemy on the reef.

"Stand by to move out!" came the order.

"What the hell," grumbled a veteran as we headed back into the scrub. "We fight like hell and reach our objective, and they order us to fall back." Others joined in the grumbling.

"Aw, knock it off. We gotta gain contact with the 7th Marines," an NCO said.

We headed back into the thick scrub. For some time I completely lost my bearings and had no idea where we were going.

Unknown to the Marines, there were two parallel North-South trails about two hundred yards apart winding through the thick scrub. Poor maps, poor visibility, and numerous snipers made it difficult to distinguish the two trails.

When 3/5, with Company K on its right flank, reached the first (westernmost) trail, it was then actually abreast of 3/7. However, due to poor visibility, contact couldn't be made between the two battalions. It was thought 3/5 was too far to the rear. So, 3/5 was ordered to move forward to come abreast of 3/7. By the time this error was realized, 3/5 had pushed 300–400 yards ahead of the 7th Marines' flank. For the second time on D day, K/3/5 was the forward-most exposed right flank element of the division. The entire 3d Battalion 5th Marines formed a deep salient reaching into enemy territory to the east coast. To make matters worse, the battalion's three companies had lost contact with each other. These isolated units were in critical danger of being cut off and surrounded by the Japanese.

The weather was getting increasingly hot, and I was soaked with sweat. I began eating salt tablets and taking frequent drinks of tepid water from my canteens. We were warned to save our water as long as possible, because no one knew when we would get any more.

A sweating runner with a worried face came up from the rear. "Hey, you guys, where's K Company's CO?" he asked. We told him where we thought Ack Ack could be located.

"What's the hot dope?" someone asked, with that same anxious question always put to runners.

"Battalion CP says we just gotta establish contact with the 7th Marines, 'cause if the Nips counterattack they'll come right through the gap," he said as he hurried on.

"Jesus!" said a man near me.

We moved forward and came up with the rest of the company in a clearing. The platoons formed up and took casualty reports. Japanese mortar and artillery fire increased. The shelling became heavy, indicating the probability of a counterattack. Most of their fire whistled over us and fell to our rear. This seemed strange although fortunate to me at the time. The order came for us to move out a short distance to the edge of the scrub. At approximately 1650 I looked out across the open airfield toward the southern extremities of the coral ridges—collectively called Bloody Nose Ridge—and saw vehicles of some sort moving amid swirling clouds of dust.

"Hey," I said to a veteran next to me, "what are those amtracs doing all the way across the airfield toward the Jap lines?"

"Them ain't amtracs; they're Nip tanks!" he said.

Shell bursts appeared among the enemy tanks. Some of our Sherman tanks had arrived at the edge of the airfield on our left and opened fire. Because of the clouds of dust and the shellfire, I couldn't see much and didn't see any enemy infantry, but the firing on our left was heavy.

Word came for us to deploy on the double. The riflemen formed a line at the edge of the scrub along a trail and lay prone, trying to take what cover they could. From the beginning to the end on Peleliu, it was all but impossible to dig into the hard coral rock, so the men piled rocks around themselves or got behind logs and debris.

Snafu and I set up our 60mm mortar a few yards behind them, across the trail in a shallow crater. Everyone got edgy as the order came, "Stand by to repel counterattack. Counterattack hitting I Company's front."

I didn't know where Company I was, but I thought it was on our left—somewhere. Although I had great confidence in our officers and NCOs, it seemed to me that we were alone and confused in the middle of a rumbling chaos with snipers everywhere and with no contact with any other units. I thought all of us would be lost.

"They needta get some more damned troops up here," growled Snafu, his standard remark in a tight spot.

Snafu set up the gun, and I removed an HE (high explosive) shell from a canister in my ammo bag. At last we could return fire!

Snafu yelled, "Fire!"

Just then a Marine tank to our rear mistook us for enemy troops. As soon as my hand went up to drop the round down the tube, a machine gun cut loose. It sounded like one of ours —and from the rear of all places! As I peeped over the edge of the crater through the dust and smoke and saw a Sherman tank in a clearing behind us, the tank fired its 75mm gun off to our right rear. The shell exploded nearby, around a bend in the same trail we were on. I then heard the report of a Japanese field gun located there as it returned fire on the tank. Again I tried to fire, but the machine gun opened up as before.

"Sledgehammer, don't let him hit that shell. We'll all be blown to hell," said a worried ammo carrier crouched in the crater near me.

"Don't worry, that's my hand he just about hit," I snapped.

Our tank and the Japanese field gun kept up their duel.

"By god, when that tank knocks out that Nip gun he'll swing his 75 over thisaway, and it'll be our ass. He thinks we're Nips," said a veteran in the crater.

"Oh, Jesus!" someone moaned.

A surge of panic rose within me. In a brief moment our tank had reduced me from a well-trained, determined assistant mortar gunner to a quivering mass of terror. It was not just that I was being fired at by a machine gun that unnerved me so terribly, but that it was one of ours. To be killed by the enemy was bad enough; that was a real possibility I had prepared myself for. But to be killed by mistake by my own comrades was something I found hard to accept. It was just too much.

An authoritative voice across the trail yelled, "Secure the mortar."

A volunteer crawled off to the left, and soon the tank ceased firing on us. We learned later that our tankers were firing on us because we had moved too far ahead. They thought we were enemy support for the field gun. This also explained why the enemy shelling was passing over and exploding behind us. Tragically, the Marine who saved us by identifying us to the tanker was shot off the tank and killed by a sniper.

The heavy firing on our left had about subsided, so the Japanese counterattack had been broken. Regrettably, I hadn't helped at all, because we were pinned down by one of our own tanks.

Some of us went along the trail and looked at the Japanese field gun. It was a well-made, formidable-looking piece of artillery, but I was surprised that the wheels were the heavy wooden kind typical of field guns of the nineteenth century. The Japanese gun crew was sprawled around the piece.

"Them's the biggest Nips I ever saw," one veteran said.

"Look at them sonsabitches; they's all over six foot tall," said another.

"That must be some of that 'Flower of the Kwantung Army' we've been hearing about," put in a corporal.

The Japanese counterattack was no wild, suicidal *banzai* charge such as Marine experience in the past would have led us to expect. Numerous times during D day I heard the dogmatic claim by experienced veterans that the enemy would *banzai*.

"They'll pull a *banzai*, and we'll tear their ass up. Then we can get the hell offa this hot rock, and maybe the CG will send the division back to Melbourne."

Rather than a *banzai*, the Japanese counterthrust turned out to be a well-coordinated tank-infantry attack. Approximately one company of Japanese infantry, together with about thirteen tanks, had moved carefully across the airfield until annihilated by the Marines on our left. This was our first warning that the Japanese might fight differently on Peleliu than they had elsewhere.

Just before dusk, a Japanese mortar concentration hit 3/5's command post. Our CO, Lt. Col. Austin C. Shofner,* was hit while trying to establish contact among the companies of our battalion. He was evacuated and put aboard a hospital ship.

Companies I, K, and L couldn't regain contact before nightfall. Each dug in in a circular defense for the night. The situation was precarious. We were isolated, nearly out of water in the terrible heat, and ammunition was low. Lt. Col. Lewis Walt, accompanied by only a runner, came out into that pitch dark, enemy-infested scrub, located all the companies, and directed us into the division's line on the airfield. He should have won a Medal of Honor for that feat![†]

Rumor had it, as we dug in, that the division had suffered heavy casualties in the landing and subsequent fighting. The

---

*Shofner had assumed command of 3/5 before the Peleliu campaign. Not only was he highly respected, but his men considered him someone special. As a captain, he had survived the fighting on Corregidor, been captured by the Japanese, escaped, and had returned to combat. He came back to the division later, and commanded the 1st Battalion, 1st Marines on Okinawa. He retired from the Corps as a brigadier general.

†Walt was the executive officer of the 5th Marines when the battle for Peleliu began. He remained with 3/5 for a few days as its commanding officer until a replacement was named. A combat Marine in the truest sense, Walt had served with the 1st Marine Division on Guadalcanal and at Cape Gloucester. He had won the Navy Cross for heroism. He went on to serve in the Korean War and later in Vietnam where, as a lieutenant general, he commanded the III Marine Amphibious Corps for nearly two years. He retired as a general after serving as assistant commandant of the Marine Corps.

veterans I knew said it had been about the worst day of fighting they had ever seen.*

It was an immense relief to me when we got our gun pit
completed and had registered in our gun by firing two or three
rounds of HE into an area out in front of Company K. My
thirst was almost unbearable, my stomach was tied in knots,
and sweat soaked me. Dissolving some K ration dextrose tablets in my mouth helped, and I took the last sip of my dwin-
dling water supply. We had no idea when relief would get
through with additional water. Artillery shells shrieked and
whistled back and forth overhead with increasing frequency,
and small-arms fire rattled everywhere.

In the eerie green light of star shells swinging pendulum-
like on their parachutes so that shadows danced and swayed
around crazily, I started taking off my right shoe.

"Sledgehammer, what the hell are you doin'?" Snafu asked
in an exasperated tone.

"Taking off my boondockers; my feet hurt," I replied.

"Have you gone Asiatic?" he asked excitedly. "What the hell
are you gonna do in your stockin' feet if the Nips come bustin'
outa that jungle, or across this field? We may have to get outa
this hole and haul tail if we're ordered to. They're probably
gonna pull a *banzai* before daybreak, and how do you reckon
you'll move around on this coral in your stockin's?"

I said that I just wasn't thinking. He reamed me out good
and told me we would be lucky to get our shoes off before the
island was secured. I thanked God my foxhole buddy was a
combat veteran.

Snafu then nonchalantly drew his kabar and stuck it in the
coral gravel near his right hand. My stomach tightened and
gooseflesh chilled my back and shoulders at the sight of the
long blade in the greenish light and the realization of why
he placed it within such easy reach. He then checked his .45
automatic pistol. I followed his example with my kabar as I
crouched on the other side of the mortar, checked my carbine,

---

*Casualty figures for the 1st Marine Division on D day reflected the severity
of the fighting and the ferocity of the Japanese defense. The division staff had
predicted D day losses of 500 casualties, but the total figure was 1,111 killed and
wounded, not including heat prostration cases.

and looked over the mortar shells (HE and flares) stacked up within reach. We settled down for the long night.

"Is that theirs or ours, Snafu?" I asked each time a shell went over.

There was nothing subtle or intimate about the approach and explosion of an artillery shell. When I heard the whistle of an approaching one in the distance, every muscle in my body contracted. I braced myself in a puny effort to keep from being swept away. I felt utterly helpless.

As the fiendish whistle grew louder, my teeth ground against each other, my heart pounded, my mouth dried, my eyes narrowed, sweat poured over me, my breath came in short irregular gasps, and I was afraid to swallow lest I choke. I always prayed, sometimes out loud.

Under certain conditions of range and terrain, I could hear the shell approaching from a considerable distance, thus prolonging the suspense into seemingly unending torture. At the instant the voice of the shell grew the loudest, it terminated in a flash and a deafening explosion similar to the crash of a loud clap of thunder. The ground shook and the concussion hurt my ears. Shell fragments tore the air apart as they rushed out, whirring and ripping. Rocks and dirt clattered onto the deck as smoke of the exploded shell dissipated.

To be under a barrage of prolonged shelling simply magnified all the terrible physical and emotional effects of one shell. To me, artillery was an invention of hell. The onrushing whistle and scream of the big steel package of destruction was the pinnacle of violent fury and the embodiment of pent-up evil. It was the essence of violence and of man's inhumanity to man. I developed a passionate hatred for shells. To be killed by a bullet seemed so clean and surgical. But shells would not only tear and rip the body, they tortured one's mind almost beyond the brink of sanity. After each shell I was wrung out, limp and exhausted.

During prolonged shelling, I often had to restrain myself and fight back a wild, inexorable urge to scream, to sob, and to cry. As Peleliu dragged on, I feared that if I ever lost control of myself under shell fire my mind would be shattered. I hated shells as much for their damage to the mind as to the body. To be under heavy shell fire was to me by far the most terrifying of

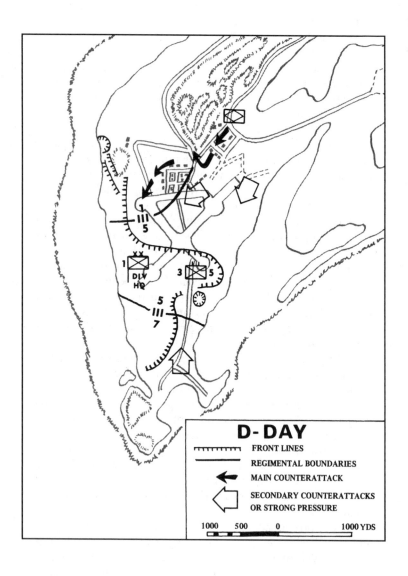

D-DAY

	FRONT LINES
	REGIMENTAL BOUNDARIES
	MAIN COUNTERATTACK
	SECONDARY COUNTERATTACKS OR STRONG PRESSURE

1000   500   0   1000 YDS

combat experiences. Each time it left me feeling more forlorn and helpless, more fatalistic, and with less confidence that I could escape the dreadful law of averages that inexorably reduced our numbers. Fear is many-faceted and has many subtle nuances, but the terror and desperation endured under heavy shelling are by far the most unbearable.

The night wore on endlessly, and I was hardly able to catch even so much as a catnap. Toward the predawn hours, numerous enemy artillery pieces concentrated their fire on the area of scrub jungle from which Lt. Col. Lewis Walt had brought us. The shells screeched and whined over us and crashed beyond in the scrub.

"Whoo, boy, listen to them Nip gunners plaster that area," said a buddy in the next hole.

"Yeah," Snafu said, "they must think we're still out there and I betcha they'll counterattack right across through that place, too."

"Thank God we are here and not out there," our buddy said.

The barrage increased in tempo as the Japanese gave the vacant scrub jungle a real pounding. When the barrage finally subsided, I heard someone say with a chuckle, "Aw, don't knock it off now, you bastards. Fire all your goddamn shells out there in the wrong place."

"Don't worry, knucklehead, they'll have plenty left to fire in the right place, which is going to be where they see us when daylight comes," another voice said.

Supplies had been slow in keeping up with the needs of the 5th Marines' infantry companies on D day. The Japanese kept heavy artillery, mortar, and machine-gun fire on the entire regimental beach throughout the day; enemy artillery and mortar observers called down their fire on amphibian vehicles as soon as they reached the beach. This made it difficult to get the critical supplies ashore and the wounded evacuated. All of Peleliu was a front line on D day. No one but the dead was out of reach of enemy fire. The shore party people* did their best, but

---

*The shore party battalion consisted of Marines assigned the mission of unloading and handling supplies and of directing logistics traffic on the beach during an amphibious assault.

they couldn't make up for the heavy losses of amtracs needed to bring the supplies to us.

We weren't aware of the problems on the beach, being too occupied with our own. We griped, cursed, and prayed that water would get to us. I had used mine more sparingly than some men had, but I finally emptied both of my canteens by the time we finished the gun pit. Dissolving dextrose tablets in my mouth helped a little, but my thirst grew worse through the night. For the first time in my life, I appreciated fully the motion picture cliche of a man on a desert crying, "Water, water."

Artillery shells still passed back and forth overhead just before dawn, but there wasn't much small-arms fire in our area. Abruptly, there swept over us some of the most intense Japanese machine-gun fire I ever saw concentrated in such a small area. Tracers streaked and bullets cracked not more than a foot over the top of our gun pit. We lay flat on our backs and waited as the burst ended.

The gun cut loose again, joined by a second and possibly a third. Streams of bluish white tracers (American tracers were red) poured thickly overhead, apparently coming from somewhere near the airfield. The cross fire kept up for at least a quarter of an hour. They really poured it on.

Shortly before the machine guns opened fire, we had received word to move out at daylight with the entire 5th Marine regiment in an attack across the airfield. I prayed the machine-gun fire would subside before we had to move out. We were pinned down tightly. To raise anything above the edge of the gun pit would have resulted in its being cut off as though by a giant scythe. After about fifteen minutes, firing ceased abruptly. We sighed in relief.

D PLUS I

Dawn finally came, and with it the temperature rose rapidly.

"Where the hell is our water?" growled men around me. We had suffered many cases of heat prostration the day before and needed water or we'd all pass out during the attack, I thought.

"Stand by to move out!" came the order. We squared away all of our personal gear. Snafu secured the gun, took it down by folding the bipod and strapping it, while I packed my remaining shells in my ammo bag.

"I've got to get some water or I'm gonna crack up," I said.

At that moment, a buddy nearby yelled and beckoned to us, "Come on, we've found a well."

I snatched up my carbine and took off, empty canteens bouncing on my cartridge belt. About twenty-five yards away, a group of Company K men gathered at a hole about fifteen feet in diameter and ten feet deep. I peered over the edge. At the bottom and to one side was a small pool of milky-looking water. Japanese shells were beginning to fall on the airfield, but I was too thirsty to care. One of the men was already in the hole filling canteens and passing them up. The buddy who had called me was drinking from a helmet with its liner removed. He gulped down the milky stuff and said, "It isn't beer, but it's wet." Helmets and canteens were passed up to those of us waiting.

"Don't bunch up, you guys. We'll draw Jap fire sure as hell," shouted one man.

The first man who drank the water looked at me and said, "I feel sick."

A company corpsman came up yelling, "Don't drink that water, you guys. It may be poisoned." I had just lifted a full helmet to my lips when the man next to me fell, holding his sides and retching violently. I threw down my water, milky with coral dust, and started assisting the corpsman with the man who was ill. He went to the rear, where he recovered. Whether it was poison or pollution we never knew.

"Get your gear on and stand by," someone yelled.

Frustrated and angry, I headed back to the gun pit. A detail came up about that time with water cans, ammo, and rations. A friend and I helped each other pour water out of a five-gallon can into our canteen cups. Our hands shook, we were so eager to quench our thirst. I was amazed that the water looked brown in my aluminum canteen cup. No matter, I took a big gulp—and almost spit it out despite my terrible thirst. It was awful. Full of rust and oil, it stunk. I looked into the cup in disbelief as a blue film of oil floated lazily on the surface of the smelly brown liquid. Cramps gripped the pit of my stomach.

My friend looked up from his cup and groaned, "Sledge-hammer, are you thinking what I'm thinking?"

"I sure am, that oil drum steam-cleaning detail on Pavuvu," I said wearily. (We had been together on a detail assigned to clean out the drums.)

"I'm a sonofabitch," he growled. "I'll never goof off on another work party as long as I live."

I told him I didn't think it was our fault. We weren't the only ones assigned to the detail, and it was obvious to us from the start (if not to some supply officer) that the method we had been ordered to use didn't really clean the drums. But that knowledge was slight consolation out there on the Peleliu airfield in the increasing heat. As awful as the stuff was, we had to drink it or suffer heat exhaustion. After I drained my cup, a residue of rust resembling coffee grounds remained, and my stomach ached.

We picked up our gear and prepared to move out in preparation for the attack across the airfield. Because 3/5's line during the night faced south and was back-to-back with that of 2/5, we had to move to the right and prepare to attack northward across the airfield with the other battalions of the regiment. The Japanese shelling of our lines began at daylight, so we had to move out fast and in dispersed formation. We finally got into position for the attack and were told to hit the deck until ordered to move again. This suited me fine, because the Japanese shelling was getting worse. Our artillery, ships, and planes were laying down a terrific amount of fire in front on the airfield and ridges beyond in preparation for our attack. Our preattack barrage lasted about half an hour. I knew we would move out when it ended.

As I lay on the blistering hot coral and looked across the open airfield, heat waves shimmered and danced, distorting the view of Bloody Nose Ridge. A hot wind blew in our faces.

An NCO hurried by, crouching low and yelling, "Keep moving out there, you guys. There's less chance you'll be hit if you go across fast and don't stop."

"Let's go," shouted an officer who waved toward the airfield. We moved at a walk, then a trot, in widely dispersed waves. Four infantry battalions—from left to right 2/1, 1/5, 2/5, and 3/5 (this put us on the edge of the airfield)—moved across the open, fire-swept airfield. My only concern then was my duty and survival, not panoramic combat scenes. But I often wondered later what that attack looked like to aerial observers and to those not immersed in the fire storms. All I was aware of were the small area immediately around me and the deafening noise.

Bloody Nose Ridge dominated the entire airfield. The Japanese had concentrated their heavy weapons on high ground; these were directed from observation posts at elevations as high as three hundred feet from which they could look down on us as we advanced. I could see men moving ahead of my squad, but I didn't know whether our battalion, 3/5, was moving across behind 2/5 and then wheeling to the right. There were also men about twenty yards to our rear.

We moved rapidly in the open, amid craters and coral rubble, through ever increasing enemy fire. I saw men to my right and left running bent as low as possible. The shells screeched and whistled, exploding all around us. In many respects it was more terrifying than the landing, because there were no vehicles to carry us along, not even the thin steel sides of an amtrac for protection. We were exposed, running on our own power through a veritable shower of deadly metal and the constant crash of explosions.

For me the attack resembled World War I movies I had seen of suicidal Allied infantry attacks through shell fire on the Western Front. I clenched my teeth, squeezed my carbine stock, and recited over and over to myself, "The Lord is my shepherd; I shall not want. Yea, though I walk through the valley of the shadow of death, I will fear no evil, for Thou art with me; Thy rod and Thy staff comfort me. . . ."

The sun bore down unmercifully, and the heat was exhausting. Smoke and dust from the barrage limited my vision. The ground seemed to sway back and forth under the concussions. I felt as though I were floating along in the vortex of some unreal thunderstorm. Japanese bullets snapped and cracked, and tracers went by me on both sides at waist height. This deadly small-arms fire seemed almost insignificant amid the erupting shells. Explosions and the hum and the growl of shell fragments shredded the air. Chunks of blasted coral stung my face and hands while steel fragments spattered down on the hard rock like hail on a city street. Everywhere shells flashed like giant firecrackers.

Through the haze I saw Marines stumble and pitch forward as they got hit. I then looked neither right nor left but just straight to my front. The farther we went, the worse it got. The noise and concussion pressed in on my ears like a vise. I gritted my teeth and braced myself in anticipation of the shock of being struck down at any moment. It seemed impossible that any of us could make it across. We passed several craters that offered shelter, but I remembered the order to keep moving. Because of the superb discipline and excellent esprit of the Marines, it had never occurred to us that the attack might fail.

About halfway across, I stumbled and fell forward. At that instant a large shell exploded to my left with a flash and a roar. A fragment ricocheted off the deck and growled over my head as I went down. On my right, Snafu let out a grunt and fell as the fragment struck him. As he went down, he grabbed his left side. I crawled quickly to him. Fortunately the fragment had spent much of its force, and luckily hit against Snafu's heavy web pistol belt. The threads on the broad belt were frayed in about an inch-square area.

I knelt beside him, and we checked his side. He had only a bruise to show for his incredible luck. On the deck I saw the chunk of steel that had hit him. It was about an inch square and a half inch thick. I picked up the fragment and showed it to him. Snafu motioned toward his pack. Terrified though I was amid the hellish chaos, I calmly juggled the fragment around in my hands—it was still hot—and dropped it into his pack. He yelled something that sounded dimly like, "Let's go." I reached for the carrying strap of the mortar, but he pushed my hand away and lifted the gun to his shoulder. We got up and moved on as fast as we could. Finally we got across and caught up with other members of our company who lay panting and sweating amid low bushes on the northeastern side of the airfield.

How far we had come in the open I never knew, but it must have been several hundred yards. Everyone was visibly shaken by the thunderous barrage we had just come through. When I looked into the eyes of those fine Guadalcanal and Cape

Gloucester veterans, some of America's best, I no longer felt ashamed of my trembling hands and almost laughed at myself with relief.

To be shelled by massed artillery and mortars is absolutely terrifying, but to be shelled in the open is terror compounded beyond the belief of anyone who hasn't experienced it. The attack across Peleliu's airfield was the worst combat experience I had during the entire war. It surpassed, by the intensity of the blast and shock of the bursting shells, all the subsequent horrifying ordeals on Peleliu and Okinawa.

The heat was incredibly intense. The temperature that day reached 105 degrees in the shade (we were *not* in the shade) and would soar to 115 degrees on subsequent days. Corpsmen tagged numerous Marines with heat prostration as being too weak to continue. We evacuated them. My boondockers were so full of sweat that my feet felt squishy when I walked. Lying on my back, I held up first one foot and then the other. Water literally poured out of each shoe.

"Hey, Sledgehammer," chuckled a man sprawled next to me, "you been walking on water."

"Maybe that's why he didn't get hit coming across that airfield," laughed another.

I tried to grin and was glad the inevitable wisecracks had started up again.

Because of the shape of the airfield, 3/5 was pinched out of the line by 2/5 on our left and 3/7 on our right after our crossing. We swung eastward and Company K tied in with 3/7, which was attacking in the swampy areas on the eastern side of the airfield.

As we picked up our gear, a veteran remarked to me with a jerk of his head toward the airfield where the shelling continued, "That was rough duty; hate to have to do that every day."

We moved through the swamps amid sniper fire and dug in for the night with our backs to the sea. I positioned my mortar in a meager gun pit on a slight rise of ground about fifteen feet from a sheer rock bluff that dropped about ten feet to the ocean. The jungle growth was extremely thick, but we had a clear hole in the jungle canopy above the gun pit through which we could fire the mortar without having shells hit the foliage and explode.

Most of the men in the company were out of sight through the thick mangroves. Still short of water, everyone was weakened by the heat and the exertions of the day. I had used my water as sparingly as possible and had to eat twelve salt tablets that day. (We kept close count of these tablets. They caused retching if we took more than necessary.)

The enemy infiltration that followed was a nightmare. Illumination fired above the airfield the previous night (D day) had discouraged infiltration in my sector, but others had experienced plenty of the hellish sort of thing we now faced and would suffer every night for the remainder of our time on Peleliu. The Japanese were noted for their infiltration tactics. On Peleliu they refined them and practiced them at a level of intensity not seen in the past.

After we had dug in late that afternoon we followed a procedure used nearly every night. Using directions from our observer, we registered in the mortar by firing a couple of HE shells into a defilade or some similar avenue of approach in front of the company not covered by our machine-gun or rifle fire where the enemy might advance. We then set up alternate aiming stakes to mark other terrain features on which we could fire. Everyone lighted up a smoke, and the password for the night was whispered along the line, passed from foxhole to foxhole. The password always contained the letter *L*, which the Japanese had difficulty pronouncing the way an American would.

Word came along as to the disposition of the platoons of the company and of the units on our flanks. We checked our weapons and placed equipment for quick access in the coming night. As darkness fell, the order was passed, "The smoking lamp is out." All talking ceased. One man in each foxhole settled down as comfortably as he could to sleep on the jagged rock while his buddy strained eyes and ears to detect any movement or sound in the darkness.

An occasional Japanese mortar shell came into the area, but things were pretty quiet for a couple of hours. We threw up a few HE shells as harassing fire to discourage movement in front of the company. I could hear the sea lapping gently against the base of the rocks behind us.

The Japanese soon began trying to infiltrate all over the company front and along the shore to our rear. We heard sporadic

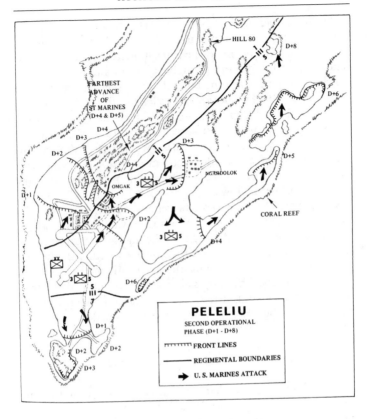

HILL 80

D+8

FARTHEST
ADVANCE
OF
1ST MARINES
(D+4 & D+5)

D+6

D+4

D+3

D+3

D+2

D+4

D+5

D+1

OMGAK

3   5

NGARDOLOK

CORAL REEF

D+2

3   5

D+4

D+6

3   5

5

III

PELELIU
SECOND OPERATIONAL
PHASE (D+1 - D+8)

⌐⌐⌐⌐⌐⌐⌐ FRONT LINES

————— REGIMENTAL BOUNDARIES

➤ U. S. MARINES ATTACK

D+1

D+2   D+2

D+3

bursts of small-arms fire and the bang of grenades. Our fire discipline had to be strict in such situations so as not to mistakenly
shoot a fellow Marine. The loose accusation was often made
during the war that Americans were "trigger happy" at night
and shot at anything that moved. This accusation was often
correct when referring to rear-area or inexperienced troops;
but in the rifle companies, it was also accepted as gospel that
anybody who moved out of his hole at night without first in-
forming the men around him, and who didn't reply immediately with the password upon being challenged, could expect
to get shot.

   Suddenly movement in the dried vegetation toward the front
of the gun pit got my attention. I turned cautiously around

and waited, holding Snafu's cocked .45 automatic pistol at the ready. The rustling movements drew closer. My heart pounded. It was definitely not one of Peleliu's numerous land crabs that scuttled over the ground all night, every night. Someone was slowly crawling toward the gun pit. Then silence. More noise, then silence. Rustling noises, then silence—the typical pattern.

It must be a Japanese trying to slip in as close as possible, stopping frequently to prevent detection, I thought. He probably had seen the muzzle flash when I fired the mortar. He would throw a grenade at any moment or jump me with his bayonet. I couldn't see a thing in the pale light and inky blackness of the shadows.

Crouching low so as to see better any silhouette against the sky above me, I flipped off the thumb safety on the big pistol. A helmeted figure loomed up against the night sky in front of the gun pit. I couldn't tell from the silhouette whether the helmet was U.S. or Japanese. Aiming the automatic at the center of the head, I pressed the grip safety as I also squeezed the trigger slightly to take up the slack. The thought raced through my mind that he was too close to use his grenade so he would probably use a bayonet or knife on me. My hand was steady even though I was scared. It was he or I.

"What's the password?" I said in a low voice.

No answer.

"Password!" I demanded as my finger tightened on the trigger. The big pistol would fire and buck with recoil in a moment, but to hurry and jerk the trigger would mean a miss for sure. Then he'd be on me.

"Sle-Sledgehammer!" stammered the figure.

I eased up on the trigger.

"It's de l'Eau, Jay de l'Eau. You got any water?"

"Jay, why didn't you give the password? I nearly shot you!" I gasped.

He saw the pistol and moaned, "Oh, Jesus," as he realized what had nearly happened. "I thought you knew it was me," he said weakly.

Jay was one of my closest friends. He was a Gloucester veteran and knew better than to prowl around the way he had just done. If my finger had applied the last bit of pressure to that trigger, Jay would have died instantly. It would have been his own fault, but that wouldn't have mattered to me. My life would have been ruined if I had killed him, even under those circumstances.

My right hand trembled violently as I lowered the big automatic. I had to flip on the thumb safety with my left hand; my right thumb was too weak. I felt nauseated and weak and wanted to cry. Jay crept over and sat on the edge of the gun pit.

"I'm sorry, Sledgehammer. I thought you knew it was me," he said.

After handing him a canteen, I shuddered violently and thanked God that Jay was still alive. "Just how in the hell could I tell it was you in the dark with Nips all over the place?" I snarled. Then I reamed out one of the best friends I ever had.

HEADING NORTH

"Get your gear on and stand by to move out."

We shouldered our loads and began moving slowly out of the thick swamp. As I passed a shallow foxhole where Robert B. Oswalt had been dug in, I asked a man nearby if the word were true about Oswalt being killed. Sadly, he said yes. Oswalt had been fatally wounded in the head. A bright young mind that aspired to delve into the mysteries of the human brain to alleviate human suffering had itself been destroyed by a tiny chunk of metal. What a waste, I thought. War is such self-defeating, organized madness the way it destroys a nation's best.

I wondered also about the hopes and aspirations of a dead Japanese we had just dragged out of the water. But those of us caught up in the maelstrom of combat had little compassion for the enemy. As a wise, salty NCO had put it one day on Pavuvu when asked by a replacement if he ever felt sorry for the Japanese when they got hit, "Hell no! It's them or us!"

We moved out, keeping our five-pace interval, through the thick swamp toward the sound of heavy firing. The heat was almost unbearable, and we were halted frequently to prevent heat prostration in the 115-degree temperature.

We came to the eastern edge of the airfield and halted in the shade of a scrub thicket. Throwing down our gear, we fell on the deck, sweating, panting, exhausted. I had no more than reached for a canteen when a rifle bullet snapped overhead.

"He's close. Get down," said an officer. The rifle cracked again. "Sounds like he's right through there a little way," the officer said.

"I'll get him," said Howard Nease.

"OK, go ahead, but watch yourself."

Nease, a Gloucester veteran, grabbed his rifle and took off into the scrub with the nonchalance of a hunter going after a rabbit in a bush. He angled to one side so as to steal up on the sniper from the rear. We waited a few anxious moments, then heard two M1 shots.

"Ole Howard got him," confidently remarked one of the men.

Soon Howard reappeared wearing a triumphant grin and carrying a Japanese rifle and some personal effects. Everyone congratulated him on his skill, and he reacted with his usual modesty.

"Rack 'em up, boys," he laughed.

We moved out in a few minutes through some knee-high bushes onto the open area at the edge of the airfield. The heat was terrific. When we halted again, we lay under the meager shade of the bushes. I held up each foot and let the sweat pour out of my boondockers. A man on the crew of the other weapon in our mortar section passed out. He was a Gloucester veteran, but Peleliu's heat proved too much for him. We evacuated him, but unlike some heat prostration cases, he never returned to the company.

Some men pulled the rear border of their camouflaged helmet cover out from between the steel and the liner so the cloth hung down over the backs of the necks. This gave them some protection against the blistering sun, but they looked like the French foreign legion in a desert.

After a brief rest, we continued in dispersed order. We could see Bloody Nose Ridge to our left front. Northward from that particular area, 2d Battalion, 1st Marines (2/1) was fighting desperately against Japanese hidden in well-protected caves. We were moving up to relieve 1st Battalion, 5th Marines (1/5) and would tie in with the 1st Marines. Then we were to attack northward along the eastern side of the ridges.

On this particular day, 17 September, the relief was slow and difficult. As 3/5 moved in and the men of 1/5 moved out, the

Japanese in the ridges on our left front poured on the artillery and mortar fire. I pitied those tired men in 1/5 as they tried to extricate themselves without casualties. Their battalion, as with the others in the 5th Marines, had had a rough time crossing the airfield through the heavy fire the previous day. But once they got across they met heavy resistance from pillboxes on the eastern side. We had been more fortunate: after getting across the airfield, 3/5 moved into the swamp, which wasn't defended as heavily.

With the relief of 1/5 finally completed, we tied in with the 1st Marines on our left and 2/5 on our right. Our battalion was to attack during the afternoon through the low ground along the eastern side of Bloody Nose, while 2/5 was to clean out the jungle between our right flank and the eastern shore.

As soon as we moved forward, we came under heavy flanking fire from Bloody Nose Ridge on our left. Snafu delivered his latest communiqué on the tactical situation to me as we hugged the deck for protection: "They need to git some more damn troops up here," he growled.

Our artillery was called in, but our mortars could fire only to the front of the company and not on the left flank area, because that was in the area of the 1st Marines. The Japanese observers on the ridge had a clear, unobstructed view of us. Their artillery shells whined and shrieked, accompanied by the deadly whispering of the mortar shells. Enemy fire grew more intense, until we were pinned down. We were getting the first bitter taste of Bloody Nose Ridge, and we had increasing compassion for the 1st Marines on our left who were battering squarely into it.

The Japanese ceased firing when our movement stopped. Yet as surely as three men grouped together, or anyone started moving, enemy mortars opened up on us. If a general movement occurred, their artillery joined in. The Japanese began to demonstrate the excellent fire discipline that was to characterize their use of all weapons on Peleliu. They fired only when they could expect to inflict maximum casualties and stopped firing as soon as the opportunity passed. Thus our observers and planes had difficulty finding their well-camouflaged positions in the ridges.

When the enemy ceased firing artillery and mortars from

caves, they shut protective steel doors and waited while our artillery, naval guns, and 81mm mortars blasted away at the rock. If we moved ahead under our protective fire support, the Japanese pinned us down and inflicted serious losses on us, because it was almost impossible to dig a protective foxhole in the rock. No individual events of the attack stuck in my mind, just the severe fire from our left and the feeling that any time the Japanese decided to do so, they could have blown us sky high.

Our attack was called off late in the afternoon, and we were ordered to set up our mortar for the night. An NCO came by and told me to go with him and about four others from other platoons to unload an amtrac bringing up supplies for Company K. We arrived at the designated place, dispersed a little so as not to draw fire, and waited for the amtrac. In a few minutes it came clanking up in a swirl of white dust.

"You guys from K Company, 5th Marines?" asked the driver.

"Yeah, you got chow and ammo for us?" asked our NCO.

"Yeah, sure have. Got a unit of fire,* water, and rations. Better get it unloaded as soon as you can, or we'll draw fire," the driver said as his machine lurched to a halt and he climbed down.

The tractor was an older model such as I had landed from on D day. It didn't have a drop tailgate; so we climbed aboard and hefted the heavy ammo boxes over the side and down onto the deck.

"Let's go, boys," our NCO said as he and a couple of us climbed onto the tractor.

I saw him gaze in amazement down into the cargo area of the tractor. At the bottom, wedged under a pile of ammo boxes, we saw one of those infernal fifty-five-gallon oil drums of water. Filled, they weighed several hundred pounds. Our NCO rested his arms on the side of the tractor and remarked in an exasperated tone, "It took a bloody genius of a supply officer to do that. How in the hell are we supposed to get that drum outa there?"

---

*Determined from experience, a unit of fire was the amount of ammunition that would last, on average, for one day of heavy fighting. A unit of fire for the M1 rifle was 100 rounds; for the carbine, 45 rounds; for the .45 caliber pistol, 14 rounds; for the light machine gun, 1,500 rounds; and for the 60mm mortar, 100 rounds.

"I don't know," said the driver. "I just bring it up."

We cursed and began unloading the ammo as fast as possible. We had expected the water to be in several five-gallon cans, each of which weighed a little more than forty pounds. We worked as rapidly as possible, but then we heard that inevitable and deadly *whisshh-shh-shh*. Three big mortar shells exploded, one after the other, not far from us.

"Uh oh, the stuff's hit the fan now," groaned one of my buddies.

"Bear a hand, you guys. On the double," said our NCO.

"Look, you guys, I'm gonna hafta get this tractor the hell outa here. If it gets knocked out and it's my fault, the lieutenant'll have my can in a crack," groaned the driver.

We had no gripe with the driver, and we didn't blame him. The amtrac drivers on Peleliu were praised by everyone for doing such a fine job. Their bravery and sense of responsibility were above question. We worked like beavers as our NCO said to him, "I'm sorry, ole buddy, but if we don't get these supplies unloaded, it's *our* ass!"

More mortar shells fell out to one side, and the fragments swished through the air. It was apparent that the Japanese mortar crew was trying to bracket us, but was afraid to fire too much for fear of being seen by our observers. We sweated and panted to get the ammo unloaded. We unloaded the water drum with a rope sling.

"You fellows need any help?" asked a Marine who appeared from the rear.

We hadn't noticed him before he spoke. He wore green dungarees, leggings, and a cloth-covered helmet like ourselves and carried a .45 caliber automatic pistol like any mortar gunner, machine gunner, or one of our officers. Of course, he wore no rank insignia, being in combat. What astonished us was that he looked to be more than fifty years old and wore glasses—a rarity (for example, only two men in Company K wore them). When he took off his helmet to mop his brow, we saw his gray hair. (Most men forward of division and regimental CPs were in their late teens or early twenties. Many officers were in their mid-twenties.)

When asked who he was and what unit he was in, he replied, "Capt. Paul Douglas. I was division adjutant until that barrage hit the 5th Marines' CP yesterday, then I was assigned as R-1 [personnel officer] in the 5th Regiment. I am very proud to be with the 5th Marines," he said.

"Gosh, Cap'n! You don't have to be up here at all, do you?" asked one of our detail in disbelief as he passed ammo boxes to the fatherly officer.

"No," Douglas said, "but I always want to know how you boys up here are making out and want to help if I can. What company are you fellows from?"

"From K Company, sir," I answered.

His face lit up, and he said, "Ah, you're in Andy Haldane's company."

We asked Douglas if he knew Ack Ack. He said, yes, that they were old friends. As we finished unloading, we all agreed that there wasn't a finer company commander than Captain Haldane.

A couple more mortar shells crashed nearby. Our luck would run out soon. Japanese gunners usually got right on target. So we yelled, "Shove off," to the driver. He waved and clanked away in his unloaded amtrac. Captain Douglas helped us stack some of the ammo and told us we had better disperse.

I heard a buddy ask, "What's that crazy old gray-headed guy doing up here if he could be back at regiment?"

Our NCO growled, "Shut up! Knock it off, you eightball! He's trying to help knuckleheads like you, and he's a damned good man."*

Each man in our detail took up a load of supplies, bade Captain Douglas "so long," and started back to the company lines. Other men went back to bring up the rest of the supplies before dark. We ate chow and finished preparations for

---

*Paul Douglas became a legend in the 1st Marine Division. This remarkable man was fifty-three years old, had been an economics professor at the University of Chicago, and had enlisted in the Marine Corps as a private. In the Peleliu battle he was slightly wounded carrying flamethrower ammunition up to the lines. At Okinawa he was wounded seriously by a bullet in the arm while carrying wounded for 3/5. Even after months of therapy, he didn't regain complete use of the limb.

Years after the war, I had the great pleasure of meeting and visiting with Senator Paul Douglas. I told him about the remark referring to him as the "crazy old gray-headed guy." He laughed heartily and expressed great pride in having served with the 1st Marine Division.

the night. That was the first night on Peleliu that I was able to make up a cup of hot bouillon from the dehydrated tablets in my K rations and a canteen cup of heated, polluted, oily water. Hot as the weather was, it was the most nourishing and refreshing food I had eaten in three days. The next day we got fresh water. It was a great relief after that polluted stuff.

Dug in next to our gun pit were 1st Lt. Edward A. ("Hillbilly") Jones, Company K's machine-gun platoon leader, and a salty sergeant, John A. Teskevich. Things were quiet in our area except for our artillery's harassing fire pouring over; so after dark obscured us from Japanese observers, the two of them slipped over and sat at the edge of our gun pit. We shared rations and talked. The conversation turned out to be one of the most memorable of my life.*

Hillbilly was second only to Ack Ack in popularity among the enlisted men in Company K. He was a clean-cut, handsome, light-complexioned man—not large, but well built. Hillbilly told me he had been an enlisted man for several prewar years, had gone to the Pacific with the company, and had been commissioned following Guadalcanal. He didn't say why he was made an officer, but the word among the men was that he had been outstanding on Guadalcanal.

It was a widespread joke among men in the ranks during the war that an officer was made an officer and a gentleman by an act of Congress when he was commissioned. An act of Congress may have made Hillbilly an officer, but he was born a gentleman. No matter how filthy and dirty everyone was on the battlefield, Hillbilly's face always had a clean, fresh appearance. He was physically tough and hard and obviously morally strong. He sweated as much as any man but somehow seemed to stand above our foul and repulsive living conditions in the field. Hillbilly had a quiet and pleasant voice even in command. His accent was soft, more that of the deep South, which was familiar to me, than that of the hill country.

Between this man and all the Marines I knew there existed a deep mutual respect and warm friendliness. He had that rare ability to be friendly yet not familiar with enlisted men. He possessed a unique combination of those qualities of bravery,

---

*Both Hillbilly and Teskevich were later killed.

leadership, ability, integrity, dignity, straightforwardness, and compassion. The only other officer I ever knew who was his equal in all these qualities was Captain Haldane.

That night Hillbilly talked about his boyhood and his home in West Virginia. He asked me about mine. He also talked about his prewar years in the Marine Corps. Later I remembered little of what he said, but the quiet way he talked calmed me. He was optimistic about the battle in progress and seemed to understand and appreciate all my fears and apprehensions. I confided in him that many times I had been so terrified that I felt ashamed, and that some men didn't seem to be so afraid. He scoffed at my mention of being ashamed, and said that my fear had been no greater than anyone else's but that I was just honest enough to admit its magnitude. He told me that he was afraid, too, and that the first battle was the hardest because a man didn't know what to expect. Fear dwelled in everyone, Hillbilly said. Courage meant overcoming fear and doing one's duty in the presence of danger, not being unafraid.

The conversation with Hillbilly reassured me. When the sergeant came over and joined in after getting coffee, I felt almost lighthearted. As conversation trailed off, we sipped our joe in silence.

Suddenly, I heard a loud voice say clearly and distinctly, "You will survive the war!"

I looked first at Hillbilly and then at the sergeant. Each returned my glance with a quizzical expression on his face in the gathering darkness. Obviously they hadn't said anything.

"Did y'all hear that?" I asked.

"Hear what?" they both inquired.

"Someone said something," I said.

"I didn't hear anything. How about you?" said Hillbilly, turning to the sergeant.

"No, just that machine gun off to the left."

Shortly the word was passed to get settled for the night. Hillbilly and the sergeant crawled back to their hole as Snafu returned to the gun pit. Like most persons, I had always been skeptical about people seeing visions and hearing voices. So I didn't mention my experience to anyone. But I believed God spoke to me that night on that Peleliu battlefield, and I resolved to make my life amount to something after the war.

That night—the third since landing—as I settled back in the gun pit, I realized I needed a bath. In short, I stunk! My mouth felt, as the saying went, like I had gremlins walking around in it with muddy boots on. Short as it was, my hair was matted with dust and rifle oil. My scalp itched, and my stubble beard was becoming an increasing source of irritation in the heat. Drinking water was far too precious in those early days to use in brushing one's teeth or in shaving, even if the opportunity had arisen.

The personal bodily filth imposed upon the combat infantryman by living conditions on the battlefield was difficult for me to tolerate. It bothered almost everyone I knew. Even the hardiest Marine typically kept his rifle and his person clean. His language and his mind might need a good bit of cleaning up but not his weapon, his uniform, or his person. We had this philosophy drilled into us in boot camp, and many times at Camp Elliott I had to pass personal inspection, to the point of clean fingernails, before being passed as fit to go on liberty. To be anything less than neat and sharp was considered a negative reflection on the Marine Corps and wasn't tolerated.

It was tradition and folklore of the 1st Marine Division that the troops routinely referred to themselves when in the field as "the raggedy-ass Marines." The emphasis during maneuvers and field problems was on combat readiness. Once back in camp, however, no matter where in the boondocks it was situated, the troops cleaned up before anything else.

In combat, cleanliness for the infantryman was all but impossible. Our filth added to our general misery. Fear and filth went hand in hand. It has always puzzled me that this important factor in our daily lives has received so little attention from historians and often is omitted from otherwise excellent personal memoirs by infantrymen. It is, of course, a vile subject, but it was as important to us then as being wet or dry, hot or cold, in the shade or exposed to the blistering sun, hungry, tired, or sick.

Early the next morning, 18 September, our artillery and 81mm mortars shelled Japanese positions to our front as we prepared to continue the previous day's attack northward on the eastern side of Bloody Nose Ridge. A typical pattern of attack in our company, or any other rifle company, went something like this. Our two mortars would fire on certain targets or areas known or thought to harbor the enemy. Our light machine-gun squads fired on areas in front of the rifle platoons they were attached to support. Then two of the three rifle platoons moved out in dispersed order. The remaining platoon was held in company reserve.

Just before the riflemen moved out, we ceased fire with the mortars. The machine guns stopped also unless they were situated where they could fire over the heads of the advancing riflemen. The latter moved out at a walk to conserve energy. If they received enemy fire, they moved from place to place in short rushes. Thus they advanced until they reached the objective. The mortars stood by to fire if the riflemen ran into strong opposition, and the machine-gun squads moved forward to add their fire support.

The riflemen were the spearhead of any attack. Consequently they caught more hell than anybody else. The machine gunners had a tough job, because the Japanese concentrated on trying to knock them out. The flamethrower gunner had it rough and so did the rocket launcher gunners and the demolitions men. The 60mm mortarmen caught it from Japanese counterbattery fire of mortars and artillery, snipers (who were numerous), and bypassed Japanese machine guns (which were common). The tankers caught hell from mortar and artillery fire and mines. But it was always the riflemen who had the worst job. The rest of us only supported them.

Marine Corps tactics called for bypassing single snipers or machine guns in order to keep forward momentum. Bypassed Japanese were knocked out by a platoon or company of infantry in reserve. Thus mortars fired furiously on the enemy to the front while a small battle raged behind between bypassed, entrenched Japanese and Marines in reserve. These Japanese frequently fired from the rear, pinning down the advance and causing casualties. Troops had to be well disciplined to function this way, and leadership had to be the best to coordinate things under such chaotic conditions. Marine tactics resembled those developed by the Germans under Gen. Erich Ludendorff which proved so successful against the Allies in the spring of 1918.

Major McIlhenny and his company commanders; 3d Bn, 5th Marines, 1st
Marine Divison. Pavuvu, June 1944. (L to R: Capt. Bishop, Capt. Neville,
Capt. McAuliffe, McIlhenny, Capt. Haldane, Capt. Crown).

An amphibious tractor burns on the beach as Marines take shelter under a
DUKW. D day, Peleliu. Private photo (Pfc. John J. Smith).

Orange Beach 3 on D day, Peleliu, to the right of where K/3/5 had landed
earlier. USMC photo.

Caliber .30 aircooled machine gun in action. Peleliu. USMC photo.

D day afternoon after Marines smashed Japanese tank attack. Peleliu. USMC photo.

Japanese soldier killed alongside his field piece. Note Japanese grenade in center foreground. Peleliu. USMC photo.

75mm howitzer of the 11th Marines fires close support for frontline troops. Peleliu. USMC photo.

Men of the 5th Marines attack across the open fireswept airfield on 16 September. Peleliu. USMC photo.

The wounded could not survive long without water in the 115° F heat. Peleliu. USMC photo.

Dead Marines lying on the north end of Airfield D-4. Peleliu. USMC photo.

81mm mortar in action. Peleliu. USMC photo.

Typical 60mm mortar section emplacement in a bomb crater blasted out of solid coral. Peleliu. USMC photo.

Assault on Ngesebus. View from amphibious amtrac while crossing in third wave from Peleliu. USMC photo.

Ngesebus: Assault troops (K/3/5) move inland. USMC photo.

Flamethrower gunner with supporting rifle fire team burns out enemy emplacement. Peleliu. USMC photo.

Corsair drops napalm on Five Sisters. Peleliu. USMC photo.

View showing the removal of a wounded Marine. Peleliu. USMC photo.

Wounded Marines being removed from the shell-blasted terrain. Peleliu. USMC photo.

Death Valley, looking north. Five Sisters on the right. Peleliu. USMC photo.

Tank infantry attack in the Horseshoe. Looking north: Five Brothers (left), Walt Ridge (right), Hill 140 (center background). USMC photo.

Col. Harold "Bucky" Harris, 5th Marines, discusses air support with some of his officers: (L to R, Lt. Col. J. R. Bailey, Harris, Maj. John "Gus" Gustafson, Lt. Col. Lewis Walt, Maj. Gordon Gayle). Peleliu. USMC photo.

K/3/5 survivors before boarding ship for Pavuvu.

A dreaded Japanese 150mm gun in its protected cave emplacement. Okinawa. USMC photo.

USS *Idaho* firing support for troops ashore. Okinawa. USMC photo.

1st Lt. Thomas "Stumpy" Stanley, CO of K/3/5, calling for artillery support.

Carrying the wounded. Okinawa. USMC photo.

Marines wait to attack as a barrage of white phosphorous shells explodes on enemy positions. USMC photo.

Gunnery Sgt. Henry A. Boyes, after the 2 May 1945 attack. Pencil indicates where an enemy bullet went through his cap. Okinawa.

Marines throwing smoke grenades to screen stretcher bearers. Okinawa. USMC photo.

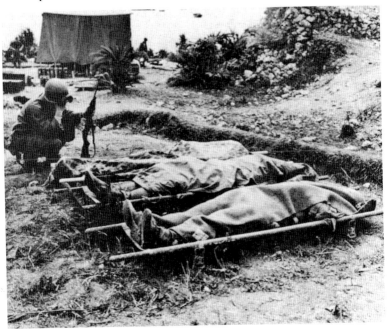

The survivor grieves. Okinawa. USMC photo.

Passing through a small village. Note split-toe tabi on dead Japanese soldier. April 1945, Okinawa. USMC photo.

Shell-blasted Wana Ridge. Okinawa. USMC photo.

Flamethrower tank cleaning out enemy. Okinawa. USMC photo.

Pfc. Paul Isen of the 5th Marines dashing across through Japanese machine-gun fire as he crosses "death valley." Okinawa. USMC photo.

Wana Ridge, Marine on left has Thompson submachine gun; his buddy has a BAR. Okinawa. USMC photo.

Collecting supplies air-dropped on Shuri Ridge after mud halted land movement to the front. USMC photo.

Rubble of the walls of Shuri Castle. Okinawa. USMC photo.

At battle's end, three weary K Company mortarmen: L to R, John Redifer, Vincent Santos, Gene Farrar. Photo by Gene Farrar.

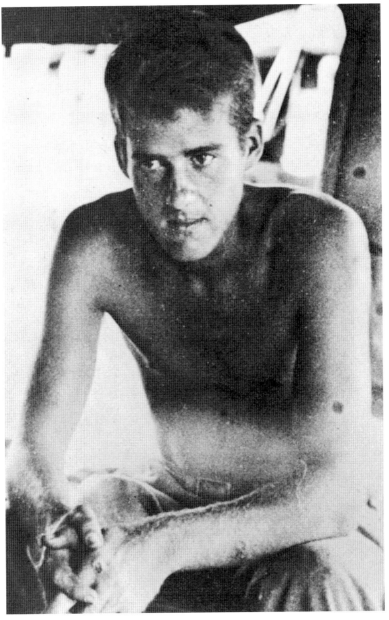
Author at the end of the campaign. Tent camp on Okinawa. Unknown photographer.

Eugene B. Sledge after return from Peking in 1946.

*

If the riflemen hit heavy opposition, our 81mm mortars, artillery, tanks, ships, and planes were called on for support. These tactics worked well on Peleliu until the Marines hit the mutually supporting complex of caves and pillboxes in the maze of coral ridges. As heavy casualties mounted, the reserve rifle platoon, mortarmen, company officers, and anybody else available acted as stretcher bearers to get the wounded out from under fire as fast as possible. Every man in Company K, no matter what his rank or job, did duty as a rifleman and stretcher bearer on numerous occasions on Peleliu and later on Okinawa.

Shelling from the ridge positions on our left slowed us down. Our planes made air strikes and our ships and artillery attacked the ridges, but Japanese shells kept coming in. The company had an increasing number of casualties. We moved our mortar several times to avoid the shelling, but the Japanese artillery and mortar fire got so heavy and caused such losses to the battalion that our attack was finally called off about noon.

On our right 2/5 made better progress. That battalion moved forward through thick jungle shielded from enemy observers, then turned east and moved out onto the smaller prong of Peleliu's "lobster claw." We moved behind 2/5 eastward across the causeway road to exploit their gain. Again shielded by thick woods, we moved away from Bloody Nose.

We pitied the 1st Marines attacking the ridges. They were suffering heavy casualties.

"The word is the 1st Marines catchin' hell," said Snafu.

"Poor guys, I pity 'em," another man said.

"Yeah, me too, but I hope like hell they take that damn ridge, and we don't have to go up there," said another.

"That shelling coming from up there was hell, and you couldn't even locate the guns with field glasses," added someone else.

From what we had seen thrown at us from the left flank during the past two days, and what I saw of the ridges then, I felt sure that sooner or later every battalion of every regiment in the division would get thrown against Bloody Nose. I was right.

The 1st Marines' predicament at the time was worse than ours in 3/5. They were attacking the end of the ridge itself, and not only received heavy shelling from enemy caves there but deadly accurate small-arms fire as well. Being tied in with the 1st Marines at the time, we got "the word" straight from the troops themselves and not from some overly optimistic officer in a CP putting pins on a map.

The word passed along the line to us told that when the men of 2/1 moved up toward the Japanese positions following preassault artillery fire, the enemy fired on them from mutually supporting positions, pinning them down and inflicting heavy losses. If they managed to get onto the slopes, the Japanese opened fire point blank from caves as soon as our artillery lifted. The enemy then moved back into their caves. If Marines got close enough to an enemy position to attack it with flamethrowers and demolition charges, Japanese in mutually supporting positions raked them with cross fire. Each slight gain by the 1st Marines on the ridges came at almost prohibitive cost in casualties. From what little we could see of the terrain and from the great deal we heard firsthand of the desperate struggle on our left, some of us suspected that Bloody Nose was going to drag on and on in a long battle with many casualties.

The troops got paid to do the fighting (I made sixty dollars a month), and the high command the thinking; but the big brass were predicting optimistically that the Japanese defenses in the ridges would be "breached any day" and Peleliu would be secured in a few days.*

As 3/5 moved eastward on 18 September, a buddy commented sadly, "You know, Sledgehammer, a guy from the 1st Marines told me they got them poor boys makin' frontal attacks with fixed bayonets on that damn ridge, and they can't even see the Nips that are shootin' at 'em. That poor kid was

---

*For nearly a week of bitter combat, Maj. Gen. William H. Rupertus insisted that the 1st Marine Division could handle the job on Peleliu alone. Only after the 1st Marine Regiment was ground down to a nub—suffering 56 percent casualties—did Maj. Gen. Roy Geiger, commander of the III Marine Amphibious Corps, overrule Rupertus and order in the U.S. Army's 321st Infantry Regiment to help the Marines.

really depressed; don't see no way he can come out alive. There just ain't no sense in that. They can't get nowhere like that. It's slaughter."

"Yeah, some goddamn glory-happy officer wants another medal, I guess, and the guys get shot up for it. The officer gets the medal and goes back to the States, and he's a big hero. Hero, my ass; gettin' troops slaughtered ain't being no hero," said a veteran bitterly.

And bitterness it was. Even the most optimistic man I knew believed our battalion must take its turn against those incredible ridges—and dreaded it.

DEATH PATROL

As we moved toward the smaller "lobster claw," Snafu chanted, "Oh, them mortar shells are bustin' up that ole gang of mine," to the tune of "Those Wedding Bells Are Breaking Up That Old Gang of Mine." We halted frequently to rest briefly and to keep down the number of cases of heat prostration.

Although not heavy, my pack felt like a steaming hot wet compress on my shoulders and upper back. We were sopping wet with sweat, and at night or during a halt in the shade our dungarees dried out a bit. When they did, heavy white lines of fine, powdery salt formed, as though drawn by chalk, along the shoulders, waist, and so on. Later, as the campaign dragged on and our dungarees caked with coral dust, they felt like canvas instead of soft cotton.

I carried a little Gideon's New Testament in my breast pocket, and it stayed soaked with sweat during the early days. The Japanese carried their personal photos and other papers in waterproof green rubber pocket-sized folding bags. I "liberated" one such bag from a corpse and used it as a covering for my New Testament. The little Bible went all the way through Okinawa's rains and mud with me, snug in its captured cover.

During one halt along a sandy road in the woods, we heard the words "hot chow" passed.

"The hell you say," someone said in disbelief.

"Straight dope; pork chops."

We couldn't believe it, but it was true. We filed past a cylindrical metal container, and each of us received a hot, delicious pork chop. The chow had been sent ashore for Company K by the crew of LST 661. I vowed if the chance ever came I would express my thanks to those sailors for that chow.*

As we sat along the road eating pork chops with our fingers, a friend sitting on his helmet next to me began to examine a Japanese pistol he had captured. Suddenly the pistol fired. He toppled over on his back but sprang up immediately, holding his hand to his forehead. Several men hit the deck, and we all ducked at the sound of the shot. I had seen what happened but ducked instinctively with an already well-developed conditioned reflex. I stood up and looked at the man's face. The bullet merely had creased his forehead. He was lucky. When the other men realized he wasn't hurt, they really began to kid him unmercifully. Typical comments went something like:

"Hey, ole buddy, I always knew you had a hard head, but I didn't know slugs would bounce off of it."

"You don't need a helmet except to sit on when we take ten."

"You're too young to handle dangerous weapons."

"Some people will do anything to get a Purple Heart."

"Is this the sort of thing you used to do to attract your mother's attention?"

He rubbed his forehead, embarrassed, and mumbled, "Aw, knock it off."

We moved along a causeway and finally halted on the edge of a swamp where the company deployed and dug in for the night. Things were fairly quiet. The next morning the company swung south, pushing through the heavy growth behind a mortar and artillery barrage. We killed a few Japanese throughout the area. Late in the day Company K deployed again for the night.

The following day, Company K received a mission to push a strong combat patrol to the east coast of the island. Our orders were to move through the thick growth onto the peninsula that formed the smaller "claw" and set up a defensive position

---

*I fulfilled that vow in July 1945 after the battle for Okinawa ended.

at the northern tip of the land mass on the edge of a mangrove swamp. Our orders didn't specify the number of days we were to remain there.

First Lt. Hillbilly Jones commanded the patrol consisting of about forty Marines plus a war dog, a Doberman pinscher. Sgt. Henry ("Hank") Boyes was the senior NCO. As with all combat patrols, we were heavily armed with rifles and BARs. We also had a couple of machine-gun squads and the mortar squad with us. Never missing an opportunity to get into the action with his cold steel, Sgt. Haney volunteered to go along.

"G-2 [division intelligence] reports there are a couple thousand Japs somewhere on the other side of that swamp, and if they try to move across it to get back to the defensive positions in Bloody Nose, we're to hold them up until artillery, air strikes, and reinforcements can join us," a veteran NCO said in a terse voice. Our mission was to make contact with the enemy, test his strength, or occupy and hold a strategic position against enemy attack. I wasn't enthusiastic about it.

We picked up extra rations and ammunition as we filed through the company lines exchanging parting remarks with friends. Heading into the thick scrub brush, I felt pretty lonesome, like a little boy going to spend his first night away from home. I realized that Company K had become my home. No matter how bad a situation was in the company, it was still home to me. It was not just a lettered company in a numbered battalion in a numbered regiment in a numbered division. It meant far more than that. It was home; it was "my" company. I belonged in it and nowhere else.

Most Marines I knew felt the same way about "their" companies in whatever battalion, regiment, or Marine division they happened to be. This was the result of, or maybe a cause for, our strong esprit de corps. The Marine Corps wisely acknowledged this unit attachment. Men who recovered from wounds and returned to duty nearly always came home to their old company. This was not misplaced sentimentality but a strong contributor to high morale. A man felt that he belonged to his unit and had a niche among buddies whom he knew and with whom he shared a mutual respect welded in combat. This sense of family was particularly important in the infantry, where survival and combat efficiency often hinged on how well men could depend on one another.*

We moved through the thick growth quietly in extended formation, with scouts out looking out for snipers. Things in our area were quiet, but the battle rumbled on Bloody Nose. Thick jungle growth clogged the swamp, which also contained numerous shallow tidal inlets and pools choked with mangroves and bordered by more mangroves and low pandanus trees. If a plant were designed especially to trip a man carrying a heavy load, it would be a mangrove with its tangle of roots.

I walked under a low tree that had a pair of man-o-war birds nesting in its top. They showed no fear as they cocked their heads and looked down from their bulky stick nest. The male saw little of interest about me and began inflating his large red throat pouch to impress his mate. He slowly extended his huge seven-foot wingspan and clicked his long hooked beak. As a boy, I had seen similar man-o-war birds sailing high over Gulf Shores near Mobile, but never had I seen them this close. Several large white birds similar to egrets also perched nearby, but I couldn't identify them.

My brief escape from reality ended abruptly when a buddy scolded in a low voice, "Sledgehammer, what the hell you staring at them birds for? You gonna get separated from the patrol," as he motioned vigorously for me to hurry. He thought I'd lost my senses, and he was right. That was neither the time nor the place for something as utterly peaceful and ethereal as bird watching. But I had had a few delightful and refreshing moments of fantasy and escape from the horror of human activities on Peleliu.

We moved on and finally halted near an abandoned Japanese machine-gun bunker built of coconut logs and coral rock. This bunker served as our patrol's CP. We deployed around it and dug in. The area was just a few feet above the water level, and

---

*During and after the war, army men told me that if a soldier got wounded and later returned to infantry duty, there was little chance it would be to his old company. They all agreed that was regrettable. They didn't like the practice, because a recuperated veteran became just another replacement in a strange outfit.

the coral was fairly loose. We dug the mortar gun pit within a few feet of the swamp water, about thirty feet from the bunker. Visibility through the swamp was limited to a few feet by the dense tangle of mangrove roots on three sides of the patrol's defense perimeter. We didn't register in the gun, because we had to maintain absolute quiet at all times. If we made noise, we would lose the element of surprise should the Japanese try to come across the area. We simply aimed the mortar in the direction we would be most likely to fire. We ate our rations, checked our weapons, and prepared for a long night.

We received the password as darkness settled on us, and a drizzling rain began. We felt isolated listening to moisture dripping from the trees and splashing softly into the swamp. It was the darkest night I ever saw. The overcast sky was as black as the dripping mangroves that walled us in. I had the sensation of being in a great black hole and reached out to touch the sides of the gun pit to orient myself. Slowly the reality of it all formed in my mind: we were expendable!

It was difficult to accept. We come from a nation and a culture that values life and the individual. To find oneself in a situation where your life seems of little value is the ultimate in loneliness. It is a humbling experience. Most of the combat veterans had already grappled with this realization on Guadalcanal or Gloucester, but it struck me out in that swamp.

George Sarrett, a Gloucester veteran, was in the gun pit with me, and we tried to cheer each other up. In low tones he talked of his boyhood in Texas and about Gloucester.

Word came that Haney was crawling along checking positions.

"What's the password?" whispered Haney as he crawled up to us. George and I both whispered the password. "Good," said Haney. "You guys be on the alert, you hear?"

"OK, Haney," we said. He crawled over to the CP where I assumed he settled down.

"I guess he'll be still for a while now," I said.

"Hope the hell you're right," answered George.

Well, I wasn't, because in less than an hour Haney made the rounds again.

"What's the password?" he whispered as he poked his head up to the edge of our hole.

We told him. "Good," he said. "You guys check your weapons. Got a round in the chamber?" he asked each of us.

We answered yes. "OK, stand by with that mortar. If the Nips come through this swamp at high port with fixed bayonets, you'll need to fire HE and flares as fast as you can." He crawled off.

"Wish that Asiatic old boy would settle down. He makes me nervous. He acts like we are a bunch of green boots," my companion growled. George was a cool-headed, self-possessed veteran, and he spoke my sentiments. Haney was making me jittery, too.

Weary hours dragged on. We strained our eyes and ears in the dripping blackness for indications of enemy movement. We heard the usual jungle sounds caused by animals. A splash, as something fell into the water, made my heart pound and caused every muscle to tighten. Haney's inspection tours got worse. He obviously was getting more nervous with each hour.

"I wish to hell Hillbilly would grab him by the stackin' swivel and anchor him in the CP," George mumbled.

The luminous dial of my wristwatch showed the time was after midnight. In the CP a low voice sounded, "Oh, ah, oh" and trailed off, only to repeat the sound louder.

"What's that?" I asked George anxiously.

"Sounds like some guy havin' a nightmare," he replied nervously. "They sure as hell better shut him up before every Nip in this damned swamp knows our position." We heard someone moving and thrashing around in the CP.

"Knock it off," several men whispered near us.

"Quiet that man down!" Hillbilly ordered in a stern low voice.

"Help! help! Oh God, help me!" shouted the wild voice. The poor Marine had cracked up completely. The stress of combat had finally shattered his mind. They were trying to calm him down, but he kept thrashing around. In a firm voice filled with compassion, Hillbilly was trying to reassure the man that he was going to be all right. The effort failed. Our comrade's tragically tortured mind had slipped over the brink. He screamed more loudly. Someone pinioned the man's arms to his sides, and he screamed to the Doberman pinscher, "Help me, dog; the Japs have got me! The Japs have got me and they're gonna throw me in the ocean." I heard the sickening crunch of a fist against a jaw as someone tried to knock the man unconscious. It didn't faze him. He fought like a wildcat, yelling and screaming at the top of his voice.

Our corpsman then gave him an injection of morphine in the hope of sedating him. It had no effect. More morphine; it had no effect either. Veterans though they were, the men were all getting jittery over the noise they believed would announce our exact location to any enemy in the vicinity.

"Hit him with the flat of that entrenching shovel!" a voice commanded in the CP. A horrid *thud* announced that the command was obeyed. The poor man finally became silent.

"Christ a'mighty, what a pity," said a Marine in a neighboring foxhole.

"You said that right, but if the goddamn Nips don't know we're here, after all that yellin', they'll never know," his buddy said.

A tense silence settled over the patrol. The horror of the whole affair stimulated Haney to check our positions frequently. He acted like some hyperactive demon and cautioned us endlessly to be on the alert.

When welcome dawn finally came after a seemingly endless blackness, we all had frayed nerves. I walked the few paces over to the CP to find out what I could. The man was dead. Covered with his poncho, his body lay next to the bunker. The agony and distress etched on the strong faces of Hillbilly, Hank, and the others in the CP revealed the personal horror of the night. Several of these men had received or would receive decorations for bravery in combat, but I never saw such agonized expressions on their faces as that morning in the swamp. They had done what any of us would have had to do under similar circumstances. Cruel chance had thrust the deed upon them.

Hillbilly looked at the radioman and said, "I'm taking this patrol in. Get battalion for me."

The radioman tuned his big pack-sized radio and got the battalion CP. Hillbilly told the battalion CO, Major Gustafson, that he wanted to bring in the patrol. We could hear the major tell Hillbilly he thought we should stay put for a couple of days until G-2 could determine the disposition of the Japanese. Hillbilly, a first lieutenant, calmly disagreed, saying we hadn't fired a shot, but because of circumstances we all had a pretty bad case of nerves. He felt strongly that we should come in. I saw several old salts raise their eyebrows and smile as Hillbilly stated his opinion. To our relief, Gus agreed with him; I have always thought it was probably because of his respect for Hillbilly's judgment.

"I'll send a relief column with a tank so you won't have any trouble coming in," said the major's voice. We all felt comforted. The word went rapidly through the patrol that we were going in. Everyone breathed easier. In about an hour we heard a tank coming. As it forced its way through the thick growth, we saw familiar faces of Company K men with it. We placed the body on the tank, and we returned to the company's lines. I never heard an official word about the death thereafter.

RELIEF FOR THE 1ST MARINES

Over the next few days, the 5th Marines patrolled most of the southern "claw." We had set up defensive positions to prevent any possible counterlanding by the Japanese along the exposed southern beaches.

On about 25 September (D + 10) the battered 1st Marine Regiment was relieved by the U.S. Army's 321st Infantry Regiment of the 81st Infantry Division. The 1st Marines moved into our area where they were to await a ship to return them to Pavuvu. We picked up our gear and moved out from the relative quiet of the beach to board trucks that would speed our regiment to a position straddling the west road. From there we would attack northward along the western side of the ridges.

As we walked along one side of a narrow road, the 1st Marines filed along the other side to take over our area. I saw some familiar faces as the three decimated battalions trudged past us, but I was shocked at the absence of so many others whom I knew in that regiment. During the frequent halts typical to the movement of one unit into the position of another, we exchanged greetings with buddies and asked about the fate of mutual friends. We in the 5th Marines had many a dead or wounded friend to report about from our ranks, but the men in the 1st Marines had so many it was appalling.

"How many men left in your company?" I asked an old Camp Elliott buddy in the 1st Marines.

He looked at me wearily with bloodshot eyes and choked as he said, "Twenty is all that's left in the whole company, Sledgehammer. They nearly wiped us out. I'm the only one left out of the old bunch in my company that was with us in mortar school at Elliott."

I could only shake my head and bite my lip to keep from getting choked up. "See you on Pavuvu," I said.

"Good luck," he said in a dull resigned tone that sounded as though he thought I might not make it.

What once had been companies in the 1st Marines looked like platoons; platoons looked like squads. I saw few officers. I couldn't help wondering if the same fate awaited the 5th Marines on those dreadful ridges. Twenty bloody, grueling, terrible days and nights later, on 15 October (D + 30) my regiment would be relieved. Its ranks would be just about as decimated as those we were filing past.

We boarded trucks that carried us southward along the east road then some distance northward along the west road. As we bumped and jolted past the airfield, we were amazed at all the work the Seabees (naval construction battalions) had accomplished on the field. Heavy construction equipment was everywhere, and we saw hundreds of service troops living in tents and going about their duties as though they were in Hawaii or Australia. Several groups of men, Army and Marine service troops, watched our dusty truck convoy go by. They wore neat caps and dungarees, were clean-shaven, and seemed relaxed. They eyed us curiously, as though we were wild animals in a circus parade. I looked at my buddies in the truck and saw why. The contrast between us and the onlookers was striking. We were armed, helmeted, unshaven, filthy, tired, and haggard. The sight of clean comfortable noncombatants was depressing, and we tried to keep up our morale by discussing the show of U.S. material power and technology we saw.

We got off the trucks somewhere up the west road parallel to the section of the ridges on our right that was in American hands. We heard firing on the closest ridge. The troops I saw along the road as we unloaded were army infantrymen from the 321st Infantry Regiment, veterans of Angaur.

As I exchanged a few remarks with some of these men, I felt a deep comradeship and respect for them. Reporters and historians like to write about interservice rivalry among military men; it certainly exists, but I found that front-line combatants in all branches of the services showed a sincere mutual respect when they faced the same danger and misery. Combat soldiers and sailors might call us "gyrenes," and we called them "dog-faces" and "swabbies," but we respected each other completely.

After the relief of 1st Marines, a new phase of the fight for Peleliu began. No longer would the Marines suffer prohibitive casualties in fruitless frontal assaults from the south against the ridges. Rather they would sweep up the western coast around the enemy's last-ditch defenses in search of a better route into the final pocket of resistance.

Although the bitter battle for Peleliu would drag on for another two months, the 1st Marine Division seized all of the terrain of strategic value in the first week of bitter fighting. In a series of exhausting assaults, the division had taken the vital airfield, the commanding terrain above it, and all of the island south and east of Umurbrogol Mountain. Yet the cost had been high: 3,946 casualties. The division had lost one regiment as an effective fighting unit, and had severely depleted the strength of its other two.

CHAPTER FIVE

Another Amphibious Assault

THE 5TH Marines now had the mission to secure the northern part of the island—that is, the upper part of the larger "lobster claw." Following that chore the regiment was to move south again on the eastern side of the Umurbrogol ridges to complete the isolation and encirclement. Most of us in the ranks never saw a map of Peleliu except during training on Pavuvu, and had never heard the ridge system referred to by its correct name, Umurbrogol Mountain. We usually referred to the whole ridge system as "Bloody Nose," "Bloody Nose Ridge," or simply "the ridges."

As we moved through the army lines, Japanese machine guns were raking the crest of the ridge on our right. The slugs and bluish white tracers pinned down the American troops on the ridge but passed high above us on the road. The terrain was flat and sparsely wooded. Tanks supported us, and we were fired on by small arms, artillery, and mortars from the high coral ridges to our right and from Ngesebus Island a few hundred yards north of Peleliu.

Our battalion turned right at the junction of West Road and East Road, headed south along the latter, and stopped at dusk. As usual, there wasn't much digging in as such, mostly finding some crater or depression and piling rocks around it for what protection we could get.

I was ordered to carry a five-gallon can of water over to the company CP. When I got there, Ack Ack was studying a map by the light of a tiny flashlight that his runner shielded with another folded map. The company's radioman was sitting with him, quietly tuning his radio and calling an artillery battery of the 11th Marines.

Putting the water can down, I sat on it and watched my skipper with admiration. Never before had I regretted so profoundly my lack of artistic talent and inability to draw the scene before me. The tiny flashlight faintly illuminated Captain Haldane's face as he studied the map. His big jaw, covered with a charcoal stubble of beard, jutted out. His heavy brow wrinkled with concentration just below the rim of his helmet.

The radioman handed the phone to Ack Ack. He requested a certain number of rounds of 75mm HE to be fired out to Company K's front. A Marine on the other end of the radio questioned the need for the request.

Haldane answered pleasantly and firmly, "Maybe so, but I want my boys to feel secure." Shortly the 75s came whining overhead and started bursting in the dark thick growth across the road.

Next day I told several men what Ack Ack had said. "That's the skipper for you, always thinking of the troops' feelings," was the way one man summed it up.

Several hours passed. It was my turn to be on watch in our hole. Snafu slept fitfully and ground his teeth audibly, which he usually did during sleep in combat. The white coral road shone brightly in the pale moonlight as I strained my eyes looking across into the wall of dark growth on the other side.

Suddenly two figures sprang up from a shallow ditch directly across the road from me. With arms waving wildly, yelling and babbling hoarsely in Japanese, they came. My heart skipped a beat, then began pounding like a drum as I flipped off the safety of my carbine. One enemy soldier angled to my right, raced down the road a short distance, crossed over, and disappeared into a foxhole in the line of the company on our right flank. I focused on the other. Swinging a bayonet over his head, he headed at me.

I dared not fire at him yet, because directly between us was a foxhole with two Marines in it. If I fired just as the Marine on watch rose up to meet the Japanese intruder, my bullet would surely hit a comrade in the back. The thought flashed through my mind, "Why doesn't Sam or Bill fire at him?"

With a wild yell the Japanese jumped into the hole with the two Marines. A frantic, desperate, hand-to-hand struggle ensued, accompanied by the most gruesome combination of curses, wild babbling, animalistic guttural noises, and grunts. Sounds of men hitting each other and thrashing around came from the foxhole.

I saw a figure pop out of the hole and run a few steps toward the CP. In the pale moonlight, I then saw a Marine nearest the running man jump up. Holding his rifle by the muzzle and swinging it like a baseball bat, he blasted the infiltrator with a smashing blow.

From our right, where the Japanese had gone into the company on our flank, came hideous, agonized, and prolonged screams that defied description. Those wild, primitive, brutish yellings unnerved me more than what was happening within my own field of vision.

Finally a rifle shot rang out from the foxhole in front of me, and I heard Sam say, "I got him."

The figure that had been clubbed by the rifle lay groaning on the deck about twenty feet to the left of my hole. The yelling over to our right ceased abruptly. By this time, of course, everyone was on the alert.

"How many Nips were there?" asked a sergeant near me.

"I saw two," I answered.

"There must'a been more," someone else put in.

"No," I insisted, "only two came across the road here. One of them ran to the right where all that yelling was, and the other jumped into the hole where Sam shot him."

"Well, then, if there were just those two Nips, what's all that groanin' over here then?" he asked, indicating the man felled by the rifle butt.

"I don't know, but I didn't see but two Nips, and I'm sure of it," I said adamantly—with an insistence that has given me peace of mind ever since.

A man in a nearby hole said, "I'll check it out." Everyone sat still as he crawled to the groaning man in the shadows. A .45 pistol shot rang out. The moaning stopped, and the Marine returned to his hole.

A few hours later as objects around me became faintly visible with the dawn, I noticed that the still form lying to my left didn't appear Japanese. It was either an enemy in Marine dungarees and leggings, or it was a Marine. I went over to find out which.

Before I got to the prone body, its identity was obvious to me. "My God!" I said in horror.

Several men looked at me and asked what was the matter.

"It's Bill," I said.

An officer and an NCO came over from the CP.

"Did he get shot by one of those Japs?" asked the sergeant.

I didn't answer, just looked at him with a blank stare and felt sick. I looked at the man who had crawled past me to check on the groaning man in the dark. He had shot Bill through the temple, mistakenly assuming him to be a Japanese. Bill hadn't told any of us he was leaving his foxhole.

As the realization of his fatal mistake hit him, the man's face turned ashen, his jaw trembled, and he looked as though he were going to cry. Man that he was, though, he went straight over and reported to the CP. Ack Ack sent for and questioned several men who were dug in nearby, including myself, to ascertain exactly what had happened.

Ack Ack was seated off to himself. "At ease, Sledge," he said. "Do you know what happened last night?"

I told him I had a pretty good idea.

"Tell me exactly what you saw."

I told him, making clear I had seen two, and only two, Japanese and had said so at the time. I also told him where I saw those enemy soldiers go.

"Do you know who killed Bill?" the captain asked.

"Yes," I said.

Then he told me it had been a tragic mistake that anyone could have made under the circumstances and never to discuss it or mention the man's name. He dismissed me.

As far as the men were concerned, the villain in the tragedy was Sam. At the time of the incident Sam was supposed to be on watch while Bill was taking his turn at getting much-needed sleep. It was routine that at a preagreed time, the man on watch woke his buddy and, after reporting anything he had seen or heard, took his turn at sleep.

This standard procedure in combat on the front line was based on a fundamental creed of faith and trust. You could depend on your buddy; he could depend on you. It extended beyond your foxhole, too. We felt secure, knowing that one man in each hole was on watch through the night.

Sam had betrayed that basic trust and had committed an unforgivable breach of faith. He went to sleep on watch while on the line. As a result his buddy died and another man would bear the heavy burden of knowing that, accident though it was, he had pulled the trigger.

Sam admitted that he might have dozed off. The men were extremely hard on him for what had happened. He was visibly remorseful, but it made no difference to the others who openly blamed him. He whined and said he was too tired to stay awake on watch, but he only got sworn at by men who were equally tired yet reliable.

We all liked Bill a great deal. He was a nice young guy, probably in his teens. On the neatly typewritten muster roll for the 3d Battalion, 5th Marines on 25 September 1944, one reads these stark words: "_____, William S., killed in action against the enemy (wound, gunshot, head)—remains interred in grave #3/M." So simply stated. Such an economy of words. But to someone who was there, they convey a tragic story. What a waste.

The Japanese who had come across the road in front of me were probably members of what the enemy called a "close-quarter combat unit." The enemy soldier shot by Sam was not dressed or equipped like their typical infantryman. Rather he wore only tropical khaki shorts, short-sleeved shirt, and *tabi* footwear (split-toed, rubber-soled canvas shoes). He carried only his bayonet. Why he entered our line where he did may have been pure accident, or he may have had an eye on our mortar. His comrade angled off toward the right near a machine gun on our flank. Mortars and machine guns were favorite targets for infiltrators on the front lines. To the rear, they went after heavy mortars, communications, and artillery.

Before Company K moved out, I went down the road to the next company to see what had happened during the night. I learned that those blood-chilling screams had come from the Japanese I had seen run to the right. He had jumped into a foxhole where he met an alert Marine. In the ensuing struggle each had lost his weapon. The desperate Marine had jammed his forefinger into his enemy's eye socket and killed him. Such was the physical horror and brutish reality of war for us.

NGESEBUS ISLAND

Early the next morning our battalion made a successful assault on a small hill on the narrow neck of northern Peleliu. Because of its isolated position, it lacked the mutual support from surrounding caves that made most of the ridges on the island impregnable.

At this time the rest of the regiment was getting a lot of enemy fire from Ngesebus Island. The word was that several days earlier the Japanese had slipped reinforcements by barge down to Peleliu from the larger islands to the north; some of the barges had been shot up and sunk by the navy, but several hundred enemy troops got ashore. It was a real blow to our morale to hear this.*

"Sounds just like Guadalcanal," said a veteran. "About the time we think we got the bastards boxed in, the damn Nips bring in reinforcements, and it'll go on and on."

"Yeah," said another, "and once them slant-eyed bastards get in these caves around here, it'll be hell to pay."

On 27 September army troops took over our positions. We moved northward.

"Our battalion is ordered to hit the beach on Ngesebus Island tomorrow," an officer told us.†

I shuddered as I recalled the beachhead we had made on 15 September. The battalion moved into an area near the northern peninsula and dug in for the night in a quiet area. It was sandy, open, and had some shattered, drooping palms. We didn't know what to expect on Ngesebus. I prayed the landing wouldn't be a repeat of the holocaust of D day.

Early in the morning of 28 September (D + 13) we squared away our gear and stood by to board the amtracs that would take us across the 500–700 yards of shallow reef to Ngesebus.

"We'll probably get another battle star for this beachhead," said a man enthusiastically.

"No we won't," answered another. "It's still just part of the Peleliu operation."

"The hell you say; it's still another beachhead," the first man responded.

---

*On the night of 22–23 September about six hundred Japanese of the 2d Battalion, 15th Regiment came down from Babelthuap and got ashore on Peleliu as reinforcements.
†Ngesebus had to be captured to silence the enemy fire coming into the 5th Marines' flank and to prevent its use as a landing place for Japanese reinforcements from the north. There was also an airfield on Ngesebus—a fighter strip —that was supposed to be useful for American planes.

"I don't make the regulation, ole buddy, but you check with the gunny, and I'll betcha I'm right." Several mumbled comments came out about how stingy the high command was in authorizing battle stars, which were little enough compensation for combat duty.

We boarded the tractors and tried to suppress our fear. Ships were firing on Ngesebus, and we saw Marine F4U Corsair fighter planes approaching from the Peleliu airfield to the south. "We gonna have lots of support for this one," an NCO said.

Our amtracs moved to the water's edge and waited for H hour as the thunderous prelanding naval gunfire bombardment covered the little island in smoke, flame, and dust. The Corsairs from Marine Fighter Squadron (VMF) 114 peeled off and began bombing and strafing the beach. The engines of the beautiful blue gull-winged planes roared, whined, and strained as they dove and pulled out. They plastered the beach with machine guns, bombs, and rockets. The effect was awesome as dirt, sand, and debris spewed into the air.*

Our Marine pilots outdid themselves, and we cheered, yelled, waved, and raised our clenched fists to indicate our approval. Never during the war did I see fighter pilots take such risks by not pulling out of their dives until the very last instant. We were certain, more than once, that a pilot was pulling out too late and would crash. But, expert flyers that they were, they gave that beach a brutal pounding without mishap to plane or pilot. We talked about their spectacular flying even after the war ended.

Out to sea on our left, with a cruiser, destroyers, and other ships firing support, was a huge battleship. Someone said it was the USS *Mississippi*, but I never knew for sure. She ranked with the Corsairs in the mass of destruction she hurled at Ngesebus. The huge shells rumbled like freight cars—as the men always used to describe the sound of projectiles from full-sized battleships' 16-inch guns.

At H hour our tractor driver revved up his engine. We moved

---

*Ngesebus was one of the first American amphibious assaults where air support for the landing force came exclusively from Marine aircraft. In earlier landings, air support came from navy and sometimes army planes.

into the water and started the assault. My heart pounded in my throat. Would my luck hold out? "The Lord is my shepherd," I prayed quietly and squeezed my carbine stock.

To our relief we received no fire as we approached the island. When my amtrac lurched to a stop well up on the beach, the tailgate went down with a bump, and we scrambled out. With its usual din and thunder the bombardment moved inland ahead of us. Some Company K Marines on the beach were already firing into pillboxes and bunkers and dropping in grenades. With several other men, I headed inland a short distance. But as we got to the edge of the airstrip, we had to dive for cover. A Nambu (Japanese light machine gun) had cut loose on us.

A buddy and I huddled behind a coral rock as the machine-gun slugs zipped viciously overhead. He was on my right. Because the rock was small, we pressed shoulder to shoulder, hugging it for protection. Suddenly there was a sickening crack like someone snapping a large stick.

My friend screamed, "Oh God, I'm hit!" and lurched over onto his right side. He grabbed his left elbow with his right hand, groaning and grimacing with pain as he thrashed around kicking up dust.

A bypassed sniper had seen us behind the rock and shot him. The bullet hit him in the left arm, which was pressed tightly against my right arm as we sought cover from the machine gun out front. The Nambu was firing a bit high, but there was no doubt the sniper had his sights right on us. We were between a rock and a hard place. I dragged him around the rock out of sight of the sniper as the Nambu bullets whizzed overhead.

I yelled, "Corpsman!" and Ken (Doc) Caswell,* the mortar section corpsman, crawled over, opening his pouch to get at his first aid supplies as he came. Another man also came over to see if he could help. While I cut away the bloody dungaree sleeve from the injured arm with my kabar, Doc began to tend the wound. As he knelt over his patient, the other Marine placed his kabar under the injured man's pack strap and gave a violent upward jerk to cut away the shoulder pack. The razor-sharp

---

*Habitually and affectionately, Marines call all U.S. Navy corpsmen who serve with them "Doc."

blade sliced through the thick web pack strap as though it were a piece of string. But before the Marine could arrest its upward motion, the knife cut Doc in the face to the bone.

Doc recoiled in pain from the impact of the knife thrust. Blood flowed down his face from the nasty gash to the left of his nose. He regained his balance immediately and returned to his work on the smashed arm as though nothing had happened. The clumsy Marine cursed himself for his blunder as I asked Doc what I could do to help him. Despite considerable pain, Doc kept at his work. In a quiet, calm voice he told me to get a battle dressing out of his pouch and press it firmly against his face to stop the bleeding while he finished work on the wounded arm. Such was the selfless dedication of the navy hospital corpsmen who served in Marine infantry units. It was little wonder that we held them in such high esteem. (Doc later got his face tended and was back with the mortar section in a matter of a few hours.)

While I did as Doc directed, I yelled at two Marines coming our way and pointed toward the sniper. They took off quickly toward the beach and hailed a tank. By the time a stretcher team came up and took my wounded friend, the two men trotted by, waved, and one said, "We got the bastard; he ain't gonna shoot nobody else."

The Nambu had ceased firing, and an NCO signaled us forward. Before moving out, I looked toward the beach and saw the walking wounded wading back toward Peleliu.

After we moved farther inland, we received orders to set up the mortars on the inland side of a Japanese pillbox and prepare to fire on the enemy to our company's front. We asked Company K's gunnery sergeant, Gy. Sgt. W. R. Saunders, if he knew of any enemy troops in the bunker. It appeared undamaged. He said some of the men had thrown grenades through the ventilators, and he was sure there were no live enemy inside.

Snafu and I began to set up our mortar about five feet from the bunker. Number One mortar was about five yards to our left. Cpl. R. V. Burgin was getting the sound-powered phone hooked up to receive fire orders from Sgt. Johnny Marmet, who was observing.

I heard something behind me in the pillbox. Japanese were talking in low, excited voices. Metal rattled against an iron grating. I grabbed my carbine and yelled, "Burgin, there're Nips in that pillbox."

All the men readied their weapons as Burgin came over to have a look, kidding me with, "Shucks, Sledgehammer, you're crackin' up." He looked into the ventilator port directly behind me. It was rather small, approximately six inches by eight inches, and covered with iron bars about a half inch apart. What he saw brought forth a stream of curses in his best Texas style against all Nippon. He stuck his carbine muzzle through the bars, fired two quick shots, and yelled, "I got 'em right in the face."

The Japanese inside the pillbox began jabbering loudly. Burgin was gritting his teeth and calling the enemy SOBs while he fired more shots through the opening.

Every man in the mortar section was ready for trouble as soon as Burgin fired the first shot. It came in the form of a grenade tossed out of the end entrance to my left. It looked as big as a football to me. I yelled "Grenade!" and dove behind the sand breastwork protecting the entrance at the end of the pillbox. The sand bank was about four feet high and L-shaped to protect the entrance from fire from the front and flanks. The grenade exploded, but no one was hit.

The Japanese tossed out several more grenades without causing us injury, because we were hugging the deck. Most of the men crawled around to the front of the pillbox and crouched close to it between the firing ports, so the enemy inside couldn't fire at them. John Redifer and Vincent Santos jumped on top. Things got quiet.

I was nearest the door, and Burgin yelled to me, "Look in and see what's in there, Sledgehammer."

Being trained to take orders without question, I raised my head above the sand bank and peered into the door of the bunker. It nearly cost me my life. Not more than six feet from me crouched a Japanese machine gunner. His eyes were black dots in a tan, impassive face topped with the familiar mushroom helmet. The muzzle of his light machine gun stared at me like a gigantic third eye.

Fortunately for me, I reacted first. Not having time to get my carbine into firing position, I jerked my head down so fast my helmet almost flew off. A split second later he fired a burst of six or eight rounds. The bullets tore a furrow through the bank just above my head and showered sand on me. My ears rang from the muzzle blast and my heart seemed to be in my throat choking me. I knew damned well I had to be dead! He just couldn't have missed me at that range.

A million thoughts raced through my terrified mind: of how my folks had nearly lost their youngest, of what a stupid thing I had done to look directly into a pillbox full of Japanese without even having my carbine at the ready, and of just how much I hated the enemy anyway. Many a Marine veteran had already lost his life on Peleliu for making less of a mistake than I had just made.

Burgin yelled and asked if I were all right. A hoarse squawk was all the answer I could muster, but his voice brought me to my senses. I crawled around to the front, then up on top of the bunker before the enemy machine gunner could have another try at me.

Redifer yelled, "They've got an automatic weapon in there." Snafu disagreed, and a spirited argument ensued. Redifer pointed out that there surely was an automatic weapon in there and that I should know, because it came close to blowing off my head. But Snafu was adamant. Like much of what I experienced in combat, this exchange was unreal. Here we were: twelve Marines with a bull by the tail in the form of a well-built concrete pillbox containing an unknown number of Japanese with no friendly troops near us and Snafu and Redifer —veterans—in a violent argument.

Burgin shouted, "Knock it off," and they shut up.

Redifer and I lay prone on top of the bunker, just above the door. We knew we had to get the Japanese while they were bottled up, or they would come out at us with knives and bayonets, a thought none of us relished. Redifer and I were close enough to the door to place grenades down the opening and move back before they exploded. But the Japanese invariably tossed them back at us before the explosion. I had an irrepressible urge to do just that. Brief as our face-to-face meeting had been, I had quickly developed a feeling of strong personal hate for that machine gunner who had nearly blasted my head off my shoulders. My terror subsided into a cold, homicidal rage and a vengeful desire to get even.

Redifer and I gingerly peeped down over the door. The machine gunner wasn't visible, but we looked at three long Arisaka rifle barrels with bayonets fixed. Those bayonets seemed ten feet long to me. Their owners were jabbering excitedly, apparently planning to rush out. Redifer acted quickly. He held his carbine by the barrel and used the butt to knock down the rifles. The Japanese jerked their weapons back into the bunker with much chattering.

Behind us, Santos yelled that he had located a ventilator pipe without a cover. He began dropping grenades into it. Each one exploded in the pillbox beneath us with a muffled *bam*. When he had used all of his, Redifer and I handed him our grenades while we kept watch at the door.

After Santos had dropped in several, we stood up and began to discuss with Burgin and the others the possibility that anyone could still be alive inside. (We didn't know at the time that the inside was subdivided by concrete baffles for extra protection.) We got our answer when two grenades were tossed out. Luckily for the men with Burgin, the grenades were thrown out the back. Santos and I shouted a warning and hit the deck on the sand on top of the pillbox, but Redifer merely raised his arm over his face. He took several fragments in the forearm but wasn't wounded seriously.

Burgin yelled, "Let's get the hell outa here and get a tank to help us knock this damn thing out." He ordered us to pull back to some craters about forty yards from the pillbox. We sent a runner to the beach to bring up a flamethrower and an amtrac armed with a 75mm gun.

As we jumped into the crater, three Japanese soldiers ran out of the pillbox door past the sand bank and headed for a thicket. Each carried his bayoneted rifle in his right hand and held up his pants with his left hand. This action so amazed me that I stared in disbelief and didn't fire my carbine. I wasn't afraid, as I had been under shell fire, just filled with wild excitement. My buddies were more effective than I and cut down the enemy with a hail of bullets. They congratulated each other while I chided myself for being more curious about strange Japanese customs than with being combat effective.

The amtrac rattling toward us by this time was certainly a welcome sight. As it pulled into position, several more

Japanese raced from the pillbox in a tight group. Some held their bayoneted rifles in both hands, but some of them carried their rifles in one hand and held up their pants with the other. I had overcome my initial surprise and joined the others and the amtrac machine gun in firing away at them. They tumbled onto the hot coral in a forlorn tangle of bare legs, falling rifles, and rolling helmets. We felt no pity for them but exulted over their fate. We had been shot at and shelled too much and had lost too many friends to have compassion for the enemy when we had him cornered.

The amtrac took up a position on a line even with us. Its commander, a sergeant, consulted Burgin. Then the turret gunner fired three armor-piercing 75mm shells at the side of the pillbox. Each time our ears rang with the familiar *wham* —*bam* as the report of the gun was followed quickly by the explosion of the shell on a target at close range. The third shell tore a hole entirely through the pillbox. Fragments kicked up dust around our abandoned packs and mortars on the other side. On the side nearest us, the hole was about four feet in diameter. Burgin yelled to the tankers to cease firing lest our equipment be damaged.

Someone remarked that if fragments hadn't killed those inside, the concussion surely had. But even before the dust settled, I saw a Japanese soldier appear at the blasted opening. He was grim determination personified as he drew back his arm to throw a grenade at us.

My carbine was already up. When he appeared, I lined up my sights on his chest and began squeezing off shots. As the first bullet hit him, his face contorted in agony. His knees buckled. The grenade slipped from his grasp. All the men near me, including the amtrac machine gunner, had seen him and began firing. The soldier collapsed in the fusillade, and the grenade went off at his feet.

Even in the midst of these fast-moving events, I looked down at my carbine with sober reflection. I had just killed a man at close range. That I had seen clearly the pain on his face when my bullets hit him came as a jolt. It suddenly made the war a very personal affair. The expression on that man's face filled me with shame and then disgust for the war and all the misery it was causing.

My combat experience thus far made me realize that such sentiments for an enemy soldier were the maudlin meditations of a fool. Look at me, a member of the 5th Marine Regiment —one of the oldest, finest, and toughest regiments in the Marine Corps—feeling ashamed because I had shot a damned foe before he could throw a grenade at me! I felt like a fool and was thankful my buddies couldn't read my thoughts.

Burgin's order to us to continue firing into the opening interrupted my musings. We kept up a steady fire into the pillbox to keep the Japanese pinned down while the flamethrower came up, carried by Corporal Womack from Mississippi. He was a brave, good-natured guy and popular with the troops, but he was one of the fiercest-looking Marines I ever saw. He was big and husky with a fiery red beard well powdered with white coral dust. He reminded me of some wild Viking. I was glad we were on the same side.

Stooped under the heavy tanks on his back, Womack approached the pillbox with his assistant just out of the line of our fire. When they got about fifteen yards from the target, we ceased firing. The assistant reached up and turned a valve on the flamethrower. Womack then aimed the nozzle at the opening made by the 75mm gun. He pressed the trigger. With a *whoooooooosh* the flame leaped at the opening. Some muffled screams, then all quiet.

Even the stoic Japanese couldn't suppress the agony of death by fire and suffocation. But they were no more likely to surrender to us than we would have been to them had we ever been confronted with the possibility of surrender. In fighting the Japanese, surrender was not one of our options.

Amid our shouts of appreciation, Womack and his buddy started back to battalion headquarters to await the summons to break another deadlock somewhere on the battlefield—or lose their lives trying. The job of flamethrower gunner was probably the least desirable of any open to a Marine infantryman. Carrying tanks with about seventy pounds of flammable jellied gasoline through enemy fire over rugged terrain in hot weather to squirt flames into the mouth of a cave or pillbox was an assignment that few survived but all carried out with magnificent courage.

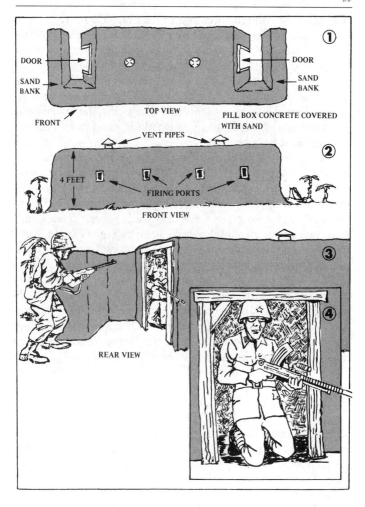

DOOR   DOOR

SAND BANK   SAND BANK

TOP VIEW

FRONT   PILL BOX CONCRETE COVERED WITH SAND

VENT PIPES

4 FEET

FIRING PORTS

FRONT VIEW

REAR VIEW

We left the craters and approached the pillbox cautiously. Burgin ordered some of the men to cover it while the rest of us looked over the fallen Japanese to be sure none was still alive; wounded Japanese invariably exploded grenades when approached, if possible, killing their enemies along with themselves. All of them were dead. The pillbox was out of action thanks to the flamethrower and the amtrac. There were seven enemy dead inside and ten outside. Our packs and mortars were only slightly damaged by the fire from the amtrac's 75mm gun.

Of the twelve Marine mortarmen, our only casualties were Redifer and Leslie Porter, who had taken some grenade fragments. They weren't hurt seriously. Our luck in the whole affair had been incredible. If the enemy had surprised us and rushed us, we might have been in a bad fix.

During this lull the men stripped the packs and pockets of the enemy dead for souvenirs. This was a gruesome business, but Marines executed it in a most methodical manner. Helmet headbands were checked for flags, packs and pockets were emptied, and gold teeth were extracted. Sabers, pistols, and *hari-kari* knives were highly prized and carefully cared for until they could be sent to the folks back home or sold to some pilot or sailor for a fat price. Rifles and other larger weapons usually were rendered useless and thrown aside. They were too heavy to carry in addition to our own equipment. They would be picked up later as fine souvenirs by the rear-echelon troops. The men in the rifle companies had a lot of fun joking about the hair-raising stories these people, who had never seen a live Japanese or been shot at, would probably tell after the war.

The men gloated over, compared, and often swapped their prizes. It was a brutal, ghastly ritual the likes of which have occurred since ancient times on battlefields where the antagonists have possessed a profound mutual hatred. It was uncivilized, as is all war, and was carried out with that particular savagery that characterized the struggle between the Marines and the Japanese. It wasn't simply souvenir hunting or looting the enemy dead; it was more like Indian warriors taking scalps.

While I was removing a bayonet and scabbard from a dead Japanese, I noticed a Marine near me. He wasn't in our mortar section but had happened by and wanted to get in on the spoils. He came up to me dragging what I assumed to be a corpse. But the Japanese wasn't dead. He had been wounded severely in the back and couldn't move his arms; otherwise he would have resisted to his last breath.

The Japanese's mouth glowed with huge gold-crowned teeth, and his captor wanted them. He put the point of his kabar on the base of a tooth and hit the handle with the palm of his hand. Because the Japanese was kicking his feet and thrashing about, the knife point glanced off the tooth and sank deeply into the victim's mouth. The Marine cursed him and with a slash cut his cheeks open to each ear. He put his foot on the sufferer's lower jaw and tried again. Blood poured out of the soldier's mouth. He made a gurgling noise and thrashed wildly. I shouted, "Put the man out of his misery." All I got for an answer was a cussing out. Another Marine ran up, put a bullet in the enemy soldier's brain, and ended his agony. The scavenger grumbled and continued extracting his prizes undisturbed.

Such was the incredible cruelty that decent men could commit when reduced to a brutish existence in their fight for survival amid the violent death, terror, tension, fatigue, and filth that was the infantryman's war. Our code of conduct toward the enemy differed drastically from that prevailing back at the division CP.

The struggle for survival went on day after weary day, night after terrifying night. One remembers vividly the landings and the beachheads and the details of the first two or three days and nights of a campaign; after that, time lost all meaning. A lull of hours or days seemed but a fleeting instant of heaven-sent tranquility. Lying in a foxhole sweating out an enemy artillery or mortar barrage or waiting to dash across open ground under machine-gun or artillery fire defied any concept of time.

To the noncombatants and those on the periphery of action, the war meant only boredom or occasional excitement; but to those who entered the meat grinder itself, the war was a nether world of horror from which escape seemed less and less likely as casualties mounted and the fighting dragged on and on. Time had no meaning; life had no meaning. The fierce struggle for survival in the abyss of Peleliu eroded the veneer of civilization and made savages of us all. We existed in an environment totally incomprehensible to men behind the lines —service troops and civilians.

*

A trip inside the pillbox by Redifer and Burgin solved the mystery of how some of the occupants had survived the grenades and shell bursts. (Burgin shot a soldier inside who was feigning death.) Concrete walls partitioned the bunker into compartments connected by small openings. Three or four enemy soldiers occupied each compartment which had its own firing ports to the outside. Each would have had to be put out of action individually had we not had the help of Womack and his flamethrower.

When our gunny came by and saw the results of our encounter with the pillbox he had thought was empty, he looked sheepish. He gazed in amazement at the enemy dead scattered around. We really razzed him about it—or rather, we gave him the nearest thing approaching the razz that we Marine privates dared hand out to the austere personage of Gy. Sergeant Saunders. I have thought often that Burgin should have been decorated for the fine leadership he exhibited in coordinating and directing the knockout of the pillbox. I'm sure men have been decorated for less.

We set up our two mortars in a large crater near the now knocked-out pillbox and registered in the guns for the night. The ammo carriers dug into the softer coral around the edge of the crater. An amtrac brought up rations and a unit of fire for the company. The wind began to blow briskly, and it got cloudy and heavily overcast. As darkness settled, heavy clouds scudded across the sky. The scene reminded me of hurricane weather on the Gulf Coast back home.

Not far behind us, the heat of the fire burning in the pillbox exploded Japanese grenades and small-arms ammunition. All night occasional shifts of wind blew the nauseating smell of burning flesh our way. The rain fell in torrents, and the wind blew hard. Ships fired star shells to illuminate the battlefield for our battalion. But as soon as the parachute of a star shell opened, the wind swept it swiftly along like some invisible hand snatching away a candle. In the few hundred yards they still held at the northern end of the island, the enemy was fairly quiet.

The next morning, again with the help of tanks and amtracs, our battalion took most of the remainder of Ngesebus.

Our casualties were remarkably low for the number of Japanese we killed.* In midafternoon we learned that an army unit would relieve us shortly and complete the job on the northern end of Ngesebus.

Our mortar section halted to await orders and dispersed among some open bushes. In our midst was the wreckage of a Japanese heavy machine gun and the remains of the squad that had been wiped out by Company K. The squad members had been killed in the exact positions to be occupied by such a squad "according to the book."

At first glance the dead gunner appeared about to fire his deadly weapon. He still sat bolt upright in the proper firing position behind the breech of his machine gun. Even in death his eyes stared widely along the gun sights. Despite the vacant look of his dilated pupils, I couldn't believe he was dead. Cold chills ran along my spine. Gooseflesh tickled my back. It seemed as though he was looking through me into all eternity, that at any instant he would raise his hands—which rested in a relaxed manner on his thighs—grip the handles on the breech, and press the thumb trigger. The bright shiny brass slugs in the strip clip appeared as ready as the gunner, anxious to speed out, to kill, and to maim more of the "American devils." But he would rot, and they would corrode. Neither he nor his ammo could do any more for the emperor.

The crown of the gunner's skull had been blasted off, probably by one of our automatic weapons. His riddled steel helmet lay on the deck like a punctured tin can. The assistant gunner lay beside the gun. Apparently, he had just opened a small green wooden chest filled with strip clips of machine-gun cartridges when he was killed. Several other Japanese soldiers, ammo carriers, lay strung out at intervals behind the gun.

A Company K rifleman who had been in the fight that knocked out the machine-gun crew sat on his helmet nearby and told us the story. The action had taken place the day before

---

*Official accounts vary somewhat as to the actual casualty figures for Ngesebus. However, the Marines suffered about 15 killed and 33 wounded, while the Japanese lost 470 killed and captured. Company K suffered the largest portion of the casualties in 3/5 by losing 8 killed and 24 wounded. This undoubtedly resulted from the presence of a ridge and caves on Ngesebus in our sector.

while the mortar section was fighting at the pillbox. The rifle-man said, "The thing that I just couldn't believe was the way those Nip ammo carriers could chop chop around here on the double with those heavy boxes of ammo on their backs."

Each ammo box had two leather straps, and each ammo car-rier had a heavy box on his back with the straps around his shoulders. I lifted one of the ammo chests. It weighed more than our mortar. What the Japanese lacked in height, they cer-tainly compensated for in muscle.

"I'd sure hate to hafta lug that thing around, wouldn't you?" asked the Marine. "When they got hit," he continued, "they fell to the deck like a brick because of all that weight."

As we talked, I noticed a fellow mortarman sitting next to me. He held a handful of coral pebbles in his left hand. With his right hand he idly tossed them into the open skull of the Japanese machine gunner. Each time his pitch was true I heard a little splash of rainwater in the ghastly receptacle. My buddy tossed the coral chunks as casually as a boy casting pebbles into a puddle on some muddy road back home; there was nothing malicious in his action. The war had so brutalized us that it was beyond belief.

I noticed gold teeth glistening brightly between the lips of several of the dead Japanese lying around us. Harvesting gold teeth was one facet of stripping enemy dead that I hadn't prac-ticed so far. But stopping beside a corpse with a particularly tempting number of shining crowns, I took out my kabar and bent over to make the extractions.

A hand grasped me by the shoulder, and I straightened up to see who it was. "What are you gonna do, Sledgehammer?" asked Doc Caswell. His expression was a mix of sadness and reproach as he looked intently at me.

"Just thought I'd collect some gold teeth," I replied.

"Don't do it."

"Why not, Doc?"

"You don't want to do that sort of thing. What would your folks think if they knew?"

"Well, my dad's a doctor, and I bet he'd think it was kinda interesting," I replied, bending down to resume my task.

"No! The germs, Sledgehammer! You might get germs from them."

I stopped and looked inquiringly at Doc and said, "Germs? Gosh, I never thought of that."

"Yeah, you got to be careful about germs around all these dead Nips, you know," he said vehemently.

"Well, then, I guess I'd better just cut off the insignia on his collar and leave his nasty teeth alone. You think that's safe, Doc?"

"I guess so," he replied with an approving nod.

Reflecting on the episode after the war, I realized that Doc Caswell didn't really have germs in mind. He was a good friend and a fine, genuine person whose sensitivity hadn't been crushed out by the war. He was merely trying to help me retain some of mine and not become completely callous and harsh.

There was little firing going on now because 3/5 was preparing to pull back as it was relieved by an army battalion. Our tanks, two of which had been parked near us, started toward the beach. As they rattled and clanked away, I hoped they weren't leaving prematurely.

Suddenly we were jolted by the terrific blast of a Japanese 75mm artillery piece slightly to our right. We flung ourselves flat on the deck. The shriek and explosion of the shell followed instantly. Fragments tore through the air. The gun fired again rapidly.

"Jesus, what's that?" gasped a man near me.

"It's a Nip 75, and God is he close," another said.

Each time the gun fired I felt the shock and pressure waves from the muzzle blast. I was terror stricken. We began to hear shouts of "Corpsman" on our right.

"For chrissake, get them tanks back up here," someone yelled. I looked toward the tanks just in time to see several wheel around and come speeding back to help the pinned-down infantrymen.

"Mortar section, stand by," someone yelled. We might be called to fire on the enemy gun, but as yet we didn't know its location.

The tanks went into action and almost immediately knocked out the weapon. Calls came from our right for corpsmen and stretcher bearers. Several of our ammo carriers went with the corpsmen to act as stretcher bearers. Word filtered along to us that quite a number of casualties had been caused by the terrible point-blank fire of the enemy cannon. Most of those hit were members of the company that was tied in with us on our right.

Our ammo carriers and corpsmen returned shortly with a distressing account of the men next to us caught directly in front of the Japanese gun when it opened fire from a camouflaged position. When I saw one of our men's face, I knew how bad it had been. He appeared absolutely stricken with horror. I often had seen him laugh and curse the Japanese when we were under heavy shelling or scrambling out of the way of machine-gun or sniper fire. Never during the entire Peleliu campaign, or later during the bloody fighting on Okinawa, did I see such an expression on his face.

He grimaced as he described how he and the man with him put one of the casualties, someone we all knew, on a stretcher. "We knew he was hit bad, and he had passed out. I tried to lift the poor guy under his shoulders, and he [pointing to the other mortarman] lifted his knees. Just as we almost got him on the stretcher, the poor guy's body came apart. God! It was awful!"

He and the man with him looked away as everyone groaned and slowly shook their heads. We had been terrified by the enemy gun firing point-blank like that. It was an awful experience. It had been bad enough on us, but it was unbearable for those unfortunates who were in the direct line of fire.

Our company had been off to one side and had suffered no casualties during the ordeal, but it was one of the more shocking experiences I endured during the war. As I have said earlier, to be shelled was terrifying, and to be shelled in the open on your feet was horrible; but to be shelled point-blank was so shocking that it almost drove the most resilient and toughest among us to panic. Words can't convey the awesome sensation of actually feeling the muzzle blasts that accompanied the shrieks and concussions of those artillery shells fired from a gun so close by. We felt profound pity for our fellow Marines who had caught its full destructive force.

During mid-afternoon as we waited for the army infantry, we sat numbly looking at nothing with the "bulkhead stare." The shock, horror, fear, and fatigue of fifteen days of combat were wearing us down physically and emotionally. I could see it in the dirty, bearded faces of my remaining comrades: they had a hollow-eyed vacant look peculiar to men under extreme stress for days and nights on end.

"Short but rough. Three days, maybe four," the division CG had said before Peleliu. Now we had been at it fifteen terrible days with no end in sight.

I felt myself choking up. I slowly turned my back to the men facing me, as I sat on my helmet, and put my face in my hands to try to shut out reality. I began sobbing. The harder I tried to stop the worse it got. My body shuddered and shook. Tears flowed out of my scratchy eyes. I was sickened and revolted to see healthy young men get hurt and killed day after day. I felt I couldn't take any more. I was so terribly tired and so emotionally wrung out from being afraid for days on end that I seemed to have no reserve strength left.

The dead were safe. Those who had gotten a million-dollar wound were lucky. None of us left had any idea that we were just midway through what was to be a month-long ordeal for the 5th Marines and the 7th Marines.

I felt a hand on my shoulder and looked up at the tired, bloodshot eyes of Duke, our lieutenant. "What's the matter, Sledgehammer?" he asked in a sympathetic voice. After I told him how I felt, he said, "I know what you mean. I feel the same way. But take it easy. We've got to keep going. It'll be over soon, and we'll be back on Pavuvu." His understanding gave me the strength I needed, enough strength to endure fifteen more terrible days and nights.

When long files of soldiers accompanied by amtracs loaded with barbed wire and other supplies came by, we received orders to move out. We were glad to see those army men. As we shouldered our weapons and loads, a buddy said to me, "Sure wish we could dig in behind barbed wire at night. Makes a fella' feel more secure." I agreed as we walked wearily toward the beach.

After crossing back to northern Peleliu on 29 September, 3/5 bivouacked east of Umurbrogol Mountain in the Ngardololok area. We were familiar with this area from the first week of the campaign. It was fairly quiet and had been the bivouac area of the shattered 1st Marines for about a week after they came off the line and awaited ships to take them to Pavuvu.

We were able to rest, but we were uneasy. As usual we asked about the fate of friends in other units, more often than not with depressing results. Rumor had the 5th Marines slated to join the 7th Marines already fighting on those dreaded coral ridges that had been the near destruction of the 1st Marines. The men tried not to think about it as they sat around in the muggy shade, brewed hot coffee in their canteen cups, and swapped souvenirs and small talk. From the north came the constant rattle of machine guns and the rumble of shells.

CHAPTER SIX

Brave Men Lost

"OK, YOU PEOPLE, stand by to draw rations and ammo. The battalion is going to reinforce the 7th Marines in the ridges."

We received the unwelcome but inevitable news with fatalistic resignation as we squared away our weapons and gear. Our information had the casualty figure of the 7th Marines rapidly approaching that of the 1st Marines. And our own regimental strength wasn't much better than that of the 7th. All of Peleliu except the central ridges was now in our hands. The enemy held out in the Umurbrogol Pocket, an area about 400 yards by 1,200 yards in the ruggedest, worst part of the ridges.*

The terrain was so unbelievably rugged, jumbled, and confusing, that I rarely knew where we were located. Only the officers had maps, so locations meant nothing in my mind. One ridge looked about like another, was about as rugged, and was defended as heavily as any other. We were usually told the name of this or that coral height or ridge when we attacked. To me it meant only that we were attacking the same objective where other Marine battalions had been shot up previously.

We were resigned to the dismal conclusion that our battalion wasn't going to leave the island until all the Japanese were killed, or we had all been hit. We merely existed from hour to hour, from day to day. Numbed by fear and fatigue, our minds thought only of personal survival. The only glimmer of hope was a million-dollar wound or for the battle to end soon. As it dragged on and on and casualties mounted, a sense of despair

---

*My memory of the remaining events of horror and death and violence amid the Peleliu ridges is as clear and distinct as a long nightmare where specific events are recalled vividly the next day. I remember clearly the details of certain episodes that occurred before or after certain others and can verify these with my notes and the historical references. But time and duration have absolutely no meaning in relation to those events from one date to the next. I was well aware of this sensation then.

pervaded us. It seemed that the only escape was to be killed or wounded. The will for self-preservation weakened. Many men I knew became intensely fatalistic. Somehow, though, one never could quite visualize his own death. It was always the next man. But getting wounded did seem inevitable. In a rifle company it just seemed to be a matter of time. One couldn't hope to continue to escape the law of averages forever.

On 3 October our battalion made an attack on the Five Sisters, a rugged coral hill mass with five sheer-walled peaks. Before the attack the 11th Marines covered the area with artillery fire. We fired a heavy mortar barrage on the company front, and the machine guns laid down covering fire.

As we ceased firing briefly, we watched the riflemen of 3/5 move forward onto the slopes before Japanese fire stopped them. We fired the mortars rapidly to give our men cover as they pulled back. The same fruitless attack was repeated the next day with the same dismal results.* Each time we got orders to secure the guns after the riflemen stopped advancing, the mortar section stood by to go up as stretcher bearers. (We always left a couple of men on each gun in case mortar fire was needed.) We usually threw phosphorous and smoke grenades as a screen, and the riflemen covered us, but enemy snipers fired as rapidly as possible at stretcher bearers. The Japanese were merciless in this, as in everything else in combat.

Because of the rugged, rock-strewn terrain and intense heat on Peleliu, four men were needed to carry one casualty on a stretcher. Everyone in the company took his turn as a stretcher bearer nearly every day. All hands agreed it was back-breaking, perilous work.

My heart pounded from fear and fatigue each time we lifted a wounded man onto a stretcher, raised it, then stumbled and struggled across the rough ground and up and down steep inclines while enemy bullets snapped through the air and ricochets whined and pinged off the rocks. The snipers hit a stretcher bearer on more than one occasion. But luckily, we always managed to drag everybody behind rocks until help came. Frequently enemy mortars added their shells in an effort to stop us.

---

*K/3/5 lost eight killed and twenty-two wounded at the Five Sisters.

Each time I panted and struggled with a stretcher under fire, I marveled at the attitude of the casualty. When conscious, the wounded Marine seemed at ease and supremely confident we would get him out alive. With bullets and shells coming in thick and fast, I sometimes doubted any of us could make it. Even discounting the effects of shock and the morphine administered by the corpsmen, the attitude of the wounded Marine seemed serene. When we reached a place out of the line of fire, the man usually would encourage us to put him down so we could rest. If he wasn't wounded severely, we stopped and all had a smoke. We would cheer him up by asking him to think of us when he got on board the hospital ship.

Invariably the not-so-seriously hurt were in high spirits and relieved. They were on their way out of hell, and they expressed pity for those of us left behind. With the more seriously wounded and the dying, we carried the stretcher as fast as possible to an amtrac or ambulance Jeep which then rushed them to the battalion aid station. After getting them into a vehicle, we would throw ourselves down and pant for breath.

When acting as a stretcher bearer—struggling, running, crawling over terrain so rugged that sometimes the carriers on one end held the stretcher handles above their heads while those on the other end held their handles almost on the rocks to keep the stretcher level—I was terrified that the helpless casualty might fall off onto the hard, sharp coral. I never saw this happen, but we all dreaded it.

The apparent calmness of our wounded under fire stemmed in part from the confidence we shared in each other. None of us could bear the thought of leaving wounded behind. We never did, because the Japanese certainly would have tortured them to death.

During the period between attacks by our battalion on the Five Sisters, our front line was formed on fairly level ground. The mortars were dug in some yards behind the line. The entire company was out in the open, and we knew the Japanese were watching us at all times from their lairs in the Five Sisters. We came under sniper and mortar fire only when the Japanese were sure of inflicting maximum casualties. Their fire discipline was superb. When they shot, someone usually got hit.

When night came it was like another world. Then the enemy came out of their caves, infiltrating or creeping up on our lines to raid all night, every night. Raids by individual enemy soldiers or small groups began as soon as darkness fell. Typically, one or more raiders slipped up close to Marine positions by moving during dark periods between mortar flares or star shells. They wore *tabi*, and their ability to creep in silently over rough rocks strewn with pulverized vegetation was incredible. They knew the terrain perfectly. Suddenly they rushed in jabbering or babbling incoherent sounds, sometimes throwing a grenade, but always swinging a saber, bayonet, or knife.

Their skill and daring were amazing, matched only by the cool-headed, disciplined manner in which Marines met their attacks. Strict fire discipline on our part was required to avoid shooting friends if the enemy got into a position before he was shot. All we could do was listen in the dark to the desperate animalistic sounds and the thrashing around when a hand-to-hand fight occurred.

No one was allowed out of his position after dark. Each Marine maintained a keen watch while his buddy tried to sleep. Mutual trust was essential. Frequently our men were killed or wounded in these nightly fights, but we invariably killed the foe.

One night so many Japanese crept around in front of the company and slipped in among the rocks and ground litter between some of the forward positions that much of the following morning was occupied with trying to kill them all. This was difficult, because in any direction one fired one might hit a Marine. The excellent discipline and control exhibited by the Marines finally got all the Japanese without any Company K casualties.

The only "injury" that occurred was to my friend Jay's dungaree trousers. Jay walked past my foxhole with a deliberate, stiff-kneed gait and wearing a wry expression on his face.

"What happened to you?" I asked.

"Aw hell, I'll tell you later," he grinned sheepishly.

"Go on, tell him, Jay," another man near him yelled teasingly.

Several men laughed. Jay grinned and told them to shut up. He waddled on back to battalion like a tiny child who had soiled his pants, which was just what he had done. We all had severe cases of diarrhea by this time, and it had gotten the best of Jay. Considering what had happened, the incident really wasn't funny, but it was understandable.

At daylight Jay had slung his carbine over his shoulder and walked a short distance from his foxhole to relieve himself. As he stepped over a log, his foot came down squarely on the back of a Japanese lying in hiding. Jay reacted instantaneously and so did the enemy soldier. Jay brought his carbine to bear on the Japanese's chest as the latter sprang to his feet. Jay pulled the trigger. "Click." The firing pin was broken, and the carbine didn't fire. As the enemy soldier pulled the pin from a hand grenade, Jay threw the carbine at him. It was more an act of desperation than anything else.

As Jay spun around and ran back toward us yelling, "shoot him," the Japanese threw his grenade, striking my friend in the middle of the back. It fell to the deck and lay there, a dud. The Japanese then drew his bayonet. Waving it like a sword, he took off after Jay at a dead run.

Jay had spotted a BARman and fled in his direction, yelling for him to shoot the enemy. The BARman stood up but didn't fire. The Japanese came on. Jay was running and yelling as hard as he could. After agonizing moments, the BARman took deliberate aim at the enemy soldier's belt buckle and fired most of a twenty-round magazine into him. The soldier collapsed in a heap. The blast of automatic rifle fire had cut his body nearly in two.

Terrified and winded, Jay had had a close call. When he asked the BARman why in the hell he had waited so long to fire, that character grinned. I heard him reply something to the effect that he thought he'd just let the Japanese get a little closer to see if he could cut him into two pieces with his BAR.

Jay obviously didn't appreciate his close call being used as the subject of an experiment. As all the men laughed, Jay received permission to go back to battalion headquarters to draw a clean pair of trousers. The men kidded him a great deal about the episode, and he took it all with his usual good nature.

During the entire period among the Umurbrogol ridges, a nuisance Marine infantrymen had to contend with was the rear-echelon souvenir hunters. These characters came up to the rifle companies during lulls in the fighting and poked around for any Japanese equipment they could carry off. They were easy to spot because of the striking difference between their appearance and that of the infantry.

During the latter phase of the campaign the typical infantry-man wore a worried, haggard expression on his filthy, unshaven face. His bloodshot eyes were hollow and vacant from too much horror and too little sleep. His camouflaged helmet cover (if it hadn't been torn off against the rocks) was gray with coral dust and had a tear or two in it. His cotton dungaree jacket (orig-inally green) was discolored with coral dust, filthy, greasy with rifle oil, and as stiff as canvas from being soaked alternately with rain and sweat and then drying. His elbows might be out, and his knees frequently were, from much "hitting the deck" on the coral rock. His boondockers were coated with gray coral dust, and his heels were worn off completely by the sharp coral.

The infantryman's calloused hands were nearly blackened by weeks of accumulation of rifle oil, mosquito repellant (an oily liquid called Skat), dirt, dust, and general filth. Overall he was stooped and bent by general fatigue and excessive physical exer-tion. If approached closely enough for conversation, he smelled bad.

The front-line infantry bitterly resented the souvenir hunters. One major in the 7th Marines made it a practice of putting them into the line if they came into his area. His infantrymen saw to it that the "visitors" stayed put until released to return to their respective units in the rear areas.

During a lull in our attacks on the Five Sisters, I was on an ammo-carrying detail and talking with a rifleman friend after handing him some bandoliers. It was quiet, and we were sitting on the sides of his shallow foxhole as his buddy was bringing up K rations. (By quiet I mean we weren't being fired on. But there was always the sound of firing somewhere on the island.) Two neat, clean, fresh-looking souvenir hunters wearing green cloth fatigue caps instead of helmets and carrying no weapons walked past us headed in the direction of the Five Sisters, sev-eral hundred yards away. When they got a few paces in front of us, one of them stopped and turned around, just as I was on the verge of calling to them to be careful where they went.

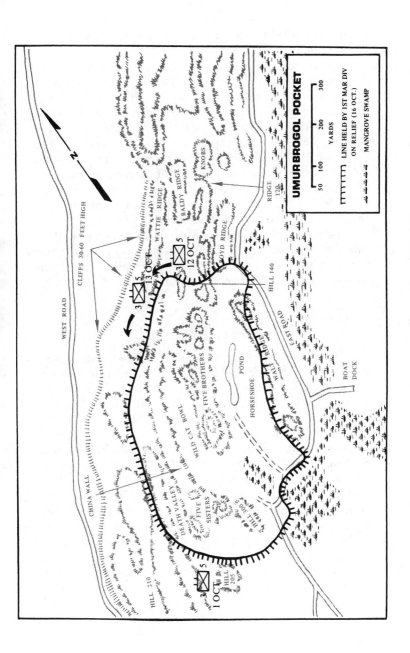

UMURBROGOL POCKET

YARDS

50 100   200   300

ᵀᵀᵀᵀᵀ LINE HELD BY 1ST MAR DIV
ON RELIEF (16 OCT.)

MANGROVE SWAMP

N

WEST ROAD

CLIFFS 30-60 FEET HIGH

WATTLE RIDGE

BALDY RIDGE

KNOBS

RIDGE 120

BOYD RIDGE

HILL 140

EAST ROAD

5
3   13 OCT

5
3   12 OCT

BOAT DOCK

CHINA WALL

POND

HORSESHOE

WALT RIDGE

WILD CAT BOWL

FIVE BROTHERS

DEATH VALLEY

FIVE SISTERS

HILL 210

HILL 205

HILL 300

5
3   1 OCT

The man called back to us asking, "Hey, you guys, where's the front line?"

"You just passed through it," I answered serenely. The second souvenir hunter spun around. They looked at each other and then at us in astonishment. Then, grabbing the bills of their caps, they took off on the double back past us toward the rear. They kicked up dust and never looked back.

"Hell, Sledgehammer, you should'a let 'em go on so they'd get a good scare," chided my friend. I told him we couldn't just let them walk up on a sniper. "Serve them rear-echelon bastards right. And they call them guys Marines," he grumbled. (In fairness, I must add that some of the rear-area service troops volunteered and served as stretcher bearers.)

In our myopic view we respected and admired only those who got shot at, and to hell with everyone else. This was unfair to noncombatants who performed essential tasks, but we were so brutalized by war that we were incapable of making fair evaluations.

A LEADER DIES

By 5 October (D + 20) the 7th Marines had lost about as many men as the 1st Marines had lost earlier in the battle. The regiment was now finished as an assault force on the regimental level. The 5th Marines, the last of the 1st Marine Division's infantry regiments, began to relieve the 7th Marines that day. Some of the men of the battered regiment would be killed or wounded in subsequent actions in the draws and valleys among the ridges of Peleliu, but the 7th Marines were through as a fighting force for the campaign.

On 7 October 3/5 made an assault up a large draw called Horseshoe Valley, known commonly as "the Horseshoe." There were numerous enemy heavy guns in caves and emplacements in the ridges bordering the Horseshoe to the west, north, and east. Our battalion was supposed to knock out as many of them as possible. We were supported by six army tanks, because the Marine 1st Tank Battalion had been relieved on 1 October to be sent back to Pavuvu. Somebody erroneously assumed there would be no further need for tanks on Peleliu.

My guess is that the 1st Tank Battalion was relieved not

because the men were "badly depleted and debilitated"—the official reason given—but because the machines were. Machines wore out or needed overhauling and maintenance, but men were expected to keep going. Tanks, amtracs, trucks, aircraft, and ships were considered valuable and difficult to replace way out in the Pacific. They were maintained carefully and not exposed needlessly to wear or destruction. Men, infantrymen in particular, were simply expected to keep going beyond the limits of human endurance until they got killed or wounded or dropped from exhaustion.

Our attack on the Horseshoe was preceded by terrific artillery fire from our big guns. The shells swished and whined toward the ridges for two and a half hours. The mortars added their bit, too. The attack was surprisingly successful. The Horseshoe wasn't secured, but many Japanese were killed. We also knocked out many caves containing heavy guns, but only after several of the tanks took hits from them.

In the estimation of the Marines, the army tankers did a good job. Here the tanks operated with our riflemen attached. It was a case of mutual support. The tanks pulled up to the caves and fired into them point-blank with their 75mm cannon—*wham bam*. Their machine guns never seemed to stop. A tank unattended by riflemen was doomed to certain destruction from enemy suicide crews carrying mines. And the riflemen got a lot of protection from the tanks.

About the only instance I know of where tanks tried to operate without riflemen in the Pacific was a case of army tanks on Okinawa. Predictably, the Japanese knocked out most of those tanks. Marine tanks always operated with riflemen, like a dog with his fleas. But with tanks and riflemen, it was mutually beneficial.

After the attack of 7 October on the Horseshoe, 3/5 pulled back some distance from the ridges. Shortly thereafter we again went up toward the northern part of the island.

Between 8 and 11 October we emplaced our 60mm mortars between the West Road and the narrow beach. We were only a few yards from the water. Thus set up, we fired over the West Road, our front line beyond, and onto the ridges. We had an observer somewhere across the road who sent us orders by the sound-powered phone.

We kept up a brisk rate of fire because Japanese had infiltrated into positions on the ridge next to the road and were sniping at vehicles and troops with deadly effect. Our mortar fire helped pin them down and clean them out. We had good gun emplacements among some rocks and were screened by a narrow strip of thick foliage between us and the road and, therefore, from the enemy in the ridge beyond.

I was extremely confused as to where we had left our company. An NCO told me our mortars were detached temporarily from Company K and were supporting another unit hard pressed by snipers. The enemy were firing from positions that were almost impossible to locate and they shot any and everybody they could—even casualties being evacuated by amtracs. More than one desperate amtrac driver, as he raced down the West Road toward the Regimental Aid Station, arrived only to find his helpless cargo slaughtered where they lay.

While we were in this position we were particularly vulnerable to infiltrators who might slip in along the beach as well as from the water to our rear. We kept watch in all directions at night; in this place, there were no friendly troops to our rear, just the water's edge about ten feet away and then the ocean-covered reef. The water was only about knee deep for quite a distance out. The Japanese would wade out, slip along the reef, and come in behind us.

One night while I was firing flare shells, James T. (Jim) Burke, a Marine we called the Fatalist, was manning Number One gun. Between firing missions, I could see him sitting on his helmet next to his gun, keeping watch to our left and rear.

"Hey, Sledgehammer, let me see your carbine a minute," he whispered nonchalantly in his usual laconic manner. He had a .45 pistol which was of little use at much distance. I handed him my carbine. I didn't know what he saw, so I followed his gaze as he pointed my carbine toward the sea. In the pale light a shadowy figure was moving slowly and silently along the reef parallel to the shoreline in the shallow water. The man couldn't have been more than thirty yards away or we couldn't have seen him in the dim moonlight. There was no doubt that he was a Japanese trying to get farther along to where he could slip ashore and creep up on our mortars.

No challenge or demand for password was even considered in a situation like that. No Marine would be creeping along the reef at night. The Fatalist rested his elbows on his knees and took careful aim as the figure moved slowly through the glassy-smooth water. Two quick shots; the figure disappeared.

The Fatalist flipped the safety back on, handed me my carbine, and said, "Thanks, Sledgehammer." He appeared as unconcerned as ever.

During the morning of 12 October, an NCO brought word that we were to take up our guns. The mortar section was to rejoin Company K. We gathered our gear and mortar. Snafu, George Sarrett, and I got into a jeep parked along a sheltered part of the road. We had to hang on because the driver took off with a lurch in a cloud of dust and drove like hell down the West Road bordered by the sniper-infested ridge. It was my first—and only—jeep ride during my entire enlistment. It was an eventful day because of that.

Shortly the driver stopped and let us off in a supply area where we waited for an NCO who was to guide us up into the ridges. Directly the rest of the Company K mortarmen arrived with directions to reach the company. We hoisted our mortar and other weapons and gear and headed across the road. We picked our way around the end of the ridge, then headed up a narrow valley filled with skeletons of shattered trees jutting up here and there on the slopes amid crazy-angled coral masses.

Johnny Marmet came striding down the incline of the valley to meet us as we started up. Even before I could see his face clearly, I knew from the way he was walking that something was dreadfully amiss. He lurched up to us, nervously clutching the web strap of the submachine gun slung over his shoulder. I had never seen Johnny nervous before, even under the thickest fire, which he seemed to regard as a nuisance that interfered with his carrying out his job.

His tired face was contorted with emotion, his brow was knitted tightly, and his bloodshot eyes appeared moist. It was obvious he had something fearful to tell us. We shuffled to a halt.

My first thought was that the Japanese had slipped in thousands of troops from the northern Palaus and that we would never get off the island. No, maybe the enemy had bombed some American city or chased off the navy as they had done at Guadalcanal. My imagination went wild, but none of us was prepared for what we were about to hear.

"Howdy, Johnny," someone said as he came up to us.

"All right, you guys, let's get squared away here," he said looking in every direction but at us. (This was strange, because Johnny wasn't the least reluctant to make eye contact with death, destiny, or the general himself.) "OK, you guys, OK, you guys," he repeated, obviously flustered. A couple of men exchanged quizzical glances. "The skipper is dead. Ack Ack has been killed," Johnny finally blurted out, then looked quickly away from us.

I was stunned and sickened. Throwing my ammo bag down, I turned away from the others, sat on my helmet, and sobbed quietly.

"Those goddamn slant-eyed sonsabitches," someone behind me groaned.

Never in my wildest imagination had I contemplated Captain Haldane's death. We had a steady stream of killed and wounded leaving us, but somehow I assumed Ack Ack was immortal. Our company commander represented stability and direction in a world of violence, death, and destruction. Now his life had been snuffed out. We felt forlorn and lost. It was the worst grief I endured during the entire war. The intervening years have not lessened it any.

Capt. Andy Haldane wasn't an idol. He was human. But he commanded our individual destinies under the most trying conditions with the utmost compassion. We knew he could never be replaced. He was the finest Marine officer I ever knew. The loss of many close friends grieved me deeply on Peleliu and Okinawa. But to all of us the loss of our company commander at Peleliu was like losing a parent we depended upon for security—not our physical security, because we knew that was a commodity beyond our reach in combat, but our mental security.

Some of the men threw their gear violently to the deck. Everybody was cursing and rubbing his eyes.

Finally Johnny pulled himself together and said, "OK, you guys, let's move out." We picked up mortars and ammo bags.

Feeling as though our crazy world had fallen apart completely, we trudged slowly and silently in single file up the rubble-strewn valley to rejoin Company K.*

So ended the outstanding combat career of a fine officer who had distinguished himself at Guadalcanal, Cape Gloucester, and Peleliu. We had lost our leader and our friend. Our lives would never be the same. But we turned back to the ugly business at hand.

THE STENCH OF BATTLE

Johnny led us on up through a jumble of rocks on Hill 140. Company K's line was emplaced along a rock rim, and we set up the mortars in a shallow depression about twenty yards behind it. The riflemen and machine gunners in front of us were in among rocks along the rim of Hill 140 facing east toward Walt Ridge and the northern end of the infamous Horseshoe. We had previously attacked that valley from its southern end. From the rim of Hill 140 the rock contours dropped away in a sheer cliff to a canyon below. No one could raise his head above the rim rock without immediately drawing heavy rifle and machine-gun fire.

The fighting around the pocket was as deadly as ever, but of a different type from the early days of the campaign. The Japanese fired few artillery or mortar barrages, just a few rounds at a time when assured of inflicting maximum casualties. That they usually did, and then secured the guns to escape detection. Sometimes there was an eerie quiet. We knew they were everywhere in the caves and pillboxes. But there was no firing in our area, only the sound of firing elsewhere. The silence added an element of unreality to the valleys.

If we moved past a certain point, the Japanese opened up suddenly with rifle, machine-gun, mortar, and artillery fire. It

*At the time of Captain Haldane's death, the bulk of Company K was operating with its parent battalion (3/5) on Hill 140 within the Umurbrogol Pocket. In an attempt to orient himself to the strange terrain his company was occupying, Haldane raised his head and looked over a ridge. A sniper's bullet killed him instantly. First Lt. Thomas J. ("Stumpy") Stanley succeeded him as commander of K/3/5. Stanley led Company K through the remainder of the Peleliu campaign and on to Okinawa the following spring.

was like a sudden storm breaking. More often than not we had to pull back, and not a man in the company had seen a live enemy anywhere.

They couldn't hope to drive us off by then or to be reinforced themselves. From that point onward, they killed solely for the sake of killing, without hope and without higher purpose. We were fighting in Peleliu's ridges and valleys, in terrain the likes of which most Americans could not even visualize, against an enemy unlike anything most Americans could imagine.

The sun bore down on us like a giant heat lamp. Once I saw a misplaced phosphorous grenade explode on the coral from the sun's intense heat. We always shaded our stacked mortar shells with a piece of ammo box to prevent this.

Occasional rains that fell on the hot coral merely evaporated like steam off hot pavement. The air hung heavy and muggy. Everywhere we went on the ridges the hot humid air reeked with the stench of death. A strong wind was no relief; it simply brought the horrid odor from an adjacent area. Japanese corpses lay where they fell among the rocks and on the slopes. It was impossible to cover them. Usually there was no soil that could be spaded over them, just the hard, jagged coral. The enemy dead simply rotted where they had fallen. They lay all over the place in grotesque positions with puffy faces and grinning buck-toothed expressions.

It is difficult to convey to anyone who has not experienced it the ghastly horror of having your sense of smell saturated constantly with the putrid odor of rotting human flesh day after day, night after night. This was something the men of an infantry battalion got a horrifying dose of during a long, protracted battle such as Peleliu. In the tropics the dead became bloated and gave off a terrific stench within a few hours after death.

Whenever possible we removed Marine dead to the rear of the company's position. There they were usually laid on stretchers and covered with ponchos which stretched over the head of the corpse down to the ankles. I rarely saw a dead Marine left uncovered with his face exposed to sun, rain, and flies. Somehow it seemed indecent not to cover our dead. Often, though, the dead might lie on the stretchers for some time and decompose badly before the busy graves registration crews could take them for burial in the division cemetery near the airfield.

During the fighting around the Umurbrogol Pocket, there was a constant movement of one weary, depleted Marine company being relieved by another slightly less weary, depleted company. We seemed to rotate from one particularly dangerous part of the line to one slightly less so and back again continuously.

There were certain areas we moved into and out of several times as the campaign dragged along its weary, bloody course. In many such areas I became quite familiar with the sight of some particular enemy corpse, as if it were a landmark. It was gruesome to see the stages of decay proceed from just killed, to bloated, to maggot-infested rotting, to partially exposed bones—like some biological clock marking the inexorable passage of time. On each occasion my company passed such a landmark we were fewer in number.

Each time we moved into a different position I could determine the areas occupied by each rifle company as we went into that sector of the line. Behind each company position lay a pile of ammo and supplies and the inevitable rows of dead under their ponchos. We could determine how bad that sector of the line was by the number of dead. To see them so always filled me with anger at the war and the realization of the senseless waste. It depressed me far more than my own fear.

Added to the awful stench of the dead of both sides was the repulsive odor of human excrement everywhere. It was all but impossible to practice simple, elemental field sanitation on most areas of Peleliu because of the rocky surface. Field sanitation during maneuvers and combat was the responsibility of each man. In short, under normal conditions, he covered his own waste with a scoop of soil. At night when he didn't dare venture out of his foxhole, he simply used an empty grenade canister or ration can, threw it out of his hole, and scooped dirt over it next day if he wasn't under heavy enemy fire.

But on Peleliu, except along the beach areas and in the swamps, digging into the coral rock was nearly impossible. Consequently, thousands of men—most of them around the Umurbrogol Pocket in the ridges, many suffering with severe diarrhea, fighting for weeks on an island two miles by six miles—couldn't practice basic field sanitation. This fundamental neglect caused an already putrid tropical atmosphere to become inconceivably vile.

Added to this was the odor of thousands of rotting, discarded Japanese and American rations. At every breath one inhaled hot, humid air heavy with countless repulsive odors. I felt as though my lungs would never be cleansed of all those foul vapors. It may not have been that way down on the airfield and in other areas where the service troops were encamped, but around the infantry in the Umurbrogol Pocket, the stench varied only from foul to unbearable.

In this garbage-filled environment the flies, always numerous in the tropics anyway, underwent a population explosion. This species was not the unimposing common housefly (the presence of one of which in a restaurant is enough to cause most Americans today to declare the place unfit to serve food to the public). Peleliu's most common fly was the huge blowfly or bluebottle fly. This creature has a plump, metallic, greenish-blue body, and its wings often make a humming sound during flight.

The then new insecticide DDT was sprayed over the combat areas on Peleliu for the first time anywhere. It supposedly reduced the adult fly population while Marines were still fighting on the ridges, but I never noticed that the flies became fewer in number.

With human corpses, human excrement, and rotting rations scattered across Peleliu's ridges, those nasty insects were so large, so glutted, and so lazy that some could scarcely fly. They could not be waved away or frightened off a can of rations or a chocolate bar. Frequently they tumbled off the side of my canteen cup into my coffee. We actually had to shake the food to dislodge the flies, and even then they sometimes refused to move. I usually had to balance my can of stew on my knee, spooning it up with my right hand while I picked the sluggish creatures off the stew with my left. They refused to move or to be intimidated. It was revolting, to say the least, to watch big fat blowflies leave a corpse and swarm into our C rations.

Even though none of us had much appetite, we still had to eat. A way to solve the fly problem was to eat after sunset or before sunrise when the insects were inactive. Chow had to be unheated then, because no sterno tablets or other form of light could be used after dark. It was sure to draw enemy sniper fire.

Each morning just before sunrise, when things were fairly

quiet, I could hear a steady humming sound like bees in a hive as the flies became active with the onset of daylight. They rose up off the corpses, refuse, rocks, brush, and wherever else they had settled for the night like a swarm of bees. Their numbers were incredible.

Large land crabs crawled all over the ridges at night, attracted by corpses. Their rustling through dry debris often was indistinguishable from prowling enemy soldiers. We responded by tossing a grenade at the sound.

In addition to rotting corpses and organic waste, the litter of smashed and worn out equipment of every type became more abundant as the battle dragged on and the size of the Umurbrogol Pocket shrank slowly. The ridges and ravines were littered with the flotsam of fierce combat. Debris of battle was everywhere and became more noticeable as the weeks dragged on.

I still see clearly the landscape around one particular position we occupied for several days. It was a scene of destruction and desolation that no fiction could invent. The area was along the southwestern border of the pocket where ferocious fighting had gone on since the second day of battle (16 September). The 1st Marines, the 7th Marines, and now the 5th Marines, all in their turn, had fought against this same section of ridges. Our exhausted battalion, 3/5, moved into the line to relieve another slightly more exhausted battalion. It was the same old weary shuffling of one tired, depleted outfit into the line to relieve another whose sweating men trudged out of their positions, hollow-eyed, stooped, grimy, bearded zombies.

The Company K riflemen and machine gunners climbed up the steep ridge and into the crevices and holes of the company we relieved. Orders were given that no one must look over the crest of the ridge, because enemy rifle and machine-gun fire would kill instantly anyone who did.

As usual the troops pulling out gave our men "the dope" on the local conditions: what type fire to expect, particular danger spots and possible infiltration routes at night.

My mortar went into a gun pit occupied by one of the 60mm mortars of the company we were relieving. The gun pit was among coral rocks about twenty yards from the foot of the ridge. An extremely youthful Marine was just buckling the leather strap around the bipod and tube of his 60mm mortar as I walked up near the position and put down my heavy ammo bag. I sat on my helmet and started talking to him as the rest of our squad moved into their positions. As the young man looked up, I was struck by the agonized expression on his face. He didn't seem happy, the way he should have, about being relieved.

"You guys watch out for the Japs at night. Two of the bastards got into this gun pit last night and cut up our gunner and assistant gunner," he said.

He told me in a strained voice that the crew was so occupied firing the mortar during the previous night that two Japanese who slipped through the line on the ridge managed to creep up close to the pit without detection. They jumped in and cut up the two men working the mortar before nearby mortar ammo carriers killed them. The wounded Marines had been evacuated, but one of them had died, and the other was in poor condition. The bodies of the Japanese had been thrown into some nearby bushes.

The man telling me of the tragedy and another crouching beside the gun pit had been ammo carriers but had now assumed new duties as gunner and assistant. I noticed that as the new gunner folded and strapped his gun to leave, he seemed reluctant to touch the bottom or sides of the emplacement. When he left and we came closer to the gun pit to set up our mortar, I saw why. The white coral sides and bottom were spattered and smeared with the dark red blood of his two comrades.

After we got our gun emplaced, I collected up some large scraps of cardboard from ration and ammo boxes and used them to cover the bottom of the pit as well as I could. Fat, lazy blowflies were reluctant to leave the blood-smeared rock.

I had long since become used to the sight of blood, but the idea of sitting in that bloodstained gun pit was a bit too much for me. It seemed almost like leaving our dead unburied to sit on the blood of a fellow Marine spilled out on the coral. I noticed that my buddy looked approvingly at my efforts as he came back from getting orders for our gun. Although we never discussed the subject, he apparently felt as I did. As I looked at the stains on the coral, I recalled some of the eloquent phrases of politicians and newsmen about how "gallant" it is for a man to "shed his blood for his country," and "to give his life's blood as a sacrifice," and so on. The words seemed so ridiculous. Only the flies benefited.

The wind blew hard. A drizzling rain fell out of a leaden sky that seemed to hang just above the ridge crest. Shattered trees and jagged rocks along the crest looked like stubble on a dirty chin. Most green trees and bushes had long since been shattered and pulverized by shell fire. Only the grotesque stumps and branches remained. A film of fine coral dust covered everything. It had been dust before the rain, but afterward it was a grimy coating of thin plaster.

The overwhelming grayness of everything in sight caused sky, ridge, rocks, stumps, men, and equipment to blend into a grimy oneness. Weird, jagged contours of Peleliu's ridges and canyons gave the area an unearthly alien appearance. The shattered vegetation and the dirty-white splotches peppering the rocks where countless bullets and shell fragments had struck off the weathered gray surfaces contributed to the unreality of the harsh landscape.

Rain added the final touch. On a battlefield rain made the living more miserable and forlorn and the dead more pathetic. To my left lay a couple of bloated Japanese corpses teeming with maggots and inactive flies who seemed to object to the rain as much as I did. Each dead man still wore the two leather cartridge boxes, one on either side of his belt buckle, neat wrap leggings, *tabi* shoes, helmets, and packs. Beside each corpse lay a shattered and rusting Arisaka rifle, smashed against a rock by some Marine to be certain it wasn't used again.

Cans of C rations and K ration boxes, opened and unopened, lay around our gun pit along with discarded grenade and mortar shell canisters. Scattered about the area were discarded U.S. helmets, packs, ponchos, dungaree jackets, web cartridge belts, leggings, boondockers, ammo boxes of every type, and crates. The discarded articles of clothing and the inevitable bottle of blood plasma bore mute testimony that a Marine had been hit there.

Many tree stumps had a machine-gun ammo belt draped over them. Some of these belts were partially filled with live cartridges. Amid all this evidence of violent combat, past and continuing, I was interested in the fact that spent, or partially so, machine-gun ammo belts so often seemed to be draped across a shattered stump or bush rather than lying on the ground. In combat, I often experienced fascination over such trivia, particularly when exhausted physically and strained emotionally. Many combat veterans told me they also were affected the same way.

All around us lay the destruction and waste of violent combat. Later, on the muddy clay fields and ridges of Okinawa, I would witness similar scenes on an even vaster scale. There the battlefield would bear some resemblance to others described in World War II. During the muddy stalemate before Shuri, the area would resemble descriptions I had read of the ghastly corpse-strewn morass of Flanders during World War I.

These, though, were typical modern battlefields. They were nothing like the crazy-contoured coral ridges and rubble-filled canyons of the Umurbrogol Pocket on Peleliu. Particularly at night by the light of flares or on a cloudy day, it was like no other battlefield described on earth. It was an alien, unearthly, surrealistic nightmare like the surface of another planet.

I have already mentioned several times the exhaustion of the Marines as the campaign wore on. Our extreme fatigue was no secret to the Japanese either. As early as 6 October, nine days before we were relieved, a captured document reported that we appeared worn out and were fighting less aggressively.

The grinding stress of prolonged heavy combat, the loss of sleep because of nightly infiltration and raids, the vigorous physical demands forced on us by the rugged terrain, and the unrelenting, suffocating heat were enough to make us drop in our tracks. How we kept going and continued fighting I'll never know. I was so indescribably weary physically and emotionally that I became fatalistic, praying only for my fate to be painless. The million-dollar wound seemed more of a blessing with every weary hour that dragged by. It seemed the only escape other than death or maiming.

In addition to the terror and hardships of combat, each day brought some new dimension of dread for me: I witnessed some new, ghastly, macabre facet in the kaleidoscope of the unreal, as though designed by some fiendish ghoul to cause even the most hardened and calloused observer among us to recoil in horror and disbelief.

Late one afternoon a buddy and I returned to the gun pit in the fading light. We passed a shallow defilade we hadn't noticed previously. In it were three Marine dead. They were lying on stretchers where they had died before their comrades had been forced to withdraw sometime earlier. (I usually avoided confronting such pitiful remains. I never could bear the sight of American dead neglected on the battlefield. In contrast, the sight of Japanese corpses bothered me little aside from the stench and the flies they nourished.)

As we moved past the defilade, my buddy groaned, "Jesus!" I took a quick glance into the depression and recoiled in revulsion and pity at what I saw. The bodies were badly decomposed and nearly blackened by exposure. This was to be expected of the dead in the tropics, but these Marines had been mutilated hideously by the enemy. One man had been decapitated. His head lay on his chest; his hands had been severed from his wrists and also lay on his chest near his chin. In disbelief I stared at the face as I realized that the Japanese had cut off the dead Marine's penis and stuffed it into his mouth. The corpse next to him had been treated similarly. The third had been butchered, chopped up like a carcass torn by some predatory animal.

My emotions solidified into rage and a hatred for the Japanese beyond anything I ever had experienced. From that moment on I never felt the least pity or compassion for them no matter what the circumstances. My comrades would field strip their packs and pockets for souvenirs and take gold teeth, but I never saw a Marine commit the kind of barbaric mutilation the Japanese committed if they had access to our dead.

When we got back to the gun pit, my buddy said, "Sledgehammer, did you see what the Nips did to them bodies? Did you see what them poor guys had in their mouths?" I nodded as he continued, "Christ, I hate them slant-eyed bastards!"

"Me too. They're mean as hell," was all I could say.

VICTORY AT HIGH COST

Twelve October continued to be an eventful day for us on Hill 140. Following Captain Haldane's death in the morning, we set up our mortars below and behind a 75mm pack howitzer tied down within Company K's lines. We were to fire our usual support for the company, but we also were to provide covering fire for the artillery piece.

Johnny Marmet was observing for us through a crack in the coral rock up near the howitzer when he suddenly called down to us that he saw some Japanese officers just outside the mouth of a cave. Apparently confident they were sheltered from American fire, they were just sitting down to eat at a table on a ledge beneath a thatched canopy.

Johnny called the range to us and the order to fire five rounds. Snafu sighted in on the proper aiming stake, repeated Johnny's range, and yelled, "Fire one." I grabbed a shell, repeated the range and charge, pulled off the proper number of powder increments from between the tail fins, put my right thumb over the safety pin, pulled the safety wire, and dropped the shell into the muzzle. Snafu realigned the sight after the recoil, grabbed the bipod feet and yelled, "Fire two." I prepared the second shell and dropped it into the tube. It went smoothly and we got all the rounds off in short order. We listened tensely for them to explode on target. My heart pounded away the seconds. It was a rare occasion to get Japanese officers bunched up and rarer indeed on Peleliu for them to expose themselves.

After seemingly endless seconds of suspense we heard the dull boom as each shell exploded over the ridge and across the valley. Something was wrong though. I heard one less explosion than the number of shells we had fired. We looked anxiously up at Johnny who had his eyes glued to the target. Suddenly he spun around, snapped his finger, and stamped his foot. Scowling down at us he yelled, "Right on target, zeroed in! But the first damned round was a *dud*! What the hell happened?" We groaned and cursed with frustration. The first shell had gone right through the thatched roof and the Japanese officers dove for the cave. But the shell didn't explode. Our remaining shells were right on target, too, smashing up and blowing apart the thatched canopy and the table. But the enemy officers were safe inside the cave. Our pinpoint accuracy had been remarkable for a 60mm mortar that normally functioned to neutralize an area with fragments from its bursting shells. Our golden opportunity had vanished because of a dud shell. We set about trying to figure out what had gone wrong.

Everybody in the mortar section was cursing and groaning.

Suddenly Snafu accused me of forgetting to pull the safety wire to arm that first shell. I was confident that I had pulled the pin. Some defense worker in an ammunition plant back in the States had made a mistake in the manufacture of the shell, I contended. Snafu wouldn't accept that, and we got into a hot argument. I was angry and frustrated enough myself. We had missed our one chance in a million to avenge the death of our CO. But Snafu was in a rage. It was a matter of pride with him, because he was the gunner and, therefore, in command of our mortar crew.

Snafu was a good Marine and an expert mortarman. His performance of his duties bore absolutely no resemblance to his nickname, "Situation Normal All Fouled Up." He felt it was a reflection on him that a chance to clobber several Japanese officers had failed because his assistant gunner hadn't pulled the safety wire on a shell. He was proud of a newspaper clipping from his hometown paper in Louisiana describing the effective fire his "mortar gun" had poured on the Japs during the bloody fighting for Hill 660 on Cape Gloucester. Snafu was a unique character known and respected by everybody. The guys loved to kid him about his intrepid "mortar gun" on Hill 660, and he thrived on it. But this foul-up and escape of those enemy officers because of a dud shell was another matter.

As we argued, I knew that unless I could prove the dud wasn't my fault, I'd never hear the end of it from Snafu and the other Company K survivors of Peleliu. Fortunately, luck was on my side. We had fired only a couple of shells to register the gun before Johnny called on us to fire on the Japanese. Consequently I had an accurate count of the number of rounds we had fired from this position. While Snafu ranted and raved I crawled around on all fours a few feet in front of the gun. With incredible good luck I found what I was seeking amid the coral gravel and pulverized plant material. I retrieved the safety wire from each shell we had fired.

I held them out to Snafu and said, "OK, count them and then tell me I didn't pull the wires on all those rounds."

He counted them. We knew that no other 60mm mortar had occupied this newly captured position, so all the wires were ours. I was angry the shell had been a dud and the Japanese had escaped, but I was delighted that it wasn't due to my carelessness. I heard no more about the dud. We all wanted to forget it.

Word also came that day that the high command had declared the "assault phase" of the Palau Islands operation at an end. Many profane and irreverent remarks were made by my buddies to the effect that our leaders were as crazy as hell if they thought that held true on Peleliu. "Somebody from the division CP needs to come up here and tell them damned Nips the 'assault phase' is over," grumbled one man.

After dark the Japanese reinfiltrated some of the positions they had been driven out of around Hill 140. It was the usual hellish night in the ridges, exhausted Marines trying to fight off incredibly aggressive Japanese slipping all around. It was mortar flares, HE shells, grenades, and small-arms fire. I was so tired I held one eye open with the fingers of one hand to stay awake while clutching a grenade or other weapon with the other hand.

The next day, 13 October, 3/5 was ordered to renew the offensive and to straighten our lines, forming a salient on Hill 140. Our battalion was the only unit of the 5th Marines still on the lines and ordered to attack. Snipers raised hell all over the place. It seemed to me the fighting would never end, as we fired covering fire for our weary riflemen. Our artillery fired heavy support. The next morning, 14 October, Corsairs made a napalm strike against the Japanese on our right. Company I made a probing attack after a mortar barrage was halted by heavy sniper fire. Companies K and L improved their positions and put out more sandbags and concertina wire.

The battalion's efforts at attacking seemed like the gasping of a tired steam engine struggling to pull its string of cars up a steep grade. We were barely making it. Rumors flew that army troops would relieve us the next day, but my cynicism kept me from believing them.

We found some Japanese rifles and ammunition in our area. Hidden under pieces of corrugated iron, I discovered two boxes containing about a dozen Japanese grenades. I suggested to an NCO that we take them in case we needed them during the coming night, but he said we could get them later if necessary. We got busy on firing missions with our mortar, and the first time I glanced back toward the boxes, the souvenir hunters had moved in and were emptying them. Another mortarman and I yelled at the scavenging pests. They left, but all the Japanese grenades were gone.

A wave of hope and excitement spread through the ranks that evening when we got solid information that we would be relieved by the army the next morning. I got less sleep that night than ever. With the end in sight, I didn't want to get my throat slit at the last moment before escaping from the meat grinder.

During the morning of 15 October soldiers of the 2d Battalion, 321st Infantry Regiment, 81st Infantry Division (Wildcats) began moving single-file into our area. I couldn't believe it! We were being relieved at last!

As the soldiers filed by us into position, a grizzled buddy squatting on his battered helmet eyed them critically and remarked, "Sledgehammer, I don't know about them dogfaces. Look how many of 'em wearin' glasses, and they look old enough to be my daddy. Besides, them pockets on their dungaree pants sure do look baggy."

"They look fine to me. They're our replacements," I answered.

"I guess you're right. Thank God they're here," he said reflectively.

His observations were correct though, because most of our fellow Marines hadn't reached the age of twenty-one yet, and army dungarees did have large side pockets.

"We sure are glad to see you guys," I said to one of the soldiers.

He just grinned and said, "Thanks." I knew he wasn't happy to be there.*

The relief, which had gone smoothly, was completed by 1100, and we were on our way to the northern defense zone of Peleliu. Our battalion deployed along the East Road facing seaward, where we were to stop any counterlanding the Japanese might try.

---

*By 15 October, the Marines had compressed the Umurbrogol Pocket to an area of about 400 to 500 yards. Yet the soldiers of the 81st Infantry Division faced six more weeks of fighting before the process of constant pressure and attrition wiped out the final vestiges of Japanese opposition.

My mortar was emplaced near the road so we could fire on the strip of mangrove swamp between the narrow beach and the sea as well as up the road toward the Umurbrogol Pocket if necessary. There was a sloping ridge to our rear along which the rest of the company dug in defensively. We stayed there from the time we came off the line until the last week of the month.

The area was quiet. We relaxed as much as we could with the nagging fear that we might get thrown into the line again if an emergency developed.

We learned that our battalion would leave Peleliu as soon as a ship was available to transport us back to Pavuvu. By day we rested and swapped souvenirs, but we had to be on the alert at night for possible Japanese movement. To the south we could hear the constant rattle of machine guns and the thud of mortars and artillery as the 81st Infantry Division kept up the pressure around the Umurbrogol Pocket.

One day a buddy told me he had a unique souvenir to show me. We sat on a rock as he carefully removed a package from his combat pack. He unwrapped layers of waxed paper that had originally covered rations and proudly held out his prize for me to see.

"Have you gone Asiatic?" I gasped. "You know you can't keep that thing. Some officer'll put you on report sure as hell," I remonstrated as I stared in horror at the shriveled human hand he had unwrapped.

"Aw, Sledgehammer, nobody'll say anything. I've got to dry it in the sun a little more so it won't stink," he said as he carefully laid it out on the rock in the hot sun. He explained that he thought a dried Japanese hand would be a more interesting souvenir than gold teeth. So when he found a corpse that was drying in the sun and not rotting, he simply took out his kabar and severed the hand from the corpse, and here it was, and what did I think?

"I think you're nuts," I said. "You know the CO will raise hell if he sees that."

"Hell no, Sledgehammer, nobody says anything about the guys collecting gold teeth, do they?" he argued.

"Maybe so," I said, "but it's just the idea of a human hand. Bury it."

He looked grimly at me, which was totally out of character for his amiable good nature. "How many Marines you reckon that hand pulled the trigger on?" he asked in an icy voice.

I stared at the blackened, shriveled hand and wondered about what he said. I thought how I valued my own hands and what a miracle to do good or evil the human hand is. Although I didn't collect gold teeth, I had gotten used to the idea, but somehow a hand seemed to be going too far. The war had gotten to my friend; he had lost (briefly, I hoped) all his sensitivity. He was a twentieth-century savage now, mild mannered though he still was. I shuddered to think that I might do the same thing if the war went on and on.

Several of our Marines came over to see what my buddy had. "You dumb jerk, throw that thing away before it begins to stink," growled an NCO.

"Hell yes," added another man, "I don't want you going aboard ship with me if you got that thing. It gives me the creeps," he said as he looked disgustedly at the souvenir.

After several other men chimed in with their disapproval, my friend reluctantly flung his unique souvenir among the rocks.

We had good rations and began to eat heartily and enjoy being out of the line as we relaxed more each day. Good water came up by jeep with the rations, and I never brushed my teeth so many times a day. It was a luxury. Rumors began to spread that we would soon board ship and leave Peleliu.

Toward the end of October, we moved to another part of the island. Our spirits soared. We bivouacked in a sandy, flat area near the beach. Jeeps brought in our jungle hammocks and our knapsacks.* We received orders to shave and to put on the clean dungarees we all carried in our knapsacks.

Some men complained that it would be easier to clean up aboard ship. But one NCO laughed and said that if our scroungy, stinking bunch of Marines climbed a cargo net aboard ship, the sailors would jump over the other side as soon as they saw us.

My hair, though it had been short on D day, had grown into

---

*A knapsack was the lower half of the two-part World War II Marine combat pack. The upper part was called the haversack. The latter half was the part a Marine normally carried with him into a fight.

a thick matted mass plastered together with rifle oil and coral dust. Long ago I had thrown away my pocket comb, because most of the teeth had broken out when I tried to comb my hair. I managed now to clean up my head with soap and water, and it took both edges of two razor blades and a complete tube of shaving soap to shave off the itching, greasy tangle of coral-encrusted beard. I felt like a man freed of a hair shirt.

My dungaree jacket wasn't torn, and I felt I must keep it as a souvenir of good luck. I rinsed it in the ocean, dried it in the sun, and put it into my pack.*

My filthy dungaree trousers were ragged and torn in the knees so I threw them into a campfire along with my stinking socks. The jagged coral had worn away the tough, inch-thick cord soles of my new boondockers of 15 September to the thin innersoles. I had to keep these until we returned to Pavuvu, because my replacement shoes were back there in my seabag.

That afternoon, 29 October, we learned that we would board ship the next day. With a feeling of intense relief, I climbed into my hammock at dusk and zipped up the mosquito netting along the side. I was delighted at how comfortable it was to lie on something other than hard, rocky ground. I lay back, sighed, and thought of the good sleep I should get until my turn for sentry duty came around. I could look inland and see the ragged crest of those terrible ridges against the skyline. Thank goodness that section was in U.S. hands, I thought.

Suddenly, *zip, zip, zip, zip*, a burst of Japanese machine-gun fire (blue-white tracers) slashed through the air *under* my hammock! The bullets kicked up sand on the other side of a crater beneath me. I jerked open the hammock zipper. Carbine in hand, I tumbled out into the crater. After all I had been through, I wasn't taking any chances on getting my rear end shot off in a hammock.

Judging from the sound made by the bullets, the machine gun was a long way off. The gunner was probably firing a burst toward the army lines over on some ridge between him and

---

*I later wore this same lucky jacket through the long, muddy Okinawa campaign. Faded now, it hangs peacefully in my closet, one of my most prized possessions.

me. But a man could get killed just as dead by a stray bullet as an aimed one. So after my brief moments of comfort in the hammock, I slept the rest of the night in the crater.

Next morning, 30 October, we squared away our packs, picked up our gear, and moved out to board ship. Even though we were leaving bloody Peleliu at last, my mind was distracted by an oppressive feeling that Bloody Nose Ridge was pulling us back like some giant, inexorable magnet. It had soaked up the blood of our division like a great sponge. I believed that it would get us yet. Even if we boarded ship, we would get jerked off and thrown into the line to help stop a counterattack or some threat to the airfield. I suppose I had become completely fatalistic; our casualties had been so heavy that it was impossible for me to believe we were actually leaving Peleliu. The sea was quite rough, and I looked back at the island with great relief as we put out for the ship.

We pulled alongside a big merchant troopship, the *Sea Runner*, and prepared to climb a cargo net to get aboard. We had done this sort of thing countless times in our training but never when we were so terribly exhausted. We had a hard time even getting started up the net because we kept bobbing up and down in the heavy sea. Several men stopped to rest on the way, but no one fell. As I struggled upward with my load of equipment, I felt like a weary insect climbing a vine. But at last I was crawling up out of the abyss of Peleliu!

We were assigned to quarters in troop compartments below decks. I stowed my gear on my rack and went topside. The salt air was delicious to breathe. What a luxury to inhale long deep breaths of fresh clean air, air that wasn't heavy with the fetid stench of death.

The cost in casualties for a tiny island was terrible. The fine 1st Marine Division was shattered. It suffered a total loss of 6,526 men (1,252 dead and 5,274 wounded). The casualties in the division's infantry regiments were: 1st Marines, 1,749; 5th Marines, 1,378; 7th Marines, 1,497. These were severe losses considering that each infantry regiment started with about 3,000 men. The army's 81st Infantry Division would lose another 3,278 men (542 dead and 2,736 wounded) before it secured the island.

Most of the enemy garrison on Peleliu died. Only a few were captured. Estimates as to the exact losses by the Japanese vary somewhat, but conservatively, 10,900 Japanese soldiers died and 302 became prisoners. Of the prisoners only 7 were soldiers and 12 sailors. The remainder were laborers of other oriental extractions.

Company K, 3d Battalion, 5th Marines went into Peleliu with approximately 235 men, the normal size of a World War II Marine rifle company. It left with only 85 unhurt. It suffered 64 percent casualties. Of its original seven officers, two remained for the return to Pavuvu.

For its actions on Peleliu and Ngesebus, the 1st Marine Division received the Presidential Unit Citation.

Even at a distance Peleliu was ugly with the jagged ridges and shattered trees. Haney came up alongside me and leaned on the rail. He looked gloomily at the island and puffed a cigarette.

"Well, Haney, what did you think of Peleliu?" I asked. I really was curious what a veteran with a combat record that included some of the big battles of the Western Front during World War I thought of the first battle in which I had participated. I had nothing in my experience to make a comparison with Peleliu.

Instead of the usual old salt comment—something like, "You think that was bad, you oughta been in the old Corps,"—Haney answered with an unexpected, "Boy, that was terrible! I ain't never seen nothin' like it. I'm ready to go back to the States. I've had enough after that."

A common perception has it that the "worst battle" to any man is the one he had been in himself. In view of Haney's comments, I concluded that Peleliu must have been as bad as I thought it was even though it was my first battle. Haney's long Marine Corps career as a combat infantryman certainly qualified him as a good judge of how bad a battle had been. His simple words were enough to convince me about the severity of the fight we had just been through.

None of us would ever be the same after what we had endured. To some degree that is true, of course, of all human experience. But something in me died at Peleliu. Perhaps it was a childish innocence that accepted as faith the claim that man is basically good. Possibly I lost faith that politicians in high places who do not have to endure war's savagery will ever stop blundering and sending others to endure it.

But I also learned important things on Peleliu. A man's ability to depend on his comrades and immediate leadership is absolutely necessary. I'm convinced that our discipline, esprit de corps, and tough training were the ingredients that equipped me to survive the ordeal physically and mentally—given a lot of good luck, of course. I learned realism, too. To defeat an enemy as tough and dedicated as the Japanese, we had to be just as tough. We had to be just as dedicated to America as they were to their emperor. I think this was the essence of Marine Corps doctrine in World War II, and that history vindicates this doctrine.

To this private first class, Peleliu was also a vindication of Marine Corps training, particularly of boot camp. I speak only from a personal viewpoint and make no generalizations, but for me, in the final analysis, Peleliu was:

- thirty days of severe, unrelenting inhuman emotional and physical stress;
- proof that I could trust and depend completely on the Marine on each side of me and on our leadership;
- proof that I could use my weapons and equipment efficiently under severe stress; and
- proof that the critical factor in combat stress is duration of the combat rather than the severity.

Boot camp taught me that I was expected to excel, or try to, even under stress. My drill instructor was a small man. He didn't have a big mouth. He was neither cruel nor sadistic. He wasn't a bully. But he was a strict disciplinarian, a total realist about our future, and an absolute perfectionist dedicated to excellence. To him more than to my disciplined home life, a year of college ROTC before boot camp, and months of infantry training afterward I attribute my ability to have withstood the stress of Peleliu.

The Japanese were as dedicated to military excellence as U.S. Marines. Consequently, on Peleliu the opposing forces were like two scorpions in a bottle. One was annihilated, the other nearly so. Only Americans who excelled could have defeated them.

Okinawa would be the longest and largest battle of the Pacific war. There my division would suffer about as many casualties as it did on Peleliu. Again the enemy garrison would fight to the death. On Okinawa I would be shelled and shot at more, see more enemy soldiers, and fire at more of them with my mortar and with small arms than on Peleliu. But there was a ferocious, vicious nature to the fighting on Peleliu that made it unique for me. Many of my veteran comrades agreed.

Perhaps we can say of Peleliu as the Englishman, Robert Graves, said of World War I, that it:

> . . . gave us infantrymen so convenient a measuring-stick for discomfort, grief, pain, fear, and horror, that nothing since has greatly daunted us. But it also brought new meanings of courage, patience, loyalty, and greatness of spirit; incommunicable, we found to later times.*

As I crawled out of the abyss of combat and over the rail of the *Sea Runner*, I realized that compassion for the sufferings of others is a burden to those who have it. As Wilfred Owen's poem "Insensibility" puts it so well, those who feel most for others suffer most in war.

*Graves, Robert, "Introduction" in *Old Soldiers Never Die* by Frank Richards, Berkley Publishing Corp., N.Y. 1966.

PART II

OKINAWA: THE FINAL
TRIUMPH

FOREWORD TO PART II

PELELIU TOOK its toll. As the executive officer and then commander of Company K, 3d Battalion, 5th Marines, I saw in the eyes of each survivor the price he paid for thirty days of unrelenting close combat on that hunk of blasted coral.

For those weary men returning to Pavuvu in November 1944, the war was far from over. Pavuvu was a better place the second time around than when we had left it. But it wasn't a rest haven. The survivors of Peleliu weren't allowed such a luxury. There was little time for licking wounds. We had to absorb a lot of new men as replacements for those lost on Peleliu and for the rotation home of the Guadalcanal veterans who by then had fought three campaigns.

Peleliu was something special for the Marines of K/3/5— for all of the 1st Marine Division. It has remained so down through the years. Yet Okinawa had its own character, more forbidding in many ways than its predecessor. There the 1st Marine Division fought a different war under a new set of rules where tactics and movement were used in a fashion previously unknown to the island-fighting Marines.

Okinawa is a large island, more than sixty miles long and from two to eighteen miles wide. It introduced the Marines to "land" warfare for the first time. Even in 1945 it had a city, towns and villages, several large airfields, an intricate road network, and a good-sized civilian population. Most important, the Japanese defended it with more than 100,000 of their best troops. Okinawa was Japanese territory. They knew it was our final stepping-stone to the home islands of Japan.

The Marines had learned a lot on the way to Okinawa. We had improved our force structure, tactics, and techniques for combat along the way. The Japanese had learned, too. On Okinawa we faced a set of defenses and defensive tactics made sophisticated by the Japanese through application of lessons learned from all of their previous losses. They also fought with an intensity born of a certain knowledge that if they failed, nothing remained to prevent our direct assault into their homeland.

179

Irrespective of the new elements, the battle for Okinawa was fought and ultimately decided the way all battles have been fought and won or lost. The men on both sides, facing each other day after day across the sights of a rifle, determined the outcome. Pfc. Eugene B. Sledge was one of those men. In this book he gives us a unique experience of seeing and feeling war at its most important level, that of the enlisted fighting man. His words ring true, clean of analysis and reaction to past events. They simply reflect what happened to him and, therefore, to all of the Marines who fought there. I know, because I fought with them.

For the men of the "old breed" who struggled, bled, died, and eventually won on Peleliu and Okinawa, Sledgehammer is their most eloquent spokesman. I'm proud to have served with them—and with him.

> Capt. Thomas J. Stanley
> U.S. Marine Corps Reserve (Ret.)

Houston, Texas

CHAPTER SEVEN

Rest and Rehabilitation

EARLY NEXT morning the *Sea Runner*, in convoy with other ships including those carrying the survivors of the 7th Marines, put out for Pavuvu. I was glad to be aboard ship again, even a troopship. I drank gallons of ice cold water from the electrically cooled "scuttlebutts."*

Most of my old friends in rifle companies had been wounded or killed. It was terribly depressing, and the full realization of our losses bore down heavily on me as we made inquiries. The survivors on board gave us all the details regarding our friends who hadn't made it through Peleliu. We thanked them and moved on. After a few of the visits and bad news about lost friends, I began to feel that I hadn't been just lucky but was a survivor of a major tragedy.

One day after noon chow a friend and I were sitting on our racks discussing things in general. The conversation drifted off, and we fell silent. Suddenly he looked at me with an intense, pained expression on his face and said, "Sledgehammer, why the hell did we have to take Peleliu?" I must have looked at him blankly, because he began to argue that our losses on Peleliu had been useless and hadn't helped the war effort at all, and that the island could have been bypassed. "Hell, the army landed troops on Morotai [Netherlands East Indies] with light opposition the same day we landed on Peleliu, and we caught hell, and the damn place still ain't secured. And while we were still on Peleliu, MacArthur hit Leyte [in the Philippines, 20 October] and walked ashore standing up. I just don't see where we did any good," he continued.

I replied gloomily, "I don't know." He just stared at the bulkhead and sadly shook his head. He was the same friend

---

*This is a naval slang word referring either to water coolers aboard ship or to rumors. Perhaps the double meaning derived from a habit of sailors and Marines of swapping rumors when gathered around a water cooler for a drink.

who had been with me the time we saw the three terribly mutilated Marine dead. I could imagine what he was thinking.

Despite these momentary lapses, the veterans of Peleliu knew they had accomplished something special. That these Marines had been able to survive the intense physical exertion of weeks of combat on Peleliu in that incredibly muggy heat gave ample evidence of their physical toughness. That we had survived emotionally—at least for the moment—was, and is, ample evidence to me that our training and discipline were the best. They prepared us for the worst, which is what we experienced on Peleliu.

On 7 November 1944, (three days after my twenty-first birthday) the *Sea Runner* entered Macquitti Bay. After passing familiar islets, she dropped anchor off Pavuvu's steel pier. I was surprised at how good Pavuvu looked after the desolation of Peleliu.

We picked up our gear and debarked shortly. On the beach we walked over to one of several tables set up nearby. There I saw—of all things—an American Red Cross girl. She was serving grapefruit juice in small paper cups. Some of my buddies looked at the Red Cross woman sullenly, sat on their helmets, and waited for orders. But together with several other men, I went over to the table where the young lady handed me a cup of juice, smiled, and said she hoped I liked it. I looked at her with confusion as I took the cup and thanked her. My mind was so benumbed by the shock and violence of Peleliu that the presence of an American girl on Pavuvu seemed totally out of context. I was bewildered. "What the hell is she doing here?" I thought. "She's got no more business here than some damn politician." As we filed past to board trucks, I resented her deeply.

Next to a table counting off the men to board the trucks stood a brand-spanking-new boot second lieutenant. He was so obviously fresh from the States and officers' candidate school that his khakis were new, and he wasn't even suntanned. As I moved slowly by the table he said, "OK, sonny, move out." Since my enlistment in the Marine Corps, I had been called about everything imaginable—printable and unprintable. But fresh off of Peleliu I was unprepared for "sonny." I turned to the officer and stared at him blankly. He returned my gaze and seemed to realize his mistake. He looked hurriedly away. My buddies' eyes still carried that vacant hollow look typical of men recently out of the shock of battle. Maybe that's what the young lieutenant saw in mine, and it made him uncomfortable.

The trucks sped past neat tent areas, much improved since we had last seen Pavuvu. We arrived at our familiar camp area to find numerous self-conscious replacements sitting and standing in and around the tents. We were the "old men" now. They appeared so relaxed and innocent of what lay ahead of us that I felt sorry for them. We took off our packs and settled into our tents. In the best way we could, we tried to unwind and relax.

Shortly after we arrived back at Pavuvu and on an occasion when all the replacements were out of the company area on work parties, 1st Sgt. David P. Bailey yelled "K Company, fall in." As the survivors of Peleliu straggled out of their tents into the company street, I thought about how few remained out of the 235 men we started with.

Dressed in clean khakis and with his bald head shining, Bailey walked up to us and said, "At ease, men." He was a real old-time salty Marine and a stern disciplinarian, but a mild-mannered man whom we highly respected. Bailey had something to say, and it wasn't merely a pep talk. Unfortunately, I don't remember his exact words, so I won't attempt to quote him, but he told us we should be proud. He said we had fought well in as tough a battle as the Marine Corps had ever been in, and we had upheld the honor of the Corps. He finished by saying, "You people have proved you are good Marines." Then he dismissed us.

We returned silently and thoughtfully to our tents. I heard no cynical comments about Bailey's brief remarks. Words of praise were rare from the heart of such a stern old salt who expected every man to do his best and tolerated nothing less. His straightforward, sincere praise and statement of respect and admiration for what our outfit had done made me feel like I had won a medal. His talk was not the loud harangue of a politician or the cliché-studded speech of some rear-echelon officer or journalist. It was a quiet statement of praise from one who had endured the trials of Peleliu with us. As far as being a competent judge of us, there was nobody better qualified than an old combat Marine and a senior NCO like Bailey, who had observed us and endured the fight himself. His words meant a lot to me, and they apparently did to my comrades, too.

One of our first activities after getting settled in our Pavuvu tents was to renew our old feud with the rats and land crabs. Our seabags, cots, and other gear had been stacked around the center tent pole while we were gone. The land crabs had moved in and made themselves at home. When several of my tent mates and I started unstacking the items around the tent pole, the crabs swarmed out. The men started yelling, cursing the crabs and smashing them with bayonets and entrenching tools. Some character sprayed cigarette lighter fluid on a crab as it ran into the company street and then threw a match at it. The flaming crab moved a couple of feet before being killed by the flames.

"Hey, you guys, did you see that? That crab looked just like a burning Jap tank."

"Good oh," yelled another man as Marines rushed around trying to find more cans of lighter fluid to spray on the hated land crabs. Men started taking orders for cans of lighter fluid and raced off to the 5th Marines PX tent to buy up all they could find. We killed over a hundred crabs from my tent alone.

One evening after chow as I sprawled on my cot wishing I were back home, I noticed one of Company K's two surviving officers carrying some books and papers down the company street in the twilight. He passed my tent and went to the fifty-five-gallon oil drum that served as a trash can. The lieutenant tossed some maps and papers into the can. He held up a thick book and with obvious anger slammed it into the trash can. He then turned and walked slowly back up the street.

Curious, I went out to have a look. The maps were combat maps of Peleliu. I dropped them back into the trash (and have since regretted I didn't salvage them for future historical reference). Then I found the book. It was a large hardback volume of about a thousand pages, bound in dark blue, obviously not a GI field manual or book of regulations.

Always seeking good reading material, I looked at the spine of the book and read its title, *Men At War* by Ernest Hemingway. This is interesting history, I thought, and was puzzled as to why the lieutenant had thrown it so violently into the trash. I opened the cover. In the twilight I saw written in a bold strong hand, *A. A. Haldane.* A lump rose in my throat as I asked myself why I'd want to read about war when Peleliu had cost us our company commander and so many good friends. I, too, slammed the book down into the trash can in a gesture of grief and disgust over the waste of war I had already experienced firsthand.

After we had been back on Pavuvu about a week, I had one of the most heartwarming and rewarding experiences of my entire enlistment in the Marine Corps. It was after taps, all the flambeaus were out, and all of my tent mates were in their sacks with mosquito nets in place. We were all very tired, still trying to unwind from the tension and ordeal of Peleliu.

All was quiet except for someone who had begun snoring softly when one of the men, a Gloucester veteran who had been wounded on Peleliu, said in steady measured tones, "You know something, Sledgehammer?"

"What?" I answered.

"I kinda had my doubts about you," he continued, "and how you'd act when we got into combat, and the stuff hit the fan. I mean, your ole man bein' a doctor and you havin' been to college and bein' sort of a rich kid compared to some guys. But I kept my eye on you on Peleliu, and by God you did OK; you did OK."

"Thanks, ole buddy," I replied, nearly bursting with pride. Many men were decorated with medals they richly earned for their brave actions in combat, medals to wear on their blouses for everyone to see. I was never awarded an individual decoration, but the simple, sincere personal remarks of approval by my veteran comrade that night after Peleliu were like a medal to me. I have carried them in my heart with great pride and satisfaction ever since.

As Christmas approached, rumor had it we were going to have a feast of real turkey. There were several days out of the year when the Marine Corps tried to give us good chow: 10 November (the Marine Corps' birthday), Thanksgiving, Christmas, and New Year's. The rest of the time in the Pacific war, chow was canned or dehydrated. Refrigeration facilities for large quantities of food were not available, at least not to a unit as mobile and as lacking in all luxuries as a combat division in the Fleet Marine Force. But the scuttlebutt was that there were frozen turkeys for us in the big refrigerators on Banika.

We had special Christmas Eve church services in the palm-thatched regimental chapel that had been constructed skillfully by Russell Island natives. That was followed by a special Christmas program at the regimental theater where we sat on coconut logs and sang carols. I enjoyed it a great deal but felt pretty homesick. Then we had our roast turkey, and it was excellent.

New Year's celebration was even more memorable for me. On New Year's Eve after chow, I heard some yelling and other commotion over at the battalion messhall. The messmen had just about finished squaring away the galley for the night when a sentry shouted, "Corporal of the guard, fire at post number three!"

I saw cooks and messmen in the messhall who were cleaning up by lamplight all rush outside to a fire burning in a grove of trees near the galley. I thought one of the gasoline heaters that boiled water in tubs where we cleaned our mess kits had caught fire. By the light of the flames I could see men running around the galley yelling, and I could hear the mess sergeant cursing and shouting orders. I also saw two figures slide through the shadows toward our company street, but paid them little heed. In a few minutes the fire was put out, just a can of gasoline some distance from the messhall that had somehow caught fire, somebody said.

A friend of mine appeared at my tent and said in a low voice, "Hey, you guys, Howard says come on down to his tent; plenty of turkey for everybody!"

We followed him on the double. As I entered the tent, there sat Howard Nease on his cot, a flambeau flickering beside him, and a towel on his lap under a huge, plump roast turkey.

"Happy New Year, you guys," Howard said with his characteristically broad grin.

We filed past him as he deftly sliced off huge slabs of turkey with his razor-sharp kabar, and placed them into our opened hands. Others came in, and we broke out our two cans of warm beer that each had been issued. Someone produced a can of jungle juice that had been "working." A guitar, a fiddle, and a mandolin struck up the "Spanish Fandango" as Howard sliced turkey until the carcass was cleaned. Then he directed the music, using his kabar as a baton. Howard told us the burning can of gasoline had been merely a diversion to distract the mess sergeant while he and a couple of other daredevils entered the galley and made a moonlight requisition of two turkeys.

We, the survivors of that recent bloodbath on Peleliu, forgot our troubles and howled with laughter at the story. Enjoying the comradeship forged by combat, we had the finest New Year's Eve party I've ever attended. The 11th Marines fired an artillery salute at midnight—as a peaceful gesture.

It was typical of Howard that he pulled off his turkey requisition so neatly and just as typical that he shared it with as many of his buddies as he could. He was one of those wonderfully buoyant souls, always friendly and joking, cool-headed in combat, and though much admired, very modest. When Howard was killed by a Japanese machine gun in the early days of the Okinawa battle (his third campaign), every man who knew him was deeply saddened. By his example, he taught me more than anyone else the value of cheerfulness in the face of adversity.

One of my most treasured memories is the mental picture of Howard Nease sitting on his bunk carving a huge turkey on his lap with his kabar by the light of a flambeau in his tent under Pavuvu's palms on New Year's Eve 1944, grinning and saying, "Happy New Year, Sledgehammer." I profited greatly from knowing him.

Our new division commander, Maj. Gen. Pedro del Valle, former commander of the 11th Marines, ordered regular close-order drills, parades, and reviews. This was better than work parties moving rotting coconuts and added a "spit and polish" to our routine that helped morale. A regular beer ration of two cans a man each week also helped. During close-order drill we dressed in clean khakis, which each man pressed under his mattress pad on his canvas bunk. As we marched back and forth on the neat coral-covered parade ground, I thought about home or some book I was reading and wasn't at all bored.

One day we had a 5th Regiment parade. Decorations and medals were awarded to those cited for outstanding service on Peleliu. Many of our wounded had returned from the hospitals by then. When the Purple Heart medal was awarded to those who had been wounded, there weren't many of us who didn't qualify for it.

During those parades we took great pride in seeing our regimental flag carried with us. Like all the regimental flags, it had a large Marine Corps emblem on it with "United States Marine Corps" emblazoned across the top. Below the emblem was "Fifth Marine Regiment."

But the thing that made our flag unique was the number of battle streamers attached at the top of the staff. These streamers (ribbons about a foot long with the names of battles printed on them) represented battles the 5th Marines had fought in and decorations the regiment had won, all the way back to Belleau Wood (World War I) and the Banana Wars (in South America). We had just added Peleliu to the World War II collection. Those streamers represented more battles than any other Marine regiment had fought in. One buddy said our flag had so many battle streamers, decorations, and ribbons that it looked like a mop—an unsophisticated yet straight-from-the-shoulder summation of a proud tradition!

After we had been back on Pavuvu several weeks, I was told one day to dress in clean khakis and to report to the company headquarters tent promptly at 0100. There was some vague reference to an interview that might lead to officers' candidate school back in the States.

"Hey, Sledgehammer, you'll have it made, being an officer and all that, wheeling and dealing Stateside," a buddy said as I got ready for the interview.

"If you're lucky maybe you can land a desk job," another said.

Some of my buddies were obviously envious as I left and walked nervously down the street. The thoughts in my head were that I didn't want or intend to leave Company K (unless as a casualty or rotated home for good) and why on earth had I been chosen for an interview regarding OCS.

When I arrived at the company headquarters, I was sent to a tent a short distance away, near the battalion headquarters. I reported to the tent and was greeted cordially by a first lieutenant. He was an extremely handsome man and, I gathered from his composure and modest self-confidence, a combat veteran.

He asked me in detail about my background and education. He was sincere and friendly. I felt he was trying carefully to determine whether the men he interviewed were suitable to be Marine officers. He and I hit it off well, and I was perfectly honest with him. He asked me why I had not succeeded in the V-12 officers' candidate program, and I told him how I felt about joining the Marine Corps and being sent to college.

"How do you feel about it now that you've been in combat?" he asked.

I told him it would be nice to be back in college. I said I had seen enough on Peleliu to satisfy my curiosity and ardor for fighting. "In fact," I said, "I'm ready to go home."

He laughed good-naturedly and knowingly. He asked me how I liked the Marine Corps and my unit. I told him I was proud to be a member. He asked me how I liked being a 6omm mortar crewman, and I said it was my first choice. Then he got very serious and asked, "How would you feel about sending men into a situation where you knew they would be killed?"

Without hesitation I answered, "I couldn't do it, sir."

The lieutenant looked at me long and hard in a friendly, analytical way. He asked me a few more questions, then said, "Would you like to be an officer?"

"Yes, sir, if it meant I could go back to the States," I said. He laughed and with a few more friendly remarks told me that was all.

My buddies asked me for all the details of the interview. When I told them all about it one said, "Sledgehammer, damn if you ain't got to be as Asiatic as Haney. Why the hell didn't you snow that lieutenant so you could go into OCS?"

I replied that the lieutenant was experienced and too wise to fall for a snow job. That was true, of course, but I really had no desire to leave Company K. It was home to me, and I had a strong feeling of belonging to the company no matter how miserable or dangerous conditions might be. Besides, I had found my niche as a mortarman. The weapon and its deployment interested me greatly, and if I had to fight again, I was confident of doing the Japanese far more damage as a mortarman than as a second lieutenant. I had no desire to be an officer or command anybody; I just wanted to be the best mortar crewman I could—and to survive the war.

There was nothing heroic or unique in my attitude. Other men felt the same way. Actually, in combat our officers caught just as much hell as the enlisted men. They also were burdened with responsibility. As one buddy (a private) said, "When the stuff hits the fan, all I have to do is what I'm told, and I can look out for just me and my buddy. Them officers all the time got to be checkin' maps and squarin' people away."

We began to assimilate the new replacements into the company, and we added a third mortar to my section. The battalion ordnance section checked all weapons, and we got new issues for those worn out in the fight for Peleliu.

There were some drafted Marines among the new replacements and also a sprinkling of NCOs who had been in navy yards and other stateside duty stations. The presence of the NCOs caused some bitterness among a few of the Gloucester and Peleliu veterans who were by then senior in their squads because of the heavy casualties on Peleliu. The latter wouldn't get promoted with new NCOs entering the company to take our leadership positions. From what I saw, however, the new NCOs were mostly men with numerous years of service, although not combat veterans. They did a good job of assuming their authority while respecting us combat veterans for our experience.

The drafted Marines took a good bit of kidding about being "handcuffed volunteers" from those of us who had enlisted into the Marine Corps. Some of the drafted men insisted vehemently that they were volunteers who had enlisted like most of us. But they were careful to conceal their records and identification, because "SS" (for Selective Service) appeared after the serial number if a man had been drafted.

The draftees sometimes had their laugh on us, though. If we griped and complained, they grinned and said, "What you guys bitchin' about? You asked for it, didn't you?" We just grumbled at them; no one got angry about it. For the most part, the replacements were good men, and the company retained its fighting spirit.

Our training picked up in intensity, and rumors began to fly regarding the next "blitz" (a term commonly used for a campaign). We heard that the 1st Marine Division was to be put into an army to invade the China coast or Formosa (Taiwan). Many of my buddies feared that we would lose our identity as Marines and that the Marine Corps would finally be absorbed into the U.S. Army (a fate that has caused anxiety to U.S. Marines of many generations, as history well documents). Our training emphasized street fighting and cooperation with tanks in open country. But we still didn't know the name of our objective. After we were shown maps (without names) of a long, narrow island, we still didn't know.

One day Tom F. Martin, a friend of mine in Company L, who also had been in the V-12 program and was a Peleliu veteran, came excitedly to my tent and showed me a *National Geographic* map of the Northern Pacific. On it we saw the same oddly shaped island. Located 325 miles south of the southern tip of the Japanese home island of Kyushu, it was called Okinawa Shima. Its closeness to Japan assured us of one thing beyond any doubt: Whatever else happened, the battle for Okinawa was bound to be bitter and bloody. The Japanese never had sold any island cheaply, and the pattern of the war until then had shown that the battles became more vicious the closer we got to Japan.

We made practice landings, fired various small arms, and underwent intensive mortar training. With a third weapon added to our mortar section, I felt as though we were Company K's artillery battery.

At this time hepatitis broke out among the troops. We called it yellow jaundice, and I got a bad case. We could look at a man and tell whether he had the malady by the yellowing of the whites of his eyes. Even our deeply tanned skins took on a sallow appearance. I felt terrible, was tired, and the smell of food nauseated me. Pavuvu's muggy heat didn't help any either. I went to sick call one morning, as other Marines were doing in increasing numbers. The medical officer gave me a "light duty slip," a piece of paper officially relieving me from the intense exertion of routine training but still making me subject to minor work parties such as picking up trash, straightening tent ropes, and the like. It was the only time during my entire service in the Marine Corps that I got out of regular duties because of illness.

Had we been civilians, I'm confident those of us with hepatitis would have been hospitalized. Instead, we received APC pills from a corpsman.* This medication was the standard remedy for everything except bayonet, gunshot, or shrapnel wounds. After several days I was pronounced recovered enough for resumption of regular duties and surrendered my cherished light duty slip to an officer in sick bay.

Training intensified. During January 1945 the company boarded an LCI† and, in convoy with other such vessels, went to Guadalcanal for maneuvers. After a division-sized field problem, we returned to Pavuvu on 25 January.

Then we listened daily with sympathetic interest to the news reports of the terrible fighting encountered by the 3d, 4th, and 5th Marine divisions during the battle for Iwo Jima that began on 19 February.

"It sounds just like a larger version of Peleliu," a buddy of mine said one day.

He didn't realize how correct he was. The new pattern of defense-in-depth and no *banzai* charges that the Japanese had tried on the 1st Marine Division at Peleliu was repeated on Iwo Jima. When that island was declared secured on 16 March, the cost to the three Marine divisions which fought there sounded like our Peleliu casualties magnified three times.

During our training we were told that we would have to climb over a seawall or cliff (exact height unknown) to move inland during the coming battle. Several times we practiced scaling a sheer coral cliff (about forty feet high) across the bay from the division's camp on Pavuvu. We had no more than two ropes to get the entire company up and over the cliff. Supposedly we would be furnished rope ladders before D day, but I never saw any.

While we stood at the foot of the cliff during those exercises, waiting our turn and watching other men struggle up the ropes to the top of the cliff with all their combat gear, I heard some choice comments from my buddies regarding

---

*A nonprescription, all-purpose painkiller containing aspirin and caffeine, among other ingredients.
†Landing Craft, Infantry; a sort of miniature LST which carried about a company of infantry plus a few vehicles.

the proceedings. The company officers (all new except First Lieutenant Stanley, the CO) were rushing around with great enthusiasm urging the troops up the cliff like it was some sort of college football training routine.

"What a fouled-up bunch of boot lieutenants if I ever saw any. Just what the hell do they think them goddamn Nips are gonna be doin' while we climb up that cliff one at a time?" grumbled a veteran machine gunner.

"Seems pretty stupid to me. If that beach is anything like Peleliu, we'll get picked off before anybody gets up any cliff," I said.

"You said that right, Sledgehammer, and them Nips ain't gonna be sittin' around on their cans; they're gonna bracket that beach with mortars and artillery, and machine guns are gonna sweep the top of that cliff," he said with melancholy resignation.

Our new mortar section leader was a New Englander out of an Ivy League college. Mac was blond, not large, but was well built, energetic, and talkative, with a broad New England accent. He was a conscientious officer, but he irritated the veterans by talking frequently and at great length about what he was going to do to the Japanese when we went into action again. We sometimes heard such big talk from enlisted replacements who were trying to impress someone (mostly themselves) with how brave they would be under fire, but Mac was about the only officer I ever heard indulge in it.

Whenever he got started with, "The first time one of our guys gets hit, its gonna make me so mad that I'm gonna take my kabar between my teeth and my .45 in my hand and charge the Japs," all the veterans would sit back and smirk. We threw knowing glances at each other and rolled our eyes like disgusted schoolboys listening to a coach brag that he could lick the opposing team single-handed.

I felt embarrassed for Mac, because it was so obvious he conceived combat as a mixture of football and a boy scout campout. He wouldn't listen to the few words of caution from some of us who suggested he had a shock coming. I agreed with a buddy from Texas who said, "I hope to God that big mouth Yankee lieutenant has to eat every one of them words of his when the stuff hits the fan." The Texan's wish came true on

Okinawa, and it was one of the funniest things I ever saw under fire.

Before the next campaign, we had to take the usual inoculations plus some additional ones. Our arms were sore, and many men became feverish. The troops hated getting injections, and the large number (someone said it was seven) before Okinawa made us crotchety. The plague shot burned like fire and was the worst.

Most of our corpsmen did a good job of making the shots as painless as possible, and this helped. But we had one arrogant corpsman who was unfeeling about other people's pain. He wasn't popular, to say the least. (I hasten to add that he was the one—and only—U.S. Navy hospital corpsman I knew in the Marine Corps who didn't conduct himself in an exemplary manner. All other corpsmen I saw were probably more highly respected by Marines—as a group, and as individuals—than any other group of people we were involved with.)

Directly in front of me as we lined up for shots was a buddy who was a Peleliu veteran. In front of him were several new replacements. The more new men "Doc Arrogant" stuck with the needle, the worse he became. He was just plain mean by the time he got to my buddy. "Doc Arrogant" was in a hurry and didn't look up to recognize my buddy as the latter stepped up to the table. It nearly cost Doc dearly. He held the needle like a dart, plunged it into my friend's arm, depressed the plunger, and said, "Move out!"

My friend didn't flinch from the painful shot. He turned slowly, shook his fist in the corpsman's face, and said, "You sonofabitch, if you want to do some bayonet practice, I'll meet you out on the bayonet course with fixed bayonets and no scabbards on the blades, and then see what you can do."

"Doc Arrogant" looked shocked. He was speechless when he realized that the arm he had punctured so roughly wasn't attached to a meek replacement but to a seasoned veteran.

Then my friend said, "If you ever give me another shot like that, I'll grab you by the stacking swivel and beat you down to parade rest. I'll whip your ass so bad you won't even be able to make this next blitz, because they'll hafta award you a Purple Heart when I finish with you, wise guy."

"Doc Arrogant" changed instantly into "Doc Meek." When I stepped up for my shot, he administered it with a gentleness that would have done credit to Florence Nightingale.

We started packing up our gear. Soon we got word that we would have more maneuvers on Guadalcanal, then shove off for our next fight—Okinawa.

CHAPTER EIGHT

Prelude to Invasion

FROM THE standpoint of personal satisfaction I've always been glad that as long as we had to pull maneuvers somewhere in preparation for Peleliu and Okinawa, this training took place on Guadalcanal. The name of that island was embroidered in white letters down the red number *One* on our division patch of which we were all very proud. Guadalcanal had great symbolic significance. I was glad I got to see some of the areas fought over by the 1st Marine Division during the campaign and got some first-hand accounts on the spot of what had taken place from veterans who had participated in making that history.

During one period of maneuvers on Guadalcanal, we stayed ashore for two or three weeks and bivouacked in an area that had been the camp of the 3d Marine Division before its troops went into the hell of Iwo Jima. We strung our jungle hammocks and made ourselves as comfortable as possible. Each day for several days we went out into the hills, jungles, and *kunai* grass fields for training. And we enjoyed a cool shower each afternoon after coming in from the field.

Guadalcanal was a big base by early 1945 and had many service troops and rear-echelon units on it. Across the road from us was a battalion of "Seabees" (naval construction battalion). Late one afternoon three or four of us went over and eased quietly into the end of their chow line. Their cooks recognized us as Marines but didn't say anything. We loaded up on real ice cream, fresh pork chops, fresh salad, and good bread (all unheard of delicacies on Pavuvu) and sat at a clean table in a spacious messhall. It sure beat C rations in a bivouac area. As intruders, we expected to be thrown out any minute. No one seemed to notice us, though.

Next afternoon we returned along with other Marines who had the same idea and enjoyed another excellent supper. Next day we tried it again, easing quietly and slowly along to the chow line, trying not to attract attention. To my amazement a large neatly painted white sign with blue letters and blue border had been placed above the entrance to the chow line since the previous evening. I don't remember the exact wording, but it went something close to this, "Marines welcomed in this chow line after all CB personnel have been through."

We were as embarrassed as we were delighted. Those Seabees had been fully aware of us all along and knew exactly how many Marines were slipping into their chow line. But they were willing and glad to share their extra chow with us as long as it lasted. The sign was necessary, because the Seabees knew we would spread the word and more hungry Marines would swarm over their chow line each day like ants.

We were elated and went through the chow line grinning and thanking the messmen. They were the friendliest bunch I ever saw and made us feel like adopted orphans. The sign may have been made earlier for 3d Division Marines who liked the Seabees' food as much as we, or it may have been put up for our benefit. In any event we appreciated the good food and good treatment. It strengthened our respect for the Seabees.

The 3d Battalion, 5th Marines had been in the assault waves at Peleliu; therefore, in the Okinawa campaign we were assigned as regimental reserve. For the voyage to the island, consequently, we would be loaded aboard the attack transport ship USS *McCracken* instead of LSTs. Such APA transports sent troops ashore in LCVPs (small, open landing craft known as Higgins boats) rather than amphibious tractors.

One afternoon following landing exercises and field problems, our company returned to the beach to await the return of the Higgins boats that would pick us up and return us to the ship. Late afternoon sunlight danced on the beautiful blue waves, and a large fleet of ships stood offshore in Sealark Channel. Dozens of Higgins boats and other amphibious craft plied from the ships to shore, loading Marines and ferrying them out to the ships. It looked like some sort of boating festival except that all the craft were military.

One by one the Higgins boats picked up men (about twenty-five at a time) from our beach area. We waited as the sun sank low in the west. The ships formed up in convoy and moved

past us, parallel to the beach. We had no rations or extra water, were tired from day-long maneuvers, and had no desire to
spend the night on a mosquito-infested beach.

Finally, as the last ship showed us its stern, a Higgins boat
came ploughing through the spray toward us. We were the
only troops left on the beach. The coxswain revved his engine,
ran the bow of the shallow-draft boat up on the beach, and
dropped the bow ramp with a bang. We clambered aboard and
someone yelled the customary, "Shove off, coxswain, you're
loaded." We held on to the bulwarks of the boat as he raised
the ramp, reversed engines, turned, and headed out at full
throttle toward the disappearing ship.

The sea was rough. As usual Snafu started getting seasick,
so he lay down on his side on the deck of the boat. We were
crowded: two machine-gun squads and two 60mm mortar
squads packed the Higgins boat, along with all our combat
gear, small arms, mortars, and machine guns.

A Higgins boat, like any powerful motor-driven boat under full throttle, normally settled down at the stern end with
bow elevated and moved easily over the water. But our boat
was so loaded with men and equipment that, even though we
crowded as far back in the stern as possible, the squared-off
bow ramp wasn't elevated sufficiently to skip over the waves.
It drove straight against some large waves, and water poured
in through an open view port. Usually, this three-foot by two-
foot panel rode well above water level. The coxswain yelled
instructions to close the folding steel shutters on the panel,
which we did as quickly as possible. But water still sprayed over
the bow ramp and in through the cracks around the panel.

In the gathering twilight we could see the stern of a transport far ahead of us. It was the last ship in the convoy that had
passed from view around the end of Guadalcanal. Our coxswain made as much speed as possible to catch the transport,
and we shipped more and more water. If we didn't catch up
with that transport before dark we didn't know when we would
get back to our ship.

Water began filling the bilges below the floor decking, so
the coxswain started the pumps to keep us afloat. We stood by
to bail with our helmets, but by the time the water rose above
the flooring where we could get at it, the boat would probably

sink because of its heavy load. The situation was grim, and I dreaded the thought of trying to swim the couple of miles through rough water to the beach. What irony, I thought, if some of us should die after surviving Peleliu by drowning on maneuvers in Iron Bottom Bay.

Slowly we gained on the transport and finally drew alongside. Towering above us, the ship was packed with Marines. We shouted up to them for help. A navy officer leaned over the rail and asked us which ship we were from. We told him we had missed the *McCracken* and requested to come aboard or we might sink. He gave orders to our coxswain to pull in close under a pair of davits. He did so, and two cables with hooks were lowered to us. Just as the hooks were fastened to rings in the floor, our Higgins boat seemed to start sinking. Only the cables held it up. A cargo net was lowered to us, and we scrambled up and aboard the ship. We were all mighty relieved to be out of that small boat.

Several hours after dark, the ship arrived at the fleet anchorage. A signalman on the bridge went to work with his blinker light sending code to other ships. The *McCracken* was located, and we were soon back aboard.

"Where the hell you guys been so long?" asked a man in my troop compartment as we fell into our racks.

"We went to 'Frisco for a beer," someone answered.

"Wise guy," he replied.

After maneuvers were completed, our convoy sailed from the Russell Islands on 15 March 1945. We were bound for Ulithi Atoll where the convoy would join the gathering invasion fleet. We anchored off Ulithi on 21 March and remained there until 27 March.*

We lined the rails of our transport and looked out over the vast fleet in amazement. We saw ships of every description: huge new battleships, cruisers, sleek destroyers, and a host of fast escort craft. Aircraft carriers were there in greater numbers

---

*Ulithi Atoll lies about 260 miles northeast of Peleliu on the western edge of the Caroline Islands. It was captured by an element of the 81st Infantry Division as a part of the Palau Islands operation. Ulithi consists of about thirty islets surrounding an enormous lagoon some nineteen miles long and five to ten miles wide. It became the major U.S. fleet anchorage in the Central Pacific.

than any of us had ever seen before. Every conceivable type of
amphibious vessel was arrayed. It was the biggest invasion fleet
ever assembled in the Pacific, and we were awed by the sight
of it.

Because of tides and winds, the ships swung about on their
anchor chains, and each day the fleet looked new and different.
When I came topside each morning, I felt disoriented. It was
a strange sensation, as though I were in a different frame of
reference and had to learn my surroundings anew.

The first afternoon at Ulithi a fellow mortarman said, "Break
out the field glasses, and let's see how many kinds of ships
we can identify." We passed the mortar section's field glasses
around and whiled away many hours studying the different
ships.

Suddenly someone gasped, "Look over there at that hospital
ship off our port bow! Look at them nurses! Gimme them field
glasses!"

Lining the rail of the hospital ship were about a dozen
American nurses looking out over the fleet. A scuffle erupted
among us over who would use the field glasses first, but we all
finally had a look at the girls. We whistled and waved, but we
were too far away to be heard.

Aside from the huge new battleships and carriers, we talked
most about a terribly scorched and battered aircraft carrier anchored near us. A navy officer told us she was the *Franklin*.*
We could see charred and twisted aircraft on her flight deck,
where they had been waiting loaded with bombs and rockets
to take off when the ship was hit. It must have been a flaming
inferno of bursting bombs and rockets and burning aviation
gasoline. We looked silently at the battered, listing hulk until one man said, "Ain't she a mess! Boy, them poor swabbies
musta' caught hell." Those of us who had lived through the
blast and fire of Peleliu's artillery barrages could appreciate well
the bravery of the sailors on the *Franklin*.

---

*During carrier raids on Japan (18–21 March), Japanese suicide planes had
crashed into the American carriers *Wasp*, *Yorktown*, and *Franklin*. The *Franklin* was the most heavily damaged of the three; her loss was 724 killed and 265
wounded. That the ship was saved at all and later towed some 12,000 miles
to New York for repairs was a tribute to the bravery and the skill of her crew.

While we were anchored at Ulithi, we went ashore on the tiny islet of Mog Mog for recreation and physical conditioning. After some calisthenics, and to the delight of all hands, our officers broke out warm beer and Cokes. We had one of the most enjoyable baseball games I ever played. Everybody was laughing and running like a bunch of little boys. It was good to get off the cramped transport, stretch our legs, and relieve the monotony. We hated to board the Higgins boats at sunset to return to the ship and our cramped quarters.

At Ulithi we received briefings on the coming battle for Okinawa. This time there was no promise of a short operation. "This is expected to be the costliest amphibious campaign of the war," a lieutenant said. "We will be hitting an island about 350 miles from the Japs' home islands, so you can expect them to fight with more determination than ever. We can expect 80 to 85 percent casualties on the beach."

A buddy next to me leaned over and whispered, "How's that for boosting the troops' morale?" I only groaned.

The lieutenant continued, "We may have trouble getting over that cliff or seawall in our sector. Also, according to G-2 there is a large Jap gun, maybe 150mm, emplaced just on the right flank of our battalion sector. We hope naval gunfire can knock it out. Be on the alert for a Jap paratrooper attack in our rear, particularly at night. It's pretty certain the Nips will pull off a massive counterattack, probably supported by tanks, sometime during our first night ashore or just before dawn. They'll *banzai* and try to push us off the beachhead."*

On 27 March the loudspeaker came on with, "Now hear this, now hear this. Special sea detail stand by." Sailors assigned to the detail moved to their stations where they weighed anchor.

"Well, Sledgehammer, they're raising the hook, so it won't be long before we're in it again ole buddy," a friend said.

"Yeah," I said, "and I'm not in any hurry, either."

---

*By this time in the Pacific war, official unit designations recognized the prevailing system of task organization for combat where supporting elements reinforced the infantry. Such units became regimental combat teams (RCT) and battalion landing teams (BLT); hence official designations were 5th RCT or 3d BLT. But the rank and file infantryman never forgot who he was. Throughout the war I never heard a Marine infantryman refer to his unit by other than its base name. We were always "K/3/5," "3d Battalion, 5th," or "5th Marines."

"You can say that again," he sighed.

The huge convoy got under way like clockwork. Just watching that host of different vessels kept my mind off what was ahead. As we proceeded I was conscious of how cool the weather had become. We had our wool-lined field jackets with us, and it was comfortable on deck, particularly at night. To those of us who had lived and fought in the sweltering tropics for months, cooler weather was very significant.

Most of our voyage from Ulithi was uneventful. Each night during the northward trip I had noticed the beautiful Southern Cross constellation slipping lower and lower on the starlit horizon. Finally it disappeared. It was the only thing about the South and Central Pacific I would miss. The Southern Cross formed a part of our 1st Marine Division shoulder patch and was, therefore, especially symbolic.

We had intense pride in the identification with our units and drew considerable strength from the symbolism attached to them. As we drew closer to Okinawa, the knowledge that I was a member of Company K, 3d Battalion, 5th Marine Regiment, 1st Marine Division helped me prepare myself for what I knew was coming.*

Okinawa is a large island, some sixty miles long and from two to eighteen miles wide. Like most islands in the Pacific, it is surrounded by a coral reef. But on the west coast that reef lies close to shore, particularly along the invasion beaches at Hagushi.

Through the center of the island runs a ridge rising some 1,500 feet in the wild, mountainous north. South of the Ishikawa Isthmus, the land levels out considerably but is cut by several prominent streams. In 1945, as it remains today, the southern portion of the island contained the bulk of the civilian population.

Of primary importance to the defense of the island were three east–west ridge systems crossing the southern part of the island. To the north and just below the invasion beaches lay the ridges

---

*Our planners still hadn't realized that this costly large-scale suicide charge tactic had been abandoned for good. The Japanese had shifted to the defense-in-depth tactic as the best means of defeating us. This tactical shift had prolonged our fight on Peleliu and had been repeated with the same murderous results against the Marines on Iwo Jima.

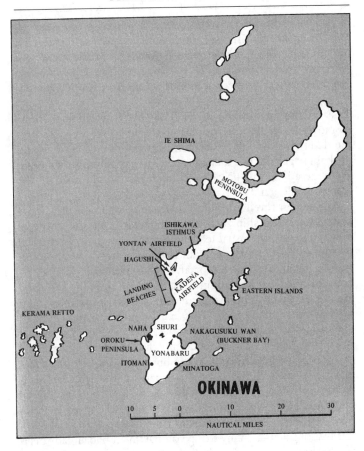

of Kakazu and Nishibaru. In the middle, running west from Shuri Castle, was the most formidable of the ridges, cut by sheer cliffs and deep draws. Above the extreme southern tip of the island lay Kunishi, Yuza-Dake, and Yaeju-Dake. Together these ridges formed a series of natural defensive barriers to the American forces advancing from the north.

Into these natural barriers, Lt. Gen. Mitsuru Ushijima threw the bulk of his 110,000-man Thirty-Second Japanese Army. Natural and man-made barriers were transformed into a network of mutually supporting positions linked by a system of protected tunnels. Each of the ridge lines was held in great strength until *it became untenable; then the enemy withdrew to the next defense line. Thus the Japanese drew on their experiences at Peleliu, Saipan, and Iwo Jima to construct a highly sophisticated and powerful defense-in-depth. There they waited and fought to exhaust the will and the resources of the American Tenth Army.*

Tension mounted on the eve of D day. We received final orders to move in off the beach as fast as possible. We were also reminded that although we were in regimental reserve, we would probably "get the hell kicked out of us" coming on the beach. We were advised to hit the sack early; we would need all the rest we could get.*

A predawn reveille ushered in Easter Sunday—April Fool's Day—1945. The ship seethed with activity. We had chow of steak and eggs, the usual feast before the slaughter. I returned to our troop compartment and squared away my ammunition, combat pack, and mortar ammunition bag. The ship's crew manned battle stations and stood by to repel *kamikaze* attacks.[†] Dawn was breaking, and the preassault bombardment of the beaches had begun. Above it I could hear the drone of enemy aircraft inbound to the attack.

I went into the head to relieve my distressed colon, cramped by fear and apprehension. On the big transport ships the toilet facilities consisted of a row of permanent wooden seats situated over a metal trough through which ran a constant flow of seawater. There were about twenty seats—no limited facilities here with Haney to delay us as at Peleliu.

Most of the men in my troop compartment had already been to the head and by then had donned their gear and moved out on deck, so I was about the last one in the head. I settled comfortably on a seat. Next to me I noticed a cagelike chute of iron mesh coming through the overhead [ceiling] near one

---

*Three/Five was scheduled to land after the 1st and 2d battalions of the 5th Marines on the extreme right of the regimental beach. It would form the right flank of the III Marine Amphibious Corps and link with the U.S. Army's XXIV Corps landing to the south.

[†]Manned suicide planes that dived into American ships. Faith in the *kamikaze*'s ("divine wind") ability to cut off the American fleet's support of the landing force ashore was an important element in the Japanese defensive scheme.

of the 40mm antiaircraft gun tubs. It extended down, through the deck, and into the compartment below.

Startled out of my wits by an incredibly loud sound of clattering, clanking, scraping, and rasping metal, I sprang up with a reflex born of fear and tried to bolt out of the head into the troop compartment. I knew a *kamikaze* had crashed into our ship right above me. My trousers around my ankles hobbled me, and I nearly fell. As I reached to pull them up, the loud clanking and clattering—like a thousand cymbals falling down stone steps—continued. I looked over at the iron mesh chute and saw dozens of empty brass 40mm shell cases cascading down from the guns above. They clattered and clanked through the chute to some collecting bin below decks. My fright subsided into chagrin.

I got on my gear and joined the other men on deck to await orders. We milled around, each man sticking close to his buddy. Higgins boats would take us to rendezvous areas and transfer us to amtracs which previously had delivered the assault waves of infantry across the reef to the beach.

The bombardment of the beach by our warships had grown in intensity, and our planes had joined in with strafing, rockets, and bombing. Japanese planes flew over the fleet at some distance from us. Many of our ships were firing at them.

An order came for all troops to go below (this was to prevent casualties from strafing enemy planes). Loaded with our battle gear, we squeezed our way back through the doorlike hatches into our compartment. Packed like sardines in the aisles between the racks, we waited in the compartment for orders to move back on deck. Sailors on deck dogged our hatches [sealed the doors by turning U-shaped handles positioned all around them]. Like men locked in a closet, we waited and listened to the firing outside. The compartment wasn't large, and the air soon became foul. It was difficult to breathe. Although the weather was cool, we began to sweat.

"Hey, you guys, the blowers [electric ventilating fans] are off. By God, we'll smother in this damn place!" yelled one man. I was next to the hatch, and several of us started yelling at the sailors outside, telling them we needed air. They yelled back from the other side of the steel door that it couldn't be helped, because the electricity was needed to operate the gun mounts. "Then, by God, let us out on deck!"

"Sorry, we've got orders to keep this hatch dogged down."

We all started cursing the sailors, but they were following orders, and I'm sure they didn't want to keep us locked in that stuffy compartment. "Let's get the hell outa here," a buddy said. We all agreed it would be better to get strafed on deck than to suffocate in the compartment. Grasping the levers and moving them to the unlock position, we tried to open the hatch. As fast as we turned each lever, the sailors outside turned it back and kept it dogged down. Other desperate Marines joined us in trying to unclamp the hatch. There were only two sailors outside, so with our combined efforts, we finally got all the clamps open, shoved open the hatch, and burst out into the cool, fresh air.

About that time other Company K men poured out of a hatch on the other side of the compartment. One of the sailors got pushed over and rolled across the deck. In an instant we were all outside breathing in the fresh air.

"All right, you men, return to your quarters. No troops topside. That's an order!" came a voice from a platform slightly aft and above us. We looked up and saw a navy officer, an ensign, standing against the rail glaring at us. He wore khakis, an officer's cap, and insignia bars on his collar, in stark contrast to us dressed in green dungarees, tan canvas leggings, and camouflaged helmet covers, and loaded with battle equipment, weapons, and gear. He wore a web pistol belt with a .45 automatic in the holster.

None of our officers was in the area, so the navy ensign had it all to himself. He swaggered back and forth, ordering us into the foul air of the troop compartment. If he had been a Marine officer, we would have obeyed his order with mutterings and mumblings, but he was so unimposing that we just milled around. Finally, he began threatening us all with courts-martial if we didn't obey him.

A friend of mine spoke up, "Sir, we're goin' to hit that beach in a little while and a lot of us might not be alive an hour from now. We'd rather take a chance on gettin' hit by a Jap plane out here than go back in there and smother to death."

The officer spun around and headed for the bridge—to get help, we assumed. Shortly some of our own officers came up and told us to stand by to go down the nets to the waiting boats. As far as I know, our breakout of the troop compartment for fresh air was never mentioned.

We picked up our gear and moved to assigned areas along the bulwarks of the ship. The weather was mostly clear and incredibly cool (about 75 degrees) after the heat of the South Pacific. The bombardment rumbled and thundered toward the island. Everything from battleships down to rocket and mortar boats were plastering the beaches along with our dive bombers. Japanese planes, their engines droning and whining, came in over the huge convoy, and many ships' antiaircraft fire began bursting in the air. I saw two enemy planes get hit some distance from our ship.

We were all tense, particularly with the intelligence estimate that we could expect 80–85 percent casualties on the beach. Although I was filled with dread about the landing, I wasn't nearly so apprehensive as I had been at Peleliu. Perhaps it was because I was already a combat veteran. I had survived the Peleliu landing and knew what to expect from the Japanese, as well as from myself. Climbing down the cargo net to the Higgins boat, I was still afraid; but it was different from Peleliu.

In addition to the invaluable experience of being a combat veteran, the immensity of our fleet gave me courage. Combat vessels and armed transports ranged as far as we could see. I have no idea how many of our planes were in the air, but it must have been hundreds.

We climbed down the net and settled into the Higgins boat. Someone said, "Shove off, coxswain, you're loaded," as the last Marine climbed into our boat. The coxswain gunned the engine and pulled away from the ship. Other boats loaded with Marines from 3/5 were pulling out all along the side of the ship. I sure hated to leave it. Amphibious craft of every description floated on the water around us. The complexity of the huge invasion was evident everywhere we looked.

Our boat ran some distance from our ship then began circling slowly in company with other boats loaded with men from our battalion. The bombardment of the Hagushi beaches roared on with awesome intensity. Sitting low in the water, we really couldn't see what was going on except in our immediate vicinity. We waited nervously for H hour which was scheduled for 0830.

Some of the ships began releasing thick white smoke as a screen for the convoy's activity. The smoke drifted lazily and mingled in with that of the exploding shells. We continued to circle on the beautiful blue water made choppy by the other boats in our group.

"It's 0830 now," someone said.

"The first wave's goin' in now. Stand by for a ram," Snafu said.

The man next to me sighed. "Yeah, the stuff's gonna' hit the fan now."

CHAPTER NINE

Stay of Execution

"THE LANDING is unopposed!"

We looked with amazement at the Marine on the amtrac with which our Higgins boat had just hooked up.

"The hell you say," one of my buddies shot back.

"It's straight dope. I ain't seen no casualties. Most of the Nips musta hauled ass. I just saw a couple of mortar shells fallin' in the water; that's all. The guys went in standin' up. It beats anything I ever saw."

Images of the maelstrom at Peleliu had been flashing through my mind, but on Okinawa there was practically no opposition to the landing. When we overcame our astonishment, everybody started laughing and joking. The release of tension was unforgettable. We sat on the edge of the amtrac's troop compartment singing and commenting on the vast fleet surrounding us. No need to crouch low to avoid the deadly shrapnel and bullets. It was—and still is—the most pleasant surprise of the war.

It suddenly dawned on me, though, that it wasn't at all like the Japanese to let us walk ashore unopposed on an island only 350 miles from their homeland. They were obviously pulling some trick, and I began to wonder what they were up to.

"Hey, Sledgehammer, what's the matter? Why don't you sing like everybody else?"

I grinned and took up a chorus of the "Little Brown Jug."

"That's more like it!"

As our wave moved closer to the island, we got a good view of the hundreds of landing boats and amtracs approaching the beach. Directly ahead of us, we could see the men of our regiment moving about in dispersed combat formations like tiny toy soldiers on the rising landscape. They appeared unhurried and nonchalant, as if on maneuvers. There were no enemy shells bursting among them. The island sloped up gently from the beach, and the many small garden and farm plots of the Okinawans gave it the appearance of a patchwork quilt. It was beautiful, except where the ground cover and vegetation had been blasted by shells. I was overcome with the contrast to D day on Peleliu.

When our wave was about fifty yards from the beach, I saw two enemy mortar shells explode a considerable distance to our left. They spewed up small geysers of water but caused no damage to the amtracs in that area. That was the only enemy fire I saw during the landing on Okinawa. It made the April Fool's Day aspect even more sinister, because all those thousands of first-rate Japanese troops on that island had to be somewhere spoiling for a fight.

We continued to look at the panorama around our amtrac with no thought of immediate danger as we came up out of the water. The tailgate banged down. We calmly picked up our gear and walked onto the beach.

A short distance down the beach on our right, the mouth of Bishi Gawa emptied into the sea. This small river formed the boundary between the army divisions of the XXIV Corps, to the south, and the III Amphibious Corps, to the north of the river. On our side of the mouth of the river, on a promontory jutting out into the sea, I saw the remains of the emplacement containing the big Japanese gun that had concerned us in our briefings. The seawall in our area had been blasted down into a terracelike rise a few feet high over which we moved with ease.

We advanced inland, and I neither heard nor saw any Japanese fire directed against us. As we moved across the small fields and gardens onto higher elevations, I could see troops of the 6th Marine Division heading toward the big Yontan Airfield on our left. Jubilation over the lack of opposition to the landing prevailed, particularly among the Peleliu veterans. Our new replacements began making remarks about amphibious landings being easy.

Lt. Gen. Simon Bolivar Buckner, Jr., USA commanded the Tenth Army in the assault against Okinawa. Left (north) of the American landing was the III Marine Amphibious Corps led by Maj. Gen. Roy S. Geiger, which consisted of the 1st and 6th Marine divisions with the latter on the left. To the right (south) landed the army's XXIV Corps commanded by Maj. Gen. John R. Hodge and

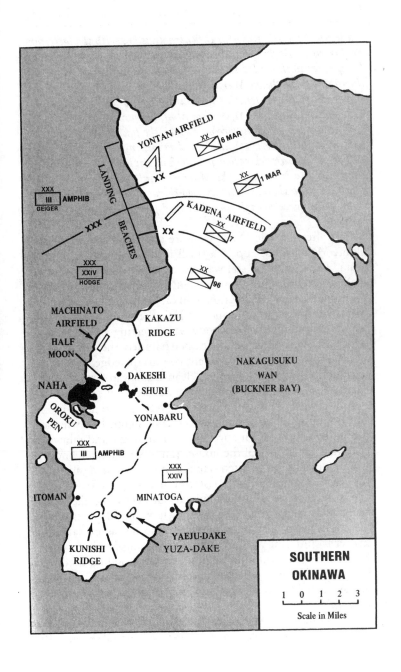

YONTAN AIRFIELD

XX 6 MAR

XX

XX 1 MAR

XXX
III AMPHIB
GEIGER

XXX

KADENA AIRFIELD

XX

XX 7

XXX
XXIV
HODGE

XX 96

MACHINATO
AIRFIELD

KAKAZU
RIDGE

HALF
MOON

DAKESHI

NAHA

SHURI

NAKAGUSUKU
WAN
(BUCKNER BAY)

YONABARU

OROKU
PEN

XXX
III AMPHIB

XXX
XXIV

ITOMAN

MINATOGA

YAEJU-DAKE
YUZA-DAKE

KUNISHI
RIDGE

LANDING

BEACHES

**SOUTHERN
OKINAWA**

1   0   1   2   3

Scale in Miles

made up of the 7th and 96th Infantry divisions with the latter on the far right. Backing up the XXIV Corps was the 77th Infantry Division with the 27th Infantry Division afloat in reserve. Across the island stood the 2d Marine Division which had conducted an elaborate, full-scale feint at the southeastern beaches. Altogether, Lt. Gen. Buckner had 541,866 men at his disposal.

Of the 50,000 troops ashore on D day, the four assault divisions lost only 28 killed, 104 wounded, and 27 missing.

The plan of attack called for the four divisions to cross the island, cutting it in two. The Marines would then turn left and move north to secure the upper two-thirds of the island while the army forces wheeled right into line and proceeded south.

By late afternoon on D day we were ordered to dig in for the night. My squad set up in a small field of recently harvested grain. The clay/loam soil was just right for digging in, so we made a good gun pit. Our company's other two mortars were positioned nearby. We registered in on likely target areas to our front with a couple of rounds of HE, then squared away our ammo for the night. Everybody was expecting a big counter-attack with tanks because of the open nature of the countryside.

Once set up, several of us went over to the edge of the field and cautiously explored a neat, clean Okinawan farmhouse. It was a likely hiding place for snipers, but we found it empty.

As we were leaving the house to return to our positions, Jim Dandridge, one of our replacements, stepped on what appeared to be a wooden cover over an underground rainwater cistern at the corner of the house. Jim was a big man, and the wooden planks were rotten. He fell through, sinking in above his waist. The hole wasn't a cistern but a cesspool for the sewage from the house. Jim scrambled out bellowing like a mad bull and smelling worse. We all knew it might be weeks before we could get a change of dungarees, so it was no laughing matter to Jim. But we started kidding him unmercifully about his odd taste in swimming holes. Jim was good-natured, but he quickly had enough and chased a couple of the men back across the field to our positions. They laughed but kept out of his reach.

No sooner had we gotten back to our foxholes than we heard the unmistakable drone of a Japanese aircraft engine. We looked up and saw a Zero coming directly over us. The fighter was high, and the pilot apparently had bigger game than us in mind. He headed out over the beach toward our fleet offshore. Several ships began firing furiously as he circled lazily and then dove. The plane's engine began to whine with increasing intensity as the *kamikaze* pilot headed straight down toward a transport. We saw the smoke where he hit the ship, but it was so far away we couldn't determine what damage had been done. The troops had debarked earlier, but the ship's crew probably had a rough time of it. It was the first *kamikaze* I had seen crash into a ship, but it wasn't the last.

In the gathering dusk we turned our attention to our immediate surroundings and squared away for the night. We each had been issued a small bottle containing a few ounces of brandy to ward off the chill of D day night. Knowing my limited taste, appreciation, and capacity for booze, my buddies began trying to talk me out of my brandy ration. But I was cold after sundown, and thought the brandy might warm me up a bit. I tried a sip, concluding immediately that Indians must have had brandy in mind when they supposedly spoke of "firewater." I traded my brandy for a can of peaches, then broke out my wool-lined field jacket and put it on. It felt good.

We waited in the clear, chilly night for the expected Japanese attack. But all was quiet, with no artillery fire nearby and rarely any rifle or machine-gun fire—stark contrast to the rumbling, crashing chaos of D day night on Peleliu.

When Snafu woke me about midnight for my turn on watch, he handed me our "Tommy" (submachine) gun. (I don't remember how, where, or when we got the Tommy gun, but Snafu and I took turns carrying it and the mortar throughout Peleliu and Okinawa. A pistol was fine but limited at close range, so we valued our Tommy greatly.)

After a few minutes on watch, I noticed what appeared to be a man crouching near me at the edge of a line of shadows cast by some trees. I strained my eyes, averted my vision, and looked in all directions, but I couldn't be sure the dark object was a man. The harder I looked the more convinced I was. I thought I could make out a Japanese fatigue cap. It wasn't a Marine, because none of our people was placed where the figure was. It was probably an enemy infiltrator waiting for his comrades to get in place before acting.

I couldn't be sure in the pale light. Should I fire or take a chance? My teeth began to chatter from the chill and the jitters.

I raised the Tommy slowly, set it on full automatic, flipped off the safety, and took careful aim at the lower part of the figure (I mustn't fire over his head when the Tommy recoiled). I squeezed the trigger for a short burst of several rounds. Flame spurted out of the muzzle, and the rapid explosions of the cartridges shattered the calm. I peered confidently over my sights, expecting to see a Japanese knocked over by the impact of the big .45 caliber slugs. Nothing happened. The enemy didn't move.

Everyone around us began whispering, "What's the dope? What did you see?"

I answered that I thought I had seen a Japanese crouching near the shadows.

There were enemy in the area, for just then we heard shouts in Japanese, a high-pitched yell: "Nippon banzai," then incoherent babbling followed by a burst of firing from one of our machine guns. Quiet fell.

When dawn broke, the first dim light revealed my infiltrator to be a low stack of straw. My buddies kidded me for hours about a Peleliu veteran firing at a straw Japanese.

RACE ACROSS THE ISLAND

On 2 April (D + 1) the 1st Marine Division continued its attack across the island. We moved out with our planes overhead but without artillery fire, because no organized body of Japanese had been located ahead of us. Everyone was asking the same question: "Where the hell are the Nips?" Some scattered small groups were encountered and put up a fight, but the main Japanese army had vanished.

During the morning I saw a couple of dead enemy soldiers who apparently had been acting as observers in a large leafless tree when some of the prelanding bombardment killed them. One still hung over a limb. His intestines were strung out among the branches like garland decorations on a Christmas tree. The other man lay beneath the tree. He had lost a leg which rested on the other side of the tree with the leggings and trouser leg still wrapped neatly around it. In addition to their ghoulish condition, I noted that both soldiers wore high-top leather hobnail shoes. That was the first time I had seen that type of Japanese footwear. All the enemy I had seen on Peleliu had worn the rubber-soled canvas split-toed *tabi*.

We encountered some Okinawans—mostly old men, women, and children. The Japanese had conscripted all the young men as laborers and a few as troops, so we saw few of them. We sent the civilians to the rear where they were put into internment camps so they couldn't aid the enemy.

These people were the first civilians I had seen in a combat area. They were pathetic. The most pitiful things about the Okinawan civilians were that they were totally bewildered by the shock of our invasion, and they were scared to death of us. Countless times they passed us on the way to the rear with fear, dismay, and confusion on their faces.

The children were nearly all cute and bright-faced. They had round faces and dark eyes. The little boys usually had close-cropped hair, and the little girls had their shiny jet-black locks bobbed in the Japanese children's style of the period. The children won our hearts. Nearly all of us gave them all the candy and rations we could spare. They were quicker to lose their fear of us than the older people, and we had some good laughs with them.

One of the funnier episodes I witnessed involved two Okinawan women and their small children. We had been ordered to halt and "take ten" (a ten-minute rest) before resuming our rapid advance across the island. My squad stopped near a typical Okinawan well constructed of stone and forming a basin about two feet deep and about four feet by six feet on the sides. Water bubbled out of a rocky hillside. We watched two women and their children getting a drink. They seemed a bit nervous and afraid of us, of course. But life had its demands with children about, so one woman sat on a rock, nonchalantly opened her kimono top, and began breast-feeding her small baby.

While the baby nursed, and we watched, the second child (about four years old) played with his mother's sandals. The little fellow quickly tired of this and kept pestering his mother for attention. The second woman had her hands full with a small child of her own, so she wasn't any help. The mother spoke sharply to her bored child, but he started climbing all over the baby and interfering with the nursing. As we looked on with keen interest, the exasperated mother removed her breast from the mouth of the nursing baby and pointed it at the face of the fractious brother. She squeezed her breast just as you would milk a cow and squirted a jet of milk into the child's face. The startled boy began bawling at the top of his lungs while rubbing the milk out of his eyes.

We all roared with laughter, rolling around on the deck and holding our sides. The women looked up, not realizing why we were laughing, but began to grin because the tension was broken. The little recipient of the milk in the eyes stopped crying and started grinning, too.

"Get your gear on; we're moving out," came the word down the column. As we shouldered our weapons and ammo and moved out amid continued laughter, the story traveled along to the amusement of all. We passed the two smiling mothers and the grinning toddler, his cute face still wet with his mother's milk.

Moving rapidly toward the eastern shore, we crossed terrain often extremely rugged with high, steep ridges and deep gullies. In one area a series of these ridges lay across our line of advance. As we labored up one side and down the other of each ridge, we were tired but glad the Japanese had abandoned the area. It was ideal for defense.

During another halt, we spent our entire break rescuing an Okinawan horse. The animal had become trapped in a narrow flooded drainage ditch about four feet deep. He couldn't climb out or move forward or backward. When we first approached the animal, he plunged up and down in the water rolling his eyes in terror. We calmed him, slipped a couple of empty cartridge belts beneath his belly, and heaved him up out of the ditch.

We had plenty of help, because Texans and horse lovers gravitated to the scene from all over our battalion, which ranged in columns along the valley and surrounding ridges. The city men looked on and gave useless advice. When we got the little horse out of the ditch, he stood on wobbly legs as the water dripped off him, shook himself, and headed for a patch of grass.

No sooner had we washed the mud off the cartridge belts than the word came to move out. We didn't get any rest during that break, and we were tired, but we had the satisfaction of knowing that little horse wouldn't starve to death bogged down in the ditch.

The clear cool weather compensated for our rapid advance over the broken terrain. Those of us with experience in the tropics felt as though we had been delivered from a steam room. The hills and ridges on Okinawa were mostly clay, but it was dry, and we didn't slip or slide with our heavy loads. Pine trees grew everywhere. I had forgotten what a delicious odor the needles gave off. We also saw Easter lilies blooming.

Completing the initial assignment of the 1st Marine Division to cut the island in two, we reached the east coast in an area of marshes and what appeared to be large freshwater reservoirs. Offshore was a bay called Chimu Wan.

We arrived on the afternoon of 4 April, some eight to thirteen days ahead of schedule. Our rapid movement had been possible, of course, only because of the widely scattered opposition. These first four days had been too easy for us. We were confused as to what the Japanese were doing. We knew they weren't about to give up the island without a fierce, drawn-out fight.

And we didn't have to wait long to find out where the enemy was. Later that day rumors began that the army divisions were meeting increasingly stiff opposition as they tried to move south. We knew that sooner or later we'd be down there with them in the thick of it.

We also learned that our namesake company in the 7th Marines had been ambushed to the north of us near the village of Hizaonna and had suffered losses of three killed and twenty-seven wounded. Thus, despite the relative ease with which our division had moved across the center of the island, the Japanese were still there and still hurting the Marines.

The 1st Marine Division spent the remainder of April mopping up the central portion of Okinawa. Elements of the division, including the 3d Battalion, 5th Marines, conducted a shore-to-shore amphibious operation toward the end of the month to secure the Eastern Islands which lay on the outer edge of Chimu Wan Bay. The purpose was to deny them to the Japanese as an operating base

*in the rear of the American forces, much the same reason 3/5 had
assaulted Ngesebus during the fight for Peleliu.*

*The 6th Marine Division moved north during April and cap-
tured the entire upper part of the island. The task wasn't easy. It
involved a rough, costly seven-day mountain campaign against
strongly fortified Japanese positions in the heights of Motobu
Peninsula.*

*Meanwhile three army divisions were coming up short against
fierce Japanese resistance in the Kakazu–Nishibaru ridgeline, the
first of three main enemy defense lines in the southern portion of
the island. Stretched from left to right across Okinawa, the 7th,
96th, and 27th Infantry divisions were getting more than they
could handle and were making little progress in their attacks.*

PATROLS

Hardly had we arrived on the shore of Chimu Wan Bay than
we received orders to move out. We headed inland and north
into an area of small valleys and steep ridges, where we settled
into a comfortable bivouac area and erected our two-man pup
tents. It was more like maneuvers than combat; we didn't even
dig foxholes. We could see Yontan Airfield in the distance to
the west. Rain fell for the first time since we had landed five
days earlier.

The next day our company began patrolling through the
general area around our bivouac site. We didn't need the mortars because of the scattered nature of the enemy opposition.
Stowing them out of the weather in our tents, those of us in
the mortar section served as riflemen on the patrols.

Mac, our new mortar section leader, led the first patrol I
made. Our mission was to check out our assigned area for signs
of enemy activity. Burgin was our patrol sergeant. I felt a lot
more comfortable with him than with Mac.

On a clear, chilly morning, with the temperature at about
60 degrees, we moved out through open country on a good,
rock-surfaced road. The scenery was picturesque and beautiful. I saw little sign of war. We had strict orders not to fire
our weapons unless we saw a Japanese soldier or Okinawans
we were certain were hostile. No shooting at chickens and no
target practice.

"Mac, where we headed?" someone had asked before we left.

"Hizaonna," the lieutenant answered without batting an eye.

"Jesus Christ! That's where K Company, 7th got ambushed the other night," one of the new replacements said.

"Do you mean us few guys are supposed to patrol that place?"

"Yeah, that's right, Hood," Burgin answered. (We had nick-named a big square-jawed man from Chicago "Hoodlum" because of the notorious gangs of John Dillinger and others in that city during the days of Prohibition.)

My reaction on hearing our destination had been to thrust my Tommy gun toward another new man who wasn't assigned to the patrol and say, "Take this; don't you wanta go in my place?"

"Hell, no!" he replied.

So, off we went with Mac striding along like he was still in OCS back in Quantico, Virginia. The veterans among us looked worried. The new men, like Mac, seemed unconcerned. Because of the strange absence of anything but scattered opposition, some of the new men were beginning to think war wasn't as bad as they had been told it was. Some of them actually chided us about giving them an exaggerated account of the horrors and hardships of Peleliu. Okinawa in April was so easy for the 1st Marine Division that the new men were lulled into a false sense of well-being. We warned them, "When the stuff hits the fan, it's hell," but they grew more and more sure that we veterans were "snowing" them.

Mac didn't help matters either by his loud pronouncements of how he would take his kabar in his teeth and his .45 in hand and charge the Japanese as soon as one of our guys got hit. The April stay of execution tended to lull even the veterans into a state of wishful thinking and false security, although we knew better.

Soon, however, our idyllic stroll on that perfect April morning was broken by an element of the horrid reality of the war that I knew lurked in wait for us somewhere on that beautiful island. Beside a little stream below the road, like a hideous trademark of battle, lay a Japanese corpse in full combat gear.

From our view above, the corpse looked like a gingerbread man in a helmet with his legs still in the flexed position of running. He didn't appear to have been dead many days then, but we passed that same stream many times throughout April and watched the putrid remains decompose gradually into the soil of Okinawa. I was thankful the windswept road with the sweet, fresh smell of pine needles filling our nostrils was too high for us to sense his presence in any way but visually.

As we patrolled in the vicinity of Hizaonna, we moved through some of the area where Company K, 7th Marines had been ambushed a few nights before. The grim evidence of a hard fight lay everywhere. We found numerous dead Japanese where they had fallen. Bloody battle dressings, discarded articles of bloody clothing, and bloodstains on the ground indicated where Marines had been hit. Empty cartridge cases were piled where various Marine weapons had been.

I remember vividly an Okinawan footpath across a low hillock where the Marine column apparently had been attacked from both sides. On the path were empty machine-gun ammo boxes, ammo clips for M1 rifles, and carbine shell cases; discarded dungaree jackets, leggings, and battle dressings; and several large bloodstains, by then dark spots on the soil. Scattered a short distance on both sides of the path were about a score of enemy dead.

The scene was like reading a paragraph from a page of a history book. The Marines had suffered losses, but they had inflicted worse on the attacking Japanese. We saw no Marine dead; all had been removed when the relief troops had come in and aided K/3/7 to withdraw from the ambush.

As I looked at the flotsam of battle scattered along that little path, I was struck with the utter incongruity of it all. There the Okinawans had tilled their soil with ancient and crude farming methods; but the war had come, bringing with it the latest and most refined technology for killing. It seemed so insane, and I realized that the war was like some sort of disease afflicting man. From my experience at Peleliu I had unconsciously come to associate combat with stifling hot, fire-swept beaches, steaming mangrove-choked swamps, and harsh, jagged coral ridges. But there on Okinawa the disease was disrupting a place as pretty as a pastoral painting. I understood then what my grandmother had really meant when she told me as a boy that a blight descended on the land when the South was invaded during the Civil War.

While a buddy and I were looking over the area, Burgin told us to check out a section of sunken roadway nearby. The sunken portion was about thirty yards long and about ten feet deep; the banks were steep and sloping. Heavy bushes grew along their edges at ground level so all we could see was the sky overhead and the sloping road in front and behind us. When we were about halfway along the sunken road, carbine shots rang out from where we had left Burgin and Mac.

"Ambush!" snarled my buddy, a veteran with combat experience stretching back to Cape Gloucester.

We went into a low crouch instinctively, and I put my finger on the safety catch of the Tommy. Hurrying over to the bank toward the sound of the shots, we scrambled up and peered cautiously through the bushes. We both knew we wouldn't have a chance if we got pinned down in that ditch-like road where we could be shot from above. My heart pounded, and I felt awfully lonely as I looked out. There, where we had left him, stood Mac in the farmyard, calmly pointing his carbine straight down toward the ground by his feet at some object we couldn't see. My comrade and I looked at each other in amazement. "What the hell?" my buddy whispered. We climbed out of the sunken road and went toward Mac as he fired his carbine at the ground again. Other members of the patrol were converging cautiously on the area. They looked apprehensive, thinking we were being ambushed.

Burgin stood a short distance behind Mac, shaking his head slowly in disgust. As we came up, I asked Mac what he had fired at. He pointed to the ground and showed us his target: the lower jaw of some long-dead animal. Mac said he just wanted to see if he could shoot any of the teeth loose from the jawbone.

We stared at him in disbelief. There we were, a patrol of about a dozen Marines, miles from our outfit, with orders not to fire unless at the enemy, in an area with dead Japanese scattered all over the place, and our lieutenant was plinking away with his carbine like a kid with a BB gun. If Mac had been a private, the whole patrol would probably have stuck his head in a nearby well. But our discipline was strict, and we just gritted our teeth.

Burgin made some tactful remark to remind Mac he was the officer in charge of a patrol and that the enemy might jump us at any time. Thereupon Mac began spouting off, quoting some training manual about the proper way for troops to conduct themselves on patrol.

Mac wasn't stupid or incompetent. He just didn't seem to realize there was a deadly war going on and that we weren't involved in some sort of college game. Strange as it seemed, he wasn't mature yet. He had enough ability to complete Marine Corps OCS—no simple task—but occasionally he could do some of the strangest things, things only a teenage boy would be expected to do.

Once on another patrol, I saw him taking great pains and effort to position himself and his carbine near a Japanese corpse. After getting just the right angle, Mac took careful aim and squeezed off a couple of rounds. The dead Japanese lay on his back with his trousers pulled down to his knees. Mac was trying very carefully to blast off the head of the corpse's penis. He succeeded. As he exulted over his aim, I turned away in disgust.

Mac was a decent, clean-cut man but one of those who apparently felt no restraints under the brutalizing influence of war—although he had hardly been in combat at that time. He had one ghoulish, obscene tendency that revolted even the most hardened and callous men I knew. When most men felt the urge to urinate, they simply went over to a bush or stopped wherever they happened to be and relieved themselves without ritual or fanfare. Not Mac. If he could, that "gentleman by the act of Congress" would locate a Japanese corpse, stand over it, and urinate in its mouth. It was the most repulsive thing I ever saw an American do in the war. I was ashamed that he was a Marine officer.

During the early part of that beautiful April in our happy little valley—while we veterans talked endlessly in disbelief about the lack of fighting—a few of us had a close view of a Japanese Zero fighter plane. One clear morning after a leisurely breakfast of K rations, several of us sauntered up a ridge bordering our valley to watch an air raid on Yontan Airfield. None of us was scheduled for patrols that day, and none of us was armed. We had violated a fundamental principle of infantrymen: "Carry your weapon on your person at all times."

As we watched the raid, we heard an airplane engine to our right. We turned, looked down a big valley below our ridge, and saw a plane approaching. It was a Zero flying up the valley toward us, parallel to and level with the crest of our ridge. It was moving so slowly it seemed unreal. Unarmed, we gawked like spectators at a passing parade as the plane came across our front. It couldn't have been more than thirty or forty yards away. We could see every detail of the plane and of the pilot seated in the cockpit inside the canopy. He turned his head and looked keenly at our little group watching him. He wore a leather flight helmet, goggles pushed up on his forehead, a jacket, and a scarf around his neck.

The instant the Zero pilot saw us, his face broke into the most fiendish grin I ever saw. He looked like the classic cartoon Japanese portrayed in American newspapers of the war years, with buck teeth, slanted eyes, and a round face. He grinned like a cat, for we were to be his mice. We were a fighter pilot's strafing dream, enemy infantry in the open with no antiaircraft guns and no planes to protect us.

One of my buddies muttered in surprise as the plane went on by to our left, "Did you see that bastard grin at us—that slant-eyed sonofabitch. Where the hell's my rifle?"

It happened so fast, and we were all so astonished at the sight of a plane cruising by at eye level, we almost forgot the war. The Japanese pilot hadn't. He banked, climbed to gain altitude, and headed around another ridge out of sight. It was obvious he was coming back to rake us over. It would be difficult to avoid getting hit. No savior was in sight for us.

As we started to spin around and rush back down the ridge seeking safety, we again heard a plane. This time it wasn't the throb of a cruising engine, but the roar of a plane at full throttle. The Zero streaked past us, going down the valley in the opposite direction from which he had first appeared. He was still flying at eye level and he was in a big hurry, as if the devil were after him. His devil was our savior, a beautiful blue Marine Corsair. That incredible Corsair pilot bore in right behind the Japanese as they roared out of sight over the ridge tops.

The planes were moving too fast to see either pilot's face, but I'm confident the emperor's pilot had lost his grin when he saw that Corsair.

On our patrols during April, we investigated many Okinawan villages and farms. We learned a lot about the people's customs and ways of life. Particularly appealing to me were the little Okinawan horses, really shaggy oversized ponies.

The Okinawans used a type of halter on those horses that I had never seen before. It consisted of two pieces of wood held in place by ropes. The wooden pieces on either side of the horse's head were shaped like the letter *F*. They were carved out of fine-grained brown wood and were about as big around as a man's thumb. A short piece of rope or cord held the pieces together across the front, and a rope across the top of the animal's head held the pieces in place on each side of the head just above the opening of the mouth. Two short ropes at the back of the wooden pieces merged into a single rope. When pull was exerted on this single rope, the wooden pieces clamped with gentle pressure against the sides of the animal's face above the mouth, and the animal stopped moving. This apparatus combined the qualities of a halter and a bridle without the need for a bit in the horse's mouth.

I was so intrigued by the Okinawan halter that I took one off a horse we kept with us for several days and replaced it with a rope halter. My intention was to send the wooden halter home —I remember that a bright piece of red cord held the front ends together—so I put it into my pack. After 1 May, however, it seemed increasingly doubtful that I would ever get home myself, and my equipment seemed to get heavier as the mud got deeper. Regretfully, I threw away the halter.

We grew quite attached to the horse our squad had adopted, and he didn't seem to mind when we slung a couple of bags of mortar ammo across his back.

When the time came at the end of April for us to leave our little horse, I removed the rope halter and gave him a lump of ration sugar. I stroked his soft muzzle as he switched flies with his tail. He turned, ambled across a grassy green meadow, and began grazing. He looked up and back at me once. My eyes grew moist. However reluctant I was to leave him, it was for the best. He would be peaceful and safe on the slopes of that green, sunlit hill. Being civilized men, we were duty bound to return soon to the chaotic nether world of shells and bullets and suffering and death.

Ugly rumors began to increase about the difficulties the army troops were having down on southern Okinawa. From high ground on clear nights I could see lights flickering and glowing on the southern skyline. A distant rumble was barely audible sometimes. No one said much about it. I tried unsuccessfully to convince myself it was thunderstorms, but I knew better. It was the flash and the growl of guns.

A HAPPY LANDING

On 13 April (12 April back in the States) we learned of the death of President Franklin D. Roosevelt. Not the least bit interested in politics while we were fighting for our lives, we were saddened nonetheless by the loss of our president. We were also curious and a bit apprehensive about how FDR's successor, Harry S. Truman, would handle the war. We surely didn't want someone in the White House who would prolong it one day longer than necessary.

Not long after hearing of Roosevelt's death, we were told to prepare to move out. Apprehension grew in the ranks. We thought the order meant the inevitable move into the inferno down south. On the contrary, it was to be a shore-to-shore amphibious operation against one of the Eastern Islands. We learned that Company K was to land on Takabanare Island, and that there might not be any Japanese there. We were highly skeptical. But so far Okinawa had been a strange "battle" for us; anything could happen.

Our battalion boarded trucks and headed for the east coast. We went aboard amtracs and set out into Chimu Wan to make the short voyage to Takabanare. The other companies of our battalion went after other islands of the group.

We landed with no opposition on a narrow, clean, sandy beach with a large rock mass high on our left. The rock hill looked foreboding. It was a vantage point from which flanking fire could have raked the beach. But all went well, and we pushed rapidly over the entire island without seeing a single enemy soldier.

After we moved across the island and found nothing but a few civilians, we recrossed the island to the beach where we set up defensive positions. My squad was situated part way up the slope of the steep rocky hill overlooking the beach. Our mortar was well emplaced among some rocks, so that we could fire on the beach or its approaches in the bay. A small destroyer escort was anchored offshore at the base of the hill. It had been standing by during our landing and remained with us during the several days we stayed on Takabanare. We felt important, as though we had our own private navy.

The weather was pleasant, so sleeping in the open was comfortable. We had few duties other than standing by to prevent a possible enemy move to occupy the island. I wrote letters, read, and explored the area around our positions. Some of the Marines swam the short distance to the ship and went aboard, where the navy people welcomed them and treated them to hot chow and all the hot coffee they wanted. I was content to laze in the sun and the cool air and eat K rations.

We left Takabanare after several days and returned to our bivouac on Okinawa. There we resumed patrolling in the central area of the island. As April wore on, rumors and bad news increased about the situation the army was facing down south. Scuttlebutt ran rampant about our future employment down there. Our fear increased daily, and we finally got the word that we'd be moving south on 1 May to replace the 27th Infantry Division on the right flank of the Tenth Army.

About mid-April the 11th Marines, the 1st Marine Division's artillery regiment, had moved south to add the weight of its firepower to the army's offensive. On 19 April the 27th Infantry Division launched a disastrous tank-infantry attack against Kakazu Ridge. Thirty army tanks became separated from their infantry support. The Japanese knocked out twenty-two of them in the ensuing fight. The 1st Marine Division's tank battalion offered the closest replacements for the tanks lost by the army.

Lt. Gen. Simon B. Buckner, Tenth Army commander, ordered Maj. Gen. Roy S. Geiger, III Amphibious Corps commander, to send the 1st Tank Battalion south to join the 27th Infantry Division. Geiger objected to the piecemeal employment of his Marines, so Buckner changed his orders and sent the entire 1st Marine

Division south to relieve the 27th Infantry Division on the extreme right of the line just north of Machinato Airfield.

During the last days of April, some of our officers and NCOs made a trip down south to examine the positions on the line that we were to move into. They briefed us thoroughly on what they saw, and it didn't sound promising.

"The stuff has hit the fan down there, boys. The Nips are pouring on the artillery and mortars and everything they've got," said a veteran sergeant. "Boys, they're firing knee mortars as thick and fast as we fire M1s."

We were given instructions, issued ammo and rations, and told to square away our gear. We rolled up our shelter halves (I wished I could crawl into mine and hibernate) and packed our gear to be left behind with the battalion quartermaster.

The first of May dawned cloudy and chilly. A few of us mortarmen built a small fire next to a niche in the side of the ridge to warm ourselves. The dismal weather and our impending move south made us gloomy. We stood around the fire eating our last chow before heading south. The fire crackled cheerily, and the coffee smelled good. I was nervous and hated to leave our little valley. We tossed our last ration cartons and wrappers onto the fire—the area must be left cleaner than when we arrived—and a few of the men drifted away to pick up their gear.

"Grenade!" yelled Mac as we heard the pop of a grenade primer cap.

I saw him toss a fragmentation grenade over the fire into the niche. The grenade exploded with a weak bang. Fragments zipped out past my legs, scattering sparks and sticks from the fire. We all looked astonished, Mac not the least so. No one was hit. I narrowly missed the million-dollar wound (it would have been a blessing in view of what lay ahead of us). The men who had just moved away from the fire undoubtedly would have been hit if they hadn't moved, because they had been standing directly in front of the niche.

All eyes turned on our intrepid lieutenant. He blushed and mumbled awkwardly about making a mistake. Before we moved to board the trucks, Mac had thought it would be funny to play a practical joke on us. So he staged the well-known trick

of pouring out the explosive charge from a fragmentation grenade, screwing the detonation mechanism back on the empty
"pineapple," and pitching it into the middle of a group of people. When the primer cap went "pop," the perpetrator of the
joke could watch with sadistic delight as everyone scrambled
for cover expecting the fuse to burn down and the grenade to
explode.

By his own admission, however, Mac had been careless. Most
of the explosive charge remained in the grenade; he had poured
out only part of it. Consequently, the grenade exploded with
considerable force and threw out its fragments. Luckily, Mac
threw the grenade into the niche in the ridge. If he had thrown
it into the open, most of the Company K mortar section would
have been put out of action by its own lieutenant before we
ever got down south. Fortunately for Mac, the company commander didn't see his foolish joke. We regretted he hadn't.

What a way to start our next fight!

CHAPTER TEN

Into the Abyss

WE BOARDED trucks and headed south over dusty roads. In this central portion of Okinawa we first passed many bivouacs of service troops and vast ammunition and supply dumps, all covered with camouflage netting. Next we came to several artillery positions. From the piles of empty brass shell cases, we knew they had fired a lot. And from the numerous shell craters gouged into the fields of grass, we could tell that the Japanese had thrown in plenty of counterbattery fire.

At some unmarked spot, we stopped and got off the trucks. I was filled with dread. We took up a single file on the right side of a narrow coral road and began walking south. Ahead we could hear the crash and thunder of enemy mortar and artillery shells, the rattle of machine guns, and the popping of rifles. Our own artillery shells whistled southbound.

"Keep your five-pace interval," came an order.

We did not talk. Each man was alone with his thoughts.

Shortly a column of men approached us on the other side of the road. They were the army infantry from 106th Regiment, 27th Infantry Division that we were relieving. Their tragic expressions revealed where they had been. They were dead beat, dirty and grisly, hollow-eyed and tight-faced. I hadn't seen such faces since Peleliu.

As they filed past us, one tall, lanky fellow caught my eye and said in a weary voice, "It's hell up there, Marine."

Nervous about what was ahead and a bit irritated that he might think I was a boot, I said with some impatience, "Yeah, I know. I was at Peleliu."

He looked at me blankly and moved on.

We approached a low, gently sloping ridge where Company K would go into the line. The noise grew louder.

"Keep your five-pace interval; don't bunch up," yelled one of our officers.

The mortar section was ordered off the road to the left in dispersed order. I could see shells bursting between us and the ridge. When we left the road, we severed our umbilical connection with the peaceful valley up north and plunged once more into the abyss.

As we raced across an open field, Japanese shells of all types whizzed, screamed, and roared around us with increasing frequency. The crash and thunder of explosions was a nightmare. Rocks and dirt clattered down after each erupting shell blew open a crater.

We ran and dodged as fast as we could to a place on a low gentle slope of the ridge and flung ourselves panting onto the dirt. Marines were running and crawling into position as soldiers streamed past us, trying desperately to get out alive. The yells for corpsmen and stretcher bearers began to be heard. Even though I was occupied with my own safety, I couldn't help but feel sorry for the battle-weary troops being relieved and trying not to get killed during those few critical minutes as they scrambled back out of their positions under fire.

Japanese rifle and machine-gun fire increased into a constant rattle. Bullets snapped and popped overhead. The shelling grew heavier. The enemy gunners were trying to catch men in the open to inflict maximum casualties on our troops running into and out of position—their usual practice when one of our units was relieving another on the line.

It was an appalling chaos. I was terribly afraid. Fear was obvious on the faces of my comrades, too, as we raced to the low slope and began to dig in rapidly. It was such a jolt to leave the quiet, beautiful countryside that morning and plunge into a thunderous, deadly storm of steel that afternoon. Going onto the beach to assault Peleliu and attacking across the airfield there, we had braced ourselves for the blows that fell. But the shock and shells of 1 May at Okinawa, after the reprieve of a pleasant April, caught us off balance.

Fear has many facets, and I do not minimize my fear and terror during that day. But it was different. I was a combat veteran of Peleliu. With terror's first constriction over, I knew what to expect. I felt dreadful fear but not near-panic. Experience had taught me what to expect from the enemy guns. More importantly, I knew I could control my fear. The terrible dread that I might panic was gone. I knew that all anyone could do under shell fire was to hug the deck and pray—and curse the Japanese.

There was the brassy, metallic twang of the small 50mm knee mortar shells as little puffs of dirty smoke appeared thickly around us. The 81mm and 90mm mortar shells crashed and banged all along the ridge. The *whizz-bang* of the high velocity 47mm gun's shells (also an antitank gun), which was on us with its explosion almost as soon as we heard it whizz into the area, gave me the feeling the Japanese were firing them at us like rifles. The slower screaming, whining sound of the 75mm artillery shells seemed the most abundant. Then there was the roar and rumble of the huge enemy 150mm howitzer shell, and the *kaboom* of its explosion. It was what the men called the big stuff. I didn't recall having recognized any of it in my confusion and fear at Peleliu. The bursting radius of these big shells was of awesome proportions. Added to all this noise was the swishing and fluttering overhead of our own supporting artillery fire. Our shells could be heard bursting out across the ridge over enemy positions. The noise of small-arms fire from both sides resulted in a chaotic bedlam of racket and confusion.

We were just below the crest of a low sloping section of the ridge. It was about ten feet high and on the left of our company's zone. Snafu and I began to dig the gun pit, and the ammo carriers dug in with two-man foxholes. Digging in Okinawa's claylike soil was easy, a luxury after the coral rock of Peleliu.

No sooner had we begun to dig in than terrible news arrived about mounting casualties in the company. The biggest blow was the word that Privates Nease and Westbrook had been killed. Both of these men were liked and admired by us all. Westbrook was a new man, a friendly curly-headed blond and one of the youngest married men in the outfit. I believe he wasn't yet twenty. Howard Nease was young in years but an old salt with a combat record that started at Cape Gloucester.

Many men were superstitious about one's chances of surviving a third campaign. By that time one's luck was wearing thin, some thought. I heard this idea voiced by Guadalcanal veterans who also had survived Gloucester and then struggled against the odds on Peleliu.

"Howard's luck just run out, that's all. Ain't no damn way a guy can go on forever without gittin' hit," gloomily remarked a Gloucester veteran who had joined Company K with Nease two campaigns before Okinawa.

We took the news of those deaths hard. Added to the stress of the day, it put us into an angry frame of mind as we dug in. Against whom should we pour out our anger while we were unable to fire at the enemy?

Most of us had finished digging in when we suddenly noticed that our pugnacious lieutenant, Mac, was still digging feverishly. He was excavating a deep one-man foxhole and throwing out a continuous shower of dirt with his entrenching shovel. While shells were still coming in, the fire had slackened a bit in our area. But Mac continued to burrow underground.

I don't know who started it, but I think it was Snafu who reminded Mac of his oft-repeated promise to charge the enemy line as soon as any of our guys got hit. Once the kidding began, several of us veterans chimed in and vigorously encouraged Mac to keep his promise.

"Now that Nease and Westbrook been killed, ain't it about time you took your kabar and .45 and charged them Nips, Mac?" Snafu asked.

Mac never stopped digging; he simply answered that he had to dig in. I told him I would lend him my kabar, but another man said with mock seriousness, "Naw, Sledgehammer, he might not be able to return it to you."

"Boy, when Mac gets over to them Nips, he's gonna clean house, and this blitz gonna be a pushover," someone else said.

But Mac only grunted and showed no inclination to charge the enemy—or to stop digging. He burrowed like a badger. Our jibes didn't seem to faze him. We kept our comments respectful because of his rank, but we gave it to him good for all the bravado and nonsense he had been mouthing off with ever since he joined the company.

"Mac, if you dig that hole much deeper they'll get you for desertion," someone said.

"Yeah, my mom use'ta tell me back home if I dug a hole deep enough I'd come through to China. Maybe if you keep digging you'll get through to the States, and we can all crawl in there and go home, Mac," came one comment accompanied by a grin.

Mac could hear us but was totally oblivious to our comments. It's hard to believe that we actually talked that way to a Marine officer, but it happened, and it was hilarious. He deserved every bit of it.

When he finally got his foxhole deep enough, he began laying wooden boards from ammo boxes over all of the top except for one small opening through which he could squirm. Then he threw about six inches of soil on top of the boards. We sat in our holes, watching him and the shelling to our right rear. When he had completed the cover over his hole, which actually made it a small dugout with limited visibility, Mac got in and proudly surveyed his work. He had been too occupied to pay much heed to us, but now he explained carefully to us how the boards with soil on top would protect him from shell fragments.

George Sarrett, who wasn't interested in the lecture, inched up the little slope several feet and peeped over the crest to see if there were any enemy troops moving around out front. He didn't look long, because a Japanese on the next ridge saw him and fired a burst from a machine gun which narrowly missed him. As the slugs came snapping over, George jerked his head down, lost his balance, slid back down the slope, and landed on top of Mac's dugout, causing the roof to cave in. The startled lieutenant jumped up, pushing boards and soil aside like a turtle rearing up out of a pile of debris.

"You ruined my foxhole!" Mac complained.

George apologized, and I had to bite my lip to keep from laughing. The other men smirked and grinned. We never heard any more from Mac about charging the Japanese line with his kabar and .45 caliber pistol. That enemy shelling had one beneficial result: it dissolved his bravado.

We got our positions squared away for the night and ate some K rations, as well as one could with a stomach tied in knots. More details reached us about the loss of Nease, Westbrook, and others killed and wounded. We regretted any American casualties, but when they were close friends it was terribly depressing. They were just the first of what was to grow into a long tragic list before we would come out of combat fifty hellish days later.*

Before dark we learned there would be a big attack the next morning all along the U.S. line. With the heavy Japanese fire poured onto us as we moved into that line, we dreaded the prospect of making a push. An NCO told us that our objective was to reach the Asato Gawa, a stream about 1,500 yards south of us that stretched inland and eastward to an area near the village of Dakeshi.

Rain ushered in a gloomy dawn. We were apprehensive but hopeful. There was some small-arms fire along the line, and a few shells passed back and forth during early morning. The rain slackened temporarily and we ate some K rations. On the folding pocket-sized tripod issued to us, I heated up a canteen cup of coffee with a sterno tablet. I had to hover over it to keep the rain from drowning it out.

As the seconds ticked slowly toward 0900, our artillery and ships' guns increased their rate of fire. The rain poured down, and the Japanese took up the challenge from our artillery. They started throwing more shells our way, many of which passed over us and exploded far to our rear where our own artillery was emplaced.

Finally we received orders to open fire with our mortars. Our shells exploded along a defilade to our front. Our machine guns opened up in earnest. Our artillery, ships' guns, and 81mm mortars increased the tempo to an awesome rate as the time for the attack approached. The shells whistled, whined, and rumbled overhead, ours bursting out in front of the ridge and the enemy's exploding in our area and to the rear. The noise increased all along the line. Rain fell in torrents, and the soil became muddy and slippery wherever we hurried around the gun pit to break out and stack our ammo.

I looked at my watch. It was 0900. I gulped and prayed for my buddies in the rifle platoons.

"Mortars cease firing and stand by."

---

*The 27th Infantry Division had been in action since 15 April. It had suffered heavily in the attacks of 19 April in capturing Kakazu Ridge, Machinato Airfield, and the surrounding area. After the 1st Marine Division relieved it, the 27th Infantry Division went north for patrolling and guard duty.

We were ready to fire or to take up the mortars at a moment's notice and move forward. Some of our riflemen moved past the crest of the ridge to attack. Noise that had been loud now grew into deafening bedlam. The riflemen hardly got out of their foxholes when a storm of enemy fire from our front and left flank forced them back. The same thing was happening to the battalions on our right and left.

The sound of the many machine guns became one incredible rattle against a thundering and booming of artillery. Rifles popped everywhere along the line, while Japanese slugs snapped over the low ridge behind which we lay. We fired some white phosphorous shells to screen our withdrawing troops. Just as we heard "Cease firing," a Marine came running through the mud on the slope to our right, yelling, "The guys pulling back need a stretcher team from mortars!"

Three other mortarmen and I took off on the double after the messenger. With bullets snapping and popping overhead, we ran along for about forty yards, keeping just below the crest of the ridge. We came to a road cut through the ridge about eight feet below the crest; an officer told us to stand behind him until we were ordered to go out and bring in the casualty. This was the exact spot where Nease and Westbrook had been machine-gunned the day before. Japanese bullets were zipping and swishing through the cut like hail pouring through an open window.

A couple of Company K rifle squads were running back toward us from the abortive attack. They rushed along the road in small groups and turned right and left as soon as they got through the cut to get out of the line of fire. Incredibly, none got hit by the thick fire coming through the cut. I knew most of them well, although some of the new men not as well as the veterans. They all wore wild-eyed, shocked expressions that showed only too vividly they were men who had barely escaped chance's strange arithmetic. They clung to their M1s, BARs, and Tommy guns and slumped to the mud to pant for breath before moving behind the ridge toward their former foxholes. The torrential rain made it all seem so much more unbelievable and terrible.

I hoped fervently that we wouldn't have to step out into that road to pick up a casualty. I felt ashamed for thinking this, because I knew full well that if I were lying out there wounded, my fellow Marines wouldn't leave me. But I didn't see how anyone could go out and get back now that the volume of fire was so intense; since most of our attacking troops had fallen back, the Japanese could concentrate their fire on the stretcher teams as I had seen them do at Peleliu. They showed medical personnel no mercy.

Our company gunnery sergeant, Hank Boyes, was the last man through the cut. He made a quick check of the men and announced—to my immense relief—that everyone had made it back; casualties had been brought back farther down the line where the machine-gun fire hadn't been as heavy.

Boyes was amazing. He had dashed out to the men pinned down in front of the ridge, where he threw smoke grenades to shield them from the Japanese fire. He returned with a hole shot through his dungaree cap (he wasn't wearing his helmet) and another through his pants leg. He had been hit in the leg with fragments from a Japanese knee mortar shell but refused to turn in.*

The officer told us we wouldn't be needed as stretcher bearers and to return to our posts. As we took off on the double to the gun pits, the shells kept up their heavy traffic back and forth, but the bullets began to slacken off somewhat with all our men by then under cover of the ridge. I jumped into the gun pit, and my temporary replacement hurried back to his hole.†

---

*Gy. Sgt. Henry A. Boyes was a former dairy farmer from Trinidad, California. He fought with K/3/5 at Cape Gloucester and landed on Peleliu as a squad leader. He won a Silver Star there and became a platoon sergeant after the assault on Ngesebus. Wounded during the fighting around the Five Sisters, he was evacuated, but returned in time for the landing on Okinawa. Wounded early in May he refused evacuation and became first sergeant of Company K. After the company commander, 1st Lt. Stumpy Stanley, was evacuated in late May with malaria, Boyes shared the primary leadership role with 1st Lt. George Loveday. A powerfully built man, Hank Boyes was stern but compassionate. No matter how low morale got, he was always there inspiring like some inexhaustible dynamo. Today he and his family run a successful logging and cattle business in Australia.

†At some time during the attack, Burgin ran out and exposed himself to heavy machine-gun fire from a weapon that no one could locate. He called back a fire mission to the mortars after he spotted the machine gun. Our mortar fire hit on target and knocked out the gun. Burgin won a Bronze Star for his actions.

We crouched in our foxholes in the pouring rain, cursing the Japanese, the shells, and the weather. The enemy gunners poured fire into our company area to discourage another attack. Word came down the line that all attacking Marine units had suffered considerable casualties, so we would remain inactive until the next day. That suited us fine. The Japanese shelling continued viciously for some time. We all felt depressed about the failure of the attack and we still didn't know how many friends we had lost, an uncertainty that always bore down on every man after an attack or fire fight.

From the gun pit, which contained several inches of water, we looked out on a gloomy scene. The rain had settled into a steady pelting that promised much misery. Across the muddy fields we saw our soaked comrades crouching forlornly in their muddy holes and ducking, as we did, each time a shell roared over.

This was my first taste of mud in combat, and it was more detestable than I had ever imagined. Mud in camp on Pavuvu was a nuisance. Mud on maneuvers was an inconvenience. But mud on the battlefield was misery beyond description. I had seen photographs of World War I troops in the mud— the men grinning, of course, if the picture was posed. If not posed, the faces always wore a peculiarly forlorn, disgusted expression, an expression I now understood. The air was chilly and clammy, but I thanked God we weren't experiencing this misery in Europe where the foxholes were biting cold as well as wet.

The shelling finally subsided, and things got fairly quiet in our area. We squatted thankfully in our holes and grumbled about the rain. The humid air hung heavily with the chemical odor of exploded shells.

Shortly, to our left rear, we saw a Marine stretcher team bringing a casualty back through the rain. Instead of turning left behind the ridge we were on, or right behind the one farther across the field, the team headed straight back between the two low ridges. This was a mistake, because we knew the Japanese could still fire on that area.

As the stretcher team approached the cover of some trees, Japanese riflemen to our left front opened up on them. We saw bullets kicking up mud and splashing in the puddles of water around the team. The four stretcher bearers hurried across the slippery field. But they couldn't go faster than a rapid walk, or the casualty might fall off the stretcher.

We requested permission to fire 60mm phosphorous shells as a smoke screen (we were too far away to throw smoke grenades to cover the stretcher team). Permission was denied. We weren't allowed to fire across our company front because of the possibility of hitting unseen friendly troops. Thus we watched helplessly as the four stretcher bearers struggled across the muddy field with bullets falling all around them. It was one of those terribly pathetic, heartrending sights that seemed to rule in combat: men struggling to save a wounded comrade, the enemy firing at them as fast as they could, and the rest of us utterly powerless to give any aid. To witness such a scene was worse than personal danger. It was absolute agony.

To lighten their loads, the four carriers had put all of their personal equipment aside except for a rifle or carbine over their shoulders. Each held a handle of the stretcher in one hand and stretched out the other arm for balance. Their shoulders were stooped with the weight of the stretcher. Four helmeted heads hung low like four beasts of burden being flogged. Soaked with rain and spattered with mud, the dark green dungarees hung forlornly on the men. The casualty lay inert on the narrow canvas stretcher, his life in the hands of the struggling four.

To our dismay, the two carriers in the rear got hit by a burst of fire. Each loosened his grip on the stretcher. Their knees buckled, and they fell over backwards onto the muddy ground. The stretcher pitched onto the deck. A gasp went up from the men around me, but it turned almost immediately into roars of relief. The two Marines at the other end of the stretcher threw it down, spun around, and grabbed the stretcher casualty between them. Then each supported a wounded carrier with his other arm. As we cheered, all five assisted one another and limped and hobbled into the cover of the bushes, bullets still kicking up mud all around them. I felt relief and elation over their escape, matched only by a deepened hatred for the Japanese.

Before nightfall we received information that Company K would push again the next day. As the rain slowly diminished and then ceased, we made our grim preparations.

While receiving extra ammo, rations, and water, I saw our company officers and NCOs gathering nearby. They stood or squatted around the CO, talking quietly. Our company commander was obviously in charge, giving orders and answering questions. The senior NCOs and the veteran officers stood by with serious, sometimes worried expressions as they listened. Those of us in the ranks watched their familiar faces carefully for signs of what was in store for us.

The faces of the replacement lieutenants reflected a different mood. They showed enthusiastic, animated expressions with eyebrows raised in eager anticipation of seeing the thing through like a successful field problem at OCS in Quantico. They were very conscientious and determined to do their best or die in the effort. To me, those young officers appeared almost tragic in their naive innocence and ignorance of what lay ahead for us all.

The new officers bore a heavy burden. Not only were they going into combat with all its terrors and unknowns for the first time—conditions even the best of training couldn't possibly duplicate—but they were untried officers. Combat was the acid test. Faced with heavy responsibilities and placed in a position of leadership amid hardened, seasoned Marine combat veterans in a proud, elite division like the First was a difficult situation and a terrific challenge for any young lieutenant. No one I knew in the ranks envied them in the least.

During the course of the long fighting on Okinawa, unlike at Peleliu, we got numerous replacement lieutenants. They were wounded or killed with such regularity that we rarely knew anything about them other than a code name and saw them on their feet only once or twice. We expected heavy losses of enlisted men in combat, but our officers got hit so soon and so often that it seemed to me the position of second lieutenant in a rifle company had been made obsolete by modern warfare.

After the CO dismissed his junior officers, they returned to their respective platoons and briefed the troops about the impending push. Mac was crisp and efficient in his orders to Burgin and the rest of the mortar section NCOs. In turn they told us what to prepare for. (It was good to see Mac divested of his cockiness.) We would get maximum support from heavy artillery and other weapons; casualties would be given swift aid. So we prepared our equipment and waited nervously.

A friend came over from one of the rifle platoons that was to be in the next day's assault. We sat near the gun pit on our helmets in the mud and had a long talk. I lit my pipe and he a cigarette. Things were quiet in the area, so we were undisturbed for some time. He poured out his heart. He had come to me because of our friendship and because I was a veteran. He told me he was terribly afraid about the impending attack. I said everybody was. But I knew he would be in a more vulnerable position than some of us, because his platoon was in the assault. I did my best to cheer him up.

He was so appalled and depressed by the fighting of the previous day that he had concluded he couldn't possibly survive the next day. He confided his innermost thoughts and secrets about his parents and a girl back home whom he was going to marry after the war. The poor guy wasn't just afraid of death or injury—the idea that he might never return to those he loved so much had him in a state of near desperation.

I remembered how Lt. Hillbilly Jones had comforted and helped me through the first shock of Peleliu, and I tried to do the same for my friend. Finally he seemed somewhat relieved, or resigned to his fate, whatever it might be. We got up and shook hands. He thanked me for our friendship, then walked slowly back to his foxhole.

There was nothing unique in the conversation. Thousands like it occurred every day among infantrymen scheduled to enter the chaos and inferno of an attack. But it illustrates the value of camaraderie among men facing constant hardship and frequent danger. Friendship was the only comfort a man had.

It seems strange how men occupied themselves after all weapons and gear had been squared away for an impending attack. We had learned in boot camp that no pack straps should be left with loose ends dangling (any such loose straps on a Marine's pack were called "Irish pennants"—why Irish I never knew—and resulted in disciplinary action or a blast from the drill instructor). So, from pure habit I suppose, we carefully rolled up the loose straps and shaped up our packs. There was always a bit of cleaning and touching up to be done on one's weapon with the toothbrush most of us carried for that purpose. A man could always straighten up his lacings on his leggings, too. With such trivia, doomed men busily occupied themselves, as though when they got up and moved forward out of their foxholes it would be to an inspection rather than to oblivion.

We were partially successful with our attack on 3 May. The knockout of the Japanese heavy machine gun by our mortars the previous day helped our company's advance to the next low ridge line. But we couldn't hold the hills. Heavy enemy machine-gun and mortar fire drove us back about a hundred yards. Thus we gained about three hundred yards for the entire day.

We moved into a quiet area back of the front lines well before dark. Word came that because of heavy casualties over the past two days' fighting, Company K would go into battalion reserve for a while. We dug in around the battalion aid station for its defense.

Our casualties were still coming back from the afternoon's action as we moved into position. Much to my joy I saw the friend with whom I'd had the conversation the night before. He wore a triumphant look of satisfaction, shook hands with me heartily, and grinned as a stretcher team carried him by with a bloody bandage on his foot. God or chance—depending on one's faith—had spared his life and lifted his burden of further fear and terror in combat by awarding him a million-dollar wound. He had done his duty, and the war was over for him. He was in pain, but he was lucky. Many others hadn't been as lucky the last couple of days.

COUNTERATTACK

We settled into our holes for the night, feeling more at ease off the line and in a quiet area. My foxhole partner had the first watch, so I dropped off to sleep, confident that we would have a fairly quiet night. I hadn't slept long before he woke me with, "Sledgehammer, wake up. The Nips are up to something." Startled, I awoke and instinctively unholstered my .45 automatic.

I heard a stern order from an NCO, "Stand by for a ram, you guys. One hundred percent alert!"

I heard heavy artillery and small-arms firing up on the line. It seemed to come mostly from the area beyond our division's left flank where army troops were located. The firing directly forward had increased, too. Our artillery shells swished overhead in incredible numbers. It wasn't just the usual harassing fire against the Japanese; there was too much of it for that.

"What's the dope?" I asked nervously.

"Beats me," said my buddy, "but something sure the hell's going on up on the line. Nips probably pulling a counterattack."

From the increasing fire, enemy as well as friendly, it was obvious something big was happening. As we waited in our holes hoping to get word about what was going on, heavy machine-gun and mortar fire broke out abruptly some distance to our right, to the rear of where the 1st Marines' line reached the sea. From our little mound we saw streams of American machine-gun tracers darting straight out to sea under the eerie light of 60mm mortar flares. That could only mean one thing. The enemy was staging an amphibious attack, trying to come ashore behind the right flank of the 1st Marines, which was the right-hand regiment on the 1st Marine Division's line.

"The Nips must be pullin' a counterlanding, and the 1st Marines' givin' 'em hell," someone said tensely.

Could our comrades in the 1st Marine Regiment stop that attack? That was the question on everyone's mind. But one man said confidently in a low voice, "The 1st Marines'll tear their ass up, betcha." We hoped he was right. With no more than we knew, it was clear that if the Japanese got ashore on our right flank and counterattacked heavily on our left and front, our entire division might be isolated. We sat and listened apprehensively in the darkness.

As if things didn't seem grim enough, the next order came along, "Stand by for possible Jap paratroop attack! All hands turn to. Keep your eyes open."

My blood felt like icewater throughout my body, and I shuddered. We weren't afraid of Japanese paratroopers as such. They couldn't be any tougher to deal with than veteran Japanese infantry. But the fear of being cut off from other U.S. troops by having the enemy land behind us filled us with dread. Most nights on Peleliu we had to keep a sharp lookout to front, rear, right, and left. But that night on Okinawa we had to scan even the dark sky for signs of parachutes.

We lived constantly with the fear of death or maiming from wounds. But the possibility of being surrounded by the enemy and wounded beyond the point of being able to defend myself chilled my soul. They were notorious for their brutality.

A couple of Japanese planes flew over during the night (we recognized the sound of the engines), and I experienced a dread I had never known before. But they passed on without dropping parachutists. They were bombers or fighters on their way to attack our ships lying offshore.

The Japanese and American artillery fire to our left front rumbled and roared on and on with frightening intensity, drowning out the rattle of machine guns and rifles. To our right, elements of the 1st Marine Regiment kept up their small-arms and mortar fire out to sea for quite some time. We heard scattered rifle fire far to our rear. This was disturbing, but some optimist said it was probably nothing more than trigger-happy, rear-echelon guys firing at shadows. Rumors passed that some enemy soldiers had broken through the army's line on our left. It was a long night made worse by the uncertainty and confusion around us. I suffered extremely mixed emotions: glad on the one hand to be out of the fighting, but anxious for those Americans catching the fury of the enemy's attack.

At first light we heard Japanese planes attacking our ships and saw the fleet throwing up antiaircraft fire. Despite the aerial attack, the ships' big guns began heavy firing against the Japanese on land. Toward our right and rear, the firing of our infantry units slackened. We learned that radio messages indicated the 1st Marines had slaughtered hundreds of Japanese in the water when they tried a landing behind our division's flank. The sound of scattered firing told us some enemy had slipped ashore, but the major threat was over.

Our artillery increased its support fire to our front, and we were told that our division would attack during the day. We would remain in position, however—an order we found most agreeable.

Word came that the army troops on our left had held off the main Japanese attack, but things were still grim in that area.

Some enemy had gotten through, and others were still attacking. While 3/5 remained in reserve, the 1st Marine Division began its attack to our front, and we heard that the opposition was ferocious. We received orders to be on the lookout for any enemy that might have slipped around the division's flank during the night. There were none.

There was a massive enemy air attack against our fleet at this time. We saw a kamikaze fly through a thick curtain of flak and crash dive into a cruiser. A huge white smoke ring rose thousands of feet into the air. We heard shortly that it was the cruiser USS *Birmingham* that had suffered considerable damage and loss of life among her crew.

The Japanese counterattack of 3–4 May was a major effort aimed at confusing the American battle plan by isolating and destroying the 1st Marine Division. The Japanese made a night amphibious landing of several hundred men on the east coast behind the 7th Infantry Division. Coordinated with that landing was another on the west coast behind the 1st Marine Division. The Japanese plan called for the two elements to move inland, join up, and create confusion to the rear while the main counterattack hit the American center.

The Japanese 24th Infantry Division concentrated its frontal attack on the boundary between the American army's 7th and 77th Infantry divisions. The enemy planned to send a separate brigade through the gap in the American lines created by the 24th Division's attack, swing it to the left behind the 1st Marine Division, and hit the Marines as the Japanese 62d Infantry Division attacked the 1st Marine Division's front.

If the plan succeeded, the enemy would isolate and destroy the 1st Marine Division. It failed when the two American army divisions stopped the frontal assault, except for a few minor penetrations, with more than 6,000 Japanese dead counted. At the same time, the 1st Marines (on the right of the 1st Marine Division) discovered the enemy landing on the west coast. They killed over 300 enemy in the water and on the beach.

CHAPTER ELEVEN

Of Shock and Shells

HEAVY RAINS began on 6 May and lasted through 8 May, a preview of the nightmare of mud we would endure from the end of the second week of May until the end of the month. Our division had reached the banks of the Asato Gawa at a cost of 1,409 casualties (killed and wounded). I knew losses had been heavy during the first week of May because of the large number of casualties I saw in just the small area we were operating in.

On 8 May Nazi Germany surrendered unconditionally. We were told this momentous news, but considering our own peril and misery, no one cared much. "So what" was typical of the remarks I heard around me. We were resigned only to the fact that the Japanese would fight to total extinction on Okinawa, as they had elsewhere, and that Japan would have to be invaded with the same gruesome prospects. Nazi Germany might as well have been on the moon.

The main thing that impressed us about V-E Day was a terrific, thundering artillery and naval gunfire barrage that went swishing, roaring, and rumbling toward the Japanese. I thought it was in preparation for the next day's attack. Years later I read that the barrage had been fired on enemy targets at noon for its destructive effect on them but also as a salute to V-E Day.

The 6th Marine Division moved into the line on our right, and our division shifted toward the left somewhat. This put us in the center of the American front. As we crouched in our muddy foxholes in the cold rain, the arrival of the 6th Marine Division plus the massive artillery barrage did more for our morale than news about Europe.

The 5th Marines approached the village of Dakeshi and ran into a strong enemy defensive system in an area known as the Awacha Pocket. Talk was that we were approaching the main Japanese defense line, the Shuri Line. But Awacha and Dakeshi confronted us before we reached the main ridges of the Shuri Line.

When our battalion dug in in front of Awacha, our mortars were emplaced on the slope of a little rise about seventy-five yards behind the front line. The torrents of rain were causing us other problems besides chilly misery. Our tanks couldn't move up to support us. Amtracs had to bring a lot of supplies, because the jeeps and trailers bogged down in the soft soil.

Ammunition, boxes of rations, and five-gallon cans of water were brought up as close to us as possible. But because of the mud along a shallow draw that ran to the rear of the mortar section, all the supplies were piled about fifty yards away in a supply dump on the other side of the draw. Working parties went off to carry the supplies from the dump across the draw to the rifle platoons and the mortar section.

Carrying ammo and rations was something the veterans had done plenty of times before. With the others I had struggled up and down Peleliu's unbelievably rugged rocky terrain in the suffocating heat, carrying ammo, rations, and water. Like carrying stretcher cases, it was exhausting work. But this was my first duty on a working party in deep mud, and it surpassed the drudgery of any working party I had ever experienced.

All ammunition was heavy, of course, but some was easier to handle than others. We praised the manufacturers of hand-grenade and belted machine-gun ammunition boxes. The former were wooden with a nice rope handle on each side; the latter were metal and had a collapsible handle on top. But we cursed the dolts who made the wooden cases our .30 caliber rifle ammo came in. Each box contained 1,000 rounds of ammunition. It was heavy and had only a small notch cut into either end. This allowed only a fingertip grip by the two men usually needed to handle a single crate.

We spent a great deal of time in combat carrying this heavy ammunition on our shoulders to places where it was needed —spots often totally inaccessible to all types of vehicles—and breaking it out of the packages and crates. On Okinawa this was often done under enemy fire, in driving rain, and through knee-deep mud for hours on end. Such activity drove the infantryman, weary from the mental and physical stress of combat, almost to the brink of physical collapse.

A great number of books and films about the war ignored this grueling facet of the infantryman's war. They gave the impression that ammunition was always "up there" when needed. Maybe my outfit just happened to get a particularly bad dose of carrying ammo into position on Peleliu because of the heat and rugged terrain and on Okinawa because of the deep mud. But the work was something none of us would forget. It was exhausting, demoralizing, and seemingly unending.

In this first position before Awacha, those of us detailed to the working parties had made a couple of trips across the shallow draw when a Nambu light machine gun opened up from a position to our left. I was about midway across the draw, in no particular hurry, when the Japanese gunner fired his first bursts down the draw. I took off at a run, slipping and sliding on the mud, to the protected area where the supply dump was placed. Slugs snapped viciously around me. The men with me also were lucky as we dove for the protection of a knoll beside the supplies. The enemy machine gunner was well concealed up the draw to our left and had a clear field of fire anytime anyone crossed where we were. We were bound to lose men to that Nambu if we kept moving back and forth. Yet we had to get the ammo distributed for the coming attack.

We looked across the draw toward the mortar section and saw Redifer throw out a phosphorous grenade to give us smoke-screen protection when we came back across. He threw several more grenades which went off with a muffled *bump* and a flash. Thick clouds of white smoke billowed forth and hung almost immobile in the heavy, misty air. I grabbed a metal box of 60mm mortar ammo in each hand. Each of the other men also picked up a load. We prepared to cross. The Nambu kept firing down the smoke-covered draw. I was reluctant to go, as were the others, but we could see Redifer standing out in the draw, throwing more phosphorous grenades to hide us. I felt like a coward. My buddies must have felt the same way as we glanced anxiously at each other. Someone said resignedly, "Let's go, on the double, and keep your five-pace interval."

We dashed into the smoky, murky air. I lowered my head and gritted my teeth as the machine-gun slugs snapped and zipped around us. I expected to get hit. So did the others. I wasn't being brave, but Redifer was, and I would rather take my chances than be yellow in the face of his risks to screen us. If he got hit while I was cringing in safety, I knew it would haunt me the rest of my life—that is, if I lived much longer, which seemed more unlikely every day.

The smoke hid us from the gunner, but he kept firing intermittent bursts down the draw to prevent our crossing. Slugs popped and snapped, but we made it across. We rushed behind the knoll and flung the heavy ammo boxes down on the mud. We thanked Redifer, but he seemed more concerned with solving the problem at hand than talking.

"Boy, that Nip's got the best-trained trigger finger I ever heard. Listen to them short bursts he gets off," a buddy said. We panted and listened to the machine gun half in terror and half in admiration of the Japanese gunner's skill. He continued to fire across the rear of our position. Each burst was two or three rounds and spaced: *tat, tat . . . tat, tat, tat . . . tat, tat.*

Just then we heard the engine of a tank some distance across the draw. Without a word, Redifer sped across the draw toward the sound. He got across safely. We could see him dimly through the drifting smoke as he contacted the tankers. Shortly we saw him backing toward us slowly, giving the tankers hand signals as he directed the big Sherman across the draw. The Nambu kept firing blindly through the smoke as we watched Redifer anxiously. He seemed unhurried and reached us safely with the tank.

The tankers had agreed to act as a shield for us in our hazardous crossing. With several of us crouching in the welcome protection it afforded us, the tank moved back and forth across the draw, always between us and the enemy machine gun. We loaded up on ammo and moved slowly across the machine-gun-swept draw, hugging the side of the tank like chicks beside a mother hen. We kept this up until all the ammo was brought safely across.

The troops often expressed the opinion that whether an enlisted man was or wasn't recommended for a decoration for outstanding conduct in combat depended primarily on who saw him perform the deed. This certainly was true in the case of Redifer and what he had done to get the ammunition across the draw. I had seen other men awarded decorations for less, but Redifer was not so fortunate as to receive the official praise he deserved. Just the opposite happened.

As we finished the chore of moving the ammo across the draw, a certain first lieutenant, who by some unlucky chance had been assigned to Company K after Peleliu, came up. We called him simply "Shadow." A tall, skinny man, he was the sloppiest Marine—officer or enlisted—I ever saw.

His dungarees hung on him like old, discarded clothes on a scarecrow: his web pistol belt was wrapped around his waist like a loose sash on a dressing gown; his map case flopped around; and every packstrap dangled more "Irish pennants" than any new recruit had in boot camp. Shadow never wore canvas leggings when I saw him. His trouser legs were rolled up unevenly above his skinny ankles. He didn't fit his camouflaged cloth helmet cover tightly over his helmet like most Marines. It sagged to one side like some big stocking cap. For some reason, he frequently carried his helmet upside down in his left hand clutched against his side like a football. On his head he wore a green cloth fatigue cap like the rest of us wore under our helmets. But his cap was torn across the top so that his dark hair protruded like straw through a scarecrow's hat.

Shadow's disposition was worse than his appearance. Moody, ill-tempered, and highly excitable, he cursed the veteran enlisted men worse than most DIs did recruits in boot camp. When he was displeased with a Marine about something, he didn't reprimand the man the way our other officers did. He threw a tantrum. He would grab his cap by the bill, fling it onto the muddy deck, stamp his feet, and curse everyone in sight. The veteran sergeant who accompanied Shadow would stand silently by during these temper displays, torn between a compulsion to reprimand us, if it seemed his duty to do so, and embarrassment and disapproval over his officer's childish behavior.

In all fairness, I don't know how competent an officer Shadow was considered to be by his superiors. Needless to say, he wasn't highly regarded in the ranks, simply on the basis of his lack of self-control. But he was brave. I'll give him that.

Shadow "pitched a fit" in reaction to what Redifer had done in facilitating our ammo transportation across the draw. It was just the first of many such performances I was to witness, and they never ceased to amaze as well as disgust me.

He went to Redifer and unleashed such a verbal assault against him that anyone who didn't know better would have assumed that Redifer was a coward who had deserted his post in the face of the enemy instead of having just performed a brave act. Shadow yelled, gesticulated, and cursed Redifer for "exposing himself unnecessarily to enemy fire" when he was throwing the smoke grenades into the draw and when he went to contact the tank.

Redifer took it quietly, but he was obviously dismayed. We looked on in disbelief, having expected Shadow to praise the man for showing bravery and initiative under fire. But here was this ranting, raving officer actually cursing and berating a man for doing something any other officer would have considered a meritorious act. It was so incredibly illogical that we couldn't believe it.

Finally, having vented his rage on a Marine who rightfully deserved praise, Shadow strode off grumbling and cursing the individual and collective stupidity of enlisted men. Redifer didn't say anything. He just looked off into the distance. We growled mightily, though.

As midday approached on 9 May, everyone was tense about the coming attack. Ammunition had been issued, men had squared away their gear and had done their last-minute duties: adjusting cartridge belts, packstraps, leggings, and leather rifle slings—all those forlorn little gestures of no value that released tension in the face of impending terror. We had previously registered our mortars on selected targets and had stacked HE and phosphorous shells off the mud on pieces of boxes for quick access.

The ground having dried sufficiently for our tanks to maneuver, several stood by with engines idling, hatches open, and the tankers waiting—waiting like everyone else. War is mostly waiting. The men around me sat silently with drawn faces. Some replacements had come into the company to make up for our earlier losses. These new men looked more confused than afraid.

The big guns had fired periodically during the morning, but then had died away. There wasn't much noise as we waited for the preattack bombardment to begin.

Then the preassault bombardment commenced. The big shells swished overhead as each battery of our artillery and each ship's guns began to shell the Japanese Awacha defenses ahead of us. At first we could identify each type of shell—75mm, 105mm, and 155mm artillery, along with the 5-inch ship's guns —as it added to the storm of steel.

We saw our planes overhead, Corsairs and dive bombers. Air strikes began as the planes dove firing rockets, dropping bombs, and strafing to our front. The firing thundered and rumbled until finally even the experienced ears of the veterans could distinguish nothing, only that we were glad that all that stuff was ours.

Enemy artillery and mortar shells began coming in as the Japanese tried to disrupt the attack. The replacements looked utterly bewildered amid the bedlam. I remembered my first day in combat and sympathized with them. The sheer massiveness of the preattack bombardment was an awesome and frightening thing to witness as a veteran, let alone as a new replacement.

Soon the order came, "Mortar section, stand by." We took directions from Burgin, who was up on the observation post to spot targets and direct our fire. Although our 60mm shells were small compared to the huge shells rushing overhead, we could fire close-in to the company front where bigger mortars and the artillery couldn't shoot without endangering our own people. This closeness made it doubly critical that we fire skillfully and avoid short rounds.

We had fired only a few rounds when Snafu began cursing the mud. With each round, the recoil pushed the mortar's base plate against the soft soil in the gun pit, and he had trouble resighting the leveling bubbles to retain proper alignment of the gun on the aiming stake.

After we completed the first fire mission, we quickly moved the gun a little to one side of the pit onto a harder surface and resighted it. At Peleliu we often had to hold the base plate as well as the bipod feet onto the coral rock to prevent the recoil from making the base plate bounce aside, knocking the

mortar's alignment out too far. On Okinawa's wet clay soil, just
the opposite happened. The recoil drove the base plate into the
ground with each round we fired. This problem got worse as
the rains increased during May, and the ground became softer
and softer.

The order came to secure the guns and to stand by. The air
strike ended, and the artillery and ships' guns slacked off. The
tanks and our riflemen moved out as tank-infantry teams, and
we waited tensely. Things went well for a couple of hundred
yards during this attack made by 3/5 and 3/7 before heavy
fire from Japanese on the left flank stopped the attack. Our
OP (observation post) ordered us to fire smoke because heavy
enemy fire was coming from our left. We fired phosphorous
rapidly to screen the men from the enemy observers.

Our position got a heavy dose of Japanese 90mm mortar
counterbattery fire. We had a difficult time keeping up our firing with those big 90mm shells crashing around us. Shell fragments whined through the air, and the big shells slung mud
around. But we had to keep up our fire. The riflemen were
catching hell from the flank and had to be supported. Our
artillery began firing again at the enemy positions to our left to
aid the harassed riflemen.

We always knew when we were inflicting losses on the Japanese with our 60mm mortars by the amount of counterbattery
mortar and artillery fire they threw back at us. If we weren't
doing them any damage, they usually ignored us unless they
thought they could inflict a lot of casualties. If the Japanese
counterbattery fire was a real indicator of our effectiveness in
causing them casualties, we were satisfyingly effective during
the Okinawa campaign.

During the attack of 9 May against Awacha, Company K
suffered heavy losses. It was the same tragic sight of bloody,
dazed, and wounded men benumbed with shock, being carried or walking to the aid station in the rear. There also were
the dead, and the usual anxious inquiries about friends. We
were all glad when the word came that 3/5 would move into
reserve for the 7th Marines—for a couple of days, it turned
out. The 7th Marines were fighting to our right against Dakeshi Ridge.

*

In the path of the 1st Marine Division, from north to south, lay Awacha, Dakeshi Ridge, Dakeshi Village, Wana Ridge, Wana Village, and Wana Draw. South of the latter lay the defenses and the heights of Shuri itself. All these ridges and villages were defended heavily by well-prepared, mutually supporting fortifications built into a skillful system of defense-in-depth. Similarly powerful defensive positions faced the 6th Marine Division on the right and the army infantry divisions on the left. The Japanese ferociously defended every yard of ground and conserved their strength to inflict maximum losses on the American forces. The tactics turned Okinawa into a bloodbath.

The battle against Awacha raged on to our left. We dug in for the night in the wet ground. Our mortars weren't set up. We were to act as riflemen and to keep watch across an open, sloping valley. Above us the other two mortar squads dug in in two parallel lines about twenty feet apart and perpendicular to the line of the crest of the embankment above us. Water and rations were issued and mail brought to us.

Mail usually was a big morale booster, but not for me that time. There was a chilly drizzling rain off and on. We were weary and my spirits weren't the best. I sat on my helmet in the mud and read a letter from my parents. It brought news that Deacon, my beloved spaniel, had been hit by an automobile, had dragged himself home, and had died in my father's arms. He had been my constant companion during the several years before I had left home for college. There, with the sound of heavy firing up ahead and the sufferings and deaths of thousands of men going on nearby, big tears rolled down my cheeks, because Deacon was dead.

During the remainder of the night, the sound of firing toward Dakeshi Ridge indicated that the 7th Marines were having a lot of trouble trying to push the Japanese off the ridge. Just before dawn we could hear heavy firing off to our left front where 1/5 and 2/5 were fighting around the Awacha Pocket.

"Stand by, you guys, and be prepared to move out," came the order from an NCO on the embankment above us.

"What's the hot dope?" a mortarman asked.

"Don't know, except the Nips are counterattacking on the 5th Marines' front and the battalion [3/5] is on standby to go up and help stop 'em."

We greeted the news with an understandable lack of enthusiasm. We were still tired and tense from the punishment the battalion took at Awacha the day before. What's more, we didn't relish moving anywhere in the darkness. But we squared away our gear, chewing gum nervously or gnawing on ration biscuits. The sound of firing rose and fell to our left front as we waited and wondered.

Finally, during the misty gray light of early morning, the order came, "OK, you guys, let's go." We picked up our loads and moved toward the front lines.

Other than occasional shells whining over in both directions, things were rather calm. Our column moved along a ridge just below the crest to the emplacements of the Marines who had been under attack. We found them assessing the damage they had done to the Japanese and caring for their own wounded. Some of the men told us the enemy had come into bayonet range before being repulsed. "But we tore their ass up, by God," one man said to me as he pointed out at about forty Japanese corpses sprawled beyond the Marine foxholes.

In the pale dawn, the air was misty and still smoky from phosphorous shells the enemy had fired to hide their approach. There was a big discussion in the ranks. Comments passed along to us from the Marines in place had it that somebody had seen a woman advancing with the attacking Japanese and that she was probably among the dead out there. We couldn't see her from our positions.

Then word came, "About face; we're moving back." In short, our help wasn't needed, so we were to be deployed somewhere else. Back through the rain and the mud we went.

All movements during most of May and early June were physically exhausting and utterly exasperating because of the mud. Typically, we moved in single file, five paces apart, slipping and sliding up and down muddy slopes and through boggy fields. When the column slowed or stopped, we tended to bunch up, and the NCOs and officers ordered sternly, "Keep your five-pace interval; don't bunch up." The ever-present danger of shells even far behind the lines made it necessary that we stay strung out. However, sometimes it was so dark that in order not to get separated and lost, each man was ordered to hold onto the cartridge belt of the man in front of him. This made the going difficult over rough and muddy terrain. Often if a man lost his footing and fell, several others went down with him, sprawling over each other in the mud. There were muffled curses and exasperated groans as they wearily disentangled themselves and regained their footing, groping about in the inky darkness to reform the column.

As soon as we stopped, the order came, "Move out." So the column always moved forward but like an accordion or an inchworm: compressed, then strung out, stopping and starting. If a man put down his load for a brief respite, he was sure to hear, "Pick up your gear; we're moving out!" So the load had to be hoisted onto shoulders again. But if you didn't put it down, chances were you missed an opportunity to rest for a few seconds, or even up to an hour, while the column halted up ahead for reasons usually unknown. To sit down on a rock or on a helmet when drunk with fatigue was like pressing a button to signal some NCO to shout, "On your feet; pick up your gear; we're moving out again." So the big decision in every man's mind at each pause in the column's forward progress was whether to drop his load and hope for a lengthy pause or to stand there and support all the weight rather than putting it down and having to pick it up again right away.

The column wound around and up and down the contours of terrain which in May and early June was covered nearly always with slippery mud varying in depth from a few inches to knee deep. The rain was frequent and chilly. It varied from drizzles to wind-driven, slashing deluges that flooded our muddy footprints almost as soon as we made them. The helmet, of course, kept one's head dry, but a poncho was the only body protection we had. It was floppy and restricted movement greatly. We had no raincoats. So, rather than struggle over slippery terrain with our loads, encumbered further by a loose-fitting poncho, we just got soaking wet and shivered in misery.

We tried to wisecrack and joke from time to time, but that always faded away as we grew more weary or closer to the front lines. That kind of movement over normal terrain or on roads would try any man's patience, but in Okinawa's mud it drove us to a state of frustration and exasperation bordering on rage. It can be appreciated only by someone who has experienced it.

Most men finally came to the state where they just stood stoically immobile with a resigned expression when halted and waited to move out. The cursing and outbursts of rage didn't seem to help, although no one was above it when goaded to the point of desperation and fatigue with halting and moving, slipping and sliding, and falling in the mud. Mud didn't just interfere with vehicles. It exhausted the man on foot who was expected to keep on where wheels or treaded vehicles couldn't move.

At some point during our moves, our mortar section completely wiped out an enemy force that had held an elongated ridge for three days against repeated Marine infantry attacks supported by heavy artillery fire. Burgin was observing. He reasoned that there must have been a narrow gully running along the ridge that sheltered the Japanese from the artillery fire. He registered our three mortars so that one fired from right to left, another from left to right, and the third along the crest of the ridge. Thus the Japanese in the gully couldn't escape.

Lieutenant Mac ordered Burgin not to carry out the fire mission. He said we couldn't spare the ammo. Burgin, a three-campaign veteran and a skillful observer, called the company CP and asked if they could get us the ammo. The CP told him yes.

Over the sound-powered phone, Burgin said, "On my command, fire."

Mac was with us at the gun pits and ordered us not to fire. He told Burgin the same over the phone.

Burgin told him to go to hell and yelled, "Mortar section, fire on my command; commence firing!"

We fired as Mac ranted and raved.

When we finished firing, the company moved against the ridge. Not a shot was fired at our men. Burgin checked the target area and saw more than fifty freshly killed Japanese soldiers in a narrow ravine, all dead from wounds obviously caused by our mortar fire. The artillery shells had exploded in front of or to the rear of the Japanese who were protected from them.

Our 60mm mortar shells fell right into the ravine, however, because of their steeper trajectory.

We had scored a significant success with the teamwork of our mortar section. The event illustrated the value of experience in a veteran like Burgin compared with the poor judgment of a "green" lieutenant.

The short period of rest in May helped us physically and mentally. Such periodic rests off the lines, lasting from a day to several days, enabled us to keep going. The rations were better. We could shave and clean up a bit using our helmets for a basin. Although we had to dig in because of long-range artillery or air raids, two men could make a simple shelter with their ponchos over their hole and be relatively (but not completely) dry on rainy nights. We could relax a little.

I'm convinced we would have collapsed from the strain and exertion without such respites. But I found it more difficult to go back each time we squared away our gear to move forward into the zone of terror. My buddies' joking ceased as we trudged grim-faced back into that chasm where time had no meaning and one's chances of emerging unhurt dwindled with each encounter. With each step toward the distant rattle and rumble of that hellish region where fear and horror tortured us like a cat tormenting a mouse, I experienced greater and greater dread. And it wasn't just dread of death or pain, because most men felt somehow they wouldn't be killed. But each time we went up, I felt the sickening dread of fear itself and the revulsion at the ghastly scenes of pain and suffering among comrades that a survivor must witness.

Some of my close friends told me they felt the same way. Significantly, those who felt it most acutely were the more battle-wise veterans for whom Okinawa was their third campaign. The bravest wearied of the suffering and waste, even though they showed little fear for their own personal safety. They simply had seen too much horror.

The increasing dread of going back into action obsessed me. It became the subject of the most tortuous and persistent of all the ghastly war nightmares that have haunted me for many, many years. The dream is always the same, going back up to the lines during the bloody, muddy month of May on Okinawa. It remains blurred and vague, but occasionally still comes, even after the nightmares about the shock and violence of Peleliu have faded and been lifted from me like a curse.

The 7th Marines secured Dakeshi Ridge on 13 May after a bitter fight. Some of the Peleliu veterans in that regiment noted that the vicious battle resembled the fighting on Bloody Nose Ridge. We could see the ridge clearly. It certainly looked like Bloody Nose. The crest was rugged and jagged on the skyline and had an ugly thin line of blackened, shattered trees and stumps.

Our company moved into a smashed, ruined village that an officer told me was Dakeshi. Some of us moved up to a stout stone wall where we were ordered to hold our fire while we watched a strange scene about one hundred yards to our front. We had to stand there inactive and watch as about forty or fifty Japanese soldiers retreated through the ruins and rubble. They had been flushed by men of the 7th Marines. But we were in support of the 7th Marines, some elements of which were forward of us on the right and left, out of our field of vision. We couldn't risk firing for fear of hitting those Marines. We could only watch the enemy trotting along holding their rifles. They wore no packs, only crossed shoulder straps supporting their cartridge belts.

As they moved through the rubble with helmets bobbing up and down, a man next to me fingered the safety catch on his M1 rifle and said in disgust, "Look at them bastards out there in the open, and we can't even fire at 'em."

"Don't worry, the 7th Marines will catch them in a cross fire farther on," an NCO said.

"That's the word," said an officer confidently.

Just then a swishing, rushing sound of shells passing low overhead made us all duck reflexively, even though we recognized the sound as our own artillery. Large, black, sausage-shaped clouds of thick smoke erupted in the air over the Japanese as each of those deadly 155mm bursts exploded with a flash and a *karump*. The artillerymen were zeroed in on target. The Japanese broke into a dead run, looking very bowlegged to me (as they always did when running). Even as they ran away under that deadly hail of steel, showing us their backs, I felt there was an air of confident arrogance about them. They didn't move like men in panic. We knew they simply had been ordered to fall back to other strongly prepared defensive positions to prolong the campaign. Otherwise they would have stayed put or attacked us, and in either case fought to the death.

More of our 155s swished over, erupting above the Japanese. We stood in silence and watched as the artillery fire took its toll of them. It was a grim sight, still vivid in my mind. The survivors moved out of sight through drifting smoke as we heard the rattle of Marine machine guns on our right and left front.

We received orders to move out along a little road bordered by stone walls. We passed through the ruins of what had been a quaint village. What had been picturesque little homes with straw-thatched or tiled roofs were piles of smoldering rubble.

After bitter fighting, the Awacha defenses and then those around Dakeshi fell to our division. Yet, between us and Shuri, there remained another system of heavy Japanese defenses: Wana. The costly battle against them would become known as the battle for Wana Draw.

CHAPTER TWELVE

Of Mud and Maggots

*T*HE BOUNDARY *between the III Amphibious Corps (Marines) and the XXIV Corps (Army) ran through the middle of the main Japanese defensive position on the heights of Shuri. As the Marines moved southward, the 1st Marine Division remained on the left in the III Amphibious Corps' zone of action with the 6th Marine Division on the right. Within the 1st Marine Division's zone of action, the 7th Marines occupied the left flank and the 5th Marines the right. The 1st Marines was in reserve.*

Beyond Awacha–Dakeshi, the Marines next faced Wana Ridge. On the other side of Wana Ridge lay Wana Draw, through which meandered the Asato Gawa. Forming the southern high ground above Wana Draw was yet another ridge, this one extending eastward from the city of Naha and rising to the Shuri Heights. This second ridge formed a part of the main Japanese defensive positions, the Shuri Line.

Wana Draw aimed like an arrow from the northwest directly into the heart of the Japanese defenses at Shuri. Within this natural avenue of approach, the Japanese took advantage of every difficult feature of terrain; it couldn't have provided a better opportunity for their defense if they had designed it. The longest and bloodiest ordeal of the battle for Okinawa now faced the men of the 1st Marine Division.

For the attack against Wana on 15 May 1945, the 5th Marines sent 2/5 forward with 3/5 in close support. The 1st Battalion came behind in reserve.

Before 2/5's attack began, we moved into a position behind that battalion. We watched tanks firing 75s and M7s firing 105s thoroughly shell the draw. The tanks received such heavy Japanese fire in return that the riflemen of 2/5 assigned to attack with the tanks had to seek any protection they could in ditches and holes while they covered the tanks from a distance; no man on his feet could have survived the hail of shells the enemy fired at the tanks. And the tanks couldn't move safely beyond

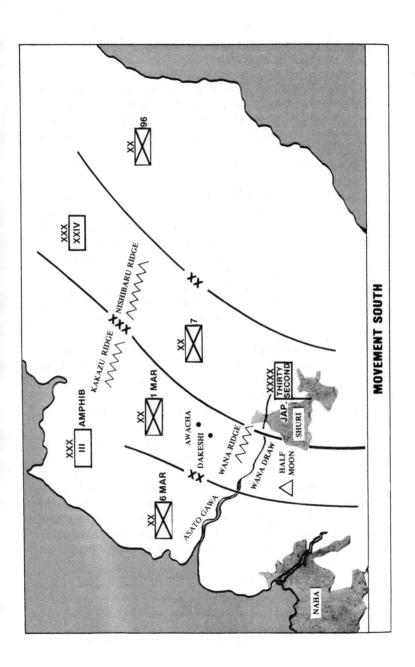

MOVEMENT SOUTH

the cover the riflemen provided because of Japanese suicide tank-destroyer teams. Finally, we saw the tanks pull back after suffering some hits. Our artillery and naval gunfire threw a terrific barrage at the Japanese positions around the draw. Shortly after that the tanks withdrew. Then an air strike was made against the draw. The bombardment of the draw seemed very heavy to us, but it wasn't anything compared to what was to become necessary before the draw was taken.

We moved from one position to another behind 2/5 until I was so confused I had no idea where we were. Late in the afternoon, we halted temporarily along a muddy trail running along the treeless slope of a muddy ridge. Marines of 2/5 moved past us going the other direction. Japanese shells whistled across the ridge and burst to the rear. Our artillery roared and swished overhead, the explosions booming and thundering out in the draw across the ridge.

Nearby our regimental Protestant chaplain had set up a little altar made out of a box from which he was administering Holy Communion to a small group of dirty Marines. I glanced at the face of a Marine opposite me as the file halted. He was filthy like all of us, but even through a thickly mud-caked dark beard I could see he had fine features. His eyes were bloodshot and weary. He slowly lowered his light machine gun from his shoulder, set the handle on his toe to keep it off the mud, and steadied the barrel with his hand. He watched the chaplain with an expression of skepticism that seemed to ask, "What's the use of all that? Is it gonna keep them guys from gettin' hit?" That face was so weary but so expressive that I knew he, like all of us, couldn't help but have doubts about his God in the presence of constant shock and suffering. Why did it go on and on? The machine gunner's buddy held the gun's tripod on his shoulder, glanced briefly at the muddy little communion service, and then stared blankly off toward a clump of pines to our rear—as though he hoped to see home back there somewhere.

"Move out," came along their file.

The machine gunner hoisted the heavy weapon onto his shoulder as they went slipping and sliding around a bend in the trail into the gathering dusk.

We were told to spread out, take cover, and await further

orders. Some of us found holes. Others scooped out what they could. Soon several Japanese shells exploded not far from me. I heard a shout for a corpsman and then, "Hey, you guys, Doc Caswell got hit!"

I forgot about the shells and felt sick. I ran in the direction of the shout to look for Kent Caswell, praying with every step that he wasn't hurt badly. Several other Marines were already with Doc, and a fellow corpsman was bandaging his neck. Doc Caswell lay back in the foxhole and looked up at me as I bent over him and asked him how he was doing (no doubt a stupid question, but my throat was constricted with grief). He opened his lips to speak, and blood trickled out from between them. I was heartbroken, because I didn't see how he could possibly survive. I feared that vital blood vessels in his neck had been severed by the shell fragments.

"Don't talk Doc, they'll get you outa here, and you'll be OK," I managed to stammer.

"OK you guys, let's get him outa here," the corpsman said as he finished his aid.

As I said so long to Doc and got up to leave, I noticed a cloverleaf of 60mm mortar shells lying on the side of the foxhole. A shell fragment had sliced a gash through the thick black metal endplate. I shuddered as I wondered whether it had passed first through Doc's neck.*

Our massive artillery, mortar, naval gunfire, and aerial bombardment continued against Wana Draw on our front and Wana Ridge on our left. The Japanese continued to shell everything and everybody in the area, meeting each tank-infantry attack with a storm of fire. A total of thirty tanks, including four flamethrowers, blasted and burned Wana Draw. Our artillery, heavy mortars, ships' guns, and planes then plastered the enemy positions all over again until the noise and shock made me wonder what it was like to be in a quiet place. We had been under and around plenty of "heavy stuff" at Peleliu, but not on nearly so massive a scale or for such unending periods of time as at Wana. The thunderous American barrages went on

---

*Some time later we learned that Doc had survived the trip to the aid station with the stretcher team and that he would live. He returned to his native Texas where he remains one of my most faithful friends from our days in K/3/5.

and on for hours and then days. In return, the Japanese threw plenty of shells our way. I had a continuous headache I'll never forget. Those thunderous, prolonged barrages imposed on me a sense of stupefaction and dullness far beyond anything I ever had experienced before.

It didn't seem possible for any human being to be under such thunderous chaos for days and nights on end and be unaffected by it—even when most of it was our own supporting weapons, and we were in a good foxhole. How did the Japanese stand up under it? They simply remained deep in their caves until it stopped and then swarmed up to repulse each attack, just as they had done at Peleliu. So our heavy guns and air strikes had to knock down, cave in, or otherwise destroy the enemy's well-constructed defensive positions.

At some time during the fight for Wana Draw, we crossed what I supposed was the draw itself, somewhere near its mouth. To get to that point, we fought for days. I had lost count of how many. Marines of 2/5 had just gone across under fire, while we waited in an open field to move across. We eased up to the edge of the draw to cross in dispersed order. An NCO ordered three men and me to cross at a particular point and to stay close behind the 2/5 troops directly across the draw from us. The other side looked mighty far away. Japanese machine guns were firing down the draw from our left, and our artillery was swishing overhead.

"Haul ass, and don't stop for anything till you get across," said our NCO. (We could see other Marines of our battalion starting across on our right.) He told me to leave my mortar ammo bag and that someone else would bring it. I had the Thompson (submachine gun) slung over my shoulder.

We left the field and slid down a ten-foot embankment to the sloping floor of the draw. My feet hit the deck running. The man ahead of me was a Company K veteran whom I knew well, but the other two were replacements. One I knew by name, but the other not at all. I ran as fast as I could, and was glad I was carrying only my Tommy, pistol, and combat pack.

The valley sloped downward toward a little stream and then upward to the ridge beyond. The Japanese machine guns rattled away. Bullets zipped and snapped around my head, the tracers like long white streaks. I looked neither right nor left, but with my heart in my throat raced out, splashed across the little stream, and dashed up the slope to the shelter of a spur of ridge projecting out into the draw to our left. We must have run about three hundred yards or more to get across.

Once behind the spur I was out of the line of machine-gun fire, so I slowed to a trot. The veteran ahead of me and a little to my right slowed up, too. We glanced back to see where the two new men were. Neither one of them had made more than a few strides out into the draw from the other side. One was sprawled in a heap, obviously killed instantly. The other was wounded and crawling back. Some Marines ran out, crouching low, to drag him to safety.

"Jesus, that was close, Sledgehammer," said the man with me.

"Yeah," I gasped. That was all I could say.

We went up the slope and contacted a couple of riflemen from 2/5.

"We got a kid right over there just got hit. Can you guys get him out?" one of them said. "There's some corpsmen set up in a ravine along the ridge there." He pointed out the location of the casualty and then the dressing station.

We hailed two Company K men coming along the ridge, and they said they would help. One ran back along the ridge to get a stretcher. We other three moved up the ridge and into some brush where we found the wounded Marine. He lay on his back still clutching his rifle. As we came up he said, "Boy, am I glad to see you guys."

"You hit bad?" I asked as I knelt beside him.

"Look out you guys! Nips right over there in the bushes."

I unslung my Tommy and, watching where he indicated the Japanese were, I talked to him. My two buddies knelt beside us with their weapons ready, watching for enemy soldiers through the brush while we waited for the stretcher.

"Where you hit?" I asked the wounded Marine.

"Right here," he said, pointing to the lower right portion of his abdomen.

He was talkative and seemed in no pain—obviously still shocked and dazed from his wound. I knew he would hurt badly soon, because he was hit in a painful area. I saw a smear of blood around a tear in his dungaree trousers, so I unhooked his cartridge belt and then his belt and his trousers to see how serious the wound was. It wasn't the round, neat hole of a bullet, but the gash characteristic of a shell fragment. About two inches long, it oozed a small amount of blood.

"What hit you?" I asked.

"Our company sixty mortars," answered the wounded Marine.

I felt a sharp twinge of conscience and thought some 60mm mortarman in the poor guy's own company fouled up and dropped some short rounds.

Almost as though he had read my thoughts, he continued, "It was my own damn fault I got hit, though. We were ordered to halt back there a way and wait while the mortars shelled this area. But I saw a damn Nip and figured if I got a little closer I could get a clear shot at the sonofabitch. When I got here the mortars came in, and I got hit. Guess I'm lucky it wasn't worse. I guess the Nip slipped away."

"You better take it easy now," I said as the stretcher came up.

We got the young Marine on the stretcher, put his rifle and helmet alongside him, and moved back down the ridge a little way to a corpsman. Several corpsmen were at work in a deep ravine cut into the ridge by erosion. It had sheer walls and a level floor and was perfectly protected. About a dozen wounded, stretcher cases, and walking wounded were there already.

As we set our casualty onto the floor of the ravine, he said, "Thanks a lot you guys; good luck." We wished him luck and a quick trip to the States.

Before we left, I paused and watched the corpsmen a moment. It was admirable how efficiently they handled the wounded, with more coming in continuously as stretcher teams left for evacuation centers with those already given field first-aid.

We split up, moved apart a little, and sought shelter along the slope to await orders. I found a commodious two-man standing foxhole commanding a perfect wide view of the draw for a long distance right and left. It obviously had been used as a defensive position against any movement in the draw and probably had sheltered a couple of Japanese riflemen or perhaps a light machine gunner. The hole was well dug in dry clay soil; the ridge sloped up steeply behind it. But the hole and its surroundings were devoid of any enemy equipment or trash of any kind. There wasn't so much as an empty cartridge case or ammo carton to be seen. But there were enemy tracks in the soft soil thrown out of the hole, tracks of tabi sneakers and hobnail-sole field shoes.

The Japanese had become so security conscious they not only removed their dead when possible but sometimes even picked up their expended "brass" just as we did on a rifle range. Sometimes all we found were bloodstains on the ground where one had been killed or wounded. They removed everything they could when possible to conceal their casualties. But when they removed even empty cartridge cases, and we found only tracks, we got an eerie feeling—as though we were fighting a phantom enemy.

During their battle on the Motobu Peninsula in April, Marines of the 6th Division had seen evidence of increased security consciousness on the part of the Japanese. But we had seen nothing like it on Peleliu, and Guadalcanal veterans had told me nearly every Japanese they "field stripped" had a diary on him. The same was said about Gloucester.

After sitting out another thunderous barrage of friendly artillery fire, the three of us shouldered our weapons and moved along the ridge to rejoin Company K. Once together, our company formed into extended file and headed westward toward the regimental right flank. (I lost track of the date, as we moved about for several days.) The shell-blasted terrain was treeless and increasingly low and flat. We dug in, were shelled off and on, and were thoroughly bewildered as to where we were, other than we were said to be still somewhere in Wana Draw. Shuri loomed to our left front.

About that time Burgin was wounded. He was hit in the back of the neck by a shell fragment. Fortunately, he wasn't killed. Burgin was a Texan and as fine a sergeant as I ever saw. He was a Gloucester veteran whose luck had run out. We would miss him from the mortar section, and were delighted when he returned later after eighteen days of convalescence.

The weather turned cloudy on 21 May, and the rains began. By midnight the drizzle became a deluge. It was the beginning of a ten-day period of torrential rains. The weather was chilly and mud, mud, mud was everywhere. We slipped and slid along the trails with every step we took.

While the 1st Marine Division was fighting the costly, heartbreaking battle against the Wana positions, the 6th Marine Division (on the right and slightly forward) had been fighting a terrible battle for Sugar Loaf Hill. Sugar Loaf and the surrounding pieces of prominent terrain—the Horse Shoe and Half Moon— were located on the main ridge running from Naha to Shuri. Like Wana, they were key Japanese defensive positions in the complex that guarded the Shuri Heights.

During the morning of 23 May, the boundary between the 1st Marine Division and the 6th Marine Division shifted to the right (west) so the latter could rearrange its lines. The 3d Battalion, 5th Marines went into line on the right to take over the extended front.

I remember the move vividly, because we entered the worst area I ever saw on a battlefield. And we stayed there more than a week. I shudder at the memory of it.

We shouldered our weapons and gear and the column telescoped its way circuitously through muddy draws, slipping and sliding along the slopes of barren hills to avoid observation and consequent shelling by the enemy. It rained off and on. The mud got worse the farther we went. As we approached our destination, the Japanese dead, scattered about in most areas since 1 May, became more numerous.

When we had dug in near enemy dead and conditions permitted, we always shoveled soil over them in a vain effort to cut down the stench and to control the swarming flies. But the desperate fighting for ten days against and around Sugar Loaf Hill and the continued, prolonged Japanese artillery and mortar fire had made it impossible for the Marine units there to bury the enemy dead.

We soon saw that it also had been impossible to remove many Marine dead. They lay where they had fallen—an uncommon sight even to the veterans in our ranks. It was a strong Marine tradition to move our dead, sometimes even at considerable risk, to an area where they could be covered with a poncho and later collected by the graves registration people. But efforts to

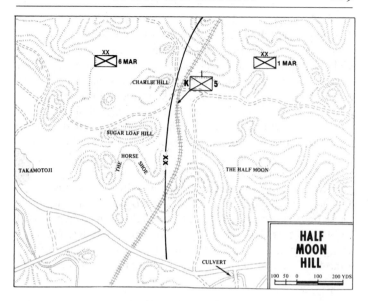

remove many Marines killed in the area we entered had been in vain, even after Sugar Loaf Hill had been captured following days of terrible fighting.

The rains had begun 21 May, almost as soon as Sugar Loaf Hill had been secured by men of the 6th Marine Division. Because of the deep mud, the able-bodied could scarcely rescue and evacuate their wounded and bring up vital ammo and rations. Regrettably, the dead had to wait. It couldn't have been otherwise.

We slogged along through a muddy draw around the base of a knoll. On our left we saw six Marine corpses. They were lying face down against a gentle muddy slope where they apparently had hugged the deck to escape Japanese shells. They were "bunched up"—in a row, side by side, scarcely a foot apart. They were so close together that they probably had all been killed by the same shell. Their browning faces lay against the mud in an even row. One could imagine the words of fear or reassurance that had been passed among them as they lay under the terror of the shelling. Each clutched a rusting rifle, and every sign indicated that those tragic figures were new replacements, fresh to the shock of combat.

The first man's left hand was extended forward, palm down. His fingers clutched the mud in a death grip. A beautiful, shiny gold watch was held in place around the decaying wrist by an elaborate gold metal stretch band. (Most of the men I knew —and myself—wore plain, simple luminous-dial, waterproof, shockproof wristwatches with a plain green cloth wristband.) How strange, I thought, for a Marine to wear a flashy, conspicuous watch while on the front lines, stranger still that some Japanese hadn't slipped out during a dark night and taken it.

As we filed past the dead Marines, each of my buddies turned his head and gazed at the horrible spectacle with an expression that revealed how much the scene inwardly sickened us all.

I had heard and read that combat troops in many wars became hardened and insensitive to the sight of their own dead. I didn't find that to be the case at all with my comrades. The sight of dead Japanese didn't bother us in the least, but the sight of Marine dead brought forth regret, never indifference.

HALF MOON HILL

While the artillery swished and whined overhead in both directions, we moved to our new positions in the westernmost extension of Wana Draw. By twos and threes, the Company K men forming the front line eased onto a barren, muddy, shell-torn ridge named Half Moon Hill and into the foxholes of the company we were relieving. Our mortar section went into place behind a low rise of ground below the ridge and about a hundred yards back of the front lines. The terrain between us and Half Moon was nearly flat. The little elevation behind which we emplaced our guns was so low that when we stood up beside the gun pit, we could see clearly up to the company's forward lines on the ridge.

Readily visible beyond that, to the left front, were the still higher, smoke-shrouded Shuri Heights, the heart of the Japanese defensive system. That ominous and formidable terrain feature was constantly under bombardment of varying intensity from our artillery, heavy mortars, and gunfire support ships. No matter, though. It didn't seem to deter the enemy observers from directing their artillery and heavy mortars in shelling our whole area frequently, every day and every night.

We faced south on Half Moon. A narrow-gauge railroad track lay a short distance to our right and ran south through a flat area between Half Moon and a ridge to our right known as the Horse Shoe. Beyond that it swung westward toward Naha. An officer told us that the ridge to our right (west) and slightly to our rear across the railroad was Sugar Loaf Hill.

Company K was on the right flank of 3/5 and moved up onto the western part of the base of Half Moon. The Japanese still occupied caves in both of the southward-pointing tips of the crescent. The right-flank foxhole of our company was dug on the crest at the western edge of the end of the base of Half Moon. Below it to the right the ridge dropped away to low flat ground.

Our company CP was situated in the sunken railroad bed to the right of our mortar section's position. A nice tarpaulin was stretched over the CP from one side of the railroad embankment to the other. This kept the post snug and dry while torrents of chilly rain kept shivering riflemen, machine gunners, and mortarmen soaked, cold, and miserable day and night in open foxholes. The rain greeted us as we moved into our assigned area.

The almost continuous downpour that started on 21 May turned Wana Draw into a sea of mud and water that resembled a lake. Tanks bogged down and even amtracs could not negotiate the morass. Living conditions on the front lines were pitiful. Supply and evacuation problems were severe. Food, water, and ammunition were scarce. Foxholes had to be bailed out constantly. The men's clothing, shoes, feet, and bodies remained constantly wet. Sleep was nearly impossible. The mental and physical strain took a mounting toll on the Marines.

Making an almost impossible situation worse were the deteriorating bodies of Marines and Japanese that lay just outside the foxholes where they had fallen during the five days of ferocious fighting that preceded Company K's arrival on Half Moon. Each day's fighting saw the number of corpses increase. Flies multiplied, and amoebic dysentery broke out. The men of Company K, together with the rest of the 1st Marine Division, would live and fight in that hell for ten days.

*

We dispersed our guns and dug gun pits as best we could in the mud. Snafu and I took compass readings and set aiming stakes based on the readings from our observer. As soon as we fired a couple of rounds of HE to register in my gun, it was obvious we had a bad problem with the base plate of our mortar being driven farther into the soft soil with the recoil of each shell. We reasoned the rain would soon stop, however, or if it didn't, a couple of pieces of ammo box under the base plate would hold it firm. What a mistake!

After digging in the gun, registering in on the aiming stakes, and preparing ammo for future use, I had my first opportunity to look around our position. It was the most ghastly corner of hell I had ever witnessed. As far as I could see, an area that previously had been a low grassy valley with a picturesque stream meandering through it was a muddy, repulsive, open sore on the land. The place was choked with the putrefaction of death, decay, and destruction. In a shallow defilade to our right, between my gun pit and the railroad, lay about twenty dead Marines, each on a stretcher and covered to his ankles with a poncho—a commonplace, albeit tragic, scene to every veteran. Those bodies had been placed there to await transport to the rear for burial. At least those dead were covered from the torrents of rain that had made them miserable in life and from the swarms of flies that sought to hasten their decay. But as I looked about, I saw that other Marine dead couldn't be tended properly. The whole area was pocked with shell craters and churned up by explosions. Every crater was half full of water, and many of them held a Marine corpse. The bodies lay pathetically just as they had been killed, half submerged in muck and water, rusting weapons still in hand. Swarms of big flies hovered about them.

"Why ain't them poor guys been covered with ponchos?" mumbled my foxhole buddy as he glanced grimly about with a distraught expression on his grizzled face. His answer came the moment he spoke. Japanese 75mm shells came whining and whistling into the area. We cowered in our hole as they crashed and thundered around us. The enemy gunners on the commanding Shuri Heights were registering their artillery and mortars on our positions. We realized quickly that anytime any of us moved out of our holes, the shelling began immediately. We had a terrible time getting our wounded evacuated through the shell fire and mud without the casualty- and stretcher-bearers getting hit. Thus it was perfectly clear why the Marine dead were left where they had fallen.

Everywhere lay Japanese corpses killed in the heavy fighting. Infantry equipment of every type, U.S. and Japanese, was scattered about. Helmets, rifles, BARs, packs, cartridge belts, canteens, shoes, ammo boxes, shell cases, machine-gun ammo belts, all were strewn around us up to and all over Half Moon.

The mud was knee deep in some places, probably deeper in others if one dared venture there. For several feet around every corpse, maggots crawled about in the muck and then were washed away by the runoff of the rain. There wasn't a tree or bush left. All was open country. Shells had torn up the turf so completely that ground cover was nonexistent. The rain poured down on us as evening approached. The scene was nothing but mud; shell fire; flooded craters with their silent, pathetic, rotting occupants; knocked-out tanks and amtracs; and discarded equipment—utter desolation.

The stench of death was overpowering. The only way I could bear the monstrous horror of it all was to look upward away from the earthly reality surrounding us, watch the leaden gray clouds go scudding over, and repeat over and over to myself that the situation was unreal—just a nightmare—that I would soon awake and find myself somewhere else. But the ever-present smell of death saturated my nostrils. It was there with every breath I took.

I existed from moment to moment, sometimes thinking death would have been preferable. We were in the depths of the abyss, the ultimate horror of war. During the fighting around the Umurbrogol Pocket on Peleliu, I had been depressed by the wastage of human lives. But in the mud and driving rain before Shuri, we were surrounded by maggots and decay. Men struggled and fought and bled in an environment so degrading I believed we had been flung into hell's own cesspool.

Not long after 3/5 took over Half Moon, several of us were on a work party, struggling through knee-deep mud to bring ammo from the rear up to the mortar positions. We passed near the company CP in the railroad bed.

"Hey, you guys, looka there; Stumpy's in bad shape!" said a Marine in an excited low voice. We all stopped and looked toward the CP. There was our CO, Stumpy Stanley, just outside the edge of the tarpaulin, trying to stand by himself. But he had to be supported by a man on each side. He looked haggard and weary and was shaking violently with malarial chills. He could barely hold up his head. The men supporting him seemed to be arguing with him. He was objecting as best he could. But it was a feeble effort, because he was so sick.

"Po' Stumpy got that goddamn bug so bad he can't hardly stand up. But looka there; he's all man, by God. He don't wanna be 'vacuated," said Snafu gravely.

"He's a damn good Joe," someone else said.

We thought highly of Stumpy and respected him greatly. He was a good skipper, and we had confidence in him. But malaria made him too ill to stay on his feet. The chilly rain, the emotional stress, and the physical exertion and strain of those days were enough to make a well man collapse. Obviously those who had malarial infections couldn't possibly keep going. So, for the second time in May, we lost our commanding officer. Stumpy was the last of our Peleliu officers, and his evacuation ended an era for me. He was the last tie to Capt. Andy Haldane. For me, Company K was never the same after that day.

As we feared, Shadow became the CO. It's best that I don't record what we said about that.

At daybreak the morning after we took over the line on Half Moon, George Sarrett and I went up onto the ridge to our observation post. Half Moon was shaped like a crescent, with the arms pointing southward. Our battalion line stretched along the crest of the ridge as it formed the base of the crescent. The arms extended outward beyond our front lines, and Japanese occupied caves in the reverse slopes of those arms, particularly the one on the left (east). They made our line a hot spot.

To our front, the ridge sloped down sharply from the crest then more gently all the way to a big road embankment approximately three hundred yards out and running parallel to our lines. A large culvert opened toward us through the embankment. The area to our front was well drained and as bare as the back of one's hand. It wasn't heavily cratered. Two shallow ditches about fifty yards apart ran across the area between the southern tips of the Half Moon. These ditches were closer to the road embankment than to our lines. The sloping area leading to the culvert resembled an amphitheater bordered by the base of the crescent (where we were) to the north, the arms of the crescent extending southward, and the high road embankment running east and west at the southern end. Our visibility within the amphitheater was perfect (except for the reverse slopes of the arms of the crescent).

Marines of 2/4 had warned us as they departed that the Japanese came out of the caves in the reverse slopes of the crescent's arms at night and generally raised hell. To combat that, our ships kept star shells aloft, and our 60mm mortars kept flares burning in the wet sky above the ridge all night every night we were there.

As the dawn light grew brighter, we could see the lay of the land through the drizzle and thin fog. So we registered the mortar section's three guns with an aiming stake on one of each of three important terrain features. We had one gun register in on the reverse slope of the left-hand extension of the Half Moon. A second mortar we registered on the reverse slope of the road embankment. We registered the third gun to cover the area around the mouth of the culvert.

No sooner had we registered the guns than we got a reaction. Big 90mm Japanese mortar shells began crashing along the crest of the ridge. They came so thick and so fast we knew an entire enemy mortar section was firing on us, not an isolated gun. They were zeroed in on the ridge and traversed along the crest from my left to the far right end of the company's line. It was an awful pounding. Each big shell fluttered and swished down and went off with a flash and an ear-splitting crash. Shrapnel growled through the air, and several men were wounded badly. Each shell threw stinking mud around when it exploded. The wounded were moved down behind the ridge with great difficulty because of the slippery, muddy slopes. A corpsman gave them aid, and they were carried to the rear—shocked, torn, and bleeding.

An uneasy quiet then settled along the line. Suddenly, someone yelled, "There goes one." A single Japanese soldier dashed out of the blackness of the culvert. He carried his bayoneted rifle and wore a full pack. He ran into the open, turned, and headed for shelter behind the tip of the southern end of the crescent arm on our left front. It looked as though he had about a thirty-yard dash to make. Several of our riflemen and BARmen opened up, and the soldier was bowled over by their bullets before he reached the shelter of the ridge. Our men cheered and yelled when he went down.

As the day wore on, more Japanese ran out of the culvert in ones and twos and dashed for the shelter of the same ridge extension. It was obvious they wanted to concentrate on the reverse slope there from where they could launch counterattacks, raids, and infiltration attempts on our front line. Obviously, it was to our best interest to stop them as quickly as possible. Any enemy soldier who made it in behind that slope might become one's unwelcome foxhole companion some night.

When the Japanese ran out of the culvert, our men fired on them and nearly always knocked them down. The riflemen, BARmen, and machine gunners looked on it as fine target practice, because we received no return small-arms fire, and the Japanese mortars were quiet.

I kept busy with the field glasses, observing, adjusting range, and calling fire orders onto the slope and the road embankment. I had the Tommy with me, but it wasn't as steady and accurate at the two- to three-hundred-yard range as an M1 Garand rifle. We had an M1 and an ammo belt in our OP, though, and I wanted to throw down that phone and the field glasses and grab up that M1 every time an enemy popped into view. As long as our mortar section was firing a mission, I had no choice but to continue observing.

The Japanese kept up their efforts to move behind the slope. Some made it, because our men missed them. Our 60mm mortar shells crashed away steadily on the target areas. We could see Japanese emerge from the culvert and be killed by our shells.

The longer this action continued without our receiving any return fire, the more relaxed my buddies became. The situation began to take on certain aspects of a rifle range, or more likely, an old-fashioned turkey shoot. My buddies started making bets about who had hit which Japanese. Lively arguments developed, but with rifles, BARs, and several machine guns firing simultaneously, no one could tell for sure who hit which enemy soldier.

The men yelled and joked more and more in one of their few releases from weeks of tension under the pounding of heavy weapons. So they began to get careless and to miss some of the Japanese scurrying for the slope. Shadow saw this. He ran up and down our firing line cursing and yelling at everybody. Then the men settled down and took more careful aim. Finally the enemy stopped coming, and I received orders to call "cease firing" to our mortars. We sat and waited.

During the lull, I moved over into the machine-gun emplacement next to our mortar OP to visit with the gunner. It contained a Browning .30 caliber water-cooled heavy machine gun manned by a gunner who had joined Company K as a replacement after Peleliu. On Pavuvu, he and I had become good friends. We called him "Kathy" after a chorus girl he knew in California. He was married and very much in love with his wife, so he bore a heavy burden of guilt because he had had an affair with Kathy on his way overseas and couldn't get her out of his mind.

As we sat alone in the machine-gun pit, he asked me whether I wanted to see a picture of Kathy. I said yes. He carefully and secretively picked up his rain-soaked combat pack and took out a waterproof plastic map holder. Folding back the canvas cover, he said, "Here she is."

My eyes nearly popped out of my head. The eight- by ten-inch photo was a full-length portrait of one of the most beautiful girls I ever saw. She was dressed, or undressed, in a scanty costume which exposed a good portion of her impressive physical endowments.

I gasped audibly, and "Kathy" said, "Isn't she a beauty?"

"She really is!" I told him, and added, "You've got a problem on your hands with a girl like that chorus girl and a wife you love." I kidded him about the possible danger of getting the letters to his wife and his girl crossed up and in the wrong envelopes. He just laughed and shook his head as he looked at the photo of the beautiful girl.

The scene was so unreal I could barely believe it: two tired, frightened young men sitting in a hole beside a machine gun in the rain on a ridge, surrounded with mud—nothing but stinking mud, with so much decaying human flesh buried or half buried in it that there were big patches of wriggling fat maggots marking the spots where Japanese corpses lay—looking at the picture of a beautiful seminude girl. She was a pearl in a mudhole.

Viewing that picture made me realize with a shock that I had gradually come to doubt that there really was a place in the world where there were no explosions and people weren't bleeding, suffering, dying, or rotting in the mud. I felt a sense of desperation that my mind was being affected by what we were experiencing. Men cracked up frequently in such places as that. I had seen it happen many times by then. In World War I they had called it shell shock or, more technically, *neurasthenia*. In World War II the term used was combat fatigue.

Strange that such a picture provoked such thoughts, but I vividly recall grimly making a pledge to myself. The Japanese might kill or wound me, but they wouldn't make me crack up. A peaceful civilian back home who sat around worrying about losing his mind probably didn't have much to occupy him, but in our situation there was plenty of reason for the strongest-willed individuals to crack up.

My secret resolve helped me through the long days and nights we remained in the worst of the abyss. But there were times at night during that period when I felt I was slipping. More than once my imagination ran wild during the brief periods of darkness when the flares and star shells burned out.

"There comes another one," somebody yelled. "Kathy" quickly stowed his picture in his pack, spun around, gripped the machine-gun handle in his left hand, poised his trigger finger, and grabbed the aiming knob with his right hand. His assistant gunner appeared from out of nowhere and jumped to his post to feed the ammo belt into the gun. I started back to the OP hole but saw that George had phone in hand, and the mortars were still "secured." So I grabbed up an M1 rifle "Kathy" had in the machine-gun emplacement.

I saw enemy soldiers rushing out of the culvert. Our line started firing as I counted the tenth Japanese to emerge. Those incredibly brave soldiers formed a skirmish line abreast, with a few yards between each other, and started trotting silently toward us across open ground about three hundred yards away. Their effort was admirable but so hopeless. They had no supporting fire of any kind to pin us down or even to make us cautious. They looked as though they were on maneuvers. They had no chance of getting close to us.

I stood up beside the machine gun, took aim, and started squeezing off shots. The Japanese held their rifles at port arms and didn't even fire at us. Everybody along our line was yelling and firing. The enemy soldiers wore full battle gear with packs, which meant they had rations and extra ammo, so this might be the beginning of a counterattack of some size.

Within seconds, eight of the ten enemy soldiers pitched forward, spun around, or slumped to the deck, dead where they fell. The remaining two must have realized the futility of it all, because they turned around and started back toward the culvert. Most of us slackened our fire and just watched. Several men kept firing at the two retreating enemy soldiers but missed, and it looked as though they might get away. Finally one Japanese fell forward near one of the shallow ditches. The surviving soldier kept going.

Just as "Kathy" got his machine-gun sights zeroed in on him, the order "cease firing" came along the line. But the machine gun was making so much noise we didn't hear the order. "Kathy" had his ammo belts loaded so that about every fifth cartridge was a tracer. He squeezed off a long burst of about eight shots. The bullets struck the fleeing Japanese soldier in the middle of his pack and tore into him between his shoulders.

I was standing directly behind "Kathy," looking along his machine-gun barrel. The tracers must have struck the man's vertebrae or other bones and been deflected, because I clearly saw one tracer flash up into the air out of the soldier's right shoulder and another tracer come out of the top of his left shoulder. The Japanese dropped his rifle as the slugs knocked him face down into the mud. He didn't move.

"I got him; I got the bastard," "Kathy" yelled, jumping around slapping me on the back, and shaking hands with his assistant gunner. He had reason to be proud. He had made a good shot.

The enemy soldier who fell near the ditch began crawling and flopped into it. Some of the men started firing at him again. The bullets kicked up mud all around the soldier as he slithered desperately along in the shallow ditch which didn't quite hide him. Machine-gun tracers ricocheted off the ground like vicious red arrows as the Japanese struggled along the shallow ditch.

Then, on one of the rare occasions I ever saw compassion expressed for the Japanese by a Marine who had to fight them, one of our men yelled, "Knock it off, you guys. The poor bastard's already hit and ain't got a snowball's chance in hell."

Someone else yelled angrily, "You stupid jerk; he's a goddamn Nip ain't he? You gone Asiatic or something?"

The firing continued, and bullets hit the mark. The wounded Japanese subsided into the muddy little ditch. He and his comrades had done their best. "They died gloriously on the field of honor for the emperor," is what their families would be told. In reality, their lives were wasted on a muddy, stinking slope for no good reason.

Our men were in high spirits over the affair, especially after being pounded for so long. But Shadow was yelling, "Cease firing, you dumb bastards." He came slipping and sliding along the line, cursing and stopping at intervals to pour out storms of invective on some smiling, muddy Marine. He carried his helmet in his left hand and periodically took off his cap and flung it down into the mud until it was caked. Each man looked glum and sat or stood motionless until Shadow had finished insulting him and moved on.

As Shadow passed the machine-gun pit, he stopped and screamed at "Kathy," who was still jumping around in jubilation over his kill. "Knock it off, you goddamn fool!" Then he glared at me and said, "You're supposed to be observing for the mortars; put that goddamn rifle down, you bastard."

I wasn't impetuous, but, had I thought I could get away with it, I would certainly have clubbed him over the head with that MI rifle.

I didn't, but Shadow's asinine conduct and comment did make me rash enough to say, "The guns are secured, sir. We were all sent out here to kill Nips, weren't we? So what difference does it make what weapon we use when we get the chance?"

His menacing expression turned into surprise and then doubt. With a quizzical look on his face, he cocked his head to one side as he pondered my remark, while I stood silently with the realization that I should have kept my mouth shut. The fine sergeant accompanying Shadow half glared and half smiled at me. Suddenly, without another glance, Shadow strode off along the ridge crest, cursing and yelling at the Marines in each foxhole as he passed them. I resolved to keep my mouth shut in the future.

As daylight waned, I looked out to our front through the drizzling rain falling through the still, foul air. A wisp of smoke rose straight up from the pack of the Japanese soldier "Kathy" had shot. The tracers had set something on fire. The thin finger of smoke rose high and then spread out abruptly to form a disc that appeared to rest on the column. So delicate and unreal, the smoke stood in the stagnant, fetid air like a marker over the corpse. Everything out there was motionless, only death and desolation among the enemy bodies.

George and I got orders to return to our mortar gun pits. Someone else would man the OP for the night. Getting back to the mortar emplacements from the company's front line was a major effort and an extremely dangerous one. From the moment we stepped to the rear of the crest of the ridge to descend the muddy slope, it was like trying to walk down a greased slide.

A large and unknown number of Japanese all over the ridge had been killed during the early counterattacks. They had been covered with soil as soon as possible. And Japanese were still being killed out front. Infiltrators also were being killed all along the ridge at night. Our men could only spade mud over them.

The situation was bad enough, but when enemy artillery shells exploded in the area, the eruptions of soil and mud uncovered previously buried Japanese dead and scattered chunks of corpses. Like the area around our gun pits, the ridge was a stinking compost pile.

If a Marine slipped and slid down the back slope of the muddy ridge, he was apt to reach the bottom vomiting. I saw more than one man lose his footing and slip and slide all the way to the bottom only to stand up horror-stricken as he watched in disbelief while fat maggots tumbled out of his muddy dungaree pockets, cartridge belt, legging lacings, and the like. Then he and a buddy would shake or scrape them away with a piece of ammo box or a knife blade.

We didn't talk about such things. They were too horrible and obscene even for hardened veterans. The conditions taxed the toughest I knew almost to the point of screaming. Nor do authors normally write about such vileness; unless they have seen it with their own eyes, it is too preposterous to think that men could actually live and fight for days and nights on end under such terrible conditions and not be driven insane. But I saw much of it there on Okinawa and to me the war was insanity.

CHAPTER THIRTEEN

Breakthrough

THE RAINS became so heavy that at times we could barely see our buddies in the neighboring foxhole. We had to bail out our gun pit and foxholes during and after each downpour or they filled with water.

Snafu and I dug a deep foxhole close to the gun pit and placed pieces of wooden ammo crates across braces set on the muddy clay at the bottom. At one end of this foxhole, beyond the extension of the boards, we dug a sump. As the surface water poured into our foxhole and down under the boards, we bailed out the sump with a C ration can for a day or two. But the soil became so saturated by continued downpours that water poured in through the four sides of the foxhole as though it were a colander. We then had to use a discarded helmet to bail out the sump, because the ration can couldn't take out water fast enough to keep up with that pouring in.

The board "floor" kept us out of the water and mud, provided we worked diligently enough at the bailing detail. Necessity being the mother of invention, we had "reinvented" the equivalent of duckboards commonly used in flooded World War I trenches. The duckboards pictured and described in 1914–18 in Flanders were, of course, often prefabricated in long sections and then placed in the trenches by infantrymen. But the small board floor we placed in our foxhole served the same function.

Continued firing finally caused my mortar's base plate to drive the pieces of wood supporting it deep into the mud in the bottom of the gun pit. We couldn't sight the gun properly. We tugged and pulled the gun up out of the mud, then it was a choice of emplacing it either on some firmer base in the gun pit or on the surface outside. The latter prospect would have meant sure death from the enemy shelling, so we had to come up with something better in a hurry.

Somebody got the bright idea of building a "footing" on which to rest the base plate. So in the bottom of the gun pit, we dug out a deep square hole larger than the base plate and lined it with boards. We next placed several helmets full of coral gravel we found in the side of the railroad bed into the footing. We set the mortar's base plate on the firm coral footing, resighted the gun, and had no more trouble with recoil driving the base plate into the mud. I suppose the other two squads in our mortar section fixed their guns' base plates in the same manner.

The Japanese infantry kept up their activity to our front and tried to infiltrate our lines every night, sometimes with success. Snafu made good about then on the threat he had made to the CP on Peleliu about any enemy headed toward the Company K CP. On Peleliu one night after we came off the lines Snafu shot two Japanese with his Thompson. He had killed one and fatally wounded the other. A sergeant made Snafu bury the dead soldier. Snafu objected strenuously because he said, and rightly so, if he hadn't shot the Japanese they would have kept on going right into the company CP. Sarge said maybe so, but the corpse had to be buried, and since Snafu had shot it, he must bury it. Snafu promised he would never shoot another enemy soldier headed for the CP.

One day as dawn broke with a thin fog and a pelting rain, Snafu woke me out of the nearest thing to sleep that could be attained in that miserable place with, "Halt who goes there? What's the password?"

Jolted out of my fatigue stupor, I saw Snafu's face silhouetted against the gray sky. Rain poured off his helmet, and drops of moisture on the end of each whisker of the thick stubbly beard on his jutting square jaw caught the dim light like glass beads. I snatched the Tommy up off my lap as he raised his .45 pistol and aimed it toward two dim figures striding along about twenty yards away. Visibility was so poor in the dim light, mist, and rain that I could tell little about the shadowy figures other than they wore U.S. helmets. At the sound of Snafu's challenge, the two men speeded up instead of halting and identifying themselves.

"Halt or I'll fire!" he yelled.

The two took off for the railroad bed as fast as they could on the slippery ground. Snafu fired several shots with his .45 but missed. Shortly we heard a couple of American grenades explode in the railroad bed. Then a buddy yelled that the Japanese had been killed by his grenades. Daylight came rapidly, so we went over to the railroad embankment to ask what had happened.

When Snafu and I got to the foxhole by the railroad embankment, we found two Marine snipers grinning and laughing. The grenade explosions had scared awake the Marines in the dryness under the tarpaulin in the company CP and had chased them out into the rain. They were drifting back to the shelter as we arrived. We waved, but got only glares in return.

We took a look at the dead enemy before returning to our foxhole. They had been wearing Marine helmets but otherwise were dressed in Japanese uniforms. A grenade had exploded in the face of one. There was no face and little head remaining. The other wasn't as badly mangled.

Snafu and I returned to our hole and got settled just in time to see Hank come stalking along from the CP. He was stopping at every foxhole along the way to find out who had been so negligent as to let the Japanese soldiers get past them and almost to the CP. Hank arrived at our foxhole and asked us why we hadn't seen the two soldiers pass if one of us was on watch as we were supposed to be.

Snafu spoke up immediately and said, "Hell, I saw 'em go right by here, but I reckoned they was headed for the company CP." (He didn't mention his challenging the Japanese or firing at them.)

Hank looked astonished and said, "What do you mean, Snafu?"

Snafu swelled with indignation and answered, "You remember when they made me bury that Nip I shot on Peleliu when them two was headed for the CP?"

"Yeah, so what?" answered Hank in a low, menacing voice.

"Well, I told them then if they made me bury 'im, then by God, next time I seen a Nip headin' for the CP I wasn't gonna' stop 'im!"

I groaned in a low voice, "Oooh, shut up, Snafu."

One didn't talk like that to a senior NCO and get away with it. Hank was a very formidable person and merited the tremendous respect we felt for him, but woe be unto the Marine who didn't do a task properly and incurred his wrath. Hank treated us with respect and compassion—if we followed orders and did our best. I had no desire to see what he would do to someone who didn't, but I thought I was about to. So I turned my head and half closed my eyes, as did all the awestruck men in the foxholes within earshot who had been watching Snafu and Hank.

Nothing happened. I glanced at Snafu and Hank as they stood there glaring at each other, a bantam rooster glaring up at a mighty eagle.

Finally Hank said, "You'd better not let that happen again!" He turned and stalked back to the CP.

Snafu mumbled and grumbled. The rest of us sighed with relief. I fully expected Hank at least to order Snafu to bury the two Japanese down there on the railroad, and then Snafu, as my corporal, would order me onto the burial detail as had happened on Peleliu. But he didn't, and someone else spaded mud over the two corpses.

Much later, when Hank was leaving Company K for home after an outstanding record in three campaigns, I asked him what he had thought about that incident. He just looked at me and grinned, but wouldn't say anything about it. His grin revealed, however, that he respected Snafu and knew he wasn't lax in any way, and probably that he himself had been ordered by some officer to look into the affair.

Because of the surroundings, our casualties during the stalemate on Half Moon were some of the most pathetic I ever had seen. Certainly a beautiful landscape didn't make a wound less painful or a death less tragic. But our situation before Shuri was the most awful place conceivable for a man to be hurt or to die.

Most of the wounds resulted from enemy shell fragments, but it seemed to me we had more than the usual number of cases of blast concussion from exploding shells. That was understandable because of the frequent heavy shellings we were subjected to. All the casualties were muddy and soaking wet like the rest of us. That seemed to accentuate the bloody battle dressings on their wounds and their dull expressions of shock and pain which made the horror and hopelessness of it all more vivid as we struggled through the chilly driving rain and deep mud to evacuate them.

Some of the concussion cases could walk and were helped and led (some seemed to have no sure sense of direction) to the rear like men walking in their sleep. Some wore wild-eyed expressions of shock and fear. Others whom I knew well, though could barely recognize, wore expressions of idiots or simpletons knocked too witless to be afraid anymore. The blast of a shell had literally jolted them into a different state of awareness from the rest of us. Some of those who didn't return probably never recovered but were doomed to remain in mental limbo and spend their futures in a veteran's hospital as "living dead."

The combat fatigue cases were distressing. They ranged in their reactions from a state of dull detachment seemingly unaware of their surroundings, to quiet sobbing, or all the way to wild screaming and shouting. Stress was the essential factor we had to cope with in combat, under small-arms fire, and in warding off infiltrators and raiders during sleepless, rainy nights for prolonged periods; but being shelled so frequently during the prolonged Shuri stalemate seemed to increase the strain beyond that which many otherwise stable and hardened Marines could endure without mental or physical collapse. From my experience, of all the hardships and hazards the troops had to suffer, prolonged shell fire was more apt to break a man psychologically than anything else.

In addition to the wounded, quite a number of men were evacuated and described in the muster rolls simply as "sick." Some of them suffered attacks of malaria. Others had fever, respiratory problems, or were just exhausted and seemed to have succumbed to the rigors of exposure and the chilly rains. There were numerous cases of pneumonia. Many men weren't evacuated, although they suffered serious ailments resulting from the cold rains and being soaking wet for more than a week.

Most of us had serious trouble with our feet. An infantryman with sore feet was in miserable shape under the best of living conditions. During a period of about fourteen or fifteen days, as near as I can calculate the time (from 21 May to 5 June), my feet and those of my buddies were soaking wet, and our boondockers were caked with sticky mud. Being up on the line and frequently shelled prevented a man from taking off his boondockers to put on a pair of dry socks. And even if he had dry socks, there was no way to clean and dry the leather boon-dockers. Most of us removed our mud-caked canvas leggings and tucked our trouser cuffs into our sock tops, but it didn't help our feet much. Consequently most men's feet were in bad condition.

My feet were sore, and it hurt to walk or run. The insides of my boondockers gave me the sensation of being slimy when I wiggled my toes to try to warm my feet with increased circulation. The repulsive sensation of slippery, slimy feet grew worse each day. My sore feet slid back and forth inside my soaked boondockers when I walked or ran. Fortunately they never became infected, a miracle in itself.

Sore feet caused by prolonged exposure to mud and water was called immersion foot, I learned later. In World War I they called the same condition trench foot. To me it was an unforgettable sensation of extreme personal filth and painful discomfort. It was the kind of experience that would make a man sincerely grateful for the rest of his life for clean, dry socks. As simple a condition as dry socks seemed a luxury.

The almost constant rain also caused the skin on my fingers to develop a strange shrunken and wrinkled appearance. My nails softened. Sores developed on the knuckles and backs of both hands. These grew a little larger each day and hurt whenever I moved my fingers. I was always knocking the scabs off against ammo boxes and the like. Similar sores had tormented combat troops in the South Pacific campaigns and were called jungle rot or jungle sores.*

Our own mail came up to us in canvas bags, usually with the ammo and rations. It was of tremendous value in boosting sagging morale. On several occasions I actually had to bend over my letters and read as rapidly as possible to shield them from the torrents of rain before the ink was smeared across the soggy paper and the writing became illegible.

---

*After the campaign on Okinawa ended, a battalion surgeon told me the sores on my hands were probably caused by malnutrition, the filth we lived in, or both. The festering sores that developed on my hands in late May didn't heal until nearly five months after we came out of combat.

Most of us received letters from family and civilian friends. But occasionally we received letters from old Company K buddies who had returned to the States. Their early letters expressed relief over being back with family or with "wine, women, and song." But later the letters often became disturbingly bitter and filled with disillusionment. Some expressed a desire to return if they could get back into the old battalion. Considering the dangers and hardships those men had been through before they were sent home, and considering our situation in front of Shuri, the attitudes of our buddies who had returned Stateside puzzled us.

They expressed themselves in various ways, but the gist of their disillusionment was a feeling of alienation from everyone but their old comrades. Although there was gasoline and meat rationing back in the States, life was safe and easy. Plenty of people were ready to buy a Marine combat veteran wearing campaign ribbons and battle stars a drink or a beer anytime. But all the good life and luxury didn't seem to take the place of old friendships forged in combat.

There was talk of war profiteers and able-bodied men who got easy duty at the expense of others. Some letters said simply that folks back in the States "just don't understand what the hell it's all about, because they have had it so easy." I heard more than one buddy express the opinion, as we sat in the mud, that civilians would "understand" if the Japanese or the Germans bombed an American city. Some men thought that would have been a good idea *if* no American civilians got killed, just scared. But nobody wanted it to be *his* hometown.

It was hard to believe that some of our old friends who had wanted so much to return home actually were writing us that they thought of volunteering again for overseas duty. (Some actually did.) They had had enough of war, but they had greater difficulty adjusting to civilians or to comfortable Stateside military posts. We were unable to understand their attitudes until we ourselves returned home and tried to comprehend people who griped because America wasn't perfect, or their coffee wasn't hot enough, or they had to stand in line and wait for a train or bus.

Our buddies who had gone back had been greeted enthusiastically—as those of us who survived were received later
on. But the folks back home didn't, and in retrospect couldn't
have been expected to, understand what we had experienced,
what in our minds seemed to set us apart forever from anyone who hadn't been in combat. We didn't want to indulge in
self-pity. We just wished that people back home could understand how lucky they were and stop complaining about trivial
inconveniences.

Siegfried Sassoon, an English combat infantry officer and
poet in World War I, experienced the same feeling when he
returned home. He summed it up in the following verse:

> You smug-faced crowds with kindling eye
> Who cheer when soldier lads march by,
> Sneak home and pray you'll never know
> The hell where youth and laughter go.*

The poet might just as well have been referring to Peleliu or
to the mudfields in front of Shuri as to France in World War I.

Some of the younger replacements who came to us then
had trouble adjusting, and not just to the shelling. That was
enough to shake up the strongest veteran, but they were utterly dismayed by our horrible surroundings. Numerous Marine replacements for combat units on Okinawa never had their
names added to their units' muster rolls, because they got hit
before notice of their transfer from their replacement draft
to the combat unit ever reached Headquarters, U.S. Marine
Corps. So they were listed on the casualty rolls as members of
various replacement drafts.

It was also common throughout the campaign for replacements to get hit before we even knew their names. They came
up confused, frightened, and hopeful, got wounded or killed,
and went right back to the rear on the route by which they had
come, shocked, bleeding, or stiff. They were forlorn figures
coming up to the meat grinder and going right back out of it
like homeless waifs, unknown and faceless to us, like unread

---

*Sassoon, Siegfried, "Suicide in the Trenches" in *Collected Poems*, Viking
Press, N.Y. 1949.

books on a shelf. They never "belonged" to the company or made any friends before they got hit.

Of course, those replacements who got hit right away with the "million-dollar wound" were actually fortunate.*

Our food usually consisted of a cold can of C rations and, rarely, a canteen cup of hot coffee. When we could brew it up, it was a treat. It was difficult to warm anything with our little heat tablets because of the almost constant rain. Sometimes I had to hunch over and shield a can of C-ration stew from the rain, because the can would fill up with rainwater as fast as I spooned the cold stew into my mouth.

We ate only because hunger forced us to do so. No other stimulus could have forced me to eat when my nostrils were so saturated with the odor of decay that I frequently felt sick. I ate little during that period, but drank hot coffee or bouillon at every opportunity.

The constant rain caused our weapons to rust. Most of us lined the holsters for our .45 automatic pistols with the green plastic covers we were issued. These came in long sleevelike pieces and could be placed over carbines, rifles, and Tommy guns. We kept a plastic hood draped over our mortar when it wasn't in use. This plastic cover was issued to be placed over ourselves while crouching down to avoid being sprayed with mustard gas, should that weapon have been used by the Japanese. We kept our weapons heavily oiled and actually had little trouble with them considering the battlefield conditions.

Field sanitation was nonexistent because of the shelling and the mud. Each man simply used a grenade canister or ammo carton and threw his own waste out into the already foul mud around his foxhole.

By day the battlefield was a horrible scene, but by night it became the most terrible of nightmares. Star shells and flares illuminated the area throughout the nights but were interspersed with moments of chilling, frightening blackness.

---

*K/3/5 landed at full strength of 235 officers and men on 1 April 1945. The company joined 250 replacements during the campaign for a total of 485 serving. Of the fifty men left at the end of the campaign, only twenty-six had made the landing.

Sleep was almost impossible in the mud and cold rain, but sometimes I wrapped my wet poncho around me and dozed off for brief periods while my foxhole mate was on watch and bailing out the hole. One usually had to attempt sleep while sitting or crouching in the foxhole.

As usual, we rarely ventured out of our foxholes at night unless to care for wounded or to get ammunition. When a flare or star shell lighted the area, everyone froze just as he was, then moved during the brief periods of darkness. When the area lighted up with that eerie greenish light, the big rain drops sparkled like silver shafts as they slanted downward. During a strong wind they looked as though they were being driven along almost horizontal to the deck. The light reflected off the dirty water in the craters and off the helmets and weapons of the living and the dead.

I catalogued in my mind the position of every feature on the surrounding terrain. There was no vegetation, so my list consisted of mounds and dips in the terrain, foxholes of my comrades, craters, corpses, and knocked-out tanks and amtracs. We had to know where everyone, living and dead, was located. If one of us fired at an enemy infiltrating or on a raid, he needed to know where his comrades were so as not to hit them. The position and posture of every corpse was important, because infiltrating Japanese also would freeze when illuminating shells lit up. So they might go unnoticed among the dead.

The longer we stayed in the area, the more unending the nights seemed to become. I reached the state where I would awake abruptly from my semisleep, and if the area was lit up, note with confidence my buddy scanning the terrain for any hostile sign. I would glance about, particularly behind us, for trouble. Finally, before we left the area, I frequently jerked myself up into a state in which I was semiawake during periods between star shells.

I imagined Marine dead had risen up and were moving silently about the area. I suppose these were nightmares, and I must have been more asleep than awake, or just dumbfounded by fatigue. Possibly they were hallucinations, but they were strange and horrible. The pattern was always the same. The dead got up slowly out of their waterlogged craters or off the mud and, with stooped shoulders and dragging feet, wandered around aimlessly, their lips moving as though trying to tell me something. I struggled to hear what they were saying. They seemed agonized by pain and despair. I felt they were asking me for help. The most horrible thing was that I felt unable to aid them.

At that point I invariably became wide awake and felt sick and half-crazed by the horror of my dream. I would gaze out intently to see if the silent figures were still there, but saw nothing. When a flare lit up, all was stillness and desolation, each corpse in its usual place.

Among the craters off the ridge to the west was a scattering of Marine corpses. Just beyond the right edge of the end foxhole, the ridge fell away steeply to the flat, muddy ground.* Next to the base of the ridge, almost directly below me, was a partially flooded crater about three feet in diameter and probably three feet deep. In this crater was the body of a Marine whose grisly visage has remained disturbingly clear in my memory. If I close my eyes, he is as vivid as though I had seen him only yesterday.

The pathetic figure sat with his back toward the enemy and leaned against the south edge of the crater. His head was cocked, and his helmet rested against the side of the crater so that his face, or what remained of it, looked straight up at me. His knees were flexed and spread apart. Across his thighs, still clutched in his skeletal hands, was his rusting BAR. Canvas leggings were laced neatly along the sides of his calves and over his boondockers. His ankles were covered with muddy water, but the toes of his boondockers were visible above the surface. His dungarees, helmet, cover, and 782 gear appeared new. They were neither mud-spattered nor faded.

I was confident that he had been a new replacement. Every

---

*The flat, muddy, cratered landscape to the west of Half Moon Hill was a no-man's-land to the railroad and beyond to the Horse Shoe and Sugar Loaf Hill, where the left flank of the 6th Marine Division was located. At no time did I see any Americans in that low, flooded ground astride the railroad. Thus a gap of considerable size existed between the 1st and 6th Marine Divisions.

An officer told me that machine guns and strong points to the right rear covered the area. He said the low flat terrain was so vulnerable to Japanese fire from the heights of Shuri that extending the lines to meet on that flooded ground would have sentenced the men involved to sure death. At night star shells illuminated the area so that the enemy couldn't infiltrate across it.

aspect of that big man looked much like a Marine "taking ten" on maneuvers before the order to move out again. He apparently had been killed early in the attacks against the Half Moon, before the rains began. Beneath his helmet brim I could see the visor of a green cotton fatigue cap. Under that cap were the most ghastly skeletal remains I had ever seen—and I had already seen too many.

Every time I looked over the edge of that foxhole down into that crater, that half-gone face leered up at me with a sardonic grin. It was as though he was mocking our pitiful efforts to hang on to life in the face of the constant violent death that had cut him down. Or maybe he was mocking the folly of the war itself: "I am the harvest of man's stupidity. I am the fruit of the holocaust. I prayed like you to survive, but look at me now. It is over for us who are dead, but you must struggle, and will carry the memories all your life. People back home will wonder why you can't forget."

During the day I sometimes watched big rain drops splashing into the crater around that corpse and remembered how as a child I had been fascinated by rain drops splashing around a large green frog as he sat in a ditch near home. My grandmother had told me that elves made little splashes like that, and they were called water babies. So I sat in my foxhole and watched the water babies splashing around the green-dungaree-clad corpse. What an unlikely combination. The war had turned the water babies into little ghouls that danced around the dead instead of little elves dancing around a peaceful bullfrog. A man had little to occupy his mind at Shuri—just sit in muddy misery and fear, tremble through the shellings, and let his imagination go where it would.

One of the very few humorous incidents I saw during those terrible days before Shuri occurred toward the end of the awful stalemate. Two Marines from the other mortar squad were dug in to the left of my gun pit. One morning at the first pale light of dawn I heard a commotion in their foxhole. I could hear a poncho being flung aside as someone began thrashing around. There were grunts and swearing. I strained my eyes through the steaming rain and brought the Tommy gun up to my shoulder. From all indications, one or more Japanese had slipped up on the weary occupants of the foxhole, and they were locked in a life and death struggle. But I could do nothing but wait and alert other men around us.

The commotion grew louder, and I could barely make out two dark figures struggling in the foxhole. I was utterly helpless to aid a buddy in distress, because I couldn't identify who was Marine and who was Japanese. None of us dared leave his own foxhole and approach the two. The enemy soldier must have already knifed one of the Marines and was grappling with the other, I thought.

The dark figures rose up. Standing toe to toe, they leaned into each other and exchanged blows with their fists. Everyone's eyes were fixed on the struggling figures but could see little in the semidarkness and pouring rain. The mumblings and swearing became louder and understandable, and we heard, "You dumb jerk; gimme that range card. It's mine." I recognized the voice of a man who had come into Company K before Okinawa.

"No it's not; it's mine. You betta gimme it. I don't take no crap from nobody." The latter was the familiar voice of Santos, a Peleliu veteran. We all started in surprise.

"Hey, you guys, what the hell's goin' on over there?" growled an NCO.

The two struggling figures recognized his voice and immediately stopped hitting each other.

"You two eightballs," the NCO said as he went over to them. "It woulda served ya right if we hada shot you both. We figured a Nip had got in your foxhole."

Each of the two battlers protested that the other was the cause of all the trouble. The light was good by then, and some of us went over to their foxhole to investigate.

"What's all the row about?" I asked.

"This, by God; nothin' but this!" snarled the NCO as he glared at the two sheepish occupants of the foxhole and handed me a range card.

I was puzzled why two Marines would squabble over a range card.* But when I looked at the card, I saw it was special and

---

*A five- by seven-inch range card came in each canister of 60mm mortar ammunition. It contained printed columns of numbers denoting range, sight setting, and number of powder increments to be attached to each mortar shell for a given range. Thus the cards were as common as ammo canisters.

unique. Impressed on it in lipstick was the ruby red imprint of a woman's lips. The men had found the unique card in a canister while breaking out ammo for the guns the previous afternoon and had argued all night about who would keep it. Toward dawn they came to blows over it.

The NCO continued to chew them out, as I handed the card back to him and returned to my foxhole. We all got a good laugh out of the episode. I often wondered what that woman back in that ammunition factory in the States would have thought about the results of her efforts to add a little morale booster for us in a canister of mortar ammo.

During the last few days of May we received several small but vicious counterattacks from the Japanese soldiers who had been occupying the caves in the reverse slope of Half Moon's left-hand arm. One morning we got a message that a large number of enemy was massing behind the crescent. I was ordered to leave the OP and return to the gun pit in preparation for a big fire mission. I moved down the ridge and across the reeking, shell-pocked wasteland to the gun pits without mishap. Once there, we squared away the three 60mm mortars to fire on the reverse slope of the left crescent arm.

The firing pattern of the mortars was arranged to box in the Japanese and prevent their escape while our three guns shelled the area heavily in an attempt to wipe them out. Consequently, we had to fire rapid-fire, searching and traversing the target area. The ammo carriers were kept busy breaking out more HE shells, but I was so busy on my mortar I didn't have time to notice them. The tube (barrel) became intensely hot. We wrapped a dungaree jacket around the lower half of it, and one of the ammo carriers poured helmets full of water taken from a shell crater over the cloth to cool the steaming barrel, while we continued rapid-fire.*

---

*I've read accounts of "mortars glowing red" when firing rapidly for long periods. They sound dramatic and impressive. But from my experience I'm skeptical that a mortar can be fired safely and accurately when its barrel is glowing red. My experience was that if a barrel got very hot from rapid fire—so hot that the surrounding air had insufficient cooling effect—it was dangerous to drop a round down the tube. The one time I did, the heat ignited the increments, then the propellant cartridge ignited before the shell slid all the way down the

We fired I don't know how many hundreds of shells before the order came to cease firing. My ears rang. I was exhausted, and had a roaring headache. Beside each of the three gun pits was a huge stack of empty HE canisters and ammo crates from the large number of shells we had fired. We were anxious to know the results of our firing. But our observers couldn't see the target area, because it was on the reverse slope of the ridge.

A few days later when our regiment went forward in the attack, we didn't move through the target area, so we still didn't see the effects of the fire mission. But one Company K NCO who did see the area told us that he had counted more than two hundred enemy dead who apparently had been trapped and killed by our fire. I assume he was right, because after our barrage, the Japanese ceased activity along the ridge.

SHURI

The rain began to slacken, and rumors spread that we would attack soon. We also heard that the main enemy force had withdrawn from the Shuri line. But the Japanese had left a strong rear guard to fight to the death. So we could expect no signs of weakness. The Japanese had been spotted retreating from Shuri under cover of the bad weather. Our naval guns, artillery, heavy mortars, and even a few airplanes had thrown a terrific bombardment into them. But withdrawal or not, Shuri wasn't going to fall easily. We anticipated a hard fight once the weather cleared.

On a quiet day or two before the 5th Marines moved out for the big push against Shuri, several Marines from the graves registration section came into our area to collect the dead. Those dead already on stretchers presented no problem, but the corpses rotting in shell craters and in the mud were another matter.

---

barrel. Consequently, the shell wobbled out of the barrel and fell short after having slid down only about half its length.

Thus, to avoid short rounds, we either had to wait for the air to cool our barrel, fire at a slower rate, or, as in this fire mission, which was an emergency, cool the barrel with water.

We sat on our helmets and gloomily watched the graves registration people trying to do their macabre duty. They each were equipped with large rubber gloves and a long pole with a stiff flap attached to the end (like some huge spatula). They would lay a poncho next to a corpse, then place the poles under the body, and roll it over onto the poncho. It sometimes took several tries, and we winced when a corpse fell apart. The limbs or head had to be shoved onto the poncho like bits of garbage. We felt sympathy for the graves registration men. With the corpses being moved, the stench of rotting flesh became worse (if possible) than ever before.

Apparently the enemy had withdrawn guns and troops from Shuri to the extent that their shelling of our area had all but stopped. A miserable drizzling rain commenced again. Almost out on my feet with fatigue, I decided to take advantage of the quiet. I unfolded an unused stretcher, set it on some boards, lay down on my back, and covered my head and body with my poncho. It was the first time in two months—since leaving my canvas rack aboard ship on 1 April (D day)—that I had been able to lie down on anything but hard ground or mud. The canvas stretcher felt like a deluxe bed, and my poncho shielded all but my mud-caked boondockers and ankles from the rain. For the first time in about ten days I fell into a deep sleep.

How long I slept I don't know, but after a while I became aware of being lifted upward. At first I thought I was dreaming, but then I awoke fully and realized someone had picked up the stretcher. Throwing the poncho away from me, I sprang off the stretcher, spun around, and saw two clean, neatly shaven Marines looking at me in utter astonishment.

Several of my grimy buddies squatting on their muddy helmets nearby began to laugh. The two strangers were graves registration men. They had picked up the stretcher thinking I was just another poncho-covered corpse. It never occurred to them that instead, I was just a weary Marine trying to catch a nap on a comfortable stretcher who had covered himself to keep off the rain. They grinned when they realized what had happened. I accused my buddies of telling the two men to pick up my stretcher, but they only laughed and asked why my nap had ended so abruptly. I was left with an eerie feeling from the incident, but my buddies enjoyed the joke thoroughly.

Dawn broke clearly without rain on 28 May, and we prepared to attack later in the morning. About 1015 we attacked southward against long-range mortar and machine-gun fire. We were elated that the opposition was so light and that the sun was shining. We actually advanced several hundred yards that day, quite an accomplishment in that sector.

Moving through the mud was still difficult, but we were all glad to get out of the stinking, half-flooded garbage pit around the Half Moon. That night we learned that we would continue the attack the next day by moving directly against the Shuri Ridge.

About midmorning on 29 May, 3/5 attacked the Shuri with Company L in the lead and Companies K and I following closely. Earlier in the morning Company A, 1st Battalion, 5th Marines had attacked eastward into the rains of Shuri Castle and had raised the Confederate flag. When we learned that the flag of the Confederacy had been hoisted over the very heart and soul of Japanese resistance, all of us Southerners cheered loudly. The Yankees among us grumbled, and the Westerners didn't know what to do. Later we learned that the Stars and Stripes that had flown over Guadalcanal were raised over Shuri Castle, a fitting tribute to the men of the 1st Marine Division who had the honor of being first into the Japanese citadel.*

We all were filled with a sense of accomplishment that night as we dug in somewhere around Shuri Castle. We in the ranks were well aware of its strategic importance to the progress of the campaign.

Although the whole place was in ruins, we could still see that the area around Shuri Castle had been impressive and picturesque before its destruction by the incessant U.S. bombardment. Shuri Castle itself was a mess, and I couldn't tell much about its former appearance. It had been an ancient stone building surrounded by a moat and what appeared to

---

*For the assault against Shuri Castle, 1/5 and 3/5 actually attacked eastward, turning approximately ninety degrees to the left of the southward-facing front. The 5th Marines thus crossed over into the zone of the 77th Infantry Division to reach Shuri Castle. The 77th Infantry Division was located north of Shuri, and a large number of Japanese were still entrenched between the army division and the 5th Marines as the latter moved eastward behind the Japanese who were blocking the 77th Division's advance.

have been terraces and gardens. As we picked our way through
the rubble, I looked at the terraced stonework and shattered
blackened tree stumps. I thought it must have been a pretty
place once.

We dug in that night with the knowledge that even though
we were at last in Shuri Castle, there were strongly entrenched
Japanese still north of us in Wana Draw, east of us, and south of
us. The lines were terribly confused to many of us in the ranks,
and we assumed that the enemy could come at us from almost
any direction. But they remained quiet during the night, except for the usual raiders.

We attacked again the next day, and got shelled badly. I was
totally confused as to where we were for several days and can't
clarify it now in my mind even after careful study of the notes
and references at my disposal.

At dusk on one of those last few days of May, we moved
onto a muddy, slippery ridge and were told to dig in along the
crest. One of the three 60mm mortar squads was to set up its
gun down behind the ridge, but my squad and the remaining squad were ordered to dig in along the ridge crest and to
function as riflemen during the night. The weather turned bad
again, and it started raining.

Mac, our mortar section leader, was nowhere to be seen.
But Duke, who had been our section leader on Peleliu and
who was by then leading the battalion's 81mm mortar platoon,
came up to take charge. He ordered an NCO to have us dig
two-man foxholes five yards apart along the crest of the ridge.
My buddy went off down the ridge to draw ammo and chow
while I prepared to dig.

The ridge was about a hundred feet high, quite steep, and
we were on a narrow crest. Several discarded Japanese packs,
helmets, and other gear lay scattered along the crest. From the
looks of the muddy soil, the place had been shelled heavily for
a long time. The ridge was a putrid place. Our artillery must
have killed Japanese there earlier, because the air was foul with
the odor of rotting flesh. It was just like being back at Half
Moon Hill. Off toward our front, to the south, I had only a
dim view through the gathering gloom and curtain of rain of
the muddy valley below.

The men digging in on both sides of me cursed the stench and the mud. I began moving the heavy, sticky clay mud with my entrenching shovel to shape out the extent of the foxhole before digging deeper. Each shovelful had to be knocked off the spade, because it stuck like glue. I was thoroughly exhausted and thought my strength wouldn't last from one sticky shovelful to the next.

Kneeling on the mud, I had dug the hole no more than six or eight inches deep when the odor of rotting flesh got worse. There was nothing to do but continue to dig, so I closed my mouth and inhaled with short shallow breaths. Another spadeful of soil out of the hole released a mass of wriggling maggots that came welling up as though those beneath were pushing them out. I cursed, and told the NCO as he came by what a mess I was digging into.

"You heard him, he said put the holes five yards apart."

In disgust, I drove the spade into the soil, scooped out the insects, and threw them down the front of the ridge. The next stroke of the spade unearthed buttons and scraps of cloth from a Japanese army jacket buried in the mud—and another mass of maggots. I kept on doggedly. With the next thrust, metal hit the breastbone of a rotting Japanese corpse. I gazed down in horror and disbelief as the metal scraped a clean track through the mud along the dirty whitish bone and cartilage with ribs attached. The shovel skidded into the rotting abdomen with a squishing sound. The odor nearly overwhelmed me as I rocked back on my heels.

I began choking and gagging as I yelled in desperation, "I can't dig in here! There's a dead Nip here!"

The NCO came over, looked down at my problem and at me, and growled, "You heard him; he said put the holes five yards apart."

"How the hell can I dig a foxhole through a dead Nip?" I protested.

Just then Duke came along the ridge and said, "What's the matter, Sledgehammer?"

I pointed to the partially exhumed corpse. Duke immediately told the NCO to have me dig in a little to the side away from the rotting remains. I thanked Duke and glared at the

NCO. How I managed not to vomit during that vile experience I don't know. Perhaps my senses and nerves had been so dulled by constant foulness for so long that nothing could evoke any other response but to cry out and move back.

I soon had a proper foxhole dug to one side of the site of my first attempt. (A few spades full of mud thrown back into that excavation did little to reduce the horrid odor.) My buddy returned, and we began to square away our gear for the coming night. There was some small-arms fire to our left, but all was quiet around us. Duke was down at the foot of the ridge behind us with a map in his hand. He called us to come down for a critique and a briefing on the next day's attack.

Glad to leave the stinking foxhole, I got up and carefully started down the slippery ridge. My buddy rose, took one step down the ridge, slipped, and fell. He slid on his belly all the way to the bottom, like a turtle sliding off a log. I reached the bottom to see him stand erect with his arms partially extended and look down at his chest and belt with a mixed expression of horror, revulsion, and disbelief. He was, of course, muddy from the slide. But that was the least of it. White, fat maggots tumbled and rolled off his cartridge belt, pockets, and folds of his dungaree jacket and trousers. I picked up a stick and handed him another. Together we scraped the vile insect larvae off his reeking dungarees.

That Marine was a Gloucester veteran with whom I had often shared a hole on Peleliu and Okinawa. He was as tough and as hard as any man I ever knew. But that slide was almost too much for him. I thought he was going to scream or crack up. Having to wallow in war's putrefaction was almost more than the toughest of us could bear. He shook himself like a wet dog, however, cursed, and threw down the stick when we got him scraped free of maggots.

Duke's group of eight to ten Marines showed their sympathy for my buddy and their appreciation of the vileness of his accident. Muddy, bearded, and red-eyed with fatigue, Duke called our attention to the map, and that helped us focus on other subjects. He showed us where we were and told us some of the plans for the next day's attack, which was supposed to break completely through the Shuri line.

I was so revolted and sickened by what had just happened and so weary that I didn't remember much of what he told us. It is a pity in retrospect, because that briefing was the only time in my combat experience that an officer ever showed a group of privates a map of the battlefield and explained recent events and future attack plans. Usually an NCO simply relayed the word to us. We then followed orders as they were given, rarely knowing what was going on.

We never knew why Duke held the little critique that night, whether he was ordered to do so or not. I suspect he did it on his own. He realized we wanted to know and understand our role in the overall plan.

It was a historic time, and we were participating in events of key importance to the American effort on Okinawa. All eyes were on Shuri. My buddies and I were key participants at a critical juncture in one of the epic land battles of World War II, and we were having our tiny role in that battle explained. Duke asked if there were any questions. A few were asked, which he answered clearly. I maintained my condition of near stupefaction through it all. Then we slowly climbed back up the filthy ridge after he dismissed us.

That night the rain came down in torrents. It was without exaggeration the most terrific deluge I've ever seen. The wind blew fiercely, slashing the rain horizontally across the crest of the ridge and stinging our faces and hands. The star shells burst but gave little illumination because they were snatched away immediately by the unseen hand of the gale. Visibility was limited to about six feet. We couldn't see our buddies in their foxholes on either side of us. What a terrible night to grapple with Japanese infiltrators or a counterattack, I thought to myself all night long.

Considerable machine-gun fire, bursts of rifle fire, and grenade explosions erupted throughout the night a short way down the line to our left. But all was mercifully quiet, albeit tense, in our immediate area. Next morning I realized why we weren't molested by the enemy as the men to our left had been. For a considerable distance to our right and left, the ridge fell away almost perpendicularly to the valley below. The Japanese simply couldn't crawl up the slick surface.

*

In the latter days of May while the Japanese held on to the center of their line around Shuri, the U.S. Army divisions to the east and the 6th Marine Division to the west (around Naha) finally made progress to the south. Their combined movements threatened to envelop the main Japanese defense forces in the center. Thus the enemy had to withdraw. By dawn on 30 May, most of the Japanese Thirty-Second Army had departed the Shuri line, leaving only rear guards to cover their retreat.

In the sixty-one days of fighting on Okinawa after D day, an estimated 62,548 Japanese soldiers had lost their lives and 465 had been captured. American dead numbered 5,309; 23,909 had been wounded; and 346 were missing in action. It wasn't over yet.

CHAPTER FOURTEEN

Beyond Shuri

W E PUSHED past Shuri over some muddy hills in the army's zone of action and came across a group of about twenty Japanese prisoners. Each man was stripped except for a G-string. They stood barefooted in the mud alongside a trail winding along the slope of a barren hill. Several dirty and battle-weary army infantrymen guarded them. The captured enemy had been ordered by an interpreter (army lieutenant) to stand off the trail so Company K's column could pass.

We slipped and slid wearily toward the sound of firing up ahead. A grizzled rifleman in front of me and I had been cursing the mud and exchanging remarks about how glad we were to be past Shuri. Suddenly a Japanese prisoner stepped in front of my friend, blocking his way.

"Get outa the way, you crazy bastard," growled the Marine.

The soldier folded his arms calmly, raised his chin, and displayed a picture of arrogance. My buddy and I heated up fast. He pushed the Japanese backward and sent him sprawling into the mud. The enemy soldier sprang up quickly and assumed his former position.

"What's that crazy bastard doin'?" I yelled as I dropped my mortar ammo bag and reached for my .45 pistol.

My buddy unslung his rifle, grasped it by the stock with his left hand and by the pistol grip with his right hand. He planted his muddy feet firmly on the trail, flexed his knees, and growled, "Git outa my way, you bastard."

Other Marines behind us had halted when we did. Seeing what was happening, they started cursing the Japanese.

"What's the hold up? Move out," someone behind us yelled.

The army first lieutenant (he was actually wearing his silver bars on his collars), clean-shaven and spotless except for muddy combat boots, came along the column to ascertain the problem. Seeing my buddy's stance and realizing he might soon have one less prisoner, he said, "You can't mistreat these men. They are prisoners of war. According to the Geneva Code,

POWs must be treated humanely." He looked desperate; the whole column of muddy, raggedy-ass Marines glared at and cursed the prisoners strung out alongside us on the trail.

"Screw the Geneva Code. If that slant-eyed sonofabitch don't move outa my way, I'll give him a vertical butt stroke in his big mouth and knock out every one of them goddamn buck teeth." My buddy slowly moved his rifle back and forth, and the enemy soldier's arrogant expression began to fade. The army lieutenant knew he had a bad problem on his hands, and he obviously didn't know how to solve it. (It was commonly said that Marines rarely took prisoners.) A couple of GI riflemen of the prisoner-guard detail stood by relaxed and grinned their endorsement of our sentiments. They obviously had been in the "meat grinder" long enough to have no more love for the Japanese than we did. The lieutenant obviously wasn't one of their officers but from some rear-echelon outfit.

Just then, one of our officers hurried up from the rear of the column. The army lieutenant was mighty relieved to see him and explained the situation. Our officers went over and quietly told my buddy to get back into ranks. He then told the army language officer that if he didn't get his prisoners out of the way, he (our officer) couldn't guarantee that some of them wouldn't get hurt. The army officer spoke kindly in Japanese to the POWs, and they all stepped farther back away from the trail, giving us plenty of room. The language officer acted and sounded more like an elementary school teacher giving little children directions than an officer giving orders to a bunch of tough Japanese soldiers.

During the whole episode, most of the Japanese never appeared afraid, merely chagrined or ashamed because they had acted disgracefully by surrendering. Perhaps the one who acted so arrogantly thought that one last act of defiance would soothe his conscience somewhat. Most Americans at the time couldn't comprehend the Japanese determination to win or fight to the death. To the Japanese, surrender was the ultimate disgrace.

We didn't feel that POWs should be mistreated or handled roughly, but neither did we feel that one should be allowed to block our path and get away with the act. My view that some language officers were often overly solicitous about the comfort of prisoners and unduly courteous to them was shared by other infantrymen in the "meat grinder." We were too familiar with the sight of helpless wounded Americans lying flat on their backs on stretchers getting shot by Japanese snipers while we struggled to evacuate them.

After the breakthrough, we moved rapidly through areas where the opposition was light or absent. Our supply lines, communications, and casualty evacuation had a difficult time keeping up with us because the mud was still such a serious problem. Although the rain fell less frequently, it hadn't ceased.

As our column moved along the base of a road embankment on one occasion, a Marine walking along the road above us carrying a field telephone and a small roll of wire shouted down and asked for the identity of our unit. His buddy followed him along the road at a little distance carrying a roll of wire. These men were clean-shaven and neat. They looked suspiciously like rear-echelon people to us.

"Hey, what outfit you guys in?" shouted the first man up on the road.

"K/3/5," I yelled.

His buddy behind him asked him, "What outfit did he say?"

"K/3/5, whatever the hell that means."

The effect on us was instant and dramatic. Men who had paid little attention to what seemed a routine inquiry looked angrily up at the man. I flushed with anger. My unit and I had been insulted. The mortarman next to me threw down his ammo bag and started up the embankment. "I'll show you what the hell it means, you rear-echelon sonofabitch! I'm gonna whip your ass."

I wasn't given to brawling. The Japanese provided me with all the excitement and fighting I wanted. But I lost my head completely. I threw down my ammo bag and started up the embankment. Other mortarmen started up, too.

"What's the dope?" I heard a man back along the column shout.

"That rear-echelon bastard up there cussed K Company," someone answered.

Immediately other Company K men started up the bank. The two men up on the road looked utterly bewildered as they saw bearded, muddy Marine infantrymen cursing, grounding their weapons, dropping their loads, and surging angrily up the embankment. One of our officers and a couple of NCOs saw what had happened and rushed up ahead of us.

The officer turned and yelled, "You people get back in ranks on the double! Move! Move!"

We stopped, each of us knowing that to disobey orders invited severe disciplinary action. The two men on the road had become frightened, and we saw them hustling along the road to the rear. They looked back anxiously several times to see whether they were being followed. We must have been an angry, menacing-looking bunch from their viewpoint. I suspect those two Marines knew the real meaning and essence of esprit de corps after that experience.

We picked up our weapons and gear and moved out again below the road only to halt shortly. The officers consulted their maps, held a critique, and decided that place was as good as any for the company to leave the muddy low ground, go up the bank, and take advantage of the coral-surfaced road (probably the east–west Naha–Yonabaru highway, a segment of which our regiment captured about then). We moved up onto the road, took off our gear, and settled onto the side of a large ridge with a wide grass- and tree-covered crest. Okinawan burial vaults and emplacements lay all along the slope of the ridge, but the Japanese hadn't left many men to defend it. However, they gave a good account of themselves before being wiped out.

Toward dusk, I was examining a Japanese 75mm dual-purpose gun which they had abandoned in perfect condition. Several of us had a lot of fun turning its cranks and wheels, which we didn't understand but which moved the big barrel up and down, right and left. Our play was interrupted by the shriek of several enemy artillery shells that exploded up on the ridge crest near a group of Company K men.

"Corpsman!"

We raced up onto the ridge, hoping no more shells came in but wondering who was hit and knowing we might be needed to help with the casualties. We could see the smoke from the shells and the Marines scurrying around to aid the casualties and to disperse.

In the gathering twilight, I ran up to a little knot of Marines bending over a casualty. To my dismay, the wounded Marine was good-natured, cigar-chewing Joe Lambert, a demolitions expert I had known so long. I knelt beside him and was distressed to see that he had multiple wounds from shell fragments in his body.

The men had eased a poncho under Lambert and were preparing to carry him down the ridge for evacuation. I wished him luck, made the usual jokes about not being too romantic with the nurses on the hospital ship, and asked him to drink a beer and think of me when he got Stateside—the usual comments one made to a badly wounded friend who had little chance.

Lambert looked up at me in the gathering darkness. With the stump of an unlighted cigar clenched in his teeth, he said with irony in his voice, "Sledgehammer, ain't this a helluva' thing—a man been in the company as long as me, and hafta get carried out on a poncho?"

I made some feeble attempts to comfort him. I knew he was going to die, and I wanted to cry.

"Wish I could light that cigar for you, Cobber, but the smokin' lamp is out."

"That's OK, Sledgehammer."

"One of those good-lookin' nurses'll light it for you," I said as they picked up the poncho and started off down the slope of the ridge with him.

I stood up and looked at a nearby group of beautiful pines silhouetted against the darkening sky. The wind blew their fresh scent into my face, and I thought how much like Southern pine it smelled. But poor, brave Lambert would never get back home again. I was thankful that when his luck finally ran out and he was fatally wounded, it happened on a high, clear, grassy ridge crest near a clump of fragrant pines and not back in the stinking muck of the quagmire around Shuri.

Corporal Lambert was a great favorite in Company K. Any of us who had fought on Peleliu's Bloody Nose Ridge had seen him numerous times standing above some Japanese cave, swinging a satchel charge of explosives on a rope until he got it just right, then releasing the rope and yelling, "Fire in the hole"—just before the muffled explosion. He would grin, then climb down and rejoin us wringing wet with sweat from his face to his boondockers. He would relight his cigar (which served in turn as a lighter for his satchel-charge fuses) and discuss the damage done to the cave. He was big, round-faced, and jovial. Rumor said that he had been scheduled to return to the States after Peleliu but refused because he wanted to remain with Company K. Not long after he was carried out, we learned that Lambert had died. It's one of the war's many personal tragedies that he was killed after having served so long and so bravely.

Next day we moved out into a wide valley below the ridge. We saw Japanese equipment and dead on several roads destroyed by the big U.S. bombardment the last week of May when the enemy had evacuated Shuri. We also encountered numerous Japanese supply dumps. Most of the food and rations didn't suit our tastes. The Japanese iron rations, which I had seen first in gauze sacs on Peleliu, tasted like dog biscuits. But I found several cans of preserved Japanese deep-sea scallops which were delicious. Several cans of these stored in my pack were a welcome change from C and K rations.

We made one rapid advance across a wide grassy valley only to be halted by snipers in some rocks on the crest of the opposite ridge. We set up the guns, registered in on the areas where snipers were, and began firing. Stretcher teams came and went up and down the slope of the open ridge. Four of us were ordered off for a stretcher team to pick up a corpsman who had been hit by sniper fire.

We went up the gently sloping, grass-covered ridge and came to the "doc." Another stretcher team passed us carrying the Marine whom the doc had been tending when he himself was wounded. The Marine had been shot by a sniper, and the corpsman had come to administer medical aid. While he was working over the wounded Marine, a Japanese shot him in the thigh. Although wounded painfully, he continued to work on his patient. Then the sniper had shot Doc in the other thigh. As we arrived, he cautioned us to be careful or we would get hit, too.

We quickly got him on a stretcher and took off as fast as possible. Doc was a fairly tall, well-built man, larger than any of us. We carried him a long distance: down the ridge and across the wide valley to a steep-sided ditch spanned by a footbridge. An ambulance jeep was waiting on the other side of the footbridge. We were all nearly exhausted from the exertions and lack of sleep of the past two weeks, and it was quite a struggle. Twice wounded though he was, he kept insisting we stop and rest for a while. But we four felt obligated to get him to the jeep and evacuated as soon as possible.

Finally, we agreed to stop for a breather. Setting the stretcher down, we fell out flat on the grass, panting for breath. Doc talked to us calmly, admonishing us to take it easy and not to overexert ourselves. I felt ashamed. That unselfish, dedicated corpsman was more concerned because we were so tired from carrying him out than he was with his own wounds.

We picked up the stretcher and got to the ditch. There on the bank I saw a bush with several small red tomatoes. I managed to grab three or four tomatoes and put them on the stretcher as we got Doc across the narrow footbridge. I told him to eat them, that they'd make him feel better. He thanked me, but said we should eat them, because he would get good chow in the hospital.

Who should walk around the jeep just as we were loading our corpsman but Doc Arrogant, notorious for painful shots on Pavuvu. "I'll take those," he said, reaching for the tomatoes.

"The hell you say!" I exclaimed, snatching them out of his hand.

One of my buddies went up to him and said, "You bastard, you'd take candy from a baby, wouldn't ya?"

Arrogant looked surly, turned around, and went back around the jeep. Our Doc handed me the tomatoes and insisted we eat them. We said we would and wished him luck as the jeep bumped off to the rear.

We recrossed the footbridge and fell exhausted onto the grass. We had a smoke, divided up the juicy little tomatoes, cussed Doc Arrogant, and voiced our admiration for all other corpsmen.

On 4 June we moved rapidly southward through open country in a torrential rain. Although the opposition was sporadic, we still had to check out all houses, huts, and former Japanese emplacements. While searching a small hut, I came across an old Okinawan woman seated on the floor just inside the doorway. Taking no chances, I held my Thompson ready and motioned to her to get up and come out. She remained on the floor but bowed her old gray head and held her gnarled hands toward me, palms down, to show the tattoos on the backs of her hands indicating she was Okinawan.

"No Nippon," she said slowly, shaking her head as she looked up at me with a weary expression that bespoke of much physical pain. She then opened her ragged blue kimono and pointed to a wound in the lower left side of her abdomen. It was an old wound, probably caused by shell or bomb fragments. It was an awful sight. A large area around the scabbed-over gash was discolored and terribly infected with gangrene. I gasped in dismay. I guessed that such a severe infection in the abdominal region was surely fatal.

The old woman closed her kimono. She reached up gently, took the muzzle of my Tommy, and slowly moved it so as to direct it between her eyes. She then released the weapon's barrel and motioned vigorously for me to pull the trigger. Oh no, I thought, this old soul is in such agony she actually wants me to put her out of her misery. I lifted my Tommy, slung it over my shoulder, shook my head, and said "no" to her. Then I stepped back and yelled for a corpsman.

"What's up, Sledgehammer?"

"There's an old gook woman in there that's been hit in the side real bad."

"I'll see what I can do for her," he said as we met about fifty yards from the hut.

At that moment, a shot rang out from the hut. I spun around. The corpsman and I went down into a crouching position.

"That was an M1," I said.

"Sure was. What the hell?" he said.

Just then a Marine emerged nonchalantly from the hut, checking the safety on his rifle. I knew the man well. He was attached at that time to company headquarters. I called to him by name and said, "Was there a Nip in that hut? I just checked it out."

"No," he said as we approached him, "just an old gook woman who wanted me to put her out of her misery; so I obliged her!"

The doc and I stared at each other, and then at the Marine. That quiet, neat, mild-mannered young man just wasn't the type to kill a civilian in cold blood.

When I saw the crumpled form under the faded blue kimono in the hut door, I blew up. "You dumb bastard! She tried to get me to shoot her, and I called Doc to come help her."

The executioner looked at me with a puzzled expression.

"You sonofabitch," I yelled. "If you want to shoot at somebody so damn bad, why don't you trade places with a BAR-man or a machine gunner and get outa that damn CP and shoot at Nips? They shoot back!"

He stammered apologies, and Doc cursed him.

I said, "We're supposed to kill Nips, not *old women*!"

The executioner's face flushed. An NCO came up and asked what happened. Doc and I told him. The NCO glared and said, "You dirty bastard."

Somebody yelled, "Let's go Sledgehammer, we're movin' out."

"You guys shove off, I'll take care of this," said the NCO to Doc and me. We ran off to catch up with the mortar section while the NCO continued to chew out the executioner. I never knew whether or not he was disciplined for his cold-blooded act.

On the right of the 1st Marine Division, the 7th Marines extended its lines to the west coast and sealed off the Oroku Peninsula. Then the 6th Marine Division came in and fought a ten-day battle of attrition to annihilate the Japanese defenders there. The division killed nearly 5,000 Japanese, taking only 200 prisoners, at a loss of 1,608 Marines killed and wounded.

On 4 June, the 1st Marines relieved the 5th Marines as the assault regiment for the 1st Marine Division's drive to the south. The 5th Marines went into reserve for III Marine Amphibious Force, a stance that still involved much danger for its weary Marines because of a mission to aggressively patrol and mop up behind the forward elements.

We dug in as a secondary line along a low ridge with some ruins of Okinawan houses behind us and a broad open valley stretching south to our front as far as we could see. The rain ended the night of 5–6 June. I'll never forget the sensation of profound physical relief when I removed my soaked, muddy boondockers for the first time in approximately two weeks. As

I pulled off my slimy, stinking socks, bits and shreds of dead flesh sloughed off the soles of my feet. A buddy, Myron Tesreau, commented on the overpowering odor, only to discover that his feet were just as bad. My socks, a pair of khaki-colored, woolen army socks (thicker and heavier than our white Marine Corps issue) were so slimy and putrid I couldn't bear to wash them in my helmet. I had traded a candy bar to a soldier for them back in April. They were my prized possession because of their comfort when wet. With regret, I threw my prize socks aside and spaded dirt over them as though covering up a foul corpse.

It was great to wash my feet, holding them up on an ammo box to let the sun shine on them while I wiggled my toes. Everybody got his feet clean and dry as soon as possible. Mine were extremely sore and red over the entire soles, almost to the point of bleeding. All of the normal friction ridges of the skin had sloughed off, and the soles were furrowed with deep, reddish grooves. But after drying them in the sun and putting on dry socks and boondockers, they soon felt better. Months passed, however, before the soles appeared normal again.

We had our mortars set up in pits at the base of the low ridge along which the Company K line was dug in. George Sarrett and I had a regular two-man foxhole on the ridge next to a road cut that came through at right angles to the ridge. During the nights we were there, we mortarmen took turns on the guns and fired flares periodically over our company area.

Between patrols and nightly vigils we began to get rested and dried out. We had air drops of supplies, food, water, and ammo. During the day we could build campfires and heat rations, which all enjoyed. We had ten-in-one rations there, always a welcome change from C and K rations. The method of air drop used to supply water had not been perfected then. The water was contained in long plastic bags, four of which were stored in a metal cylinder attached to the parachute. Quite often the impact of the cylinder hitting the deck caused one or more of the bags to break, and some or all of the water in it was lost.

We always had a lot of fun when supplies were air-dropped to us, even though it was hard work running through the mud collecting up the ammo, rations, and other supplies attached to the brightly colored chutes. Most of the time Marine torpedo bombers made the drops while flying low over us. Their accuracy was remarkable. During the periods when deep mud covered much of the battlefield we always welcomed a clear day, not only because we hated the rain, but because it meant our planes could be up and supply us with air drops. Otherwise supplies had to be manhandled miles through the mud.

While we were in reserve, another mortarman and I were sent on a routine mission to carry a message to the west coast regarding supplies. It was the kind of ordinary thing every infantryman was called on to do many times. Typically, it was good duty, because we were temporarily out from under the eagle eye of the company gunny sergeant, could move at our own pace, and do a little sightseeing along the way through areas already fought over and secured. It wasn't considered hazardous.

Our instructions were straightforward. Our company gunny, Hank Boyes, told us to keep on the main east–west road all the way to the beach and back. He told us who to contact and what to ask for. Then he warned us against screwing around souvenir hunting and cautioned us about the possibility of by-passed enemy.

We started off in high spirits for what we thought would be an interesting jaunt into the area south of the Oroku Peninsula. We had gotten cleaned up by then. Our dungarees had been washed, and our leggings and boondockers were dry and scraped clean of mud. We carried the usual two canteens of water. We also had ration chocolate bars because we would be gone several hours and could eat those on the move. My buddy was armed with a carbine. I carried the Tommy and my .45 pistol. The weather had dried out, and it was an ideal day for a little harmless diversion from the patrols we had been making.

After we moved out of our battalion area and onto the road, we saw almost no one. As we walked along the silent road, the only sounds in our immediate surroundings were our own voices, the crunching of our boondockers on the road, the muffled sloshing of the water in our canteens, and the occasional thump of our weapons' stocks against our canteens or kabar scabbards. We moved in that silent world that characterized the backwash of battle.

The area was replete with the flotsam of war. The storm front had passed, but its wreckage was left behind. Our experienced eyes read the silent signs and reconstructed the drama and pathos of various life-and-death struggles that had occurred. We encountered numerous enemy corpses, which we always passed on the windward side. We saw no Marine dead. But a bloody dungaree jacket here, a torn boondocker there, a helmet with the camouflage cloth cover and steel beneath ripped by bullets, discarded plasma bottles, and bloody battle dressings gave mute testimony of the fate of their former owners.

We passed through an embankment for a railroad track and entered the outskirts of a town. All buildings were badly damaged, but some were still standing. We stopped briefly to explore a quaint little store. Displayed in its window were various cosmetics. In the street in front of the store lay a corpse clad in a blue kimono. Someone had placed a broken door over the pathetic body. We speculated he had been the proprietor of the little shop. We passed a burned-out bus station with the ticket booth still standing in front. To our right and distant the battle rumbled and rattled as the 6th Marine Division fought the enemy on the Oroku Peninsula.

Without incident we continued through the ruins toward the beach when an amtrac came rattling toward us. The driver was the first living soul we had seen. We hailed him, and it turned out he was expecting us at the beach but had started along the road hoping to locate us. After receiving the information about our unit, he spun his amtrac around and headed back toward the beach. With our mission completed, my buddy and I started back along the road through the ruins.

We passed the little cosmetic shop and the dead Okinawan covered by the door and approached the bus station on our left. A gentle breeze was blowing. Only the clanking of a piece of loose tin on the ruined bus station roof broke the silence. If I blotted out the distant rumble of battle, our surroundings reminded me of walking past some deserted farm building on a peaceful spring afternoon back home. It seemed like an interesting place to take ten, explore the bus station, and eat our ration bars. We had saved time by meeting the amtrac, so we could stop for a while.

The harsh snapping and cracking of a long burst of Japanese machine-gun bullets zipping chest high in front of us sent my buddy and me scrambling for cover. We dove behind the concrete ticket booth and lay on the rubble-strewn concrete, breathing hard.

"God, that was close, Sledgehammer!"

"Too damned close!"

The enemy gunner had been zeroed in perfectly on his elevation, but he had led us too much. The bullets ricocheted and whined around inside the burned-out bus station. We heard the tinkle of glass as the slugs broke windows among the burned-out buses.

"Where the hell is that bastard?" asked my buddy.

"I don't know, but he's probably a couple of hundred yards away from the sound of the gun."

We lay motionless for a moment, the silence interrupted only by the peaceful, lazy clanking of the tin in the breeze. Cautiously I peered out from behind the base of the ticket booth. Another burst of slugs narrowly missed my head and went clattering through the building after striking the concrete alongside us.

"That bastard's zeroed in on us for sure," groaned my buddy.

The ticket booth in front of the building was surrounded by an open expanse of concrete in all directions. The gunner had us pinned down tightly. My buddy peeped around his side of the narrow booth and got the same reception as I had. The enemy machine gunner then fired a burst across the top of the concrete portion of the booth, shattering what was left of the windows in the upper part of the booth. We were sure that the Nambu gunner was up on the south side of the railroad embankment.

"Maybe we can get back among them buses and out of sight and then slip out of the rear of the building," my buddy said. He moved slightly to one side to look behind us, but another burst of fire proved his plan faulty.

"I guess we'll hafta wait it out till dark and then slip out of here," I said.

"Guess you're right. We sure as hell ain't gonna get outa

here during the daylight without gettin' hit. He's got us pinned down tight. Sledgehammer, after all the crap we've been through, damned if we ain't between a rock and the hard place. Goddamit to hell!"

The minutes grew into lonely hours as time dragged by. We kept a sharp lookout in all directions in case other Japanese might slip in behind us while we were occupied by the machine gun.

Toward late afternoon we heard a burst of M1 rifle fire over in the direction where the enemy gunner was located. After a few minutes we peeped out. To our delight we saw a group of four or five Company K Marines striding along the road from the direction of the road cut.

"Look out for that Nambu!" we yelled, pointing back toward where the fire had been coming from.

A grinning Marine held up the machine gun and yelled, "Rack 'em up. You guys OK? The gunny figured you'd run into trouble when you didn't come back and sent us out to look for you."

By mid-June familiar faces were scarce in Company K and in all the infantry units of the 1st Marine Division. On 1 June the company lost thirty-six men to enemy action. Ten days later, twenty-two men left with immersion foot and other severe illnesses. Despite midmonth replacements, Company K moved toward its final major fight with about one hundred men and two or three officers—only half of whom had landed at Hagushi two and a half months earlier.

CARNAGE ON KUNISHI RIDGE

Toward the middle of June we began to hear disturbing rumors about a place south of us called Kunishi Ridge. Rumors circulated that our division's other infantry regiments, the 7th Marines and later the 1st Marines, were involved in bitter fighting there and would need our help. Our hopes began to fade that the 5th Marines wouldn't be committed to the front lines again.

We continued our patrols. I enjoyed my canned Japanese scallops and hoped there was no such place as Kunishi Ridge.

But, the inevitable day came with the order, "Square away your gear; we're movin' out again."

The weather turned dry and warm as we moved south. The farther we proceeded, the louder the sound of firing became: the bumping of artillery, the thudding of mortars, the incessant rattle of machine guns, the popping of rifles. It was a familiar combination of noise that engendered the old feelings of dread about one's own chances as well as the horrible images of the wounded, the shocked, and the dead—the inevitable harvest.

Following the retreat from Shuri, the Japanese defenders of Okinawa withdrew into their final defensive lines along a string of ridges near the southern end of the island. The western anchor was Kunishi Ridge. In the middle was Yuza-Dake. Farther east was Yaeju-Dake.*

Kunishi Ridge was about 1,500 yards long, a sheer coral escarpment. The Japanese dug into caves and emplacements on its forward and reverse slopes. The northern frontal approaches to Kunishi lay wide open: flat grasslands and rice paddies across which the Japanese had perfect fields of fire.

On 12 June the 7th Marines made a predawn attack and captured a portion of Kunishi. The Marines were on the ridge, but the enemy was in it. For four days, the Marines of the 7th Regiment were isolated atop the ridge. Air drops and tanks supplied them, and tanks removed their dead and wounded.

On 14 June the 1st Marines attacked portions of Kunishi and suffered heavy losses for their efforts. On the same day, the 1st Battalion—led by Lt. Col. Austin Shofner (former CO of 3/5 on Peleliu)—attacked and captured Yuza-Dake but suffered terrible casualties from the Japanese defenders there and from intense fire sent over from Yaeju-Dake.

Into the hellish confusion we went on 14 June with the words still ringing in our ears, "The 5th Marines may not be committed again." We plodded along the sides of a dusty road, next to tanks and amtracs moving forward and a steady stream of ambulance jeeps returning loaded with the youthful human wreckage of the battle for Kunishi Ridge.

---

* *Dake* means "hill" in Japanese.

That afternoon our company deployed along a row of trees and bushes on the south side of the road. We saw and heard heavy firing on Kunishi Ridge across the open ground ahead. My mortar section dug in near the road with our guns adjusted to fire flares over a picturesque bridge that remained intact over a high stream bank.

A couple of us went to look at the bridge before dark. We walked down to the stream on a trail leading from the road. The water was crystal clear and made a peaceful gurgling sound over a clean pebbly bottom. Ferns grew from the overhanging mossy banks and between rocks on both sides. I had the urge to look for salamanders and crayfish. It was a beautiful place, cool and peaceful, so out of context with the screaming hell close above it.

The next morning we relieved 1/1 on Yuza-Dake. As we moved up along a road, we passed a small tree with all the limbs blasted off. So many communication wires hung from it at all angles that it looked like a big inverted mop. A ricocheting bullet whined between me and the man in front of me. It raised a little dust cloud as it smashed into a pile of dry brush by the roadside. Back into the meat grinder again, I thought, as we moved up toward the sound of heavy firing.

Yuza-Dake looked terrible to me. It resembled one of the hellish coral ridges on Peleliu. We could see Kunishi Ridge on our right and the Yaeju-Dake escarpment on our left. Army tanks were moving against the latter while machine guns and 75mm cannons hammered away.

For the first time in combat I heard the wailing of sirens. We were told that the army had put sirens on their tanks for the psychological effect it might have on the Japanese. To me the sirens just made the whole bloody struggle more bizarre and unnerving. The Japanese rarely surrendered in the face of flamethrowers, artillery, bombs, or anything else, so I didn't understand how harmless sirens would bother them. We got mighty tired of hearing them wailing against the constant rattle of small arms and the crash of shell fire.

While we were on Yuza-Dake under sporadic enemy fire, 2/5 joined the 7th Marines in the bitter fighting to capture the rest of Kunishi Ridge. The Japanese emplacements and caves received terrific bombardment by mortars, artillery, heavy naval gunfire, and air strikes consisting of twenty-five to thirty planes. It reminded me more and more of Bloody Nose Ridge on Peleliu.

The 2d Battalion, 5th Marines gained some ground on Kunishi but needed help. Company K was attached to 2/5 and arrived just in time to help that battalion fight off a company-sized night counterattack on 17 June. Later that night we heard that our company would attack the next morning to seize the remainder of Kunishi Ridge in the 5th Marines' zone of action. Once again we would enter the abyss of close combat.

We learned that we would move out well before daylight and deploy for the attack, because we had to move across a wide open area to get to the ridge. An officer came along giving us what sounded like a pep talk about how the 5th Marines could finish the job on Kunishi Ridge. (We all knew that the 1st Marines and the 7th Marines had already been terribly shot up taking most of the ridge.)

Moving in the darkness was something the old salts of Gloucester and Peleliu didn't like at all. We were stubborn in our belief that nobody but the Japanese, or damned fools, moved around at night. The new replacements who had come into the company a few days before seemed so pitifully confused they didn't know the difference. But moving up under cover of darkness was the only sane way to approach Kunishi Ridge. The 1st Marines and the 7th Marines had already found it necessary to move that way to get across the open ground without being slaughtered.

We moved slowly and cautiously across dry rice paddies and cane fields. Up ahead we saw shells exploding on and around the ridge as our artillery swished overhead. We heard the familiar popping of rifles, rattle of machine guns, and banging of grenades. Enemy shells also exploded on the ridge. We all knew that this was probably the last big fight before the Japanese were wiped out and the campaign ended. While I plodded along through the darkness, my heart pounding, my throat dry and almost too tight to swallow, near-panic seized me. Having made it that far in the war, I knew my luck would run out. I began to sweat and pray that when I got hit it wouldn't result in death or maiming. I wanted to turn and run away.

We came closer to the ridge silhouetted against the skyline.

Its crest looked so much like Bloody Nose that my knees nearly buckled. I felt as though I were on Peleliu and had it all to go through over again.

The riflemen moved up onto the ridge. We mortarmen were positioned to watch out for Japanese infiltrating from the left rear. We didn't set up our weapons: the fighting was so close-in with the enemy on the reverse slope and in the ridge that we couldn't fire high explosives.

Our 105mm artillery was firing over Kunishi Ridge while we moved into position in the dark. To our dismay, a shell exploded short in our company's line. The company CP alerted the artillery observers that we had received short rounds. Another 105 went off with a terrible flash and explosion.

"Corpsman!" someone yelled.

"Goddamit, we're getting casualties from short rounds!" an officer yelled into his walkie-talkie.

"What's the word on those short rounds?" the company executive officer asked.

"Says they'll check it out."

Our artillery was firing across the ridge into and around the town of Kunishi to prevent the enemy from moving more troops onto the ridge. But each time they shot, it seemed that one gun fired its shells in a traversing pattern right along the ridge in Company K's lines. It was enough to drive anyone into a state of desperation.

The Japanese were throwing grenades all along the line, and there was some rifle and machine-gun fire. On the right we began to hear American grenades exploding well within our lines.

"Hey you guys; Nips musta gotten hold of a box of our grenades. Listen to that, wouldja?"

"Yeah, them bastards'll use anything they can get their hands on."

During the next flurry of grenades, we heard no more U.S. models explode within our area. Then the word came along in the dark to be sure all the new replacements knew exactly how to use grenades properly. One of our new men had been discovered removing each grenade canister from a box of grenades, pulling the sealing tape from the canister, and then throwing the unopened canister at the enemy. The Japanese opened each canister, took out the grenade, pulled the pin, and threw the deadly "pineapple" back at us. The veterans around me were amazed to find out what had happened. The incident, however, was just one of many examples of the poor state of combat readiness of the latest group of new replacements.

With daylight I got a good look at our surroundings. Only then could I appreciate fully what a desperate, bitter battle the fight for Kunishi Ridge had been—and was continuing to be. The ridge was coral rock, painfully similar to Peleliu's ridges. But Kunishi was not so high nor were the coral formations so jagged and angular as those on Peleliu. Our immediate area was littered with the usual debris of battle including about thirty poncho-covered dead Marines on stretchers.

Some of our riflemen moved eastward along the ridge, while others moved up the slopes. We still didn't set up our mortars: it was strictly a riflemen's fight. We mortarmen stood by to act as stretcher bearers or riflemen.

Snipers were all over the ridge and almost impossible to locate. Men began getting shot one right after another, and the stretcher teams kept on the run. We brought the casualties down to the base of the ridge, to a point where tanks could back in out of the view of snipers on the ridge crest. We tied the wounded onto the stretchers and then tied the stretchers onto the rear deck of the tanks. Walking wounded went inside. Then the tanks took off in a cloud of dust along a coral road to the aid station. As many men as possible fired along the ridge to pin down the snipers, so they couldn't shoot the wounded on the tanks.

Shortly before the company reached the east end of the ridge, we watched a stretcher team make its way up to bring down a casualty. Suddenly four or five mortar shells exploded in quick succession near the team, wounding slightly three of the four bearers. They helped each other back down the ridge, and another stretcher team, of which I was a member, started up to get the casualty. To avoid the enemy mortar observer, we moved up by a slightly different route. We got up the ridge and found the casualty lying above a sheer coral ledge about five feet high. The Marine, Leonard E. Vargo, told us he couldn't move much because he had been shot in both feet. Thus he couldn't lower himself down off the ledge. "You guys be care-ful. The Nip that shot me twice is still hiding right over there in those rocks." He motioned toward a jumble of boulders not more than twenty yards away.

We reasoned that if the sniper had been able to shoot Vargo in both feet, immobilizing him, he was probably waiting to snipe at anyone who came to the rescue. That meant that anyone who climbed up to help Vargo down would get shot instantly. We stood against the coral rock with our heads about level with Vargo, but out of the line of fire of the sniper, and looked at each other. I found the silence embarrassing. Vargo lay patiently, confident of our aid.

"Somebody's got to get up there and hand him down," I said. My three buddies nodded solemnly and made quiet comments in agreement. I thought to myself that if we fooled around much longer, the sniper might shoot and kill the already painfully wounded and helpless Marine. Then we heard the crash of another 105mm short round farther along the ridge—then another. I was seized with a grim fatalism—it was either be shot by the sniper or have all of us get blown to bits by our own artillery. Feeling ashamed for hesitating so long, I scrambled up beside Vargo.

"Watch out for that Nip," he said again.

As I placed my hands under his shoulders, I glanced over and saw the entrance of the sniper's small cave. It was a black space about three feet in diameter. I expected to see a muzzle flash spurt forth. Strangely, I felt at peace with myself and, oddly, wasn't particularly afraid. But there was no sound or sight of the sniper.

My buddies had Vargo well in hand by then, so for a brief instant I stood up and looked south. I felt a sensation of wild exhilaration. Beyond the smoke of our artillery to the south lay the end of the island and the end of the agony.

"Come on Sledgehammer. Let's move out!"

With another quick glance at the mouth of the small cave—puzzled over where the sniper was and why he hadn't fired at me—I scrambled back down the rock to the stretcher team. We carried Vargo down Kunishi Ridge without further incident.

After bringing down another casualty, I passed our company CP among some rocks at the foot of the ridge and overheard one of our officers talking confidentially to Hank Boyes. The officer said his nerves were almost shattered by the constant strain, and he didn't think he could carry on much longer. The veteran Boyes talked quietly, trying to calm the officer. The officer sat on his helmet, frantically running his hands through his hair. He was almost sobbing.

I felt compassion for the officer. I'd been in the same forlorn frame of mind more than once, when horror piled on horror seemed too much to bear. The officer also carried a heavy responsibility, which I didn't have.

As I walked past, the officer blurted out in desperation, "What's the matter with those guys up on the ridge? Why the hell don't they move out faster and get this thing over with?"

Compassion aside, my own emotional and physical state was far from good by then. Completely forgetting my lowly rank, I walked right into the CP and said to the officer, "I'll tell you what's the matter with those guys on the ridge. They're gettin' shot right and left, and they can't move any faster!"

He looked up with a dazed expression. Boyes turned around, probably expecting to see the battalion or regimental commander. When he saw me instead, he looked surprised. Then he glared at me the way he did the time I had too much to say to Shadow back on Half Moon. Coming quickly to my senses and remembering that a private's advice to first lieutenants and gunny sergeants wasn't considered standard operating procedure in the Marine Corps, I backed away quietly and got out of there.

Toward afternoon, several of us were resting among some rocks near the crest of the ridge. We had been passing ammo and water up to some men just below the crest. A Japanese machine gun still covered the crest there, and no one dared raise his head. Bullets snapped over the crest and ricochets whined off into the air after striking rocks. The man next to me was a rifleman and a fine Peleliu veteran whom I knew well. He had become unusually quiet and moody during the past hour, but I just assumed he was as tired and as weary with fear and fatigue as I was. Suddenly he began babbling incoherently, grabbed his rifle, and shouted, "Those slant-eyed yellow bastards, they've killed enougha my buddies. I'm goin' after 'em." He jumped up and started for the crest of the ridge.

"Stop!" I yelled and grabbed at his trouser leg. He pulled away.

A sergeant next to him yelled, "Stop, you fool!" The sergeant also grabbed for the frantic man's legs, but his hands slipped. He managed to clutch the toe of one boondocker, however, and gave a jerk. That threw the man off balance, and he sprawled on his back, sobbing like a baby. The front of his trousers was darkened where he had urinated when he lost control of himself. The sergeant and I tried to calm him but also made sure he couldn't get back onto his feet. "Take it easy, Cobber. We'll get you outa here," the NCO said.

We called a corpsman who took the sobbing, trembling man out of the meat grinder to an aid station.

"He's a damn good Marine, Sledgehammer. I'll lower the boom on anybody says he ain't. But he's just had all he can take. That's it. He's just had all he can take."

The sergeant's voice trailed away sadly. We had just seen a brave man crack up completely and lose all control of himself, even to the point of losing his desire to live.

"If you hadn't grabbed his foot and jerked him down before he got to the crest, he'd be dead now, for sure," I said.

"Yeah, the poor guy woulda gotten hit by that goddamn machine gun; no doubt about it," the sergeant said.

By the end of the day, Company K reached the eastern end of Kunishi Ridge and established contact with army units that had gained the high ground on Yuza-Dake and Yaeju-Dake. Mail came up to us along with rations, water, and ammo. Among my letters was one from a Mobile acquaintance of many years. He had joined the Marine Corps and was a member of some rear-echelon unit of service troops stationed on northern Okinawa. He insisted that I write him immediately about the location of my unit. He wrote that when he found out where I was, he would visit me at once. I read his words to some of my buddies, and they got a good laugh out of it.

"Don't that guy know there's a war on? What the hell does he think the First Marine Division is doin' down here anyway?"

Someone else suggested I insist not only that he come to see me at once, but that he stay and be my replacement if he wanted to be a true friend. I never answered the letter.

A small patrol from the 7th Marines came by, and we talked with an old buddy. He said his regiment had been in terrible fighting for the several days it had been on Kunishi Ridge.

Then we sat silently, ruefully watching a group of Marines far over to the right get shelled by large-caliber Japanese artillery. Word came along the line about the death earlier in the day of the U.S. Tenth commander, General Buckner.*

Not long after we were relieved on Kunishi Ridge (in the afternoon of 18 June), I asked Gy. Sgt. Hank Boyes how many men we had lost fighting on Yuza-Dake and Kunishi. He told me Company K had lost forty-nine enlisted men and one officer, half of our number of the previous day. Almost all the newly arrived replacements were among the casualties. Now the company consisted of a mere remnant, twenty-one percent of its normal strength of two hundred and thirty-five men. We had been attached to 2/5 for only twenty-two hours and had been on Kunishi Ridge for less time than that.

* Gen. Simon Bolivar Buckner, USA, had come up to the front lines to watch the 8th Marine Regiment, 2d Marine Division, in its first combat action on Okinawa. He was observing from between two coral boulders when six Japanese 47mm artillery rounds struck the base of the rocks. Hit in the chest, he died shortly thereafter. Lt. Gen. Roy S. Geiger, USMC, III Amphibious Corps commander, took command of the Tenth Army and carried through to the end of the fighting a few days later. To this date in 1981, Geiger remains the only Marine officer to command a force of army size.

CHAPTER FIFTEEN

End of the Agony

FROM 11 to 18 June the fierce battle for the Kunishi–Yuza–Yaeju escarpment cost the 1st Marine Division 1,150 casualties. The fight marked the end of organized Japanese resistance on Okinawa.

The battle for the Kunishi escarpment was unforgettable. It reminded many of us of Peleliu's ridges, and we still weren't used to the fact that night attacks by Marines had played a significant role in capturing the difficult objective. Among my friends in the ranks, the biggest surprise was the poor state of readiness and training of our newest Marine replacements, as compared to the more efficient replacements who had come into the company earlier in the campaign (they had received some combat training in the rear areas before joining us). But most of the new men who joined us just before Kunishi Ridge had come straight from the States. Some of them told us they had had only a few weeks training or less after boot camp.

It's no wonder they were so confused and ineffective when first exposed to intense enemy fire. When we had to evacuate a casualty under fire, some of the new men were reluctant to take the chances necessary to save the wounded Marine. This reticence infuriated the veterans, who made such threats against them that the new men finally did their share. They were motivated by greater fear of the veteran Marines than of the Japanese. This isn't to reflect on their bravery; they simply weren't trained and conditioned properly to cope with the shock, violence, and hellish conditions into which they were thrown. The rank and file, usually sympathetic toward new replacements, simply referred to them "as fouled up as Hogan's goat," or some other more profound but profane description.

With a feeling of intense relief, we came down off Kunishi Ridge late in the day of 18 June. After rejoining the other companies of 3/5, we moved in column on a road cut through the ridge. As we wound south, we talked with men of the 8th Marines who were moving along the road with us. We were glad to see a veteran Marine regiment come in to spearhead the final push south. We were exhausted.

The veterans in our ranks scrutinized the men of the 8th Marines with that hard professional stare of old salts sizing up another outfit. Everything we saw brought forth remarks of approval: they looked squared away, and many of them were combat veterans themselves.*

I talked to a 60mm mortarman who was carrying almost an entire cloverleaf of HE shells on a backpack rig. Asking why he was so overloaded, I was told his battalion commander wanted the mortarmen to try the arrangement because they could carry more ammo than in a regular ammo bag. I hoped fervently that none of our officers saw that rig.

I also saw a machine-gun squad with "Nip Nemesis" stenciled neatly on the water jacket of their .30 caliber heavy machine gun. They were a sharp-looking crew.

We passed a large muddy area in the road cut. In it lay the body of a dead Japanese soldier in full uniform and equipment. It was a bizarre sight. He had been mashed down into the mud by tank treads and looked like a giant squashed insect.

Our column moved down into a valley at five-pace intervals, one file on each side of the road. An amtrac came clattering slowly along, headed toward the front farther south. It passed me as I was daydreaming about the delightful possibility that we might not get shelled or shot at anymore. But my reverie was terminated rudely and abruptly by *whiz . . . bang! whiz . . . bang!*

"Disperse!" someone yelled. We scattered like a covey of quail. About ten of us jumped into a shallow ditch. The first enemy antitank shell had passed over the top of the amtrac and exploded in a field beyond. But the second shell scored a direct hit on the left side of the amtrac. The machine jolted to a stop and began smoking. We peeped out of the ditch as the driver tried to start the engine. His crewman peered back into

---

*The 8th Marines came up from Saipan to reinforce the 1st Marine Division in the final drive on Okinawa. Among the many streamers on its regimental battle color flew one for Tarawa.

the cargo compartment to assess the damage. Two more shells slammed into the side of the disabled amtrac. The two Marines in the cab jumped out, ran over, and flopped down, panting, into the ditch near us.

"What kinda cargo is in there?" I asked.

"We got a full unit of fire for a rifle company—'thirty' ball, grenades, mortar ammo—the works. Boy, she is gonna blow like hell when that fire gets to that ammo. The gas tanks are hit so bad there's no way to put it out." The driver crawled off along the ditch to find a radioman to report that his load of ammo couldn't get through to the front.

Just then a man crawled over next to me and stood upright. I looked up at him in surprise. Every Marine in the area was hugging the deck waiting for the inevitable explosion from the amtrac. The man was clad in clean dungarees with the new sheen still on the cloth, and he displayed the relaxed appearance of a person who could wash up and drink hot coffee at a CP whenever he was in the mood to do so. He carried a portable movie camera with which he began avidly filming the billow of thick black smoke boiling up from the amtrac. Rifle cartridges began popping in the amtrac as the heat got to them.

"Hey mate," I said. "You'd better get down! That thing is gonna blow sky high any minute. It's loaded with ammo!"

The man held his camera steady but stopped filming. He turned and looked down at me with a contemptuous stare of utter disdain and disgust. He didn't demean himself to speak to me as I cringed in the ditch, but turned back to his camera eyepiece and continued filming.

At that moment came a flash accompanied by a loud explosion and terrific concussion as the amtrac blew up. The concussion knocked the cameraman completely off his feet. He was uninjured but badly shaken and terribly frightened. He peered wide-eyed and cautious over the ditch bank at the twisted amtrac burning on the road.

I leaned over to him and said pleasantly, "I told you so."

He turned his no longer arrogant face toward me. I grinned at him with the broadest smile I could conjure, "like a mule eatin' briars through a barbed wire fence," as the Texans would say. Speechless, the cameraman turned quickly and crawled off along the ditch toward the rear.

Four or five Marine tanks were parked close together in the valley downhill from us about one hundred yards away. Their heavily armored fronts faced up the valley to our left. The crewmen had been alerted by the first enemy round fired at the amtrac; we saw them swinging their 75s toward our left and closing their turret hatches. Not a moment too soon. The entire Japanese 47mm gun battery opened rapid fire on the tanks. Too bad the movie cameraman had felt the call of duty summon him to the rear after the amtrac exploded, because he missed a dramatic scene. The enemy guns fired with admirable accuracy. Several of their tracer-like armor piercing shells hit the turrets of the tanks and ricocheted into the air. The tanks returned fire. In a few minutes, the Japanese guns were knocked out or ceased firing, and everything got quiet. The tanks sustained only minor damage. We went back onto the road and moved on south without further incident.

Until the island was secured on 21 June, we made a series of rapid moves southward, stopping only to fight groups of diehard Japanese in caves, pillboxes, and ruined villages. The fresh 8th Marines pushed south rapidly. "The Eighth Marines goin' like a bat outa hell," a man said as news drifted back to us.

We were fortunate in not suffering many casualties in the company. The Japanese were beaten, and the hope uppermost in every weary veteran's mind was that his luck would hold out a little longer, until the end of the battle.

We used loudspeakers, captured Japanese soldiers, and Okinawan civilians to persuade the remaining enemy to surrender. One sergeant and a Japanese lieutenant who had graduated from an Ivy League college and spoke perfect English gave themselves up in a road cut. Just after they came out and surrendered, a sniper opened fire on us. We eight or ten Marines took cover next to the embankment, but the Japanese officer and NCO stood in the middle of the road with the bullets kicking up dirt all around them. The sniper obviously was trying to kill them because they had surrendered.

We looked at the two Japanese standing calmly, and one of our NCOs said, "Get over here under cover, you dumb bastards."

The enemy officer grinned affably and spoke to his NCO. They walked calmly over and got down as ordered.

Some Company K men shot the gun crew of a 150mm howitzer emplaced in the mouth of a well-camouflaged cave. The
Japanese defended their big artillery piece with their rifles and
died to the last man. Farther on we tried to get a group of
enemy in a burial vault to surrender, but they refused. Our
lieutenant, Mac, jumped in front of the door and shouted in
Japanese, "Do not be afraid. Come out. I will not harm you."
Then he fired a complete twenty-round magazine from his
submachine gun into the door. We all just shook our heads
and moved on. About a half hour later, the five or six Japanese rushed out fighting. Some of our Marines behind us killed
them.

Our battalion was one of the first American units to reach
the end of the island. It was a beautiful sight even though there
were still snipers around. We stood on a high hill overlooking the sea. Below to our left we saw army infantry advancing
toward us, flushing out and shooting down enemy soldiers
singly and in small groups. Army 81mm mortar fire kept pace
ahead of the troops, and some of our weapons joined in coordination. We got a bit edgy when the army mortar fire kept
getting closer and closer to our positions even after the unit
had been apprised of our location. One of our battalion officers became furious as the big shells came dangerously close.
He ordered a radioman to tell the army officer in charge that if
they didn't cease fire immediately, our 81s would open fire on
his troops. The army mortars stopped shooting.

The night of 20 June we made a defensive line on the high
ground overlooking the sea. My mortar was dug in near a coral
road and was to illuminate or fire HE on the area. Other guns
of the section covered the seaward part of the company's sector.

Earlier we had seen and heard some sort of strange-looking
rocket fired by the Japanese from over in our army's sector. The
projectiles were clearly visible as they went up with a terrible
screaming sound. Most of them exploded in the 8th Marines
area. The things sounded like bombs exploding. A call came
for every available corpsman to help with casualties resulting
from those explosions.

The Japanese on Okinawa had a 320mm-spigot-mortar
unit equipped to fire a 675-pound shell. Americans first encountered this awesome weapon on Iwo Jima. I don't know

whether what we saw fired several times during the last day or two on Okinawa was a spigot mortar, but whatever it was, it was a frightful-sounding weapon that caused great damage.

The night turned into a long series of shooting scrapes with Japanese who prowled all over the place. We heard someone coming along the road, the coral crunching beneath his feet. In the pitch dark, a new replacement fired his carbine twice in that direction and yelled for the password. Somebody laughed, and several enemy started firing in our direction as they ran past us along the road. A bullet zipped by me and hit the hydrogen cylinder of a flamethrower placed on the side of the adjacent foxhole. The punctured cylinder emitted a sharp hissing sound.

"Is that thing gonna blow up?" I asked anxiously.

"Naw, just hit the hydrogen tank. It won't ignite," the flame-thrower gunner said.

We could hear the enemy soldiers' hobnailed shoes pounding on the road until a fatal burst of fire from some other Company K Marines sent them sprawling. As we fieldstripped them the next morning, I noted that each carried cooked rice in his double-boiler mess gear—all bullet-riddled then.

Other Japanese swam or walked along in the sea just off-shore. We saw them in the flarelight. A line of Marines behind a stone wall on the beach fired at them. One of our men ran up from the wall to get more carbine ammo.

"Come on Sledgehammer. It's just like Lexington and Concord."

"No thanks. I'm too comfortable in my hole."

He went back down to the wall, and they continued firing throughout the night.

Just before daylight, we heard a couple of enemy grenades explode. Japanese yelled and shouted wildly where one of our 37mm guns was dug in across the road, covering the valley out front. Shots rang out, then desperate shouts and cursing.

"Corpsman!"

Then silence. A new corpsman who had joined us recently started toward the call for help, but I said, "Hold it Doc. I'll go with you."

I wasn't being heroic. I was quite afraid. But knowing the enemy's propensity for treachery, I thought somebody should accompany him.

"As you were, Sledgehammer. Ya might be needed on the gun. Take off, Doc, and be careful," an NCO said. A few minutes later he said, "OK, Sledgehammer, take off if ya wanta."

I grabbed the Tommy and followed the corpsman. He was just finishing bandaging one of the wounded Marines of the 37mm gun crew when I got there. Other Marines were coming over to see if they could help. Several men had been wounded by the firing when two enemy officers crept up the steep slope, threw grenades into the gun emplacement, and jumped in swinging their samurai sabers. One Marine had parried a saber blow with his carbine. His buddy then had shot the Japanese officer who fell backwards a short distance down the slope. The saber blow had severed a finger and sliced through the mahogany carbine forestock to the metal barrel.

The second Japanese officer lay dead on his back next to the wheel of the 37mm gun. He was in full-dress uniform with white gloves, shiny leather leggings, Sam Browne belt, and campaign ribbons on his chest. Nothing remained of his head from the nose up—just a mass of crushed skull, brains, and bloody pulp. A grimy Marine with a dazed expression stood over the Japanese. With a foot planted firmly on the ground on each side of the enemy officer's body, the Marine held his rifle by the forestock with both hands and slowly and mechanically moved it up and down like a plunger. I winced each time it came down with a sickening sound into the gory mass. Brains and blood were splattered all over the Marine's rifle, boondockers, and canvas leggings, as well as the wheel of the 37mm gun.

The Marine was obviously in a complete state of shock. We gently took him by the arms. One of his uninjured buddies set aside the gore-smeared rifle. "Let's get you outa here, Cobber."

The poor guy responded like a sleepwalker as he was led off with the wounded, who were by then on stretchers. The man who had lost the finger clutched the Japanese saber in his other hand. "I'm gonna keep this bastard for a souvenir."

We dragged the battered enemy officer to the edge of the gun emplacement and rolled him down the hill. Replete with violence, shock, blood, gore, and suffering, this was the type of incident that should be witnessed by anyone who has any delusions about the glory of war. It was as savage and as brutal as though the enemy and we were primitive barbarians rather than civilized men.

Later in the day of 21 June 1945, we learned the high command had declared the island secured. We each received two fresh oranges with the compliments of Admiral Nimitz. So I ate mine, smoked my pipe, and looked out over the beautiful blue sea. The sun danced on the water. After eighty-two days and nights, I couldn't believe Okinawa had finally ended. I was tempted to relax and think that we would board ship immediately for rest and rehabilitation in Hawaii.

"That's what the scuttlebutt is, you guys. Straight dope. We're headed for Waikiki," a grinning buddy said. But long conditioning by the hardships that were our everyday diet in a rifle company made me skeptical. My intuition was borne out shortly.

"Get your gear on; check your weapons. We're moving back north in skirmish line. You people will mop up the area for any Nips still holding out. You will bury all enemy dead. You will salvage U.S. and enemy equipment. All brass above .50 caliber in size will be collected and placed in neat piles. Stand by to move out."

A FINAL CHORE

If this were a novel about war, or if I were a dramatic storyteller, I would find a romantic way to end this account while looking at that fine sunset off the cliffs at the southern end of Okinawa. But that wasn't the reality of what we faced. Company K had one more nasty job to do.

To the battle-weary troops, exhausted after an eighty-two-day campaign, mopping up was grim news. It was a nerve-wracking business at best. The enemy we encountered were the toughest of the diehards, selling their lives as expensively as possible. Fugitives from the law of averages, we were nervous and jittery. A man could survive Gloucester, Peleliu, and Okinawa only to be shot by some fanatical, bypassed Japanese holed up in a cave. It was hard for us to accept the order. But we did—grimly. Burying enemy dead and salvaging brass and equipment on the battlefield, however, was the last straw to our sagging morale.

"By lawd, why the hell we gotta bury them stinkin' bastards after we killed 'em? Let them goddamn rear-echelon people git a whiff of 'em. They didn't hafta fight 'em."

"Jeez, picking up brass; that's the most stupid, dumb jerk of a order I ever did hear of."

Fighting was our duty, but burying enemy dead and cleaning up the battlefield wasn't for infantry troops as we saw it. We complained and griped bitterly. It was the ultimate indignity to men who had fought so hard and so long and had won. We were infuriated and frustrated. For the first time, I saw several of my veteran comrades flatly refuse to obey an order. If some of us hadn't prevailed on them to knock off arguing hotly with an NCO, they would have been severely punished for insubordination.

I'll never forget cajoling, arguing with, and begging two veteran buddies to be quiet and follow orders as I unstrapped my entrenching shovel from my pack. We stood wearily in a trampled cane field beside a bloated Jap corpse. Both buddies were three-campaign men who were outstanding in combat but had reached the end of their ropes. They weren't about to bury any stinking Japanese, no sirree. I prevailed, however, just as Hank Boyes came over grim-faced and yelling at them to turn to.

So we dragged ourselves back north in skirmish line. We cursed every dead enemy we had to bury. (We just spaded dirt over them with our entrenching shovels.) We cursed every cartridge case "above .50 caliber in size" we collected to "place in neat piles." Never before were we more thankful to have the support of our tanks. The flame tanks were particularly effective in burning out troublesome Japanese in caves.* Fortunately, we had few casualties.

In a few days we assembled in an open field and fell out to await further orders. The weather was hot, so we all took off our packs, sat on our helmets, drank some water, and had a smoke. We were to be there for several hours, an NCO said, so we got the order to chow down.

---

*The total number of Japanese killed by the five American divisions during the mop up was 8,975, a large enough number of enemy to have waged intense guerrilla warfare if they hadn't been annihilated.

A friend and I went over to a little wooded area near the field to eat our K rations in the shade. We walked into a completely untouched scene that resembled a natural park in a botanical garden: low graceful pines cast dense shade, and ferns and moss grew on the rocks and banks. It was cool, and the odor of fresh pine filled the air. Miraculously, it bore not a single sign of war.

"Boy, this is beautiful, isn't it, Sledgehammer?"

"It looks unreal," I said as I took off my pack and sat down on the soft green moss beside a clump of graceful ferns. We each started heating a canteen cup of water for our instant coffee. I took out the prized can of cured ham I had obtained by trade from a man in the company CP. (He had stolen it from an officer.) We settled back in the cool silence. The war, military discipline, and other unpleasant realities seemed a million miles away. For the first time in months, we began to relax.

"OK, you guys. Move out. Move! Move! Outa here," an NCO said with authority ringing out in every word.

"Is the company moving out already?" my friend asked in surprise.

"No, it isn't, but you guys are."

"Why?"

"Because this is off limits to enlisted men," the NCO said, turning and pointing to a group of officers munching their rations as they strolled into our new-found sanctuary.

"But we aren't in the way," I said.

"Move out and follow orders."

To his credit, the NCO appeared in sympathy with us and seemed to feel the burden of his distasteful task. We sullenly picked up our half-cooked rations and our gear, went back out into the hot sun, and flopped down in the dusty field.

"Some crap, eh?"

"Yeah," I said, "we weren't even near those officers. The fighting on this goddamn island is over. The officers have started getting chicken again and throwing the crap around. Yesterday while the shootin' was still goin' on, it was all buddy-buddy with the enlisted men."

Our grumblings were interrupted by the sound of a rifle shot. A Marine I knew very well reeled backward and fell to the ground. His buddy dropped his rifle and rushed to him, followed by several others. The boy was dead, shot in the head by his buddy. The other man had thought his rifle was unloaded when his young friend had stood over him and placed his thumb playfully over the muzzle.

"Pull the trigger. I bet it's not loaded."

He pulled the trigger. The loaded rifle fired and set a bullet tearing up through the head of his best friend. Both had violated the cardinal rule: "Don't point a weapon at anything you don't intend to shoot."

Shock and dismay showed on the man's face from that moment until he left the company a few weeks later. He went, we heard, to stand a general court-martial and a probable prison term. But his worst punishment was living with the horror of having killed his best friend by playing with a loaded weapon.

While the company was still sitting in the field, five or six men and I were told to get our gear and follow an NCO to waiting trucks. We were to go north to a site where our division would make a tent camp after the mop-up in the south was completed. Our job was to unload and guard some company gear.

We were apprehensive about leaving the company, but it turned out to be good duty. During the long and dusty truck ride to the Motobu Peninsula, we rode past some areas we had fought through. By then we could barely recognize them—they were transformed with roads, tent camps, and supply dumps. The number of service troops and the amount of equipment was beyond our belief. Roads that had been muddy tracks or coral-covered paths were highways with vehicles going to and fro and MPs in neat khaki directing traffic. Tent camps, quonset huts, and huge parks of vehicles lay along our route.

We had come back to civilization. We had climbed up out of the abyss once more. It was exhilarating. We sang and whistled like little boys until our sides were sore. As we went north, the countryside became beautiful. Most of it seemed untouched by the war. Finally our truck turned off into a potato field not far from high rocky cliffs overlooking the sea and a small island which our driver said was Ie Shima.

The land around our future campsite was undamaged. We unloaded the company gear from the truck. The driver had picked up five-gallon cans of water for us. Plenty of K rations had been issued. We set up a bivouac. Corporal Vincent was in charge, and we were glad of it. He was a great guy and a Company K veteran.

Our little guard detail spent several quiet, carefree days basking in the sun by day and mounting one-sentry guard duty at night. We were like boys on a camp-out. The fear and terror were behind us.

Our battalion came north a few days later. All hands went to work in earnest to complete the tent camp. Pyramidal tents were set up, drainage ditches were dug, folding cots and bed rolls were brought to us, and a canvas-roofed messhall was built. Every day old friends returned from the hospitals, some hale and hearty but others showing the effects of only partial recovery from severe wounds. To our disgust, rumors of rehabilitation in Hawaii faded. But our relief that the long Okinawa ordeal was over at last was indescribable.

Very few familiar faces were left. Only twenty-six Peleliu veterans who had landed with the company on 1 April remained. And I doubt there were even ten of the old hands who had escaped being wounded at one time or another on Peleliu or Okinawa. Total American casualties were 7,613 killed and missing and 31,807 wounded in action. Neuropsychiatric, "nonbattle," casualties amounted to 26,221—probably higher than in any other previous Pacific Theater battle. This latter high figure is attributed to two causes: The Japanese poured onto U.S. troops the heaviest concentrations of artillery and mortar fire experienced in the Pacific, and the prolonged, close-in fighting with a fanatical enemy.

Marines and attached Naval medical personnel suffered total casualties of 20,020 killed, wounded and missing.

Japanese casualty figures are hazy. However, 107,539 enemy dead were counted on Okinawa. Approximately 10,000 enemy troops surrendered, and about 20,000 were either sealed in caves or buried by the Japanese themselves. Even lacking an exact accounting, in the final analysis the enemy garrison was, with rare exceptions, annihilated. Unfortunately, approximately 42,000 Okinawan civilians, caught between the two opposing armies, perished from artillery fire and bombing.

The 1st Marine Division suffered heavy casualties on Okinawa. Officially, it lost 7,665 men killed, wounded, and missing. There were also an undetermined number of casualties among the replacements whose names never got on a muster roll. Considering that most of the casualties were in the division's three infantry regiments (about 3,000 strength in each), it's obvious that the rifle companies took the bulk of the beating, just as they had on Peleliu. The division's losses of 6,526 on Peleliu and 7,665 on Okinawa total 14,191. Statistically, the infantry units had suffered over 150 percent losses through the two campaigns. The few men like me who never got hit can claim with justification that we survived the abyss of war as fugitives from the law of averages.*

IT WAS OVER

As we finished building our tent camp, we began trying to unwind from the grueling campaign. Some of the Cape Gloucester veterans rotated home almost immediately, and replacements arrived. Ugly rumors circulated that we would hit Japan next, with an expected casualty figure of one million Americans. No one wanted to talk about that.

On 8 August we heard that the first atomic bomb had been dropped on Japan. Reports abounded for a week about a possible surrender. Then on 15 August 1945 the war ended.

We received the news with quiet disbelief coupled with an indescribable sense of relief. We thought the Japanese would never surrender. Many refused to believe it. Sitting in stunned silence, we remembered our dead. So many dead. So many maimed. So many bright futures consigned to the ashes of the past. So many dreams lost in the madness that had engulfed us. Except for a few widely scattered shouts of joy, the survivors of the abyss sat hollow-eyed and silent, trying to comprehend a world without war.

In September, the 1st Marine Division went to North China on occupation duty, the 5th Marines to the fascinating ancient city of Peking. After about four and a half months there, I rotated Stateside.

My happiness knew no bounds when I learned I was slated to ship home. It was time to say goodbye to old buddies in

---

*The 1st Marine Division received the Presidential Units Citation for its part in the Okinawa campaign.

K/3/5. Severing the ties formed in two campaigns was painful. One of America's finest and most famous elite fighting divisions had been my home during a period of the most extreme adversity. Up there on the line, with nothing between us and the enemy but space (and precious little of that), we'd forged a bond that time would never erase. We were brothers. I left with a sense of loss and sadness, but K/3/5 will always be a part of me.

It's ironic that the record of our company was so outstanding but that so few individuals were decorated for bravery. Uncommon valor was displayed so often it went largely unnoticed. It was expected. But nearly every man in the company was awarded the Purple Heart. My good fortune in being one of the few exceptions continues to amaze me.

War is brutish, inglorious, and a terrible waste. Combat leaves an indelible mark on those who are forced to endure it. The only redeeming factors were my comrades' incredible bravery and their devotion to each other. Marine Corps training taught us to kill efficiently and to try to survive. But it also taught us loyalty to each other—and love. That esprit de corps sustained us.

Until the millennium arrives and countries cease trying to enslave others, it will be necessary to accept one's responsibilities and to be willing to make sacrifices for one's country—as my comrades did. As the troops used to say, "If the country is good enough to live in, it's good enough to fight for." With privilege goes responsibility.

A Roll of Honor
Peleliu Veterans with K/3/5 at the End of Okinawa

1. James Allen
2. Charles Anderson
3. James C. F. Anderson
4. Franklin Batchelor
5. Henry (Hank) Boyes W/NE
6. R. V. Burgin W/R
7. J. T. Burke
8. Guy E. Farrar
9. Peter Fouts
10. G. C. Gear
11. Anton Haas
12. Julius (Frenchy) Labeeuw
13. Les Land
14. Thorkil (Toby) Paulsen
15. Les Porter
16. Bobby Ragan
17. John Redifer
18. D. B. A. Salsby W/R
19. Vincent Santos
20. George Sarrett
21. Henry K. Schaeffer
22. Merriel (Snafu) Shelton S/R
23. E. B. Sledge
24. Myron Tesreau
25. Orly C. Uhls
26. W. F. Vincent

Note: W/R—wounded returned to duty; W/NE—wounded not evacuated; S/R—sick returned to duty.

Of the approximately 65 Peleliu veterans who landed with the company on Okinawa, only the above survived death, injury or illness, and were present at the end of the battle. Many of the above had been wounded on Cape Gloucester or Peleliu.

Bibliography

The books and documents listed here are not the only accounts and references to the battles of Peleliu and Okinawa, nor should the reader construe them to be suggestions for further reading. My story is personal. It relates what I saw and knew. I used the following references to check my facts for the few pieces of connecting tissue I've included to orient the reader to the larger war that raged around me and to be sure I had the names and places right.

Appleman, Roy E., *et al. Okinawa: The Last Battle*. Washington: Historical Division, Department of the Army, 1948.

Davis, Burke. *Marine! The Life of Lieutenant General Lewis B. (Chesty) Puller*. Boston: Little, Brown and Company, 1962.

Davis, Russell. *Marine At War*. Scholastic Book Services, N.Y., 1961.

Falk, Stanley. *Bloodiest Victory: Palaus*. New York: Ballantine Books, 1974.

Frank, Benis M. *Okinawa: Touchstone to Victory*. New York: Ballantine Books, 1974.

Frank, Benis M. and Henry I. Saw, Jr. *Victory and Occupation: History of Marine Corps Operations in World War II*, Vol. V. Washington: Historical Branch, G-3 Division, Headquarters, U.S. Marine Corps (hereinafter HQMC), 1968.

Garand, George W. and Truman R. Strobridge. *Western Pacific Operations: History of U.S. Marine Corps Operations in World War II*, Vol. IV. Washington: Historical Division, HQMC, 1971.

Heinl, Robert D., Jr. *Soldiers of the Sea: The United States Marine Corps, 1775–1962*. Annapolis: United States Naval Institute, 1962.

Hough, Maj. Frank O. *The Assault on Peleliu*. Washington: Historical Division, HQMC, 1950.

Hunt, George P. *Coral Comes High*. New York: Harper and Brothers, 1946.

Isley, Jeter A. and Philip Crowl. *The U.S. Marines and Amphibious War*. Princeton, NJ: Princeton University Press, 1951.

James, D. Clayton. *The Years of MacArthur*, Vol. II, 1941–45. Boston: Houghton Mifflin, 1975.

Leckie, Robert. *Strong Men Armed: The United States Marines Against Japan*. New York: Random House, 1962.

Mayer, S. L., ed. *The Japanese War Machine*. Secaucus, NJ: Chartwell Books, 1976.

McMillan, George. *The Old Breed: A History of the First Marine Division in World War II*. Washington: Infantry Journal Press, 1949.

Moran, John A. *Creating a Legend*. Chicago: Publishing Division, Moran/Andrews, Inc., 1973.

Morison, Samuel Eliot. *The Two-Ocean War*. Boston: Little, Brown and Company, 1963.

Moskin, J. Robert. *The U.S. Marine Corps Story*. New York: McGraw-Hill Book Company, 1977.

Muster Roll of Officers and Enlisted Men of the U.S. Marine Corps: Third Battalion, Fifth Marines, First Marine Division, Fleet Marine Force. From 1 September to 30 September, 1944, inclusive; from 1 October to 31 October, 1944, inclusive; from 1 April to 30 April, 1945, inclusive; from 1 May to 31 May, 1945, inclusive; from 1 June to 30 June, 1945, inclusive. Washington: History and Museums Division, HQMC.

Nichols, Charles S., Jr., and Henry I. Shaw, Jr. *Okinawa: Victory in the Pacific*. Rutland, VT: Charles E. Tuttle Company, 1966. Originally published in 1955 by the Historical Branch, G-3 Division, HQMC.

Paige, Mitchell. *A Marine Named Mitch*. New York: Vantage Press, 1975.

Shaw, Henry I., Jr., Bernard C. Nalty, and Edwin T. Turnbladh. *Central Pacific Drive: History of U.S. Marine Corps Operations in World War II*, Vol. III. Washington: Historical Branch, G-3 Division, HQMC, 1966.

Smith, S. E., ed. and comp. *The United States Marine Corps in World War II*. New York: Random House, 1969.

Steinberg, Rafael. *Island Fighting*. Morristown, NJ: Time-Life Books, 1978.

Stockman, James R. *The First Marine Division on Okinawa: 1 April–30 June 1945*. Washington: Historical Division, HQMC, 1946.

Time Magazine, 9 October 1944, p. 29; and 16 October 1944, p. 38.

Toland, John. *The Rising Sun*. New York: Random House, 1970.

United States 1st Marine Division. Operation Plan 1-44. Annex A, B Serial 0003 over 1990–5–80 over 458/332; dated 15 Aug 1944.

———— Palau Operation, Special Action Report, Serial 0775 over 1990–5–80 over 458/390; dated 13 Sept 1944.

———— Field Order No. 1–44 through 9–44. Serial 1990–5–80 over 458/332; dated 20 Sept, 21 Sept, 22 Sept, 25 Sept, 2 Oct, 5 Oct, 8 Oct, 10 Oct, and 13 Oct 1944.

FLIGHTS OF PASSAGE

REFLECTIONS OF A
WORLD WAR II AVIATOR

Samuel Hynes

For John Graves and Les Conner

PREFACE

Every generation is a secret society. The secret that my generation—the one that came of age during the Second World War—shared was simply the war itself. We grew up on active duty. I entered Navy Flight School when I was eighteen, and I was not twenty-one until two weeks after the war ended, and most of the young men I flew with were roughly my age. The years that in peacetime we would have spent in college, we spent instead first in learning to fly, and to fight a flying war, and then in fighting it. Our secret made us different from those who were older or younger than ourselves, or who were not in the war. I can't formulate the differences in terms that seem adequate to the experience, but perhaps I can recover something of the experience itself.

This is the story of a fairly ordinary flying war—of the training and the fighting, and of the growing up that went with it. I have tried to tell it with the voice of the young man who lived it, and to see it with his eyes, and not to impose upon it the revisionary wisdom of age. I have not improved upon events, but have told them, insofar as memory allows, as they happened. Only here and there have I changed a name, or disguised a circumstance, where not to do so might have troubled an old companion.

Sequences from this book have been published in *Four Quarters*, *TriQuarterly*, and *The Sewanee Review*, and I thank John Keenan, Reginald Gibbons, and George Core, the editors of these journals, for their help, and for permission to reprint those pieces.

Princeton, New Jersey

Chapter One

M**Y FATHER** was a tall, country-looking man. When he walked, with his long farmer's stride, he swung his hands with the palms facing back, so that he seemed to be paddling his way through some fluid more resistant than air. Because his arms were long, and his overcoat was cheap, a good deal of wrist protruded from his sleeves, making his enormous hands look even more like paddles. As he walked beside me that cold night in March 1943, through the empty Rock Island station and onto the platform, he seemed to be propelling himself forward swiftly but against his will, toward the edge of his familiar world, where he would have to stop, but I would step over.

He had missed his own war—had been drafted in 1918 but left waiting in a New Jersey camp until it was all over. I remember the pictures in the family photograph album—a yellowing snapshot of a smiling young man in a private's uniform, sitting in the doorway of a tent, and another, a posed portrait taken by the town photographer in LaPorte, Indiana, of the same young man standing stiffly at attention, looking very determined, but still a farmer dressed up as a soldier. Now he was too old to fight, though at fifty-six he was bigger, stronger, handsomer, and more eager than I would ever be. He loved his country in a simple, old-fashioned way, and he loved his sons; it must have been almost unendurable for him that they should go off to war, and he remain at home. Still, he would go down to the station with me, though he wouldn't say much, certainly wouldn't kiss me goodbye, or express any feelings right out.

The platform was dark, except at intervals where standing lamps shed pale disks of light at their bases, and as we moved from dark into light and back to dark our shadows slipped back and forth, before and then behind us, his tall, mine shorter and slighter. At the end of the platform, under a lamp, a yeoman was reading orders from a clipboard, and boys in civilian clothes were shuffling into crooked lines. I stopped awkwardly and shook my father's hand. It was the first time I had ever done that; a boy didn't shake hands with his own father. He put his other huge hand on my shoulder, as though he would still protect me while he could. Then he let go, and I went on and joined a line with the others. The yeoman began to call muster: '. . . Baird, Berg, Eichman . . . Johnson, Milch, Spitzenberger . . .' The names were midwestern-sounding, German and Scandinavian, most of them, the kind of names you'd expect to find in Minneapolis. I had grown up with such names, and I felt a little reassured by their familiarity. I picked up my suitcase and went to board the train. On the steps I paused to look back. My father was far down the platform, his long arms swinging, his head bent a little, moving rapidly away through the spots of light and shadow toward the dark street.

I don't remember feeling any particular vocation for flying, or any sense that flight school was where I belonged. I was not one of those kids who built model airplanes, I never ran around with my arms stuck out, making engine-noises, I never put goggles on the helmet that I wore to school in the winter. I read *G-8 and His Battle Aces* like everybody else, but I didn't imagine myself in those Spads and Nieuports, shooting down Huns and winning medals. I don't think I imagined myself as anything at all.

Still, in the thirties airports were romantic, and drew boys to them. None of the kids I knew had ever been in a plane, or expected ever to be in one; planes were for watching, not for riding in. On sunny Saturday mornings my friends and I would make sandwiches and fill our sour-smelling Boy Scout canteens, and ride our bikes out through the thinning Minneapolis suburbs and between the first farms, to the airfield. Along the highway, just before you came to the commercial part of the airport, there was a sign pointing down a narrower road to the Naval Reserve Air Station, and we turned there and rode toward a tin-roofed hangar with U.S. NAVY painted on the roof in big yellow letters.

Across the road from the hangar a small hill had been partly dug away—perhaps for gravel or fill—leaving a grass-covered knob, like a head with hair on it, with its sandy face toward the field. We lay on the grass on the top of that slope and ate our sandwiches and watched the Navy biplanes landing and taking off. If the wind was right they would take off over our heads, passing so close that we could see the grease and oil streaks on the cowlings and the spurts of flame from the exhaust stacks, and could watch the wheels draw up as the planes roared over us. It made us feel daring, to be lying there in the path of the booming planes.

When we had eaten we sometimes went down onto the field and hovered around the hangar. (There never seemed to be any guards to chase small boys away.) Inside it was cool and shadowy. I remember the light coming down, soft and unfocused from the high ceiling, and the soft cries of the swallows that nested in the roof beams, and the smell of hydraulic fluid and oil. Planes in for repair were scattered around the hangar floor, half-dismantled, surrounded by cowlings and tools, and mechanics worked beside the open engines. Sometimes one man would speak a word or two to another, or tap a tool on an engine, but the sounds were muted and lost in the tall emptiness under the roof; and the effect was of a careful quietness, as though the hangar were a church, and the mechanics priests engaged in some ritual that we were too young, and too earthbound, to understand.

But for all the romance of the Navy field, I didn't want to be a pilot. All I wanted, when I rode out to the airport on those distant Saturdays, was the presence of that romance. I wanted to hear the engines and see the planes climb out of sight, and to watch the mechanics at their priestly tasks. I was not, even in imagination, a pilot; but I was a true believer in the religion of flight.

The young men on the train that night were from Minnesota and the states around. Most of them came from farms, or from little towns, places I had never heard of like Blue Earth, Minnesota, and Bonesteel, South Dakota. The most citified were, like myself, from Minneapolis, which was not much more cosmopolitan than Bonesteel. We were all yokels. For many of us it was the first time away from home, the first time out of the home state, the first time in a Pullman car. Everything was new and strange—the berths with their green curtains, already made up for the night, the smoking room at the end of the car, the yeoman with his clipboard giving orders. We were subdued by it all, and there was none of the shouting and singing and drinking that a troop train would have had. We were shy of each other, and nervous about behaving properly (none of us knew how an aviation cadet was supposed to act), and frightened by the mystery into which we were moving.

Among all those strangers were two boys I had known in high school and during my few months at the university. They became my friends, but that night on the train they were only familiar faces, comforting simply because I had seen them before. I knew Joe Baird because he was an athlete. He had played end on the university's freshman football team. He was tall, and so broad-shouldered and narrow-hipped that he looked top-heavy. When he moved, he moved very delicately, walking on his tiptoes, carefully, as though holding back his great energy and strength out of a protective concern for the world. His friend Wally Milch was a straw-haired, pink-faced Minneapolis Swede—the kind of boy who at eighteen still hadn't shaved, and didn't look as though he'd ever have to. He had the face of a sweet-tempered child, and that's what he was. Like Joe, he was kind and generous by instinct—it seemed easy for him to be a nice guy—and funny out of simple good feeling.

The three of us crowded together onto a lower berth for a while, talking and giving each other such encouragements as we had, and I went to bed feeling a little better, and a little sad for the others, the country boys in their plaid mackinaws, with their high-sided haircuts and their shy manners, who were absolute strangers that night. But though I was better off than they were, my own apprehensiveness would not go away entirely, and I lay awake for a long time, watching the snow-patched Minnesota fields and the dark, lonely little towns pass, and trying to imagine what was coming. The life of flying was so mysterious that I could not construct an image of it; I couldn't even visualize it enough to imagine failing at it. It was as though the darkness through which the train rolled would go on forever.

We were headed south, to Texas and Oklahoma. There we would be scattered among little towns, each of which had a college of sorts and an airport. At the college we would be instructed in subjects thought suitable for pilots—physics and aerology and military history—and at the airport we would be taught to fly Piper Cubs. We weren't exactly in the Navy yet—the program we were entering was called *Civilian*

Pilot Training—but we weren't exactly civilians either. If we passed this first testing period, the yeoman on the train explained, then we would be sent on into the real Navy flight training; 'But if you wash out,' he went on, 'it's Great Lakes!' To 'wash out' meant to fail; it sounded as though you turned colorless and just faded away, like a guilty spirit. Great Lakes was the Navy training station where such failures were reassigned, and would-be flying officers turned into enlisted men. I didn't yet know how to fail, but I had learned the vocabulary of failure.

Early in the morning of the second day we stopped somewhere in Oklahoma, and Wally and Joe and some other boys got off. I heard Joe ask the name of the college they were going to.

'Panhandle A&M.'

Joe laughed his whinnying laugh. 'You're kidding.' And it certainly did sound like a joke, a made-up name for the worst school in the world. But it was a real place.

The rest of us went on, across the flatness of north Texas, to Dallas, and changed to another, dustier, older, and pokier train, and crept back north a bit, and stopped at last beside a station with a sign that said 'Denton.' 'Fall out!' the yeoman shouted, and we stumbled out of the train onto the platform, and stood blinking in the bright sunlight. From around the corner of the station a man appeared dressed in the uniform of a Navy lieutenant junior grade. He was, apparently, our Commanding Officer; but even in the uniform he looked like a schoolteacher. He stood still for a moment, staring abstractedly through his glasses, as though he were running over in his mind a speech that he hadn't memorized. 'Ten-shun,' he said apologetically. 'This way—uh—cadets, for the bus to North Texas State Teachers College.' It sounded a little better than Panhandle A&M. But not much.

Everything about Denton, Texas, and the life we lived there was strange to us; we lived in strangeness as though it were an environment, or a climate. Perhaps that is why memory offers only fragments and images of that time—often very vivid, but only bright, broken pieces. The town itself was strange, like no town that any of us had known back home. It spread out around us in a random-looking sprawl of one- and two-storied buildings, dust-colored and flattened-looking, as though the weight of the Texas sky had pressed it down into the earth. The trees were different from the ones back home, and the flowers bloomed too early, and the soil was the wrong color—reddish and sandy and dry. The people we met spoke a soft-slurring speech that at first we couldn't understand. Shopkeepers welcomed us as though we were old friends, and when we left they said, 'Y'all hurry back, heah?' The black shoeshine boy who kept his stand on the main street grinned and greeted us cheerfully, and played a jazz tune with his rag on our shoes. Pretty girls smiled as they passed. It was all very friendly—friendlier than it would have been in Minneapolis or Bonesteel—but it was unfamiliar, a foreign country in which we were only tourists. I felt more at home back in my dormitory room, where Midwestern was spoken.

But even there life was strange. I had never slept in a room with anyone but my brother, and now I shared one with three strangers—Ike, Bergie, and Johnson. There were common showers and common toilets, and a common mess hall where we ate together at long tables. It was all pleasant enough, and I suppose it wasn't much different from life in a college dormitory, but I hadn't lived in a college dormitory, and for me the abrupt loss of privacy and family, both at once, was a shock.

Our airport was a sheep pasture on the edge of town, which we shared with the sheep. It had no runway, only grass, which the sheep kept trimmed. It was not even flat—it sank in the middle and rose steeply at the far side, where it ended in a grove of trees. At the corner of the field by the road was a small hangar and a shed that was called the Flight Office; beside the hangar four or five Piper Cubs were parked. That was all the equipment there was, except for a windsock, once red and yellow but faded now to an almost invisible gray, which drooped on a staff near the fence. It wasn't much of an airport, or much of a school, but I took my first flight there, and soloed there, and I have the sort of affection for the place that I have for other beginnings—for the first girl, the first car, the first drink.

First flight: what images remain? I am in the rear seat of a Cub, and my instructor is taxiing to the takeoff position. The wheels of the plane are small, and it rides very low, so that I seem to be sitting almost on the ground, and I feel every bump and hollow of the field as we taxi. The wings seem to flap with the bumps, and the whole machine seems too small, too fragile, too casually put together to be trusted.

The instructor turns into the wind, runs up the engine, and I feel the quick life of the plane. It begins to roll, bumpily at first, as though we are still taxiing. The nose is high, I can't see around it, and I have a panicky feeling that we are rushing toward something—a tree or a sheep or another plane; and then the flow of air begins to lift the wings, the tail comes up, and the plane moves with a new grace, dancing, touching the rough field lightly, and then not touching it, skimming the grass, which is still so close that I can see each blade, and I am flying, lifted and carried by the unsubstantial air.

At the end of the field the grove of trees is first a wall, a dark limit, and then sinks and slides, foreshortening to a green island passing below us. The plane banks and I can see the town and the college—but below me, all roofs and tree-tops —and beyond it there is distance, more and more distance, blue-hazy and flat and empty, stretching away to the indistinct, remote horizon. The world is enormous. The size of the earth increases around me, and so does the size of the air; space expands, is a tall dome filled with a pale, clean light, into which we are climbing.

Below me the houses, each in its own place, look small and vulnerable on the largeness of the earth. I stare down at first like a voyeur, looking into other people's lives. A truck drives along a road and turns into a yard; a woman is hanging out clothes; she stops and runs to the truck. Should I be watching? Does she feel me there above her life? The world below exposes itself to me—I am flying, I can see everything!

I don't remember doing any flying myself on that first flight. I must have tried, and I could invent what the instructor said and what I did, but I don't remember it. What I remember is the way the world changed from the familiar, comfortable space I had always lived in to the huge, empty world of the flier.

As the days of marching and flying and just hanging around passed, the strangers in my room became my friends. Ike, a big, gentle, countryish boy from South Dakota, was like my father, and that made friendship easy. He walked with long, galumphing strides (it came from walking between the corn rows, Johnson said), and he talked like a yokel in a movie. He was the only person I ever knew who really said 'Golly.' (But it was more like 'Gawlly'—he always spoke as though his mouth was full of water, and he didn't want to spill it.) He didn't talk much, though; he was ill at ease with words. He communicated in other ways—by smiling, or by touching. He would put his arm around a friend's shoulder without embarrassment, in a way that the rest of us couldn't. I envied him his natural affection.

Bergie came from South Dakota too—from a town larger than Ike's, he explained, though in South Dakota that didn't seem to make much difference; they all seemed like country boys to me. He was as tall as Ike, but slender and dark where Ike was blond and broad; and he had a small, deeply seamed face, as though he had been born smiling and had never stopped smiling long enough for the furrows to smooth out. He spoke in a rapid tumble of words that were sometimes hard to separate; but when he sang, which he did whenever he wasn't required to be silent, his voice was pure and clear, and very high, almost like a boy soprano's. Even on first meeting, he looked and acted like a friend—so open, so decent. I liked him at once.

Johnson was a smoother character than Ike. Like almost everyone else in the group he was blonde, but he had not allowed his hair to be cut in the standard crew cut; it was parted high up on the side, and slicked back. He knew the current slang, and the campus fashions; and he had a worldly, knowing smile (Ike's smile was all trusting innocence). He would have been a city slicker—the kind who swindles rubes like Ike—if he had come from anywhere but South Dakota. How, I wondered, could you be a city slicker in a state that had no cities? But Johnson had been to the state university there, and he had been in a fraternity (he even wore his pin on his khaki shirt until the C.O. noticed it). He regarded the country boys with pitying disdain—hayseeds, he said, with the cow shit still on their shoes.

After a week or so we trusted each other enough to bring out the pictures of our girls that we'd been hiding in our dresser drawers. Ike's was a cheerful-looking, long-faced girl with an elaborate movie-star hairdo. 'She runs the beauty parlor,' he explained, 'back in Bonesteel.' Johnson had two— a Pi Phi, he said, and a Tri Delt. I brought out my picture of Alice. She was a girl I had met during my first week at the university. She was pretty and in a sorority (both good), but she was a Catholic (bad). We had been going steady for a couple of months, and the night before I left we had sat in my father's car parked on a bluff by the river, necking a lot—but not going-all-the-way (whatever *that* was)—and talking romantically about our future. She was my girl, and I assumed that I'd marry her some day. Right now I didn't want to— what I wanted to do was to take all her clothes off, look at her, touch her, and find out what going-all-the-way meant—but I expected to want to later on. I wasn't sure that her picture would impress my roommates, but Johnson examined it with an experienced eye, and said she reminded him of an Alpha Phi he knew, and Bergie raised his eyebrows, making the furrows in his brow even deeper, and whistled appreciatively. Ike said 'Golly!'

On the other side of town, at Texas State College for Women, hundreds of girls lived lives made celibate by the draft and gas-rationing. TSCW had been the traditional territory of boys from Texas A&M, and those boys were now out of reach. We rode past the campus every day in the bus that took us to the airport, and looked at the girls, moving in twos and threes along the campus paths under the trees that were just coming into leaf. Sometimes we waved, or shouted something, and they waved back, some cheerfully, some wildly, as though they were drowning and we were the lifeboat crew. It was a little scary, seeing them so eager; I wasn't sure that the things I had learned about girls back in Minneapolis would be adequate for this situation.

After a couple of weeks of training we were given a Saturday-night liberty, and Ike and Johnson and I caught a crosstown bus for TSCW. None of us was quite sure what we should do when we got there, and for a while we just walked around, sticking together like a rifle platoon. But finally we spoke to a girl, and she had friends, and in a few minutes we were paired off.

At first my new date seemed very different from what I was used to. She had more names, for one thing—her name, she said, was Jo Belle (or maybe it was Mary Beth, or even Lalla Rookh), and when she spoke her voice was like home-made fudge. But beyond those variations she was just another middle-class American college girl.

Where should we go? We could go into town to a movie, she said, or we could dance at the Union. But I said I only had until eleven, so we had a coke and went out onto the dark campus. There was an outdoor theater nearby, Jo Belle said, that was right pretty.

It was still March, but the evening was warm, and we sat on the grass at the back of the theater, under some bushes. Jo Belle was soft and warm, and soon we were lying back, kissing and whispering. But we were still strangers, and we were shy of each other. I wasn't sure how much groping she would tolerate, and she wasn't sure how far I expected to proceed. So it was mostly fumbling there under the bushes, and 'No' and 'Please' and more 'Nos.' I suppose all that she wanted, really, was just to touch a young male, to be assured that at eighteen she was pretty and desirable. I wanted to be led into a darkness that I didn't understand. You could call it sexual need, all right, but it was more than that. It was a desire to know, not to be ignorant of what was there, under a girl's clothes. Sex was a journey of exploration. Girls were Africa and I was Stanley. Which way to the Congo? And what did you do when you got there? Adults knew. I wanted to know too.

Then it was ten-thirty, and I was back on the bus with Ike and Johnson, remembering how her body felt under the starched cotton, and lying about how I had made out, and all the time my genitals feeling like cannonballs. I was no more ready for women than I was ready for war. Sex was another military skill that I hadn't yet acquired.

I didn't advance my knowledge of sex much at Denton, but I learned a little about flying. My teacher, a man named Moreland, was one of three flight instructors—leathery-faced, laconic Texans, cropdusters, I suppose, in peacetime, or dollara-ride fairground fliers. You'd find them, when they weren't flying, lined up in chairs propped back against a sunny wall of the hangar, watching the planes take off and land, and occasionally making a terse comment: 'Should'a used some power there,' or 'He done landed ten feet in the air.' If you were scheduled for a flight, you'd find your instructor in his chair, and he'd tilt forward and rise, and stand for a minute looking at the sky, as though the thought of flying hadn't struck him until right then, and he'd walk out to the Cub, and you'd trail along behind him.

The Piper Cub, with its large square wing and slender fuselage, is like a kite with a small engine in it; it will float on an air-current, settle lightly to the ground with no power at all, and bounce forgivingly away from a bad landing to give you a chance to try again. In heavier planes the engine dominates, pulling the plane along, but in a Cub it is the wings; the engine seems to do no more than hold you hovering in space. It was a wonderful plane to begin with, friendly and safe.

At first we did simple things—turns and climbs and gentle glides. I was all right while the plane was flying straight and level, but I felt insecure and vulnerable when it banked, and I could feel myself leaning away from the turn, trying to keep my body vertical to the ground, as though I might get some support from the earth if I were loyal to it. 'Relax, son,' Moreland would say, 'fly with the plane. The ground ain't no use to you up here.' And gradually I learned to move instinctively with the plane, and to let the world tilt as it would. For, once you are really flying, it is the world that tilts, not the plane; it's the horizon that tips up when you turn, and settles back when you roll out, sinks when you climb, and rises when you dive. The plane remains a steady thing, a part of yourself, or so it seems—and you are not really flying the plane, you are flying the world.

'Now you take it,' Moreland would say, and he'd let go of the stick, and I'd clutch it with my right hand, grab the throttle with my left, and shove both feet onto the rudder pedals, and the plane would jerk and yaw about the sky. 'E–e–e–easy movements,' Moreland would plead, 'easy movements, that's all she needs,' and I would try to relax, and move the stick gently forward, and the nose would sink, back and it would rise, left and the left wing would drop. It wasn't exactly the feeling of flying that I was getting then; it was the feeling of mutual responsiveness, my life touching and merging with the life of the plane.

Once I could perform these simple flying movements we went on to the next step, which is a kind of nonflying, or antiflying—stalling the plane, so that it virtually stops in the air. You pull the nose high; the earth and the horizon disappear, the airspeed drops, and you hold the stick back and wait for the shudder; and the nose falls heavily earthward like a stone, or something dead, and you recover speed and are flying again. Or at the top, at the moment of stalling, you kick the rudder in, and the plane falls in a twisting stall that is a spin, and you are looking down at the earth, rotating like a dream of falling, and you *are* falling, and then the recovery, the plane begins to live again, the horizon settles into a reasonable place, and it is like waking after a sickness. I learned to do these things because I had to, but I hated them; they seemed a violation of the plane and of the life of flying.

When we had learned one set of skills, or at least had flown the prescribed number of hours, there were check-rides, to determine whether we were ready for the next set. These were tests, but not like any test that I had taken at school or university. You couldn't cram for it, and you couldn't fake it. You weren't even being tested on something that you had studied, really, but on what you were. If you were a flier, you passed; if you weren't, you washed out—fell out of the air, and became a lower order of being.

It became clear that some people were natural fliers, and some weren't. The athletes usually were; they used their bodies easily and naturally, and they seemed to make the plane a part of themselves. Ike was one of those. He didn't enter a plane so much as put it on, like an odd suit of clothes, and you could see already that the only trouble with the Cub was that it was too small for him, that he belonged in a full-sized, serious plane, like a Corsair or an F6F.

I wasn't a natural pilot—or an athlete. I had to think about flying all the time—left aileron, don't forget left rudder, back on the stick, keep the horizon there, watch the airspeed—all this to make a simple 360° turn. But Ike did it all intuitively: 'I just roll her over,' he'd say, 'and around she goes.' I wondered if it was significant that the plane was a female for him, and only an *it* for me.

I wasn't a natural, but I learned to control the plane, and myself with it. But there were some young men for whom even this was impossible. In some, fear of the air was as deep and as irrational as fear of water or of the dark is in others; it kept them tense and helpless in flight, jerking the plane about with sudden, desperate gestures, skidding into turns, overcorrecting mistakes, bouncing on landings, never making those easy movements that are all she needs. One cadet, a big, stolid farmer who was older than the rest of us, was airsick on every flight. He returned each day, grimly, to try again; but he never got over whatever it was that gripped his belly, never reached the point at which movement in the air, you and the plane moving together, becomes a liberating, joyous action. I remember Ike walking back from the flight line with him, his arm around the sufferer's shoulders, saying, 'Golly, it's not so bad,' and the farmer's face sweaty and strained and despairing. Then one day he was gone, washed out and shipped off to Great Lakes.

But the rest of us, those who had not failed, began to enter the pilot's world, a world in which weather is an environment, clouds are three-dimensional landscapes, and the earth is— not exactly two-dimensional, but panoramic, patterned, and expansive. We began to get a pilot's sense of the earth, how it goes out to horizons beyond horizons, how it is marked by man and nature—the straight lines of roads and fields and railroad tracks, the irregular lines of rivers, the dark patches of woods—and how, in spite of those marks, earth can deny location and leave a flier lost above unknown landmarks.

I asked Moreland one day if we could climb to ten thousand feet. To be two miles above the earth seemed to me something remarkable, something more than merely flying. It was a fine, clear day—it must have been in April—and as we climbed, slowly because the Cub engine didn't have much power, the earth opened out farther than I had ever seen before, extending in a vast circle, hazy at the edges and, it seemed, faintly curving away toward the horizon. I thought, if Columbus could have climbed two miles high he'd have known that his theory was true, and he could have saved himself the trip to America.

Since we were over Texas, the most striking thing about that expanding circle below us was its sameness. To the southeast lay Lake Dallas, and still farther off I could see the smoke of Fort Worth, but in every other direction the land spread its redundant flatness unbroken to the horizon. And since it was all the same, there was no knowing how far away that horizon was; we might have been looking north all the way to Canada, it would have looked the same. It was just earth, and space, and weather.

Weather is the pilot's nature, air is his ocean, winds are his waves and streams. Wind makes the plane fly—the flow of air over the wing literally holds it in the air—but it also blows you off course, tosses a light plane about in a landing run; it can get you lost, or kill you. When the northers blew down across those flat Texas fields, planes like ours could take off and land almost vertically, but they could also get hopelessly lost downwind, blown like a bird or a scrap of paper out of sight. On the windiest days we kept the Cubs tied down, rocking and bouncing against the ropes. But off to the east of us, at the Army field where artillery spotters were being trained, the little observation planes would go on flying, barely moving into the wind and, when they put their enormous flaps down, seeming to land moving backwards. And then they too would be grounded, and the sky would be empty, swept clean by the streaming wind.

By early May we had all finished the CPT course. We could get a Cub into the air and back down again; we could march together if the commands weren't too complicated; we had a smattering of knowledge of aeronautics and weather. We were ready to graduate, and like any graduating class we gathered to have our picture taken on the steps of our dormitory. The boys in that picture look tanned and fit, and much too young for a war. Some of them are grinning into the camera, some are clowning around. It's the sort of picture that you might find in a high-school yearbook—the baseball team, or a fraternity. Nobody seems to regard the occasion as a very solemn one. After all, we weren't really in the Navy yet.

*

It seemed a million miles from Texas to Georgia, and every mile just the same. I remember sitting in a hot, stationary train, looking out the window at a cotton gin and a mule and a pine tree, while we waited for a more urgent train to pass; but I don't know whether we were in Louisiana or Mississippi or Alabama or Georgia. It was May, and already it was like high summer back home. A black man sat on a wagon, waiting like us for the train to pass; he looked back at me, but without interest. I had seen the cotton gin and the mule and the man on the wagon a hundred times in the two days that it took us to ride that slow southern train from Dallas to Athens, Georgia. It was like a punishment in some myth: we were condemned to ride forever through the same southern landscape.

Athens, in its way, was like another myth—the fall of Icarus, if he had landed on red Georgia dirt. For a few weeks we had been pilots—well, sort of pilots—and now we were back on the ground, at a place called a *pre*flight school, as though in the Navy's eyes we not only weren't pilots, we never had been pilots. As we rode into the school's grounds we passed a symbol of our situation; a worn-out fighter plane had been set in concrete in front of the administration building. It was the only plane in the place, and it looked sad and humiliated, grounded and stuck there as a decoration, far from any airfield.

The school occupied part of the buildings and grounds of the University of Georgia. Our quarters were in two converted girls' dormitories that faced each other across what had been a lawn, but was now a grassless, pounded parade ground. The architect of these buildings had obviously been much influenced by *Gone With the Wind*, and had designed two Taras, with tall white columns and a commanding sweep of steps (and after all, what else would you build for southern coeds?). But there was nothing romantic, or collegiate, and God knows nothing coeducational, about the life we lived there.

I felt at once, almost before I had unloaded my gear, that this was a place dominated by two qualities: it was very military, in an oddly phony way, and it was very tense. On the baked clay between the two Taras cadets were marching as we arrived, practicing for a parade. We had marched and paraded at Denton, but never like this, not rigid with concentration, eyes staring forward, arms swinging, sweating in the Georgia sun. A lot seemed to be at stake. As we carried our bags into the barracks, a voice came down from a window across the way: 'You'll be sorry!' It was what old hands always shouted to new ones, but this time it seemed to be more than that, as though he really knew that we would be, that what would happen to us there would make regret a certainty.

Later, at our first muster, we got the official version of that warning. We stood on the parade ground in platoon formation, and above us, at the top of the steps between the white columns, an officer stood and told us how the next three months would be, and why.

'We're here,' he shouted, 'to prepare you to be naval officers. You'll be taught things in ground school that we think an officer should know, and you'll learn the discipline of close-order drill. But most of all we'll be seeing if you can take it. If you can't take it, now's the time to find out, not when you're Out There, with lives depending on you.' He spoke with feeling, and you could almost forget for a moment that he was a schoolteacher or a football coach dressed up as an officer, and think that he must have been at Midway or the Coral Sea, that he knew what he was talking about. He stood silent for a time, running his eyes back and forth along our ranks, as though watching for someone to speak or move, or perhaps looking for weaklings, the ones who couldn't take it. Then he barked 'DIS-missed,' and the echo bounced back from the other Tara, '-missed,' and we turned slowly back into human beings.

Back in the barracks I found some of the boys who had left Minneapolis with me. Joe Baird and Wally were there, full of unlikely stories about Panhandle A&M, the flying and the Oklahoma girls, and I told them a few lies about Jo Belle and Denton. But then we were scattered again, shoved once more into rooms with strangers. I had a roommate from New Orleans, one from Virginia, and one from New Hampshire. I knew nothing about any of these places, and I had no way of understanding what these strangers were like. I couldn't read the Virginia or the New Hampshire signs of background or class or manners, and they couldn't read my Minneapolis signs. We circled each other cautiously, like sniffing dogs. But though we shared nothing of the past, we shared everything in the present—a room, toilets, mess hall, classrooms, parade ground. And more than that we shared a hatred of the whole program, and a determination to survive it.

At preflight we stopped being half-civilians and became a military unit, the Twenty-fifth Battalion. We were given regulation short-back-and-sides haircuts, and regulation uniforms: khaki for working days, whites and blues for dress, like officers; and our civilian clothes were packed and sent home. We posed for official pictures in our new whites, and the Navy sent them to hometown papers, and they came back as newspaper clippings stuck in our parents' letters: 'Local Boy Begins Pre-flight Training.'

Ground school began ('*Ground* school,' Joe grumbled, 'it's always *ground* school, as though we ever got *off* the ground in this place'), and we learned how to behave in a military classroom. You sat and waited for the instructor, and when he entered, the first cadet who saw him coming yelled 'ten-SHUN!' and you jumped to your feet and stood stiffly until the instructor said 'At ease,' and you could sink back into your seat. If the instructor called on you, you jumped to attention again and began your recitation with 'Sir!'—an exclamation more than a form of address. 'Cadet, what is the armament of the Scharnhorst-class cruiser?' (Leap to attention) 'Sir! The armament of the Scharnhorst-class cruiser is. . . .'

I suppose it all must have been modeled on the customs of the Naval Academy at Annapolis, and perhaps it worked there; but it seemed extravagant and a little comical to be always leaping up for these schoolteachers, and to stand backed stiffly up against the wall whenever one of them walked down the hall. This was called 'bracing the bulkhead.' The terminology was part of the nautical atmosphere, and part of the joke—the wall of a converted women's dormitory at the University of Georgia being called a 'bulkhead,' for God's sake!

The whole of the life was like that. We never walked anywhere, we marched—to meals, to classes, to church on Sunday (where we sang the hymn about God protecting those in peril on the sea), even to the movies. And we drilled, close-order drill, hour after hour on the fierce parade ground in the sun. If you were a great success at drilling you might get to lead a platoon or even a company; or you might even be made

Cadet Commander and run a whole parade. But that glory went mostly to cadets who had been in ROTC or had gone to military school; the rest of us stayed in the ranks, and tried not to fall down, or turn right when everybody else turned left. Because you could wash out just as easily for bad drilling as for bad flying; the football coaches believed that if you couldn't drill you were uncoordinated, and if you were uncoordinated you obviously couldn't fly.

Sport was another, even better test of coordination, and in that steaming Georgia summer we competed with each other in every kind of sport. We played football and ran races, both dashes and distance; we boxed and we wrestled, slipping from each other's sweaty grips like wet soap. They were all *games* when other, ordinary people played them, but for us they were Tests. Every competition was Judgment Day, and if you lost it seemed a moral failure, a revelation of a weak character that would make you useless, dangerous even, 'Out There.' It wasn't, of course, *The* Test—that would come at the heroic moment, the true and final occasion for action. I felt —surely we all felt—a boy's desire to do that one thing that really mattered, that was adult, that required courage and skill. I was being trained for it, the Navy would see that I was ready for it (or would cast me aside because I wasn't), and when it came I would move through it easily and without anxiety, and would come out the other side into an eternal state of hero-ism, which would also be adulthood. Flying would provide and demonstrate the skill, flying in combat would show the necessary courage; but only the successful attack—the bomb well placed, the enemy plane destroyed by accurate gunfire —would be the true consummation. Sometimes I had secret doubts: Would I ever be ready? Would I know when I was? The Navy's endless Tests were there to reassure me. I was passing, I was winning—surely it was all preparation, it was all right and necessary.

Not everyone could win, of course, not everyone would get his wings and his commission and fly into combat; there had to be losers, and so, though we liked each other, we began to look on even our best friends as competitors, as opponents. I boxed with my roommate, and though I didn't want to hurt him, be-cause I liked him, I found myself pressing in, pounding at his guard, hitting harder and harder because an officer was scoring us, and one of us would win; and afterward I felt ashamed that friendship had been weaker than the need to win, to pass the Test.

Not everybody minded it. Joe Baird, who could do anything effortlessly, and who never lost his temper, ran and boxed and climbed ropes all day, and would come into my room afterward, still on his tiptoes, to joke and chatter, as though the whole ordeal was just a summer camp. And Ike was the same: he just went on smiling and saying 'Golly,' and doing what was required of him with placid ease. The actions that for the rest of us were torments of physical strain and psychic tension were for them simply exercise. Their bodies had been lean and fit at the beginning, and they simply stayed that way, while their friends grew thinner and more irritable by the day, and more daunted by the effort that tomorrow would demand. But it was more than just physical conditioning. Joe and Ike were serenely happy people, *above* the Test; whatever the competition was, they simply weren't in it. I admired and envied their state of mind, but I never attained it.

What I dreaded most was the obstacle course, a race run over, under, and through various painful difficulties. The obstacles included most of the things I couldn't do—a long rope to climb, a log over a ditch, which had to be inched across straddling (it was known as the Nutcracker), a high wall to be scaled. I would lie awake at night thinking, Tomorrow is Thursday, I'll have to run the obstacle course, and this time I won't make it. And when I slept I would run it in my sleep, and fail at The Wall.

There was only one way to get over the wall (which was probably about eight feet high, though it seemed higher). You had to run at it full tilt, leap and catch a momentary foothold on its smooth side, grasp the top before your foot slipped, and hurl yourself headfirst over, turning in midair to land on your feet. If you failed to do this perfectly there was nothing to do but go back and start your run over again, while all your friends and opponents dashed past and over it and out of sight. It was humiliating, and I think that's why it was there—to make defeat seem worse than anything, worse than dying. The obstacle course was a moral exercise. It tested your willingness to undergo any strain, any effort, for the sake of a chance at a commission, and to avoid the shame of losing.

I made a new friend at the wall when, as I was hanging head-first over the top, gasping for breath, I heard an angry southern voice say, 'Aw, fuck it!' and saw a cadet named Taylor walk around the wall and jog off toward the next obstacle. I knew he could have got over—he was a good athlete—but he'd had enough; he just didn't see the sense of it. This approach to life made Taylor good and consoling company during those trying months. He would collapse on my bunk after a day of unreasonable trials and groan, 'Every muscle in muh fuckin' body is screamin',' and then he would go over the day's activities in vivid, angry detail—the recognition class on Italian fighter planes ('*Italian* fighter planes, for Christ sake! There *ain't* any Italian air force except on those goddamn slides'), the signal-flag practice, the lecture on saluting, the film on venereal disease titled *She May Look Safe, But*. . . . It was all chicken shit to Taylor. 'Old Taylor,' some other southerner said, 'he thinks like a nigger. Even walks like a nigger. Maybe he *is* a nigger.' But he said it with a kind of admiration. He saw that Taylor was a born outsider, a natural anarchist caught in a system that had nothing for him, and that his anger and his sly evasions were the only self-defense he had.

I thought I had no memories of that time, because it had nothing to do with flying, and because I hated it so; but names and faces come back: the roommate from Virginia, with his soft Tidewater accent, who said 'hah-oos' for 'house'; the methodically tidy New Englander whose housekeeping got us past a white-glove inspection; Hawk Henry, an ex-enlisted man who was the only cadet in our platoon who could give orders with style. ('Eyes in the boat!' he would shout as we marched past the C.O., 'Eyes in the boat!' It seemed a very salty way of telling us not to gawk around.)

One evening remains, still evocative of how it felt to be young then, and going, however slowly, toward war. We had been marched across the campus, down a cinder trail through a pine wood, to the university's auditorium to see a movie. We sat by battalion, and while we waited for the film to begin we chanted, battalion by battalion, how long we had to go: 'Twenty-third, one more week!' 'Twenty-fourth, three more weeks!' We were the Twenty-fifth—five more weeks! Then the movie started. It was *Casablanca*.

When we returned late to our barracks, marching along the dark path through the pines, no one talked, but every once in a while someone would whistle or sing a phrase from 'As Time Goes By.' We were not so much thinking about the film as floating on its emotions, feeling the sadness of Humphrey Bogart, who had given up Ingrid Bergman for the Cause. We didn't really understand what the Cause was, exactly, what high principles linked the French at Casablanca to us at Athens, Georgia. But we felt the emotional link; it had to do with separation and loss, and at eighteen, in a strange place among strangers, we knew something about that. In the barracks we went quietly to bed. There still wasn't much talking, but as I fell asleep I heard one last cadet, alone in the shower, singing, 'You must remember this, a kiss is just a kiss. . . .'

The days of those painful months will not separate themselves into this day or that one. But I remember the weather. There were two kinds. Rain: it fell heavily from purple-black, low, pregnant-looking clouds, straight down, windlessly, for days at a time. The red dirt of the parade ground was marched and kneaded into mud like dough, and puddles stood in the paths between the buildings. We were wet from morning until night, and the next morning our clothes had not dried, and it would still be raining, and the voice of the Officer of the Day would come over the barracks loudspeaker: 'Now hear this. The uniform of the day will be raincoats, with condom-type cap covers.' And we would hunch out into the waiting rain for muster. And sun: it burned down, indifferently, out of a coppery, cloudless sky that seemed to be stretched very low, just over the parade ground and the football field. It burned through clothes, it burned through short Navy haircuts, into the scalp, into the skull, and made your brain feel hot and dry. I played a sixty-minute football game under that sun, and it was like a year on Devil's Island.

But then, the whole thing was a kind of penal servitude, three months at hard, meaningless labor. Far from increasing our endurance, preflight drained it. Our faces grew tanned, and our bodies lean, but we were strained and tense, keyed up beyond any useful level. It was an ordeal that did nothing for us, certainly didn't make officers, or even men of us, a pointless ritual to a god called 'Attitude.' I sensed this, and resented it, though I didn't understand what was wrong with it then. But my resentment must have surfaced, because the football coach who commanded my company called me into his office to say, with loathing in his voice, 'Cadet, you'll never make an officer. Your Attitude's all wrong.' Perhaps it was. Certainly it was different from his.

The most surprising thing about preflight school is that we managed to survive it, and as friends. I don't think we learned much there, but we did learn one lesson that was valuable to us all. We learned to hate our enemies—not the Germans and the Japanese (nobody ever mentioned them), but the nonflying, Attitude-talking martinets who commanded us, and the military system that they represented. After preflight we would never quite join the Navy; we had joined instead a smaller, more independent and anarchic group, the community of fliers. The Navy was our antagonist, muscle-bound and dumb like those football-coach officers; but because it was dumb we could beat it. With a little imagination we could circumvent, muddle, and exploit the regulations, and we could fly. 'Fuck the Navy,' Taylor said as we packed to leave Athens. 'That's all, just fuck the Navy.' We were moving on, out of the chicken shit, back to our proper element, the air.

Chapter Two

MEMORIES OF flying are almost always memories of land-scape. It isn't that you think *I am flying over this state or that one*, but that you are moving above a landscape pierced by a mountain, or patched with woodlands, or edged by the sea. The earth is always there below, apart and beautiful (no land is ugly from the air), revealing its private features in a way that it never does to the traveler on its surface. A pilot can see where a road goes, what is over that hill, the shapes of lakes and towns; and I suppose this knowledge of the earth's face is a part of the feeling of dominion that a pilot feels when his plane reaches a commanding altitude and he looks down on the world that stretches out beneath him.

At the Naval Air Station at Memphis there was, most of all, the river, a broad presence lying to the west of the airfield: black in the morning light, a vast reflector at sunset, gray when the sky was gray, but always there. The impression it gave, from the air, was of absolute flatness—an odd impression, perhaps, for what would you expect a river to be except flat? Still, the earth from the air retains its contours and remains three-dimensional (it never really looks like a map or a patchwork quilt); but the river was relentlessly two-dimensional. It didn't seem to move or to have any irregularities at all—it just lay there, like an old mirror, revealing nothing, only reflecting.

Beside the river, the Naval Air Station looked temporary, raw, and ugly. A year before it had been a Tennessee farm, with a big old frame house surrounded by oaks, and a pond where cattle stood and drank. Bulldozers had come in, and the trees and the pond were gone. In their place were rows of impermanent-looking gray buildings and two paved circular landing mats, and around the whole Station a high wire fence, along which military police patrolled with guard dogs. It was a place without a single thing to please the eye, and I was always glad to take off from it and to see the river and the farmland outside.

Life at the Air Station was lived in the constant presence of planes—the sound of engines testing, warming up, taking off. There were planes overhead all day; and at night, as you walked back from the movie or a beer at the Slop Chute, red and green running lights passed in the dark sky, and the flicker of exhaust flames. You went to sleep to the sound of flying, and woke to the first morning takeoffs. Planes became a part of your subliminal life, only thrusting up into consciousness when an engine faltered, and you rushed to a window or stepped in the street to look up at trouble.

At Athens we had lived four in a room in our women's dormitory with the columns. But Memphis was a real naval base, and we were housed there in regulation enlisted-men's barracks, barnlike two-story frame buildings with one long room on each floor. In each of these rooms double-decked bunks were lined up symmetrically on either side of a central aisle —room for eighty cadets, maybe more. It didn't seem possible that I could ever fall asleep in a room with eighty people, and at first I lay awake at night after the lights were out, listening to the sounds—the street sounds, the airfield sounds, and the sounds of sleeping. The dim exit light at the end of the room only made the shadows deeper, the sounds more anonymous and remote. Then I was sleeping too.

In a barracks, life begins anonymously. Every bed is like every other bed, lockers are identical, all arrangements are symmetrical (hang your towel, folded once vertically, on the lefthand end of the foot of your bed; do not display personal photographs; shoes must be placed in the locker in pairs, toes in). There is one common toilet room (no doors on the stalls) and one shower room. No individual is to be distinguished from another.

But gradually personality seeps in and fills the spaces between the identical beds, and makes the barracks into a human community, and the anonymous others into people. So I remember how, first of all, there were only the individual voices: a drunk Georgia cracker at the other end of the long room, babbling to himself in a shrill, incomprehensible whine; a couple of country boys on their bunks harmonizing a mournful church song; a Texan telling a long dirty story. Then, after a while, some of the voices became persons, and some of these became my friends.

In the service, friends often come by the accidental conjunctions that the system imposes. Because my name came between the next-to-last of the H's and the first of the I's I got to know Spanish John (above me in the double-decker bunk) and T (on my left). The three of us became friendly, took our liberties together, got drunk together, shared our money and our news from home, encouraged each other when the work or the flying got tough. Once, while drunk in Memphis, we had our portrait taken together by a classy photographer, and there we still are, looking young, and soberer than we were, with faces like blank pages.

T became my close friend, and remained so. He was an odd-looking guy—short, thin, and undernourished looking, nothing like what you'd expect an Aviation Cadet to be. He carried his shoulders hunched forward, and his head slightly on one side, as though he had been interrupted in a shrug. His walk was a kind of shuffling dance; he seemed to hear a jazz tune that nobody else heard, and he sang wordless Louis Armstrong riffs to himself as he walked—'bah-bah zoo-zee bah, yeah, yeah.' He looked frail, but he could do everything that I could do, and slightly better. When we boxed he landed three punches while I was landing two, when we swam he finished his laps first, and when we flew he seemed always to pass his check-flights sooner and with less trouble. But though he was good at what the Navy demanded of him, he never seemed altogether involved in the business of being military; even in the middle of a platoon he didn't seem to be actually *marching*. Like Taylor, he had a streak of the born anarchist in him; perhaps he had learned it from the southern blacks who played the music he heard in his head.

Spanish John wasn't really Spanish; we took the name from a petty gangster in a story by Damon Runyon, because John seemed to us like that kind of guy. He was a tough kid from a New Jersey slum, and he seemed to know more about adult life, or at least the drinking and the sex parts, than the rest of us did. He regarded us as childish innocents, and his mouth wore an habitual smile of disdain; his eyes were restless and watchful, alert for an opportunity to outsmart authority and to beat the system. I didn't like him as I liked T, but I was

impressed by his city-shrewdness, and I accepted the compan-
ionship that the alphabet had imposed.

Another new friend was the story-telling Texan, who was
called Rock, no doubt because his face looked as though it
had been carved in red sandstone—or perhaps not carved, but
simply eroded. The skin of his forehead and cheeks was red and
dry looking, and scored with deep lines, like a dry gully, and his
nose thrust sharply outward, and then turned suddenly down
and slightly to one side, like a crooked beak. I asked him about
the nose. 'Met a Mexican once,' he explained. 'Meaner than
me.' Rock had endless stories to tell, about Texas, about his
college years at A&M, about women and drinking. He would
flop down on his bunk, drop his shoes on the floor, and remark
that that reminded him of the time he bought a pair of twenty-
dollar boots and then got drunk. 'Got me to bed, and in the
middle of the night I had to piss so bad, and was so drunk,
that I *dreamed* I got up and went to the can, and went back
to sleep. Woke up in the morning, and there was my twenty-
dollar boot, full of piss right up to the top.'

Sometimes you would meet someone just by accident,
hanging around the flight line waiting for a flight, or over a
beer, or in the barracks. Bud was an accidental friend; we had
been at the same university the fall before, but we met for the
first time in a chow line in Memphis. Bud had an ironic view
of life that was a great consolation in the military world. He
didn't expect life to be rational, or effort to be rewarded;
he didn't expect success, I don't think he even wanted it. He
was content if the human comedy was occasionally funny. Bud
was incapable of assuming a military posture, or a military appearance; however he was dressed—in flight gear or in dress
whites—he looked like a lost Marx Brother. Such a guy is a
natural subversive; Bud denied and defeated the Navy way of
doing things, simply by existing. And he helped his friends to
preserve their individualities, because he would only deal with
the world in individual terms.

Bud was much preoccupied with sex. His problem, as he
saw it, was a simple physiological one: 'My balls are too big,'
he explained. But though he was interested, the girls weren't,
and his life at Memphis was a long series of failed conquests.
Perhaps because he found the sex so elusive, he also found it

poetic, and he spoke of sexual matters in lyric metaphorical terms. The female organ was 'the bearded clam' or 'the mossy doughnut,' and when I came in from a date he would look up brightly and ask: 'And did you soak the social sausage?'

I don't think Bud's metaphors were obscene—he really was a sexual poet. But much of what we all said and sang *was* obscene. Obscenity was a kind of intimacy, a shared language like the common toilet and the single room we slept in, a step past conventional reticences. We took that step because we had to live an intimate collective life, and this was one way of accepting it. Our common vocabulary connected us with each other, and separated us from the world out there, and Back Home. There were limits, though. You used obscenities with each other, but not too freely; you could call your friend a bastard, affectionately, but you couldn't call him a shit. You never used any really obscene terms when you were speaking of people you were fond of—your family, for instance—and never in the company of girls, unless they were clearly tramps. And you didn't use it indiscriminately. Fucking couldn't *always* be the adjective; that was the way enlisted men talked, and we were going to be officers.

Obscenity was masculine; anyone who objected to it, or simply didn't use it, must therefore be feminine—a queer, a pansy. In a bunk just down from mine lived a gentle, Bible-reading Georgia boy named Newton. He was the politest cadet I ever met, in that formal, old-fashioned way that some southern country folk have, and the most fastidious. He would wait until midnight to go to the toilet or take a shower, so that he could be alone there, and he would leave the room when the talk got too coarse. He must have hated us and the way we lived; but he wanted to belong, too, and so he kept coming back, and hanging around. We teased him, called him 'Newt the Fruit,' and hinted, if he seemed to have made a friend, that unnatural acts took place in the shower after lights out. The mood was meant to be joking, and I think many of us felt some fondness for him, but his manner was outside the limits of our world, and so we had to keep him outside, too. I don't think he was homosexual, what we took for femininity was simply his gentleness (T said he was just a Good Ol' Boy who loved his mamma). But we were beginning to think in a—what shall

I call it?—a military way; perhaps we had learned the preflight lesson after all, and were developing the right Attitude. We didn't actually persecute poor Newton, but we despised him, and that is worse than persecution when you're nineteen, and want to belong.

The planes at Memphis were Stearman N2S's, open-cockpit biplanes that were painted yellow and were known as 'Yellow Perils.' In fact they were anything but perilous; they were probably the safest and strongest airplanes ever built. They could be flown through acrobatic maneuvers that would disintegrate a fighter, they could be dropped to a landing from a stall twenty feet in the air, and they could be ground-looped with no more damage than a bit of scraped paint. I did all these things to the planes, and they (and I) survived. And in the process I learned a bit more about flying.

What I learned, first of all, was the intense delight of flying an open plane. I'm not sure that I can explain why it is so different from a closed cockpit, but it has to do with the intimate presence of the air itself, the medium you fly in, streaming past and around you. You can thrust your whole arm out into the slipstream and press back against the flow of air; you can lean to the side, and the air will force the tears from your eyes and rush into your lungs. And you can look straight into space, down to the earth and up to the sky, with nothing between you and the whole world. The plane is not a protective shell, as an automobile is, but an extension of your own body, moving as you move; and your head is the brain of the whole stretched and vibrating organism. Flying alone in an open plane is the purest experience of flight possible.

But from the Navy's point of view our learning was a bit more programmed and less lyrical than that. Each of us was assigned to an instructor, a flying officer whose task it was to guide his pupil through the stages of the training program and to prepare him for the periodic Tests, the check-rides. The instructors were flying tutors, each with his own style, though with one common syllabus.

Primary flight instructors were of two kinds. One lot had been private pilots before the war—amateurs, mostly, who had flown light planes on weekends. They had been hustled into the flight program and assigned to bring beginners like ourselves up to roughly their own level of competence. So long as they did this more or less efficiently, they would be allowed to remain where they were; but they would never be promoted to *real* planes, the combat planes that we aspired to, they would never join the fleet, they would never do any fighting. Pilots in this category had a special designation—they were called Voluntary Reservists (USNR–V) rather than simply Reservists, like the rest of us. They were on the whole a complacent lot, content to fly all day and then go home to their wives and children like any bank clerk; they were easygoing and undemanding in the air, asking only that you did nothing while flying that might get them, and you, killed. You could recognize them by their expression, and by their generally unmilitary bearing.

The other kind were pilots who had been through the same program that we were in—had gone all the way through Pensacola or Corpus Christi and had been commissioned like any service pilot, and then, instead of going on to operational training and fleet duty, had been sent back to a primary base to instruct novices in Yellow Perils. These men—at least the ones I came up against—were angry and bitter; they hated their job, and the cadets they taught, and the fat, comical-looking airplanes they flew. They seemed sadistically demanding, especially in check-rides, and we feared them, without really respecting them (after all, they had never flown fighters).

Ensign Dewberry, my instructor, was USNR–V. He had a round face that always seemed to be freshly polished, and he smiled a lot, not at anything in particular, but as though he had been smiling a while ago and had forgotten to stop. When he flew he wore a flying suit that was too short in the arms and legs, so that his khaki pants and shirt sleeves stuck out at the ends. The effect was oddly temporary, as though he was only playing at flying for a minute or so, and would then revert to something more appropriate and civilian.

We met each day at the schedule board in the hangar, where flight assignments were posted. He would be standing there, with his parachute slung over one shoulder by the leg straps (something we were told we must never do), staring dreamily at the board, and when I approached and saluted he would turn, still smiling but without any sign of recognition, and say 'Hi.' Usually he forgot to salute. We would drift out to the flight line, and he would comment vaguely on the weather, and ask me what we were supposed to be doing on this flight.

There was no radio in the N2S, and once in the air we could communicate in one direction only, through a tube that ran from a mouthpiece attached to Dewberry's helmet, down inside the fuselage, and up to earpieces on my helmet. As I took off I could hear Dewberry humming to himself as he gawked around at the sights, like a yokel on his first five-minute ride at the state fair. Sometimes he'd point to something that had caught his eye, and look up in the mirror above his head, and I'd nod furiously to show that I saw what he saw. It was all very amiable, but sometimes I felt that I was teaching myself to fly, while in the front seat a cheerful but simpleminded stranger nodded encouragement.

Together Dewberry and I rode through twenty-five or thirty flying hours. We began with the basic things that I thought I had already learned in the Cubs at Denton—takeoffs and landings—but now we did it differently, because this was *Navy* flying. Some of us would fly from carriers some day, and so we learned to get the plane into the air fast—no more of those long, tail-in-the-air rushes, like a galloping cow, that had been the CPT style—and we learned to land in a full stall, the tail wheel touching the ground first, so that the landing hook (if we had had one) would always catch the arresting wire (if there had been an arresting wire on the Memphis mat). Between flights, back in the barracks, T would explain how it should be done. 'Puh-TOW,' he would say, flapping one hand down on the other, heel-end first, 'that's all you got to do, just puh-TOW!' It looked easy, but it wasn't; but after a while I could do it, and it was very satisfying to feel the plane stop flying just as you touched the mat. Puh-TOW!

Then we went on to an altogether new kind of flying—acrobatics. Acrobatic flying is a useless skill in its particulars —no combat pilot will ever need to loop or slow-roll—but it is one that extends your control of the plane and yourself, and makes extreme actions in the sky comfortable. In acrobatics the sense of flying is extended to its extreme limit; flying a plane through a loop or a Cuban-eight is the farthest thing possible from simply driving it. When you reach the top of a loop, upside-down and engine at full throttle, and tilt your head back to pick up the horizon line behind you, you are as far outside instinctive human behavior as you can go—hanging in space, the sky below you and the earth above, inscribing a circle on emptiness. And then the nose drops across the horizon, your speed increases, and the plane scoops through into normal flight, and you are back in the normal world, with the earth put back in its place. It's that going out and coming back that makes a loop so satisfying.

After a while, that is. At first it was terrifying, like being invited to a suicide that you didn't want to commit. 'This is a loop,' Dewberry said casually. He lowered the nose to gain airspeed and then pulled sharply up. The earth, and my stomach, fell away from me, and we were upside-down, and I could feel gravity clawing at me, pulling me out into the mile of space between me and the ground. I grabbed at the sides of the cockpit and hung on until gravity was on my side again. Of course I knew that I had a safety belt that would hold me in my seat; but my body didn't know it—*if you're upside-down in space*, my body said, *don't be a fool, hang on!*

'You seemed a little nervous that time,' Dewberry said, when the plane was right-side up again. 'You've got to have confidence in that seat belt or you'll never do a decent loop. So this time, when we get on top, I want you to put both arms out of the cockpit.' And I did it. It was like stepping off a bridge, but I did it, and the belt held, and the plane came round. And after that I could fly a loop. It was, as I said, satisfying.

Not always, though. There was an instructor named Harris who was famous for his fondness for loops. It was said that if you could do a good loop for him you could pass any flight test, whether it was supposed to involve loops or not. He would fly you through one of his own beautifully executed maneuvers, and as he pulled out he would say through the speaking tube, with evident self-approval, 'And that, cadet, is how a loop should be flown.' Since the speaking tube was only one-way, the cadet couldn't reply, but he was expected to assume an expression of reverent admiration. Then he could try one himself. One day the cadet in the back seat forgot to fasten his safety belt, and at the top of the loop he fell out. Harris pulled the plane on through, and began his speech: 'And that, cadet, . . .' glancing up in his mirror for the appropriate look of admiration. No cadet. He turned and flew sorrowfully back to the field, wondering how to break the news to the C.O. that he had dropped a student. By the time he had landed the cadet was trudging toward the hangar, carrying his opened parachute.

The next time out, Harris drew a student from my barracks called Gus. Gus was the shortest cadet in the Navy, and he flew with his seat raised all the way to the top (you could raise and lower it like a barber's chair). Harris began his favorite maneuver, first diving to pick up airspeed and then pulling up sharply. As he did so, the ratchet on the back seat slipped, and centrifugal force thrust Gus forcibly down to the bottom of the cockpit, where the seat stuck. Harris completed the loop, and once more began his routine: 'And that, cadet. . . .' Meanwhile Gus was bent over, groping for the seat lever. Harris glanced at his mirror. My God! He had lost another one!

I found all acrobatic maneuvers pleasurable: the slow-roll, in which the plane is rolled around its length-wise axis; the snap-roll, a quick rotation that has a wonderful suddenness; the Immelmann, the first half of a loop with a half-roll at the top. The more things you can make a plane do, the more you are flying it; though that's not quite right—you don't make a plane roll, you coax it, ease it, fly with it through the whole maneuver. It becomes a natural series of muscular adjustments, like walking or running, but more conscious.

For some acrobatics instructors these natural movements were no longer enough; they were decadents, bored with ordinary maneuvers, only thrilled by exotic variations. They would fly a loop wrong-way-round, beginning upside-down and reaching the top right-side-up—a maneuver that put the pilot on the *outside* of the circle and forced the blood to his head, and that would tear the wings off a less sturdy plane. Or they would fly outside snap-rolls, a much more violent version of the ordinary kind. Or they would ride a falling-leaf—a sort of controlled stall that loses altitude very fast—too close to the ground, and come out with a roar just over the trees. I found all these maneuvers perverse, contrary to the nature of both planes and pilots; but I could understand why some instructors did them. The bitter ones knew that the war would be fought and finished some day and that they would still be there, in the Yellow Perils, and that we wouldn't. We would go on to fly the fighters and the bombers, to see Pacific islands and learn what combat was like, and whether we could pass the Test. But they would never know. Like most perversions, theirs was the product of despair at never knowing the real thing.

Time passed, and we began to have some feeling for the movement of the plane, some sense of the harmony that exists between a pilot's body and his machine—what pilots mean by 'flying by the seat of your pants.' We had come to be at ease in space, even when upside-down, and we had learned to return to the surface of the earth without anxiety and without disaster ('it ain't the air that kills you,' the old-timers told us, 'it's comin' back to the ground'). There was only one natural threat left—the night.

In darkness, instincts weaken. The horizon is scarcely there, up is less certainly up, and down may not be exactly down. The earth, which by daylight offers a comforting variety of possible emergency landing fields, becomes threatening at night. Darkness hides hills and trees, and swallows every flat surface. There is no hope for you down there at night, and it is reasonable that you should feel fear, flying in darkness.

I didn't know anything about that kind of fear yet when I reported for night flying at Memphis; it was just one more preliminary Test, one more way of eliminating the unworthy. The exercise was simple, Dewberry had said, anyone could do it. You simply took off between rows of lights, followed the taillight of the plane ahead of you around the traffic pattern, and landed. Then you taxied back to takeoff position and did it again. The only trouble was that you did it in the dark, and so everything had to be learned anew. The cockpit, which by day had become a familiar, secure place, at night was a black hole. Engine instruments showed only as dim greenish lines of phosphorescence; switches were invisible, and had to be found by touch. Just getting the engine started was a new and difficult process, and taxiing was a game of blindman's buff. Then you had to take off without swerving into a runway light, and find and follow the taillight ahead of you. But the night sky is full of lights, and if you chose a star instead of a taillight (and occasionally someone did), you would fly in a straight line forever, waiting for it to turn.

Darkness, which makes most of your familiar plane invisible, makes one feature dramatically visible. The exhaust stacks, which in daylight are just pipes sticking out of the right-hand side of the engine, are red mouths spitting fire at night. If you're flying in a left-hand landing pattern you'll be looking over the left side of the cockpit and won't notice the stacks; but one cadet looked over the other side, saw those streams of flame and thought his plane was on fire, and bailed out. The plane went on without him until it ran out of gas and crashed in Arkansas.

On my first night solo flight the darkness seemed immense and hostile, and the spots of light scattered across it were mysterious and uncomforting. Memphis was a dim halo that seemed to come out of the earth itself, the airport beacon winked and went dark, and the solitary lights below me seemed lonely and apart. Even the red and green running lights at my wing tips seemed separate from me, and a long way off. There were no certain distances, either on the earth or in the air, I wasn't sure where I was, and the plane was a stranger that made odd noises that it didn't make in the daylight. I was eager to be back on the ground.

Not eager to land, though; landing at night was the worst part of night flying. It was like jumping into a dark pool, when you just have to take it on faith that there's really water down there. The runway—the hard, paved, comforting reality—was invisible; there were only the two rows of lights and a black space between them. As you turn into the landing approach the lights run together and form two perspective lines, and you thump down between them; but for me that last moment, when I cut the power and waited for the thump, was a moment of complete despair. My confidence as a flier fell from me, I wasn't flying the plane, I didn't know where the ground was; the plane would just have to get down on its own.

During those months in which we were learning to fly the Navy way, we were also learning what it meant to be cadets. It meant, among other things, being a segregated minority, separated both from the enlisted men and from the officers. We ranked neither above the one group (enlisted men did not

salute us or address us as 'Sir,' and they made a considerable
show of their contempt for our ambiguous status) nor below
the other (officers were more our elders than our betters, since
we would eventually join their ranks). We were just apart. It
was impossible to imagine hanging around with either an enlisted man or an officer; we hung around only with each other,
lived together, ate together, flew together. I cannot recall one
instant of that time when I was not with another cadet, except
when I was flying solo, and occasionally when I managed to be
with a girl, nor one instant when I was with an adult male who
was neither a cadet nor an instructor.

Our segregation was extraordinarily complete. Even when
we went on liberty we moved in cadet groups; every liberty was
a party, and it was always an all-cadet party. There had naturally
been no parties at preflight school. We were given no time off
there and were never allowed off the grounds, and anyway we
were always too tired to do anything very riotous, even if pleasure had been allowed. But now our lives were different. We
had our evenings and our Saturday nights, and Memphis was
a wild liberty town within easy reach. And we were recovering
our energies and our sexual appetites.

A party really began in the barracks head, with the shower-
ing and the shaving lotion and the dress uniforms, everybody changing—changing his clothes and his frame of mind,
thinking about drinking and girls instead of flying. It was like
Saturday night in a fraternity house, I imagine, or in a college dormitory. Then the liberty bus into town, through the
dejected little town of Flemington, on past the fields and the
unpainted sharecroppers' shacks, and into Memphis—first
the shanty town of Negro houses and finally, at the center,
the white, romantic city.

The bar of the Peabody Hotel would be full of Navy uniforms, and there you might meet some friends or try to pick
up an enlisted Wave. The Waves seemed safer than the civilian
women, who might be whores (we remembered the admoni-
tions of *She May Look Safe, But* . . . , the Navy's cautionary VD
film), and we assumed, or pretended to assume, that because
they were Waves they must be easy and experienced. There
must have been Wave officers around, too, but I never met
one; they wouldn't have associated with cadets, and anyway

they were probably too old (I had just turned nineteen, and I was easily frightened by 'older women' over twenty-one).

On an upper floor of the hotel there was a Service Club, where you could buy setups for the bottle you had bought (blended whiskey, most likely, unless you had taken a cab out into the Negro district, where liquor stores sometimes still had a bottle of Scotch on the shelf), and where you could dance with the Wave you had picked up, and try to get her drunk before you passed out yourself. Or you could wander the streets and find other places, where there was music and dancing, or go down to the other hotel, an ancient antebellum pile beside the river called the Gayoso, where there was usually a party going on in someone's room.

The parties passed in a blur of drunkenness and confusion. I am in a room with twin beds and a large number of cadets and girls. There are bottles and a bowl of melting ice-cubes on the dresser, and glasses on every table. All the glasses have been used, and have yellow dregs of drinks and cigarette butts in the bottom, but you can always empty them out the window and make another drink. A girl has locked herself in the bathroom, and her date is asking people what to do. At the window Gus is dropping paper bags of water onto passersby on the sidewalk below. Taylor lies on a bed with a girl who is drunk, but not drunk enough to be seduced in a room full of people. She has smeared her brown leg-makeup onto the legs of his white trousers. T is sitting on the floor, backed into a corner, with an inverted wastebasket between his knees, drumming softly on it with his fingertips, and humming a jazz tune, almost inaudibly —'If you see me comin', hise yo' window high. . . .' At the door Spanish John explains to the house detective that it's all right now, and gives him some money. Then I am on the bus again, and the shacks pass in the cold half-light, and I am walking up the company street toward the barracks, trying not to stagger, and over on the airfield engines are beginning to warm up for the first morning flight.

One photograph survives from these Memphis nights. It is one of those large, glossy pictures that wandering photographers used to take in night clubs: a party picture, with a table full of bottles and drinks in the middle, and all around it people facing the camera, trying to look as though they're having a good time. The photograph has dimmed and darkened with time, so that it has a remote, underwater look, but I can still make out the faces: three rather ugly Waves, in uniform, looking hearty, as though they might burst into a sea-shanty at any minute; Spanish John, eyeing one of them hungrily; Bud, owlish and melancholy, even though he is smiling; and myself, grinning foolishly around the stem of a brand-new pipe. We are in the Creole Room of the Hotel Peabody. The Waves are going to drink more than we can afford. It will only be worth the effort and expense if they sleep with us. Why else would you spend money on a Wave? They know that, and are determined to leave us at the party's end, broke but un-screwed. Spanish John is optimistic; he believes that no girl can resist him for long. I am hopeful, but uncertain about how the act is actually performed. Bud sees it all—that we will try, that we'll fail, and that it doesn't make any difference.

There were nice girls in our lives, too. Being middle-class is more than a social station, it's a kind of destiny. A middle-class boy from Minneapolis will seek out nice middle-class girls, in Memphis or anywhere else, will take them out on middle-class dates and try to put his hand inside their middle-class underpants. And he will fail. It was all a story that had already been written.

I picked up a pretty girl who worked in a record store, and made a date with her, feeling rather wicked and dashing because I was moving so fast—a seducer at work, a carefree, careless Navy man ruining a virtuous maiden. I should have known when I called for her that I had already lost. The white frame house, the dress with the flouncy skirt, the introduction to the folks ('Don't be too late, dear')—it was all like an Andy Hardy movie. I took her to a beer cellar where there was music, and we drank and danced, and while the jukebox played 'Pistol Packin' Mama' I tried to play the role of the irresistible lover. She drank her beer calmly and without apparent effects, and said over and over, 'No, let's dance,' patiently and without rancor, as though I were subnormal, or a child, but not dangerous.

Our courtship went on all that fall, and I grew quite fond of her, but I never came near reaching the goal that I had imagined, that first afternoon in the record shop. We didn't

go off to the Gayoso, or even into the back seat of a parked
car; we danced, and though I wasn't very good at that either,
at least I had done it before. I suppose I had known all the
time that I wouldn't make her. That's really why I went back,
because I knew that she wouldn't let me reach the Test, the Big
Sex Game where I would have to perform, and would know
whether I was a winner or a loser.

At the same time, like everyone else, I went on writing to
Alice, the girl back home, letters that I hoped were full of pas-
sion and erotic stimulation; and she wrote cheerful, but not
very erotic, replies. One of the things that girls from back
home did was to come and visit you. It gave you a kind of
status among the other cadets if a reasonably pretty girl would
make a trip just to see you, and to be paraded around. Every
weekend you would see cadets, dressed in careful whites, walking awkwardly around the base showing the sights to girls in
frilly dresses. And to their mothers; there were always mothers,
it was a chaperoning time. So I invited Alice down from Minneapolis, and she (and her mother) came.

They stayed at the Peabody, in a double room. I had a room
on the floor above. My plan of action was simple: get rid of
the mother, take Alice to my room, and pass the Test. But
first there were the formalities. I took them both to dinner, on
the roof of the hotel—the Starlit Roof, it was called. A band
played, and a master of ceremonies sang and told off-color
stories, which Alice's mother received with thin-lipped disapproval. We ate. And drank—not too much, though, I mustn't
appear out of control, I mustn't let my lechery show. I danced
with Alice, and felt her mother's eyes follow us around the
floor. (Was I dancing too close? Were my intentions obvious?)
I even danced with the mother, steering her stout, corsetted
form like a wheelbarrow among the other dancers. At last the
band played 'Goodnight, Sweetheart' and the mother, who
had her own sense of fair play, said she would be off to bed.
But she would stay awake until Alice came in, that was clear.

But why go on, when the rest of the story is so predictable?
—how we got to my room, how we fumbled and embraced,
how she would go *that* far (after all, she'd come all the way
from Minneapolis, she must have had something in mind herself), but no further, how she struggled, how I pleaded and

lost, and at last sullenly delivered her at her mother's door. It
had all been a charade, an acting out of middle-class morals, an
allegory. I represented Lust, Alice was Innocence (or maybe
True Romance), and her mother was the dragon Virtue. Alice
went as she had come, a good girl. 'How'd you do, man?' Bud
asked me when I saw him on the flight line. 'Did you get into
Alice's Chalice?' But he knew the answer already; her Chalice
was still the Holy Grail.

As I approached the end of the training program at Memphis, I began to believe that I would make it all the way to the
end—through Pensacola, to a commission, wings, a squadron,
even to the ultimate Test of combat. Before, these had all been
insubstantial fantasies, but now, gradually, they were becoming real and possible. And as success became imaginable, the
meaning of failure also became clearer. After a check-ride the
instructor would walk silently back to the scheduling board in
the hangar and would enter the result with an arrow beside
the student's name. An Up ↑ meant that you had passed; a
Down ↓ meant failure. Maybe the symbolism had been borrowed from the Roman emperors in the Colosseum; certainly
a Down seemed as final and as fatal to us as thumbs down was
to a gladiator. But the symbolism had another, more obvious
significance: Up pointed to the air, where we wanted to be,
and Down condemned you to the earth. The more I flew, the
more I wanted to go on flying, and the more terrible it seemed
to fail.

When a friend did fail, it was like a death in the family. Bud,
the sad-eyed ironist, washed out on acrobatics—he was just
too sensible, he said, to learn to fly upside-down—and left for
Great Lakes. And a Dartmouth man failed to master small-field
landings and also left, though instead of Great Lakes he went
to train in blimps, and even got a commission, which we all
thought was all right, because he had been to Dartmouth. I
was fond of them both, but when they walked out of the Station gate they left my life as totally as if they had died. And in
a way they had; they weren't pilots anymore.

When I first came to Memphis it was late summer, and
the fields lying eastward from the river were green. The cotton was being picked, and bits of white lay along the road-
sides like blown snow. The sun was hot on the landing mat,

and even high in the air it was warm. As I went through the training program, autumn came, the fields turned brown and wet, and the days grew shorter. At the end of my time there, in November, darkness fell so early that it overtook the last flight of the afternoon. It was on one of those late flights that I learned a new thing about flying—that it makes the approach of night different. It was late as I flew back from some practice solo, and the sun was nearly set, but the air was still warm and bright. The flight must have gone well, and I was feeling at ease with the plane and, in spite of the engine's steady racket, quiet and peaceful. Below me lights began to come on in houses and farms, and everything that was not a light became dark and indistinct, so that the ground was almost like a night sky. But still I flew on in sunlight. The surface of the plane seemed to absorb and hold the light and color of the sunset; brightness surrounded me. It was as though the earth had died, and I alone was left alive. A sense of my own aliveness filled me. I would never die. I would go on flying forever.

Chapter Three

I WENT HOME that fall, after I had finished the course at Memphis, to see my father. He and my stepmother had moved from Minneapolis to a grim industrial suburb of Chicago, where my father had a job in a factory that made military engines. It was shift work, and it was hard on him at his age, but it was 'helping the war effort,' and he was the kind of man who accepted such slogans. Maybe he had had trouble finding work; it wasn't the kind of thing we would have talked about in our family. Reticence was a primary virtue in our house, above cleanliness and godliness even.

His shift was off at four in the afternoon the day I arrived, and I walked down to the factory to meet him. I was wearing my Navy blue cadet uniform, and I thought I looked pretty good, almost like an officer. I stood near the factory gate, waiting and eyeing the stream of young girls coming out as the shift changed. Then I saw my father, his handsome, ruddy face and soft white hair tall above a circle of girl workers. They were giggling and flirting with him, and he was smiling and teasing back, in his gentle, courteous way. I waited for him, and for them, too; after all, I was nearly an officer, and in uniform. But they never turned, they just went on flirting, and finally he saw me and came over, picking his way gently among the girls, as though they were flowers he didn't want to step on.

I stayed at home for nearly a week. We talked—'had a good visit' was the family phrase—and we ate the familiar, wholesome, country-style meals, and we listened to the news. Montgomery was moving against Rommel in North Africa; the Nazis were stopped at Stalingrad; Marines were attacking in the Solomons. My father listened in strict, attentive silence, as though the broadcast were a sermon, and I knew that he was wondering where the war would be when I got to it, and that further back in his mind, too far back really to be a thought, was the question of whether I would be killed.

On the last day, my stepmother took a photograph of my father and me standing together in the front yard. I look self-conscious and a little vain in my uniform; my father looks proud but ill-at-ease, as though he is wearing the wrong clothes for a formal occasion, and knows it. Then I caught the train back south.

For many of us, Pensacola was the first experience of a living past. Bonesteel has no history, and Minneapolis hasn't much. We had lived our lives in a floating present, where nothing was very old, nothing expressed past values or recalled past events, and achievement was what you did today. In our brief Navy lives we had moved through a series of hastily improvised installations—a state teachers' college in Texas, a women's dormitory at the University of Georgia, and the raw and ugly Air Station at Memphis. None of these places had had any dignity or any feeling of tradition. They were makeshift, and we regarded them all with disappointment and distrust. Perhaps the resistance that most of us felt to becoming entirely absorbed in Navy life was partly a feeling that we would be joining this makeshift Navy, a system as temporary and ugly as the towns most of us came from.

And then we came to Pensacola, and there was the Navy's past: old buildings—a round powder-magazine that had served naval vessels a century before, and rows of sedately beautiful old houses where the senior officers lived—old, moss-stained walls, old live oaks hung with Spanish moss. The Naval Station had been there a long time. This, I thought, is what tradition means. The past is all around me; the Civil War was fought from here, the first Navy fliers learned to fly here. The atmosphere of the place made the Navy seem as permanent and as value-filled as a national church, or a parliament. At nineteen I didn't analyze or debate the values of military tradition and elitism; I simply surrendered to the tranquillity of the Station.

I suppose there is another, even simpler explanation of my response. I was a midwestern boy, coming in November to the Gulf Coast, where the sun shone on the bay, and palm trees lined the Station streets, and the earth was sandy and warm under the feet. Some of the serenity of my image of Pensacola comes from the fact that in memory it is always warm and soaked in sunlight, and there is always the flash and sparkle of light on water. Pensacola was a place that seemed to promise a warm civility, a life that would be happier than it was in my Middle West.

And I was happy there. I was doing what I liked to do—flying—with young men who became my friends. I had no responsibilities, except to fly and to study flying. No one was dependent on me, and I was dependent on no one. A hostile definition of the military life is that in it everything that is not required is forbidden. But there is another way of putting it. At Pensacola everything that I had to do, I wanted to do, and there was nothing I wanted to do that I couldn't do. It was a simple, preadult state in which we were suspended, but while it lasted it was joyous; like childhood, it remains in the memory as a good, uncomplicated time.

I reported first to the old Main Station, 'Main Side,' driving in a cab from the town railroad depot along a causeway over the lagoon (the image of bright water comes first from that drive), past the Main Side airfield, with its old-fashioned circular landing mat, and into the Station. Planes took off and landed at the field, and there were always planes in the air, but they didn't disturb the serenity of the Station; their engines were only a background humming, like bees in the warm sunlight. Sailors and officers and cadets walked or marched along the streets, and jeeps and trucks passed; but there seemed room enough to absorb them all, and the effect remained of a quiet, spacious place.

When I checked in at the Transient Quarters, some of my friends were already there: Joe and Wally had settled into the next room, Ike was down the hall, T came in as I unpacked. I felt a pleasure that was also a kind of relief at being back with them. To be with my father, and to feel that strong, steady flow of inarticulate love, was painful; I didn't know what to do with it, and I felt restless and clumsy and resentful. But these young pilots were my *real* family. I was easy with them, we understood each other, they didn't *want* anything.

We shared the Transient Quarters barracks with graduating cadets who were waiting there to be commissioned. And so we saw the rewards—the new uniforms, the wings, the gold bars, all those symbols of the success we aspired to—before we met the obstacles. If this was the Navy's conscious strategy, it was a clever one. The graduates looked much like us; they walked, talked, drank, and played poker like anyone else; but they were different, touched somehow by their achievement.

They had made it, they were really naval aviators. We gaped and envied and were condescended to; we listened to their stories and asked respectful questions. But, inside, each of us was thinking: *He's nothing special. I can do it if he did.* We knew at the beginning that there would be no challenges at Pensacola that we couldn't meet.

After a few days we moved out of Main Side to an outlying training field, and out of that remembered sunlight into winter rain. Whiting Field was a new field, a few miles inland from Pensacola, and very different from the Main Station. It had been built, in obvious haste, in the middle of bleak pine woods, near a sad little town called Milton—the kind of southern town where the telephone switchboard is in somebody's bedroom, and the post office is in the general store. It was a town nobody stopped in—why should you? There was nothing there that could possibly be regarded as interesting. It simply existed there at the entrance to the Station to remind us of where we were—not at Pensacola, on the Gulf of Mexico, in the sunlight, but in a Florida piny woods, in the winter, in the rain. Milton existed, T said, for only one purpose: to make sure that the cadets of Whiting Field were always depressed.

Whiting itself had its own kind of depression. It was as temporary-looking as Memphis had been, but whereas Memphis had seemed threatening and prisonlike in its bare ugliness, Whiting was only melancholy. Being new, it was unfinished in all but the meagerest essentials; the buildings were full of the resinous smell of unfinished pine boards, and the interiors were unpainted. The same pine wood stood all around outside, too; the view in every direction ended in a wall of thin, dejected-looking trees. Whatever on the Station had not been paved was still raw earth, and since the winter rains began as we arrived, and continued (or so it seemed) all the time we were there, we lived in mud—red, glutinous mud. We marched through mud to meals, and straggled through mud to the flight line. We followed mud paths to the Slop Chute, and came back, precariously drunk, along those paths in the dripping dark. Mud entered the barracks and the hangars, and even the cockpits of planes. I remember Whiting as a landscape as boring as the time I spent there: gray cloud above, wet red earth below, and between, endless and identical, the impoverished black pines.

At Whiting I learned to fly by instruments, in SNV's, training planes that were neither honest antiques like the N2S's, nor honestly modern like the planes we went on to, but in-between, low-winged, with cockpits that closed, but with fixed landing gear and a shuddering, whining engine—transitional trainers, and like everything else in the world that can be called transitional, profoundly unsatisfactory. They were called Vultee Vibrators, and I never met anyone who enjoyed flying in them.

On an instrument hop you take off with an instructor, climb a bit, and go 'under the hood.' A canvas curtain is drawn between you and the world outside, cutting off all sight of earth and air, and leaving you with only the inscrutable, indifferent instruments to look at. You learn how to tell the altitude of the plane by the indicators before you—airspeed, turn-and-bank, altimeter, artificial horizon—and to fly by referring to them instead of to the horizon, as you naturally do in flight. But you don't learn to trust the instruments, because they contradict the information that your own body gives you. Without the testimony of the horizon line, and the solid and visible earth, the exact location of up and down becomes uncertain. Your body says you are leaning, but the turn-and-bank says you are upright. Your body is wrong, and the instrument is right, but it is difficult, perhaps really impossible, to remove the body's message from your mind. If you could do that, you'd separate the mind's experience from the body's in a way that would be psychologically very disturbing. What you learn to do is to suppress the body's version of your attitude, and base your actions on the instruments, and that is what we did, hour after hour, out there above the piny woods. We learned to fly the plane in intricate patterns, at set altitudes; we learned to fly radio-ranges, and to make a landing approach without seeing the field we were approaching; and we learned how to get out of trouble, when the body's bad advice had got us into it.

Trouble, on instruments, is not knowing what you are doing in relation to the earth—how high you are, which way the earth is, what attitude the plane is in. You can get into this kind of trouble very easily in clouds, or in a storm, or at night—any time when the earth is hidden from you—and it will very quickly kill you, spinning you out of the bottom of a cloud, flying you into a hill that you thought was below you or somewhere else, tearing at the plane so violently that it will break. And so we were trained in a new necessary kind of fear, called 'Unusual Attitudes.' In this exercise the instructor puts you under the hood and then pulls the plane through one violent maneuver after another, while you snap and jerk around the back cockpit like dice in a box, and then says into your earphones: 'O.K., cadet, it's all yours.' Are you turning or level? Diving or climbing? Right-side-up or inverted? Your senses are so disturbed by the shaking that you don't know, and you must remake your own equilibrium by reading the instruments and doing what they tell you to do. Like all instrument flying, Unusual Attitudes was unnatural, a violation of your reasonable assumption that the ground will always be below your feet, that the earth, at least, can be trusted. But because the exercise was violent and extreme, it made the unnaturalness especially intense, something that took place in the pit of the stomach; it was a nightmare of insecurity, in which earth and air fell, spun, would not stay in place, and in which you were left, blind and alone in chaotic space, to make your world orderly again.

Instrument flying is one kind of flying that can be simulated. In the Link Trainer, a mechanical cockpit with all the instruments and controls of an airplane, you can do anything that a plane can do except take off and crash. At Whiting we spent hours in the Link building, hooded in these nonplanes, struggling with airspeed and direction and altitude, while alongside on glass-topped tables, mechanical crabs traced out our errors and instructors recorded these as passes or failures. It didn't feel like flying—there is no machine that can simulate the flow of air over control surfaces, or the sound of the wind, or the way the stick feels—and it never touched any emotion except anger, and maybe boredom. I remember waiting outside one of the Links while inside, under the hood, Taylor fought the machine, jerking it about as though he would wrestle it into doing what it was supposed to do. The instructor watched his instruments impassively, and finally picked up his microphone: 'Cadet,' he said, 'you are now two thousand feet underground.'

The Link might be boring, but there was one machine in that building that was exciting—the Simulated Aerial Combat Machine was like a booth at a fun-fair. It was set up in a room of its own, a cavernous, shadowy chamber like a movie theater. At one end was an elaborate mock-up of a fighter plane's cockpit, with a windshield, a gunsight, and all the flight controls. At the other end was a screen, on which films of attacking enemy planes were projected. As you moved the controls of the mock-fighter, the enemy planes moved on the screen, until you got one in your gunsight and squeezed your trigger. All this was accompanied by very satisfying, realistic sound effects —the diving, screaming planes and the chatter of the guns when you fired—and it was impossible not to be drawn into the excitement of the game, not to fly at those twisting images with a hot determination that turned them into realities, and the sound track into bullets. Then it was over, and the house lights went up, and you were left with a score—the number of unbullets that you had fired into the enemy unplanes. The Simulated Aerial Combat Machine was a marvelous, elaborate American game. It made the business of shooting men out of the sky seem a harmless game of skill, something you might do in a pinball palace to pass the time, and win a Kewpie doll.

I learned one other thing at Whiting that had nothing to do with instruments or flying. It was a lesson in the hostilities of ordinary people. Ted Williams, the baseball player, was a cadet in instrument training then. We all knew who he was; we had read the sports pages, and followed the batting averages, like other boys our age. I remembered him from Minneapolis, when he played AAA ball for the Millers before the war; others knew him as a home-run hitter for Boston. He was our first celebrity. He didn't want to be that; he clearly wanted to be just another cadet and to live a military life of perfect ordinariness, but there he was, in the next barracks room or on the flight line, a tall thin guy in a flight jacket, one of us. We all wrote home that we were flying with Ted Williams, and felt a little more important because of him, even if we never spoke to him (I never did).

An interviewer from a Boston paper came to Whiting to interview Williams, and got from him the quite reasonable statement that he wanted to be a fighter pilot, and a story of some small flying mistake—he hadn't lowered his flaps for a landing, something like that. When the piece appeared in the Boston paper, it carried the headline 'Teddy Wants a Zero,' and reported his 'close brush with death.' Somehow a copy of the article reached Whiting—I suppose one of those proud parents in Boston, somebody whose son was flying with Ted Williams, sent it—and was stuck up on the mess hall bulletin board. That evening, when Williams entered the mess hall for supper, a chant began: 'Teddy wants a Zero, Teddy wants a Zero,' on and on, louder and louder, until Williams left his food uneaten and stalked angrily out.

It wasn't his fault, and we all must have known that it wasn't. Sports writers did things like that to decent athletes. What were we punishing him for, then? For being famous? For having an existence out there, outside the Navy? Or simply for being somebody, a person with an identity, when we were all kids, just ciphers?

Though the rain fell, we took our hours of liberty, and went damply into Pensacola, in raincoats and condom-type covers. Pensacola was a small southern town that tried to look Spanish. It had the railroad tracks running through the middle of town, the dejected-looking stores with their wooden awnings over the sidewalk, the black ghetto that you would see in any Alabama or Mississippi town of that size; but it also had a sort of plaza, or maybe it was a boulevard, where the architecture was white stucco and red tile, and there were rows of damp, spindly palm trees. It was also a Navy town, the first I had seen—a place packed with sailors, every other store a uniform tailor, and the ones in-between bars, with a few taxis to drive drunks back to the Station, and a hotel with a whore for the sexually necessitous.

I knew only one cadet who ever patronized the hotel whore. He was an earnest, business-like person from Brooklyn named Green, who went to the whore in a business-like way, as he might have gone to a dentist. He was also the kind of guy who came back to the barracks at Whiting and told us about it. The whore, he said, was busy; it was Saturday night, and the bellhop who provided her customers could bring them up as fast as she could deal with them. When Green walked into her room, she fell on her back almost before the bellhop had closed the door, and lay there waiting, like a side of beef waiting for the butcher. Green prepared himself carefully; he was entering where hundreds had gone before him, and he didn't want to spoil his Navy career with a dose. Once he had mounted her, he was determined to stay; he had paid his five dollars, and he wanted his money's worth. So he hung on for all he was worth, thinking of the cash value of what he was getting in dollars-per-minute, making it last. The whore grew impatient, tried her erotic skills, such as they were, heaved and groaned, but Green rode on. She lost her temper, cursed and raged: 'Come on, damn you, *come*! You're costing me money!' But Green was unmoved, until in his head a meter clicked over at $5.00. Then he withdrew, in a dignified way, he said, leaving the whore exhausted and defeated.

We all professed to be amused, but I think the episode, and Green's triumphant telling of it, as though it had been a clever business deal, struck most of us as gross and ugly—the sort of thing you might expect of a guy from New York, who had gone to CCNY and wore a lavender sweatshirt. We were puritans; it didn't matter where we had come from, the whole country between the two coasts shared that tradition of severity, work, and repression. Certainly middle westerners and southerners were alike in taking sex and liquor as two forms of sinfulness, to be indulged in, usually at the same time, and to be punished for, but not to be taken lightly, and certainly not as a business deal with a whore. We probably all wanted sex as much as Green did, but we wanted it in the form of seduction, or true love (which was another name for the same thing), with plenty of emotion, and a lot of guilt afterward. Green had shaken our romanticism as well as our puritanism.

There were, of course, exceptions, cadets who had somehow escaped our puritanical rearing—like Spanish John, whose working-class industrial town in New Jersey was a different world—young men who had had girls early and easily, and whose lives seemed to the rest of us vivid and depraved. We heard their stories of callous seductions restlessly, but with helpless fascination. There was a cadet who, when a girl wrote to him that she was pregnant, and would kill herself if he didn't marry her, replied that Yes, that would probably be the best thing to do. When he heard from her again a few weeks later, he was very annoyed: 'That bitch,' he complained, 'she didn't kill herself!' We all knew that, in that situation, each of us

would have married her and ruined our lives. For the Navy for-
bade cadets to marry, and anyone who did and was found out
was washed out of flight training and sent to Great Lakes, to
become—most ignominious of conditions—a married enlisted
man. So the cold-blooded seducers and the Greens seemed
free, in a way that we could never be—free of the consequences
of their sexual needs.

Sometimes hometown girls came to visit at Pensacola, as they
had at Memphis, and stayed at the whore's hotel, and sometimes they were conquered there, by drink and the sentimentality of wartime, or perhaps by the atmosphere of continuous
fornication, and went away pregnant, and then the frightened
cadet would go home on leave and arrange a back-street abor-
tion. Even the few cadets who were secretly married were
afraid of having a child, afraid that somehow the Navy would
discover it and would throw the father out of flight school, and
so even legitimately conceived babies were aborted, to save the
father's flying career. A Good Ol' Boy I knew from Birmingham did that, took his young wife to a Negro woman with a
knitting needle, and then had to return to Pensacola while she
nearly died of infection, back home.

If you were afraid of whores, and had no girl, you could take
a bus to Mobile, and there pick up country girls who had come
to the city to work in the shipyards, and were careless with
their favors. You met them in Constitution Square, an agree-
ably old-fashioned place then, with its elegant old hotel and
its rows of canopied shops. The girls would be walking, two
or three together, around the square, looking into the shop
windows and chattering in their up-country voices, or simply
standing under the street lights, like torch singers about to
break into 'My Man.'

Your approach didn't have to be polished; you simply invited
a couple of them to have a drink. After the drink you'd find a
cab, and ride out into the anonymous small streets of Mobile,
to the girls' apartment—it would be two rooms in the cellar of
an old house, or the back half of a bungalow that you entered
from the alley, or rooms above a store. The cabdriver would
overcharge you because you were drunk, and then you'd be
alone in the dark, wondering if you had a rubber, worrying

about the clap, while in the other room some friend was fumbling with the other girl, indistinguishable from yours.

That's how it happened, the Big Test, as casually as that. I guess I passed it, in the sense that I was able to perform; but I couldn't have given that girl much pleasure, and I certainly felt none myself. I don't remember her name or her face— I probably had forgotten both the next morning—or what she said or what I said. I only remember the room—a sun porch at the back of the house, shut off from the next room by double glass doors that were covered by curtains, a room so small that a bed filled it, and the girl fell back on it as soon as we entered, and lay there silently in the dark. What did she feel? Hope? Curiosity? Boredom? Despair? I don't know, she was scarcely there for me; I only know what I felt—a kind of numb fatalism, that it was too late now to change my mind.

I could hear my friend in the other room, and I suppose he could hear us, and afterward we were both embarrassed, though the girls weren't, and we joked too much and said good-bye hastily, and were back in the drab street, empty at 2 A.M., no cabs anywhere then, walking back toward the square, sober and depressed. For the next couple of weeks we were anxious, too, nervously watching for the signs of infection that we had seen in the VD movies. It had all been necessary, we all agreed on that, you had to have girls, it was something important, like a part of our training; but I had found less pleasure in it than I did in flying, and I wasn't any good at it, and I think this was true of most of my ignorant friends, too.

Memories of those liberty nights have faded. I don't remember the girls of Mobile, and the nights have run together into one montage of drunkenness, fumbling, and the loneliness of late streets. But I remember standing in a barracks room back at the Main Station, with instrument school finished and the last stage of training about to begin, and hearing someone say, 'Smith got killed yesterday.' It wasn't, of course, Smith—I've forgotten what his name was—but I knew him. He had been with me at Memphis, and I could picture his face and recall his voice; he was an actual person out of my life. Somewhere in the building someone was playing a piano, and the sound of the music is a part of the story as I remember it: how he had been dogfighting with another student pilot, each maneuvering his plane to get behind and below the other, as fighters would do in actual combat, and how the planes had collided, and one pilot had bailed out, but the other had been caught in his spinning plane.

The reality of death comes to you in stages. First it is an idea—all men are mortal, as in the syllogism. Then it is something that happens to strangers, then to persons you know, but somewhere else, and at last it enters your presence, and you see death, on a runway or in a field, in a cloud of dust and a column of smoke. Though even that doesn't make your own death conceivable. There were times when I was afraid in a plane, when I knew I was in trouble, but I never believed that I would die *then*—it was always something that would happen later. But after that moment in the barracks while the piano played I realized that some of the men I knew would die, that they would be killed by planes, by bad luck, by their own errors. At that moment the life of flying changed.

Pilots are always fascinated by accidents. Any sound of a plane in trouble, a sudden change in an engine's note, a cough or a burst of power or a silence, will bring a whole ready room to the windows. There was a French cadet at Whiting who sat every day in the ready room in total silence. No one had ever heard him speak a word, and we only knew he was with the Free French because he wore an enormous beret with a red pom-pom. One day a plane taking off made an odd, whining sound, and the Frenchman rushed to the window. 'Aarrh,' he exclaimed, 'I thought he was takeeng off in high peetch!' Then he returned to his French silence.

Any story of a crash was listened to avidly, as though it were scandalous gossip, and accident reports were read like novels. The Navy in those days published a monthly magazine that contained accounts, sometimes with photographs, of the month's accidents in Naval aircraft, and we all turned to those pages first. What were we looking for? Some sort of magic, perhaps, by which we might avert disaster by experiencing it vicariously? Or the reassuring feeling that this was one accident that had already happened, and to somebody else? Or did we look for reasons to believe that the difference between those pilots who had accidents and the rest of us who didn't were absolute—differences of intelligence or skill or luck that would protect us? Most of the reported accidents were caused by pilot error, as most flying accidents always have been; and it was clear, from those reports, that most of us could stay alive, at least until we got into combat, simply by not being dumb.

The military life doesn't offer a man many real choices, but at this point in our training the Navy offered two: What kind of planes do you want to fly? And do you want to fly with the Navy or with the Marines? The first choice was easy, or seemed so to the cadets I knew best: to choose any course except single-engined planes—the route to fighters and dive-bombers —would have seemed cautious, unromantic, almost middle-aged, like wearing your rubbers or voting Republican. The second choice was only difficult if you thought about it: if you surrendered to your impulse, you at once chose the Marines. Marines were tough, romantic, and elitist; virtually all Marine officers got into combat, and though they were supposed to be officers and gentlemen, they were, in our minds, fighting men first. I don't think most of us really saw ourselves as fighting men, but it was tempting to think that other people might if we wore the right uniform. For me it seemed a good way of fighting my father's war in his style; he'd like having a son in the Marine Corps. My closest friends—Joe, Wally, T, Rock, Taylor—all made the same choice. We were sent to finish our training at Bronson Field, an outlying field west of Pensacola, near the Alabama line, where cadets were turned into Marine fighter and dive-bomber pilots.

Like the Air Station at Memphis, Bronson Field had been built on the site of an old southern farm. The road to it, off the highway, was like a farm road, between a pine wood and a pasture, and the field itself had a quiet, sun-baked rural feeling, even with the planes. The farm buildings were gone, and only one reminder of the old life remained; on the other side of the field, out by the gunnery butts, there was a little family graveyard—just six or eight graves, weed-grown and untended, with a wrought-iron fence around them. The graveyard provided instructors with a tired joke, and occasionally it seemed a bit macabre, there at the end of a runway; but most of the time

I liked it being there, untouched by our busyness, a continual silent recitation of private human history.

Perhaps it was that we had made the same choice of duty, and held a future in common, or perhaps it was simply the natural selection of like-minded young men; whatever it was, the move to Bronson was the beginning of an intimacy among us so close that I find it difficult to put a name to it. For this final training cadets were divided up into six-man flights, and T and Rock and Taylor and I were all in the same one. We flew together, we took our check-rides together, and we went to ground school together. We shared our barracks rooms, and when we went on liberty we went together. We were responsible for each other—to see that the others got up in the morning and got to meals, that they came back from liberty, that no one missed a flight. We wanted our flight to finish the course with a perfect record—no Downs on check-rides, no flying missed. If we did, we would be allowed to fly together to New Orleans ('the birthplace of Louis Armstrong,' T said reverently). But it was more than that; we wanted our record to be perfect, because the flight itself, the way we felt about each other when we flew together, seemed perfect. So we worried about each other, and even Taylor, the wildly irresponsible Taylor, would turn up to rouse us if the weather changed. I remember waking on a morning that should have been rainy to find him standing in the center of my room shouting, 'Come on, you guys, it's blue as shit out there!'

When the time came to buy our officers' uniforms we went together to the expensive, dishonest uniform shops of Pensacola, and there we bought greens and tans and trench coats, all said to be tailor-made but in fact mass-produced in New York. When we got them back to Bronson we immediately dressed up for each other; there was no point in pretending to be modest, we all felt exactly the same extravagant pride in what we were about to become. For the moment, in that barracks room in our ill-fitting new uniforms, we felt transformed—elegant, romantic, elite; surely when we were at last made officers, and put on these clothes for good, we would be changed as completely as our uniforms changed, we would be different people, we would be adults. It was like the feeling I had when I was a child, of what it would be like to become twenty-one. It would be like walking through a door, and closing it behind you.

We went on liberty together, and drank and pursued girls, abetted each other's attempts at seduction and helped each other home when we got drunk. It was all a collective activity, like formation flying. After one trip to Mobile I developed the symptoms of gonorrhea, and the whole flight was worried, not about my health ('Shit, man,' Taylor assured me, 'a dose of the clap ain't half as bad as piles') but about the flight. 'If you turn yourself in,' T said, 'they'll ground you, and what'll *we* do?' The flight was a unit, and it couldn't function as a flight with one member in the clap shack. But if I didn't turn myself in I would become sterile, blind, palsied, and insane, like the guys in the VD movies. I reported to the sick bay, and was grounded as T had predicted, and lay in my bunk for a whole day, sweaty with fear, while I waited for the results of the test. I didn't sleep, I didn't read, I just lay there. I would be dropped from the flight program—that was clear. What would I tell my father? I would be sent to Great Lakes. I thought about the outer darkness into which I would be hurled—the strangeness, the statusless obscurity, the boredom of being an ordinary seaman. In flight school I belonged—to the world of fliers, and to my flight; I knew what to do there, I lived in an agreeable, entirely familiar world. But out in the drab world of enlisted men I would be a stranger, a nobody, ignorant and alone, and, worst of all, grounded.

But it wasn't the clap, after all. The doctor said it was only overexertion, and he advised me to stay out of Mobile for a while. That night I bought beer for the flight at the Slop Chute, and T explained to the other cadets that I had just passed through a medical crisis.

At Bronson we flew SNJ's—training planes that were like real combat planes, but slower, smaller, and safer. They had, most importantly, retractable landing gear. When a plane takes off and the wheels come up, it has cast off its connection with the earth and become adapted to the air (birds do the same thing with their legs). The pilot can't see that the wheels are up, but knowing it makes a difference. The SNJ also had a closed cockpit, like a fighter, and it could be mounted with a machine gun, and could carry toy-like practice bombs. It could execute any maneuver that a fighter could, and it was an excellent acrobatic plane. Because it had a variable-pitch propeller, it even sounded like a fighter—it took off with a whine that faded in the air to a sort of stammering whisper—wh–wh–wh–wh. Flying SNJ's was like trying on officers' uniforms; it made us feel almost like adults.

The sudden Gulf Coast spring came as we began to fly from Bronson. Wisteria bloomed on the houses in the little towns, and the air was soft. We seem, in memory, always to have been high in a sky of tropical blueness, with perhaps some bright fair-weather clouds below us. We are making gunnery runs on a towed sleeve, or diving on a target at the edge of the sea, or we are tail-chasing, playing like children or birds, up the sides of tall clouds that are blinding-white in the sunlight. I remember flying alone among cumulus clouds on a fine day, and hearing two of the Mexican students who also trained at Pensacola talking on the radio, one calling, 'Hey, Cisco, where are you?' and Cisco: 'I'm over here, behind thees leetle cloud. Come chase me.' It was all like that, like play, *Come chase me*; it was games, and we were children. Gunnery and bombing were only follow-the-leader; you kept score, and somebody won and somebody lost, but nobody got hurt.

In gunnery practice one member of the flight takes off towing a canvas sleeve at the end of a long cable. The rest follow him to a proper altitude, and make attacks on the sleeve as though it were an enemy plane. A gunnery run is a beautiful gesture, as graceful as a ballet movement—a long descending S–curve from a position above and to the side of the target that brings you into position, and ends in a burst of firing. As plane after plane repeats it, it seems choreographed, symmetrical, aesthetically perfect.

To the pilot in the towplane, the experience is not quite so aesthetic, though. He can see the planes entering their runs, can hear their guns and see the tracers' tracks. And when an attacker gets too intent on the target, and slides round behind the sleeve, the towpilot can feel the tracers reaching for his own plane, and his own vulnerable flesh. And it's his own friends who are back there, taking shots. I remember the voice of Taylor, plaintively: 'Hey you guys, stop shootin' up mah ass!'

Bombing was another kind of game, a sport rather like throwing darts—the same target of concentric rings, the same scoring according to how close you came to the bull's-eye. You approached the target in a steep glide, weight thrown forward against your seat belt, the plane bucking as it accelerated, wind screaming a higher note, earth rising toward you. As you dived you had to bring the target into your bombsight, jerking the plane over with stick and rudder, holding it for an instant to drop your bomb, and then pulling up in a steep bank to look back and see the puff of smoke that showed where the bomb had hit. The dive was like taking a dare, and the pullout was safety, the dare taken, the Test passed.

That spring at Bronson was full of games; flying, together or alone, we seemed possessors of the empty, golden air. But the emptiness wasn't always joyous. Once, flying alone, I wandered above a bank of cloud, and learned how it feels to be separated completely from the earth, how anonymous and signless clouds are, and how uncomforting the sun is when it shines down on unbroken, trackless whiteness. This kind of experience, of separation from the comfortable and the familiar, is a part of the price of flying. The pilot has to accept the stretches of loneliness and isolation, when the earth is erased by cloud or darkness, or is facelessly strange or hostile, when his will to fly has thrust him into void space.

I felt this separation most intensely on the navigation flights that were a part of the final training program. First we flew, in flights of three planes, out over the Gulf on a triangular course that, if we were proper navigators, would return us precisely to the field. Since there were other planes involved, this was not really a separating experience, though it did offer one new kind of feeling that was disquieting—the feeling you get when the last bit of land disappears behind you, of the shapelessness and endlessness of space. Below you is the flat and uninformative sea; all around you the air extends its emptiness. Why go one way rather than another, when it is all the same, and goes on forever? People have committed suicide by flying straight out to sea, and I can understand that it could have a right feeling, that it would be a gesture that would express the feeling of suicide, as well as a way of dying.

The other navigation flight was flown alone, and overland.

This time, too, the pattern was a triangle—inland to one town, across to another, and back. No doubt the solitariness was a part of the flight's strange feeling, but it was more than that. I was flying over the pine woods of Florida and south Alabama, a surface that stretched unbroken to the horizon, as flat and featureless as the sea. The Gulf behind me became what the land had been before, a friendly and familiar landmark. When I lost sight of it I felt as though I had flown out of measurable space into the boredom of infinity.

I could see the shadow of my plane sliding along below me on the tops of the trees, and its insubstantial, steady movement seemed a part of the emptiness. Occasionally a railroad track appeared, making a diagonal mark across the pines; but railroads are as identical as pine trees, and it did nothing to alter my mood. I checked the calculations on my plotting board, and I watched the clock on the instrument panel, and at the predicted time the right town appeared, an island of tin roofs and a water tower floating in the sea of pine trees. But I could feel no necessity in that appearance; it might as well have been some other town, or no town at all. I turned, found the second landmark, and headed south. When I could see the Gulf once more beyond the trees I felt that I was reentering the real, distinguishable world.

At the end of our training we came again to that other kind of unreality, night flying. It was even more alarming at Bronson Field than it had been at Memphis, because we took off over the Gulf, and so had no comfortable human lights below us, but only a darkness more absolute and bottomless than the sky. A few lights—a town, scattered farms, a car on a road —would have given some sense of depth, of where the earth was; but in that blind blackness the earth seemed to have fallen away, and left below me the other side of the sky.

Our instructions were to leave the traffic pattern and fly away from the field, into the outer training space called simply 'the area,' and then to return, reenter the pattern, and land. I flew cautiously out over what I thought must be the south end of Alabama—though it was alien and unidentifiable—and when enough time had passed, turned back toward the flashing beacon that was home. But nothing looked the same, the approach was different at night, none of the usual landmarks were helpful, and I reached the field in a state of disorientation and uncertainty. But it was the field, all right, and I swung round the pattern and began my landing approach. Lights seemed to flash from all directions, and the radio sputtered bursts of hysterical static in my ears, but I couldn't understand what was said because of a horn that was blowing somewhere behind my head. Then I touched down—not with a bounce and a roll, but with a screaming, scraping cry of anguished metal that ended suddenly as the plane stopped. Then there was only the horn blowing, and the siren of the crash-truck approaching. I had landed wheels-up. The horn I had heard was the warning horn, which blew if you cut off power before you lowered your wheels, the lights were signal lights from the tower, the radio hysterics had all been for me. But I had simply concentrated them all out of my consciousness, and I had wrecked my first plane.

The consequences were complex, but not particularly unpleasant. By a curious piece of official reasoning it was decided that I had not failed the flight, since my task had been to leave and reenter the pattern, and I had done that quite satisfactorily; so there was no downward-pointing arrow on the flight-board, and our flight still had a perfect record at Bronson, and would get the cross-country flight to New Orleans. But if I didn't get a Down, what was to be done with me? Clearly the Navy couldn't simply ignore that wrecked plane. I was sent to a Navy psychiatrist.

The psychiatrist was a disappointment. I had been reading Freud, evenings in the barracks, and I knew what to expect: a beard, a German accent, and a lot of questions about sex and dreams. But this one looked like a farmer and talked like a Georgia cracker. He peered at me gloomily through his gold-rimmed spectacles for what seemed to me a long time, and then said: 'Cadet, Ah don't want to know why you didn't put your wheels down. Ah want to know why all those other guys *did*.' I had no answer; it seemed unreasonable to me, the way the whole night-flying system was arranged, that anybody should have thought to lower his wheels, ever, and I said so. The psychiatrist brooded over that for a while. 'But it works for everybody but you.' I had to admit that that seemed to be so.

'If Ah was to make a report on you,' he said at last, 'you know what would happen—Great Lakes, and the night run to Murmansk.' I tried to imagine that fate. 'Cain't do that.' He looked up and smiled. 'Mah professional advice to you, cadet, is—put your goddamn wheels down. Dismissed.'

There was nothing very memorable about the flight to New Orleans—we simply flew over, landed and looked around for a while, and flew back. But it felt memorable. We were flying to somewhere, and this was the first time any of us had ever done that. Up until now, the planes we flew had not been vehicles for transportation, we had never gotten anywhere in them, except back where we started. There was always the invisible elastic, one end attached to the plane, the other firmly fastened at the field; and though you could stretch it out for an hour, it then snapped you back and landed you where you had begun. But now we were in transit, flying from Florida, first over Alabama and then Mississippi, and landing in Louisiana. Mobile Bay, and then Mobile passed below us, Biloxi was off to our left, the coastline curved away to the south, and then we could see Lake Pontchartrain, and the Naval Air Station, New Orleans.

The other thing I felt during that flight was how large and empty the air is, away from a flying field. We didn't see another plane after we left Pensacola, and our little flight of four seemed tiny and vulnerable in all that space. If a plane slid away from the formation, it immediately became very small, a speck you could lose if you took your eyes from it. I thought for the first time of what it would be like to be flying like that, so separate and exposed, out where the war was, where the speck at the far end of a vision might be a Jap fighter. Vaster and emptier than the widest prairie, the air offered no place to hide, nowhere to run to. But our air remained empty, and as we returned the elastic began to pull once more. We were reentering the familiar: Mobile Bay appeared, Perdido Bay was just ahead, we began to respond to habit, wheels went down, and we swung in a stretched-out file around Bronson and landed.

It was our last flight as cadets, and I climbed down from my plane a little sadly, and stood for a moment, looking at the place where I had found such content. High up, over the field, two planes were dogfighting; at that distance it seemed a desultory, leisurely activity, a kind of slow-motion dance in the air. Across the field, beyond the graveyard, cadets were firing machine guns into the butts, making an irregular crackling sound. Everything seemed warm and comfortable in the sun, and everybody seemed happy. 'Come on,' Taylor said, 'I'll buy you a fuckin' beer. To celebrate.' I wasn't sure a celebration was the right thing for that moment, but I picked up my parachute and walked back with him across the mat toward the hangar. We might as well have a beer.

Chapter Four

AFTER THE ambiguous life of a cadet, the life of an officer promised to be simple: money, status, and freedom would be ours, the high living come at last. An officer could marry and move off the Station, or he could live in Bachelor Officers' Quarters, where black servants would make his bed and clean up after him. He could give orders to enlisted men, and he could drink in the Officers' Club. Enlisted men would salute him. And women—women would fall on their backs before him, stunned by his golden glory. We left Bronson and moved back to Main Side for the last time in a state of dazed expectation, and when the day came we dressed in our new green uniforms, pinned on the bars and the wings, and marched off to be transformed.

The commissioning ceremony at Main Side was more like a high-school commencement than seemed quite right, everyone dressed up in unfamiliar costumes, and the Commanding Officer like the high-school principal, making a speech about duty, and handing out diplomas and shaking hands. One striking difference, though, was that Tyrone Power, the movie actor, was in this class—he had been training in multiengined planes while we were training for fighters—and so there were photographers and reporters around, but not for us. 'Shit,' Rock said angrily, 'I can fly better than him. Take *my* picture, you bastards!'

We felt a little superfluous until the ceremony was over; our new glory had been diminished before we got it. We walked together back to the barracks, Rock and Taylor and T and I, and enlisted men saluted us along the way, and I felt embarrassed, saluting back, as though I had been caught doing in earnest what we had played at, back at Bronson. It still seemed like a game, that diploma and handshaking hadn't changed anything. No door had closed behind me; I didn't feel like an adult.

The flight was breaking up, going on to different operational training stations, some to fighters, some to bombers. We had had to make a choice, back at Bronson; and most of my friends had applied for fighters—naturally enough, I suppose, that was where the excitement and the glory were —and some of them were ordered to Jacksonville to train in Corsairs. But others were disappointed, and would be training in dive-bombers with me. I hadn't even tried to be a fighter pilot, and I'm not sure why I hadn't. Perhaps I didn't think I was good enough for Corsairs. They were said to be very hot, very hard to fly—if you stalled in your landing approach you rolled over, or so the old-timers told us, and you couldn't get them out of an inverted spin. Or perhaps it wasn't that, exactly; maybe I just didn't see myself as that heroic figure the Fighter Pilot. Whatever the reason, I decided that the fighter test was one I didn't have to take, and I chose dive-bombers without pausing, as though there was no choice to make.

Before we reported to our new stations we got a few days' leave, and the whole flight went to Birmingham to T's wedding, traveling together up from Pensacola in a Greyhound bus that meandered through the Alabama spring as though it had no certain destination. The trip was a ritual, we all felt it, it was like the flight to New Orleans. It was the last time we would all be together, and the last time we would all be bachelors. I wondered which would divide us from each other more, the different combat roles we'd play, or the entrance of wives into our world. When we thought ahead, the game-playing days seemed to be ending, we could see responsibilities coming. An officer was supposed to be a leader, to care for his men, to share in the conduct of the war. And if he were also a husband? It began to seem that what the Commanding Officer had handed out to each of us was an assignment to adulthood, ready or not.

T's sister Liz met us at the bus station. She was wearing a dress with Degas dancers on it, and she was like a dancer, too, pretty and gay, and light in her movements. She laughed and teased her brother, and she greeted his friends prettily; and when she turned, her hair swung, and the Degas dress swirled to her body. It was all like a dance. And she was very Southern, with her formal manners and her soft speech that seemed to be all vowels. I had never met anyone like her in Minneapolis.

Nor like her family—her mother, who was friendly and fussed, and said 'I swanee,' and 'Our fathers!,' and her grandmother, a matriarch with the commanding presence of a

Confederate general, and her stepfather, who was fat and easy, and spent most of his time calming his wife down, saying 'Now 'Lizbeth, now 'Lizbeth.' Nor like her town, so hot in April, so leafy and blossoming, the streets so crowded, so many Negroes everywhere. There was too much life there; I was charmed but I was also confused by it all.

That first night there was a bachelor party for T, and we all got drunk and made speeches about how great it had been, and how we would always stick together; but even drunk we knew that only the first part was true. The next day we went to the wedding, in a Methodist church that was all varnished pine and ugly red and blue windows, and I was Best Man. Through the ceremony I felt hung over and distracted, and while the preacher rambled I stared absently at the window above the al-tar. It was Christ the Good Shepherd, and the lamb in it looked like somebody I knew back home, but I couldn't remember who. Alice's mother? Then the ring part of the ceremony came, and I couldn't find the ring in my pockets, but then I did, and it was all right.

In the evening we went, rather self-consciously, to the Bir-mingham Officers' Club, the first Officers' Club that any of us had ever been to. I took T's sister, and we danced and drank and talked, the way you do on a first date with a nice, pretty girl (and especially if her brother is there). The next day I rented a car and we drove around town, to the pool and the country club, and she showed me the statue of Vulcan and the steel mill where her uncle worked, and when we stopped at night we held hands and kissed. It was very romantic. I was a flier on the way to war, and she was a Southern belle. Our roles seemed fixed, as though we had been cast in a sentimental movie, or a story by Scott Fitzgerald. We were convinced that we felt deeply about each other.

Then the leave was over, and I was in another train, with T and Taylor and the others, moving on to another airfield, sentimentally sad, but relieved to be out of the civilian world of mothers and relations and fond neighbors, and even of dates with nice girls. We sat in the dusty, red-plush coaches, sweating into our new uniforms, down the length of Alabama to Flo-maton, that odd, obscure intersection in the piny woods that all Southern trains seem to reach sooner or later, and across to Jacksonville, where the Corsairs were, and where Ike left us, and then south again, down the east coast of Florida. The land turned from red clay to bright sand, and sometimes the train ran so close to the shore that we could see the wide white beaches and the breaking waves, like pictures on travel posters, indolent and inviting. I had never seen the Atlantic Ocean before—or any other ocean—and I tried to respond to it; but there was too much of it, I couldn't think of anything to think about it.

Toward afternoon the train turned inland and stopped at Deland, a town twenty miles or so from the coast, behind Daytona Beach. It was a small college town—very pretty, I thought, with its Spanish-style buildings, and its palm trees and little ponds; it seemed very green and cool-looking after the bright coast. I thought of Denton, the other college town, and wondered if I had changed enough since then. Would I be any better with the Jo Belles of this place?

The Naval Air Station at Deland was neither green nor cool-looking. It was sun-baked space in the woods, with a plain, functional airfield in it. As we drove in I saw only standard Navy buildings, a single long landing strip, and a tower, and parked by the tower, rows of SBD's—no other kind of plane, just SBD's. NAS Deland existed for one purpose—to teach new pilots like us how to fly those planes.

Assignment here, to dive-bomber training, had been a furious disappointment to guys like Taylor, who dreamed of flying Corsairs and thought of fighter pilots as the aristocrats of the air; but I didn't feel like an aristocrat, and I felt pleased and easy when I saw the planes in their rows. The SBD was a slow, sturdy, dependable plane that I thought I could probably fly well enough. Old-timers said that you could lose a cylinder, or two feet of wing, and still get it home. It had no particular style, and you certainly wouldn't call it beautiful; but it had its own aura of achievement. It had been the Navy's dive-bomber through most of the early part of the war, and Marines had flown it at Guadalcanal. It worked well, carried the bombs (slowly) to the targets, could be dived with great accuracy, and would then fly you back. I didn't think I wanted anything more than that from the plane I flew into combat. 'But Christ,' Taylor said, '*look* at it! It looks like a pickup truck. But a Corsair, man, that fuckuh's *beautiful*!' And of course he was right, that fucker was beautiful, and the SBD wasn't. Still, I was content with its plainness—a matter of temperament, I guess.

The planes on the flight line were old; they had come from fleet duty, and they were still painted in what was then the standard fashion for naval combat planes—the upper half dark blue, the lower half a blue that was nearly white. The theory was that this scheme camouflaged the plane when seen either from above (against the dark water) or from below (against the light sky). I don't think it worked any better than gray or brown or white would have—I certainly never had any trouble seeing a plane against either the sea or the sky—but it seemed symbolically right for Navy fighting planes to be painted the colors of the sea and sky, and I liked the look of it. It seemed serious and warlike.

Like the planes, our instructors were combat veterans, and they too made the field seem closer to the reality of war. These were the first pilots I had met who had been to the Pacific theater, had seen the islands, and Japanese planes in the air, had dropped real bombs on real enemy targets, and had been shot at. They had passed the Test. All the excitement that I had gotten from movies and stories hung about these men, and made the plainest and quietest of them extraordinary, touched by heroism and romance. When they talked about the 'Canal or the Coral Sea, it was like Spanish John talking about sex —they had been somewhere, and had had feelings there, that were beyond my imagining. I couldn't conceive how it would feel to be at fifteen thousand feet, above a ship or an island, and then to dive through the antiaircraft fire toward the target, and drop and pull away. But I knew it would be a great thing, and that it would make me different.

I met the Navy lieutenant who was to be our instructor sitting in the bar of the BOQ, sipping Southern Comfort through a straw. He was a Cherokee Indian from Oklahoma, and he had a profile like the Indian on the penny; like every Indian in the service, he was called 'Chief.' The Chief had flown dive-bombers at Midway, and he was a good, intelligent pilot. He led our flights carefully, and taught us how to approach a target, the best position from which to enter a bombing run, how to dive. He dropped his bombs accurately, and he taught us how he did it. And he also taught us how to pull out, how to take evasive action and get the hell out of there. There were two goals in his flying—to carry the bomb to the target, and to carry himself back home—and he was good at both of them, but his flying had no personal style; he was like a driver who has never had an accident, but doesn't like to drive. Perhaps the experience of combat, early in the war when losses were high and achievements were low, had taken the joy of flying out of him. He didn't talk much about it, or the war, or anything else. He just sat in the bar when the day's flying was over, quite friendly if you approached him, but content to be alone, as though he were waiting for it all to end, patiently, but without much hope, sipping his Southern Comfort. Strictly speaking, this was illegal. Indians weren't allowed to drink liquor; there was a Federal law against it. But the lunacy of denying alcohol to a man who was fighting your war must have struck the local bartenders, and the Chief was never refused a drink.

The main thing the Chief had to teach us was to dive an airplane straight toward the earth, and to drop a bomb while diving. This is the most unnatural action possible in a plane, a kind of defiance of all life-preserving instincts. As a maneuver it is no more difficult than a loop or a slow-roll, but psychologically it is a violation of life. You begin a dive-bombing attack in an echelon, a diagonal line of planes stretched out and back from the leader, letting down from twelve or fifteen thousand feet in a steady, accelerating glide. Then the leader signals, pulls up sharply, rolls, and drops suddenly, like a bird shot in flight, and each plane follows, rolling nearly over at the start, so that the pilot pulls the nose of his plane onto the target from an inverted position. The plane is diving vertically now, or nearly so, and your weight is no longer on your back and seat, but forward, against your seat harness, and on your feet on the rudder pedals. You have your dive-brakes open to make the descent slower, but still the earth that you see through your bombsight seems to rise to meet you very fast. As speed builds up, the flight characteristics of the plane change, the target slides away from your bombsight, and you have to fly the plane back to it while holding the dive. The sudden change of altitude hurts your ears, and you yell to relieve the pressure, and to help the psychological pressure that is also building up. You glance at your altimeter, which is unwinding swiftly toward zero, kick the plane onto the target, press the button on the control stick that releases the bomb, and pull out, banking up so that you can see where your bomb fell.

Diving was a violent experience, always. You could burst an eardrum in a dive (I saw T walk back from the flight line after a flight, with blood seeping from his ear); and you could lose consciousness in the pullout, when the force pulling the blood from your brain was many times the force of gravity. But what made dive-bombing sometimes fatal was not the dive, but the target. Down there below you was a bull's-eye pattern of concentric circles painted on the ground, and up here, on the bombsight set in your windshield, was a similar pattern drawn in lines of light. The problem was to bring them together, so that one was centered on the other, and then to drop. But air and airplane conspired to make this difficult and momentary, and the pilot might try again and again to get on target, slide away, try, slide, and dive into the center of the target still trying.

In Florida in 1944 one dive-bomber pilot died every day. We heard about them at dinner, in the officers' mess—a guy at Jacksonville, someone we had known in flight school killed at Vero Beach, another at Lauderdale. The account of every crash was embellished with details: how the plane buried itself in the bull's-eye, how the wreckage covered the target, how the body was gathered up in a bushel basket and sent home in a coffin that had to be loaded with engine parts to give it sufficient weight. It was a kind of accident that any of us might have, a momentary hypnosis that no intelligence or skill seemed proof against.

As any war movie will tell you, the prospect of sudden death draws men together. Those of us who had been friends before—Joe and T, Rock, Taylor, Wally, and I—were closer still at Deland. It was partly, perhaps, because of the way dive-bombing is done. A dive-bombing attack is always a group attack, and we flew constantly at each other's wing-tips, followed each other in dives, rendezvoused after the attack, flew back together in divisions of V's. So bombing became a form of comradeship; you had a good feeling about those other planes strung out below you in the dive, joining up in sections as you pulled out.

So the old friends became closer, and we made some new ones—pilots who had trained at Corpus Christi instead of Pensacola, or had simply been in another flight at Bronson, partygoers, drinkers, comedians, eccentrics. Taylor found a wild accomplice in a Portuguese from New England called Puta. And T and I took up with a guy who had played shortstop for the Saint Paul Saints. I liked him because he could talk about Minneapolis, and T liked him because he was an athlete and could talk comically about life in the minor leagues, and we both liked and trusted him because he was a good, steady flier.

The pilots in the flight who couldn't fly—who were too stupid, too clumsy, or too frightened—became outsiders and enemies. We had one such in particular, a faded-looking Southerner with hair so pale that he was called Cottonhead. It wasn't exactly that Cottonhead couldn't fly, of course—he had graduated from flight school, and he could get the plane off the ground and down again—but he flew as though he or the plane were spastic, skidding and jerking, slowing and speeding in unpredictable and unnerving ways. Taylor, who often flew with Cottonhead, would throw his helmet into his locker after a flight and rage, 'That fuckuh. I look at him up there and I think, "He's gonna kill me if I ain't careful,"' and he would itemize Cottonhead's misdeeds for the day—the sudden throttling back, the ungainly roll into the dive, the slow, stretched-out approach to a landing. It was like living with a bomb, Taylor said. Our distrust of Cottonhead in the air made us avoid him on the ground, as though he carried danger with him everywhere, and might explode or crash into us at mealtimes, or in the bar. He must have lived a lonely life at Deland, but there was nothing to be done about it; he was excluded by an instinct below self-preservation, the same instinct that made the rest of us closer than friends. In the squadron photograph that was taken at the end of our training there, we stand in an informal group in front of an SBD; it is clear that we are friends, that there was joking going on when the picture was taken, that as soon as the posing is over we'll all go to the bar. All except Cottonhead, who stands at the edge of the picture, not far from the rest, but separated, like a man with a smell, or a fatal disease.

Another kind of fellow-feeling developed from the fact that the SBD was a two-man plane, which in combat carried a gunner. We began to fly with an enlisted crewman in the rear seat, and occasionally flew gunnery flights in which he fired his machine gun at a sleeve, while we simply drove. We had all flown other people before, but they had always been instructors or other student-pilots—people who could fly, and who had a set of controls to fly with, if necessary; but now we had men riding with us who had no controls, and wouldn't have been able to use them anyway, and who depended on us to keep them alive. They weren't our own crewmen yet. All the names in my logbook are different, and occur only once—Nugent, Redlinghafter, Beeken, Poe—and there was no sense of a common enterprise. I simply felt responsible—to them, to their mothers, to life.

May passed into June, and the Florida sun burned down. The concrete of the runway and the flight line burned, the air quivered with heat above the burning earth, and when we took off to eastward, over the beach and the ocean, the water below was metallic and blinding, the color of heat. A cockpit was a furnace. Every metal surface was hot to the touch, and the engine blew back parched air that smelled of burning gasoline. We flew in nothing but our cotton flight suits, and whenever we weren't at high altitude we were sweating; the suits became black with sweat-stains, and rotted from our shoulders, and our cotton helmets shone with sweat.

In the afternoons thunderstorms built up and swept across the field and erased it in pelting rain. Coming back from a flight over the ocean, we would maneuver among the storms to find that the field was hidden at the bottom of a dark column of rain that seemed to hang like a curtain from the bottom of a thunderhead. We would fly around and wait for the storm to pass, circling aimlessly out over the piny woods in the burning, improbable sunshine. When we landed, the field would be bright with sun, and the strip already steaming; the earth would be hot as ever, and the sweating would begin again.

But it wasn't really enervating, it wasn't like that other summer in preflight school. We were not held in the heat, made to bear it incessantly as though it were a moral exercise. When we had flown, we could go back to our quarters in the BOQ, shower, have a drink, and lie around half-dressed and talk. T and I had a phonograph in our room, and some jazz records, and we would lie there, cooling off, and listen to that music: the Benny Goodman Quartet playing 'Runnin' Wild,' Nat Cole's 'Sweet Lorraine,' Mezzrow-Ladnier's 'Comin' On With the Come On,' Peck Pecora and his Back Room Boys. And eat oranges. The country around Deland was orange-growing country, and you could buy a tall sack for a dollar just outside the Station gate. There was always a sack in the closet, and orange peelings under the bed. There were black enlisted men, called mess-boys, whose job it was to clean out the peelings, but if they came in while we were there they would mostly just hang around, listening, and have a drink if we were having one (it was part of the resistance to Navy Regs to assume that a mess-boy who appreciated jazz wasn't a mess-boy). And sometimes when I came in from a flight the phonograph would be playing, a blues, maybe, 'Don't the moon look lonesome . . . ,' and one of the mess-boys would be sitting alone there on the edge of a bed, or leaning on a broom among the unswept orange peelings, listening, and maybe thinking of other places, better times.

When the sun went down and the air cooled, we went sometimes to Daytona Beach. It was a good time to go to a resort: civilians had no gasoline and no time for holidays, and the hotels and bars were nearly empty. And it was off-season, early summer then. There were girls around, though: Waves from the air stations, casual party girls, even a few nice girls. The shortstop from Saint Paul met one of the nice ones, and dated and courted her, and got no further than the rest of us did with nice girls. I remember him coming into the room late one night after a date, and T asking, 'How was it, man? Did you get in?' 'Ah,' said the shortstop sadly, 'it's always the same with me. Cheek-cheek-forehead, that's all I get, just cheek-cheek-forehead.' He's one of us, I thought, even if he did play shortstop for the Saints.

The steaming summer air seemed to create an atmosphere of feverish sexuality. There was a Wave from the Air Station who took a leave and spent the whole time in a hotel room in

Daytona, taking on all comers, or so the story went. Taylor and his pal Puta had found her, and told us about her. 'Shit, man,' Taylor said, 'she ain't very good-lookin', not what you'd call a beauty. In fact'—he began to laugh his high-pitched, wild-man laugh—'she's downright ugly. But who cares?' Puta said nothing, but made an obscene Portuguese gesture, winked, and laid an index finger alongside his nose—a movement that apparently expressed satisfaction.

We went to see her, as you might go in a party to the zoo to look at a rare new species; five or six of us trooped into the room in the cheap tourist hotel, and had a drink, and just looked at her. There she was, in bed all right. She was a big, husky girl, and Taylor was right—she wasn't very good look-ing. She might have been a farm girl or a singer in a church choir, except for the look that never left her face—a despairing, defiant look, the look of someone who had got to a place too far to come back from. She lay in the bed, her big body cov-ered by a sheet, and stared back at us. Nobody touched her or suggested any sexual act. Partly we were shy in front of each other, I suppose, but it was something else, too. I remember what the atmosphere was like, now; it wasn't like a zoo—it was like a sick room in a hospital. We were visiting a patient, she was sick and we were all well, and we drew back from her sickness. It wasn't a matter of VD, but of the look on her face. When we had finished our drinks and clowned around self-consciously a little, we left. I looked back from the door and she was just lying there, watching us go, not saying anything.

The hard-drinking, all-night Daytona parties usually ended on the beach. The sand would still be warm from the sun, and it never rained at night. You could go down there with a bottle and a girl and fall asleep under a pier, or just on the sand of the beach, and wake to see the sun rising red and burning out over the ocean, and feel the day's heat beginning. And you'd stand up and brush the sand from your clothes, and start back toward the base, feeling a little stiff, and emptied of feeling and desire. If Taylor went along, the trip back was part of the party, though, and he would touch even the morning quiet with wildness. I remember walking with him in the Daytona dawn toward the bus station. Ahead of us an all-night cafete-ria still had its blinking neon sign on, though it was already daylight, and Taylor began chanting in time with the flashing light—'Eat! Eat! Eat!'—until his shouts woke the sleeping citizens, and heads were stuck out of windows to protest. Taylor shouted obscene replies, and we went on, contemptuous and free, along the hot and empty street.

Daytona was like an occupied city. There seemed to be no laws that governed the behavior of Marine pilots; nothing was prohibited; there were not even any proprieties. Many of the girls there were camp-followers, sluttish and obliging. It was said that an enlisted man had gotten syphilis in his big toe while sitting in a booth of a beach-side bar opposite such a girl in a bathing suit. Hotel clerks would register any couple under any name; bartenders were always willing to ignore the fact that none of us was old enough to drink legally; the police might scold, but they never arrested us. Taylor once destroyed the awning of a store while trying to climb it to get to a second-story window where he had seen a girl. No one suggested that he should pay for the damage, and certainly such a thing didn't occur to him. The town had surrendered to a barbarian invasion.

For me it was a disturbing life—too free, too irresponsible, too wild. I was frightened by a world without rules. I wanted to be middle-class again. Others among us must have felt the same, because after a while nice girls began to appear, back-home girls, mostly, and the parties changed into dates, and we all felt more secure. T's wife came down and found an apartment in Daytona, and his sister Liz came to visit, and I began to take her out. It was fun, it was innocent, it was like a game —to dress up like adults and go out to order meals and drinks in grown-up places. We were both nineteen, and we knew no more of the world than any sheltered child does. We scarcely knew what drinks to order, and it seemed impertinent to say to an adult bartender, 'Two gin rickeys' or 'A sloe gin fizz, please.' Most of the time we behaved like nineteen-year-olds; we lay on the beach all day, or played in the surf, or dawdled along the boardwalk. Sometimes if it rained we browsed in bookshops, and tried to be literary. I bought Virginia Woolf's *Haunted House* there, and felt rather avant-garde. At night there were hotels—old-fashioned, clapboard-sided places, short on their usual resort customers, and happy to receive whoever turned up. An ocean wind blew all night long through the open windows, lifting the curtains and cooling us where we lay. In the dark there, with the wind blowing, there seemed to be no time, no future, no war, no adults, and no children. Only two people touching, entering that dark world that was beyond my imagination, and altogether different from it.

In the evenings we went to the Casino on the Daytona Pier, and danced and courted. The Casino was an old barn of a place, thrust out over the ocean and open on three sides so that the ocean breezes could cool the dancers. A band played the tunes that Glenn Miller was playing then, and we danced, or sat at a table in a corner and held hands and looked out at the dark water. We were sitting there one night when a sudden roar of engines drowned the band, and I looked out and saw the running lights of three planes coming toward me up the beach out of the darkness, and low—lower than the level of the casino floor. It was like looking down the barrel of a loaded gun. They would certainly hit the casino; they were too low, too close to pull up; we'll be killed, I thought angrily, just when I've met this marvelous girl. And then they were up and over our heads in a shaking roar, and I could see their taillights through the opening at the other side of the casino, receding up the beach. It was Taylor and a couple of friends, just saying hello.

It began to be clear that our flight was divided into the Sane and the Crazy. The Crazies buzzed the Casino at night, or flew night-time tail chases, or tried night loops; the Sane flew their flights as they were instructed to, and tried not to kill themselves. Perhaps it was a distinction between the frustrated fighter pilots, who flew suicidally to prove to themselves that they should have been chosen for Corsairs, and the rest of us, who flew because we liked to, but also flew to stay alive. Or maybe it was something else. Maybe we were afraid, and they weren't. Taylor often said that he *knew* nothing would happen to him, and whatever crazy thing he tried, nothing did; he was a brilliant pilot, but he seemed to be protected by something more than his brilliance. I wasn't brilliant, and I didn't feel, ever, that I could take chances. Or maybe they were afraid, too, but in a different way, of different things. Death isn't the only terror. I don't know; I never understood the Crazies, though they were my friends.

Two planes crashed in the swamps during our training at Deland—one flown by a Sane, one by a Crazy. We were practicing carrier-landings, using a landing strip out in the pines as the carrier. An area the size of a deck was marked out on the strip, and at the end of it a Landing Signal Officer stood with his paddles and steered you slowly in to a heavy, thudding landing. Then you took off again, followed the plane ahead of you out over the swamp, and in your turn made another approach and thumped down again. It was all low, slow, wheels-down flying; and in that heat, with those old, combat-tired planes, there were bound to be engine failures.

The Sane was a sober-sided young man from Yale named Stanley. He was the only Ivy Leaguer I ever met in the Marine Corps, and he seemed out of place, as though he had wandered in while looking for Naval intelligence. His manners were correct, and rather formally old-fashioned, and he was always clean and pressed and well-groomed. He was the sort of young man who manages always to look as though he gets more haircuts than you do. I liked him well enough; he just seemed a little exotic, that's all. Stanley was on the downwind leg of the pattern when his engine stopped. He made the classic emergency landing, as described in all the manuals, and in many lectures that we had heard—straight ahead, full-stall in to the tree tops, shoulder harness secure, canopy open. He walked briskly away from it, and was brought back in a jeep to the ready room, where we were all anxiously waiting for news. 'Christ,' Joe said, 'what will Yale say if we've killed their only Marine?' Stanley began his account as though he were back at Yale, delivering a lecture on crash-landings: 'I perceived that my oil pressure was dropping, and so I immediately set about preparations for. . . .'

The Crazy, in the same predicament, settled toward the trees, but at the last moment decided, as he put it, that 'those bastards were wrong' in the emergency instructions they gave, and pushed the nose of his plane down into the trees instead of stalling in flat. He ploughed through an acre or so of pines, and was knocked in the head by a trunk before what was left of the plane came to rest. He climbed out, carrying with him his cockpit microphone, and was found, after a good deal of searching, stumbling through the swamp shouting curses into the mike—at God, the C.O., and the designer of the SBD. When he was brought back in the ambulance, he was still clutching the microphone, and as he passed us at the BOQ he hung out of the ambulance window and shouted a reporter's account of his exploit, like H. V. Kaltenborn. He was kept in the sick bay for a couple of days for observation, but the doctor concluded that though he was crazy, he wasn't any crazier than before the crash. When he was released he immediately drove his car back to the wreck and siphoned a tank full of gasoline out of it. He had no other closed containers to fill, but there was all that gas, and it was rationed, so he found a washtub somewhere and put it in his trunk, and filled that too, and drove back to the airfield with a tub of high-octane gasoline sloshing about in the back of the car. He said it made his engine run a hell of a lot better than the SBD's did.

In the end the Marine Corps seemed to recognize the Sane-Crazy distinction. When we had finished our training at Deland and were certified dive-bomber pilots, we were given two kinds of assignments. The Crazies were sent to another Florida training station, where they were assigned to fly target planes for night-fighter training. It was like being sent to Siberia. They would not be preparing for combat, and they had no prospects of ever joining a combat squadron. They would simply be tools for the training of luckier pilots, who would pass on to the world we all wanted to inhabit—a fighting squadron in the Pacific war.

The rest of us, the Sanes, had orders to California, 'for aviation duty with MarAirWingSoPac.' That last word was what we wanted—duty with the Marine Air Wing, South Pacific. We were going West, to where the real squadrons were put together. It was hard on the Crazies, some of whom were marvelous natural pilots, and I wanted to say something to them, but there wasn't anything to say, really. Taylor was sitting in the BOQ bar when I left, and I went in and just said so long. 'So long, man,' he said. 'Don't crash and burn.' I could hear his high, cackling laugh as I walked down the path to the waiting jeep.

Chapter Five

WE WERE on our way to the real war, but first we were given a leave, and I went to see my father. The visit wasn't a success. I had decided that I was going to marry T's sister before I went overseas, and I knew I couldn't tell my father. I was only nineteen; I had less than a year of college, and no prospects after the war; I had known her only a few months, neither of us had any money or any expectations of it —the sensible arguments against such a foolish act were over-whelming. And the arguments for it didn't exist.

It wasn't that I thought I would die in combat; I knew that pilots were killed out there, but I didn't believe, couldn't even imagine, that I would be the one who would meet the anti-aircraft burst, the one in the spinning, burning plane. So I wasn't rushing into marriage before I died, nothing so foolish and romantic as that. No, I think I saw marriage as simply one more Test that stood between me and adulthood, or man-hood, or whatever that state was that lay on the other side of innocence. I had passed one Test. I was a Marine officer and a pilot. If I were also married, then there would be only one Test left—the Test of combat. The girl I had chosen was pretty, and we were happy together, but I didn't expect that marriage would be like the days at Daytona. I had seen the way it was for my parents and their friends, I knew that it was bills and de-cisions and children and quarrels, and above all being respon-sible for somebody else—a voluntary abandoning of freedom. And I was nineteen years old; I had only just begun to know what freedom offered. Still, I was determined that I must be a married man.

And so I moped around home, and had another picture taken with my father, in front of the house. In this one I am wearing my new Marine uniform; the blouse is too long—the shoulders fit all right, but it was obviously made for a taller man—but it looks new and pressed, and the gold bars are bright on the shoulders. My father is in his shirt sleeves, taller than me, white-haired. He has one hand on my shoulder, in a gesture that was meant to be affectionate, but looks a little threatening, as though he might lift me into the air, or press me down into the ground with one powerful movement. It is a picture of deep, clumsy love.

Then I went back to Birmingham, and we told Liz's parents, and there was a lot of weeping and talk, and Aunt Sister came in and wrung her hands, and then we were married, in the Methodist church at the corner, with the flowers left over from somebody else's wedding. After the ceremony I sent my father a terse, embarrassed telegram; I knew that nothing I could say would explain what I had done, or ease his puzzled disappointment. Liz's family gave us a wedding supper, and we spent our wedding night in the Tutwiler Hotel, and the next day T and I set off by train for California.

Almost immediately (I think it was in New Orleans) I knocked a suitcase against my ankle and did something to a bone. While we rolled through Texas in a hot, crowded train, my ankle swelled. By the time we had reached New Mexico, I couldn't walk; I had to hop to the toilet, and I could only stand in line for meals by leaning on T, using him as a crutch. At night I sat with my foot propped on the opposite seat, not sleeping, just hurting and worrying. I worried about what I had just done—the marriage that I had committed. Suppose Liz was pregnant? I'd have a child before I was twenty-one. How would I support it and her? And myself, for that matter? I had never had a full-time job; I had only been a college freshman in that other world back home. Alone there in the night, rolling through the darkness that was New Mexico or Arizona, the comfortable present-tense security of the military life fell from me, and I looked bleakly beyond, into a gray civilian future. This was what being grown-up was like. It still seemed an imperative that I couldn't dodge; but I wished I had not rushed toward it so eagerly.

I worried about military matters too, as the train swayed and my swollen ankle responded with a jab of pain. What would the doctors do to me in California? Would I be put into a cast? Would I lose my place in the squadron? Would my friends go off to the war and leave me on crutches? I hobbled off the train at Los Angeles in more anxiety than pain.

Railroad stations and bus stations: they were the sad places of the war, the limbos of lost souls. All those troops, far from their hometowns, and miserable-looking in their new uniforms, and the sad, young country girls, pregnant or holding babies, not looking around much, just standing, waiting. Lines everywhere. There was no place you could go that you didn't have to stand in a line first. Piles of duffel bags. And MP's with their white leggings and night sticks, patrolling, representing discipline, *being* discipline in their stiff postures and their sharp uniforms. War could do worse things than this to plain people, but for a sense of the ordinary outrages of life in a country at war, the stations were the place to go.

T helped me through the Los Angeles station and onto a train for San Diego, and off at the other end, and found the liberty bus for the Marine Corps Air Depot at Miramar. People in the stations stared as I hobbled past, and perhaps wondered vaguely if I had been wounded in action; but they had their own problems, and they turned back into themselves. I had my problem, too, and I brooded on it as we rode out of San Diego and up into the hills. I had to get checked in at this new base without revealing that I was crippled, and I had to cure myself before I was discovered. I couldn't go to the doctor at the sick bay, for fear he'd ground me, and I didn't know how to treat myself, or even exactly what was wrong.

When we got there, T did it all. He installed me at the BOQ bar with my foot up on a cushion, and checked me in by proxy ('My buddy ain't feelin' so good,' he'd say, 'it was a little rough in L.A. last night, y'know'), and he wangled a crutch from a sympathetic corpsman. I was safe until the next orders came.

Miramar was a staging base, just a collection of barracks and mess halls—that was all—on a bare, treeless hill above San Diego. If you entered or left California, in either direction, you had to go through Miramar, and while you were there you did nothing except wait. Orders came, and you went, or they didn't come, and you waited, and drank, and tried to make long-distance phone calls home. In the bar you met pilots on their way to the war, pilots who had just come back, and pilots like us, passing through to California bases for still more

training, before we could join those enviable guys who were
on their way out.

We must have been impatient, but I don't remember impatience. Or not the kind you feel in ordinary life, when a letter
doesn't come, or a girl is late. There were always parties; we
carried our permanent party with us, and you could go to the
club and drink anytime. But, more than that, existence itself
was exciting. Just waiting on that bare California hill was odd
and exhilarating. Most of us had never been to California before; it was new, it wasn't like Minnesota, or even like Florida.
And the old hands around us in the bar were always willing to
tell us war stories. It was there that I first heard the romantic
island names: Rabaul and Munda and Bougainville, Espiritu
Santo, Emirau. The tellers were like old explorers, or like the
sailor in that painting of the boyhood of Sir Walter Raleigh,
and we were the listening boys.

It was a whole life, at Miramar—insulated, alcoholic, and
idle, but in its way complete. You could go into town on liberty if you wanted to, but not many people did. I think everyone felt superstitious about leaving the base; if you went
away, your orders would come and you'd be left behind. And
anyway, San Diego wasn't much of a liberty town. Once T and
I did make the trip to Los Angeles, on the fancy train that runs
up the coast from San Diego; we found that the crutch and
the hobble got us onto the train ahead of the mob of waiting
sailors and Marines, and we sat in the soft seats of the club car,
and drank and looked at Southern California. I suppose it was
beautiful, but its mountains and rocks and dry hillsides were
too alien still to register as landscape. It looked like a bad place
to crash-land in, that was all.

In a couple of weeks our orders came, and by then I could give
a fair imitation of a man with two legs, and I was sure I could
fly. We rode up the coast again, past Los Angeles this time, to
the Marine Corps Air Station at Santa Barbara. It was the first
all-Marine field we had seen, and it was different. The Marines
are administratively attached to the Navy, but no Marine likes
to admit it, and the Navy is generally regarded (by Marines,
that is) as a softer, more gentlemanly, less belligerent service. Of
my flight school friends it was certainly true that the well-bred

ones tended to take Navy commissions; and those like myself who felt provincial, or common, or underbred, chose the Marine Corps, where those qualities wouldn't show. The Marines that I knew, both the officers and the enlisted men, seemed to be mainly southerners and midwesterners—country boys, rednecks, and yokels. I don't think I ever met a Marine from New York or San Francisco, or a rich one.

The base at Santa Barbara was small, new, and temporary-looking, with nothing like the old-school elegance of Pensacola; but that seemed right for Marines. As we drove along the flight line we could see that each area, with its hangars and Quonset huts, housed a real fighter or bomber squadron, with a number—Marine Fighter Squadron 122—on a sign by the road, and sometimes a squadron insignia, a bolt of lightning, or an ace of hearts, a symbol that you could imagine painted on the side of a fighter plane, beside a row of little Jap flags, for the planes it had shot down. The numbers and the insignias, and the rows of fighting planes, made the whole place seem very real, as though the war was being fought nearby, just over the horizon.

Our squadron was VMTB-943, which means V—heavier-than-air-craft, M—Marine Corps, TB—torpedo bombers. The planes we would fly were TBM's, the model that the Navy had chosen to replace the disastrous Douglas Devastators, the torpedo bombers that had been shot out of the air at Midway. The TBM was a big plane—the biggest single-engine plane ever built—and a good one. It could carry a ton of bombs (the SBD carried only 1,000 pounds), and had a range twice that of the SBD, and greater speed. Because it carried the bombs internally, in a closed bomb bay, it had a curious, sagging look along its belly; and to keep this sag off the ground, it had a very long landing gear, which were attached close to the fuselage, so that they seemed to be a pair of long, awkward legs. It looked, on the ground, like some barnyard fowl, and pilots called it the Pregnant Turkey.

Any plane looks awkward on the ground. A plane's environment is the air, and it becomes itself when the air begins to flow over its surfaces, and it responds to the controls; but the Turkey looked as clumsy in the air as it did on the ground. It really did look like a turkey taking off, and whatever you did with it in the air, that thick, pregnant body moved effortfully. It was only beautiful to the men who flew it; for it was a beautifully functional plane. It did what it was designed to do; it had no tricks, would not stall or spin off in a landing approach (as a Corsair would), would fly heavily but steadily through bad weather or through enemy fire. There was no glory in flying Turkeys, but there was a good deal of flying pleasure.

There was pleasure, too, in flying them in a real squadron. It made our activities seem more significant, and our relationships—in the air as well as on the ground—formal, and directed toward a war. I can think of no analogy for the feeling of belonging to a squadron. It wasn't like being on a team. Nobody ever did anything for the good of the squadron, that I heard of; nobody talked about winning, or about loyalty or spirit. It wasn't like a private club—I'd have happily blackballed some of my fellow-pilots, if I could. Perhaps it was more like a family than anything else, with the C.O. for the father, and the Adjutant, fussing over his records, for Mom. As in a family, everyone moved in his own sphere, was free to dislike and fight with the other members, but yet acknowledged that there were bonds that linked him to this group of human beings, and excluded all others. In the club in the evenings, squadron members would drink together, and I often found myself joining someone I didn't even like because he was in my squadron, rather than drink with an outsider. It wasn't a hostile exclusiveness, just a recognition that ties existed. Ours wasn't even a combat squadron, it was only for training; but still it was a squadron: it had senior pilots who had been in the Pacific, and it could, if required, have gone into combat. It was a whole fighting unit, with a function and a collective set of skills.

The presence of experienced fliers—not as instructors, the way they had been at Deland, but simply as fellow-pilots—made the greatest difference in the atmosphere of Santa Barbara. The fighter ace Joe Foss was there with a fighter squadron, and his presence made the Corsairs on the field seem more serious, machines made for killing men and destroying other machines, and when I passed them on the field I was aware of the machine guns poking from the wings. You could stand beside Joe Foss at the BOQ bar and listen to him making flat, sane conversation. Because he was one of the Sanes, one of the best of them. He was a famous fighter pilot, maybe a great one, because he had studied his plane, and his enemies, and had used the odds carefully. From him you could learn how to survive. But his very sanity made him drab and unheroic, like a schoolteacher or a successful businessman. It was exciting to stand beside a man who had shot down so many planes, but the man himself was colorless. Without his record he would have been invisible.

We stood at the bar in the presence of Joe Foss and told each other stories about another fighter pilot, Pappy Boyington. If Foss was the greatest of the Sanes, Pappy was the greatest Crazy. He was one who would fly over a Japanese base on a quiet day and invite opponents up to fight with him, as though he were a knight in some old poem. Only a world crazy with war could have supported a man like Boyington; yet for us he was the Hero, and I'd have liked to talk with him and drink with him. Foss was there in the BOQ bar, but there seemed no point in actually meeting him. What could he say?

Certainly it is the Crazies in our lives who charm and seduce us. They live their lives free of the restraints, the fears and prudences, that limit our own actions. They gamble with death and scandal, and seem to thrive on the troubles and turmoil that we spend our lives avoiding. They seem, to the Sane, continuously careless; carelessness seems a necessary element in whatever they do, a seasoning to the sauce, an excitement. So the Crazies become legends, and we talked about them by the hour, there in the BOQ bar when the flying was done. We talked about the guy, whose name no one could remember, who had spent all his training time at Santa Barbara flat-hatting his TBM along the coast highway. Flat-hatting is simply flying very low, the lower the better. Your sense of speed increases as you come nearer to the ground, objects flash by faster, and you get a feeling of domination and power, as though you are defeating the friction of the earth's surface. Your sense of danger also increases as you get lower, and that is why flat-hatters are Crazies.

This Crazy had begun to fly low along the coast, over the flat shelf that lies between the mountains and the sea. He would go out on a flight—navigational practice, perhaps, or a gunnery hop—and would spend the time roaring up and down the beach, or inland, over the undulating foothills. Gradually this palled, and he began to concentrate on the highway. Drivers headed south for Los Angeles would meet him headed north, bearing down on them apparently at their own level, and he would thunder over their heads with a roar, so close they could see the streaks of oil along the bomb-bay doors, and the scared face of the radio man at the tunnel window. Sometimes a driver would try to avoid what seemed a certain collision, and would weave frantically back and forth across the road, or drive into the ditch, and when this happened the Crazy was especially pleased. He seemed to have taken it as his mission to empty the highway of cars, to make the world safe for low-flying airplanes.

Complaints began to reach his Commanding Officer. Even in wartime you can't terrorize civilians, unless they are enemy civilians, and the Crazy clearly had to be dealt with. The C.O. might have court-martialled him, and thrown him in the brig; but he did a more sensible thing—he sent his Crazy overseas to a combat squadron, arguing that that kind of behavior might perhaps have good results out there. At least that's the story we heard in the Santa Barbara BOQ bar. There were various versions of what happened then, and you can take your choice: the Crazy became a hero, attacking and sinking enemy ships against impossible odds; or he crashed on a takeoff and was killed; or he went out of his mind (*further* out of his mind, some would have said) and is still confined to a naval hospital for the incurably insane. I favor the second version—Crazies are careless, and carelessness will kill you in an airplane, sooner or later.

On the flight line, in the ready room, and in the bar we began to get acquainted with the other pilots in the squadron. The most important man in 943 was Jimmy, a sweet-faced captain who looked about sixteen, but had already had one tour of duty in TBM's, and had a Distinguished Flying Cross. His title was Operations Officer, but in fact he was C.O. and Executive Officer and everything else in the squadron. He planned everything, he trained all the new pilots, and he told the vague-minded C.O. what to do. Jimmy had been on the famous torpedo run to Rabaul, and he told us about it, one night in the bar.

'Fucking MacArthur,' he began. Marines who had been to the Pacific hated MacArthur; he was the Supreme Commander out there, and Marines believed he had exploited them, gave them the worst and most dangerous assignments, wasted Marine assault troops on unimportant islands, and squandered Marine pilots and planes attacking targets that the Air Force was afraid to hit. MacArthur had got the idea of hitting the ships in Rabaul harbor with torpedoes.

The harbor, Jimmy explained, was shaped like a teacup— no, more like a cream pitcher, round, with steep sides, and one narrow entrance like the spout. If you wanted to drop torpedoes, what you had to do was sneak in over the edge of the pitcher—at this point Jimmy began to fly the strike with his hands—and drop down low over the water, and then fly straight-and-level, at not more than a hundred and fifty knots, for not less than one minute, and *then* release your torpedo. If you weren't flying flat and slow when you dropped, the torpedo would porpoise—he made an up-and-down, plunging movement with his hand—or break up when it hit the water. Then you had to fly out the spout.

So there they were, sixteen planes trying to sneak up on Rabaul because MacArthur thought it was a good idea, and the Japs had them on the radar all the way; and when they came over the hill and dropped down to the bay every gun in the place was on them, and they couldn't even take evasive action until they'd dropped. Then they went corkscrewing out the harbor mouth, and when they got outside there were only four of them left. 'Just me and George,' Jimmy said, 'and Black Mike Savino, and Junior Ransom.'

Joe wanted to know what they had hit; I could see that he was imagining himself there.

Jimmy didn't know. He'd been too busy trying to get out of there to look back, but George thought they must have hit *something*, there was all that black smoke. But the smoke could have been the other twelve planes, of course.

Not everybody talked about flying. I met a first lieutenant named Harry who talked mostly about sex. He was tan and blond, and very muscular—the weight-lifting type; you could imagine him on a beach, flexing his biceps, or in an ad for a muscle-building course. All his free time was spent chasing women, and when he couldn't chase them he liked to remember conquests from his past. He was a raconteur of bedroom anecdotes, all of which he claimed had happened to him. While we were in Santa Barbara he established a liaison with a dentist's wife, and he entertained us at the bar with stories of her sexual enthusiasms, until one day the doctor came home early from his office, and the affair ended. According to Harry, the dentist walked into the bedroom while his wife was engaged with Harry in a particularly unusual sexual act. Harry looked up, saw the dentist in the doorway, and said: 'Don't you know enough to knock before you enter a room?' 'Excuse me,' the dentist said, and withdrew, closing the door behind him. This seemed very sophisticated stuff to us, and it was somehow all right to laugh, because the husband was a dentist.

There was another first lieutenant who had been a baseball player; a lot of ball players turned up in the Marine Corps, though I can't explain why. Ken Kelleher was a Boston Irishman who had pitched for some team in the International League, and he was full of stories about how he had gone twelve innings against Montreal, and how his knuckleball had mystified the batters. He would go out behind the ready room when he wasn't flying and pitch to anyone who would catch for him. He liked it if you talked to him while he pitched, like a pro: 'Come on, Ken baby, chuck me that old apple,' stuff like that. Ken was the squadron philosopher, and he had a philosophical aphorism for every occasion. If you complained about some official order he would say, in his Boston accent, 'Don't fight it, you cahn't shovel shit against the tide.' We all adopted his sayings, long *a*'s and all, and they became a part of the squadron's language.

All of these guys were likable, even Harry was entertaining. But no squadron is made up entirely of likable guys. There was, for example, Sly. He must have had a first name, but it is an indication of his status in the squadron that nobody wanted to know him well enough to know what his first name was, and he was always referred to as just Sly. He was a big, flabby man, with thinning sandy hair, and a lumpy, shapeless sort of face.

To compensate for his general unimpressiveness he had tried to grow a mustache, but his facial hair, like the hair on his head, was thin and limp, and the mustache was never more than a straggly shadow on his upper lip. 'Makes his mouth look like a pussy,' Rock said. (Rock was growing a handlebar mustache that gave him the look of a Texas sheriff.) Sly was unpleasant to look at and he was a bore, and to my mind he was a mediocre pilot; but he too was a member of the squadron, and we flew with him, drank with him, and listened to his boring obscenities. It was all part of squadron life.

The field at Santa Barbara lay north of the town, between the ocean and mountains. Both sea and mountains became important in our lives. The mountains were simply there, a solid obstacle always, lifting their jagged tops toward the vulnerable belly of your plane, denying the possibility of a safe landing if your engine failed. They were like reality, or death—unavoidable, always there. In darkness, or in bad weather, they were especially threatening, for their presence bent the radio range signals and made it difficult to approach Santa Barbara on instruments. But, whatever the weather, I felt mortal when mountains were below me.

From the sea came afternoon fog that lay offshore, solid and definite as a gray blanket, and then drew in over the field as the earth cooled. From the air you could watch it moving, first the offshore islands gone, then the beach, then the ocean-end of the landing strip. It would get that far and still the mountain-end would be perfectly clear, and you could still land there, and roll out toward the sea, into the thick mist. But once the fog had slid on over the entire strip the field would be closed for the night, and planes caught above it would have to find other landing places.

In the autumn the fogs were frequent, and moved in very quickly, as though the earth were pulling a blanket up to its chin in preparation for a cold night. One day, at the end of October, a quick fog nearly caught a whole flight of us too far from the field to get home. We turned and ran, and all of us made it except one. A pilot we called Frenchy had fallen behind, and as we landed we could hear him on the radio, caught above the fog, asking the tower for directions to a field that was clear. He seemed miles away, up there on top in the sunlight while we taxied slowly and nervously through the luminous wetness toward the flight line. We heard him get a heading for El Centro, the Marine field on the Salton Sea, a hundred miles inland behind the mountains, and we heard no more. We kept in touch with El Centro, but he didn't arrive, and after a few hours, when his fuel supply would have run out, we had to assume that he was down somewhere, perhaps dead in the mountains. Weeks passed, and the squadron was ordered to another station, and there was still no word of Frenchy. He had simply disappeared, as though dissolved, plane and all, by the fog.

Those of us who were married had left our wives behind when we came to the west coast; there was no time for domesticity, we thought, on the way to a war. But we were nevertheless newlyweds, and it was impossible to pretend to be bachelors again. On weekends we went to Los Angeles in a bunch, some married, some single, and got rooms at a shabby hotel across the street from the Biltmore ('next to the best hotel in town,' Rock said). We would sleep there, we thought, but we'd live at the Biltmore, where there was an officers' club and a fancy bar, and a lot of women seemed to be coming and going. Toward the end of the afternoon we strolled into the club. The room was already full of officers and women, some of them in uniforms of the Waves or the woman Marines (called BAMS, meaning Broad-Assed Marines), others pretty clearly local camp followers. The married men huddled together at the bar, in a circle, like a wagon train protecting itself against marauding Indians; the bachelors drifted off after women. I watched Puta moving from one girl to another at the other end of the room. He would approach one, speak low for a moment, watch her face, and pass on with a shrug. Some of the faces looked startled, some angry, one or two laughed. In a few minutes he left with a BAM. The rest of us went on drinking.

When we came out onto the street it was dark, and we were drunk. We must have eaten; I only remember a long taxi ride to Hollywood, where, T said, you could hear great jazz. And he was right. All along Sunset Boulevard, in little clubs, were the jazz musicians I had been listening to on records—Illinois Jacquet, Teddy Bunn the guitarist, Howard McGhee—each in a trio or a quartet, up behind the bar. We drank a good deal more, going from club to club, and my memories are blurred; at one point T was singing with a band, in his husky, Louis Armstrong voice, and somewhere else he was playing drums, and we were all cheering him. The musicians didn't seem to mind.

The next day, on the way back to Santa Barbara, I asked Puta what he had said to those girls in the officers' club. 'Me, I got a very straightforward approach,' he said. 'I go up to a girl, an' I say, "Hey, honey, do you fuck?" Mostly they say "No," but the thing is, see, I don't waste no time.'

'And what did the BAM say, the one you went out with?'

Puta laughed. 'She said, "I sure do, you smooth devil!"'

On another occasion Puta and Rock and a friend called Mac went hustling at the Biltmore, but could only manage to pick up one girl. 'Never mind,' Puta said, 'I got a system. You guys go back to the hotel and hide in the john. I'll take her in and screw her, and then I'll say, "Honey, I got to go to the toilet," and one of you come back and have a piece, and do the same thing.' And that's what they did. It worked all right the first time; Rock was about Puta's size, and had a crew cut like Puta's, but Mac was heavier, and had long curly hair, and when he climbed aboard the girl sensed something had changed. She turned the light on, and found the stranger sprawled in her lap, and she began to cry, more and more hysterically. Puta and Rock had to come out of the bathroom and try to calm her before the house detective heard her. Finally her sobs subsided, and she got up and began to dress. As she opened the door to leave she turned to the three still naked culprits sitting on the edge of the bed: 'That's the trouble with you fucking Marines,' she said, 'you don't know how to treat a lady.'

As the autumn passed, and we stayed on at Santa Barbara, those of us who were married began to imagine living a married life there. We could send for our wives, we said, though when we said *wives* it didn't somehow seem like the right word. Liz was my wife all right, but when I thought of her it was more as though she were still my best girl, my steady date. But maybe if she and all the other girl-wives came out and actually lived with us we'd all learn how to feel married. Maybe we'd even become adults. I went down the hall to the phone and called his wife in Birmingham, and then I called Liz. Of course we were married, and we should live together for as long as we could, though none of us had any real notion of what living together meant, except from watching our parents, and you can't learn much that's useful about married life from observing your elders.

Joe sat silently on his bunk for a while, which wasn't like him, and then said, 'I'm going to call Bev and tell her to come out here and get married, too.' And he went down the hall.

The BOQ phone was hung on the wall of the corridor, next to the head. Joe was shy and didn't want us all to hear him proposing marriage, and so he dialed, and then took the phone around the corner of the door, into the room where the toilet stalls were. Wally crept after him, listened, and when Joe had his girl on the phone, slipped behind him and began to flush the toilets. The room was filled with the rush and gurgle of water, louder and louder as Wally moved along the row of stalls. By the time he had flushed the last one, the first was ready again, and he kept the uproar going, a complex counterpoint of flushing. Joe shouted, turned back to the phone, pleaded, returned to soothe his puzzled girl, and finally began to laugh. Wally was roaring with laughter, too, flushing and shouting, and waving his arms like a mad conductor; and we all came down the hall to watch, laughing too, hanging onto each other helplessly. Eventually Joe managed to shout his speech over the noise, and his girl accepted. We went back to the room and had a drink to celebrate. Joe said Wally was a very funny guy, and made him his Best Man. Somebody said they should be married in the head, with the crappers providing the wedding march.

Liz was on her way, her train already rolling across Texas, or maybe New Mexico by now, and I didn't have a home for her to come to. It was obvious that that was what a husband did, he *provided*; but I didn't know how to go about it, and I faced the problem in a helpless daze—I suppose I saw it as the first in a lifelong series of duties to be done, a process by which I somehow became my father, and I knew that I wouldn't handle the others any better than I was handling this one. Santa Barbara was crowded already with young people like us, every spare room seemed to have a newlywed couple in it. But, even if I could find a room, was that what I wanted? Was that the way to begin being married? Wouldn't it be like living with your in-laws? But if a room wouldn't do, how did I find something better, like a regular house? So I sat around the BOQ moping and doing nothing, until T came in with the answer.

He had found a house, he said. A big one, and expensive; but we could manage it if we got Bergie to come in with us. It had three bedrooms—well, really *two* bedrooms and a sun parlor off the living room—and two bathrooms; we could fit in all right. Spanish-style, he said, a regular hacienda. Even the address was fancy—Calle Boca del Cañon. I thought it sounded fine. Beginning marriage in the company of other beginners didn't seem so embarrassing as with strangers, or in-laws, or just any other adults.

The house in Calle Boca del Cañon was much grander than anything any of us was used to. The living room had a high, beamed ceiling and a stone fireplace that covered a whole wall, and there was a balcony at the end with a view across the roofs of the town to the mountains. On the upper floor was a round bedroom, with a round bed in it, and another balcony. The idea of sleeping in a round bed struck us all as very sexy, the sort of thing that Rita Hayworth might do in a movie, and we flipped coins for that room. T won, and his first child was conceived there. I came third in the toss and got the sun parlor. Liz and I would never be able to go to bed until everyone else did, but it was all right—we had a home.

While we waited for our wives, we moved our possessions out of BOQ and into the house. The possessions were mostly pieces of Marine equipment, the steel helmets and carbines and .38 revolvers and bayonets that had been issued to us at Miramar, for no reason that any of us could work out. There was no place to store all the gear, so we put it in the fireplace. It made the house look like a guerrilla headquarters, or a set from *For Whom the Bell Tolls.*

Then the wives arrived—three tired nineteen-year-olds, none of whom had ever been to California, or traveled that far on a train before (I don't suppose Bergie's wife Fran had ever been out of South Dakota), or run a house—and we began our collective life. It was pleasant, and sometimes even domestic-looking, but it never seemed more than playing at marriage. We were all too young, we had no idea of what marriage meant; it was all laughter and parties and clumsy love-making. The girls wore their college-girl clothes—bobby sox and big sweaters and loafers with pennies in them—and ran out to meet us when we came home, looking like the girls at a sorority house greeting a carload of SAE's. After work we strolled through the shops of the town, and bought things that made us feel adult and married—ashtrays, and potholders and towels. Liz and I found a secondhand bookstore, and bought the complete works of Thomas Wolfe, and T bought some old issues of *G-8 and His Battle Aces*, and read them aloud to us after supper. There was a copy of *Lady Chatterley's Lover* in the house, and Liz read that, too, but she didn't say much about it. I was too shy to read it; I guess I was afraid that if I read it, we'd have to discuss it. Sometimes we went out to a dinner, to a Mexican restaurant called El Paseo, where a marimba band played, and people who knew how to rumba danced. It was like the evenings in Daytona Beach, part of the game we were playing, called Grown-ups.

Nobody made any plans. I think we were all frightened at the thought that the war might end, and then we'd have to start being grown-ups in earnest, with children and mortgages and debts. We had learned that much about marriage from our parents. But in the meantime we could have this long house-party in a romantic town with a view of the mountains, in a romantic place where none of us had ever been before.

T came home one day driving an old Ford that he had bought from an enlisted man. We could drive it to the squadron every morning, he said. But in the morning it wouldn't start; and in spite of our efforts it never would under its own power. Every morning the girls had to come out of the house in their house-coats and push us off down the hill, and at the end of the day we would get a mechanic to bring a starting truck from the flight line and get the car going for the drive home. Bergie, the cautious, practical father of the house, couldn't understand how T could have been slickered so completely. 'Well,' T explained, 'that ol' boy was smilin' and thinkin', and I was just smilin'.'

While we stayed in Santa Barbara we had squadron parties in our Spanish house. They were like fraternity parties, mostly drinking and singing. All the junior flying officers came—those who were new second lieutenants like ourselves, and the slightly older first lieutenants who had had one tour of duty in the Pacific. Senior officers—the C.O. and the Exec—and the nonflying administrators never came; I never once had a drink with a Commanding Officer, anywhere. We took this to be a matter of rank, of our seniors preserving their dignity; but probably it was simply a difference in age. The college boys drank with the college boys, and the adults drank with the adults.

Wives came too, all of them young and newly married. Jimmy brought his new wife, a Navy nurse who ran the medical ward at the Station hospital. Liz met a young war widow who lived across the street, and brought her over to meet Nick Nagoda, one of the squadron bachelors; and she seemed interested, but Nick wasn't. Sometimes a bachelor brought his own girl. Wally invited a girl out for a visit from Minneapolis, and they came one evening, and stood around shyly, as though it was their first date, or even their first party.

Those parties differed in one way from fraternity parties (or at least what I had heard about them)—there wasn't much sexuality at ours. Everyone drank a lot, and there was a good deal of stumbling affection, but not sex. What there was mostly was singing; we were never too drunk to sing, and the singing seemed more important than the drinking, which was more important (and less threatening) than sex. The songs we sang were the ones that had been brought back from the war, a separate repertoire of songs suitable for Marines to sing while drunk. Pilots had learned them at Ewa or Santos or Bougainville, or on rest leave in Australia; none had ever been written down, I'm sure, and many had been remade to fit new circumstances. They were a genuine oral tradition, like folk ballads. Most of them were about sex or death, though a few were devoted to despising senior officers and the military life. All were comic, or were intended to be.

Some of these songs had been picked up from British or Australian troops, and were not entirely comprehensible to us, though we liked them. I didn't know, for example, what it meant when I sang:

> *I don't want to be a soldier,*
> *I don't want to go to war;*
> *I'd rather be around*
> *Piccadilly Underground,*
> *Living on the earnings of a high-class lady.*

Where was Piccadilly? Why did the guy in the song want to live underground? How was it that a high-class lady earned money?

Others, or parts of others, seemed to have nothing to do with war and soldiering, and for all I know they might have come from any tradition, and almost any date. A song, for instance, that began with this stanza:

> *The captain he rides in his motor-boat,*
> *The admiral rides in his gig;*
> *It don't go a goddamn bit faster,*
> *But it makes the old bastard feel big*

was in the anti-senior-officer tradition; but it went on in this rather different vein:

> *Here's to the sex life of the camel,*
> *It's stranger than anyone thinks;*
> *In a moment of amorous passion*
> *He tried to make love to the Sphinx.*
> *Now the Sphinx's posterior anatomy*
> *Is clogged by the sands of the Nile;*
> *Which accounts for the hump on the poor camel's back,*
> *And the Sphinx's inscrutable smile.*

And what has that got to do with war, or flying, or Marines? But we sang it, and everyone joined in the choruses, which were mostly 'toora-looras' and 'Sing tiddly-aye–o's.' Even the wives sang—or at least the party girls among them did. The shy ones sat, holding untasted drinks, and looked at each other or at the floor, waiting for their husbands to take them home. You could see, if you looked at them, the women they would be in twenty years, living lives devoted to not enjoying themselves.

Joe Baird became the squadron song-leader, a sort of mnemonic curator of the collection. He had no particular singing voice—he could carry a tune, like the rest of us, but no more than that—but he loved to sing. I think he felt the community of the singing more strongly even than the rest of us, how affection flowed among young men when they threw their arms around each other's shoulders and sang a roaring bawdy song. It isn't easy for young American males to express feelings for each other, but on those occasions, when we were together—all pilots, all drunk, shouting indecencies to music and laughing—it was all right; and Joe, who had a deep, easy capacity for love, was our natural leader. With a glass swinging in his hand in time to music, and a happy grin on his face, he would finish one song and begin another, all night, inexhaustibly. 'There were *cats* on the roof,' he would begin, and we'd be singing

> *And cats on the tiles,*
> *Cats with the shits*
> *And cats with the piles,*
> *Cats with their a—a—ass ho—o—o—les*
> *Wreathed in smiles,*
> *As they revelled in the joys of fornication.*

Where did that one come from, I wonder? Joe sang it with great feeling. There were, of course, a great many more verses, including some vivid ones on the sex life of the armadillo. Even the sweet-faced Wally would join in, and Bergie, too, with his high pure voice like a choirboy's (T called it his 'church-in-the-wildwood tenor'), soaring up easily above the rest of us. It was possible, then, to feel comradeship, to be happy together without being emotional, or not visibly, and thus unmanly. They were good parties.

I said that we were playing at being Grown-ups, but that wasn't entirely true. Fran and Berg weren't playing. It was simply in their natures to be an adult married couple, and as the weeks passed they gradually became the father and mother of the house, taking responsibilities and making decisions. Bergie mended broken fixtures and made sure that the phone bill was paid, and Fran cooked most of the meals (neither of the other girls knew how). It was easy to imagine them together after the war, in some little South Dakota town, with a houseful of growing kids—two solid, church-going, tax-paying citizens, as happy with each other as they were now. For the present, their cheerful maturity made it easier for the rest of us to go on being adolescents.

As domesticity flourished in Santa Barbara, as the squadron dug in and made a stable life, other pilots sent for their girls back home, and were married. One of these was a pleasant, rather remote guy from Minneapolis who was considered eccentric because he was a composer. He would sit in the ready room, waiting for a flight, with a sheet of music paper in his lap. Puta, seeing him thus, asked, 'Whatcha doin', Gordon?' Gordon said he was writing music. 'Aw, how can you be writing music? You ain't got no pianna!'

As the date approached for his girl's arrival and the wedding, Gordon became more and more nervous and remote, and took to going on long walks into the hills above the town. On one of these he wandered into some poison oak, and his legs were soon covered with an itching rash. We sent him off to the sick bay, and there he made the mistake of explaining to the corpsman that he was getting married in a few days and had to get the itching stopped before then. The corpsman replied that there was only one possible cure, and painted Gordon from his ankles to his crotch with gentian violet. And so he was married, in purple.

It reminded Rock of a story. 'This guy comes into a hardware store and asks for a can of green paint, and a can of red paint, and a hammer.' 'Whadya want that for?' the hardware guy asks. 'Well,' he says, 'I'm getting married tomorrow. So I'm gonna paint one ball green and the other one red. And if my wife says, "That's the funniest looking pair of balls I ever seen," I'm gonna hit her with the hammer.'

'Poor old Gordon,' T said. 'He'll be too embarrassed to take his pants off. He's so shy, I bet he'll put his foot in the toilet and piss down his leg, just so he won't make any noise.' But the marriage seemed to go all right, the gentian violet faded, and Gordon went on composing music in the ready room.

The ready room was our environment, our club, our sanctuary. Every ready room that I was ever in was just like every other one, yet each was unique—the domain of a particular squadron, the place where the pilots spent their time. They were all fitted with the same furniture—red plastic easy chairs with wooden arms, and seats that were always collapsed onto the springs, so that you sat deep down in them, almost on the floor, and green lockers along the walls for flying gear, and metal-and-plastic card tables. On one of these there was always an acey-deucey board. Acey-deucey was the naval pilot's game —a game something like backgammon that can be played for money, if you have any, or just to pass the time if you're broke. Not a great game, not even a very interesting one, but played in ready rooms, ritualistically. There was a Coke machine in a corner, and a blackboard where flight schedules were posted, and messages written. On one wall an aeronautical map of the area was mounted, with a worn, smudged place where the local field was. The other walls were covered with Dilbert cartoons.

Dilbert was a cartoon character invented, I think, by Robert Osborn. He was the image of an incompetent, careless, stupid flier; and his misdeeds were represented in cartoons that amused pilots, at the same time—or at least that was the theory —that they instructed. 'Dilbert,' the caption would read, 'always believed in stretching a glide,' and Osborn's cartoon would show a plane, stretched out over a boundary fence like a piece of bubble gum, with Dilbert's complacent lunatic face thrust from the cockpit. In time Dilbert's name entered the vocabulary of naval pilots and attached itself to every incompetent flier, and every squadron that I was in had one. Nobody had a special name for the brilliant pilots. But the brilliant ones weren't going to kill you.

In the ready room pilots waited for their flights. When it rained, they waited for the rain to stop. If they weren't flying, they just hung around—partly because there wasn't anywhere else to go, but partly because it was a pilot's place. You could watch planes take off and land, and you could talk to pilots who had just flown, or were on their way to fly. You could read about accidents in the *BuAerNews*. If you couldn't be flying, the next best things were watching it, talking about it, reading about it.

Failing that, you could get into a card game—the endless poker games, or, if Wally was there, pinochle, the only game folks played back home, he always explained. He was very good at it and liked to play for money. 'I've heard of pool hustlers,' Rock would say, 'and I've heard of poker hustlers. I've seen a man get shot for hustlin' at pool. But Wally's the only pinochle-hustler I ever heard tell of.'

Still, we were a training squadron, and we were expected to train. On wet mornings we were turned out of the ready room by the Training Officer, whose job it was to get us to do things that could be put in his records and sent to Washington, as evidence that we were improving our combat readiness. We might drift down the flight line to the Link building and practice instrument flying under the hood, or draw the ready-room blinds and sleep while an enlisted man ran training movies— *What to Know About Air Masses* or *How to Survive in the Jungle* —or go out into the fog and mist and play volleyball with a ball that was clumsy and slick with the dampness. On the coldest, bleakest mornings we were sent to the swimming pool; and there, in that chill chemical bath, we passed endurance tests, swimming round and round the pool (it was understood that it was not cheating to stand up and walk when you came to the shallow end), or practicing how to swim through burning oil, or how to take your pants off in deep water and make them into water wings. ('But think of the embarrassment,' Wally said, 'our ship is sunk, the rescue ship comes up, and there we all are, floating around in our underpants.') It was all training for extreme, but possible situations. Pilots did go down at sea, carriers were set afire. But I found them hard to imagine as I swam up and down (being sure to walk round the shallow end) and waited for 4:30, when we could get the car started and go home. The hint of danger made our lives exciting, but the danger wasn't a reality, not yet. I wanted to get into combat, and in my fantasies I did heroic things, but the Test would not happen today or tomorrow. Today and tomorrow we would go on training, and there would be a party at night, or a movie.

When the weather cleared, we trained in the air. We practiced formation-flying and navigation, we bombed and strafed, and we started night-flying; and in the process of learning to do all these things in TBM's we had a run of accidents. They were mostly of the usual kinds—a pilot lost control in a landing, and ground-looped, and scraped a wing; an engine failed on take-off, and the plane slid to a stop, wheels up, off the end of the runway; a pilot hit his brakes too hard while taxiing, and the plane nosed up—the sorts of accidents you have when you're new and uncertain in a plane. Once, while we were practicing bombing runs on an offshore rock, someone dropped a water-filled bomb—weighing maybe a hundred pounds—through another plane's wing, and I heard the offended pilot's rage on the radio. For a moment I felt that shameful excitement that you feel in the presence of a disaster that is close, but isn't happening to you—there was going to be a crash, reality had entered our bombing game. But the wing held together, and the pilot flew back to the base and made an ordinary landing.

One dark, wet morning in October we drove out to the squadron to meet muster. There had been night-flying the night before, but we didn't expect to fly that day. An overcast hung down along the mountainsides like a heavy, torn curtain, and the wind blew gusts of sudden, vicious rain across the field. But we had to muster anyway. When we were together in the ready room, Jimmy came in and told us that Wally was missing. He had been night-flying the night before, had taken off, Jimmy said, at a quarter to seven. At eight o'clock all planes were ordered to return to the field—aerology said there was fog coming in. Wally was the only pilot who didn't acknowledge the order, and didn't come back. Radar stations along the coast had been alerted, but hadn't picked up any signals. By now the plane was down somewhere, probably in the sea. Wally might be alive, in a life raft or floating in his Mae West. Or there might be wreckage, or an oil slick. We would have to fly a search for him.

We would be scanning the sea and the beach, under a ceiling that sometimes came down to a few hundred feet above the water, below the minimums allowed for visual flight. Visibility would be poor, and the flying dangerous, and there seemed little chance that we would find anything. A plane that goes down at sea, unless it breaks up on impact, simply goes to the bottom and leaves no trace. But a search like this for a lost friend was not a search so much as it was a ritual for the dead. We dressed silently in the ready room. I noticed that Wally's flight was still on the schedule board. Beside it he had left a message for somebody: 'Don't forget the pinochle game.'

I took off with T in the rain and turned north along the beach. We were to search from the Air Station to Cape Lobos, a stretch of about twenty-five miles. The clouds lay low and ragged over the water, and drooped along the hills. We flew just below the cloud base, scanning the surface of the sea and the beach for wreckage. There was only the gray water and the featureless rocks. As we flew the weather got worse, the clouds lowered until we were flying in a thin and narrowing wedge of rainy air just above the waves. We would have to pull up, climb above the clouds, and return to the field; it just wasn't flying weather, hadn't been, really, when we took off. Still, we went on for a while, all our attention now on flying—clearing the sudden outcroppings of rock that jutted from the coastline, maintaining a little altitude, a hundred feet or so now, keeping each other in sight. Finally we quit, deciding at once and without words, and began to climb together.

I felt a mounting uneasiness as we climbed through clouds that seemed threatening and endless. T's plane on my wing was an indistinct shadow, and I was afraid I'd lose sight of it, and then fly into it. The clouds were dark and full of turbulence, and the planes bucked and tossed, and instrument needles swung erratically. Then it became lighter, there was sunlight above us, and I felt an impulse to pull back on the stick, to plunge up to that light; but still we went on in mist, watching the airspeed, the tilting horizon-indicator, the rate-of-climb. When we had burst out at last, into the light, the sky was burning blue above us, and the tops of the clouds were an unbelievable white that was like light itself. It was like flying out of death into life. Wally was dead, but we had performed our ritual of grief. We flew back in a tight two-plane formation, one plane's wing stuck in the space between the other plane's wing and tail, two friends being skillful together, being pilots, being alive.

Chapter Six

IN NOVEMBER the squadron moved to El Toro, a Marine field that lay in a broad, shallow valley south of Los Angeles and inland from Laguna Beach. It was a bigger field than Santa Barbara, and a better one to fly from. The mountains were higher, but they were farther away. You could see their snow-covered tops in the distance to the east when you took off, and the land around the field was flat enough to crash-land on if you had to. And because the sea was beyond the low line of hills to the west, there were no sudden fogs to catch you in the air, the way Frenchy Brelet had been caught. No one knew why we were sent there. Some said it was only an excuse for delaying our assignment to combat; pilots were not dying in the Pacific as rapidly as had been expected.

T and I came into Laguna Beach on a rainy Sunday night. We had ridden down from Los Angeles on a bus to see whether we could find a place for Liz to live (T's wife was pregnant, and had gone home to her mother in Birmingham). The town had the shut-down look that resort towns have out of season; not only was it closed, but it would be closed tomorrow and the next day and the rest of the winter. The lights were out on the movie marquee and on the gas pumps at the corner. Nothing moved on the main street, not a car, not even a dog or cat, and there was no sound except the hush and shuffle of the sea on the beach; the water must be close, just behind that row of stores.

The only lighted door was a storefront USO, and we went in, feeling a little ill at ease (the USO wasn't for officers, or at least we didn't think it was). A girl of perhaps nineteen or twenty was sitting at a desk, looking as though nothing had happened for quite a while. She was tall and blond, the kind who would be handsome when she was thirty; but at nineteen she was too big and definite to be pretty, and she was simply friendly looking. Her name was Torchy, and she was the daughter of a local dentist. We both liked her at once, and if either of us had been alone with her, he'd probably have flirted a bit, though she seemed too nice to get very far with, and I thought she'd probably be too tall when she stood up. But we were brothers-in-law, and the ground rules weren't clear yet, so we talked about housing, and I got a couple of addresses, and then we went back into the rain, feeling gloomy and married. Knowing one friendly girl seemed to make the town lonelier. We caught the last bus through the canyon to the Air Station, to report for duty.

The duty was more training. By now we were easy in TBM's, but we weren't very skillful in them yet. We began to work seriously at bombing, getting the angle right, dropping, pulling up, and getting the hell out; and we practiced formation-flying. Tactically, good formations were part of good bombing procedures—the better the formation was in an attack, the sooner all the planes would get onto the target and away again—but we began to fly together for other reasons, for the pleasure and satisfaction of it. Turkeys weren't stressed for acrobatics; you couldn't Victory Roll one low over the strip, or loop to a landing, as I once saw somebody do in a Corsair; but they were marvelous for precision flying, being heavy, stable, and powerful. If you were any good you could put your plane two feet from another one and stay there all day.

We began to work especially on formation approaches to landing—the only kind of flying in which we might look better than the fighter pilots (and right over the field, where they could see the show). A group of TBM's would approach the field in a column of three-plane V's, in very tight, very symmetrical formation, the wingmen's propellers inches from the leaders' wing-tips, and as they crossed the downwind end of the runway the lead plane could break away suddenly, up and to the left, into a sweeping vertical bank, lowering wheels in the turn, holding the bank through a full circle, and rolling out just over the runway in time to make a heavy, full-stall landing on one side of the strip, and already the second plane rolling out to touch down on the other side, and the third plane coming in behind the first, until the whole flight was on the runway, alternatively left and right, and the leader was just turning off onto the taxiway. It was a beautiful and astonishing thing to watch, and it was very satisfying to do, all together, like a team or an orchestra.

Section takeoffs, though less commonly done, were also pleasurable. I think the greatest satisfaction I ever got from flying an airplane was taking off in section (T was on the other wing) on a rather doltish captain in the squadron. He wasn't much of a flier, but his phlegmatic calm was just right for the occasion. He rolled stolidly down the runway and into the air, while we, on either wing, held position as though we were a single, three-fuselaged machine. It was two or three minutes of absolutely flawless flying, the sort of pure act of skill that stays in the mind, in detail as clear as a sharp photograph—the three planes, rising smoothly in the steady air, the flat land below, the clear sunlight.

Our usual bombing target was a circle of whitewashed stones on a bare hillside some miles south of the field. We went back to it day after day, watching our scores, comparing our hits. It began to seem easy, a daily routine that we would do forever, while the war went on without us. Then on a single day two planes crashed on the target, and killed eight men—the two pilots, their crews, and a couple of extra men who had gone along to get their flight time. Both pilots were experienced, both had been in combat, neither should have died. The first dove straight into the ground on a bombing run—fascinated by the target, perhaps, concentrating on making the drop perfect, or maybe just careless about his altitude. There's no way of knowing. He was Nick Nagoda's friend, and Nick volunteered to help the ambulance crew reach the wreck. He flew above them as they crept up the dirt roads, some of them scarcely more than tracks, that led from the highway into the hills, and when they came to an intersection, he dove to show them which way to go, pulled up into a steep turn, and stalled. The plane rolled on its back and plunged into a ravine and burned. I flew over the target a few days later. The two wrecks were still there, very near each other. They looked small, just two tangles of metal, each in a burned spot on a hillside. They didn't seem big enough to have killed eight men. After a while the wrecks were cleared away, but we could still see the burned spots when we used the target. Two dumb mistakes. Even a good pilot like Nick, an intelligent, quick man, could do something dumb in a plane, and when he did, it would kill him.

About this time we finally heard the end of the story of Frenchy. When he found himself caught above the fog, that day at Santa Barbara, he had asked for a heading to El Centro —we had heard that much on our own radios. But either the controller made a mistake or Frenchy did. Instead of flying on a course of 080 degrees, East, he had flown on 180, which carried him due South, still above solid fog, into Mexico. When the fog began to break up, he saw below him the western side of a body of water. It was the Gulf of California; but he took it to be the Salton Sea, and since he was nearly out of gas he made a wheels-up landing on the beach. Then he wrote a letter to his mother and left it in the cockpit of the plane, with an airmail stamp on it, and set out to walk north along the beach to the town that his map showed was not far away. He left all the emergency rations and water in the plane, perhaps because the town looked so close. But there was no town. The Mexican Army tracking party that finally found him said that he had walked along the beach for a couple of days, then turned to wander inland, returned to the beach, wandered back again into the trees, until at last he fell. 'He was found in the surrounding desert,' the official report said, 'dead and mutilated. The numerous wild birds and small animals existing in the vicinity probably were responsible for the mutilation.' The body could only be identified by checking Frenchy's Navy dental charts. 'Christ,' T said, 'he was eaten by wolves.'

That month the Navy took away half the squadron's TBM's, and gave us SB2C's instead. These were the Navy's new dive-bomber, bigger and faster than the SBD's I had trained in, but in every other way less satisfactory. The SBD was named the Dauntless, though I never heard it called anything but Speedy–D, and it *was* dauntless; some public-relations man had decided to call the SB2C the Helldiver, and it was as showy and as phony as the name, like a beach athlete, all muscle and no guts. It was a long, slab-sided, ugly machine, with a big round tailfin. Unlike most service planes, it was entirely electrically operated (others had hydraulic systems for wheels, flaps, and wing-folding), and the circuits were very undependable, so that you might approach for a landing, flip the switch that activated the flaps, and find that only one flap opened (which would probably roll the plane on its back a hundred feet from the ground); or only one wheel would retract on takeoff; or circuits would get crossed, and the wheels would drop when you wanted to turn on your bombsight. We were all afraid of the SB2C's, and we flew them as though they were booby-trapped. On dive-bombing flights, nobody dived; we settled for gentle glides toward the target, and even gentler pull-ups. And we landed like the Air Force—far apart, flat in the approach, and with plenty of power. 'That thing looks like a coffin,' Rock said, 'and it flies like a coffin. It ain't worth a pot of cold piss.'

In the end it wasn't the power system's failings that saved us, but those big tails. The squadron's Executive Officer was sitting in an SB2C one morning, pretending to warm it up, but actually using the cockpit oxygen mask to breathe a little pure oxygen, which was very good for hangovers. While he was sitting there, breathing deeply and running the engine at screaming full throttle, the tail of the plane fell off. It just fell off, and blew across the mat, with the mechanic running after it. We all went out from the ready room to look at the plane, sitting there, tailless and disgraced, with the Exec standing by it, looking as though his hangover was worse, and each of us was thinking, *Jesus, that could have happened while I was flying it*. So they were all grounded, and after a while they were taken away, and we went back to TBM's, the planes that we trusted and knew how to fly.

Though VMTB-943 was by official designation a torpedo-bombing squadron, and though we were once more flying torpedo bombers, none of the junior pilots had ever seen a torpedo, let alone dropped one. The C.O. decided that we must go, a few at a time, to San Diego, to the Naval Air Station on North Island, to be instructed. I went in a flight of six, and almost at once the flight leader's radio failed, and he returned to El Toro, and left me, flying behind him, to lead the flight. The route looked easy—down the valley to Capistrano, past the church the swallows were supposed to come back to, and then south along the beach, over San Clemente, a boom-town real estate gamble of the twenties that had failed. It was a good landmark. From the air you could see the grid of unused streets, and here and there a sad, fraudulent-looking Spanish-style house, with white walls and a red tile roof, and all around it fields of weeds. Then the coast curved, and we slid out to sea and headed for Point Loma, the northern arm of San Diego harbor. I was rather pleased with myself, leading my flight so neatly and efficiently. Then, as we approached Point Loma, little white clouds began to appear in the air to the left of us —the puffs that bursting antiaircraft shells make. Someone was shooting at us. I swung away from the coast and pulled out my maps. I had just led my flight through a restricted zone, a practice area for antiaircraft crews. 'Some flight leader,' T said when we had landed at North Island. 'Ain't everybody can lead a flight into combat in southern California.' But nobody was really upset; it was another part of the game, a joke, something to kid me about. It was still impossible to believe that those white puffs might be fatal.

San Diego was in some ways like Pensacola—an old established Naval Station with a serenely permanent look. But it was different. The harbor was a deep-water anchorage, and when you flew over the bay you could see combat ships entering and leaving, and convoys gathering in the waters offshore before sailing to Pearl Harbor and the islands beyond. In moorings along the edge of the North Island Air Station, carriers with famous names were tied up—the *Enterprise*, the *Saratoga*, the *Ticonderoga*—and we looked at them with reverence as we passed, as though they were heroic monuments of battles fought long ago. You felt, in San Diego, that the serious war began here.

The town was rougher than Pensacola had been, full of sailors just in from the fleet, who were sometimes brutally violent when drunk; a fighter pilot I knew had his face ripped open with a broken bottle in a brawl there, and the bars were full of fights and club-swinging shore patrolmen. But the Air Station was calm, secure in the presence of its own past. The landing field was a circular mat, like the one at Pensacola's Main Side, perhaps fifteen hundred feet across, put down in the thirties; it had been big enough for the biplanes of those days, but it wouldn't do for modern fighters, and so a straight strip had been added at the side. But the presence of that outmoded mat, and of the old hangars beside it, and the seaplane ramps along the beach was all part of the special quality of North Island, the feeling it always gave me of a tradition in Navy flying. It wasn't a long tradition—there had been Navy pilots then

Contra Costa County Library

Pleasant Hill

2/28/2024   2:23:23 PM

- Patron Receipt -

ID: 21901026947279

1:

Transaction Type: Charged

Title: World War II memoirs : the Pacific Theate

Item #: 31901069708644

Call #: 940.54817 WORLD

Charge/Request Date: 2/25/2024

Due/NNA Date: 3/19/2024

Return Date:

Amount Due:

Account information, library hours,
 nd upcoming closures can be found
  https://ccclib.org/contact-us/,
   by calling 1-800-984-4636.

for about thirty years—but still I liked the sense of the past I
got when I read above a hangar door a sign that said Bombing
Squadron Two; it was a designation from the twenties.

We went to classrooms in one of the hangars for ground
school—the structure of the aerial torpedo, the technique of
torpedo attack—taught by a man who had taught me freshman English in college. He invited me home for dinner, and
showed me his newborn daughter; and I felt for a little while
out of the flying world, and in a world where people read serious books, thought serious thoughts, and in general took life
more seriously than Marine pilots did. We ate and drank and
talked about Keats, and I had a good time, but I found the
presence of the baby disturbing; it seemed a threatening part
of the seriousness, a responsibility that lay in wait. They were
already entangled in their future, and in time I would be, too.

In the same hangar I met Bud, my melancholy friend from
my Memphis days, now a seaman pushing a broom. We went
out together that night, and listened to Stan Kenton in a San
Diego bar, and drank Irish whiskey. We were still friends, and
he was still funny, but we were a little stiff and awkward together. Life had confirmed his melancholy, and his war was a
long boredom, something to be expected and endured. But
my war was just about to begin, and boredom was a state I
knew nothing about.

Next day our planes were loaded with dummy torpedoes,
and we were sent out to make practice runs on an elderly World
War I destroyer that was operating among the islands off the
mouth of the harbor. The point of the attack was to approach
the destroyer from the side, flying low and level just above the
water (like Jimmy and George at Rabaul), and drop your torpedo fifty to a hundred yards from the target. If you dropped
correctly, the torpedo would fall flat into the water—it was
like dropping a telephone pole on its side—and the propeller
at the back would begin to turn and drive the torpedo toward
the ship. The dummies contained no explosives, but they were
still big, heavy hunks of steel; and the destroyer skipper was
apprehensive and kept his ship heeling and turning evasively as
we approached. We launched our attack, raggedly. Some torpedoes fell too far out and never reached the target; others fell
crookedly, and sank, or crossed ahead of or behind the ship.

Joe, at the end of the flight, was determined to get a hit. He bore in close, diving toward the ship, delaying the drop until he was sure of his aim. The torpedo struck the water just short of the ship, in exactly the right spot. But it struck at an angle, submerged, and a moment later burst from the water like a porpoise, in a leaping arc that carried it across the destroyer's deck, past the astonished crew, and into the water on the other side. The skipper immediately radioed that he was suspending operations, and the destroyer wheeled and steamed for home, smoke pouring from all four stacks.

We turned to antisubmarine warfare, first lectures, and then a practice flight, to drop dummy depth-bombs on a training submarine off the coast. We circled offshore, watching the surface. The sub was to cruise, just underwater; we were to spot the dark shadow and straddle it with our harmless bombs, thus learning both to locate a submerged sub and to drop on it. But we came upon it unawares, just as it was surfacing, and began our attack as the conning tower rose from the water. By the time the sub was fully surfaced, and had its tower open, the bombs were splashing alongside and the air was full of TBM's. The submarine submerged in a crash-dive, and lay under the water, sulking, and refused to play, or even to answer our radio pleas. We decided we must be qualified antisub pilots; after all, Joe said, we had nearly sunk the goddamn thing. We returned to North Island.

Back at El Toro we found a new Commanding Officer in charge, a fierce, stiff, academy-trained Lieutenant Colonel— a professional son-of-a-bitch, as Rock put it, with a ramrod up his ass. He was the kind of Regular who is sent to over-relaxed outfits run by Reservists, to bully them into shape. He had swept into 943 during our absence, and had found everything out of order. The Sergeant Major had been lax in his record-keeping, and he was now on his way to the war; officers weren't being trained, and so a new training program had begun. There was no one at all in the ready room when I came in that first morning; either all the pilots were somewhere being trained or they were hiding from the Colonel. The clerks in the squadron office were starched and barbered, and seemed in a state of shock.

The next day, taxiing in from a flight, I followed a lineman's signals, swung my plane around to park it in front of the hangar, and ran the tail into the hangar door. I was annoyed as I shut the engine down—the goddamn lineman should have been more careful—and I was prepared to climb down and give him hell, but I saw that this wouldn't be necessary. There was already an officer standing beside him, and though I couldn't hear what was being said, the lineman seemed to be shriveling.

By the time I had gotten down the Colonel had gone, but the lineman was still fixed to the spot. He stared at me as he might have stared at a man on the gallows. 'The Colonel wants to see you,' he said. 'Jeez, is he pissed off.'

He was right. The Colonel was pissed off all right. While I stood as stiffly at attention as I could manage, he paced his office and as he marched up and down he poured over me a cold stream of furious abuse. I was a destructive idiot; I had damaged valuable Marine Corps property (much more valuable, it was clear, than I was); I was a disgrace to the squadron, to the Air Group, to the Wing, to the Marine Corps past and present (in the Halls of Montezuma, angels turned their backs and wept), to my nation, my parents, and myself. I realized all this time that, although I was standing still and he was moving, he nevertheless managed to be more at attention than I was. At last he stopped, turned full at me, and delivered the sentence: 'You're grounded, Lieutenant. I'm going to send you down to Pendleton for two weeks, to find out what being a Marine is all about.'

The old anxieties came flooding back. I was going to be left out. While I was at the infantry camp at Pendleton, the squadron's orders would come; everyone else would go into combat; I'd be left behind. And it would all be my fault. Goddamn the lineman, goddamn the hangar door. And most of all, goddamn the sadistic Colonel, whose harsh face had cracked into a smile of cold satisfaction. I went home gloomily to explain to Liz that she would be a widow for two weeks while I learned to be an infantryman.

With me the Colonel sent, for no reason that either of us could figure out, a big, ugly, cheerful man from the squadron named Steve Bakos. Steve and his wife lived near us in Laguna, and he drove us down the coast to Pendleton the next Sunday night. In the back of his car was all the useless gear that we had been lugging around with us since we came to the west coast in August, the stuff that had been in the fireplace at Santa Barbara—fatigue uniforms, carbines, helmets, canteens, bayonets, webbed belts. We had never worn any of it and could never have any possible use for it. Some of it I didn't even know how to wear; but it had been issued to us at Miramar, and we were responsible for it all each time we moved. It was like having an idiot-child, Steve said, or a senile grandmother —just one more set of worries.

Dressed in this comical gear, I felt like a character in a play, or in a recruiting movie, Freddy the Fearless Leatherneck. I could even imagine my dialogue: 'Just let me at them Japs!' and 'Don't worry, men, the odds are only ten-to-one against us,' and 'Tell Mom that. . . .' I tried to look casual, but the stuff was all brand new, and the fatigues crackled when I walked, and I couldn't keep my pants stuffed down into the leather leggings that were attached to my boots. After a while, when we had marched cross-country for a whole day, the crackling stopped, and I began to feel that I was wearing my own clothes, though I never got used to wearing a helmet. I even began to enjoy the course, without understanding the point of it.

It was one more summer camp, a last version of military training as a game. One night we played No-Man's-Land, a game in which you crawl on your belly in the dark from one trench to another, across a space that is strung with barbed wire. As you crawl along, machine guns fire tracer bullets above you, to encourage you to keep your bottom down, and here and there along the way explosives are detonated in the earth to simulate shell explosions. With the tracers and the noise and the smell of powder it was quite realistic—as realistic, probably, as the trench scenes in *All Quiet on the Western Front*. But it was still a game. Like the Simulated Aerial Combat Machine, it could momentarily persuade you, but in the end, safe in the other trench, you knew that the real thing would be different, and that this wasn't really much help.

Another night we played Commando Raid, crossing a shallow pond in rubber boats, and stumbling around a lot among reeds and mud. The water was cold—even in southern

California nights are chilly in November—but the game was fun. We were told that we had lost, but since I had not understood what winning involved, I wasn't disappointed.

Steve and I were both entertained by our two weeks of pretending to be infantrymen, and we went home feeling easier about fatigues and carbines and web-belts, but without really knowing much more about our remote allies, the ground Marines. When we got back to the squadron, nothing had happened except that the Colonel had left for a higher echelon job, and the new Sergeant Major that he had demanded had turned up. There were still no orders, and the squadron was still training, though now that the Colonel was gone there were more pilots in the ready room, and the acey-deucey board was out again.

The new Sergeant Major was in fact an old one, one of the prewar breed of Marines, a veteran of the Nicaragua campaign and of China duty. He had the typical bulldog look, heavy-set and jowly, and a voice like an angry bass fiddle. He was punctilious about his military courtesies, but he had small regard for the young flying officers around him. 'Goddamn it, Lieutenant!' he would growl when he met a young pilot about to walk out the door carrying a bottle of whiskey, 'you can't do that!' And he would find a piece of wrapping paper or a paper bag, and cover it up properly.

The Sergeant Major was old, in our eyes. He had been in the Corps all his adult years, and he had no other life. He had never married, and seemed to have no family, and it was said that he had not left the Station since he arrived there. He spent his free time in his barracks room, so the story went, polishing his shoes and his insignia. But he was aging, and his health was failing, and he would be forced to retire soon—943 was his last billet. One night he went into the squadron office, sat down in the Commanding Officer's chair, and shot himself in the head with the C.O.'s 45. The second lieutenant who was Duty Officer that night was quite upset. There was nothing in the regulations to cover an event like that, and Christ, what a mess it made.

Weeks passed, it was December 1944, and still the squadron stayed on at El Toro. We began to evolve a permanent-feeling life. Liz and I had a little apartment in a house at the top of

a canyon in the Laguna hills. I came home at night like any
married man, and we walked together in the town, or along
the beach, and had parties with other young couples. On wet
evenings we went to movies—romantic ones like *Now, Voyager*
and *Laura* and *To Have and Have Not*—and held hands in the
dark, as though we were on a date. We climbed on the rocks
along the coast, and found shells and starfish. I have a photograph of Liz fooling around, like a kid, with Steve Bakos; Steve
is holding two starfish to his chest, like a stripper's bra, and
they're both laughing. The picture has the spirit of that time,
as I remember it—being young and happy and silly.

Not always happy, though. In Santa Barbara we had been
cushioned from the most fundamental of marriage-truths—the
endless intimacy of two—by the company of the other couples
in the house. That life had been more like a long college party
than like a marriage. But in Laguna we were alone in our two
rooms together, and the fact that we were still very ignorant of
each other became clear. We were not, for one thing, from the
same America. I found Liz's easy southern ways charming, but
sometimes maddeningly irresponsible and vague; she found my
midwestern puritanism strict and cold. So there were quarrels,
and cruel words, and tears. But we learned, each of us, who it
was that we were married to, and so gradually became what
the certificate said we already were—a married couple. And the
two rooms in the canyon became a home, a place I came back
to for comfort, a refuge.

We spent our first Christmas together in Laguna. The
weather was warm and hazily sunny, and we walked down
into the town and had dinner at a French restaurant that we
thought was a very good one; perhaps it was, we had no way
of judging—everything tasted good, everything was sophisticated to us. It seemed funny, spending Christmas in shirt-
sleeves in the sun, a part of the whole unreality of the game
of marriage that we played there. But the next day it was cold
and damp again, and as I waited by the canyon road for a ride
to the squadron I felt like a commuter going to work too early
in the morning.

On New Year's Eve we were with Steve and his wife, in their
house high up on a hill over the town. Jane was pregnant,
and very big; and she moved clumsily but happily around the

rooms, in a domestic dream. Steve was happy and proud of her and the baby. He seemed more married than the rest of us, a man cut out for family life. He was a good, dependable flier, as he would have been a good truck driver or a good doctor; but he wasn't in love with flying, the way the rest of us were. The center of his life was in that small house, with his wife and his child. That night we ate, and drank a little—but not too much, because of Jane—and talked about home, about what high school was like, the dances and the music and the clothes we wore, and for a while the war didn't exist. Except for Jane's pregnancy, we might have been two young couples on a double date, or two pairs of newlyweds in some suburb in a time of peace.

When midnight came, we went out to stand on the porch. It was a cold, clear night, and we could see lights far down the beach, and along the road that led up into the canyon. There were distant sounds of celebration, and one church-bell ringing. So much for 1944, I thought. A year ago I was in a barracks at Whiting Field, listening to the rain—a cadet, single, a kid. I hadn't even met Liz. Now I was married, and an officer. Where would I be in another year? Would I be alive? Liz said she was cold, and there really wasn't much point in standing out there in the dark. We went in and had another drink, and walked home through the dark, quiet streets.

January passed, alternately hazy and warm and wet and cold. We flew when we could, but restlessly; the squadron felt trained, and we wanted to get out, before the war ended. In the Philippines the invasion was going well, and when that was over the next one might be the Japanese mainland. If we missed that, we'd have missed the war. But no orders came, and we went on flying, and living our little domestic lives. Other pilots in the squadron met girls, or sent for their hometown sweethearts, and married them, and moved "ashore": even the unlovable Sly got married.

For most of us, the private, physical side of marriage was a mystery, partly sacred and partly embarrassing, that we never mentioned to each other. But Sly had no such reticence about it; he dragged his sex life into squadron conversations as though it was a dirty joke that he'd just heard, that was too good to keep to himself. He would go home for lunch, and then come back and buy a sandwich at the PX, and eat it in the ready room. 'Going home for lunch sure gives a man an appetite,' he would say with a leer. 'Shit,' Rock said, 'a guy like Sly gives fuckin' a bad name.'

We flew at night, out of sheer restlessness, in wandering section-flights up and down the coast. Laguna, with its curve of bay and its one lighted street, looked like a necklace, with a pendant stretching out into the canyon toward El Toro. Los Angeles was a vast saucer of lights. Long Beach was a bright patch. Inland, a vast darkness seemed to stretch out forever, the darkness of the whole American continent; and westward was another and larger void, the dark Pacific. We were impatient to leave that continent for that ocean, but up there at night, alone in the dim light of the cockpit, both directions seemed alien and fearful, and we held to a course along that thin band of familiar lights that was the coast.

When we didn't fly at night there were parties. We met in bars and sang drunkenly with bands, or by ourselves if the band wasn't playing. Joe sang, with great feeling, a ballad about a girl who married a man who had no testicles, and we all roared out the chorus:

> *No balls at all,*
> *No balls at all,*
> *A very short peter*
> *And no balls at all,*

while the proprietor looked uneasily around at his other customers. Sometimes we ran through the endless choruses of 'Fuck 'em All,' though in public we made a concession, and changed the refrain to 'Bless 'em All.' Some of the bachelors rented an apartment in Laguna—it was known as Shades-down Chateau—and had parties there, and got drunk, and sang, and seduced girls. One of the squadron's most aggressive lovers boasted that he had seduced Torchy, the friendly girl from the USO. I felt sad about that—it was like another rainy night in a strange town, a loss.

At the end of the month our orders came; twenty-eight of us were to report to Miramar on February 8, 'for further assignment.' We were on our way out, somewhere. I took Liz up to Los Angeles and put her aboard a train for Chicago. My father would meet her (he had never seen her) and take her to the train for Birmingham. I knew how it would be—he, who had never had a daughter, would sweep through the crowd and wrap his big arms around her; and she, who had no father, only a stepfather, would feel at once secure and protected by him. With a daughter he could express the feelings that he couldn't show for a son. I felt full of love for them both as I caught my own train, south, for San Diego.

Chapter Seven

M IRAMAR AGAIN. I was exhilarated but apprehensive. This was what I wanted, what we had aimed for all these months; it was the dream of success, like marrying money. But, like marriage, it was the beginning of another, unknown life, a step into experience that I knew nothing about, and couldn't imagine, and that all the stories of the veterans couldn't help me to feel. What would it be like, flying from a Pacific island, diving on a real target, being shot at, shooting back? It wasn't exactly fear that I felt, not fear of any specific thing, not death or wounds or even being a coward; it was vaguer than that, an emptiness at the center, a void, a drawn breath in a dark room.

There was nothing to do at Miramar until embarkation orders arrived, but no one left the base. We spent our time in the BOQ bar, drinking and making those quick, temporary friendships that you make in bars. A middle-aged intelligence officer was always there, and he taught us to drink French 75's. The French 75 is a drink invented—or so the intelligence officer said—by American troops in France during the First World War. A mixture of champagne and brandy, it makes you very drunk. 'But you'll never have a hangover from French 75's,' the intelligence officer said. 'I know that to be a fact, based on years of research.' Nevertheless, we all did. If he didn't, it may have been because he kept a bottle of whiskey under his bunk. I roomed with him, and he insisted on having the lower bunk, because otherwise he couldn't reach the bottle in the morning while lying down.

As we got drunker, we sang our songs, and the intelligence officer added one that stayed with us. We were between songs, just sitting there, sort of limply, the way you do when you're halfway to being really drunk, and have plenty of time, when the intelligence officer raised his French 75 in the air and began:

> *Here's to Marianne, queen of all the acrobats,*
> *She's a big fat slob, twice as big as me,*
> *Pimples on her ass like cherries on a tree.*

There were other, more scatological choruses, and it ended

> *She's the kind of girl that will marry—*

The intelligence officer looked around, and spotted Harry, the squadron seducer.

> *—that will marry Harry here.*

A great joke, we thought, Harry married to a big fat slob, and we sang the song again and again, changing the name at the end sometimes, when somebody else came into the bar.

A pilot just back from the South Pacific taught us a ballad that he had learned from an Australian, about a man who went out with a bloody great rod and came back with a bloody great cod. There was a chorus, 'Singing ee–iy—ee–iy—ee–iy—o,' something like that. The pilot went on:

> *He didn't have a place to put the bloody fish,*
> *So he put it in the pot where the old girl pissed.*
> (chorus)
> *In the middle of the night she got up to take a squat,*
> *And the codfish crawled up you know what.*
> (chorus)
> *They worked it out with the handle of a broom,*
> *And they chased it around and around the room.*
> (chorus)
> *There's a moral to the story, and the moral is this—*
> *Always look into the piss-pot before you take a piss.*
> (chorus)

We all learned it, and it joined the repertoire. Joe liked to act it out, especially the part about the broom, and he would get to laughing so hard at his pantomime that he couldn't sing.

From time to time someone would leave the bar and try to place a long distance call. Not that there was anything to say, but it seemed a thing that you did before you went overseas. There was always a wait—the operator would intone through her nose, in an automatic way, 'There will be a four-hour delay'—and so the caller would return to the bar, have another French 75, sing another song, until at last, when his mother was on the phone, he'd be too drunk to say anything except 'Hello, Ma.'

Even the bar and the songs got boring. I got a jeep, drove to a nearby Navy field, and scrounged a hop in a PB4Y, the Navy's version of the B–24 bomber. A flight in a four-engined plane would be something different, at least. Pilots tend to feel about new planes the way lechers feel about women—every one is a new experience, it's all interesting, any flying is better than no flying. But this time it was pretty dull, just flying around, like a long ride on a Greyhound bus. Only the landing was really interesting; getting all that heavy clumsiness down and stopped seemed a difficult and delicate operation, the only part of the flight I wasn't sure I could do. But I was relieved to get in the jeep and hurry back to Miramar to see if the orders had come while I was gone.

They hadn't, but eventually they did, covered with 'SECRET' stamps, and written in the odd, condensed language of official military bureaucracy, but saying, when we'd worked it all out, that we would go to Pearl Harbor, and there would be assigned to a working squadron somewhere in the South Pacific. So we were going to make it to the war. We had a last, all-night party in the BOQ, packed our gear into trucks, and were driven, in the half-light of early morning, down to the San Diego docks.

Our transport was a Liberty ship called the *Lavaca*. Rock said it meant 'cow' in Mexican, and that seemed appropriate for such a lumpish, uninteresting-looking vessel. Still, going on board was exciting; I had never been on an oceangoing ship before. As the *Lavaca* left the harbor I stood on deck with T, feeling sentimental and a little scared as we left the familiar places—past the moored carriers, past North Island, where F6F's were taking off, and a P–boat was drifting down to a landing, past Point Loma, where I had led my flight through the antiaircraft range, past the offshore islands, where we had almost sunk the submarine. In open water outside the harbor the ship joined a convoy, and began to pitch and roll. Gun crews uncovered their guns and test-fired them. Off our beam destroyers slid by, covering the perimeter of the convoy. The war was still a long way off, but we were entering its atmosphere.

Hawaii would be the first strange place, the edge of a world that was not like anything back home. No one I knew had ever been there, except maybe a few Marines, and it existed in my imagination as a mixture of myths. The beach at Waikiki was a part of the romantic mythology of Minneapolis, a place taken out of a song, like Paris in the spring—it was all leis and hula girls and ukuleles. But Pearl Harbor was a part of that mythology, too; it was the stab in the back, the day that would live in infamy, columns of black smoke and diving planes. I couldn't put the two together into one place.

We hung around on deck all morning, the last day out, waiting for signs. First came patrol planes, like the first birds, signifying land ahead, and then picket boats, circling around us suspiciously. Then tugs pulled the antisubmarine nets open, and we entered the roadstead. Somebody on the deck recognized Diamond Head, and for a moment the mood was that of a cruise ship. We were seeing the sights, but as we steamed on we could see the inner harbor ahead, where the superstructures of the sunken ships still thrust up out of the water, with their trapped dead below, and our holiday mood faded. We moved slowly in past the wrecks, and I thought of the dead men's bones, down there in the sunken hulls, so many of them, all white and fleshless now. We had reached the real edge of the war.

'Come on,' Rock said. 'We've got one day to spend in this town. Let's spend it.' And we did, the way any tourist would. We went to the Royal Hawaiian Hotel at Waikiki, because we had heard of it, and had a drink. We swam on the beach (it was surprisingly stony), watched a couple of surfboard riders (and speculated as to why they weren't in the army), and went back into Honolulu. For a famous city it had a disappointingly small-town look ('nothin' but Amarillo with a beach,' Rock said); the streets were narrow and crowded, and the buildings were low and temporary-looking, as though they might have all been built to last only for the duration of the war, or were a set for a war movie. We couldn't think of anything to do there. I found one bookstore—not a very good one—and after a good deal of deliberation I bought a book to last me for a while, *War and Peace*.

For lunch we chose the most Hawaiian-looking restaurant we could find, a place that was all bamboo and palm leaves, with a sort of a hut at one end of the room, where a band in flowered shirts played Hawaiian guitars. 'Mainland rum or island whiskey?' the waiter asked. Those were the only options, and we chose the island whiskey—what was the point of being in the islands if you didn't share their customs? It was made from pineapples, the waiter said, and one swallow sent a pain through my head that was like being shot, a sort of instant hangover.

Honolulu, like its whiskey, was a failure. Perhaps no place could have been exciting enough just then, or at least no place that wasn't in the middle of war—London or Paris, maybe, or Berlin. But Honolulu on the last day of February in 1945 was only another crowded Navy town, much like Pensacola or San Diego, full of sunlight and sailors and bad liquor. We took our island hangovers back to the Marine base at Ewa, and lay around the pool there and waited to move out. At the pool side there wasn't much difference between being where we were and waiting on some other base. It was just another station where nothing was happening.

The flight from Honolulu to Ulithi atoll in the Western Carolines took three days—three days of almost total emptiness, empty air around us and the vacant sea below. I began to get a sense of the enormous expanse of the Pacific. We sat in bucket seats along the sides of the Navy transport plane, with our feet on the cargo that was stowed down the middle, and tried to read or sleep, or talked about where we were going. It took four hours to reach the first crumb of land—Johnson Island, a landing strip and a couple of buildings and nothing else, not even a tree to shelter you from the baking sun, and all around, stretching to the horizon, the empty, featureless, blinding sea. We ate a hasty lunch there, and were off again for seven more hours' flying to the next island, Majuro. It was night by then, and we landed in moonlight.

Majuro was a perfect coral atoll, a serene lagoon circled by a ring of islands set with palm trees. When we had carried our gear to the Transient Officers' Quarters we went to the officers' club and got cans of beer and took them out onto the beach. The moon was rising across the lagoon, making a bright track on the water, and the palm trees on the far islands were black silhouettes. It was a scene that demanded sentiment, and I knew that I should have feelings about it, sad romantic yearnings for the far-off beloved, something like that. But how

could I have any real response to a tropical island in the moonlight? It was too damn much, too like a movie with Dorothy
Lamour; and I could only feel the way I did in movies like that
—charmed, but disbelieving. We all sat a little uncomfortably,
looking at the moon on the water, overwhelmed by the actual
existence of romance, drinking our beer. Then we went in to
the mess hall to supper.

On the wall where the chow line formed was a bulletin
board, and the first notice that caught my eye was a report of a
court-martial: Seaman Second Class Somebody-or-Other had
been found guilty of sodomy. How, I wondered, could there
be only one sodomist? And which one was he? His sad crime
made more sense than the moonlight and the palm trees, and I
felt a little sorry for him, out there in that empty beauty in the
middle of nothing.

In the morning we moved on again, first to Kwajalein and
then to Eniwetok. Of these islands, touched only for an hour
or so while we refueled, two impressions remain—of the litter
that war leaves, and of the sun. Both islands had been bitterly
fought over, and both were very small. There seemed to be
nothing left on the surface of either except ruined blockhouses,
burnt-out planes, and a few splintered trees, and around the
edges a ring of wrecked landing craft left to rust in the surf.
They were violated places, torn up and left to bleed in the sun.
You felt the sun always, not hot but burning, and the light—
pure white, colorless, intense, pouring down from the sky and
reflected up from the coral sand, from the heat-dazzled runways, from the sea. Under that sun you felt naked and exposed;
there was no shade to escape into on those ravaged islands.

In the afternoon we flew on, to Guam, which was bigger,
less distinct, and less memorable. There was a club there, and
we all got drunk, and I fell and cut my hand—a coral cut that
instantly became infected, and made my whole hand an angry red by the next morning. Christ, I thought, I'm poisoned;
they'll cut my whole arm off, I'll never fly again; and I felt the
old anxiety, the fear and rage at being left behind when the
Test came. But it healed all right in a couple of days. By then
we had flown the last leg of our journey, a short hop south
from Guam to Ulithi. From San Diego we had come six thousand miles. All that way to find a war to fight in.

Ulithi is said to be the best anchorage in its part of the Pacific. It can shelter a thousand ships in its vast lagoon, and there were nearly that many when we got there, early in March, just before the fleet left for the attack on Okinawa. It was the ships that I saw first—black dots and dashes scattered densely over the surface of the sea, so many, over such an area, that the distant ones faded into the horizon's haze. As we flew closer, the near islands of the atoll became visible, first as arcs of a thin broken circle that enclosed the ships, then as narrow strips of bright sand and palm trees. They looked less substantial than the dark fleet that they protected. This ring of fragile islands, set in the vast Pacific emptiness, was land, a habitation for men, the sight that sailors thirst for. But the sea diminished it, and made the earth seem trivial. Out here the ocean distances commanded space, and the atoll was a meager refuge, a dot on the vast surface, something you could miss, or lose.

It was hard to see how any of these islands could hold an airfield large enough for our transport to land on; but the plane was banking and settling, the wheels dropped, and we were sinking toward water and then, when it seemed we would touch the surface of the lagoon, a strip of white coral sand slipped under our wheels, and we were rolling to a stop. On either side of the plane there were palm trees, and as the plane turned to taxi back I could see that we were at the water's edge —the strip used up the whole length of the island, and if you overshot, you swam. The plane stopped at a Quonset hut beside the strip, and the pilot shut down the engines. We climbed out into the white sunlight, and stood gawking and uncertain, like immigrants in a strange country.

And it was strange—it was a new world, unfamiliar in every particular, with an unexplained code of behavior, full of puzzles and mysteries. Where would we live? Where did you go to the toilet? What were those white canvas bags, hanging like udders from the wooden frames? Could you eat the coconuts? Were there natives? It was like my first day at Boy Scout camp —a mixture of excitement, shyness, and anxiety. The possible ways of doing something wrong seemed infinite.

Back among the trees, half-hidden in shadow, I could see tents—big ones for storage, and smaller ones for the men— and a couple of Quonset huts, and men moving about among them wearing shorts and naked to the waist. Taxiways just wide enough for a plane had been cut back into the trees (was that a jungle, I wondered?), and in revetments along the sides Corsairs and F6F nightfighters and TBM's were parked, some with the cowlings off, and mechanics working on them. An engine coughed to life, and the noise rose slowly to a full-throttled scream, like a bandsaw going through a log, and then dropped suddenly to a guttural mutter that was like silence.

The Adjutant came out of a tent, took our orders, and shook hands all around. 'Officers' Country is over there,' he said, 'across the strip. Find a tent with an empty cot, and just move in.'

Opposite us, in a stand of palm trees between the runway and the beach, I could see pyramidal tents scattered, half-hidden among the trees. They were raised on pilings, and had screened sides that were open to the wind, and they looked cool and separate and private, like summer cottages by a lake, back home. I could see no human figures among them; nothing moved except the shadows of the palms on the tent roofs; and there were no sounds.

I rode across in a jeep with Rock and T, and we found a tent that looked mostly empty, and lugged our gear in. A very tanned young man was dozing on a cot at the far side. He was wearing only shorts—cut off, very carelessly, from a pair of khaki pants—and sandals that had once been high-top field shoes. He gave us a languid greeting. 'You must be the new guys. Now maybe we can go home.' His name, he said, was Telikoff, but we could call him Telly. Then he dozed off again.

In front of the tent was one of those frames with the dangling udders. It was a lister bag, a canvas sack with a tap at the bottom, full of water that oozed enough through the fabric to evaporate and keep the contents cool. Further on was a frame privy, clean and screened, and with a good view of the strip, and next to it a makeshift but workable shower. The building at the end of the area was the Officers' Club, where we would eat our meals and do our drinking. It was made of rough stained boards, and had a wide veranda on the ocean side, hanging out over the beach; it might have been a Minnesota hunting lodge, or the clubhouse of a small-town country club.

Officers' Country was a cool, quiet, shadowy place. The earth under the trees was soft sand, scattered with fallen coconuts, and bare of any undergrowth. A kind breeze blew from the sea, and rustled the stiff leaves of the palms. It would be easy to sleep all day here, like Telly. Only the airstrip was a violent brightness; when we came onto it from the shadows under the trees, it was like entering a noisy room. The real activities of the island would be conducted out there, in the insistent sunlight, but back here, in the shadows, it was lotus-land.

Ulithi was an unreal world that never became familiar or habitual. The sun was always warm, and the breeze was always an ocean breeze. Wherever the island came to an end there was a spotless coral beach, with a lazy surf breaking. Wherever you stood on the island, and whatever direction you looked, the sea was always in the background, at eye-level because the island was so low, a winking blueness behind everything. On the sand among the tents, coconuts lay waiting to be opened and eaten and drunk from. It was like Eden. And the life we lived was as easy and as pleasant as it should have been in such a place. After a day's flying—never very demanding—you could swim, shower, and go to the club for a cold beer. After supper you could sit on the veranda and drink and watch the tropical night come suddenly out of daylight, without any dusk at all, and then drift off to bed. The next day would be the same—from tent to mess, to ready room, and back at the end to the club, the veranda, and bed.

We were on an island called Falalop, a triangle three thousand feet long on its longest side. It would have been easy to walk around it in half an hour, but I never did. I stayed in Officers' Country, on the long side of the triangle, and never entered the country on the other side of the runway except to fly. Partly I felt that that was the enlisted men's world, and private to them, as our side was to us. The landing strip ran between us like a class barrier, as fundamental a reality of the island as the sea around us. But part of my reluctance to explore came, I think, from a feeling that my presence on the island was temporary, and that it would somehow be wrong to become too familiar with it, to try to settle in here.

So I only walked along the beach a little way, up past the club, to where the only native building on the island stood. It was an open-sided thatched house, not much more than a frame of coconut logs, empty now, but with a waiting dignity. Out of that house the handful of natives must have thronged to gape at the United States Army, storming ashore in force from landing craft to capture the island the year before. The Army had expected resistance, but there were only the natives. And now they were gone, sent away, for our convenience, to other islands. They had not left many evidences of their lives behind them—their lives were not the kind that mark the earth with signatures—only this house with the steady, gentle wind blowing through it, on the beach beyond Officers' Country.

I saw those people only once, on a reconnaissance flight to Fais and Sorel, the islands south and east of Ulithi to which they had been exiled. 'Just go down there,' the Operations Officer said, 'and look around. You won't see anything, nobody ever does. But it's part of the job.' I didn't know what I was supposed to be looking for; but I flew out, found the two tiny islands, and flew up and down their beaches for a while, looking in at the thatched huts under the trees, and at the people who came shyly down to the water's edge to stare as I rumbled past. I couldn't see anything that looked threatening. In the water offshore an outrigger canoe bobbed, and two men seemed to be fishing. I flew over, low, and looked back to see them rising from the floor of the canoe. Could I make them jump out? I wondered. I made another pass, lower, and another, lower still, down on the waves this time, and when I pulled up and banked, I could see two heads in the water. I felt suddenly awful, like a bully or a cop, and I flew over at a safe altitude, and waggled my wings to say that I hadn't meant it, that I was sorry. Then I went back to Ulithi, to the squadron life.

The squadron we had joined was VMTB–232, an outfit that called itself, when anyone thought of it, the Flying Red Devils. It was one of the old Marine squadrons. It went back to Bombing Squadron Two in the twenties, and it had a traditional pride in itself, like an old regiment that remembers its heroic days. The squadron had been at Ewa when the Japanese attacked Pearl Harbor, and a detachment of its enlisted men had fought in the defense of Wake Island. It had had a tour of duty in SBD's at Guadalcanal, and had gone back to the Solomons in 1943 to fly strikes on Rabaul, to sink ships (and lose planes and pilots), and to go on wild shore leaves in Sydney.

By the time we reached Ulithi, half of the squadron there had departed, as the forward echelon for a move to an unspecified new base—somewhere nearer Japan, we were told, somewhere where a real war was going on, or about to start. The half that remained behind was waiting, for us and for the orders to move. In the meantime, they flew milk-runs.

The squadron's assignment was simple—to provide a dawn-to-dusk antisubmarine patrol around the anchorage; to bomb Yap, a by-passed island to the west, often enough to keep its airstrips neutralized; and to fly reconnaissance flights over the other islands of the group. These were all boring, minor-league jobs, and the old pilots disliked them. And, besides, the men who had been out for a year or more had had enough; they had lost interest in the war. They were tired and undisciplined and hard-drinking, and they had gotten careless in the air. They had lost three planes since they came to Ulithi, all of them in unnecessary accidents. Two pilots had sunk a midget submarine together, and somebody had bombed and killed a whale (which looks rather like a submarine submerged), and that was the sum of their action. You could feel the boredom and lethargy all around you. You could see it in the way the old pilots dressed—like Telly, with his cutoff shorts and his sandals—and in the way they lounged from their cots to the flight line, from the flight line to the mess, and back to their cots. They seemed to sleep for astonishing portions of every day, and yet when I got to the bar at the end of the afternoon they were always there, already half-drunk, and singing.

They sang songs we hadn't heard before, songs brought up from other islands, other club-bars, or from Sydney; and Joe added them to his repertoire, and was very contented, singing and keeping time with a sloshing can of beer. If it was a slow song he would make it sound like a hymn, or a choral work for a hundred voices; it didn't matter how dirty it was, it came out like the songs we had all sung in Sunday school. 'I love to see Mary make water,' he would sing, with tender yearning in his voice,

> *She can pee such a beautiful stree—ee—ee—eam.*
> *She can pee for a mile and a quarter* (long pause)
> *And you can't see her ass for the steam!*

Rock told him he would have made a great Texas evangelist, singing and drinking the way he did.

The squadron doctor was usually there, drinking steadily but without apparent effect, and recalling difficult operations that he had performed back in Denver. He was a surgeon whose greatest glories were the incisions he had made and the organs he had removed. On Ulithi he got nothing in his sick bay except athlete's foot and coral cuts to treat, and he had gotten so bored and so hungry for surgery that one night, after a couple of drinks, he circumcised himself. Or so the story went. Harry, the squadron's lover, saw an opportunity to settle a question that had been bothering him. 'Listen, doc,' he began nervously one evening, sitting on the club veranda, 'listen, how many orgasms has a guy got in his life? I mean, a healthy guy, well, a kind of a stud, you might say.' Doc had a pull at his beer, and was studiously silent for a minute, as though he was doing a multiplication problem in his head. 'Well, now, Harry,' he said at last, 'it all depends, but I guess maybe ten thousand might be possible.' Harry rose unsteadily to his feet and threw his arm melodramatically across his forehead. 'My God,' he muttered, 'I'm finished.' He lurched off toward the bar. The doctor went on drinking; he seemed as bored by Harry as he was by athlete's foot.

Here and there, an officer had adjusted himself to boredom in an individual way. In the tent next to ours a guy who had been out for a year passed the time by writing pornographic novels. He didn't aim to have them published; there was no commercial motive at all. It was just a hobby, like Sunday painting. He would lend one to you if you asked, and would lovingly describe the plot-line to see that you got one to your tastes. He thought I'd like *Two Blondes in One Bed*. 'There's this guy who's married to this gorgeous blonde,' he said, 'and he makes her bring him his dinner stark naked. Well, she meets another blonde who looks just like her, and they decide. . . .' By the end of the story he had worked in sadism, lesbianism, and transvestism, as well as a great deal of ordinary screwing. 'You'll like it,' he beamed, 'it's one of my best.'

Clearly we had joined a collection of odd characters, but no one could call them a combat-ready squadron. This fact was made clear to me on the second day I was on the island.

After breakfast the new pilots all reported to the ready room—
a Quonset hut on the other side of the strip—for flying assignments and an introductory lecture by the Operations Officer.
As we hung around outside the hut, waiting for the lecture to
begin, a TBM from the day's first antisubmarine patrol landed
and rolled to a stop just in front of us. The pilot reached for the
lever that would raise his flaps and got the wheel lever instead.
Slowly the long legs of the landing gear spread, and the plane
settled, gently and carefully, like a fat lady sitting on a small
chair, until the wheels had disappeared into the wing wells, and
the plane rested on its belly on the runway. The propellers of
the slowly idling engine dug into the coral surface and stopped,
and the plane leaned slightly on one wing-tip, as though to be
more comfortable in its humiliation. The pilot in the cockpit
did not move, except to clutch his head in his gloved hands.
Then the crash horn began to sound, equipment—a fire engine
and a crane—appeared on the runway, and the pilot climbed
down, and came toward where we were standing in the ready
room door.

'This is Captain Childers,' the Operations Officer said to me.
'You'll be flying wing on him.'

'Cain't understand how it happened,' Childers said. He went
on into the hut.

Billy Childers was a regular Marine from backwoods Mississippi who had been an enlisted pilot before the war. When
the war began, he was given a temporary commission, and
he had risen, in the automatic way of wartime promotions,
to the rank of temporary Captain. He was a tall, bony man,
with a face that was at once weather-beaten and pale—I never
understood how that could be true, but it was—and his eyes,
which were always moving, were so light-colored that they
seemed to have no pupils. (T, who flew on his other wing,
said he had eyes like Little Orphan Annie.) Billy seemed to
live at the edge of the squadron's life. He didn't drink beer at
the club, or at least I don't remember him there, and he was
never a part of the talk and the horseplay in the ready room.
Maybe, I thought, that was because he was older; or maybe
his years as an enlisted man had made him suspicious of officers. Or maybe, I added nervously, the other pilots mistrusted
him. Maybe that dumb stationary accident of his was typical

of the way he handled airplanes. And I was to fly wing on him, in combat.

To make this ragged gathering of misfits ready for combat, the Marine Corps had sent most of the old squadron home and had brought in a new C.O. We called him simply The Major. Like the fierce Colonel at El Toro, he was a Regular and an Academy graduate (every other pilot in the squadron was a Reservist except Billy Childers). He had been a tank officer —in Samoa, as I remember—had gone through flight training, and was taking his first command. He seemed, to the rest of us, rigid, aloof, and impersonal, a guy who knew what he wanted and would quietly annihilate anyone who didn't co-operate. He started issuing orders on the day he arrived. The uniform of the day would be issue khaki, with fore-and-aft cap; the cut-off shorts and the baseball caps disappeared at once. All officers would appear at meals clean-shaven and in the proper uniform: goatees went, sandals went. Pilots would fulfill the squadron's combat assignment: strikes began to take off daily for Yap, reconnaissance flights to Fais and Sorel went regularly, antisubmarine hops left before dawn and landed after dusk. The pilots grumbled—you always got chicken shit like this, they said, when a Regular took over—but they began to look like officers and to fly like a squadron.

In the air the change came mainly from the new replacements. We were still held in the discipline of our state-side flying, and eager to show the old hands that we were as good as they were (secretly we thought we were better). We made our formation-flying even tighter, and our division landing approaches steeper, faster, and—in the language we used —'hairier,' dropping planes on alternate sides of the runway so closely spaced that a whole flight of six would be landed and rolling before the flight leader turned off. On a three-thousand-foot strip this took a good deal of skill and some nerve. Navy pilots, in from the carriers in the lagoon to touch earth and drink our beer, would come out of the club, beer cans in hand, to watch the squadron land. 'It isn't so much a landing pattern,' one of them said, 'it's more a controlled group-crash.' They regarded us as crazy and dangerous, but that was a kind of admiration. It was better, anyway, than being patronized.

Plane-watching is always fascinating for pilots. We would rather drink facing the strip, if there was anything doing, than face the other way, where there was only sun and water. If somebody was in trouble, all the better—that was like reading about a good accident in *BuAerNews*. One stormy day, when the wind was blowing hard at ninety degrees to the runway, instead of straight down the length as it did in fine weather, I saw Tyrone Power make five passes in an R5C before he got it down safely. Every pilot on the island seemed to know that a movie star was at the controls, and they came out in the rain to watch him and to take pleasure in his troubles. He was being a good and careful pilot, making a cautious approach, applying power when he felt the wind drifting him into the palms, and going around to try again. A strip like Ulithi's didn't allow for carelessness. It really didn't allow for a crosswind, certainly not in a lumbering transport that had a weathervane tail and not enough power. But he was Tyrone Power, the guy who had stolen our commissioning ceremony, someone who existed in the world outside. And who were we?

The Major believed in flying—any kind of flying was better for a pilot, he said, than sitting on his ass in the ready room, or lying around in his sack getting fat. We began a daily weather hop, which took off before dawn and reported the weather up to twenty thousand feet. And we took over the island mail flight. It wasn't ordinary mail, not the letters from home that came in by transport plane from Pearl Harbor, but the official mail—pouches marked SECRET that were carried around the islands of the atoll by an official Navy messenger. He traveled his daily circuit in a light observation plane, and somebody, the Operations Officer explained to me, had to fly it.

The mail plane was a sort of overgrown Cub, with a high, broad wing and flaps as big as barn doors—the sort of plane that the Army had flown near us back in CPT in Texas. It could take off and land at 35 mph, which was a good thing, since the landing strips on the other little islands of the atoll were sometimes only 300 feet long. I tried out the plane a couple of times on the main strip at Falalop, and as near as I could judge I got it down inside 300 feet. It didn't seem too difficult. So I picked up the messenger, a Navy Lieutenant with glasses and a nervous CPA's face, and took off for Mogmog, the next island. It seemed only fair to prepare my passenger for what was coming. I turned around in my seat and said, as reassuringly as I could, 'I've never landed here before, but it'll be all right. If other guys can do it, why can't I?' He said nothing, just sat there clutching his official pouch and looking down at the waves below.

The trick was to drop full flaps, get low and slow, and drag around to the end of the strip as though you were landing on a carrier. As soon as you were within gliding distance of the strip, but before you were actually above it, you cut the throttle and held the airspeed steady while you settled—if you had judged everything correctly—to a three-point landing on the first ten feet of land. Then you got on the brakes to stop the plane's roll before you reached the water at the other end of the strip.

Mogmog was fine. We stopped, my passenger surrendered his pouch and got another just like it, and we took off for the next spot of land. There the strip was even shorter, and I tried to lower the flying speed a knot or two on the approach. We touched down nicely, very close to the end, and I tromped down hard on the brakes—and there weren't any. Something had happened to the brake lines on that last landing. I fishtailed the rudder to lose speed, but we were still rolling briskly along when we ran out of runway. I did the only thing I could do—I gave the engine a burst of power and held full left rudder. The tail swung around with a rush, the right wing dipped but didn't touch, and we were stopped. But there had been a sinister thump as we swung, and I climbed down to see what had happened. Just at the edge of the runway a palm log lay, with a rough end sticking out onto the runway. The tail had hit it, just below the stabilizer, and the log had torn into the fabric covering. Christ, I thought, another tail. But at least there was no Colonel watching this time, only a very old native chief, the only native left on the atoll. He drifted up from nowhere, wearing a sort of a sarong, and stood looking sadly at the damage. His look was kind and sympathetic, as though he knew how I must feel—I had punctured my canoe. I shook his hand warmly, and he smiled a wide brown smile. Together we detached the airplane from the palm log. Then I climbed back into the plane. The Navy messenger was sitting still, as I had left him, his pouch in his lap, his gold-rimmed spectacles shining. He had neither spoken nor moved during the incident, but he looked at me as a condemned man might look at his executioner. I could see what he was thinking: Why me? and What a way to die! We flew silently back to Falalop, and I landed, carefully keeping the tail up as long as I could, in case it fell off when I touched it down. I reported to the Operations Officer that I didn't seem to have the hang of the mail plane. The messenger at my elbow agreed that this did seem to be true. The next day he had a new pilot, and I was back in a TBM.

From this time on my logbook customarily lists, under 'Passengers,' the same two names for every flight—Edwards and Campbell. They weren't passengers; they were my crew, though much of the time they did no more than just ride along. Edwards was a thin-faced, sardonic Texan, intelligent and capable, with that strong sense of self-preservation and self-interest that an intelligent enlisted man has, especially if he's a Reservist. It wasn't his war, and it wasn't his Marine Corps. He did his job well when it needed doing, but he did it for Edwards, not for glory. He was my radio- and radar-man. He rode in the belly of the plane, aft, in a dark cylindrical space called the tunnel, with his electronic gear around him. At the back end of the tunnel, under the tail, a thirty-caliber machine gun, the stinger, was mounted, and Edwards was also the tail gunner. Campbell was quieter and less distinct—dark, from Pittsburgh, very young-looking (though none of us was over twenty). He was turret gunner, and rode in a glass bowl on the backbone of the plane, with a fifty-caliber machine gun.

These two were my constant companions all the time I flew in the Pacific, but I have almost no memories of either. They rode with me on every flight, but they were back there in the guts of the plane, out of sight, two people I was responsible for, but didn't really need, or not very often. Flying in the same plane with them was not at all the bond that flying beside other pilots was. The pilots were my friends, but the crew was just a responsibility, like relatives or debts. On the ground we separated at once, to our segregated quarters, two areas that were as remote and isolated from each other as two countries that have cut off diplomatic relations. I never saw where my crew lived, and they never came to my tent. We never ate a single meal together. We never discussed any human problem. They simply rode at my back, prepared to fight off the attacking planes that never came, bored, reading their comic books, I suppose—though I realize now that I don't even know what they did read.

The first flight that Edwards and Campbell flew with me was a bombing attack. 'Strike on Yap,' my logbook reads, 'pier and shore installations—strafing—4 × 500.' Yap, a hundred miles west of Ulithi, had been bypassed when Ulithi was taken. It was of no strategic importance, except for its airstrip, which was pitted and broken by many bombings; but it was still occupied by a Japanese garrison. Looking at aerial photographs of Yap, our intelligence officers had persuaded themselves that in an inlet there might be facilities for docking submarines. Our planes were loaded with 500–pound bombs, and we took off to destroy the dock and to strafe whatever we saw.

I flew on Billy's wing out over the fleet, and beyond, until Ulithi was lost behind us, and there was nothing in sight but water and the empty air. Without visual references, we seemed to hang motionless above the sea, which seemed motionless too, while the minutes passed. Then an island appeared, first a low darkness on the horizon, then a green mass of palm trees. We circled over it, looking for the target, and the greenness became palm trees, each one a green asterisk on a lighter ground. The island had been bombed again and again, and in among the trees where bombs had fallen there were spots of exposed white sand, like pockmarks on dark skin. The airstrip was full of craters, and looked abandoned and desolate, a place where planes had once flown. Along the sides were the remains of wrecked and burnt-out planes, and one or two that seemed to be dummies, knocked together to tempt strafing planes down where the waiting guns could find them.

Nothing moved below us. Nothing suggested any life at all there. I saw no installations, no people, not a hut or a kitchen garden. The island seemed uninhabited and forlorn. We flew lower, across the inlet that Intelligence had marked. I thought I saw a fence strung across it—a few strands of barbed wire, perhaps—but I could see nothing else. We circled again and made our bombing runs. As I dropped my bombs I could hear the hard rattle of Campbell's gun, and the high, tinny popping of Edwards' thirty-caliber. What the hell were they shooting at, I wondered. Just shooting, because they were in combat now.

I pulled away from the island and joined the formation. That was my first attack on the enemy, and I felt sour disappointment. Was that all there was to combat? No antiaircraft shells bursting, no fierce defenders at their guns, nothing exploding, no columns of smoke visible for miles. I had expected flame and ruin, but even our own bombs had gone off squashily, blowing up mud and water, destroying nothing (except maybe a barbed-wire fence). I didn't feel any different; I hadn't been initiated into manhood; I hadn't even seen the enemy. I flew disconsolately back to Ulithi.

The enemy was there, though; there were both men and guns on Yap. They bided their time and only took the easy shots, but they were there. The following week they shot a wing off a strafing plane, and it crashed and burned near the other wrecks along the ruined airstrip. The pilot who was killed had been Torchy's lover, back in Laguna. I thought of him as her seducer; but then I had liked her on that wet night in November when T and I met her in the USO, and I didn't much like him.

Even after that first death in action, Ulithi seemed a pastoral, innocent place, a long way from the real war. American troops were fighting in the Philippines, and the Marines were just cleaning up on Iwo, but we were thousands of miles from either battle, with only a bypassed island for an enemy. We went on living our simple life in our open tents, under the palms that dropped their nuts quietly, with a muffled swish and thud, through leaves to the sandy earth. We swam from the beach behind Officers' Country. Waves broke on a reef offshore in a fine show of foam, but within the reef the water was calm and clear, and the sand was clean and free of any flotsam. I suppose there was no place for anything to float from, out there in the empty ocean. I always felt when I swam there that no one had ever gone swimming on that beach before; it was sort of a Robinson Crusoe feeling, of being outside human existence, and alone.

Although it was February, the sun was hot, and our bodies grew tanned and our hair bleached, and our khaki shirts and trousers turned white in the sun. Sometimes we swam naked, and once Rock took a naked sunbath, fell asleep, and burned his buttocks so severely that he had to spend three days lying facedown and naked on his cot. His bottom turned scarlet and swelled so tight that if you flipped it with your finger it thumped like a drum. The doctor came round to look at the damage, but he couldn't find anything to operate on. 'It could have been worse,' he said as he left. 'You could have been sleeping on your back.'

Out in the lagoon the warships gathered and waited, but as we flew over them, coming and going on our solitary patrols, they did not look like menacing machines designed to burn and drown men, but like delicate abstractions—slender, tapered shapes at rest on the smooth bright water, part of the static pattern of our lives. And so when the air-raid sirens began to howl one evening in the early dark, we took it for a drill. After all, the nearest Japanese planes were away off in the Philippines, and there weren't many of them left even there. As the island lights went out, we left the club and gathered curiously at the lagoon-end of the landing strip, and watched the fleet black out—a ship here, a ship there, one or two of the big ones delaying, and then suddenly blinking out, until at last the whole lagoon was dark. Not a very successful drill, I thought; it had been far too slow.

And then, astonishingly, antiaircraft guns began to fire, and tracers sprayed up into the darkness, as though the lights that had burned across the waters of the lagoon were being hurled into the sky. I began to feel exposed, standing there on the runway while the guns fired; but no one else moved, so I didn't. Across the lagoon a plane screamed into a dive, higher and higher pitched, and there was a flash and an explosion, and an instant later another explosion in what seemed the center of the moored ships. Then darkness and silence, until the all-clear sounded, and lights began to come on in the harbor again.

It had been a kamikaze raid. The Japanese planes had flown all the way from the main islands, touching at the Philippines. They had planned to refuel at Yap, and then fly on to attack the fleet at Ulithi; but bad navigation, bad weather, bad luck, whatever it was, had delayed them, and sent some planes back. Others had crash-landed on the Yap beach. Only three reached Ulithi. One was shot down; one crashed into the deck of the

carrier *Franklin*, where the crew was crowded into the flight
deck watching a movie; and one, taking an island for a large
ship, dove on Mogmog and blew up a kitchen.

The whole lasted perhaps fifteen minutes. We were excited
by it—perhaps *entertained* is a more precise word—it was a
spectacle, like a *son et lumière*, with noise, light, explosions.
We didn't know what was happening to human lives while we
watched, but even if we had, I wonder if it would have mattered. We were a mile or so from the *Franklin*, and perhaps
a mile is too far to project the imagination to another man's
death. We took it as a sign that the war was still with us, that we
still had an enemy, and went to bed heartened by the incident.

Because the *Franklin* was damaged, her planes were catapulted and flown to Falalop to wait while repairs were done on
the ship. The *Franklin* had just come back from a raid on Japan, where her planes had flown strikes against Tokyo, and the
pilots were inclined to strut a little. They had bombed Tokyo,
we bombed Yap. We couldn't blame them for feeling superior,
but we didn't like it, and a couple of fights blew up in the club
bar, and I had to restrain Joe. To amuse themselves, the Navy
squadron flew a strike on Yap, and lost two planes to the invisible antiaircraft fire there. After that they were more restrained
in the club, and we got on better.

March passed. We flew our desultory strikes, and our interminable antisubmarine patrols. Ulithi was a natural target for
subs, and every day, all day, our planes flew out from the atoll
on triangular tracks, watching by eye and by radar for enemy
vessels. It was different, flying over water there, from what it
had been at Pensacola or at Santa Barbara. At those bases you
couldn't really get lost, or not for long; there was always a
direction to fly that would take you back to land. But when
the land is an island three thousand feet long, in the middle of
the world's largest ocean, no course is sure. Even in the best
weather Ulithi was hard to see (it was maybe ten feet out of
the water at its highest point); and in the worst weather it was
impossible. I would work out my navigation, fly out along the
charted track, turn at the proper time, fly, turn again, and then
at the predicted moment I would look round for home. Occasionally I missed, dropped down through cloud cover where
the island should have been, and found the ocean empty, the

island anywhere but there. Then I'd turn to Edwards for help
—'Find me a course, for Christ sake!'—and Edwards would
use his radar, offer a heading, and lead us home.

On a low, overcast day, like the day after Wally died, we
heard that a carrier pilot had been lost near Ulithi, and I flew
once more in a ritual search, this time alone. The clouds hung
in a solid layer that seemed to slope down at the horizon into
the sea, like an inverted saucer, so that my plane was suspended
in a shallow wafer of space between the gray above and the
gray below, a space entirely one color, and without a landmark
or a point of reference. As I flew the set search-pattern the
plane seemed not to move at all, everything in sight remained
the same. It was an experience of total, gray isolation, in a space
without life or identity or particularity, like some extreme psychological state—looking for a dead man in a dead space, without any hope of finding him, and in the process losing contact
with, almost losing belief in, the reality of any solid object.
The thought of being lost at sea became a new nightmare, the
worst form of dying.

Late in March the orders came. We would be the first
land-based bomber squadron in the attack on Okinawa. The
forward echelon was already there, lying offshore with the invasion fleet, and would go ashore on D–plus–five. Those of
us at Ulithi would fly the squadron's planes to join them, and
begin combat operations. No one had heard of Okinawa. Intelligence knew nothing about it except that the natives were
called Hairy Anus (many obscene jokes) and that the island
was infested with poisonous snakes. We all drew combat boots,
the kind with leather puttees attached. We had shots for every
known disease, and were feverish, or fainted, and couldn't raise
our arms. Then we packed up the squadron and waited.

The battle of Okinawa began on Easter Sunday, April 1st.
We heard about it at Ulithi, standing around outside the ready
room, where a loudspeaker had been hung on a palm tree.
Tokyo Rose told us that the assault forces had landed, but had
been repulsed; many ships had been sunk. On the second day
she addressed our squadron specifically; she knew that 232 was
coming, she said, but they would be ready for us. I felt ri-
diculously melodramatic, standing there being threatened on
the radio; it was like stumbling onto the set of a B-grade spy

movie, where an Oriental hisses, 'Yankee dog, you die!' But I also felt a bit important—at least in Tokyo they had heard of us. It made up a little for not having bombed Tokyo with the Navy.

We were eager to move—D–plus–five was only three days away—but there were delays. The attack, we were told, was going well, but the weather was bad, the sea was too rough to land enough aviation gasoline to supply us. Finally, on the fifth, we left. It was the first time that I had seen all of the squadron's planes in the air together, and as we gathered into formation I felt a strong emotion that I couldn't define—Was it pride? Affection?—for that pattern of planes. It was *my* squadron, I belonged to it, I was in my place, and we were headed for combat. It isn't a surprising emotion. Men have always felt pride when they could for their military units, their regiment, their ship. But I hadn't felt it until then. Looking across from my plane I could identify some of my friends in the others, even at a distance, by the way they sat, the style of their flying. There was T, small, crouched forward, his head cocked, as though he was listening (to Louis Armstrong, maybe); Joe beyond him, very tall, very straight in the cockpit; Rock, solid-looking, like his name. The planes didn't look clumsy, but beautiful and intent, flying toward the war.

Chapter Eight

WE FLEW into Saipan on the fifth of April—the day on which, if the battle plan had been working, we would have landed at Okinawa. We knew that storms were battering the Okinawa beaches and delaying the landing of supplies, but there was another kind of delay that we didn't know about. The Japanese were sending suicide planes against the fleet, hundreds of them in those first days, and were sinking ships; and the constant raids, even when they weren't successful, kept ships' crews at their battle stations and interrupted unloading operations. Back in Saipan we weren't told about the kamikazes, and we expected to take off in a day or two, as soon as the weather cleared. All we had to do was to kill a little time.

Time died hard on Saipan. We lived together in a hot, crowded Quonset hut on a bare hill by the airstrip, and much of the time those first days we just hung around the hut, lying on our cots, reading if we could find anything to read, waiting for our orders, afraid to leave in case they came. It was like Miramar, in a way, but worse. At Miramar we were at the gateway to the whole Pacific war, and surrounded by men who had been there; there was excitement in the air, but no anxiety —we were all going to get there, to the war. But at Saipan we were isolated and immobilized, and raw with impatience to move on to the particular war that was waiting for us, like a birthday party that we'd been invited to, and would miss if we didn't hurry.

I had only one book with me—the *War and Peace* that I'd bought back in Honolulu—and I tried to read it; but I couldn't keep all those Russian names straight, and after a while I'd give up, wander outside, and just look around. Not that there was much to look at. Saipan itself was just one long, treeless hill, a hog's back that ran the length of the island, north and south, with a meager flatland around the edge, like a narrow brim on a hat. In the distance I could see Tinian, the nearest island, a rocky hill like Saipan, thrusting up out of the sea. Steve Bakos' squadron was stationed there, flying antisubmarine patrols. I thought how much I'd like to see him again, but of course

489

I couldn't leave Saipan because the orders might come. So I stood around, and if there was any flying going on I watched that, and then I went back into the hut and tried Tolstoy again.

A loudspeaker had been attached to the front of the hut, and at noon and six P.M. we could hear the news broadcasts from the island radio station. We listened for word of the battle of Okinawa, and were told that it was going well (but still we didn't move up). And it was there that I learned of the death of Franklin Roosevelt. I remember hearing the news, standing in the sun there, looking out across the sea toward Tinian, thinking The President is dead, and not feeling anything. I couldn't remember when he hadn't been the President. I had seen him once, in the thirties—it must have been during the 1936 presidential campaign—driving down Nicollet Avenue in Minneapolis in an open car, smiling and waving. But he wasn't a person; he was an institution of government, like the Constitution or the Supreme Court. I was surprised, I think, that he had died—institutions don't die. But his death would change nothing out here, the war would go on, planes would fly. It was nothing to me.

I heard of another death at about that time. From Tinian word came that Steve Bakos had flown on a patrol and hadn't come back. Steve, the ugly, happy family man with the pretty wife, and a small child by now, the man for whom the war was only an interruption in a peaceable life, was lost in the sea (that terrible way to die). I tried to imagine what had happened—engine failure, perhaps, a water landing, and the long waiting to be found? Or something else? A fire? Or a navigational error that ended with a dead engine and a drop into darkness? No other details came across from his squadron; he was just dead, that was all.

Days passed, no orders came, and our restlessness got worse. No one had any duties, and there was no flying to do. We waited in that Quonset hut on the hill, and the time dragged by. During those empty, fretful days I learned a basic truth about military life: that it's only the *doing*—the fighting, or just the drilling and the routine—that makes it endurable. Freed from the discipline of flying, we found that it was the only discipline we had. We missed the flying, but not out of love alone; partly we were lost without the shape that it gave to our lives.

When time is empty, it stops; and every hour is just the past hour over again, and just as meaningless.

Old Regulars will tell you that the thing to do when you hit a temporary Station is to dig in as though you might be there forever. After all, they say, the Navy might lose your records. We began to think that we had been misplaced, that in the official, bureaucratic Navy there was no 232, and that we would be found, to everyone's astonishment, still sitting on that goddamn hill when the war was over. So we looked around the place we were stuck in, for ways to pass the time.

There were, it seemed, only two things to do: you could go sightseeing or you could bar-hop among the officers' clubs around the island. Saipan had been in American hands for about six months when we arrived, and it had already been transformed into a sort of temporary Navy town—Pensacola without the Spanish architecture and the whores. Along the road that followed the west coast of the island a string of little camps had sprung up, each the headquarters of a naval unit, each with its docks and its supply dumps, its Post Exchange and its club. The whole stretch looked like a third-rate resort, a string of crummy bars along a beach road.

But there were signs of war, too. Below our hill, between the beach road and the sea, was the first military cemetery I had ever seen. We went swimming there, on the sandy beach where the graves ended. Behind us a vast space was symmetrically patterned with rows of regular markers that ran back out of sight over the hill. At one side were the graves of some Japanese soldiers, and I was surprised to find them there, treated so courteously. Why didn't I expect so small a gesture of magnanimity from my own countrymen? I suppose because back home the Japanese were the yellow devils of propaganda, not men like ourselves who could die on a Saipan beach, and be buried like other men. Along the beach and out in the shallow water you could see the usual debris of a beach assault—the shattered masonry of the defenses, the rusting hulks of landing craft, the abandoned equipment. All that, out there in the slow surf, had made these regular, monotonous rows of identical graves.

To get beyond the Quonset and the beach, to go drinking in all those promising bars, and to see the rest of the island, we had to have transportation. There was a motor pool from which we were entitled to draw jeeps, when there were any; but there never were. The obvious thing to do was to steal one. Stealing was not, of course, called *stealing*; you called it *scrounging*, and nobody had any qualms about doing it. In a world where everything belonged to the government, nothing belonged to anybody, and we quickly lost our back-home sense of the inviolability of personal property. If an object was portable and no one was guarding it, it was as much yours as anybody else's. And there were lots of jeeps sitting around unguarded.

We agreed that it would be wise not to steal a jeep if it had four stars painted on it, or one that seemed to be attached to an important command. We tried instead to concentrate on chaplains and on the minor functionaries of lower-level units (Joe always said that a laundry officer was the ideal victim—nobody could have less influence than a laundry officer, not even a chaplain). And if we thought of it, and weren't too drunk, we took the jeeps we had borrowed back where we had found them.

One day, in a Catholic chaplain's jeep, we drove the length of the island, up the west beach road all the way to the northern tip. Along the beach we passed the ruins of the island's sugar factories. Sugar had been a major industry on Saipan before the invasion, but it was dead now, and the factories were clusters of roofless shells. It felt wrong to me, that the war should have passed through this place where something useful had been done. The other islands I had seen that had been fought over had been nothing to begin with—a few palm trees, a few natives, maybe, and a Japanese garrison—ideal empty spaces to fight for. But this island had been a real community, with roads and factories, little towns, docks. What I was feeling, I suppose, was that it was like home, or a possible home, a place that my imagination could populate and live in, and that the ruined buildings were wounds in a real landscape. We drove on, through fields now; but there were no crops, no natives (they had been driven together into compounds), no life. We only saw other Americans, moving about in their American trucks and jeeps, each in its cloud of dust, and American camps, and supply dumps, and ships unloading still more American supplies.

The steep backbone of the island was always on our right, a single long ridge of rock. Japanese soldiers were still hidden up there, emerging sometimes at night to snipe into some American camp and, so one story went, to watch the outdoor movies that every camp had. I felt a shiver that was not quite fear, or even anxiety—just a feeling that up there, among those bare rocks, there were men who would kill me if they could, and whom I would have to try to kill if I met them. I had never been on the same piece of earth with an enemy before.

To the north the island was less crowded and less Americanized, and you could still see here and there the remains of a farmer's house and the unmarred shapes of his fields. At the very northern point, where the rocky central escarpment broke into the sea, the ruin of a Japanese blockhouse stood in a field. We stopped the jeep and walked across to look at it. I climbed in through the ruined door, and scuffed my foot around in the rubble on the floor, hoping I'd find a souvenir there. In the dust was a Japanese shoe, the kind with a separate toe, like a mitten. It still had a foot in it.

Back at the airfield, Joe found a headquarters squadron that had a few fighter planes, but no pilots. The planes were old ones, castoffs from the fleet. (A headquarters squadron, being mainly an administrative unit, is the sort of place where such odds and ends are assigned, when no one can think of what else to do with them.) But now that the planes were there, and had been tinkered with, they had to be tested, and Joe and I volunteered as test pilots. Neither of us had ever flown a fighter, we had never even been close enough to one to look in the cockpit. But Joe was confident: 'Planes are like women,' he said, 'you fly one, you've flown 'em all.' I was sure he didn't know much about women—he was a very monogamous man—but he might be right about airplanes. And we were bored. So we lied to the Operations Officer of the headquarters squadron, and were assigned to fly a row of F6F's and F4F's.

Ordinarily when you fly a strange plane you first read the pilot's manual, a book that explains how everything works and where it is. You sit for a while in the cockpit with the book open and find the levers for wheels and flaps, and the switches, and figure out how to start the engine and turn on the radio. But we couldn't ask for a manual—that would have exposed our inexperience—and so we had to sit in the cockpits and figure out how to fly the planes just by looking and groping. I was still peering around, muttering to myself 'Mags, wheels, flaps, radio,' when Joe started his engine, waved cheerfully, and taxied his F6F onto the runway. I got mine started in a billow of smoke and followed him apprehensively. What was I doing here, in a fighter?

The F6F was a boring plane, efficient enough but without any character. Flying it was like driving the family car on a Sunday afternoon. Even Joe, who loved flying so much that he even liked Links, was unimpressed. We circled the field for an hour, as we were instructed to do—you were supposed to be within gliding distance on a test hop, in case the engine failed —and landed. Nothing had happened; it was like being alone with a girl you don't like.

But the F4F Wildcat was marvelous—very small (so small that it seemed you could reach out from the cockpit and touch both wing-tips), simple, maneuverable, and delicately responsive to the controls. After the TBM, which needed hydraulic boosters to be flown at all, and the humdrum F6F, the Wildcat was like a toy designed especially to please pilots. It did acrobatics as though it wanted to, and had been hoping you'd try one; and when you did, it flew you through the most intricate maneuver in a cooperative, friendly way.

Joe and I would take off, soberly and separately, and rendezvous high above the island, and chase tails, or dogfight, or just drift around, one flying wing on the other, looking down at the military busy-ness going on below us. On our second flight Joe slid up into formation on my wing flying upside down. He had found a manual, and had discovered that the Wildcat had a pressurized oil system and could fly inverted without the engine seizing up. He flew along, head down, roaring with laughter, as though he were playing a great joke on gravity. For a while I led him in gentle turns and climbs, and he stayed there in position, flying as well upside down as I did rightside up.

I felt so much at home in a Wildcat that I even ventured a Victory Roll, the fighter pilot's grandstand maneuver. Approaching the field for a landing, I dived toward the runway, building up speed, and pulled up in a slanting slow-roll to the left. Beneath me as I rolled, five or six hundred feet below, I could see some of the squadron playing softball on a field behind the Quonset hut. Then the plane was rolling out, scooping a little, but safe; and I swung around into the downwind leg, and swept in to a landing. I was scared when I entered the roll—I remember thinking, This is the kind of dumb showing off that gets guys killed—and I was even more scared afterward, when I thought about it. Still I was glad I had tried it, even though T said that it didn't look so hot from second base.

Saipan was a good place to fly. After the insignificance of Ulithi, the island had a secure solidity; it looked like the kind of island that you might lose and find again. And the flying we did in those old Wildcats was good, too—free and spontaneous. I remember those bright days as I do some in flight school, as days that held the true feeling of flight, the way it ought to be —two friends, easy in the air and with each other, just fooling around.

But we couldn't spend all our time testing those few tired planes. In the evenings we couldn't go sight-seeing either; there was nothing to do but party. It was easier to steal a jeep at night—chaplains didn't seem to do much after supper—and the clubs were livelier then. Sometimes you could even see a woman in one, a Navy nurse or a Red Cross girl; and though it never seemed worthwhile to enter into competition for such a rarity, it was pleasant to look at them. Joe, I noticed, censored his songs when there was a woman at the bar, even though some of them looked as though they could match him, obscenity for obscenity, and win.

One of the pilots in the squadron—a guy who fancied himself a great lover—went courting. Somewhere on the island he found a Red Cross hut, one of those places where you can get free coffee and writing paper from a girl in a uniform, and stare at her breasts under the starched cotton. He met a girl there who was willing to have a date with him in a couple of days, and we heard all about his worries and preparations. He would lie on his cot at night in the Quonset hut and worry out loud to his friend in the next cot. 'Christ,' he would say, 'what if we get our orders tomorrow? What if we have to leave before I get a chance to fuck her? I should have made the date for tonight.' And 'Should I get a new rubber? How long are rubbers good for? This one might be no good.' And he would remove from his wallet a dirty little envelope, take out the Trojan inside and unroll it, and hold it dangling before his eyes, examining it for flaws. Or he'd review his strategy, how he wouldn't move in too fast, would talk first, maybe even dance, be a nice guy even if she *was* ugly, and then. . . .

It was a relief when the night of the date came. At least we wouldn't hear any more plans when we were trying to sleep. The cocksman came back late, slapping the screen door open and stumbling in the dark among the rows of sleeping men. He sat on the edge of his cot, shook his friend by the shoulder, and launched at once into an account of the evening—first the pre-liminaries, how he had gotten her drunk at a club, had danced, and at last had driven her to a secluded beach in her jeep. He had put his arm around her, made a few speeches, and kissed her. 'And do you know what she said? Right then, when I'd just kissed her once? She said, "Why honey, it's lucky I wore my diaphragm tonight!" What do you think? She must be some kind of tramp, a girl who'd say a thing like that.' And then the guilt began: 'I shouldn't have done it, should I? I mean, I'm married. What would my wife think?' Sleepers woke, cursed him and his date and his fucking wife, but he seemed not to hear them. He was alone with his libido and his guilt.

We had been on the island for more than a week, and had exhausted the nearby clubs. One night we set out, six or eight of us in one borrowed jeep, to look for a P–boat base some-where on the northern end of the island, where the club was said to be especially fine and private. After some time and a lot of drinks on the way, we found it, and it was as good a place as we'd heard it was—well-designed, even landscaped, with a garden and a view of the bay, and a vast supply of liquor. Rock said it reminded him of the country club back in San Antonio. I thought it was more like some place in the movies, the Riviera, maybe. It even had gambling machines, one-armed bandits lined up along one whole wall. We felt very pleased with ourselves for having found it, and we all had a drink to congratulate ourselves. Joe sang his version of 'Casey Jones':

> *He was found in the wreck with his hand on the throttle,*
> *And his airspeed reading forty knots.*
> *They searched all day for the poor pilot's body,*
> *But all they could find were spots.*
> *Hundreds and hundreds of spots.*

And we sang the chorus:

> *Ten thousand dollars going home to the folks.*
> *Ten thousand dollars going home to the folks.*
> *Oh won't they be delighted!*
> *Won't they be excited!*
> *Think of all the things that they can buy!*

The officers of the P–boat squadron didn't join in and didn't seem pleased to have us in their club. Gradually they drifted off, until we were the only customers. We drank beer, and when each can was empty the drinker bent it in half and put it on the table. It wasn't so easy, in those days, to bend a can with one hand; it was a modest feat of strength, that's why you did it. Another test.

The pile of bent cans grew, covered the table, and spilled clanking to the floor. Between beers we began to play the slot machines, but without much luck. Joe in particular lost steadily, and badly; he seemed to think the machines were part of a Navy plot against him, or perhaps against the entire Marine Corps. The machines would never pay off for him, he was being robbed, the whole place was a trap for the gullible. I thought we'd better leave, and I began to shove people out the door, toward our chaplain's jeep. But it was gone; somebody had stolen it. We stumbled about in the darkness, muttering and complaining: 'Steal a man's jeep, goddamn Navy bastards. . . .' There was only one jeep in the lot, and we climbed aboard it. Joe was still in the club, but in a minute he appeared, staggering, his arms wrapped in a bear hug around a slot machine. He had decided to take it with him; it was what they deserved, fucking Navy. It was no use arguing with him; we tried to make the machine inconspicuous in the back seat, and set off for the Station gate. The guard there was unfriendly and full of questions. Why were we driving the C.O.'s personal jeep? Where had we come from? Where were we going? And eventually, he asked; what was that in the back? We were in trouble.

The Major summoned us all the next morning, and he was not happy. He had been on the carpet before an Admiral. Why shouldn't his officers be court-martialed? What did they think this was, a goddamn house party? You goddamn Marines think you own the Navy, well, he'd show . . . and so forth. You couldn't blame the Major for being sore. But he had defended us—we were restless, eager to get to war, a good combat squadron, morale was high, spirits were volatile. He had managed to delay the formal hearing, but if we hung around much longer we'd have to go before the court. He was to have another meeting with the Admiral the next day.

We followed the Major's negotiations with nervous interest, and discussed our prospects over the piled-up bent beer cans in various Navy clubs. Kelleher, the philosophical knuckle-baller, was gloomy: 'We haven't got a chance,' he said. 'No more than a fart in a windstorm.' But after all, Joe remarked, looking on the bright side, What could they do to us? Send us overseas? We went on drinking; we even stole a jeep or two to show each other that we were not downhearted. But the party spirit had gone flat, like last night's beer. Nobody wanted to be drunk any more. We wanted to move; our battle was already being fought, had been for two weeks now, and we weren't in it. We were afraid it might end before we got there, that the war would be over and we'd still be sitting on Saipan, drinking and getting court-martialed.

Then the orders came, and in a day we were off. We had stayed on Saipan for fourteen days, had been drunk and disorderly almost every night, and had left behind us a large number of misplaced jeeps, some angry Navy officers, and, on the Admiral's desk, court-martial papers that would never be served.

Chapter Nine

IWO JIMA was an island so dead and uninhabitable that it seemed wrong to call it an island: it was a blasted, charred heap of sand, as littered and abandoned as a public beach after the Fourth of July. Except that this beach was black—a coarse volcanic sand that grated like cinders under the feet, on which nothing would grow. When we landed there, on April 19, the battle was over, the airstrips had been repaired, and fighter squadrons were flying from them to cover B-29's on raids to the Japanese mainland. But enemy troops were still alive in the caves and tunnels at the north end of the island, and emerged sometimes at night to hurl suicidal attacks on planes and guns, and on the tents of sleeping men. The night before we landed, a single Japanese soldier had run through the company street of a fighter squadron, tossing hand grenades into the tents until he was shot by sentries. One pilot had been killed, others were wounded. It was an unpleasant feeling, to be walking about, eating and sleeping there, while in their tunnels underground the enemy, like hunted nocturnal animals, waited for night. The squadron stayed at Iwo for three days while we waited for a storm to end. These days were as dead and empty as the island—fearful days, everything unnatural, even the ways men died, blown up at random in the night, or burned out of holes in the ground, or buried alive. I was relieved to take off for Okinawa; I didn't think I could have fought my war on Iwo.

We approached Okinawa through gray, broken clouds beneath a high overcast. The sea was gray, too, and empty at first; then I saw one picket ship, then more and more ships, all kinds of ships, and then the dark bulk of the island. It was the first place I had seen where a war was actually going on, and I looked down when I could as our flight swung round the southern end of the island, staying well out to sea, because it was the end that the Japanese held. I could see nothing very clearly, only wooded hills across which artillery smoke drifted like low clouds, but I knew that it was enemy earth down there. There could be nothing familiar about it.

We flew past the island, and over the fleet, where there was more drifting smoke from the guns of battleships and cruisers, and then turned back toward the island and began our landing approach. As we descended and crossed the beach, I saw the part of the island that American troops controlled, and familiarity returned. It looked more like a construction site or a highway project back home than like a battlefield—slashes of raw earth everywhere, bulldozers, steamrollers, cities of tents and temporary buildings, heaps of supplies. Seabees were building roads and airstrips, and the scene was full of American energy and bustle. It was only when we had landed and I was standing uncertainly on the flight line waiting for orders that I became aware of the presence of war—a distant rumbling, like a trolley-car passing late at night, that was the sound of guns.

Trucks took us and our gear to the squadron's area on a low hill near the strip, and I found a tent and moved in with Rock and Joe and T and Bergie. Officers' Country was the top of a rise in what had been a wheat field, and the tent stood in the spring crop of young wheat; under my cot the grain was still growing. I threw the parachute bag that held all my possessions down on my cot and went out to look around. At the end of the officers' street—only a dirt path between the rows of tents—and on either side behind the tents, the ground fell away sharply into narrow little valleys, gullies almost. The officers' toilet had been built in the valley behind our tent, and I walked down that way, past the toilet and on up the valley. In a hundred yards or so it came to an abrupt end, and there, set into the steep hillside, were fan-shaped walls of masonry that I knew must be tombs—each with a terrace in front, and a low, narrow entrance to the vault. I was a little afraid, alone there among the tombs—there might be a leftover Jap alive in one of them, or a booby trap—but I went nearer. The tombs had been broken open, and shattered funeral urns and bits of bone were scattered about. No doubt some Marine had hoped there would be something worth taking there; but these were poor people, and they had buried nothing but their dead. I crept inside one of the tombs and found in the stooping darkness only dust and fragments and dry, dead air. It didn't even feel like a special place, the way cemeteries back home did; war had robbed it of its reverence.

From our hill we could see the whole of Kadena airfield—fifteen hundred feet of runway, with a bright yellow bulldozer parked across one end to encourage short landing runs, and a makeshift tower. Taxiways led from the runway to banked revetments where the planes were parked, and a dirt road ran up the hill to the squadron camp. On the far side of the field was a gravel pit, from which all day trucks carried gravel to build more taxiways, and an extension of the runway, down beyond the parked bulldozer. To the north was Yontan, once the principal Japanese airfield and now a Marine base, spread out across the top of a low plateau a couple of miles away; to the south, three or four miles off, we could see the hills where the Marines and the Army were attacking the main Japanese defensive line. We could stand at our tent doorway and watch the battleships that lay just offshore shelling Shuri Castle, the Japanese strong point, and could even see the shells arcing through the air, changing color from white to red as they cooled.

But before we could watch the war we had to build foxholes, to hide in when the war came too close for watching. There are no conventions in foxhole design; you dig according to your energies, and cover according to the materials at hand. Down in the valley by the tombs Joe and Bergie had found a rusting pile of railroad tracks, and we used them for our roof-beams. The hole we dug was U–shaped, with the longest section at the base. We laid the lengths of track across the long part, and covered them with sandbags to make a cave, for which the two ends of the U were entrances, opening at the two back corners of our tent. We figured we would be up from a sound sleep and into the hole in under one minute. My cot was nearest to one entrance, and to make my own retreat even faster I placed a pair of rubber boots, with my pants stuck over them fireman style, beside my cot. I was going to be the first man in the hole every time.

But when the first air raid came, late in the night, I woke slowly and confusedly, and I was still trying to get my legs through the mosquito netting and into my boots when Rock shot past me, fully clothed, with a flashlight in his hand and his .38 revolver strapped across his chest, and plunged into the foxhole entrance. I had just managed to stand up in the boots, and was pulling up my pants when the sound of six rapid revolver shots burst from the hole, accompanied by dazzling flashes of light. Rock had fired all six of the tracer bullets in his gun.

'Christ,' Joe yelled, 'there's a Jap in the foxhole!' He began groping for his own .38. I sat back down again. It looked as though it might be safer to stay in bed. Down on the runway the air-raid siren was still wailing, up and down. Rock appeared in the foxhole entrance, and when I shone my flashlight on him he blinked and looked dazed.

'It was a rat,' he said. 'Big as a shoat. Right there in the corner, just starin' at me. I got him, but them tracers will blind a man.' He stood, filling the entrance, squinching up his eyes, trying to get his vision back.

'Either get in or get out, for God's sake,' Joe said. 'There's an air raid on, and you're standing there blocking the whole goddamn hole!' Rock drew back in, and we tumbled after him. But when we had flashed our lights around the hole, there was no dead rat there, only a bit of the corner crumbled where the bullets had hit, and the smell of burning.

'I be damned,' Rock said. 'I don't see how I could of missed him.'

'Next time there's a raid,' Bergie said, 'you leave that gun in your sack. I know you're not going to shoot a rat, and you probably couldn't hit a Jap, but you might just hit one of us.'

That was the only time any of us ever fired a pistol, though we all went on carrying them when we flew.

At that time, early in the battle, the Japanese were sending desperate waves of planes down from the main islands, and we spent a good deal of our time hiding. The sirens would wail, we would throw ourselves into the hole, and then if the guns around us didn't begin to fire we'd peer out, cautiously at first, and then more boldly, and finally climb onto the roof for a better view. The air raids became a spectacular show, and the roof of our foxhole was our box seat. From there, one night, I saw a Japanese bomber (the twin-engined type called a Betty) fly the length of the island along the west side, held in the searchlights all the time, and in a network of tracers and exploding shells, and when he was over the fleet, at the point of fiercest fire, do a perfect, insolent slow-roll and fly on out of range. It was a beautiful gesture, the pilot up there with his lost war, showing his skill, being a pilot still.

Once a raid came suddenly in the twilight and caught me sitting contemplatively in the officers' head, down in the little valley behind the tents. There was nothing to do, no point in running up to the foxhole; I simply sat there with my pants around my ankles, and went about my business. It was very quiet, and then, with a sudden ripping sound, a Japanese fighter swept over the trees by the mess hall, very low. I could see the blinking of his machine guns as he rushed toward me and then swung toward the parked planes on the field. Then he was gone. Not a single gun had fired at him. I had the feeling that no one had even seen him but me. I pulled up my pants and walked up the valley to the tent. Only then did I think how embarrassing it would have been to die down there, on the toilet, with my pants down.

As time passed and the Japanese expended their experienced pilots and their best planes, they began to send beginners, in anything that would fly. One night we saw, caught in an intersection of searchlights, a biplane, a trainer much like the Yellow Perils of our primary training. The lights, like long clutching fingers, held it almost motionless in the center of brightness, No guns seemed to be firing at it, there were no explosions of shells, no tracers, only the fragile plane alone in the light. Then it began to spin, slowly, never picking up much speed, down out of the lights into the darkness beyond Naha. Some kid, not used to night-flying, had been dazzled by the lights and had spun in. It wasn't a kill, it wasn't a credit to anybody—just a flight accident, the kind we used to read about in *BuAerNews*. *Poor bastard*, I thought, remembering my own night flights, *so scared, so unready for war, and now so dead.*

Our own losses began too, almost at once, though they were less spectacular than the deaths of the Japanese pilots. I had been on the island only three days when a pilot named Fox died. He was one of the old hands of the squadron, who had left Ulithi with the forward echelon before we arrived, so I hardly knew him. He didn't even have a first name for us yet, and when Joe came into the tent to tell me about it he said simply, 'Fox is down.'

Fox had been flying an artillery spotter around over the front lines. It was a job that we all did, but that nobody liked

—flying back and forth across the island, low and not too fast, while the spotter looked for gun flashes and radioed their locations to his own guns. It was at once boring and dangerous. The air was full of shells, the Japanese gunners were accurate at low altitudes, and yet there was nothing to see, and nothing to do except drive, like a chauffeur. Shuri Castle was down there, at the center of the front, and two armies were struggling for it, but you didn't notice it. You only saw guns winking, tanks breathing flames like dragons, maybe a patrol running across a field, but nothing more, nothing that looked like a big war.

That's what Fox was doing when his plane was hit. An Army artillery captain saw it happen and wrote a report. The plane was flying at about 250 feet, he said, when it was hit—by a 'high trajectory shell,' so it must have been one of our own mortars, lobbing shells over the line, maybe a mortar that the Captain commanded. The plane crashed on our side of the front, and the Captain got to the wreck within ten minutes of the crash. There was, he said, no sign of life in the area.

Three days later Bergie took off on the same kind of flight and simply disappeared. This time there was no eyewitness, and though later a rumor reached us that a plane had been hit by mortar fire that day, it was never verified, and no wreck was found. Our friend Bergie—the church-in-the-wildwood tenor, the gentle husband, the 'father' of our Santa Barbara family —had simply vanished from our lives. There was no body, no grave, and no funeral, no one, it seemed, to mourn for. T and Joe and I put his possessions together—there was almost nothing worth saving—and gave them to the Adjutant to send home, and took his cot apart and moved it out of the tent. For a while there was a patch of dead wheat where the cot had been; but gradually it was worn away, until it was like the rest of the tent floor.

When you have flown from an airfield for a while, the landscape around it becomes as familiar as a neighborhood. You know where you are by the pond there, the hill over there, the highway, the smoke of the town. But at first it is strange, and no feature is yet a landmark. At Kadena the land was even more alien. It was a foreign place, with tiny fields and tombs, but with no railroads or water towers or highways; and it was a battlefield, devastated and smoking. In the island's principal town, Naha, there was only one wall standing—not a single entire building, just that one white wall (it looked as though it might have been a public building, perhaps a school), rising uselessly from the ruins. All the villages had been destroyed, and the people who lived in them killed or driven into camps. The only signs of human life that you saw from the air were military signs—the supply dumps along the beaches, the air-fields, and the columns of trucks creeping along dirt roads toward the front.

I still had this sense of an unknown landscape below me when I flew my first strike at Okinawa. Our target, we were told, was a set of torpedo launchers, thought to be hidden on the eastern shore of the island. We flew there and circled in formation, in over the beach, out over the anchored fleet, and back again to the shore. Pine trees grew to the edge of the water there, and it looked quiet and pleasant, the sort of place where you might stop for a swim or have a picnic. It would also have been a good place from which to launch torpedoes against the motionless ships in the bay, but we couldn't find any launchers.

From my position as wingman in the rear section, I couldn't even look for them; I had to watch the planes ahead of me, and I had only a vague sense of where we were—now over water, now over land. As we turned in over the beach for maybe the tenth time I looked along my port wing toward my section leader, watching him, working to hold my position, and there on the wing surface, a few feet out from where I sat, a row of holes appeared, suddenly and almost unobtrusively. We flew on, I kept my position in the flight, we swung once more out over the bay; the holes seemed to have nothing to do with anything. I had been hit, that was all. Not as dramatic as losing your virginity, not even like a first drink; just four or five holes the size of quarters in the smooth dark metal.

We gave up looking for the rocket launchers and turned across the island toward Naha, where the Japanese still held the bombed and shattered airfield. We had to do something with our bombs, so we would attack the gun-emplacements there. The air over Naha was full of Navy planes and confusion. It seemed as though all the failed strikes for that morning had come to the same place to unload. We circled, waiting for an opening in the traffic, and then swung into attack formation. The flight leader peeled off and dived, and when my turn came I followed, trying to remember all the things I should do: bombsight on, bomb bays open, bombs armed, machine guns armed (don't forget to fire them!). I could see the other planes of the flight spread out in a loose diagonal below me and to the left. Some AA fire was rising from somewhere on the field, spotting the sunshine with little clouds of smoke; but in the flurry of my preparations I couldn't see the guns.

Bombs began to explode, scattered randomly over the field. I was nearly at the point where I had to drop, and I hadn't found anything to drop on, hadn't even had time to look for a target. Then, in the right angle where two runways crossed, I saw the gun emplacement, with tracers rising out of it like roman candles. But it was too late, I couldn't turn, the altimeter read 2,000 feet, then 1,500, I had to pull out. I dropped my bombs—just threw them away like rubbish, something to be got rid of—and pulled out and to the right, across the beach and out over the fleet, and joined up with the rest of the flight. Two years' training, I thought gloomily, for this—this aimless attack on nothing. I had come at last to the Big Test, the moment of action in the real war, but somehow I had missed it, or it had missed me.

This sense of the aimlessness of the war never quite left me, though later strikes were sometimes more comprehensible, as the squadron found its special mission. We began to fly attacks in support of the infantry—low-level precision bombing of enemy positions just in advance of our troops. We'd circle over the lines, and a controller on the ground would give us our target: 'Do you see a hill with a road running up it? We're marking it with blue smoke. There's a gun in a cave at the top, to the left of the road.' The strike leader would find the target, drop on it, and we'd drop on his explosion. The system worked pretty well, though one hill with a road up it looked very much like another, and the Japanese sometimes confused things by firing blue smoke back into our own lines, so that occasionally we dropped on the wrong troops, and an angry complaint would come to us from an infantry commander. But our own soldiers were not much more real to us than the enemy. If they were in the Army they were called Doggies, which was short for Dog-faces, and Marines despised them, along with their commanders. (Marines taught Okinawan children to stand by the road when Army units passed, shouting 'General MacArthur eats shit!' They thought it meant 'Give me a cigarette.') Even our own Marine infantrymen were a different species, called Gravel-crunchers or Crunchies—remote allies, at best. And anyway, they were all down there on the ground, invisible except when they did something spectacular, like attacking with flamethrowers or tanks; and we were up here, separated from them by the supporting air.

After each strike there was a debriefing session with the squadron intelligence officer. You gathered around his desk and told him, one at a time, what you thought you had seen and what you might have hit, and he turned it all into extravagant claims of destruction and pinpoint accuracy, and put it in the squadron war diary. If anything had really been achieved, he sent a news item back to Washington, which sent it to your hometown paper, which might run it, especially if it was a small town, maybe even with your picture; and then the cuttings would come back, from McComb, Mississippi, or Albany, Minnesota, and we'd sit around with some beers and the mail and laugh about what the folks back home thought we were doing. Once the intelligence officer sent the same item out for every pilot in the squadron, about what a great job we were doing, and mine got to a brewery in Chicago that had a Hero of the Week award. My name was mentioned on the radio, and my father got a certificate suitable for framing. He was very proud of the certificate, but he wouldn't frame it because it came from a brewery.

Slowly life at Kadena began to take shape, and our squadron camp became a sort of village. The road down the hill to the strip was our main street, and along it a village life moved. At the top on one side of the road was Officers' Country, and on the other side the squadron mess hall. Downhill from the mess hall were the enlisted men's quarters, rows of tents like the officers' but closer together, and with more men in each tent. A Quonset hut across the road was the Operations office and also the village post office, a place you could just drop in to when you were passing by, to talk and listen to the latest rumors. A little farther down, two tents together were the offices of the Commanding Officer and the Adjutant, a sort of town hall. At the bottom of the road, beside the strip, were the squadron shops: tents for armament, for radio and radar, and for the quartermaster's supplies. On an ordinary day men moved up and down the street or stopped in little groups to talk and laugh, jeeps threaded among them, and from below the sounds of men working drifted up—the clanking and hammering, and the rise and fall of engines being tested.

It was an odd community—a village with no women or children, in which only one business was conducted—but it had a wholeness, and it felt familiar and comfortable and not, like the rest of the island, exotic and foreign. Everything you wanted (except women, children, and peace) you could get there: clothes at the quartermaster's store, food at the mess hall, your mail at Operations. The Red Cross tent down by the strip provided tobacco and writing paper, and sometimes a brown rocklike substance called Tropical Chocolate, which would not melt, and had to be pulverized between the teeth. Back of the tents in Officers' Country there was a tub for washing clothes, and a shower-bath made from an oil drum; you could build a fire under it and have a hot shower, if you wanted one.

There was even a village movie theater on the hillside behind Operations. It was primitive and uncomfortable—you sat on cartridge cases in the open air—but it completed village life, and made it more like life back home. A movie began every night as soon as it was dark enough, just about when the first nightfighters took off. It usually began with a newsreel, edited to give an encouraging view of the war, and a short, which always seemed to be Lawrence Tibbett singing 'The Road to Mandalay,' and then the feature film. Most nights we didn't get through the whole program, though; the feature would start, and then the air-raid sirens would begin to wind up to a howl, and the screen would go blank and dark, and the ninety-millimeter gun on the hill behind Officers' Country would begin to fire. I saw the beginning of a Spencer Tracy–Katharine Hepburn movie five times, and never saw the end; they were together in a buggy, and he was courting her—and then the sirens would blow.

In the residential section of our village, domestic improvements continued. Joe and I walked up the road, away from the airfield, and found a ruined house that must have been an impressive place before it was shelled. It had a tiled roof, now mostly blown off, and many rooms. In one was a sort of toilet, apparently designed to save human excrement for fertilizer. In another stood an elaborately lacquered dresser. The drawers were all gone—perhaps the inhabitants had simply seized them and run off with the contents—but the frame remained, with flat surfaces where the drawers had been, which could be used as shelves. It was beautiful, even in its devastated form, and we carried it back to our tent. It looked a little odd there, on the dirt floor, stuffed with khaki pants and T-shirts, but it made us feel settled.

Rock built a floor lamp out of two-by-fours, with a helmet liner for a shade, and T constructed a primitive brazier out of a gasoline can. It was filled with broken roof tiles, and you doused the tiles with gasoline and lit them, and you could make coffee. Once T heated a can of soup on it, but neglected to open the can. It exploded and covered our cots, our mosquito nets, and the walls of our tent with Campbell's tomato. Liz sent me two photographs of herself, and I asked a maintenance man to make frames for them. He made them out of cockpit plexiglass, in two panels, hinged like a book, and painted them with blue airplane paint, like the TBM's on the line. I put them on top of the Japanese dresser—two pictures of the smiling, pretty girl who was my responsibility.

In the evenings junior officers took turns doing the dreariest of squadron jobs—censoring the letters that the enlisted men wrote. Most of the men were not very literate, and their letters home were composed of clumsy expressions of affection and preposterous lies about their military exploits. They knew that we censored their letters, and some of them resented it and played a game with us, trying to sneak information past us, to hint by some elaborate circumlocution where the squadron was and what it was doing. Our part of the game was to snip out whatever seemed too obvious, but never to report a man to the C.O.

Sometimes their amorous feelings for their wives and sweethearts were expressed with a forthrightness that seemed pornographic to middle-class young men like us. We'd be sitting in the tent, each with a pile of letters to be censored, and someone would begin to laugh: 'Hey, listen to this guy,' and he'd read out some mechanic's fancy, addressed to his wife, of what he'd do to and with her when he got home. It was funny, and it was astonishing, that there were marriages in the world in which a man said *cunt* to his wife, and in which sexual relations were apparently conducted with such violent and inventive enthusiasm. Men like that mechanic made censoring an endurable and sometimes an educational activity.

For one pilot in the squadron it was different. In the tent opposite mine lived a gentle, priest-like Catholic boy named Feeney. He never spoke above a murmur, he didn't drink with us, and he lived in general the life of a seminarian. Feeney was a good pilot and a nice guy, and we all liked him, but he wasn't like the rest of us. Eventually, in the rotation of censorship duties, he came upon one of the pornographic mechanic's letters, and was horrified, so horrified that he summoned the man to his tent. We hovered outside and heard this interview:

Lt. Feeney: 'Sergeant, you can't do this.'

Sergeant: 'Do what, sir?'

Lt. Feeney: 'Write a letter like this to your wife.'

Sergeant: 'What about it, sir?'

Lt. Feeney (nervously): 'Well, you say you're going to fuck her cross-eyed. That's no way to talk to your wife.'

Sergeant: 'Why not? She's my fucking wife, ain't she? Sir?' Feeney could find no answer for that one, and the Sergeant continued to embellish his descriptions of his return home with sexual fantasies.

The shock that Feeney felt we all shared. But still, we expected that sort of thing from the enlisted men. Yet it was surprising and upsetting when one of our own talked that way. I remember walking down the road to Operations one day with Jimmy and Sly. Sly was telling a long, boring story about something that had happened at El Toro, but I wasn't really listening. It was a sunny spring day, early May probably; and I could see that the low hills beyond the strip, where the fighting was still going on, were beginning to turn green, in spite of the war.

Jimmy seemed distracted, too, walking along, hands in pockets, scuffing his feet like the small boy he seemed to be; but Sly bored on relentlessly. 'I remember, it was January. . . . No, it must have been December. Anyway, it was raining, and I was home fucking my wife. . . .' Jimmy stopped short on the road and turned. 'Goddamn you, shut up!' His face was white with anger. 'Don't ever talk that way about your wife, not in front of me,' and he stalked away into Operations. Sly stared, and his mouth beneath the limp mustache gaped open, but he didn't say anything. I don't think he understood, even then, that though Marines did talk about women that way some-times, a wife was different—even the wife of a man like Sly.

Air raids continued, but more sporadically now—a single plane at night, high in the lights, or a crackle of AA fire over the fleet. We woke in the dark, sometimes to the mournful howling of the sirens, sometimes to the cough of the ninety-millimeter behind the hill; and crowded, half asleep, into the open ends of the foxhole; and stood there, shoulder-deep in the earth, to see what was happening. We were standing that way one night in May when the darkness over Yontan lit up like a Fourth of July show. Bright fingers of searchlights probed and crossed the sky, and guns sprayed tracers into the dark. Guns in the fleet began to fire, too, and then our own guns at Kadena, and others, until it seemed that every battery on the island and in the anchorage was hurling a converging fire at Yontan. As we watched, the guns' trajectories gradually low-ered, until they were firing nearly horizontally, a dense criss-cross of fire that was almost solid.

Up from the net of fire a sudden ball of flame rose, and a moment later we heard the explosion, and then another and another. Something was burning, a plane probably, and other fires started and rose up, filling the sky with flames that were brighter than the tracers' tracks. What possible attack could be taking place there, a mile or two away? We could see noth-ing except the tracer fire and the flames, and we knew nothing except what we saw. The defensive fire seemed desperate and irrational—they must be firing into their own positions—as though the attacker were something monstrous and inhu-man, that could not be fought in a customary way. Then the gunfire began to subside, and for a time there were only the tall flames, and scattered explosions, tardy-sounding after all that noise. And then the flames died, very slowly at first, and then they were gone, and the night was dark and silent.

The next day we heard the story. The Japanese had sent seven bombers, loaded with troops, in a suicide raid against Yontan. The planes were to crash-land on the runways, and the troops, armed with explosives, would leap out and destroy the aircraft parked on the field. Three of the bombers were shot down by nightfighters before they reached the island, but four got through and approached the field, coming in low over the trees in the darkness. The horizontal gunfire we saw had been directed at them, and three were shot down in the last seconds before they landed; the first flames we saw were those exploding planes.

Only one pilot managed to land and to get his load of troops out onto the runway. They ran among the parked planes, throwing grenades and firing machine guns, until they were killed by rifle fire. When daylight came, the field at Yontan was scattered with smoking wreckage and bodies. Forty planes had been destroyed or damaged, seventy thousand gallons of aviation fuel had been burned, and two Marines had been killed. The control tower was flattened, and the runway was blocked by the burned-out Japanese plane. In the three crashed bombers, and scattered in ones and twos along the strip, were sixty-nine dead Japanese. No one could say how many of the burned planes had been hit by the Japanese raiders, and how many by the wild AA fire, or whose bullets had killed the two Marines (they were in the tower, and were caught in the crossfire).

The raid had no effect on the progress of the war. How could it? We had more planes and more Marines; we could pile a field with wreckage, burn a gasoline dump, and go on fighting without an interruption. The men in those dark bombers must have known that, and the men who sent them certainly did. Yet the raid came. By happening at Yontan, up there on the next rise where we could watch the whole spectacular madness of it, it forced upon us the strangeness of the people we were fighting.

For in an air war you are not very conscious of your enemies as human beings. We attacked targets—a gun emplacement, a supply dump, a radar station—not men, and succeeded or failed in terms of the things we destroyed. I flew more than a hundred missions during the Okinawa campaign and never saw a single Japanese soldier on the ground. If I thought of the men down there at all, I thought of them as ordinary, like us—men who ran supply dumps and radar stations, and who manned their guns and shot at us when we attacked them; the rules of war, I thought, were the same. But the raid on Yontan was different; it wasn't something we could have done. It was not concerned, as our raids were, with destroying, but with dying. It seemed to me then that the true end of war for the men I was fighting against was not victory, but death. And spectacular death, fire and explosions, the body bursting in a terrible, self-destroying orgasm. One of the Japanese at Yontan had held a grenade in his belly and blown himself up.

Later that month I woke in the night to the sound of a shout and then a burst of automatic rifle fire. There were hurrying footsteps in the company street, and voices, and when I looked out people were running past with flashlights. I ran, too, in my rubber boots. At the end of the row of officers' tents, where the hill dropped off sharply, a sentry was posted; and it was his voice that I had heard, and his rifle. Someone had crept up the gully below and had begun to climb the hill toward him. He shouted once, as the regulations told him to, and then fired a whole magazine, point-blank.

The body lay at the bottom of the hill. It was the first dead man I had ever seen. After all that dying, the friends lost, the wrecked planes crumpled on the bombing target, this was the first time that actual and particular death had reached me. I went down the hill and pointed my flashlight at the body. It didn't look like a man who had just been alive. It didn't look like a man at all. The clothes seemed to have neither color nor shape, not to be clothes at all; it was a bundle of rags that lay at my feet, just rags without even the shape of a human being. Perhaps he wasn't even a Jap, only an Okinawan, hiding and hungry, not murderous but only desperate with hunger and fear. I felt revulsion at his deadness, so ugly, sprawled and defaced by the bullets that had killed him, but no fellow-feeling at all. He might have been a dead dog, hit by a car and thrown to the side of the road. We all turned away and left him there, and went back to bed.

The next morning T and I went to see Billy Childers in his tent, to talk about something to do with our section—the next strike, probably, or a problem of armament. When we came in, Billy rose from his cot, put his hand slowly into his pocket, and brought out a dirty handkerchief. Slowly, carefully, he unwrapped it, holding it on one palm while he turned back the handkerchief with the other. Then he looked up proudly. On his extended palm, on the handkerchief, lay the dead man's ear. 'Got me a souvenir,' Billy said.

That was the only dead man, but there were many deaths, and the images of those deaths come back like film clips. We are watching a movie on the makeshift screen near the strip. A nightfighter pilot, approaching to land, mistakes the lights of a road for a row of landing lights and settles to a perfect three-point landing between the road and the strip, in the gravel pit. The plane explodes, and a sudden ball of fire rises into the night. The movie is stopped until the darkness settles again, and then continues. I sit in my plane on the taxiway at Yontan, waiting for clearance. A Corsair damaged in a fight approaches for an emergency landing; it levels off, stalls, a wing drops, and it flips over to crash beside the runway. From my foxhole I see Japanese planes hit; they blossom in flames; are shot to pieces, crash.

I remember a day in May—a warm, sunny, still day. I was lying naked in the sun, stretched out on a canvas cot reading not very attentively one of those odd-shaped, lengthwise paperbacks that the Army distributed to the troops. The day seemed peaceful, though the war was there, if you listened for it. A mile or so offshore, the *Missouri* was still shelling Shuri Castle, and the sound of the firing and the detonations of the shells reached me as a dull, monotonous rumble, like the sound of a factory making something heavy but uninteresting. But where I lay the earth was silently, soporifically hot, and I might have been on any beach back home, sunburned and sweating and thinking about nothing.

On a cot next to mine Rock was lying propped on his elbow; we were probably talking about girls, or the wild parties he'd known back at A&M. But at the sound of planes we stopped and watched a flight of Turkeys come rumbling over the field. They looked as they always did in the air, cumbersome and tired, as though they didn't like flying very much and weren't much good at it; but they were in good formation, a tight V of V's, trying to look as much like the fighters as their ungainly shapes would allow. They flew the length of the strip and began to peel off for landing, and as they did, I counted them. There were only eleven; one was missing.

I tried to remember who had gone on the strike and where they had gone, but I couldn't. None of my close friends, anyway. We watched the formation break into a stretched-out string of separate planes, watched the wheels and flaps come down as one by one they turned to touch down.

Then I saw the other one approaching from the south, flying low and slow. It passed over us, so close and so slow-moving that I could look up into the ragged hole that gaped in the belly of the plane, just aft of the wing. And I could see that the gunner's door, toward the tail, had been jettisoned; there was someone in the open doorway, motionless, facing out.

The plane made a slow circle of the airfield and once more headed down the strip. *The radio must be out*, I thought; *he's looking for a green light from the tower.* We could see the controller in the tower raise his signal light. The pilot began to rock his wings, slowly back and forth, to acknowledge the controller's signal.

Then, from the open door, something fell. Slowly, as though the sunlit air were bright water, it sank toward the earth, turning and turning, very slowly. It struck the airstrip near the tower and bounced, suddenly and surprisingly high. And as it bounced, it opened, and became a spread-eagled man, and fell again to the earth and lay, once more a lump, a something. The plane, as though relieved of an intolerable burden, circled more swiftly and prepared to land. On the strip near the tower there was a sudden flurry of jeeps, an ambulance, and men running, but there was no sound—I particularly remember that there was no sound—except for the quick bass roar as the pilot changed to low pitch for his landing.

The ambulance began to move slowly up the strip toward the sick bay, and the jeeps and men scattered as quickly as they had come. The strip was empty except for the plane rolling slowly and clumsily to a stop. Even the sky was empty, not a plane or even a cloud in sight.

The plane had been hit by groundfire, and a shell had exploded inside the fuselage, somewhere behind the wing. It had knocked out the radio, killed the turret gunner, and wounded the radio operator. The wounded man couldn't talk to the pilot with the radio out, and he could see the great hole in the fuselage, so he tried to bail out, but fainted in the doorway. When the plane tilted over the strip, he fell, and died. Of all the deaths in the squadron, his was the only one I actually saw.

It must have been about that time that Dick Whitfield got lost over clouds on an antisub patrol, and radioed in to Ground Control for a heading, but never reached the field. For a while he could be heard on the radio, reporting in, flying the heading and complaining that he hadn't reached the field yet. Then he faded out. Three or four days later we heard what had happened, how he had been given, not the correct heading to the base, but its reciprocal (an error that's easy to make if the plane is close overhead, as Dick's was). He had, on instruction, flown directly away from the field until his gas was almost gone. Then through a hole in the clouds he saw an island and began an approach. But it looked unfamiliar, and after consulting his maps he concluded, correctly, that he was preparing to land on a Japanese-held island several hundred miles east of Okinawa. He turned round and flew back west until he ran out of gas. Then, with a dead engine, he began a descent through clouds, and skillfully made a smooth, power-off landing in the sea. It was early afternoon. He and his crew unloaded their survival gear—the two rafts that the TBM carried, Mae Wests, rations, everything—and had the rafts inflated and were aboard them before the plane sank. Then they rigged a sail and set out to sail home, or to survive until they were found.

That afternoon they heard a plane fly over, but it was out of sight in the overcast. Later another appeared, this time lower. It was Japanese. They lowered their blue sail and hid under it until the plane flew away. As night fell the wind rose and the sea became rough. Whitfield took down the sail and improvised sea anchors to hold the raft into the wind and keep it from capsizing. On the second day it was the same—the storm continued and planes passed high up in the overcast.

The weather improved on the third day, and the clouds lifted. They saw an American transport overhead and signaled with flares and mirrors, as the survival instructions directed, but got no response. Other planes passed, and finally someone in a flying boat saw their blinking mirror, and circled over the raft, waggling its wings. It didn't land, though, but flew off toward where they imagined Okinawa must be; there was a Very Important Person aboard, and the pilot wouldn't chance a landing in that high sea. But he did radio the position of the raft, and in an hour or so another flying boat appeared.

That plane (now this is Dick's story) landed heavily into the waves and taxied to pick them up. Dick climbed aboard last —he had a feeling the officer in command was supposed to be the last to leave the ship—and with relief turned and stuck his sheath knife into the raft, and let it sink. 'I wouldn't have done that, if I were you,' the pilot said. 'When we landed just now we sprung all the plates in the bow. We may sink.' The plane didn't sink, but it couldn't take off in that sea, and so Whitfield and his crew were taxied the hundred miles home. It took twelve hours. They had been at sea for more than three days.

A message came from the taxiing plane that the rescue had been accomplished, and we began to prepare a welcome for him. We removed from his tent every object that was his—his clothes, his footlocker, his cot, every single possession. Then we waited. Days passed. Where was he? It turned out that he had been taken to a naval hospital for examination, which revealed that the three days in the raft had given him a case of the piles. A doctor (no doubt another rusty surgeon, like the one at Ulithi) operated at once, and when he found that his patient had not been circumcised, he performed that operation as well, 'as long as I'm in the neighborhood,' as he put it. Whitfield came out of anesthesia unable to lie either on his back or on his stomach; he felt, he said, a lesser man.

At last he returned to the squadron, where he was met with feigned embarrassment. 'Gosh, Dick,' Kelleher said, 'who'd have thought you'd survive? We drank your whiskey at the wake. You'd have liked that wake.' 'Clothes?' another tentmate added. 'Shit, they were worn out anyway. We couldn't even give 'em back to the quartermaster. Chaplain gave 'em to some gooks.' 'Letters? You don't mean those were *love* letters? I sent them to your mother.' Whitfield had been erased. He got quite upset about it, standing there in his tent looking at the bare place where his cot had been. He said he sort of knew now what being dead would be like, and it wasn't worth a shit. So we gave him back his possessions and put his cot together again for him, and then we drank all his whiskey, and after a while he felt better and told us the whole story, except about the circumcision. Rock said he didn't want to hear about cutting a piece of a man's cock off while he was drinking. Whitfield was unique—the only dead man who was ever restored to us alive —and the way we responded was cruel, but understandable. It was a chance to exorcise death by parodying it.

As the campaign continued, 232 began to fly more and more antisubmarine patrols; probably some of the Navy carrier squadrons had been withdrawn from the area. It was boring flying, and nobody ever saw anything. I generally took my mail and a cigar with me, and I would put the plane on automatic pilot, tune the radio to Shanghai if I could, and listen to music that was like the crashing of garbage-can lids while I read and smoked. Once I ran a tank dry while I was dozing along that way, and it took a while to get the engine started again, and Edwards and Campbell were quite annoyed. I suppose I had waked them up. Sometimes an air raid would come while I was on a patrol, and the radio would begin to sputter warnings and instructions—'Bandit in your section' or 'Remain clear of fleet anchorage, where a kamikaze might be attacking'—and the air would be full of AA fire.

I saw an attack happen only once while I was flying. I was out over the water west of the island, patrolling, when Ground Control reported that a Japanese bomber had just dropped a Baka bomb and that it was in flight somewhere between me and the island. (*Baka* means stupid or crazy in Japanese. A Baka bomb was a tiny suicide plane, powered by a rocket engine and carrying in its nose an armed bomb. It had no landing gear, no armor or defensive armament, no radio, and almost no instruments. It was carried into attack position by a bomber and dropped. The pilot then fired his rocket and flew the bomb into the largest enemy ship he could see. In a revetment near Yontan there was a captured Baka—stubby-winged, fragile-looking, like a toy. It made me sick to look at it. A machine for killing pilots.)

Control said I was to continue my patrol and stay away from the island. But this time I turned and flew back, searching the sky. It was one of those warm, hazy spring days, when there is no horizon, just one curve of gray from the sea beneath you right round to the sky above. The island was an indistinct dark mass in the distance, and though I knew the fleet was off to my right, in the anchorage around Kerama Retto, I could only see a few of the closest ships, dark streaks on the gray water. The Baka appeared first as a dark line of smoke drawn diagonally downward across the grayness, from high on my left, descending toward the shrouded fleet on my right. Then I could see the little plane, looking like a model a child might make, moving very fast, nearly in front of me now, in a steep glide. Ahead of the plane AA shells from the ships below began to burst, silently, leaving small white puffs of smoke that hung against the darker haze like bits of cotton wool. I armed my guns, flipped on the gunsight, and began an intercepting turn, the kind of maneuver I had learned on gunnery sleeves in flight school. But a Baka is faster than a gunnery sleeve, and Turkeys are slow; my target fled past me as I turned, and disappeared into the haze and smoke over the fleet, leaving behind his scrawled trail, like a derisive message written on the air.

I felt foolish and let down. Of course you couldn't catch a Baka with a TBM; and why was I trying, anyway? Fighters chased their targets through friendly AA fire, and sometimes out again, but why behave like a fighter pilot? And especially *now*, at the end of a war that was already won. Yet, when the word about that Baka came, I turned. Perhaps the indoctrination had worked, after all, and I was like the third-string quarterback, running onto the field for his chance in the Big Game.

Ground Control for the antisub patrols was handled by our own pilots. Once every week or so you would have to spend a day in a dark, cavelike control room at Yontan, watching a radar scope and directing your friends around their patrol areas. That part of the job was dull, but the room itself was very exciting. This was where all planes in the air over Okinawa and to the north were tracked, where enemy raids were first noted, and fighters sent against them. So that while the antisub controller's job was simply to see that his man wasn't shot down, he could watch the drama of fighter interception on the screen before him and follow the action on his earphones.

The visual part of this show was tense and dramatic. The intruding spot of light showed first on the rows of radar scopes before which the controllers sat. It was then transferred to a large transparent screen as a fluorescent spot of crayon located on a map of the area. As the enemy plane flew on toward the island, the bright spots followed it, making a track on the screen, and our fighters left their own trails of light as they moved to an intersection; and then, if the controlling had been good, the intruder's trail stopped, and a circle on the screen marked the place where he had been shot down into the sea.

It should have been a silent show, but unfortunately the Navy had written dialogue for these occasions. There was a whole arch vocabulary for communicating a few simple facts: an enemy plane was a 'bandit' or a 'bogey'; altitude was given in 'angels' instead of thousands of feet; and a kill was supposed to be reported in the laconic line 'Splash one bogey.' And of course you said Roger and Wilco and Over and Out all the time. It always seemed to me melodramatic and phony and unnecessary. Who were we supposed to be fooling, saying angels for altitude? And all that understatement, it was straight out of the movies—the influence of Gary Cooper and Bogart on American military procedures. The true line would have been, 'Hey, you guys, I just shot a fucking Jap.' But the script read, 'Splash one bogey.' Very phony.

It was while I was on my way to Ground Control duty that I suffered my only war wound. I was driving a squadron jeep, and I was late, and I drove along the empty Okinawa lane at pretty near top speed, which was probably around fifty in that jeep. The lane was narrow, and sunk between banks higher than my head, but there was no traffic, and I hurried along, not thinking about much, probably wishing I was in the air instead of down there in all that dust. A blind corner was coming up where another sunken lane crossed the one I was driving in, but my road was empty, the other one must be, too. I shot into the intersection. In from my left rumbled an amphibious landing craft—one of the kind that the Marines called Ducks. On land it was clumsy, like its namesake, but it was also tall and massive-looking as it bore down on me. I braked and swerved away, and the driver of the Duck braked and slammed into the back of my jeep, lifting it into the air, and tossing it head-first into a ditch. I gripped the steering wheel and hung on, like an unskilled rider on a mean horse, and I stayed in the seat; but my head snapped forward when I hit the ditch, and my forehead struck the screw-and-bar device that opens the windshield. I climbed out, feeling stunned but as far as I could tell unhurt, and scrambled up out of the ditch. There, looking down at me, was a frightened-looking pfc. 'O my God,' he moaned when he saw me, 'I've killed an officer.' I realized then that my forehead was cut and that blood was pouring down my face and onto my shirt.

The jeep wasn't damaged, only bent here and there where it didn't seem to matter; the Duck wasn't damaged, and the pfc wasn't hurt. And it was my fault. The important thing, then, was that the pfc shouldn't get into trouble. So we found a first-aid kit, put a patch on my head, and agreed that nothing had happened—neither of us had ever been there, there had been no accident. Then we hauled the jeep out of the ditch and I drove on.

At Yontan I went first to the sick bay. There was no doctor on duty—probably out circumcising somebody—and the corpsman was dubious about treating me. A flap of skin and flesh had been torn loose, and hung on my forehead like a small red tongue. It should be sewn up, but the doctor wasn't there, and the corpsman couldn't sew up a head. Finally he said, 'Well, I can't sew it up, but I can cut it off.' He took a huge pair of scissors, snipped off the flap, poured on Merthiolate, and bandaged me up. I went to the control room, thinking that when people asked me how I got the scar on my forehead, I could say, 'I was hit on Okinawa.'

In May we began to fly at night—solitary flights over the Japanese lines that were meant to disturb the enemy's sleep and to prevent him from moving supplies. Any light—a truck's headlights, a fire, a lighted doorway—was to be fired on. It was the kind of flying that I hated, hovering around at a thousand feet, above invisible watchers, a target for any gun. And because I hated it, I did it; you could only evade what you weren't afraid of—that was understood.

The strip, with its rows of flickering flare-pots, was dark and unsubstantial-looking; but once I was in the air I could see lights all around—the fleet lit up for miles on both sides of the island, Yontan with its rotating beacon, the lights of camps, jeeps moving along the roads. It might have been California, or Memphis, or Pensacola. But the lights stopped suddenly in a ragged east-west line below Naha, and from there south the island was as black as a night sea. It was like an allegory—the good side full of light, and the evil side covered in darkness.

I flew out over the eastern bay, and south, and swung in toward the dark land. The observer riding with me began to scan the ground below us for gun flashes. I looked around for something to attack, somebody boiling a pot of tea or lighting his way to the toilet, but I could see nothing. To the north, across the lines, Army artillery was firing sporadically, lobbing mortar shells onto some Japanese position. It was one of those guns that had killed Bergie. Poor me. The island below remained black and inscrutable, a shadow over waiting men. I flew on, waiting, too. Nothing happened, there were no lights, no guns were fired, and I didn't drop a bomb or fire a single round. Then on my radio I heard my relief report himself airborne, and I turned back toward the lights, toward possible life.

Because Yontan had a beacon and electric landing lights, and Kadena had only flare-pots, we returned from these night flights to Yontan, and hung around there until dawn. There was a mess hall near the ready room that was open all night, like a highway diner, and the cook could do something with Spam and powdered eggs that made them taste reasonably good, at least after a night hop. So we hung around there, eating and drinking coffee, and listening to the stories of the night pilots as they came back. Sometimes the stories seemed a bit doubtful, the kind of yarn you'd spin for the intelligence officer. One pilot—not a guy I liked or trusted very much—claimed he had attacked twenty soldiers who were trying to launch a boat and had sunk the boat and killed all the soldiers. His description of the bodies floating in the water was very vivid, but it was hard to understand how he could have seen such detail at night, when I couldn't even see the ground. Kelleher told us how he had been in the air over the southern end of the island when an air raid began, and how every time he tried to come home and land his own AA guns started shooting at him. The Turkey had about four-and-a-half or five hours of gas in it, but Kelleher stretched his to five-and-a-half ('I could hear that engine sucking the last drops,' he said, 'like drinking a soda through a straw') before he was finally allowed to land.

Joe, the man things happened to, was hit by a shell on one of these night flights. It knocked out his hydraulic system, and he had to make a no-flaps, wheels-up landing in the dark. He did it perfectly, and the plane was repaired and flew again. Joe told the story, sitting there in the mess hall at three in the morning, eating Spam-and-eggs and laughing, as though it was a good joke on him. The next night the same thing happened to another pilot, but he wasn't the flier that Joe was, and though he survived, the plane was destroyed.

It was on one of those night-heckler hops that one of our pilots—his name was Fred Folino—shot a Jap plane down. He was down there at the southern end of the island, strafing up and down in the dark, when an air raid began. Control told him to clear the island at once and orbit to the southwest, but as he did he saw another plane ahead of him, its exhaust flames just visible in the darkness. He complained to Control: why was he being sent off the island into a boring orbit, when this other guy was allowed to stay here just flying around? You idiot, Control replied, that's the bandit.

By this time Fred was closing in on the plane and could see it more clearly. It was a float plane, with two pontoons, and it was flying straight and level at about his altitude, and on the same course. He slid into position astern, armed his guns, and turned on his gunsight. But then, he said, he couldn't see the Jap, he couldn't see anything but the bright bull's-eye of the gunsight. So he turned it off again and tried a burst in the dark. The tracers fell short. He added all the power he had, and slowly began to overtake the plane ahead, and when he thought he had gained some distance, he tried another little squirt, but he was still too far back. All this time the Jap didn't seem aware that he was being followed and shot at; he flew on on a straight course, Fred and his TBM grunting and straining behind.

At last, Fred said, he was sure he was close enough; the twin floats seemed to be sticking into his propeller. He took careful aim and squeezed the trigger. Nothing. He had run out of ammunition. But Fred was a calm man, and he considered what was left to him. He was carrying rockets, four on each wing, to be fired in pairs against ground targets. He armed them and fired the first two. They swished past the Jap, just below his wings, and now he knew he was being hunted, and he rolled into a diving turn. Fred followed, took a lead on his target, and squeezed off the second pair of rockets. There was a bright flash, and debris flew past his plane. He reported his achievement to Control. Control told him to get back on station where he belonged.

It was the only plane destroyed by a member of the squadron, and as far as I know the only one ever shot down at night with rockets. We were proud of old Fred, and of the little Jap flag that was painted on the fuselage of his plane the next day. It was something to show the fighter pilots.

Not all the action took place at night. Feeney, the gentle censor of enlisted obscenities, was attacked by a Japanese fighter plane one afternoon on a patrol. He told the story with a mild astonishment, as though it were an account of bad manners. 'I was out on this ASP,' he said, 'just drifting along below the overcast, thinking about Boston, and letting my radar man do the looking—and all of a sudden there was this Irving making a head-on run at me!' ('Irving' was the American name for a kind of Jap fighter.)

'So you made a 180 and fired both fifties and shot him down, right?'

'Are you kidding? I pulled up into the overcast and began evasive maneuvers. At least I thought they were evasive, but the Jap kept finding me again. I couldn't see much—my engine was throwing oil—and my compass was swinging, so I wasn't too sure where I was going, but I just kept on twisting and turning and trying not to spin out, and the Jap kept coming back and losing me in the clouds again. Once he flew right over me, maybe twenty or thirty feet above, and never saw me.

After a while he quit. I guess he was disgusted with me for not being more gung-ho.'

Two or three days later another ASP plane met a fighter, and wasn't fired on, and a few days after that a Tony made a head-on run on somebody else, and again didn't fire. Three interceptions in a row, and not a shot fired—it was very odd. The Japanese pilots seemed uncertain, as though they hadn't been told what to do if they met an American plane, or they had been given some other, quite different mission that was preoccupying them. I suppose most of them had been sent down to crash into ships and not to waste themselves on single aircraft. None of them ever shot at one of our planes, and except for Fred Folino's rocket shot, none of us ever hit any of them. 'You'd think we were fighting in different wars,' Feeney said wonderingly, 'the way we just pass and nod to each other.' And certainly it seemed that whoever our squadron was fighting —and I didn't usually have much feeling that we were fighting anybody in particular—we weren't fighting the Japanese air force.

The strain of combat flying began to tell on some pilots. One night-fighter pilot I knew had three consecutive engine failures (maybe he was hit by ground fire or by a Japanese plane, maybe the engine just stopped, I've forgotten) and had to land three times in the sea in the darkness. He didn't seem affected by these experiences—his conversation was normal, though he talked about water landings a good deal—but he began to paint things blue. Everything: his Mae West, his helmet, his flying suit, finally his tent—all blue. His C.O. concluded that the man needed a rest, and so he sent him back out of the action, but only as far as Saipan (we had been envying him a trip to Honolulu). In a week or so he was back with his squadron, supplied with a new helmet (beige) and a new Mae West (yellow). He seemed to be recovered—at least he went back to night-flying.

Nobody in our squadron seemed especially disturbed by the life we were leading, flying day and night and meeting Jap fighters; nobody went noticeably crazy, nobody painted anything blue. Still, someone must have thought that we were showing signs of weariness, and we were sent, a half-dozen at a time, to a rest camp farther north on the island, away from the fighting. The camp was nothing much—a few tents to sleep in, a small mess hall, and some cases of beer—but the setting was beautiful and restful—a pine grove on a rocky promontory, looking over a small, untroubled bay. Pine woods always have a tidy feeling, of being empty and just swept, a feeling that I associate with Japanese orderliness and Japanese gardening and painting; and in that camp I felt as though we had been allowed into the best part of our enemy's world, a place that expressed his sense of beauty. Out in the center of the little bay there was a cluster of jutting rocks, and on the largest was a torii, one of those formal arches that you see outside Japanese temples. It was the only Japanese structure I ever saw on the island that was intact, and it seemed serene and eternal, out there on the rock, away from the war.

At the rest camp we got up when we felt like it, lay about reading and drinking, and in the afternoons climbed down the steep face of the promontory to swim and lounge on the rocks at the edge of the bay. Among the rocks and trees on the opposite promontory, a Japanese sniper was hiding, though our troops had long since passed him by and had gone on up the island. Sometimes while we were swimming he would lob a few rifle shots at us, just to show us that he was still resisting, I suppose, and to keep his courage up. We would hear the distant crack of his rifle, and a plunk where the bullet struck the water. I rather admired his lonely, stupid defiance over there.

It was obviously a good life up there at the camp, just what we needed, but it felt strange, and we were restless and ill-at-ease. We weren't used to unscheduled time, and whole days without duties made us feel disoriented. And it was so quiet —there were no engine sounds, and we had been living with airplane engines for years, and got a feeling of security from hearing them in the night. Everything that was energetic in our lives—all the noise and the bustle—was absent in the pine-wood hush, and we were homesick for it. Three days was all we could stand, and we piled into the trucks that would take us back to Kadena like schoolboys at the end of term, headed for their vacation.

We went back to flying strikes, and I learned, one day, what I had not known before, that it is possible to feel pity for a machine. It was one of those on-the-island strikes, and we were loaded heavily: four five-hundred-pound bombs, eight rockets, full machine-gun ammunition. I taxied into position in my turn, ran up the engine, and released the brakes. The plane began to roll, ponderously at first; then as the speed increased the tail came up, the plane felt lighter on the stick, it was nearly flying. I reached for the wheel handle; I would pull up the wheels as I left the ground, a foot or two in the air. It was a way of showing off for the fighter pilots—like our landings, a foolish demonstration that we were hot pilots, too. I raised the handle, and the wheels began to fold up into the wings. And the plane began to settle. The throttle had slipped back, the power had dropped, I was no longer flying. The plane touched the runway with a scream of offended metal, a blade of the propeller broke away and skittered across the runway, and we skidded to a stop, one wing down, in a cloud of dust. I sat in the cockpit, helpless with misery. I had busted another one. At this rate, I thought, I'll be a Japanese ace before the war is over. Then the crash truck was there, and I climbed out. Far down the runway I could see Edwards and Campbell still running; they must have jumped before the plane stopped sliding to have got that far. Then I realized that I had crashed with all those bombs and rockets, and I wanted to run, too. But it didn't seem right, after I'd wrecked that poor plane, to run away from it. I waited for a jeep and rode back to the squadron in wretched silence.

The C.O. dealt with my misdeed in what seemed then, and seems now, an exemplary way. He grounded me for a week and put me to work salvaging the wreck with a couple of mechanics. I tore up my knuckles taking off spark plugs, I covered myself with grease and oil, and I learned a good deal about how a TBM is put together. It was like sending a hit-run driver to work in a hospital. By the end of the week I was so sorry for that dead plane that I'd have given it a funeral if I could. I said as much to Kelleher. 'Forget it,' he said, 'it's over. Never look up a dead horse's ass.'

The rains began in late May. Clouds slid in from the China Sea, and lay low and motionless over the island, and the rain fell heavily and ceaselessly, day after day. I would wake at night and hear the rain droning on the tent roof, and wonder if it would ever stop, and fall back asleep to the dull sound of the rain, and wake to find that it was morning—dark, gray, and the rain still falling.

We lived in a world of water and mud. The company street ran first in rivulets, then streams, until it became a bog of gluey mud that sucked at your feet as you walked. Tent roofs sagged with the wet, and dripped where you touched them, and tent floors were slick with mud. Foxholes filled slowly, like bathtubs. We were always wet. Bedding never dried, and clothing never dried, so that night and day our bodies were always in contact with something damp and unpleasant to the touch. When we went out we wore suits of Navy rain gear—rubberized parkas and baggy pants that were clammy and cold, and high rubber boots; but the rain found entrances, streamed down our faces and necks, and in at our sleeves. Rain became the medium we lived in, a part of our air.

In the rain the airstrip looked like a dirt road to nowhere. Water stood in ponds on the runway, and the taxiways were rivers. Nothing was flying, no planes moved on the flight line, and no human beings were in sight. Our Turkeys sat in rows with their wings folded, like wet, melancholy birds. The air-raid sirens were silent—the Japs were grounded, too, and were not even sending suicide attacks against the fleet. It was as though man's gift for flight had been withdrawn from him, and he had been returned to earth and water, and to primeval mud.

The roads on the island quickly became impassable, slippery in the high places and flooded in the hollows. Every road to the front was jammed with stalled trucks, tanks, and jeeps, mile-long lines of them, motionless and abandoned. Only the shelling went on, very muted and distant in the rain, but audible, if you listened—the rumble of shells from the fleet, and the more staccato sound of the field artillery. Sometimes at night, even through the rain, you could see the flicker of shellfire along the southern horizon, like summer lightning.

As the rain continued and the roads remained clogged with mired vehicles, the troops in the line began to run short of supplies. Our squadron was given the task of delivering those supplies by parachute drops over the lines, and for nearly a month we delivered everything that reached the front lines: food, water, ammunition, medical supplies, even a telephone switchboard.

We would take off in the rain, splashing through puddles that threw sheets of water back over the cockpit, and climb to the base of the hanging clouds—five or six hundred feet, most days—and slide into a loose formation and head south, toward the lines. There a controller on the ground took over by radio and directed the flight toward the drop area, where a colored panel spread in a field or a smudge of colored smoke identified the exact place for the drop. As we rumbled along over the low hills, I looked down into what seemed the ruins of an ancient, peaceful world—tiny fields and old stone walls, deep, narrow lanes lined with gnarled old trees, a heap of stones where a house had been, all very close under our wings, everything clearly visible, even in the rain. I wondered where it ceased to be American-held, and became enemy territory, and what the Japs would do to me if I were shot down there.

When the flight leader had located the marker, the flight would string out into a long column and the leader would begin his pass. His bomb-bay doors would open, and as he passed over the marker the bundles of supplies would tumble out and behind him the parachutes would open—bright-colored, like flowers against the dark, wet earth, settling gently toward the ground—and more and more chutes as the other planes followed.

To drop supplies this way successfully you must fly over the target low and slow, and in a level straight line. If you fly too fast, the chute will split when it opens; if you aren't straight and level, it may entangle itself in the bomb bay. You must calculate the wind and correct for it, or you may deliver your supplies to the wrong army. You settle into your run, the marker ahead and just to one side. It slides under your nose, and you open the bomb bays and begin to count. You feel exposed, the plane maybe five hundred feet from a Japanese gun, the belly open, the airspeed dropping. It seems that a Jap with a good throwing arm could hit you with a rock. You wait, counting. Now! The weight drops free and the plane lifts, you throw the throttle forward, the plane surges, and you swing north, away from trouble, and head for home. It has all taken less than an hour.

The squadron flew nearly five hundred of those drops during that rainy stretch; my logbook says that I flew nine in the first five days of June. It was surely the most useful thing we did during the whole campaign.

While the rain fell, air raids ceased, but in their place we began to have shelling. One gun, hidden from the spotting planes during the good weather, could now be run out of its cave, fired for a few minutes, and hidden again before it could be located. The shelling could come at any time—in the night, while we were at lunch, or just as we taxied out to fly a para-chute drop. There was no warning—just the first whuff of the distant gun, the descending shriek of the shell, and the explo-sion. Other shells would follow as the gunner worked his way around Kadena, aiming blind and changing direction slightly for each firing. We called him Pistol Pete, and his presence, down there in the hills in the rain, became a part of existence.

Pistol Pete caused two kinds of fear. One was the steady, subliminal fear that you felt when he wasn't shelling, the fear that soon, now—right now—as you crossed the road, exposed and helpless, the shriek would sound and the shell would fall, carrying your death. It was a terrible game that we all played. *Now!* (walking down the hill to the head). No, *now!* (sitting at dinner). No, *now!* Always the thought that at this very mo-ment you might have finished all your living. The other kind was the fear that came while the shells were falling. It was deep and clutching, like a seizure. I sat in the foxhole with Rock during a shelling, and though he was a brave man he was shak-ing uncontrollably. None of us was surprised or shocked; we all felt the same, though it had not seized our bodies that way. And we were right to be frightened; before Pete was silenced he had wounded seven of our men.

The rain ended; it was June, summer weather, flying weather. The squadron grew restless. For two months we had been fly-ing hard—two or three hops, some days—but they had been local, unspectacular flights—a strike against a cave or a hidden gun, supply drops, antisubmarine patrols. In one month we had flown a thousand combat missions and had dropped a hundred tons of supplies. We had delivered mail, sprayed the island with DDT, dropped propaganda leaflets behind the enemy lines. These had been useful services, and we might have argued that 232 was the most useful squadron on the island; but usefulness is only a military virtue among the upper echelons—generals cherish it, but second lieutenants don't. We had been raised on movies like *Dawn Patrol* and *Wings*, and for a year or more in flight school we had been handed the Navy's literature—all those glossy leaflets with titles like 'Winning Your Wings of Gold.' Military flying, these sources agreed, was bombing and shooting, sinking carriers and sending planes down in flames; it was daring, not utility, that counted. After all those services we wanted a bit more daring in our lives.

Down at the southern end of the island our strikes were less and less necessary as the Army and Marines tightened their ring around the last defenders. The Japanese fought on, but the battle was really over; they had no more guns, and their caves and tunnels were blasted and burned out one by one. Shuri Castle had fallen. There was nothing left but the killing, and the infantry could do that. We flew our last strike on the island against some trivial target on June 19th; Joe came back to assure the intelligence officer that he had got a direct hit on a three-hole privy. On the 21st Admiral Nimitz, commander of the combined attack forces, announced that organized resistance had ended and that the island was secure. We heard stories, afterward, of what those last days had been like for the defenders, and of how at the end the senior officers had ceremoniously committed suicide. But we didn't know enough about the defense to know that it had been brilliant and courageous. All I felt when I heard those stories was incomprehension: How could men behave like that, when they had lost?

We began to fly strikes against neighboring islands—to Miyako and Ishigaki, south of us toward Formosa, and north to Kikai Jima and Amami o Shima. This was more like what we had expected—the massed flotilla of attacking planes, rumbling in formation toward the invisible target, the high, nervous movements of the fighter cover, nothing else in sight but water and clouds. And then the island appears ahead, the planes slide into attack formation, the high-speed descent begins, the first plane peels off, and you really see the island for the first time, in your bombsight—a grove of trees on the right, an airstrip, a few buildings—and the tracers begin to rise lazily toward you, and little clouds of AA bursts hang in the air as you dive past, and you have dropped and are pulling away, over the trees toward the beach and safety.

They were classic, beautiful strikes, the feeling of planes and men relating in the intricate choreography of a strike-formation, the gut-knotting climax, and the long, calm return. What memory returns to me is images. On a flight to Ishigaki I look out over the formation, the planes invisibly linked together, a squadron, and the weaving fighters above us, and I feel the sun warm on my cockpit canopy, and I am content to be there; and a later moment, an image not of contentment but of heightened life—diving, the plane bucking in the troubled air, and the tracers rising.

But that strike, though it offers me such images, was the grimmest one I flew on. We returned to Kadena to learn that the fighters had lost planes—five? ten? I have forgotten how many—and all to stupidity. Some of the Corsairs had carried bombs with proximity fuses. Once such bombs are armed (a wire is removed from the fuse) a small propeller on the nose begins to turn. When it has turned a certain number of revolutions, the bomb begins to send out radio impulses, and when they return, bounced back from some solid surface, the bomb explodes. If you arm the bomb as you attack, and drop it, its impulses will bounce back as it nears the ground, and it will explode in the air and scatter shrapnel; it is therefore useful against troops, parked planes and vehicles, and supplies. But these bombs had been rigged incorrectly, the arming wires had dropped out in flight, and the bombs began transmitting impulses too soon, before they were dropped. When those impulses returned, bounced from another plane, the bombs exploded, and plane after plane was blown from the sky. I saw none of this—the bomb-carrying Corsairs were either ahead or behind our formation—but we heard the story when we landed, and felt the rage that other pilots felt, that a fool of an armament officer, who never left the ground to get shot at, should have killed good men.

The beauty and the stupid deaths are both parts of the whole. I grieved for the dead men, and I hated the unnecessariness of their dying. But the images that the mind cherishes remain beautiful.

We flew a strike against Amami, and there I got the only certain direct hit on anything that I can remember—two bombs dropping precisely through the roof of a building, and quite effectively destroying it. But what was in the building? Radar equipment, we were told, and certainly there was an antenna near by; but it might have been a barn or an abandoned warehouse, or almost anything. It might have been a barracks; perhaps there were men in it, but I don't think so, and of course I want not to think so. Being a bombing pilot, I had never had to set out to kill anyone, or to think of human beings as my target. I discouraged my gunners from firing at random when we flew against little islands like Amami, which lay so peacefully in the summer sea, and looked as though it must be occupied by peaceful people—a few farmers, maybe, and a couple of radar men who kept a garden, and wrote haiku about loneliness.

Kikai, across a narrow strait from Amami, was more military —it had a bombed-out airstrip, and the guns around the strip were manned by skillful gunners. Like the gunners back at Yap, they conserved their ammunition, only fired at sure targets, and never used tracers; so you never knew that you were being shot at until you felt the shells hitting your plane. We flew strikes against Kikai occasionally, bombing the strip just to keep it out of operation, but we were cautious there—get in, drop, and get out, away from the hidden guns.

As the strike targets were extended, our ambitions grew grander. Shipping was reported near the China coast. Why not a torpedo attack? After all, we had lugged torpedoes with us all the way from the far south, from somewhere before Ulithi (nobody in the squadron was sure exactly where we had acquired the damn things). It would be a long flight, very near the limit of our range, but it would be glorious—a chance to sink ships. But when the armament officer examined the torpedoes, he found that they were all dry—someone had drunk the fuel (they ran on alcohol). And before bombs could be substituted, the flight was cancelled; maybe the ships weren't really there, or maybe they were sunk by the Navy. They might even have been our own.

We returned to our bombing attacks against nearby islands. On one of these Joe took a bullet through his engine cowling that hit an oil line, and on the way home he gradually lost oil pressure until, as the flight crossed the eastern coast of the island, his engine stopped dead. Below him was a new airstrip, just being finished, and he glided down and made a fine dead stick landing there. He came back to Kadena later that day in a jeep, in very high spirits; he had spoiled the Colonel's Grand Opening, he said, and the Colonel was very pissed off. It had been arranged that the Colonel commanding our group would land the first plane on the new field the next day, thus officially opening it; but Joe had got there before him. Still, as Joe said, the Colonel would be the first to land a plane with its engine running.

The next day the squadron was told to prepare to leave Kadena. Henceforth we would operate out of Awase, the new field that Joe had just initiated. His forced landing seemed an appropriate beginning to a new kind of life.

Chapter Ten

MOVING FROM Kadena to Awase was like moving from the frontier to the suburbs. Kadena had been built in a hurry, while the war was being fought a mile or two away, and it had a hasty feeling, even after months of village life. The tents still had dirt floors, and every tent had its foxhole; the shower was still an oil drum, and officers and enlisted men still ate together in one mess tent. It was an agreeable kind of place, and I was happy there. But it was primitive—there was no denying that—and we moved to Awase with a sense of upward mobility.

Awase had been built like a real-estate development. Along the beach, at the edge of the eastern anchorage called Buckner Bay, ran the airstrip—new, hard-surfaced, and longer than we were used to. The Air Force had installed a P-51 squadron there, on the east side, by the water; we were to have the west side. Inland from the strip the land rose steeply in irregular, treeless hills. Roads had been built up into these hills, and the squadron quarters were scattered along the roads, like development houses. The roads even had development-sounding names—Roosevelt Road, Admiral Something Street, General Somebody Boulevard. They had been named, we were told, by the former congressman from Minnesota who commanded the base.

Our squadron area was high up, on a hilltop with a view of the field and the harbor. We had Quonset huts, tents with floors and screens, a mess hall with a separate officers' mess and an ice machine, electric lights, a hot-and-cold shower, even a laundry, staffed by flat-faced, gold-toothed, grinning native women. There were no foxholes, and we didn't dig any; it would have been like digging a foxhole in Edina, or Great Neck. It was summer 1945, the island was secure; it was a time and a place to be soft. We lay in the sun, drank in the evenings, and flew uneventful antisub patrols and mail runs, and occasionally an unnecessary strike to neutralize an already bombed-out island. It was like summer vacation, when we were kids

—the sun always shining and hot on the skin, nothing much to do, the rhythm of life slowed.

For the moment our war had ended, and we lived a pleasant, suspended life while we waited for it to begin again somewhere else. The next assault, we knew, would be against the home islands of Japan; and we had heard from someone in group headquarters, who had it from someone in the wing, that our squadron would be the first bombing squadron to be based on Kyushu, as it had been the first one on Okinawa. When I thought about what that would be like, I felt doomed, with a Japanese fatalism. I imagined the desperate defense of the homeland, the suicide attacks, the fierce concentrations of AA fire. The whole population would fight against us. In my imagination farmers attacked with pitchforks, crying 'Banzai!' and geisha girls held grenades between their inscrutable thighs; every object was a booby-trap, and all the roads were mined. We would all be killed, I thought, by fanatics who had already lost their war. We would die a month or a week before it was all over; come all this way and die at the end of it, stupidly.

But now it was summer, and we lived a summer life. We wandered the hills above the camp, and found in the highest hill a tunnel, cut through the rock of the hill's core, that led to a chamber with gun ports overlooking the valley. Japanese defenders had crouched here with their weapons, scanning the valley, waiting for an attack that came another way. Looking through those slits in the rock was like looking through their eyes—you could imagine the expected battle, the machine-gun fire pouring down on troops as they toiled up the slope below. And you could imagine the lone despair of waiting, guarding those empty hillsides against an enemy who never came. Now the tunnel and the room at the end were empty too; only a sad dampness, the smell of cellars and funeral vaults, filled it. This one defensive post was the only sign around us that Japanese soldiers had lived here, that a war had been fought on this ground. All the other evidences had been erased, swallowed by the American suburb in which we lived and waited.

In our suburb the new mess hall with its officers' section and its ice machine was our country club; it was inevitable that we should have a Saturday night dance there. Women existed on the island; a few men had even seen them—nurses, mostly, in the hospitals that the war had filled. An invitation was sent, and on the Saturday night busloads of women appeared. They were of all sizes and shapes and ages, most of them rather plain-looking. I was surprised that after all these months away from women I still thought these plain; the myth of the Pacific war was that after a while even the natives turned white and became beautiful. A band began to play, drinks were poured, dancing began. I remember Sly engaged in an intricate bit of jitter-bugging with a stout nurse—and how comical her sensible nursing shoes seemed in those steps.

But most of us just stood around, watching. Nobody competed for the women—there were far fewer of them than of us, but we seemed to sense who wanted them most, and the rest of us drifted away after a while, up the hill to the Quonset hut, and started a card game. I could hear the dance music through the open door, like the sound of peacetime, the sound of our world before the war. I remembered Spring Lake Casino at Lake Minnetonka, and how when you walked with your girl along the beach the music followed across the water, all those songs that seemed so tender then—'Green Eyes,' 'I'll Never Smile Again,' 'Perfidia'? We sat there, in the hut, and down the hill the band played; but we didn't go back to the dance. Nobody wanted to fight for a dance with a plain stranger; nobody wanted to make love to one.

We had been away from women then for nearly a year, yet I felt no sexual need and neither, apparently, did anyone else. In all those months I could only remember two incidents that were explicitly sexual—the quiet man at Ulithi who wrote pornography, and the stud's guilty night with the Red Cross girl at Saipan. We were young men at the peak of our sexual powers, but those powers slept. The native Okinawan women—grinning, gold-toothed, perhaps obliging for all I know—were not looked upon as sexual partners at all (though there was a story around that some enlisted entrepreneur had established a makeshift brothel somewhere); and though the nurses had been at hand for months, no one had sought them out until the dance. Is it really true, then, that sex is a form of aggression like war, and that one form drives out the other? Were we living our sexual lives in the bombing and strafing? Or in the comradeship of the all-male, committed life of the squadron?

I only know that for nearly a year we lived like monks—hard-drinking, obscene monks, but poor, obedient, and chaste.

Being Americans, with time on our hands, we set about to furnish and domesticate the camp, as we had done at Kadena, but this time in a more suburban way. The squadron's radar officer, our best scrounger, appeared one day with a truckload of plywood. He didn't particularly want plywood; nobody in the squadron wanted plywood; but if you were a good scrounger you scrounged first, and then found a use for whatever you turned up. We decided to build a sort of barroom at the end of our Quonset hut BOQ. The plywood made a dividing wall and covered the sides and the end. Somebody borrowed a blow torch and ran the flame over the plywood walls, giving, he claimed, a desirable decorator's effect of knotty pine (actually it looked more like burned plywood than anything else). A bar was built in one corner, and a poker table in another, covered with a green blanket that looked, to the casual eye, like green felt. We had everything we needed for a club except liquor.

The quartermaster solved that problem. He heard of an Air Force squadron based in the Philippines that was going home, and he bought the entire contents of their club bar.

'A bargain,' he assured us. 'You put up ten bucks, you get five bottles. If you don't want it, trade it for souvenirs.'

'Five bottles of what?' Rock asked suspiciously.

'How do I know? Whatever the Air Force drinks. Don't worry, it'll make you drunk.'

Eventually the stock arrived, and was delivered, rather ceremoniously, by the quartermaster and a couple of enlisted men. Box after box marked FRAGILE—GLASS was unloaded outside the Quonset, and as the stock grew we began to feel like millionaires, with all that booze. Then the divvying-up began. There was, we discovered, almost no whiskey; the Air Force types had drunk that before they left. What there was was rum, sauterne, sherry, crème de menthe, curaçao, crème de cacao. Rock got kümmel, in a bottle shaped like a sitting bear. Joe drew rock-and-rye, and stood holding the bottle up to the light, staring in a baffled way at the lumps of rock candy inside.

Some of these liquors we had never seen before, except maybe behind a bar, and we didn't know how you drank them.

But they were all we had, and we settled down to find out. The party that night was memorable. There was a poker game that lasted until breakfast, and a fight in the course of which three cots were broken, and Joe invented two new choruses of 'Bless 'em All.' Even Billy Childers came, with his five bottles, and joined in the singing. When we sang one of our familiar songs, he would decorate the pauses between the choruses with traditional witticisms from his Mississippi country past. We'd be singing, say, a chorus of the endless limerick song, maybe the one about the man from Saint Paul, who went to a fancy-dress ball, and Billy would come in at the end, very drunk, with 'Do you wet yo'r hair in the morning, daughter?' 'No, mother, I pee through a straw,' or 'Don't cut no firewood tonight, mother—I'm comin' home with a load.' And then he'd look around, smiling, as though he'd said something original and funny. It seemed to be a part of the ritual of collective drunkenness, as practiced in Mississippi.

Next morning most of the new stock of booze was gone. Joe's rock-and-rye bottle had only some sticky lumps in the bottom, and the sitting bear, empty now, was on the Quonset hut roof. What was left was mainly things like green crème de menthe, liqueurs that even a drunk man could see weren't drinkable in large quantities. Later on, when there wasn't anything else to drink, we tried the crème de menthe poured over the shaved ice that we got from the mess hall ice machine— Billy called the drink a 'green frappie,' said it was like what he used to get in the drugstore back home—but nobody could bear to drink enough of it to do him any good.

We went on flying. Sometimes it seemed that we flew simply because we always had flown; that we were a machine that couldn't run down. We flew strikes against islands that now are only names—Gaga Shima, Kume Shima. We hunted Japanese radar installations on the little islands that ran north in a chain toward Kyushu, and attacked buildings and antenna towers with bombs and rockets. We went on flying the interminable antisub patrols, and never saw a sub, though Feeney found a small boat full of men, dropped a depth charge, the only bomb he had, and blew the boat in two. The men were wearing green hats and trousers, he said, but not shirts; but they must have been soldiers, trying to escape from the island, didn't we think so? He was very worried that they might have been civilians, just trying to get away from the Americans, or going fishing or something. We said they were almost certainly escaping Japs. The intelligence officer was pleased to have something new to report, and wrote in his log: 'Approx. seven (7) bodies were left lying motionless in the water.'

The impulse to do something spectacular, which had almost sent the squadron ship-hunting in the China Sea, was still strong in us. If not ships, well then, the Japanese mainland. Kyushu was barely within range of our planes, and we'd have to hit the extreme southern tip if we were to get back to Okinawa, but we could do it, and we'd have bombed Japan. A target was chosen—an airfield on the southern coast of the island—and a strike was launched. There was no particular reason to bomb that target. Surely the Navy and the Air Force's B-29's had been hitting it for months, and anyway the Japanese were virtually out of aircraft, and their fields were no serious threat to us. The strike wasn't really an attack; it was a sightseeing expedition, something to tell the grandchildren; it was as though we were getting ready, now that the war was near its end, to become boring old soldiers, full of interminable war stories and lies.

Everybody was excited by the plan, everybody wanted to go, and I was disappointed and angry when I wasn't chosen, and even felt a touch of satisfaction that the weather was going to be awful; with a little luck, I thought, they won't even find Kyushu. They did, but under a storm front that covered the island with low, solid cloud. They couldn't find their target, headed for another field, couldn't find that one either, and were about to head for home when someone saw an airfield through a hole in the clouds. Any target was better than lugging the bombs home again, and they straggled through the hole and dropped. They had bombed Japan, but nobody could be much more precise than that.

In mid-July the squadron tried another strike against Kyushu. This one was to be led by Jimmy, and all my friends—Rock, T, Joe—went, but once more I was left out. This time there would be an elaborate fighter cover, forty-eight Corsairs over the twelve TBM's; it was going to be a show, something to remember. The fighters took off first and circled in divisions of four, stacked up in the blue summer air above the field. Our planes were delayed, and by the time they were airborne the fighters didn't have enough fuel left to make it to Kyushu and back; and so the strike was diverted to the airstrip at Kikai. We had flown an eighteen-plane strike there the week before, and there couldn't be anything left that was worth bombing, only the patient gunners waiting for a sure shot. But once you have started such an elaborate operation you have to send it somewhere, if only to get rid of the bombs, and Kikai was handy.

I hung around on the hill, watching the squadron take off. It was hot and sunny, and after they had joined up and left I took off my shirt, and brought a chair out into the sun and tried to read. But I couldn't. It was too quiet on the hill—everyone else seemed to be on the strike—and I felt restless, up there alone, waiting for my friends to come back. The ordinary air traffic moved around the field—a P-51 took off, sounding like an intent insect; a night-fighter landed. Down on the line a mechanic ran up an engine, up and up to a high scream like pain, and then suddenly back to a hoarse whisper. Then there was silence, only the hum of summer, and I waited in the sun.

I heard the flight before I saw it, a steady rumble out of the north, and then I could see them, first only a line, at eye level from where I stood on the hill, then separate planes, in tight formation, a column of three-plane V's, close, steady, and formal-looking. But in the last V there were only two planes, and the empty space seemed an enormous emptiness, like a catch in the breath, a skipped heartbeat. One plane was down somewhere—in the sea, or wheels-up on a beach, or crumpled in the rubble at Kikai field.

I waited. I could have gone down to the Operations tent and heard the story, but I stayed on the hill, and put off knowing. The pilots would land, they'd be debriefed by Intelligence, and then they'd come up to their quarters, and I'd hear then.

It was Joe who was missing, and he was dead. He had dived in his turn over the target, and had flown straight into the ground. Not even the beginning of a recovery, just straight in. He must have been killed in the air, Jimmy said, shot dead as he flew; otherwise he'd have got the plane somehow into level flight, and out to sea, as good a pilot as he was. There had been no explosion when he hit, and no fire—just the smash, like a car against a wall, or a tree falling.

In a month the war was over. The atom bombs were dropped, though we got only sketchy and confusing reports of what the bomb was exactly, and what it did to Hiroshima and Nagasaki. We were relieved; we told each other, drinking in our plywood bar, that we were relieved. But we were saddened, too, though we didn't talk about that. Our common enterprise had come to an end; the invasion of Kyushu, and our flaming deaths in combat, would not take place.

Our war ended officially on August 12th, and that afternoon we launched every plane that would fly in what my logbook calls Victory Flight, a sweep out over the fleet anchorage in a huge V–formation. The bay was crowded with ships, motionless at anchor; they looked very peaceful and tranquil in the August sun, as though they would never steam out to sea again, or fire a shell, or spray up tracers against attacking planes. It was a painting of a fleet that we flew over that hot, late-summer day; the fleet itself belonged to the past. We finished the sweep and turned, and the flight leader signaled us into a column. We dove back toward the ships below us, as though in an attack, and then, to my astonishment and alarm, the lead plane pulled suddenly up and heaved itself over into a portly barrel-roll—a sort of parody of a fighter pilot's Victory Roll. It was like seeing a fat lady somersault—it seemed impossible, it was certainly unwise, but she was doing it. The second plane followed, and the next, and it was my turn.

The TBM was not built for acrobatics: the wings would not bear negative stress, and if I faltered in the roll while the plane was upside down I would surely pull both wings off, and plunge into the bay. I told my crew to hang on, pulled the nose up sharply, and rolled. The plane seemed to resist at first, and then resignedly entered the roll. A year's accumulated rubbish flew up from under the floorboards, and I could hear loose gear rattling around in the tunnel behind me; I wondered how poor Edwards was surviving back there. Then we were rolling out, swooping up toward level flight, the horizon returned to its proper place, and I joined up on the plane ahead of me. So much for Victory.

It was a stupid thing to have done, but I understand why we did it—why it was, in a way, necessary. We were giving Death the chance that he'd missed at Kyushu. We had survived a war, and all the ways that airplanes can kill you, and we were going one step further, stretching our luck. Some of the sadness was in it, too; from now on our lives would never be daring and foolhardy again.

That night every gun—every AA gun, every machine gun, rifle, and pistol—seemed to be firing into the sky. Everyone was out in the company streets, outside tents and Quonset huts, firing into the air, drinking and yelling and firing the shells and bullets that they'd never need again. The air was full of noise and the red tracks of tracers, and falling shrapnel. It wasn't safe to be out there, and some prudent pilots crawled under the Quonset hut, regretting that they hadn't dug fox-holes. I was ashamed to be so chicken, but I lay inside on my cot, listening to the spent bullets dropping on the tin roof, and thinking how ironic it would be to be killed tonight. Three or four men were killed before the night was over, most of them accidentally, but one—an unpopular Sergeant Major—almost certainly by intention, shot in the back in the uproar. It was an hysterical, frightening night, a purging of war's emotions.

The war was over, but the flying wasn't. The Navy's PBY's, which had flown the night-time antisub patrols, were sent to Japan to fly American prisoners out, and we took over their patrols. Some subs, we were told, were still at sea, hadn't heard that the war was over, might yet sink an American ship. The Seventh Air Force sent down ambiguous instructions—we were to continue to fly armed, but were not to attack unless fired upon, and were not to take shots at Japanese planes or attack ground targets. It was odd, like being halfway in and halfway out of war.

Night searching was a gloomy, fearful business. The weather had turned hot and stormy, the way it does sometimes in August, and every night there were squalls and thunderheads over the sea. The nights were black, without moon or stars or horizon line; even the lightning, which lit the piled clouds with a cold white light, didn't reach the darkness of the sea. My sector was a long triangle over the China Sea—west toward China, then north, then back to the island. As soon as the plane was airborne the lights of the island disappeared, and we entered the blackness. I reported on station, and the voice of the controller came back, but so broken by crashing static that though

it was audibly human, it spoke in meaningless syllables: 'Hel
. . . Four . . . ver. . . .'

I flew among the thunderheads as I would among mountains, watching ahead when the lightning flashed, altering
course to avoid the mountains and fly the valleys. (A tall thunderhead is full of violent vertical currents; it will tear a plane
apart, hurl the pieces up and down, and scatter them over the
sea.) In the tunnel Edwards searched with his radar for submarines, but among such storms it was a useless exercise; only the
thunderheads appeared on his scope, as bright as battleships,
and more dangerous. In that electric atmosphere the plane itself became charged, and balls of Saint Elmo's fire rolled up
and down the wings, and whirled on the propeller. Lightning
flashed, and for a time after each flash I could not read my
instruments, and had to fly blindly, holding the plane on its
course by feel until sight returned.

I was more afraid that night than I have ever been in the air.
Fear is probably always there, subliminally, in an experienced
pilot's mind; it is a source of that attentiveness that keeps you
alive. But only rarely does it thrust itself into your consciousness. This never happened to me on a strike—I felt keyed up,
tense, abnormally aware of the plane, but not exactly afraid
—but it happened on those night patrols over the China Sea.
I felt fear then; but I also felt something else—resentment,
outrage that I was out there, with the war over, alone and
half-blind with lightning and blackness, that I might die out
there, on a pointless exercise in the dark.

I flew my last night patrol on my birthday, August 29th; and
when I got back, toward midnight, we had a party—liquor
had become a little easier to find by then—and I got pretty
drunk. I was twenty-one, I kept telling everyone, and I was
old enough to drink. I guess I must have used that line too
often, or maybe it was something else, but at the end of the
evening I found myself fighting with Rock. We struggled up
and down the Quonset hut, over people's cots, and sometimes
under them, wrestling (we couldn't really have hit each other),
grunting, cursing, until at last he won, and sat straddling my
chest the way a fight used to end in school. Then we got up
and had a drink. If you have a fancy for symbolism, you could
find some there; I had reached manhood and lost a fight on the

same night; or, the war was over, and friends turned to fighting each other. Probably either reading would be a bit heavy, but I was sorry I had that fight. I don't think I cared about losing it, much.

Summer turned into fall. The trees on the hillsides above the strip turned brown and gold, and the nights were cooler, but the days were fine and clear, only with that metallic look that blue skies have in autumn. Our lives were aimless, without the momentum of war, and we spent our time mostly just waiting for the orders that would send us home. Flying was only another form of idleness—flying around and around the field testing an engine, or to another field on the island to deliver some mail, or for no reason at all, just to be doing something. Some pilots I knew flew to Japanese-held islands, and landed, and were received with formal courtesy; and there were several round trips to Kyushu, to the airfields we had never been able to find. But I didn't go on any of these tourist trips; I had had enough of islands.

In that fine autumn weather I might have taken a good look at the island on which I had lived for nearly six months. I could have walked over the ruins of Shuri Castle, or I might have driven north, into the steep, quiet valleys that the war had never reached. But I didn't; I stayed there in our tent at Awase, doing nothing, feeling emptied of all motives. A squadron of F7F's arrived—the first we had seen—and I went down to the line to look one over, but I didn't try to wangle a checkout flight. I went on flying Turkeys some, but there wasn't much fun in it anymore. The machine had run down at last.

The Navy announced the system by which we would be returned to the States. It involved an elaborate counting of points —so many for each month overseas, so many for each medal, so many for each dependent. The junior officers in the squadron had all come to the war together, so there was no competition there. And we all had the same medals, earned the same way— five strikes for an Air Medal, twenty for a Distinguished Flying Cross. It was embarrassing to get medals for such humdrum, unheroic actions; but each medal was worth five points in the system. The only variable among us was the number of dependents. Some of us were married and got points for that. A few, like T, had a child (a son, born to his wife in Birmingham in

June), and that put them ahead of the rest. It seemed a good enough system, and nobody complained. We just calculated our scores, figured the order of departure, and waited.

Senior pilots began to leave; there were drinking parties in their tents, and then they were gone, and we became senior, and moved into the tents they had vacated. T and Rock and I moved together, and got a fine tent, with a wooden floor and sides, screens, and electricity—more like a cottage than a tent, with a view of the bay. I thought of the first tent we had shared at Kadena—the dirt floor, the wheat under the cots, the kerosene lantern. Now Bergie and Joe were dead, the war was over, and we had a wooden floor. We found a new partner, an amiable giant from Mississippi named Ed, and settled in to wait for orders.

In the meantime we made ourselves comfortable. That is, we began again the process of accumulating and homemaking, partly for comfort's sake, but partly to create a special place to exist in, a place that was marked by the persons who lived there, that wasn't simply something that had been issued. Rock appeared one day with a Seth Thomas clock; he had traded a fifth of whiskey for it, so it must have been important to him. Once it had decorated an Okinawan shop, or perhaps a government office. It had a loud, imperative tick, and was always right, though it never really looked at home hanging on a post in a tent. I found a phonograph, and I traveled the island's chaplains' offices begging phonograph records, 'to help the troops pass the time.' I accumulated quite a large selection, very random, since I followed the first rule of scrounging and never refused a record; but I remember only one song, Billie Holiday singing 'Travellin' Light.' We made a bookcase out of shell-cases, and filled it with books. Most of them were government-issue paperbacks, often very peculiar choices for the circumstances (what committee had decided that the troops would want to read Joseph Hergesheimer's *Three Black Pennys?*); but we had a few hardcover books, too, my *War and Peace* from Honolulu, a copy of *The Fountain-head* that Liz had sent me, and a New Testament with a steel cover (you carried it in your breast pocket, and Jesus stopped the bullets, but we kept it in the bookcase).

September passed. The days were sunny, and warm at noon, with a haze at the horizon—like good fall days at home. We took books out into the sun, and talked instead of reading, and watched the planes around the field. The P-51's still flew a lot—obviously it was more fun to play at dogfighting and acrobatics in a fighter than to lumber around in a TBM—and we watched them idly, out over the bay, twisting and diving, catching the autumn sun on their silver wings. Two began a dogfight, and we stopped talking to follow their maneuvers, crossing, turning steeply, and diving back toward each other, neither getting an advantage, weaving back and forth as in a formal dance. And then they hit. There was no noise, no explosion or any of the accompaniments of violence; they simply seemed to enter each other for a moment, and to emerge broken. One plane dropped gently into a shallow dive, and flew at that exact and careful angle into the sea; as it dove, a figure fell free, and a parachute whipped out behind it, but the chute did not open, and the figure dropped with the chute-lines streaming, into the shallows of the bay. The other plane broke apart; a wing, separated from the body, fell slowly and weightlessly, like a falling leaf, turning over and over; the rest of the plane began to spin, winding tighter and tighter, the engine winding, too, in a rising whine until it struck the mud flat at the edge of the strip. The water and the mud received the wreckage and the bodies, and in a minute there was nothing to show that two men had died there. Nobody said anything. We had thought the casual dying was over.

On one of those fall days I flew to Kikai to look for the wreckage of Joe's plane—and to say goodbye to him. It was an odd, uncomfortable feeling, to approach that hostile island, and to fly low and slow over the gun emplacements from which my enemies, the careful gunners, had looked up at my squadron's planes, and had killed my friend. The airstrip had not been repaired, it was still what it had been, a heap of useless, broken concrete; but the camouflaged guns had been uncovered, and I was struck by how many there were, a ring of them around the field. As I flew slowly across the field, a man came out of a shed and waved. I rocked my wings. Hell, the war was over.

I found the wreck just south of the field, not far from the beach. The engine was buried in the earth—he must have hit at a steep angle, and at high speed—and the tail stood up in the air, like a monument. The wings had crumpled with the impact, but I could read the number painted on the tail; it was Joe's plane, all right. I felt I should do something; but I didn't know how a man grieves. The reticence that made my father so inarticulate in his loving—I had it too; it was as much a part of my inheritance as my name. I waited for my body to instruct me—to burst into tears, or a howl or a moan of misery—but it did nothing but fly the plane. Down there, under that wreckage, was the disintegrated body of a friend I had loved, a part of my life before the war, and all through it. I felt that part as a vacancy, but I couldn't express how that vacancy felt. There was nothing that I, up there in the plane, could do for him, down there. I flew around the wreck once or twice, very carefully (Nick Nagoda had killed himself flying around the wreckage of his friend's plane), and then turned south and headed home.

Along the northern coast of Okinawa I flew in close to the shore; I would probably never see that part of the island again. It was just as I had first seen it, a bit of peaceful northern landscape—rather like Norway as I imagined it—that had not been touched by the war; its steep wooded hills and narrow valleys were too rugged and too small-scale to interest generals or contain armies. I turned up a narrow, wooded valley, and saw a small house by the stream, and two or three people working in a garden. They looked up, as though they had never seen a plane before, and stood with their hands shading their eyes and watched me out of sight. I went on to Awase and landed, making the squadron approach automatically, the dive to the strip, the steep, impossible-looking bank, wheels and flaps down in the turn, the sharp, last-minute rollout as the plane stalled to the strip. It was still pleasing to land in that extravagant way—if you could make a Turkey behave like a fighter, you could really fly. But there really wasn't any point, any more.

Later on we heard from a Navy unit that had landed on Kikai—maybe to accept the Commanding Officer's sword or something, I suppose somebody had to go round to all those little islands so that they could surrender—anyway, someone had been there, and had seen Joe's grave. The Japanese had removed the bodies from the wreck, had given them a decent burial, and had placed above the graves a marker that read: 'In Memory of the Brave American Fliers.' That seemed right.

We woke one morning in late September to the sound of wind, the tent flapping, guy wires whistling. It was the typhoon season in the China Sea, and a storm was moving up from Formosa. Aerology said it would reach us in the early afternoon, but it never did, quite, though the edge of the storm that we got was violent, howling, and wet. It broke up some of our planes and beached some small boats; but we rode it out all right, our tent survived intact, and the squadron planes were repaired in a couple of days. Once the sky had cleared and we had dried out, we felt rather proud of ourselves, coming through a typhoon so easily—we were seasoned, Old China hands.

Three weeks later the real storm hit us. It began in the night, with a long, drenching rain; and then the wind began, driving the rain horizontally, with the force of buckshot. We closed and tied down the tent flaps and walked down to breakfast, leaning into the hard, punishing wind, hunched down in our foul-weather clothes. Afterward we sat in the tent, trying to think of what we could do, to be ready. This one was going to be a fierce one, and Aerology predicted that the eye of the storm would pass directly over the island. Already rain was driving in around the tent flaps. We went out into the gale and nailed the flaps to the frame. But still the rain came in, until the wooden floor was slick with mud and drops of water covered the blankets of our bunks like a fine dew. In the bookcase the books warped and swelled. The electric light flickered, brightened, and went out. Somebody stopped at the door to tell us that the anemometer on the control tower was reading one hundred knots and that the planes, which had been tied down facing into the wind, were actually airborne on the gale.

By mid-afternoon the tent was rocking on its pilings, like a small boat in a storm, and we were out in the storm again, putting up braces, ropes, and guy wires to hold the tent down.

And still the wind rose—we couldn't tell exactly what velocity it reached, but someone said the anemometer had been registering a hundred and fifty knots when it blew away. The wind was strong enough by then to peel sheets of corrugated tin off the Quonset hut roofs and hurl them through the air like whirling machetes. It could snatch up a tent and whip it off into the storm, and then tear away the plywood flooring and send it spinning after.

Visibility was down to a few yards—our world was our own tent and the Executive Officer's tent next door. Then his went, opening in the air like a parachute and disappearing downwind. The Exec grabbed what he could save and started toward us, and as we watched his progress through the storm the entire plywood floor lifted behind him and struck him to the ground. The giant Ed plunged out into the wind, lifted the flooring, and carried the Exec into our tent. He lay for an hour on a bunk, unconscious, while the wind howled and the rain came in. There was no way of getting him to a doctor, or a doctor to him.

The force of the wind had separated the threads of the canvas in the tent roof without tearing it, and you could stand inside the tent and look up and see a dim light from the sky. Rain soaked in, everything was wet—our beds, our clothing, all the books—the very air inside the tent was a mist of rain. But the tent still stood. We would not have been much worse off without it, but it seemed important that we should win against the storm. The guy wires twanged, and the tent shifted on its pilings; but it stood. It was still a tent and not a scrap of blown canvas; it was the place we had made for ourselves.

When the weather cleared, ours was the only tent in sight. Where the others had stood there were only the pilings of the floors and a few tent pegs. The Quonset hut where we had built our bar had slid down the hill twenty or thirty feet, and lay there at an angle, like a ship aground. The squadron buildings —supply tents, repair facilities, ready room, Operations—were all gone. Of our twenty-four planes, only five were flyable, and some of the others were beyond repairing. The airstrip was littered with wrecked planes and rubbish. Along the edge of the bay, naval vessels and flying boats were beached, some of them wrecked. All communication lines were down; the east coast of the island could not reach the west coast, and we couldn't even speak to our flight line.

The island was once more like a battlefield, the scene of a battle fought against wind and rain. But there was an odd exhilaration in the experience; officers and men had moved together into the mess hall and were sleeping there on the tables and on the floor, and there was only food enough for two meals a day, but nobody complained. The violence of nature was somehow amiable compared to the violence of war, even though ten men had died in the storm. To survive a war, and then two typhoons—there was a kind of immortality in that.

Ed stole a gallon of airplane paint, and we began to make our tent waterproof again. As I stood on a ladder painting the roof, I thought of the night-fighter pilot and his madness; I too had been driven to paint my tent blue.

My orders came a week later: 'When directed by the Commanding Officer, Marine Wing Service Squadron–2, you will stand detached from your present station and duties, and will proceed via first available government transportation to the United States.' But there was no transportation—it was on the beach at Buckner Bay, or blown out to sea. We went on waiting —excited at first to be going home, then indifferent, bored, just waiting for the Navy to do something with us, as we had waited so many times before. When a transport ship at last appeared, and we were ordered aboard, the excitement was gone; it was just another move.

There were ten or twelve of us on the orders—married men with two DFC's, I suppose, and no children. We had a party, and the radar officer gave me his last bottle of whiskey as a farewell present, and I was surprised and touched. But it wasn't much of a party. We were ordered to report somewhere at five A.M.—it struck me as a nice Marine Corps touch that my last orders should involve such an unreasonable hour—and we sat up through the night, drinking a little, dozing, feeling bored, and depressed to be bored when we were going home. It was still dark when we drove away from the squadron camp, down Eisenhower Boulevard (or was it Admiral Spruance Drive?) to the coast road, and on south to the landing area.

The ship, we were told, was a converted United Fruit banana boat. The conversion consisted of stacking bunks nine-high in the hold for the enlisted men, so close together that a man had to get into a horizontal position first in order to get into bed, and three-high, nine to a cabin, in the officers' quarters. We mustered, marched aboard, and waited. And after some delays and confusion, and a lot of roll-calling, the ship sailed. I have no memory at all of the sailing, no nostalgic images of Okinawa receding in the distance, nor even any feelings about the occasion. We just left. But my island had already ceased to exist —it was the island at war, the strikes, the gunfire to the south, Joe Baird laughing and singing, the feeling of a good, working squadron. That was all gone now. I wasn't leaving anything.

The ship was headed east, but nobody knew our exact destination, though there were many rumors. We were going to Pearl Harbor, and would have shore leave there. We were headed directly for San Francisco. We would sail through the Panama Canal and dock in Norfolk. One day followed another, and the ship rolled and pitched in the long Pacific swells, lifting its screw from the water with every swell, so that the ship shuddered and rattled (troops were not as heavy as bananas, though they were packed in nearly as tightly). Everyone was seasick, which was just as well, since there wasn't enough food to satisfy appetites of all the men on board. Officers were all right; we sat down three times a day to well-cooked meals, served on tables with linen cloths and silver cutlery. But the enlisted men were limited to two meals a day, often eaten standing up, or sitting on the deck. Junior officers were assigned as 'Mess Control Officers' to see that the men didn't eat more than one serving per meal, or take an extra orange. I took my turn with the rest of the second lieutenants, but I couldn't do the job conscientiously. I just stood at the mess-hall door and tried to look severe as the men came and went, but I never stopped anyone, not even the ones with two oranges.

We were at sea for seventeen days. We didn't stop at Pearl, and we didn't go through the Canal. We went back into the port from which we had left—San Diego. Point Loma on the left, North Island on the right, the circling planes, the berthed carriers, and then the dock—it was all the same, the film run backwards. As the ship tied up, music on the dock below began to play. We surged to the starboard rail, and there below us was a uniformed band and a drum majorette. She marched and twirled and threw her baton in the air, while the band played

'From the Halls of Montezuma.' It was as though we had won the war all by ourselves. More and more of the troops on board crowded to the rail to see the show. The ship began to list. Over the ship's loudspeaker an official voice spoke: 'Now hear this. Now hear this. The starboard head is flooded. The starboard head is flooded.' We were moved back away from the rail, the band stopped playing, and the drum majorette moved off to her next docking. We were home. And the starboard head was flooded.

Once more we returned to Miramar. In many ways it was still the same. I roomed with another drunk, who might have been the intelligence officer who introduced me to French 75's, but wasn't. I drank in the bar and tried to put through telephone calls to Liz and to my father, but couldn't, and went on drinking, and went back into the booth from time to time to quarrel with the long-distance operator. The same San Diego tramps were there, in the same low-cut dresses, drinking and talking in low voices to strangers. But it was profoundly different, too. There was no excitement now, no one waiting for orders to the war, no eager young men hanging around some veteran while he told them how it had been at Rabaul. We had all been there, somewhere, and we were through with it. It was like a locker room after a game, a game that you've lost. Or like the morning after a party, when you wake up and realize what you did last night, and how much of it can't be undone, ever.

In a week or so new orders came, and Rock and I and some other pilots checked out and went up to Los Angeles for one last party. Everything was familiar and stale; it was like starting a big evening with a hangover; it was the end of something that had been good, perhaps like the breaking up of a marriage. The train we rode was the same one I had traveled on the year before, with my crutch and my fat ankle; it was just as crowded, with what seemed to be the same people. Sailors sat on their seabags in the aisles and drank from whiskey bottles, and passed them along; babies cried. In Los Angeles the hotel was the same—the Santa Rosa, next to the best in town. We went out to Hollywood, and the same bands were playing in the bars. We drank a lot, and told people that we had just come back from the war, and I tried to teach a bartender to sing 'The Fucking Great Wheel.' Then I was on the street somewhere, explaining to a Shore Patrol why I was not in the proper uniform, telling him about the two typhoons, and how my dress greens had blown away (a lie, but easier than the truth, when you're drunk). Later we were together in a hotel suite, but it wasn't ours at the Santa Rosa. Everyone was drinking, and there were some girls in the other room. The girls were unhappy, they had expected a party; they wanted to go home, and somebody was saying, in a tired voice, 'All right, then, go home. Fuck you.' And the girls were crying.

Then it was dawn, another drunk dawn—How many dawns had I been drunk in?—and I was walking alone down some anonymous Los Angeles street that seemed to go on forever. The streetlights were going out along the block, and now and then a car passed, but there weren't any taxis, and I went on walking in the cold November morning.

It was hard to get out of Los Angeles then. The commercial airlines were filled with high-priority bigshots, and every military airbase had a mob of returned troops waiting around for a seat on a cargo or a transport plane going anywhere east. I found another pilot who was headed east, and together we managed to get a two-berth compartment on a train for Chicago. We had no dress uniforms, only our unpressed khakis and flight jackets, and we looked and felt like aliens in that elegant train. But we had our wings, and some ribbons now; and we wore them all above our shirt pockets, as witnesses that we had been there, and were coming home. The working clothes seemed to us worthy. Apparently they impressed others, too; my compartment mate met a California congressman's wife in the compartment next door, and disappeared for the rest of the journey.

I rode out from Chicago on the El, over the slums and the flat empty lots through the gray afternoon, to my parents' factory-town suburb, and took a cab to their house. I hadn't told them I was coming. I imagined a scene of surprise and joy as I turned up unexpectedly, just in time for a home-cooked American supper. But they weren't at the house. It was empty, and their name was gone from the mailbox; they had moved the day before, nobody seemed to know where.

When at last I found the new house, dinner was over, and they were sitting together amid the disorder of packing, looking tired and disoriented. I had to climb over rolled-up rugs and around furniture to reach them. My stepmother kissed me, and my father gripped my hand and said, 'Well. Well, well. You're back.' Then my stepmother flustered into the kitchen, where everything was still in boxes, and produced my first home-cooked meal—fried Spam. I ate it among the boxes and the piled dishes, while my parents told me that I was looking well. Then we sat in the living room for a while. The furniture was the same stuff I had grown up with—I remembered the sofa, and the oak rocking chair, and the pictures leaning against the wall—but it had grown unfamiliar in this new place. After a while we put a bed together and found some bedding, and I left them sitting there and went to bed.

In the day or two I spent there, my father tried to tell me his feelings. 'Son—' he would begin, but then he'd stop. A lifetime of not talking about feelings was too strong a habit to overcome. But I showed him the medals, and he was pleased, almost as pleased, I think, as if he'd won them; and I got out some photographs, and they seemed to make the war more actual for him, and my life credible. Nothing got said, but he managed, just by putting his big hand on my shoulder and saying, 'Son—' to express love and pride. We never played the homecoming scene that I had imagined, but it was all right.

But the house wasn't my house, and the town wasn't my town. And I was married. I caught a train for Birmingham, for the other reunion.

Because Liz was waiting in Birmingham, I chose to be discharged from active duty at Pensacola, and we rode down from Birmingham together, on the same slow, dusty train, stopping, as you always did, at Flomaton, and on down to the Gulf. But it wasn't simply convenience that had brought me back to Pensacola. I wanted to return just once, just for a few days, to that place where I had learned the only skill I had, and where I had been happy in that timeless world of young men, before the dying began. Perhaps the impulse to return is a sign that one has grown up, an acknowledgment of the way the good times pass us. We go back in space because we can't go back in time.

Pensacola was peaceful-looking in the winter sunshine; everything was bright with sun—the white-painted buildings, the sandy earth, the palm trees, the quiet waters of the bay. In that mild stillness the sound of planes was as distant and peaceful as the buzzing of insects on a summer afternoon. It was as if the whole place knew that the war was over, that there was nothing urgent left to be done.

I was still on flight orders, and entitled to flight pay if I flew four hours in a month; so when I had reported in I went over to the Main Side hangar to look for a plane. There I found another Marine pilot on the same errand, and one plane—an N2S Yellow Peril, the kind I had learned to fly in, back at Memphis. One tank of gas would last, if we stretched it, for just about four hours. We didn't know each other; neither had any particular reason to trust the other's flying; we had nothing to do and barely enough gas to do it; but we took off together to fly somewhere, anywhere, for four hours.

My companion climbed carefully over the lagoon and took a cautious, level course north, over the piny woods. It was the same featureless landscape over which I had navigated two years before, and I felt the same withdrawal from the actual world. He flew on for an hour, made a cautious turn, and flew back toward the field. When it came in sight I took over the controls and headed back out over the pines again. Time passed with excruciating slowness; there was nothing to see but the lengthening shadows of the pines, and we could not communicate from one cockpit to the other, even if we had had anything to say. The plane seemed to move as slowly as the hands of my watch.

As the end of the four hours approached, I turned toward the field, checking my watch nervously against the fuel gauge. It looked as though we could make it, but without much gas to spare. I circled the field, using up the last few minutes. By then it was evening, and the hangar cast a long shadow across the landing mat, and the water of the lagoon was dark. I began an approach to landing, letting down out of the last late sun into the twilight, and landed in shadow, and taxied to the parking ramp and shut down the engine. We both got out and walked silently to the hangar, and separated with scarcely a word. I think we must have had the same feelings. It was all over now, we were at the end of the adventure; we had become men with families and responsibilities and futures. The end of flying had made us mortal.

CROSSING THE LINE

A BLUEJACKET'S ODYSSEY
IN WORLD WAR II

Alvin Kernan

For my children

CONTENTS

INTRODUCTION

My qualifications for writing an introduction to Alvin Kernan's frank, vivid, and moving description of his experiences in the navy during World War II are as follows. After serving in several ships from a destroyer to a battleship, I too ended up, like Kernan, in an escort carrier in the western Pacific off Japan. We were both part of the Seventh Fleet, which was the greatest battle fleet ever assembled, under the command of Admiral Nimitz, and the most amazingly efficient organization I have ever seen in my life. My aircraft carrier, HMS *Chaser*, had been sent to serve in the Pacific, partly to help the Americans but mostly to make sure that, in a fit of anticolonial enthusiasm, they did not give Hong Kong back to the Chinese at the end of the war. In this we were successful, being the first ship to enter the harbor after the Japanese surrender.

Kernan and I joined our respective navies from noticeably different backgrounds. He was abruptly wrenched out of civilian life on a remote, isolated ranch in Wyoming and thrown into the traumatic experience of boot camp. I was similarly wrenched out of civilian life, but in my case this meant cozy rooms, good food, and a servant to wait on me, all of which were provided to prewar students at Oxford University. After boot camp at Shotley and nine months on the lower deck of HMS *Fiji*, I was sent back home for officer training and thereafter served in the comfortable, if alcoholic, atmosphere of a British naval officers' wardroom.

Kernan saw much action, exhibited great bravery, and was many times very nearly killed; once he even had to abandon his sinking ship. Although I was involved in several dangerous operations, including two convoys to Malta and two to Murmansk, my life was in imminent danger only once. Kernan served as a gunner on a plane, frequently in fierce combat, while I sat in a windowless office as senior aircraft controller, directing planes like his to their missions. But as I read his story, again and again I find myself thinking, yes, this is exactly how it was.

The author encapsulates the culture and ideology of the U.S. Navy of that time in a series of shrewd observations. For example, "Cleanliness was not next to godliness in the United States Navy; it was godliness." Boot camp, with its endless drill on the "grinder," was designed to force you "to put your individuality in storage. . . . Reasonable excuses were not part of this life." For me, on the other hand, the benefits of low cunning were also part of boot camp. I soon made an arrangement with the chief petty officer by which I would take charge of our squad after 1600, leaving him free to go home. In exchange, he left me alone all day—time which I spent reading Proust in the laundry (the only place where I could be both warm and safe from discovery). The culture of the U.S. Navy as described by Kernan is identical with that to be found in the British navy of the same period. More remarkable is the similar inefficiency of our navies' planes and, especially, the torpedoes with which both fleets were provided in the early stages of the war. (When I complained to a senior officer, he retorted that British torpedoes were excellent in peacetime—that is, on maneuvers—since they could be relied upon to come to the surface after firing and so to be used again!) Only the Japanese and the Germans seem to have been able to manufacture effective torpedoes. In the end, victory came from the sheer volume of military hardware, plus advanced radar, success in decoding, and, as at the Battle of Midway, to which Kernan devotes a riveting chapter, a lot of luck.

Kernan notes the brutality of life as a seaman during wartime, a life he describes as "healthy but in many respects like a chain gang." He reminds us that in times of crisis all hands were on four-hour shifts (four on, four off) throughout the day and night, so that one was perpetually tired. He also remembers the torments of heat rash in the tropics. Nor does he ever forget that "death lived on an aircraft carrier operating in wartime conditions." One day a plane would crash on takeoff; the next day a plane would crash on landing. And it was all too easy for one of the flight deck crew to take a false step and get chewed up by a propeller.

Sometimes "planes went out on patrol and were never heard of again." This was particular agony to me, as I called the plane for hours on the radio and listened as the signals became fainter and fainter, ending in a total silence. Kernan rightly lays great stress on the sheer boredom of life during the long stretches between the brief moments of sheer terror. He describes how the Americans spent their time playing cards for money, often all day long. It was mostly poker, and the gambling was for high stakes. The British did the same, but the stakes were very much lower. We could never have pulled off Kernan's last financial coup. We tended to play liar's dice, the loser buying drinks all round, and for a while we played endless games of Monopoly. The conversation, such as it was, was mostly about sex and girls, if only because they were in such short supply.

The author deals discreetly but frankly with the sexual problems and temptations for young sailors on periods of leave. Prostitutes were readily available in every naval base, but they were not always free from venereal disease. I do not know what happened in the Pacific theater, since our rear base was Sydney, Australia, but in the Mediterranean theater—in Algiers, Naples, Rome, etc.—the U.S. Army tried to deal with this problem by organizing medically supervised brothels, some for officers and others for enlisted men, as so vividly described in Joseph Heller's *Catch-22*. A young man has to lose his virginity sometime, and Kernan observes that "sex and war really initiate us into society," while the former provides some intense pleasure "in a world that offers a lot of dullness and pain."

But Kernan does not fail to mention the good times and the nobler aspects of a sailor's life in wartime. For example, "the instant love affair" with whatever ship one happened to be assigned to. He observes, correctly, that "to a young man war is exciting." At that age—eighteen, nineteen, twenty—we all thought that we were immortal. It was only the older men, worried about a wife and children, who were constantly afraid of death. There was no great hostility toward the Japanese, who, rightly, "were regarded as a worthy foe." Taken all in all, "we saw the war as a natural and rare chance to live life at least close to something great." The Seventh Fleet off Japan was one of the most amazing sights we would ever behold—a gigantic armada spread out over miles and miles of ocean, the vast assembly all dedicated to the destruction of Tokyo and Japan. At night, the phosphorescence of the water all around us was all that was visible of this stupendous array of warships.

This "handbook to life" is a brilliantly evocative, scrupulously honest, and extremely well-written description of naval life on the lower deck in World War II, comparable only, so far as I know, to the equally distinguished memoir of another aviator turned scholar, Samuel Hynes. If anyone wants to know what it was really like to serve in the U.S. Navy in World War II, these are the books to read.

Lawrence Stone

The first publication of *Crossing the Line* in 1994 brought a flood of welcome letters from people who remembered the events I described as intensely as I did. "How young we were," said most, and some brought me new information, such as how Al Capone's bullet-proof Cadillac limo got to Shanghai to provide transportation for the commanding officer. Others had different views of events from those I remembered. An intelligence officer wrote that my story about the plans for Midway circulating by scuttlebutt on the *Enterprise* a month before the battle simply could not have been true since it was the war's best-kept secret. I could only reply that on this matter my memory was firm and clear. Years afterward a discussion of the matter on the online Battle of Midway Round Table revealed that numerous people knew that we had the names of the Japanese ships and the battle plans. Cincpac, authorized by Admiral Nimitz, before the battle had sent out both an ULTRA radio communication and a standard coded description of the Japanese battle plans. The information was discussed at meetings in wardrooms, published on bulletin boards, and given to flight crews.

Vice Admiral William D. Houser, USN (Ret.), wrote that he had been in the antiaircraft batteries on the USS *Nashville* when it fired on the Japanese picket boats encountered as the *Hornet* was about to launch the Doolittle raiders on Tokyo. I had referred to the failure of a thousand six-inch shells to sink the pickets as "disgraceful." Vice Admiral Houser took exception to this term, explaining that "*Nashville* opened fire at long range on the wildly tossing craft and scored a number of hits. The gunfire straddled the small wooden ship but the shells were all armor piercing (AP) and thus hits passed through without exploding." Vice Admiral Houser also sent a copy of his letter and my book to Rear Admiral Harry Mason, USN (Ret.), who just happened to have been the fire control officer on the *Nashville* that day. He thought my story sounded like it had been told by Sinbad the Sailor or by my old ordnance chief, Murphy, befuddled by drinking his "moosemilk" compounded of coffee and bombsight alcohol.

In time the mail brought a book, too, Steve Ewing and John Lundstrom's *Fatal Rendezvous: The Life of Butch O'Hare* (1997), containing a thorough investigation of the night-fighter flight on which O'Hare was killed. Over the years a story had grown that I had shot O'Hare down, but Ewing and Lundstrom concluded that he had fallen to enemy fire. Understandably, this greatly relieved the guilt that I had carried over the years about the possibility that I had hit the group commander while firing at the Japanese intruder.

Most of the communications came from shipmates of half a century ago who had stored away in their heads some of the same scenes I had in mine. Imagine opening a letter to read, "I recall you and I up on the hangar deck of CV-8 [the sinking *Hornet*] waiting to climb down the cargo net to the deck of the DD410, *Hughes*. I recall, while in line, you asked me if there was anything I wanted from my locker. I said, 'Kernan, I wouldn't go back for anything.' You insisted on going —you came back with a pillow cover with my gear." This was my old shipmate Dan Vanderhoof, not seen or heard from for fifty years. Some voices came back from the dead. I had written about three bodies stretched out on the deck of the USS *Suwanee* after one of their own hundred-pound bombs hung up, armed in their bomb bay, and exploded on landing. Then came a letter from Dick Morrow, the gunner, who had spent a long and prosperous life directing a fashionable dance band in the suburbs of Detroit: "I had no idea what had happened until the flames began to burn me. . . . I remember releasing the turret window latch and fell out. . . . I also remember hearing over the ship's loudspeaker 'Taps' at the moment Obie [the pilot, Lt. (jg) O. B. Slingerland] was being buried at sea. . . . Then while on a landing barge I heard a medical corpsman exclaim that [the radioman] Jim Joyce's tongue was swollen and he had passed away."

Often children whose fathers had mentioned only brief events in the war wrote to find out what it had actually been like the day the *Hornet* sank, or what the scene looked like when Lieutenant Collura went down on the way back from Ishigaki. Occasionally relatives who had never heard how men

I mentioned had died wrote to ask for information: "I am the widow of John Wiley Brock, who was . . . in VT-6 on the old *Enterprise*, and was killed in 1942 at Midway. . . . What I would like to know is do you remember him? I have never found anyone who did. I would like this information for our son . . . who never knew his father."

This book was originally published by the Naval Institute Press in 1994, in paper in 1997. I am most grateful to the Institute for the fine treatment they gave the book and the skill with which they promoted it over the years. Largely because of the responses to the book like those described above, I was unwilling, however, to see it go out of print, and the Naval Institute very generously returned the copyright, making it possible for me to publish this new edition with Yale University Press. I want to thank the Naval Historical Center for many of the illustrations, which they generously have placed in the public domain.

CHAPTER ONE

Snow

IN THE winter of 1940–41, I stood in the deep snows of the mountains of southern Wyoming and realized that it wasn't going to work. Our ranch was five miles from the nearest neighbor, and during the winter months we had to snowshoe or ski that five miles, leaving the car where the county snow-plow had stopped, carrying in packs or pulling on sleds whatever was necessary until the next month, when we would go to town again—Saratoga, about twenty miles away. We would cut enough wood in summer to keep the stoves burning and store enough staples in a frost-proof cave dug into the mountainside to see us through the winter. There was no electricity or running water. The horses were driven down the valley and boarded for the winter with people who lived out of the shadow of the mountain, where the snows were the heaviest. The cats were brown and singed on their sides from spending their days trying to keep warm curled around the stovepipes that came out of the roof.

The ranch had been one of the last homesteads taken out and "proved up," 640 acres in a canyon near the head of South Spring Creek, 8,500 feet high, a few miles east of the crest of the Continental Divide. The stream flowed down into the valley of the North Platte and into the young river that comes out of the Colorado mountains. It was a very real place—water, sagebrush, rocks, pine trees—but the ranch was also a dream, my stepfather's dream, after he lost his work in the Depression, that a Wyoming dude ranch would provide a wonderful life for all of us and eventually make us rich. As in many other American families during the Depression, conversations frequently began with, "When we get rich . . ." The ranch had made us neither rich nor happy, and there was never the slightest chance that it would, with no building capital, few fish and little big game, and no dudes with enough money or interest to find their way to a small rundown ranch forty miles from a railroad or a main highway. My stepfather couldn't see it, of course; he had no place else to go. But my sense that things were going wrong had been growing since the evening of September 1, 1939, when we listened to the news, on a radio powered by an old car battery, that Hitler had invaded Poland, and that Britain and France had declared war. We knew, sadly, far away though it was, that it would affect us, and that life would never again be the same. But nothing much changed until I graduated from high school in 1940. I had boarded in town while I went to school, but now, unable to get a job, I was staying on the ranch alone, taking care of things, and had to face the question of how I was going to live my life. My stepfather was away in the East looking for work, my mother with him.

In early November, I got a heads-up about how life really works. The snows had held off longer than usual, and I had delayed taking the horses down below. One day an old car, a Star coupe, a model by then no longer sold or familiar, pulled up and stopped in front of the fence, waiting. No one got out for a while. In that time and place it was not thought polite to be too forward, and I waited before going down to lean on the fence, establishing ownership, and say hello. By then two men and a pregnant woman had gotten out of the car. They wanted to know the condition of the road above our ranch, a road that ran for about ten miles through the Medicine Bow National Forest up to South Spring Creek Lake. The lake was in the core of an old volcano with one side blown out, Mount Saint Helens fashion, out of which ran South Spring Creek down the canyon in which our ranch was located. The road, built years ago and poorly maintained, was at the best of times un-improved, running over big rocks, through swamps, dugways nearly washed away in the side of mountains, across rotting log bridges, and, in places, up 40-degree slopes. I told the strangers that the bridges, though shaky, had all still been there a week ago when I had gone deer hunting up that way, but that they would need something powerful and high centered to get up the road, all things their antique car was not. They went off together and talked for a while, and then came back and asked if I would take them by wagon to an old mine up on the shoulder of Mount Vulcan, rising high on one side of the lake. They were out-of-work miners, hoping to find a mine and work it for enough ore to sell to a smelter in Colorado to keep going, always with the hope of a real strike. We were all dreamers then.

The weather was not good: the snow was likely to begin any time, which I explained to them, adding truthfully that once it began at this time of year, you could get snowed in all winter. They still wanted to go, and I sensed that there might be real money in this job, so I gulped and said I would go for ten dollars. I had never had ten dollars at once, and they too were impressed with the big bucks we were talking. Since they were nearly broke, they bargained hard, starting at five dollars, moving to seven, and agreeing to ten only when I, knowing nothing about bargaining, remained adamant, on condition that I feed them, let them sleep there that night, and allow the pregnant woman to stay in the cabin while we were gone.

Feeling like a real trader, I had the old team hitched to the wagon the next morning before light, with some oats for them in a sack, and off we went, with the smell of snow in the air. We jolted along, and I worried about whether my stepfather would ever find out, and if he did, whether he would want half of the money for wear and tear on the horses and the wagon, or whether he would just be plain mad about my doing something with his property without permission. He and I didn't agree about a lot of things.

With enough snow on the ground to make the rocks slick, the going was slower than usual, and at that time of year dark came in the deepening canyon by four in the afternoon. Shortly after a lunchless noon, we got stuck in a narrow place trying to turn between some rocks. The wagon box was sixteen feet long and firmly wedged; a shorter one would have been much better for this work. After some geeing and hawing it was clear that the only way to get out of there was to unhitch the horses, take off the wagon box, disassemble the wagon, and put it together facing the opposite way, downhill and back toward the ranch. The miners weren't happy with this. "Isn't there some way to get to the mine and get the drills without using the wagon?" There was a back trail leading directly to the mine, up the ridge and across the shoulder of the mountain; but the only way to bring the heavy drills out would be to hook them to the harness traces on the horses and drag them along, bouncing up and down on the rocks, careering down the slopes. "That's okay; rock drills are tough anyway." So up through the fading light, soft snow drifting down, high up on the shoulder of the green mountain, we made our way through the pines to the old mine. A spooky place, abandoned years ago, leaving behind a diesel engine, compressor, drills, and a lot of other equipment. We hooked a drill to each horse and started back down the mountain. Dark set in and the snow increased, big heavy wet white flakes, not quite a blizzard, but not reassuring either.

By the time we got back to the wagon it was pitch dark, and time for the strenuous work of getting the wagon, locked into the rocks in the big pine grove, apart and back together facing the other way. We should have done it before going up the mountain, but the miners had been in a hurry. Now it had to be done in the dark. The miners wanted to build a fire and get warm, but I argued that things were getting tight, and it was time to work hard and get the hell out of there. They went ahead building a fire, saying that they had hired me and the wagon, and it was my problem to get them back. Angry enough to be able to do it, I got the box out of the bolsters onto a rock, took the reach out, reversed the wheels, and put the box back in.

The miners got in sullenly and hunched down in their coats. I couldn't see a thing, and let the horses find the way, which was fine until we came to a bridge they didn't like. They spooked, backed and snorted, the harness rattling and jangling, and wouldn't go on. I got down and took hold of the mare's bridle and led them across the bridge. It seemed easier on foot, so I continued walking, leading the horses and talking to them. About eleven at night we got back to the ranch. The miners went up to the cabin, and I took the horses to the barn. By the time I had unharnessed and fed the horses, the miners and the woman were piling things in the car, saying they wanted to get out of there before the snow—by then about six inches deep —made it impossible to get up a steep hill on the only road out of the canyon. That was fine with me, I had seen enough of them, but nothing was said about the ten dollars as they piled into the car. I was prepared to fight for it after the day I'd just had. In fact, I was going to make it impossible for them to get out of there, and they must have felt the growing tension, for at the last minute they handed over an old, dirty ten dollar bill, got in the car, and roared out.

The futility of it all was underlined the following summer, after I was gone, when they came back with an old Fordson tractor with a compressor on the back that they were taking up to the mine, planning to work it. They stopped to talk to my stepfather for a while, and he heard for the first time what had happened the winter before, but when they got ready to go, the hand-cranked tractor wouldn't start. They cranked it for a day and a half, no exaggeration, taking turns, before it fired. Then they clanked out, but about a hundred yards up the road the steering gear broke in a deep rut. There was a power reel on the front of the tractor with a hundred feet of cable, and from there on—the whole ten miles or so up that canyon, over those rocks, to the mine—they reeled out the cable, fastened the end to a tree, then winched the tractor up by its own boot-straps, as it were, to the tree, where the same job began all over again.

These later disasters merely drove home what the miners had already taught me on that long November day about the futility of life lived with old, broken-down equipment, about foolish ideas that have no chance of succeeding. In a world where disaster is always ready to happen, it is best to look for something that has a chance of working. And after the miners left the winter came on in earnest. A wind that would knock you off your feet, snow eight feet deep, and weeks of below zero weather put a still finer edge on my thinking. Seventeen years old, no job, no prospects, I knew how to do only one thing, the same thing all inland mountain boys do, go to sea. I think my parents were glad to see me go; one less pair of hands but also one less mouth to feed—one less worry, it seemed at the time, about what was going to happen. They were a little ashamed of not having been able to send me to college or provide a paying job for me, but nobody had helped them out, and they were, I thought, glad I had relieved them of their vague feelings of guilt and responsibility.

And so one day in March, with heavy snow clouds hanging gray over the ranch, I borrowed five dollars—having long ago spent my profits from the trip to the mine—and got a ride down to Cheyenne. A ground blizzard was blowing on U.S. 30

from Rawlins to Cheyenne. Blazing bright sunlight and blue sky above, snow blowing a few inches above the ground so thickly that it was as impossible to see the road as it was to see my future.

I found the recruiting center in the Cheyenne post office and signed up for a minority enlistment (until I was twenty-one years old) in the United States Navy. The train went down to Denver that evening. There, in a room in Union Station, about a hundred young men were assembled from all over the Rocky Mountains to take the oath. We were young—seventeen, eighteen, nineteen—and for the most part, kids who couldn't get jobs. Here and there were men in their twenties, jobless workers at the end of their rope, or incorrigible "fuck-ups" who had gotten into some kind of trouble at home once too often and had been given the ancient choice by the judge of going to jail or joining one of the services. Most of us were from small towns, often from broken families, notable for bad teeth and worse complexions, the marginal American products of more than ten years of the hardest of times.

After the oath we went out to the cold platform and into the warm cars. Not expecting anything other than coaches, we murmured our pleasure at the sleeping berths the navy provided its newest members. The yellow Union Pacific train, with its streamlined engine and coaches, snaked through long curves out of the Colorado and New Mexico plateaus, across the mountains, to stop in the bright sunshine of California on the second morning. The warmth itself was luxurious after the cold of the mountains, and the orange groves and Spanish architecture seemed to promise the freedom and pleasure that I had longed for in the deep snows of Wyoming. A glimpse of Los Angeles, Union Station, and then the train rounded a bend and there was the Pacific Ocean, blue and infinite, the sea of adventure and excitement, stretching out to the horizon and beyond: Hawaii, the Philippines, Indonesia, China, and Japan. I would see them all, I was sure, and in time I did, but not quite as I imagined them in that moment of wild surmise.

CHAPTER TWO

Boots

THE U.S. Naval Training Station, San Diego, was in 1941 the boot camp for all those who enlisted in the mountain region and the West Coast. Stuck out next to the marine boot camp on a beach extending in a westerly curve to Point Loma, forming the northwestern shore of San Diego Bay, the camp faced the Naval Air Station on North Island across the water. The huge harbor and its shores were the training center for the Pacific Fleet, which was now home ported at Pearl Harbor in the Hawaiian Islands. Inside the main gate of the training station two-story stucco barracks with arcades stretched out in long rows to the blacktop "grinder," the drill field where we would spend most of the next few months learning the naval axiom that military duties take precedence over trade skills by marching as a company, under arms, back and forth, up and down, on the oblique, to the rear, rear, rear, march!

Soft warm air, light breezes, and the lift that intense sunlight gives: the climate had a holiday feel even in those strenuous first days of boot camp, which began with a physical exam, where the city boys laughed at those of us from the country still wearing long underwear. Since my long johns came only to the waist, with a T-shirt above, I thought myself quite sophisticated, but this was still far from the West Coast jockeyshort style, and I was glad to package the underwear with my other clothes—the Hart, Schaffner, and Marx suit bought as a high school graduation present, my stepfather's cut-down topcoat, the gray hat—to be sent home. Civilian identity vanished with the clothes, and, naked, we were initiated into our new identities, which were minimal, by probing, poking, testing, shooting. The barbers sheared off almost all our hair, leaving only an inch on top, bare on the sides. For some the loss of long, carefully groomed hair was as painful as it was to Samson, but to most of us it was only a necessary part of becoming a sailor.

Once out of the barbershop we counted off, and when the number reached one hundred, two chief petty officers advanced purposefully and claimed us as a company. Chief Dahlgren was a gunner's mate, tall, tolerant, composed, Nordic. Chief Bilbo was a short, stocky, fiery, Sicilian and truly dangerous to disappoint. Company 41-39 was the thirty-ninth company formed at San Diego in 1941, and after being assigned a barracks it was marched off to stores, where the navy issued the clothes and equipment needed to live in and work with from then on.

Whap! The heavy canvas hammock landed on the brightly polished, red linoleum deck (no longer a floor) in front of each man, who then dragged it along in front of the counters where endless items were called out—"Two undress uniforms, white, one pair of leggings canvas, khaki"—and thrown on the hammock. Sea bag for all clothing, ditty bag for toilet gear and personal possessions. Dress blues (one) with a white watchstander's qualification stripe around the right shoulder to identify you as a deckhand, not a red-striped engineer, and one white tape around the cuffs to mark you as the lowest of all beings in the navy, an apprentice seaman. Black silk neckerchiefs (two) to be folded into a long flat ribbon and tied around the neck with a square knot exactly at the bottom of the vee in the blouse. Undress blues, no tape on collar and uncuffed sleeves; dungarees for work details; white caps and blue wool flat cap; pea coat (to be paid for from pay in installments); one pair of low dress shoes. "What's your size?"

The pile on the hammock grew mountainous: smallclothes (underwear), line for lashing hammock, cord for hanging washed clothes up to dry, a flat mattress and two covers, pillow, shoe brush and dauber, socks, black and white. At the end of the line two sailors grabbed the hammock, folded it double, put the rings on either end in your hand and hoisted it onto your back. Bent double with this huge white hump on your back, you followed the arrows and your company number chalked on the sidewalk to the barracks, where you were assigned to a double-deck bunk and began to fold, tie, and store your clothing in your sea bag.

There was little personal gear. The navy did not encourage private possessions. A pocketknife was allowed, as were scissors, toothbrush, razor, soap, shoe polish, and some writing materials. These were kept in the ditty bag tied to the side of your bunk. There wasn't room for anything else and no place elsewhere to stow anything. In time, on shipboard, the sea bag and ditty bag gave way to a small locker, but in training the Old Navy tradition of little gear packed compactly in tight quarters survived. Clothing was folded and stored. Each piece, from jumpers to skivvies, was folded in a particular way, rolled tightly, and then tied with white clothes stops, square knotted at a prescribed point, the cord ending in a brass collar just at the knot. No "Irish pennants" (loose ends) allowed here. The folds for storage gave the uniforms their distinctive appearance when worn, like the three ridges on the collar of the blue-and-white jumpers or the inverse seam on the trousers from being stored inside out.

No dirt. Cleanliness was not next to godliness in the United States Navy; it was godliness. Everything in the barracks was constantly shined to a high gloss, from the red linoleum floors to the brass work on the fire hose fittings. Shoes were a brilliant deep black, in contrast with the unspotted white uniforms that we scrubbed every day, kneeling with a stiff brush and harsh soap on the cement platforms provided for that purpose in the rear of the barracks.

Men were expected to be as clean as their quarters and equipment, and most were so by easy choice. Company 41-39 contained, inevitably, one of those odd people encountered here and there in every walk of life who not only smell foul by nature, it seems, but nurture the smell by keeping themselves and their clothes as dirty as possible. Pigpen in the comic strip "Peanuts" is an attractive version of this human oddity. Our Pigpen stuffed his sea bag with dirty clothes, never brushed his teeth or washed, and lay in his bunk with one hand under the blanket (forbidden by unwritten rule), giggling, reading a comic book. The remedy was gleeful and brutal. From time to time he was stripped and put in the wash trough, surrounded by jeering recruits, secure in their own cleanliness, who washed him down with a gritty sand soap and then scrubbed him with stiff long-handled brushes. The process, which involved a lot of hitting with the brush handles, was painful, a form of running the gauntlet, but it never had the slightest effect. Nowadays he would have sued the navy, but when I last saw Pigpen he was lying in his bunk, smelling horrible, one hand under the blanket, giggling and reading the same page of the comic book he had been looking at when I first staggered into the barracks under my load of equipment. I thought then that he must always have been there, and he probably still is, some old Adam who haunts all the navy's efforts at cleanliness, positive thinking, and order.

We were children still—astonishingly stoical, self-reliant, tough children, but children still—and, like all children, fascinated with killing. The guns drew us like magnets when they were given to us one afternoon in the huge, cool armory, filled with the odor of greasy brown cosmoline, where each of us was issued, and signed our life away for, a rifle. Stands of boarding cutlasses still stood as ornaments next to the cases of rifles, but so innocent were we that we thought boarding enemy vessels—just like Errol Flynn in the movies set on the Spanish Main—was still a part of naval warfare and were disappointed when we had to be satisfied with only a murderous sixteen-inch bayonet.

Springfield rifles, 1903, .30 caliber, were the standard issue, but every seventh unlucky company (and the lot fell on 41-39) was given British-made long Enfields from the First World War. The Enfield weighed three pounds more than the Springfield, and we soon found out just what those three pounds meant at the end of a long, hot ten hours on the grinder. Not only that, you lived with that heavy rifle in boot camp, using it in morning calisthenics, running around the grinder with it at high port for punishment, slamming it around your head and shoulders with one hand while going through the manual of arms. In the end you were stronger for having lugged that extra three pounds about with you, but Atlas could have been no gladder to get rid of his load than we were when we finally gave those huge, heavy guns back to the armory.

The grinder was where we learned the really hard lesson of military life: putting your individuality in storage and moving as a group. On ten or more acres of baking black asphalt, shimmering with heat waves in the hot afternoon sun of the Mexican border, the company marched as a unit—white hats turned down to protect nose and neck from sunburn—five days a week, inspection on Saturday, up and down, by the right flank, by the left flank, to the rear, march! Eyes right, eyes left, eyes front, right shoulder arms, left shoulder arms. In four columns, tallest men at front. Blessed were the shortest, for no one marched behind them; they were always getting out of step and scraping their well-polished heels with the out-of-step toes of their shoes. Not only was it infuriating, hot, and exhausting to be stepped on by some bastard who couldn't keep step—and there were those congenitally unable to do so—but it also scuffed the backs of the shoes, making it impossible to polish them smoothly and deeply again, which led to trouble at the next inspection. Reasonable excuses were not a part of this life. The company would be moving smoothly along, the Olympian Dahlgren at front, a sword on his shoulder, Bilbo at the rear, shouting time: "Hut, two, three, four, and your left, your right, your left, goddammit!" Then a shout, "You dirty son of a bitch," and turmoil would break out in the middle of the ranks, a few blows. Someone had, once again, stepped on somebody's heels "for the last time." The company would halt, order would be restored, punishments handed out, and off we would go, "Your left, your right, your left, hold up your fucking heads."

After fifty years, the only name I remember from this group with whom I lived so intimately for three months is Mudrick, the man who marched immediately behind me, had trouble keeping step, whined a lot, and filled my heart with red murder on those blazing afternoons when he stepped on my heels again and again and snickered when I muttered oaths. Years later there was a cross-grained literary critic named Marvin Mudrick, whom I never knew, but whom I loathed on the unlikely suspicion that he must be the same man, up to his old trick of being out of step.

Money was no problem because we had none. The few coins that everyone hoarded were saved for cigarettes—it was part of manhood to smoke at that time—which could be bought during a once-weekly few minutes in the ship's store at the duty-free price of five cents a package. There was no time to smoke during the day, and the smoking lamp was always out in the barracks. But during the evening while outdoors washing clothes, the fortunate few with cigarettes could light up. Their pleasure was lessened a great deal by the envious faces that peered at them as intently as begging dogs. As soon as they took the pack out of the sleeve of the skivvy shirt, where it was twisted up to keep the cigarettes from being dampened by sweat, a loud cry of "butts" would come from the throat of some wretch whose need for nicotine had overwhelmed self-pride. The cry was privileged, and as soon as the first smoker had smoked his fill, he had to turn over the butt to the man who had claimed it rather than putting it in the sand bucket. Usually the man who had been "butted" couldn't take the hungry look of the "butter" and smoked the cigarette down only halfway before giving up in disgust. As time passed between paydays and fewer had cigarettes, the sound of "butts" would be followed by the desperate call of "butts on the butts!" "Butts on the butts on the butts" was only a joke, but there were those who would have tried it if social opinion would have tolerated it.

"Twenty-one dollars a day, once a month" was the refrain of an old song, and twenty-one dollars a month was the pay of apprentice seamen. The navy didn't bother paying at the end of the first month in boot camp, on the theory that you had no need of money since you couldn't go on liberty until the end of the second month. But at the end of the second month the solemn naval ritual of payday began with the posting of the pay lists a few days before payday. All to be paid were on the list with first, second, and third names. If you lacked a middle name, the navy, sure that all humans needed a middle name for purposes of identification, supplied one: None. None was the most frequent middle name in the navy, and Samuel None Jones or Fred None Smith would be followed by the amount the navy figured it owed you after all the deductions were made. A legendary recruit joined the navy with only the name J. B. He soon became Jonly Bonly.

The amount was always less than the sailor calculated he had coming to him. This was why the lists were posted beforehand, so that the arguments could be sorted out before you passed, neatly dressed in the uniform of the day, in alphabetical order down the line in front of the yeomen and that august figure, the warrant paymaster. If you were going home on leave after boot camp, money was deducted to pay for your train ticket, the heavy pea coat, and any fines or punishments.

Also allotments. You wouldn't think there would be anything to spare out of twenty-one dollars minus deductions, but there were men whose families were so poor that they would send them ten dollars, or even more, every month. And then, at the end of the line, looking particularly grim, Bilbo and Dahlgren would be standing behind the Red Cross and the Navy Relief representatives, each of whom had to be given a dollar if you wanted to avoid getting on the company's permanent shit list, which brought all kinds of drab extra work. Lifelong dislikes of the Red Cross were born in front of the superior-looking, elegantly uniformed lady who disdainfully took your dollar while chatting with one of the supervising officers. But Navy Relief, which provided for families of enlisted men fallen on hard times, was accepted as a tax on life. The families of enlisted men in peacetime had an Appalachian quality to them at best, so grim as to make us both sorry for them and determined while in service to avoid marriage and children at all costs.

There were always navy ships in San Diego Harbor, and on the first liberty, Saturday from noon to ten o'clock, they drew me, along with many others, across the bay to the North Island docks to spend a fireman's holiday going from one great ship to another. The aircraft carrier *Lexington*, blocks long and tall as a hotel, was irresistible. We asked the officer-of-the-deck permission to come aboard—"Permission granted"—and saluted toward the rear of the ship, where the flag was flown at anchor, in the manner we had learned in *The Bluejackets' Manual.* With a few smiles at our oversize boot uniforms and rounded hats, we were allowed to wander about looking at the planes on the hangar deck and the guns, small and large, around the immense flight deck. The high smokestack with ladder rungs welded to the side was so tempting that I climbed up to near the top, getting more and more scared at the height, until someone called from below telling me to get the hell off.

The streetcar clanged back to "Dago" where the streets were filled with sailors on liberty. The bars, with someone sitting on a stool at each door to examine your liberty card to make sure you were twenty-one, stood with their doors open and the jukeboxes blaring out "Hut sut rawson on the rilliraw" and "Drinking rum and coca cola, Working for the Yankee dollar." Neon lights flashed over "The Arabian Palace

Hotel" and "Intimate Nights," where the Shore Patrol stood
on the sidewalks swinging their clubs and looking mean,
and the smell of Lysol hung in the air. In the tattoo parlors,
open to the street, sailors were getting dragons, daggers, and
"Death before Dishonor" worked in vivid color on their arms
and backs, the bright inks mixed with sweat and blood standing in pools, shining in the bright lights. Of all the walkers on
the streets, only the boots with floppy white-issue uniforms
and broad white hats sitting squarely on the head, the brim
flaring wide out, neckerchiefs tied at the vee of the jumper
rather than at the throat, looked like real rubes. Everyone else
looked in the know: tight uniforms, campaign ribbons, old
chief boatswains' mates from the Asiatic station, and long-
term hands with rows of hash marks on their sleeves.

There was real, vulgar joy among so much life ordered by a
symbology of hierarchy and skill that flashed along the streets.
Petty officers with rating badges displayed on the left arm for
the trades, on the right for those who worked on deck like
quartermasters, gunners, and coxswains. Red hash marks on
most, gold hash marks after twelve years of consecutive good
conduct. White uniforms, dress blues, khakis, and greens here
and there on the aviation chiefs. Lots of sailors were in civvies,
usually a garish Hawaiian or Philippine shirt, with tight trousers and cheap boots that were kept, along with a bottle, in
locker clubs, where for a few bucks you could drink, shower,
and change clothes for liberty. Selling uniforms and badges
was big business. Outside each clothing store an affable man
called out, "Hey, chief!" to every sailor who walked by, trying
to lure them into buying tight-fitting tailor-made uniforms,
gold dragons stitched into the silk lining of the panel above the
crotch. "Liberty" was the right word for it. It was an enlisted
man's world on the streets; the officers, unenvied, stayed with
their strained-looking women in the hotels or in Coronado in
one of the officers' clubs.

In time basic training ended. Those who were going straight
to the fleet without further training to become deckhands
and firemen were given a ten-day leave, and with any luck had
saved enough money to pay for a train ticket home. The rest
of us went off to another three months in a training school
to learn a trade. It was necessary to pass some rudimentary

exams to be accepted for one of the training schools, but since promotion came more rapidly to those with a trade and the work was easier, schools were thought desirable. The great reason for joining the navy in those Depression days was to learn a trade. But it wasn't anything so practical that directed my choice. Out of all the useful skills I could have learned—radio, electricity, motors, signaling, navigation, even boiler making —I, wild about flying and airplanes, chose aviation ordnance, bombs, aerial torpedoes, machine guns, and other instruments of destruction. This was thought a good route to flying as a gunner or an observer, even to pilot training, and this is what I was after.

With our sea bags lashed up in our hammocks and on our shoulders, looking like real seamen for the first time, we walked up the hill to the holding barracks for the long row of training schools. Here you stayed until enough people arrived in your specialty to form a class, and in the meantime the navy found work to busy idle hands. The barracks were new and built about three feet off the ground on spaced cement pilings. Someone had had the idea that it would be good to fill the empty space with dirt dug from the clay hill behind the barracks. Just why was never explained. The dirt was dragged in baskets by hand to the center of the area, dumped, and pushed back.

It was dirty and hard work, and I was delighted when the chief in charge of the barracks selected me and one other young sailor to clean his room. The room was only about ten by six, with a bunk, a chair, and a locker, and one person, let alone two, could have kept it spotless working about half an hour a day. Innocent as lambs, both of us looking very young, the other sailor and I never questioned our good fortune, slicking up the room, running a few errands, and then loafing in the ship's store or reading in out-of-the-way areas. I don't think I had ever heard of homosexuality, and when the chief, having sent the other cleaner off on an errand, made his smiling, good-natured move, I was so aghast that I jumped without thinking in one giant leap out the open window, which fortunately was on the first floor. No hard feelings, but within the hour I was back on the dirt gang with the worst job, at the front of the line pushing the dirt by hand close to the barrack's floor.

In a few days the class for aviation ordnance school filled up, and we moved to another barracks, double-decker bunks on each side, with a long desk made of two planks, with fixed benches, running down the center for study. Light and clean, simple but efficient, it was a pleasant place to spend the late summer and fall of 1941. The course itself was easy—a few simple facts about electricity and some rudimentary chemistry, learning the difference between one type of bomb rack and another, some information about various explosives and the fuses used to ignite them, how to break down, clean, and adjust machine guns, pistols, and rifles. Probably the most complicated mechanism was the aerial torpedo, which ran on an ingenious little steam engine fired by alcohol and contained a lot of complex gyroscopes and settings to control depths and angles. At the Battle of Midway I would learn that our aerial torpedo, Mark 13, Mod. 1, was deeply flawed, seldom running hot and true and regularly failing to explode. But like all the fairly crude weaponry we worked on, it seemed to be the latest martial technology, to be studied with care.

We saw no real airplanes in training school; instead, we bore sighted machine guns (that is, aligned them to converge their fire at a certain number of yards in front of the plane) on a frame model of an old plane. Learning on a mock-up to synchronize machine guns so that they could fire through a turning propeller without hitting the blades, we made a gambling game out of whether the firing solenoid clicked on empty space or on an old propeller turned slowly by hand.

Twelve-hour liberties were given on three out of four weekends. On the fourth your section had the watch. By now we had become second-class seamen, with a pay raise from twenty-one to thirty-six dollars a month, which meant that for the first time we had some real money left over after deductions when we were paid every two weeks. Everyone bought a small black wallet designed to tuck without much bulge into a uniform waistband or into the small breast pocket on the jumper.

Before the war the navy had the quaint custom of paying in two-dollar bills, perhaps because no one else wanted them, but the sailors all said it was because two dollars was what they charged in the whorehouses in Dago. In a small town crowded with sailors, life moved from the bars to the whorehouses and back to the bars. Eighteen-year-olds like myself, with little cash, were not very welcome in either, even with doctored identification, but no one really worried much, and sooner or later you could work your way into a bar to sit with your friends, eight or ten in a booth, and tell stories about what a good job you had had back in civilian life, how much money you had made, your flashy clothes and car, the adoring and obliging girlfriends. Having had none of these I listened happily to the more polished liars, kept time to the music of the jukebox, and basked in the sense of being one of a group of real men of the world.

The local beer was the drink, cheap and sufficient for inexperienced drinkers like myself, but sometimes money would be pooled to buy a pint of some bright-colored gin—sloe, mint, apricot—more memorable for its vividness coming up than its pleasure going down, and with this in a paper bag we would sit on the curb, or, sometimes, five or six together, take a room in one of the whorehouses. A quirk of the law required them actually to rent rooms, which they did for a few dollars, and groups of sailors would take one to sit in drinking and talking to the whores, strongly perfumed, who came in from time to time for a drink and to see if there was any business.

You could also sit in the parlors for a limited time looking at the girls in scanty costumes who displayed themselves provocatively, and then move on to another house, and another. It was all incredibly garish and tawdry; most people would probably think the strong sounds and smells vulgar, even disgusting, but to young men in their late teens, with their experience of women limited for the most part to a few awkward pawings in a parked automobile, their glands in an uproar, and their sexual urgencies flowing full tide, it looked like Babylon itself, the harem of the sultans, the paradise of the true believers. The Oriental motif carried on to a pale, slender young girl called Cleo, who with good humor and real tenderness took me through my sexual initiation on a sagging old bed in a quiet room, jukebox music in the distance and a cool breeze playing gently over our bodies from the electric fan. It was not a romantic setting, far from it—sensible and workmanlike, rather —but it was not brutal or degrading for anyone.

Later, on the stairs going out, I heard a drunken sailor who had gotten into an argument with a whore cursing the madam. She screamed back at him, "You want to hurt someone? You fucking cocksucker. Come on and fuck me, and I'll show you how to hurt someone fucking." This had nothing to do with me or the sex I had just found in Cleo's thin arms, and I hurried on out to the bus back to the base, where, after the liberty card was deposited in the box, reality spoke up again in the prophylactic station where you were required to pump some stinging brown liquid up your cock—sometimes fainting when you did so if you had had too much to drink—washed, and used an antiseptic cream. Gonorrhea was endemic in the fleet, and fearful tales went around of syphilis picked up in the Orient, requiring long, painful treatment and spinal taps and eventuating in various kinds of rot and disintegration.

For someone with a good memory and a feel for simple systems, the training school was easy, but for others it was a slow drudgery, involving sitting up in the heads all night to try to get the facts down for one of the dreaded weekly exams. Not everyone in the school was a genius. One sailor was a boxer, and he practiced sometimes by sparring with one of the iron support posts in the middle of the barracks. He would get very excited at times, so much so that he would bang his head on the post until one of us told him to break, that the round had ended. He and some others flunked out, but most passed, and all through the war I ran into them in odd places in the Pacific, filling practice bombs with sand on Guadalcanal, caring for ammunition storage depots on Ford Island, taking the temperatures in the bomb magazines of aircraft carriers like the *Hornet*, cleaning machine guns on a racetrack in New Caledonia, and loading bombs in Okinawa.

I was the honor man of the class, not because of my mechanical skills—I was a bit clumsy—but because of the written tests. The chief in charge of our class arranging graduation ceremonies had never laid eyes on me and did not know my name, so when he called it out to tell me to go up on stage, he had to ask someone, "Who is he?" This was a mark of great success to me and to my friends: you did your work and got ahead but remained totally anonymous. This is how you survived in the navy and most other places in the world before the modern triumph of the cult of personality. At those graduation ceremonies on October 21, 1941, I shook hands for the first time with a commissioned officer, creatures seen only from a distance theretofore. Captain Henry Gearing was the commander of the U.S. Naval Training Station, San Diego, a grizzled old sea dog, at least in appearance, bluff, tall, commanding. When he saw me on the stage, small and thin and still very young-looking, he leaned over and whispered as he gave me the diploma, "My God, boy, how old are you?" I thought I had set his concerns entirely at ease by truthfully answering, "Eighteen," having reached that advanced age in June, and went out to the tune of "Anchors Aweigh" for fifteen days of leave at home.

Two days of sitting up on a train so packed there was not even any standing room left returned me to the cold of Wyoming. Rawlins, where the train stopped, is sixty miles from our ranch across the bleak desert of south-central Wyoming. Up in the mountains a few inches of snow had already fallen by the end of October; the yellow leaves were all gone from the aspens, and at the line where they ended and the green pines began the dark and cold of winter were already to be felt. The mountains rose up and up through the pines to the bare space above timberline. Their bald peaks dominated our ranch, loomed over everything with menacing size and durability. They set the scale of reality here, of things as they permanently are, and against them everything else seemed ephemeral and puny. The new cabin with the stone fireplace, for the dudes who would never come, the ranch itself and all the hopes invested in it, the faraway sunniness of California, where nature seems to promise a lot, and even the might of the United States Navy were emptied of reality by those monstrous mountains and the oncoming winter.

I had expected to return a hero, and the dog was glad to see me, and my mother fussed over me and listened with real interest to my stories. My stepfather, who had not seen service in the First World War, felt somewhat threatened by my military authority and constantly told me there wouldn't be a war. But my life and interests had migrated elsewhere, and, half aware of it, I had some guilt for not feeling the old loyalties. A brief trip to Saratoga, where nothing had happened since I left and where no one was interested in my adventures, was only awkward.

That was the last time I saw my mother alive, and as I write this, almost exactly fifty years later, I am troubled by how little I can remember of her, barely able to see her worried face in the lamplight or hear her words of good advice as I left. The big snows held off, and in early November 1941 they drove me back to the train that took me to the bustle of San Diego and on to Pearl Harbor and the other side of the world.

[TOP] Main Street, Saratoga, Wyoming: pop. 650, ca. 1933.

[LEFT] Frank and Kate Kernan, stepfather and mother, 1937.

[BOTTOM] Wyoming snow: on the way to the navy, age seventeen, winter 1941.

Paul Cadmus, "The Fleet's In," 1934, oil on canvas, Navy Art Gallery, Washington, D.C., 34-5-A.

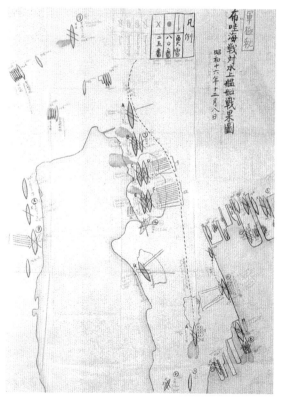

Sketch of the Japanese attack on Pearl Harbor, made by the Japanese air commander, Mitsuo Fuchida, for Emperor Hirohito. Parallel lines indicate torpedoes; "X" indicates a hit.

Slow, steady, and low: Torpedo 6, Douglas Devastator, TBD, the Midway torpedo plane, dropping a tin fish.

TBF-1: the Grumman Avenger, a new torpedo plane used after Midway.

USS *Hornet*, under air attack and sinking at the Battle of Santa Cruz, October 26, 1942.

[TOP, LEFT] On leave, March 1943, wearing the new tailor-made uniform bought with my anchor-pool winnings.

[TOP, RIGHT] The schoolmarm: Ruth Emery, a romance that never bloomed.

[BOTTOM] Dick Boone (*Have Gun, Will Travel*), Jim Gaffney, me, and Ed Dutcher in a San Diego bar, 1943.

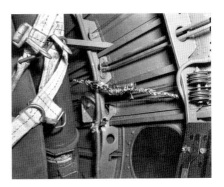

Ed Sullivan's elevator-cable splice, Butaritari, Gilbert Islands, 1943

[ABOVE] Night-fighter radar plane crew: me, Hazen Rand, Ed Sullivan (on wing), and Lt. Cdr. John Phillips.

[RIGHT] Lt. Cdr. Edward H. "Butch" O'Hare, Congressional Medal of Honor, 1943.

Overboard: Ens. Robert Dyer, me, and Moon Mullins after crashing off the catapult of USS *Suwannee*, 1945.

Recreation at Mog Mog, Ulithi Atoll, 1945.

Free beer: Torpedo 40 in Guadalcanal, 1945.

Torpedo 40 aircrew: Mullins, Dyer, and me.

Chief Petty Officer Kernan back from the war before my discharge.

Much later, talking to the brass: my wife, Suzanne, and me with Adm. Jay L. Johnson, CNO, 1997.

CHAPTER THREE

Pearl

THE USS *Procyon*, a military cargo vessel, sailed from San Diego to Pearl Harbor in mid-November 1941, loaded with various stores and machines and packed with sailors being sent out to the fleet, many of us recruits going overseas for the first time. The strictest seniority is the navy's operating rule, and what this means in practical terms is that all the menial jobs that have to be done every day to keep things running fall to the newest and the lowliest in rank. My introduction to this rule came at once and in the classic way—as "captain of the head." The moment I stepped aboard, I was assigned to keep spotless and shined to a high gloss the decks, the showers, the basins, and the troughs of running seawater in several heads. I craned my neck out of a porthole to see Point Loma, the dangling peninsula that protected San Diego harbor, known to generations of sailors as "Point Hard-On" because of its shape and its effect on those returning from—not going on —long voyages overseas. Once around Point Loma and into blue water the ship began to pick up speed, and as she did, she began to pitch and roll. My stomach, never having been at sea before, heaved for a while and then groaned for a day or two while I swung the heavy swab to clean the head until my appetite came back and my sea legs set. I was never seasick again in my life.

Five days out we came in the early morning around Diamond Head and went down the shore opposite Honolulu and then through the nets and buoys into the narrow entrance to Pearl Harbor. The water formed a ring around Ford Island, the pearl in the center of the anchorage, the naval air station where the patrol squadrons of PBYs, the Catalina flying boats, were based and where the squadrons from the aircraft carriers operated while they were in port. The *Procyon* tied up in the navy yard, and immediately a swarm of motor whaleboats arrived to pick up the personnel assigned to the various ships and deliver them to their new homes. The air was electric: the

589

tropical surroundings and soft smells, the huge and busy naval base, the ships of all kinds—battleships, aircraft carriers, submarines, cruisers, destroyers, minesweepers. If you were of a warlike turn of mind, this was the place, fairly breathing the invincible power of the United States Navy.

Still eager to work with airplanes, I considered it a stroke of good luck that I had been assigned to Torpedo Squadron 6, part of the air group on the USS *Enterprise* (CV-6), one of three carriers in the Pacific Fleet at that time, along with the older *Lexington* and *Saratoga*. The sister ship of the *Enterprise*, the USS *Yorktown* (CV-5), was on her way to the Pacific. The *Enterprise* was tied up on the western side of Ford Island taking on supplies, and as the motor whaleboat came up under her counter on her seaward, port, side, she towered a hundred feet above us, grayish white, nearly nine hundred feet long, beautifully proportioned despite her size. The squadron was in barracks ashore with the planes, but I was assigned a bunk on ship and given an hour to wander around, staring with wonder at the complicated machinery, elevators, and spare planes tied up in the overhead of the vast hangar deck. It was all very busy, the sailors—a crew of two thousand—in spotless white shorts and T-shirts rushing here and there, the public-address system constantly blaring out bugle calls, the shrill of the boatswain's whistles, and unintelligible orders to "hear this" or "hear that," or that sounded something like, "Flemish down the bosun's lines." Mine was a total and instant love affair with this great ship, never lost and never experienced again in quite the same way with another.

The *Enterprise* became the most famous of American warships, in all wars. She was in eighteen major actions, hit by bombs many times but never by a torpedo; she downed 911 enemy planes with her guns and planes. Her planes sank 71 enemy ships and damaged or destroyed 192 more. When she was about to be broken up for scrap after the war, there was a national campaign to raise money to save her as a museum. I thought about it but decided not to contribute because I didn't want to think of her sitting around in some backwater, being exploited in unworthy ways. Better by far, I thought, to leave her to the memory of those who had served on her when she was fully alive, vibrating under full steam at thirty-two knots, the aircraft turning up, guns firing, heeling over so sharply that the hangar deck took on water to avoid the bombs. Others must have felt the same way, for the funds fell short, and having gone through nearly every major engagement on the long road to Tokyo, she was broken up for scrap. Better that, I still think, than to be like the *Intrepid* in New York Harbor, where the school groups clatter and squeal, the professional veterans come to be photographed, and the politicians make patriotic speeches on holidays.

I was brought down to earth that afternoon by being put on the anchor chain work detail. Life on board ship is a constant battle with rust, in which the weapons are the chipping hammer, the wire brush, red lead, and gray paint. The anchor chain is always rusty and while in port is regularly taken out of the chain storage and laid out in a barge alongside the ship, each huge link more than three feet in length. The trick is to chip off all the old paint, wire brush the rust off down to bare pitted metal, and put on a priming coat of red lead followed by two or three coats of navy dark gray paint. Hard work, dirty, tiring, hot, and totally unrewarded unless by knowing that you had done a good job. The members of the air group, called Airedales by the rest of the crew, were normally exempt from this kind of ship's work, but the real king of the ship, Jocko— a boatswain's mate first class, the ship's master-at-arms, a kind of chief of police-cum-ward politician—was happy to hold transfers like me in his transit group as long as possible to supply manpower for such jobs.

After a few days the ground crews of the air group came back aboard in preparation for sailing, and Murphy, the chief of the ordnance gang in the torpedo squadron, instantly reclaimed me on the usual grounds that he was already shorthanded and needed every trained man he could get. The deck crews regarded this as bushwa, just a plausible Airedale excuse, but the ship officially recognized the airplanes as her primary armament and gave priority to their operation. I was overjoyed to be given a bunk in the squadron compartment, made known to the leading chief and the yeomen who kept the records, and, above all, given a place, however low, in the ordnance gang, which meant a coffee cup and the right to sit around in the ordnance shack, a wire-mesh enclosure suspended just below the flight deck where tools were kept. Here Murphy and his leading petty officer, Freddy Moyle, a refugee from the British navy, kept court, quietly and happily buzzed all day long on "moosemilk," a mixture of coffee and bombsight alcohol of 99 percent purity used for cleaning the Norden bombsights, the supply of which was fortuitously in Murph's charge.

Ordnancemen worked in pairs: an experienced petty officer and a striker, the navy's name for an apprentice, like me, learning the ropes. Each pair was responsible for three planes, seeing to it that the guns were kept clean and adjusted, the bomb racks working, the torpedo gear ready to go when needed, and so on. Much of the work was more communal, involving the whole ordnance gang: belting ammunition, bringing bombs up from the magazine and fusing them, hauling the torpedoes out on long hydraulic trucks to the planes and loading them, changing bomb racks so that different weights of bombs could be carried. It required a lot of running about and a lot of savvy, which came only with practice.

The torpedo squadron of eighteen planes at full complement, which was seldom, was one of four making up the air group. Besides the "fish" there were two identical squadrons of eighteen dive-bombers, one specializing in scouting (VS-6), and one in dive-bombing (VB-6). Providing cover for the ship and protection for the torpedo planes and bombers was a squadron of eighteen fighter planes (VF-6). Together these seventy-two planes were judged able to deliver a deadly coordinated attack against any naval target, the fighters flying protection overhead, the dive-bombers going in first from high altitude, followed at sea level by the torpedo planes to deliver the coup to the enemy ships. To me, with my limited conceptions of warfare, it all looked like the most up-to-date and modern technology, Buck Rogers himself. The officers who flew in the squadrons and ran the ships were as naive about their equipment and tactics as I was.

The torpedo plane came from the mid-thirties. The TBD-1, translated "torpedo bomber, made by Douglas Aircraft, model 1," was obsolete. Designed to carry three men—pilot, observer-bomber in the center, and radioman gunner in the rear—it could do only about a hundred knots with a torpedo, a fatally slow speed for escaping shipboard antiaircraft gunners and fast fighter planes. It was not much faster with a load of two five-hundred-pound bombs, or eight one-hundred-pounders, and used with these bomb loads as a high-level bomber with the Norden bombsight it was long out of date. Its armament was extremely modest: one .30-caliber fixed machine gun synchronized to fire forward through the propeller and one free .30 caliber in the rear fired by the radioman. Later there were two guns in the rear, but the increase in fire power was offset by the awkwardness of handling their weight in the slipstream. About all you could say in praise of the old "Devastator," as it was styled, was that with its huge wingspan, it seldom crashed, and it floated onto the deck at a nice slow landing speed. But to me it looked like some spaceship ready for Mars, and I polished up all the ordnance gear on my planes daily, disassembled the guns down to the smallest parts, cleaned them, and adjusted the headspace far more often than was needed.

The dive-bomber, the SBD Douglas "Dauntless," was the top of the line and would become the primary naval aircraft during the first two years of the war. The fighter plane, the F4F-3, the Grumman "Wildcat," was new and powerful but definitely inferior to the Japanese fighter, the Zero, that would be its primary opponent in 1942 at the Coral Sea, Midway, and the Solomons.

The demand for labor of the most basic kind was endless on board ship, and a sailor's first year or two in the fleet was usually spent going from one kind of scut work to another. As the lowest in the squadron pecking order, I was soon off to the plane-handling crews, a life that was healthy but exhausting. My days from before dawn until after dark were spent on the flight deck, wearing a dark blue T-shirt and a canvas helmet dyed the same color buckled tightly under the chin, pushing planes at a dead run back and forth on the flight deck and the hangar deck. There was barely enough room on the two decks for all the planes after space was left for landing or taking off, and they had to be spotted with the greatest skill, like the puzzles with moveable pieces and only one empty space. When planes were about to land, all the planes on the flight deck had to be pushed forward to leave enough room aft. Those for which there was no space were pushed onto one of the three elevators and taken down to the hangar deck, where other crews picked them up and moved them around that deck. When planes were taking off, the process was reversed, with all the planes to be launched spotted aft on the flight deck with clear space in front of them. Then, as the ship turned into the wind and went to high speed to provide the greatest possible wind speed over the deck, the plane taking off went to full power with the brakes on, released them suddenly, and used the combination of its forward speed and the wind to lift it (usually) into the air by the time it reached the forward end of the deck.

As soon as the planes were off, the blue plane handlers leaped out of the catwalks alongside the flight deck, where we had been waiting, and began to re-spot the deck for the next planes coming in to land. In the days before tractors were used to pull the planes, all of this complicated maneuvering was done entirely by man power. Since the battle effectiveness of the carrier depended on the speed and efficiency with which it moved its planes for launching and landing, keeping the deck as prepared as possible to launch an attack, this was a high-pressure business, with a lot of shouting and running all day long, a lot like athletic teams. Except for lunch, you never left the deck from the time flight operations began, before light, until they ended, after dark, and any moment of rest was passed sitting at the side of the island, asleep in an instant, so that you could be there immediately if needed. Lots of military drills are more show than reality, but this one was in dead earnest, timed with a stopwatch. In the coming war, battles were lost and won by the plane-handling on the carriers. The Japanese lost the Battle of Midway in large part because of a systematic failure to handle their planes properly.

The *Enterprise* left Pearl Harbor at the end of November, loaded with, in addition to her own air group, the fighter planes of a marine squadron that was to be taken to Wake Island and flown off to the landing strip there. Wake was the closest of our bases to Japan, and the faces of the pilots were grim when they flew off to the island. In a few weeks they had all been captured or killed, including a boy named Bobby Mitwalsky, who had gone to school with me and joined the marines when I went into the navy. I remembered him most for a leather jacket he had with panels of admirable blue fur.

The clouds were heavy all the way back from Wake and the storms continuous, waves breaking over the flight deck when the bow dipped deep. The other ships in the task force, cruisers and destroyers, began to make heavy going of it, and the task force slowed down, delaying its entrance into Pearl Harbor from the night of December 6 to sometime in the morning of the 7th.

Whenever the *Enterprise* went into port, because she could not launch or land aircraft while tied up, the planes were flown off to a land base for as long as we were in harbor. Early on the morning of the 7th our air group took off for Ford Island. The ship was empty, without its planes, and everyone was getting ready for docking in Berth 1010 alongside the navy yard and the starboard watch going ashore for liberty. But before 0900 hours, general quarters was sounded—a clanging bell followed by a boatswain's pipe and a stirring bugle call. A stern voice ordered, "All hands man your battle stations," at the sound of which all hell broke loose, and thousands of sailors ran to their assigned battle stations. You had to race up ladders and down passageways to get through before all watertight doors and hatches were closed and dogged down. No one was surprised —submarine scares were common—but this was different. A huge battle flag was broken out and streamed down the deck. The captain came on the public address system to announce that Pearl Harbor had been bombed and that we were now at war with the Japanese. This was followed by the reading of the Articles of War, a long list, I thought, of the many reasons for which the navy could imprison you for life or shoot you. It spoke of no rewards.

I didn't worry about being killed, but I did wonder how long I was going to have to stay in the navy now. We all disliked the Japanese and the Germans in a general kind of way, not really knowing much about them. But I never saw a newspaper, only the daily mimeographed sheet put out aboard ship with ball scores and a few headlines, and I knew nothing of how oil embargoes and blocked finances had brought us to war. I knew that the Japanese had invaded China long ago and were still fighting there. Everyone knew the Japanese hated us, even as we despised them, and the old Asiatic hands told stories of Japanese sailors lining up at the rail and shouting, "Yankee, we sink you," when they passed in port. So, really, it was no surprise, somehow expected and taken for granted for a long time, though the reasons were beyond us.

The ship stayed at general quarters; we were only a few miles south of the entrance to Pearl Harbor, and the scuttlebutt (named after the water cask on the old ships where sailors getting a drink of water exchanged gossip) began to circulate that the Japanese had landed on Oahu, taken San Francisco, and on and on. Rumor is a remarkable thing, a free play of the imagination, but the truth was that after two air strikes the Japanese planes went back to their carriers north of Oahu, which turned at high speed and went back to their home ports. We looked for the Japanese fleet in an unlikely direction, southwest, and fortunately never found it, for although some of our planes had returned to the ship—others had gotten mixed up in the battle and been shot down—a single carrier with few planes aboard would have been no match for the enemy's six carriers.

Fuel was low in all the ships in the task force, and we had to go into port in the late afternoon of December 8, fueling that night and putting to sea by dawn. Rumors of new attacks were everywhere, and since no one knew where the attack had come from, there was fear that it might come again. Everyone was keyed up and the ship remained at general quarters, which meant that I was on the flight deck, where I could see everything in the fading light. The smells came first as we moved slowly through the nets guarding the channel, smells of fuel oil, burned paint and canvas, hot steel. Fires were still burning, and a heavy cloud of smoke hung over ships that had looked so bright a week earlier. It was eerie, the huge ship moving painstakingly slowly into the harbor through what had always been a narrow channel, now made much narrower by a battleship half in the mud on the port side, its stern sticking well out into the channel. The *Nevada* had managed to get under way during the attack but began to founder going out of the channel. The captain, realizing that if his ship sank in the channel it would block the Pacific Fleet from entering or exiting, beached her on the western side, leaving just enough room for the big carrier and her escorts to maneuver around him at painfully slow speed.

After inching around the *Nevada*—oh, how slow it was when all we wanted to do was get it over with and get out of there—the *Enterprise* turned a few points to port and started down the anchorage between battleship row to port and the dockyard and submarine base to starboard. At the naval yard, aft of a huge drydock containing the battleship *Pennsylvania*, were the cruiser *Helena* and the minesweeper *Oglala*. Japanese intelligence had predicted that the aircraft carrier *Enterprise* would be in this position on December 7, and a torpedo intended for her smashed into the smaller ships. The entire front of the navy yard, including the immense drydock with the *Pennsylvania* inside, accompanied by a badly hit destroyer, was blasted and strewn with rubble of broken ships and installations. But for some reason the Japanese had neglected to bomb the all-important fuel storage tanks on the hill beyond the yard. The operation of the fleet depended on this fuel.

It was on the port side, however, that the real devastation was visible, beginning with wrecked hangars and seaplanes on the tip of Ford Island, then, one after another—broken in two, turned over, canted crazily, lying under water with only the upper masts showing, burned, smoking, and smoldering—the long row of battleships, two by two, the main battle force of the Pacific Fleet and the U.S. Navy. The attack announced in a violent way that the day of the battleship was gone, that it had been replaced by aircraft carriers like the one that was now picking her way daintily, almost disdainfully, down the harbor past the smoking hulks of the old navy devastated by planes from foreign aircraft carriers.

The meaning extended even further, for the carrier-based Japanese planes not only sank the American battleships, they sank at the same time all the huge battleships that the Japanese Imperial Navy had been building for many years. The Japanese would emphasize the lesson on the other side of the Pacific Ocean when off Malaya they sank the British battleships *Prince of Wales* and *Repulse* with land-based torpedo aircraft as the ships were under way and combat ready, not tied up. Having seen the mighty effects of air power, I was stunned, and more than a little frightened, by this sudden destruction of what had seemed invincible a week earlier. There was no

question of losing the war, but how would we win it? Surely
not with a few aircraft carriers like the *Enterprise*, but there
wasn't anything else.

One dreary scene succeeded another, and as night fell we
inched in slow motion around the northern end of Ford Island, like some skulking mourner at a ghastly funeral. Loud
voices called out from shore: "You'd better get the hell out of
here or the Japs will get you too." And "Where in hell were
you?" A few guns went off here and there, and machine-gun
tracers rose in the air from time to time as nervous gunners let
loose at their fears and confusion. Then, to port, we passed the
old target battleship *Utah*, with her bottom turned up to the
sky, and we tied up just beyond her. The fuel lines came aboard
in an instant, and all hands that could be spared from battle
stations, which included me, formed lines down the gangways
onto Ford Island to pass the supplies that were waiting there
for us into the ship.

Each sailor was given postcards to send home: two with the
printed message "I am well and will write soon," another two
with "I am wounded and will write details as soon as possible." We joked that there should be a third message, "I am
dead." Laughter aside, at this point a fatal train was lighted that
would explode months later in my family's mountain ranch.
Two cards meant one for the family and one for the girlfriend
all sailors claimed to have. I did not have a girlfriend, wasn't
even sure I wanted one, but you had to live up to the heroic
moment, which required a girlfriend, so I sent my second card
off to a girl in Saratoga whom I much admired but who was
indifferent to me. The cards became separated in transit, and
the card to the girl arrived first, while the one to my family was
delayed. The ranch was snowed in, but someone trudged the
four miles through the snow to tell my parents that Jane had
heard from me and I was safe. My mother was relieved, but,
suffering already from depression, which had been intensified
by my going overseas and the beginning of the war, she concluded that I no longer cared for her and had transferred my
loyalties to a girl she didn't like. She assumed that I had had
only one card and had used it to write to Jane, and when her
card arrived a week or two later, it made no difference to her
feelings about my disloyalty.

By three or four in the morning the ship was loaded, many of the supplies still on the hangar deck waiting to be stowed below. The lines were cast off, and the *Enterprise* began to edge her way out the harbor, down the channel, through the nets, and into blue water, picking up speed as she went, the sun rising, the water beginning to hiss alongside, and the smell of oil, charred paint, bodies, and defeat left far behind. Our air group landed aboard later, and the war had begun.

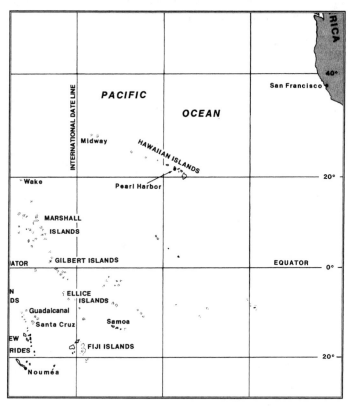

We cruised in the first year of the war across the date line and below the equator.

CHAPTER FOUR

Cruising

To a young man war is exciting, and few wars can have looked more promising at the beginning than the naval war in the Pacific Ocean between the United States and Japan from December 1941 to September 1945. The ocean itself was vast and filled with mysterious places whose exotic names now became as familiar to me as the little towns in Wyoming where I had grown up—Medicine Bow, Rawlins, Encampment, and Laramie—once had been. Now the names were Truk (the major Japanese base in the Marianas Islands), Cavite and Bataan, the Java Sea and the Coral Sea, Guam and Wake Island, Mindanao and Balikpapan, New Caledonia and Guadalcanal.

Great fleets steamed across vast spaces of water at high speed, surprising the enemy with sudden raids and then disappearing into the emptiness extending from the Aleutians and the Bering Strait in the north to Port Moresby and New Zealand in the south, from the California coast to the Indian Ocean. The ships were fast, heavily armed, and technically advanced; never before tried in combat, they were now about to develop by trial and error a new kind of war of aircraft carriers: ship-based aircraft fighting with other ship-based aircraft for control of the air and sea.

The crews on both sides at that early point in the war were professional and volunteer; everyone was there because he had wanted, or at least agreed, to be there, and as a consequence the morale was high, as were the skills of the combatants. It was a war both navies had wanted for a long time, and, tired of messing with each other, they went at it with a lot of energy. We despised the Japanese at first, and it took a lot of failures to realize that at the beginning of the war theirs was a better navy than ours: better aircraft, better trained personnel, better night training, better torpedoes by far. We improved rapidly, but in the end we overcame them by sheer weight of equipment and men. They remained to the end a worthy foe—courageous, skilled, tenacious, gallant in their strange way—whom we had seriously underestimated. Never after the first days of the war did the sailors in our fleet look down on "the Japs" or speak contemptuously, like our yellow press, of the cowardice of the enemy.

Most of us on the *Enterprise* assumed after Pearl Harbor that the ship and the other carriers in the Pacific would be sent at once to relieve the Philippines and to break up the attack on Wake Island. Our admiral, William F. "Bull" Halsey, a real fire-eater, thought so too. His quarters were just down the passageway, beneath the flight deck and the island, from our ordnance shack, and when we went down to try to wheedle fresh fruit from his mess attendants we could hear him thundering away, cursing Washington and the shore-based navy for their cowardice. The only reason we could think of for not being sent to sink the Japanese fleet forthwith—this is how we thought in our innocence—was that nearly all our battleships were lying broken and burned on the mud bottom of the anchorages alongside Ford Island. But Adm. Chester Nimitz, soon to be the commander of the Pacific Fleet, must have had some understanding of what Pearl Harbor meant for the long run, for later, when he was assembling the fleet to fight the Battle of Midway, he left out several seaworthy battleships that were assembled in San Francisco.

Wisely, no one ordered us to fight our way to Manila, Truk, or Yokosuka, and we were kept on patrols during December and early January, guarding the approaches to the Hawaiian Islands, going back and forth across the 180th meridian, the International Date Line. On December 24, 1941, with a satisfactory kind of black humor, we crossed the dateline to the west at midnight, going straight to December 26, never missing Noel and God Rest You Merry Gentlemen.

The American carriers—there were only three, *Lexington*, *Yorktown*, and *Enterprise*, after the *Saratoga* was hit by a torpedo in early January—operated separately, each the center of a task force completed by heavy cruisers and destroyers. Standard watches were Condition Three (four hours on duty and eight off) and Condition Two (four hours on and four off), with most watertight doors and hatches dogged closed. It was difficult to move about the ship, and everyone was always tired. Reveille came before sunrise so that general quarters could be sounded in time for everyone to be at their battle stations at sunrise. Sunrise and sunset were considered the two most dangerous moments, when submarine or airplane attacks could be made out of the sun. Six fighter planes would be launched just before sunup to fly combat air patrol (CAP) over the task force, and soon after a number of dive-bombers and torpedo planes armed with aerial depth charges would be sent up to fly searches out a hundred miles (ASP) or more looking for submarines or surface vessels. After the planes were off the deck and general quarters secured, the smoking lamp was lit, and breakfast was served. Coffee and beans, sometimes Spam, occasionally dried eggs, dry cereal with powdered milk, prunes, or some other kind of dried or canned fruit. Oranges or apples if you had been in port recently. Then the day's work began, cleaning and polishing, repairing the equipment for which you were responsible, belting ammunition, providing working parties for one job after another, and the dreaded chipping detail. Peacetime navy ships were beautifully painted inside and out, and the lower decks were covered with thick red linoleum kept at a high shine. The Pearl Harbor attack, however, had shown that paint and linoleum burn fiercely, giving off a heavy toxic smoke, and so after December 7 ships were ordered to get rid of all the interior paint, except in the light-green officers' quarters, and all the linoleum.

The interior of a carrier, like that of other warships, is a maze of hatches, welded supports, air ducts, cables, and pipes, all covered generously with several coats of white paint, and to chip it all off, flake by flake, with a chipping hammer—a flat iron bar, bent at a right angle two inches from one end, and sharpened on both ends—was a labor of the damned. It was hot inside the ship, and the men stripped to their skivvies, rags around their heads, chipping away—clink, clink, clink, sonofabitch!—hour after hour. It was maddening work, difficult, endless, seemingly pointless, and when it was finished, after many months in which it took up every spare hour, and the linoleum ripped off the rusty decks, the compartments with their raw, rust-pitted bulkheads were as depressing as if the ship had been burned out.

Watching the task force spread out over the ocean never ceased to be interesting, even after months of steaming. The carrier was in the center, and the cruisers *Salt Lake City*, *Northampton*, *Chester*, and *Pensacola* plunged steadily along on both sides. Ten or twelve destroyers raced about on the flanks, ahead, and to the stern, listening for submarines, transferring material and personnel, and serving as plane guards to pick up the crews of crashed planes.

We refueled at sea, and occasionally a big tanker named after a faraway American river—the Platte or the Cimarron—would come alongside, some fifty feet away, and with both ships still under way, pitching and rolling toward each other, these thousands of tons of mass would send rubber hoses across and pump fuel and aviation gas out of the tanker into the carrier. Sometimes, as we became more adept, a cruiser or destroyer would get fuel at the same time on the other side of the tanker, or would take fuel from the carrier herself on the side away from the tanker. During this operation the waves between the ships were huge, and standing on the deck of the carrier you could watch the great bulk of the tanker rise up above you and then crash down. It was blue-water seamanship at its best, always pleasant to watch how smartly it was done. It permitted our ships to stay at sea much longer and to operate while there without having to run at slow speeds to conserve fuel. It also meant that, keeping radio silence, you could disappear in the distances of the ocean, to appear suddenly somewhere you weren't expected or wanted.

At the beginning of February 1942, the *Enterprise*, on the first major American carrier raid of the war, appeared out of the blue in this way to attack Kwajalein Atoll in the Marshall Islands. We had been down to Samoa escorting troop ships and looking longingly at the green tropical islands off in the far distance. The *Yorktown* had come around from the Atlantic, and after we joined her, we had moved north together. The run in to the islands began at high speed in the evening and continued all night long. For the first time, we sweated through the night before the battle. The crew's compartments were aft, where, lying in your bunk with the whole stern of the ship vibrating from the propeller shafts turning at high rpms below, sleep was fitful. There was a general uneasiness, which the crew, restless with the noise and rattle, the shush of the air ducts bringing fresh air to compartments in which all portholes had been covered, communicated by endless nervous shifting in the bunks and constant movement back and forth to the heads in the red glare of the night-lights. During battle conditions the red lights went out, and the blue battle lamps here and there created an eerie, never-to-be-forgotten spooky feeling, as the sweat dripped down into your eyes from under your gray steel World War I helmet, the stale camphor smell of the fireproofed canvas covers of the bulky gray kapok-filled life jackets tied tightly up under your chin.

Reveille was a relief. We rushed to get up to the deck, hoping to see the islands we were attacking, but there were only the familiar blue water and the escort vessels. Kwajalein Atoll was still many miles away, attacked but never seen by the carrier's crew. The strike force—a few torpedo planes carrying bombs for a high-level attack, some dive-bombers each carrying a yellow five-hundred-pound bomb under the fuselage, and a handful of fighters to provide air cover—went off about 0500, and the cruisers moved in to shell the landing fields. At that time it seemed a mighty air armada to us, who had not yet seen the sky filled from horizon to horizon with carrier planes on their way to the Japanese mainland. I was released from plane-pushing duties to help load bombs onto the torpedo planes, hoisting them up and locking them on the bomb rack, inserting the fuses and threading the long copper arming wire through the holes in the fuse vanes, tightening up the sway brackets.

Off in the distance the strike group was no bigger than a fist held up in the sky, and the *Enterprise* was still with her planes gone. Everyone waited nervously to see whether we had been spotted by the enemy. Ship's radar was primitive in those days, but we did have it, and the Japanese did not—one of our few advantages—and this morning it kept telling us that the skies were clear. The Japanese planes had been caught on the ground with their ships in the anchorage inside the big atoll. Then the wait began for the return of our own planes, and about mid-morning a few fighters came back, then some dive-bombers, and at last the torpedo planes. All eyes tried to count to see how many planes had been lost. Only a few, it turned out, not more than three or four.

The *Enterprise* turned into the wind, picked up maximum speed, cleared the flight deck, and raised the arresting cables to catch the planes' tailhooks. The hydraulic crash barriers three-quarters of the way up the deck came up with a swoosh, and the carrier was ready to take her strike group aboard. The planes roared by in loose formation on the starboard side, a few hundred feet up, and as they passed the ship, they began to peel off, one by one, to their port, flying around the ship and coming in low and aft, following the wake onto the deck. The landing signal officer stood at the rear on the port side, facing aft, with two yellow paddles, one in each hand, giving visual signals to the incoming plane. Up a little, a bit to port, less power, cut.

The plane hit the deck heavily, and its hook grabbed one of the elevated arresting wires and jerked it out until the plane came to a stop. Men raced out to release the arresting wire, the tailhook retracted, the crash barriers went down, the plane taxied forward at high speed, then slammed on the brakes, and the barrier came back up just as the next plane was landing. It was a tricky and a dangerous business, and everything depended on doing it fast and doing it well. In peacetime the navy was miserly about every piece of equipment, but in wartime a badly damaged plane went over the side instantly to clear room for the following plane.

How effective the strike had been no one seemed to know, and if they did, no one bothered to tell the crew, who filled what later times would call an information gap with scuttlebutt about monstrous battleships sinking in the channel, hundreds of planes exploding from direct hits while taxiing out to take off, and disgraced and distraught Japanese admirals committing hara-kiri in the control tower to apologize to the emperor. Quite satisfying stuff, which made the morning seem extremely worthwhile, though in fact the few planes with their light bomb loads had done little harm.

After a small follow-up strike was launched, we were told to rearm all the torpedo planes with torpedoes, which were considered, as the Japanese had demonstrated at Pearl Harbor, the right weapons with which to sink warships. Quick, an older ordnanceman, and I were moving one of the stubby two-thousand-pound aerial torpedoes on a hydraulic lift across the oily, slippery hangar deck. Suddenly the five-inch antiair-craft guns on the after starboard sponson above began firing, and the deck heeled sharply up fifteen degrees on that side as the ship turned abruptly to port to evade an attack. The PA blared, STAND BY TO REPEL ENEMY AIR ATTACK. My first im-mediate experience of a shooting war! A big Japanese patrol plane had found us. The steep angle of the deck caused the heavy torpedo to slide down toward the port side, carrying us with it. We lowered the hydraulic skid to the deck, but it continued sliding on the oily steel until secured to a ring in the deck used for tying down planes. There we stood, frozen, two sailors with a lashed-down torpedo, in the middle of the vast, empty hangar deck, which was shifting rapidly from one crazy angle to another. I wanted to get the hell out of there, but we couldn't leave the torpedo for fear it would break loose and smash into a bulkhead and explode. The progress of the attack could be measured, even when you couldn't see anything, by the number and caliber of guns firing. As long as only the five-inchers were booming, the enemy was still high and far away, but when the small-caliber guns cut in (first the four-barreled, deliberate one-point-ones—bang, bang, bang, bang—and then the .50-caliber machine guns along the catwalks), it was time to put your head down. When someone ran out on the deck and began firing a handgun, which occasionally happened, the at-tack was really closing in. After the fifties cut in water splashed in one of the openings of the hangar deck from a near miss. In a few minutes it was all over.

The *Enterprise*, undamaged, was on her way back to Pearl Harbor one bright blue day when one of our torpedo planes flying a search vector failed to return. We waited for it and the three men aboard for hours until we were certain that it must have run out of gas in an area where there was no place to land except on the deck of the *Enterprise*. Search planes went out, and destroyers patrolled for miles in all directions, but no trace of the plane was found, and the men were assumed lost. When they turned up in Pearl Harbor about two months later, we were all astounded. They had spent thirty days on their small yellow rubber raft, all three of them, with no rations or water, having lost everything when they ditched. Rainwater, seabirds, and fish kept them going until, purely by chance in all that vastness, they washed ashore on a small island, losing their raft getting across the coral reef.

The March 23, 1942, issue of *Time* magazine referred to the pilot, an enlisted chief aviation pilot named Harold Dixon, as "a man that Bligh would fancy," and encouraged by this double-edged praise, he published a book, *The Raft*, with the aid of a ghostwriter who made him quite a hero. The writer had him saying, for example, when his crew lay exhausted, emaciated, and dehydrated on the beach of the island, "If there are Japs on this island, they'll not see an American sailor crawl. We'll stand like men-of-warsmen." Everyone hooted at this, and the squadron wits did some very funny acts standing like "men-of-warsmen," a role no one had heard of for years. Tony Pastula, the middle-seat man, told us that Dixon had failed to make a crucial turn on the patrol, and when the radioman, Aldrich, told him that the ship's homing signal was getting weaker, Dixon told him to shut up, that he had been flying by the seat of his pants longer than Aldrich had been a radioman. In the end they ran out of gas and took to their raft, and after Aldrich, not Dixon, dragged them out of the surf, they were saved by the natives and some nuns. The raft went into the U.S. Naval Academy Museum, where it is still displayed, and the book made a lot of money, but the ghostwriter and Dixon cut Pastula and Aldrich out of the deal. Tony said that they had been conned into signing a paper to surrender their rights to the story in return for five hundred dollars each. But at least they became members of the "Sea Squatters," a club organized by Kidde, the company that made the small CO_2 bottles that inflated the navy rafts and Mae Wests.

Entering Pearl Harbor after the Marshall raid may have been the most moving moment of the war for me, far more than seeing Nagasaki, which was hard to take in, or Tokyo Bay, which was anticlimactic. We were in whites, lined up at quarters on the flight deck, and as we came down the channel, the sunken and burned battleships in plain sight along Ford Island, the crews of the anchored ships, at quarters themselves, their white uniforms showing up against their gray ships, cheered us, one after another, again and again. The frustration of defeat and helplessness after Pearl Harbor, while the Japanese overran the entire western Pacific and sank our ships wherever they found them, in the Philippines and Indonesia, was enormous. The raid on the Marshalls, followed by other raids on small islands like Wake and Marcus, was the first successful action by an American ship; small, yes, but it was enough to give the fleet a lift.

The feeling of being a hero didn't last long. I had already been a plane handler, but that was a noble occupation compared to mess cooking: three months in the galleys, literally, peeling potatoes in enormous machines, washing huge pots and pans, serving food to endless lines of sailors making nasty remarks about what you gave them. Mess cooking was exile. You had to move to the mess halls with your sea bag, stow your hammock in the nets there, and sleep in it at night, one of the few places in the navy where hammocks were still used. The food-serving operation ran night and day, with watches coming on and going off duty every four hours, and only the exhaustion after long days of heavy labor made sleep possible in compartments where the lights were never out and noisy people came and went constantly.

One of the most disagreeable jobs was handling the huge galvanized garbage cans filled to the brim with slops to be dumped over the side. It took two men to get them up the slippery, narrow ship's ladders, step by painful step, with some inevitable spillage, to where they could be emptied over the side, to leeward, of course, which was not always an easy place to find in the dark if the ship was maneuvering and the wind was shifting. The job was made more difficult by the fact that it had to be done after darken ship to avoid showing a trail in the ocean until the fish had a chance to clean up after us. One night my fellow garbage handler, Whitey, and I fell on a steep ladder. In a failed attempt to keep the can from spilling, Whitey slipped and hit his mouth on the edge of the can, knocking out one of his upper front teeth. The ship's dentist did only fillings and extractions, no cosmetic work, and so Whitey spent his next few liberties—we got liberty only every month or two when we came into Pearl—going to a Honolulu dentist to get a false tooth. This was both a joyless and expensive way to spend what little liberty and money he had, even though by that time we were seamen first class, making all of fifty-four dollars a month, and I used to argue with him long and earnestly, in the way that only a young man who knows nothing about the matter could, that it was pointless to waste his time and money in this fashion. Better to wait until the war was over and you knew whether you would survive to use a false tooth, ran my foolish and boring refrain.

But Whitey was not only stubborn, he was, it turned out to my vast surprise, hugely vain, and though small and non-descript physically, like the rest of us—we did not look at all like the sailors we occasionally saw gaily dancing their lives away in movie musicals!—he could not bear the thought of being what he considered mutilated. He was right, I suppose, but there was something to be said for my perception. After he became an apprentice cook Whitey was killed by an armor-piercing bomb that exploded in the *Enterprise*'s chiefs' galley the following October at the Battle of Santa Cruz.

Honolulu in those days, where we took our brief, eight-hour liberties, was more out of Somerset Maugham than Gauguin, but it seemed a proper setting for the old salts we thought we were by that time. Dressed in fresh white uniforms, we rushed onto the buses and roared down to Canal Street. A few min-utes were spent in the New Congress Hotel where the "French line" went up the long wooden stairs on the right, and the "old-fashioned" line ascended the left staircase. Such sophis-tication! Going through both lines—take your choice of the order—was considered a sign of super manhood. Weaker spir-its were likely to wander off to have a few beers before going through the line, but older hands knew from experience that the unspeakable local brew, Primo Beer, which was loaded with saltpeter—at least so it was said—would douse the flames of lust faster than a fire hose.

I fancied myself quite a dancer at the time, and I found my way in time to the servicemen's club—the USO that had just been opened—to dance with the local Portuguese girls who volunteered to mingle with the sailors. Honolulu was an old liberty port, long familiar with naval antics ashore, and while nothing we did could any longer surprise the outrage-hardened citizenry, they wanted as little to do with us as possible. In par-ticular, they did not want us even to look at their daughters. Unaware of the reputation of sailors in Honolulu, though, I thought I cut quite a fine nautical figure and was crestfallen when I tried to make a date with a beautiful Portuguese girl, only to learn that her father would rather see her date one of the lepers from Molokai than a sailor. But my heart was not broken.

On to the honky-tonks with the jukeboxes, the fights between sailors from different ships, and several bottles of the abominable Primo, no hard liquor being sold. Dirty, bedraggled, and obscenely noisy, we made our way back to the navy yard by late afternoon, ran the gauntlet of the marine guards at the gate who took out their frustrations, with clubs, on sailors looking for a fight, and then crowded into the fifty-foot motor launches that took us at last back to ships with names as epic— *Enterprise, Yorktown, Salt Lake City, Northampton*—as those at Trafalgar or Jutland. Weighed soberly, Honolulu liberty was not much, but it had the effect of making us glad to be, as sailors always are, aboard ship and at sea again.

In April we put to sea and to our surprise went north for a change. Morale dropped with the news that Bataan had surrendered. As it became cold and colder, woolen watch caps and winter uniforms, long stowed away in storage lockers, appeared. White water broke over the flight deck as the ship rose and fell in heavy seas. One morning there was another carrier, the USS *Hornet* (CV-8), younger sister ship of the *Enterprise*, running alongside us, about a hundred yards away. Instead of the usual pale-blue-and-white naval aircraft, her deck was loaded with twin-engine army bombers, Mitchell B-25s, from a point forward of the island all the way to the stern. We assumed that they were intended for delivery somewhere in the Aleutians, but the public address system soon announced (there was no need for secrecy since there was no one we could tell and no way we could tell them) that this was an army squadron commanded by Col. James Doolittle, to be launched for an attack on Tokyo after we took it to a point five hundred miles off the Japanese mainland. The *Enterprise* was to provide combat air patrols and antisubmarine patrols for the *Hornet* since she could launch none of her own planes while the Mitchells filled her flight deck.

We were excited not only at the idea of hitting Tokyo itself but also at the danger of going so close to Japan. But we were technicians, and it was the technical problem that really intrigued us. Could the heavy planes with a bomb load of four five-hundred-pounders, even when stripped of guns and armor, get to Japan and then make it to the nearest safe landing point in China? Even before that, could such heavy planes, designed for long airfields, get off a short carrier deck? The B-25s spotted farthest forward had a run of only about three hundred feet, which was about the minimum run needed for even the much smaller carrier planes designed for this work. Sailors, like stockbrokers, work everything out by betting, and there was soon heavy money down on both sides: would they make it, would they not? The odds were that the B-25s wouldn't have been on the *Hornet* if there had not been successful tests somewhere, but with all the skepticism of an old salt about anything the services did, I put down ten dollars at even money that less than half of them would get into the air.

April 18 was a cold and windy morning: near gale-force winds with high green foam-flecked waves and the taste and smell of the northern ocean. We were spotted some six hundred miles off the Japanese coast by fishing boats serving as patrol craft. The light cruiser *Nashville*, with fifteen six-inch guns in five turrets, three forward and two aft, looked the picture of naval warfare in the age of steam as she came up to flank speed—about thirty-five knots—turned sharply to port, and began firing. Signal flags crackled as they ran up and down on the halyards, black smoke blew in the wind, yellow flashes came out of the gun barrels, and salvo after salvo missed the little boats bobbing on the waves, now in sight, now hidden. They were not easy targets, and the rounds that hit were armor piercing and went through the wooden hulls without exploding. The *Nashville* sailors stubbornly denied over the years that their gunnery had failed and that the transfer of their ship to the Aleutians soon afterward was a removal to a less critical area, but it looked like a big failure to the sailors on other ships.

It was assumed that the Japanese had radioed alerts to Tokyo, though they hadn't, and although the range was a hundred miles or so too long for the B-25s, the decision was made to risk it and launch anyway. So turning into a wind that was now close to forty knots, which helped the launch, the *Hornet* began to send the bombers off. The first plane, Doolittle's, didn't even use up the available deck. So powerful was the effect of the wind added to the full speed of the ship—about seventy-five knots total—that the B-25s needed only to get up about thirty knots' speed to float off the deck like great kites, only slowly moving ahead of the ship, which seemed to remain almost stationary below them. One after another the entire squadron went off, and we all cheered loudly and choked down a few patriotic tears. I thought my ten dollars well lost in a good cause, as if I had actually contributed the money to success in the war. We turned back at once to get out of range of Japanese aircraft, and although we were told that Doolittle had bombed Tokyo, we heard no details about how most of the planes made it to China until years afterward, when the entire story of the minor damage, but heavy blow to Japanese pride, became public.

Within a few days it was warm again, and after another brief stop at Pearl we departed, still with the *Hornet*, for the southwest Pacific, where the battle to contain a Japanese drive to the south and the east—Australia, New Guinea, and the Solomon Islands—was shaping up. Task forces centered on aircraft carriers maneuvered to locate the enemy and get in the first strike before being discovered. Two of our fleet carriers in the Pacific, the *Lexington* and *Yorktown*, were already in the Coral Sea, off the eastern end of New Guinea, trying to block two Japanese fleets coming at them from opposing directions. We were being sent to equal the odds and coming in from the east to surprise a Japanese two-carrier task force coming south from Truk.

Wartime cruising now became a routine in which boredom and tiredness ate away at the usual good nature of sailors. Stripped of paint and linoleum, rusting everywhere, hot from cruising near the equator, with only a few air blowers open below deck, shuddering from high-speed maneuvers in a way that knocked over anything set on shelves and tables, the ships and the life aboard them began to get to us. Fresh food lasted only a few days after we had been in port; we washed and shaved in salt water, our skin irritated by sandy saltwater soap; work and catnaps filled up the days. Dungarees and blue work shirts, the standard uniform of the day, were never ironed, only washed and dried all together in a great bag that had to be rummaged through to find the pieces with your name stenciled on them. Put on clean and dry, they were soaking wet from sweat in a few minutes. White hats were dyed an anemic purple, and white socks were forbidden so as to avoid flashes of white on the flight deck that would betray the presence of the ship to snooper aircraft. Heat rash tormented everyone, particularly around the waist, where several layers of wet clothing twisted and scraped inside a belt. A story circulated that you would die when the heat rash—a quarter of an inch high and several inches wide, red and angry—had girdled your waist. No one believed it, but everyone kept a careful eye on the progress of the rash around his middle. Every free moment was spent somewhere the cooling breeze could blow over the rash and the sun could dry it out. Lacking any movies, radio, or music to entertain us, we gambled. It became the only relief from the tedium of what was now becoming not weeks but months at sea without even a sight of land in the distance. I was a more enthusiastic than skillful poker player, but I loved the game, as I did bridge, and even though I regularly lost my money in small games in out-of-the-way compartments around the ship, the first glimpse of the five cards in draw poker or the hole card in stud poker were the highest moments, ironically, of days that were routinely filled with accidents and sometimes death.

Death lived on an aircraft carrier operating in wartime conditions. One day a plane would crash taking off, and a lucky pilot lost no more than an eye on the telescopic sight mounted in front of him. The next day a plane landing on deck would drop a wheel strut into the catwalk and run screeching up it for a hundred feet. A mangled crewman who had been watching the landing would be carried away. A thoughtless step backward on the flight and hangar decks where the planes were turning up led to decapitation and gory dismemberment by a propeller. Planes went out on patrol and were never heard of again. Death took many forms, but I think I first really came to know him on a day when I was standing on the flight deck and a Dauntless dive-bomber flew across the ship to drop a message. Once ships had put to sea, strict radio silence was maintained except for certain high-frequency TBS (short-range Talk Between Ships). Beanbags trailing long red streamers were used by planes for message drops in order to preserve radio silence.

As the dive-bomber came across the ship at about 120 knots, with the starboard wing sharply down to give the radioman an open field to throw the message bag on the flight deck, the down wing caught, ever so slightly, just a tick, the railing of the catwalk at the very edge of the ship. It was enough. In an instant the plane was in the water off the starboard side, broken in half between the radioman and the pilot, neither of whom, knocked out by the crash, heads hanging limply forward, moved. Then in an instant both pieces were gone, the water was unruffled, and the ship sailed on. How quickly life swooping along in the graceful plane disappeared as if it had never been! It was the instantaneous succession of quite a lot of something and nothing that focused my attention, and like some eighteen-year-old ancient mariner, I went around for days trying to tell people what had really happened, how astounding it was. The response was polite; death was a grave matter and never lightly dismissed. But no one, quite rightly, wanted to philosophize or make too much of what was common and likely to be the end of all of us, much sooner than later.

CHAPTER FIVE

Midway

THE EMBERS of fear of death that never left us were fanned to life a few days later when we heard that the *Lexington*, commissioned in the early 1920s, had been sunk and the *Yorktown* damaged by aircraft in the Battle of the Coral Sea, the first of the great carrier battles of the Pacific war. The *Lexington* was a "good ship," as was said in the navy—while her sister ship, the *Saratoga*, was not, for unknown reasons—and the news of her sinking was felt as a personal blow, particularly by the many aboard the *Enterprise* (a relatively new ship, commissioned in 1938) who had served on the "Lady Lex." Felt too because she was the first American fleet carrier to go down —CV-1, the old *Langley*, had been sunk in Indonesia, but she was only a converted coal carrier—making clear our own vulnerability by increasing the ratio to six Japanese carriers against only three American.

Our desire for revenge was thwarted when the *Enterprise* and *Hornet* turned and began making a high-speed run back to Pearl Harbor. It seemed to us like craven cowardice, once again, and there was a good deal of muttering. But as we approached Pearl, where there was, we were told, to be no liberty this time, scuttlebutt began to whisper a fantastic story. We had broken the Japanese code, it was said, and learned that their fleet was about to attack Midway Island, with a diversionary move on the Aleutians. We were going to lie off Midway and ambush them. I remember the exact occasion on which I was told, with plentiful details about ships and dates, about the coming battle, but intelligence officers still insist that secrecy on this critical matter was carefully maintained. Everyone who has been in the service, particularly the navy, can testify that it is impossible to keep a secret, no matter how big—messages have to pass through too many hands and be seen by too many eyes—and I repeat that among the enlisted men it was widely known before Midway that we had broken the Japanese code, and the strategy and tactics for the coming battle were learnedly discussed by the admirals of the lower deck, who were, on the whole, of the opinion, as always, that the officers would screw it up.

A few days out of Pearl a destroyer came alongside with the mail that was our lifeline to familiarity. Several hours later the letters worked their way down to the divisional compartments and were passed out by the mail orderly who stood cracking jokes in the center of an anxious circle of impatient sailors: "Smith, she's run off with a marine." My best letters came from my mother, who was a good correspondent, typing long and interesting letters about the dogs, cats, and horses on the ranch, telling me about the neighbors and the plans for the spring and new buildings. I saved her letter for later and opened first a letter from my stepfather (he did not often write), dated April 28, 1942. The words hit me like a hammer: "I am writing this in Saratoga on Sunday morning following the funeral of our Dear. . . . I went over to get in the wood and do the chores. The door was locked. My first thought was it was a joke. I called to her and no answer. Then I tapped the door with my overshoe and asked to be let in. No answer. Then I got alarmed and kicked the door in. Mother was laying in the dining room Dead. I ran to her and felt her pulse. She was cold as marble. I felt her head and it was likewise. She had shot herself in the temple with the 22 pistol you gave her. I did not touch the gun. The whole sight was one awful shock and I will not describe the scene further in this letter. I hunted for a note for a few minutes and then lit out for town. I ran until I was ready to keel and then got control of myself to go into a walk."

The old letter still has burns from when I crumpled it and put it in a bulkhead ashtray before I finished reading, only to return to dig it out, smoldering, and go through each of the awful details. I opened the letter from my mother later, hoping for some clue to what had happened. It was written a few days before her suicide on April 22 and gave no indication that anything in particular was wrong. Apparently she had bottled up whatever it was, as she always had. In all the old photos she was always hard to spot in the group, lurking in the background, away in the corner. Her suicide was, of course, ultimately rooted in despair, despair over all the many things that had gone wrong in her life and could never be put right,

ALVIN KERNAN

despair from living on an isolated ranch with no company; but I hunted for particular reasons, blaming myself for having left her and sending Jane the other postcard.

The telegram telling me of Mother's death arrived in the mail months later. On a ship in the middle of an ocean, on the way to a great battle, trying to deal with a faraway death, the body already buried a month earlier, creates overwhelming emotional pressure. Having to do something, I blundered down into the pale-green officers' quarters, where enlisted men were prohibited without a pass, and found my way to the Catholic chaplain's rooms. I was not devout, but I had been raised a Catholic, and now seemed the time, if ever, to call on religion for help not to be found elsewhere. The chaplain was napping. Startled to see a tearful young sailor, he asked first if I had a pass to be in officers' country, which I did not. Being young, I expected help, and insisted that he provide it in some tangible form like getting me leave to go home, which he could not, of course, arrange.

The chief of the ordnance gang, Murphy, sipping his customary moosemilk, was more sympathetic and more practical. He took me off mess cooking—sending some other poor devil down to the galleys—and gave me a day off, which I spent sitting on a sponson and staring at the ocean rolling by and trying to think of some answer to my sorrow. I slept unexpectedly well that night, which made me feel guilty but began in the way of living things to heal my grief.

A second day off was not thought good for me by the assembled wisdom of the ordnance gang, sitting in solemn conclave like a consistory of cardinals, wearing the red-cloth helmets, that were the symbol of our trade. So somber but glad to have escaped from mess cooking, I was put to work again along with everyone else, getting ammunition up from the magazines, taking it out of its wooden boxes, opening the greased tin inner containers and paper cartons, and then using hand- and automatic belting machines to shove the bullets into the connecting metal links to feed the machine guns of the planes in the coming battle. Black tips were armor piercing; blue, incendiary; red, tracer; and plain, ball. We made up different combinations for different purposes, using more tracer where it was important to be able to see from the burning base of the bullet where the fire stream was going, more armor piercing and incendiary for the hits, and ball to keep the barrels of the guns from burning out too quickly with all this hard, hot stuff.

While I was working away, eating, sleeping, and in a short time talking and joking with the rest of the ordnance gang, my mother's death drifted away from consciousness. I found, like many another, that we are much simpler mechanisms than we think, preserving life and accepting whatever shreds of meaning we can find in it. The dead must bury the dead because the living do not—cannot—pause long enough to do so. Guilt for the dead, especially a suicide, is powerful, but the danger, I soon found, is in feeling that you cannot move away from it and thus letting deep emotions become too tangled.

On May 26 we were back in Pearl. Halsey, who had been standing for weeks on the bridge in his skivvies trying to cool the allergic rash that was covering his body—he must have been more nervous than he appeared to be—went to the hospital on shore. He had become a hero to the crew by then, for no apparent good reason except that he was gruff and outspoken, and his departure seemed ominous. Nimitz came aboard, and we all stood to quarters to watch medals presented to various worthies. Later, Spruance, not an aviator, came aboard as the new admiral commanding Task Force 16, built around the *Enterprise* and *Hornet*, for the Battle of Midway.

Though no one else got liberty, someone saw fit to give me a two-hour compassionate liberty after we reached Pearl, enough time to race into Honolulu in a taxi to the Mackay office (naval communications were never used for personal matters—maybe for officers, I wouldn't know, but never for enlisted men) to cable some borrowed money home to help with funeral expenses and let my stepfather know that his letter had been received, that grief had spread as far as it was likely to for this death. The brass would never have let me off the ship, let alone into a cable office, if they thought I or anyone else had the slightest knowledge about the Japanese plans and the coming battle. How astounded they would have been to learn that everyone in the crew knew about the code and the plans! All precautions were taken to seal off the ship lest something leak out somehow, and I was always grateful to whoever made the eloquent argument that must have been necessary to get me ashore under those tense circumstances.

The time in port was short, two days, and filled with all-hands details: provisioning the ship, filling the magazines, getting stores and fuel aboard. Despite the blackout, bright floodlights burned all night as one lighter after another came alongside, while workmen installed new guns and equipment. But no one complained, for once, about extra duty, and excitement shone in everyone's eyes. By the late morning of the 28th of May, barges alongside still casting off, we, along with the *Hornet*, were under way, steaming once again out of that deep channel that leads south out of the big harbor at Pearl to open water. The *Yorktown* was still being patched up in the dry dock at Pearl and would follow in a few days to complete the American fleet. Though we were unaware of it, at the same time (May 29, Japanese time), the commander of the Japanese Imperial Fleet, Isoruku Yamamoto, on his flagship *Yamato*, the largest ship in the world—seventy thousand tons, nine 18.1-inch guns—was taking the Japanese fleet out of Yashiro-jima through the Bungo Channel on the way to Midway, twenty-five-hundred miles to the east.

Once under way, we continued belting machine-gun ammunition obsessively, like some rite of war, piling up huge mounds ready for use in the planes. We also piled up an enormous amount of trash that had to be burned: long tow targets filled with pasteboard cartridge cartons pulled like Chinese festival dragons laboriously down the passageways and ladders to the ship's incinerator to be burned at night, when the smoke would not give away the position of the ship to submarines or scout planes. Someone had to shovel this mountain of trash into the incinerator far below decks, and perhaps because of recent favors shown me I was dispatched to shovel tons of paper into the incinerator all night long. The job required two sailors, dressed only in skivvies in the boiling heat that was filled with the stale smell of trash, flames weirdly lighting the small space. The cardboard contained bullets here and there that had been missed in the sorting, and after these had lain in the hot fire for a time they exploded. Since they had no backing when they went off, the bullets lacked the force to go through the insulated steel sides of the furnace, but if by chance one came through the door of the incinerator when it was open, it would maim anyone it hit. One man opened the door of the furnace and ducked while the other sailor threw a shovel load in the furnace and then quickly dropped to the deck to avoid any rounds that might have cooked off since the last shovelful was thrown in. The pops were loud and frequent, and shovel-drop-pop from sunset to sunrise jangled the nerves. We were under heavier fire than the rest of the crew, but the frustration of being occupied with trash disposal while going into what we all knew would be one of the big naval battles of all time kept us from feeling heroic.

After burning trash all night, I went up to the ordnance shack on the morning of June 4 to help put the torpedoes on the planes. Incinerator or not, I wasn't going to miss out on this one. This was the big day when U.S. naval air tactics that had been developed over twenty years were at last going to be put into practice. Knowing that the Japanese fleet intended to attack and take Midway to prevent Doolittle-type raids and draw out our fleet for the big surface battle they believed would end the war, the three American carriers—the *Enterprise*, the *Hornet*, and the battered *Yorktown*, all sister ships and the only American carriers left in the central Pacific—had steamed more than a thousand miles and joined to the north and east of Midway at the aptly named Point Luck. Though we were apprehensive, the Japanese were completely unaware of our presence. Having beaten us so easily for so long, they were careless with their scouting and launched half of their planes for a land attack on Midway. Their position was established just after dawn by PBY Catalinas flying out of Midway. Our carriers turned into the wind, and the *Enterprise* and *Hornet* began to launch their strike at about 0700. The *Yorktown* held back its strike for an hour until it was sure that there were not other Japanese carriers shadowing the main force.

All the ground crew, aware that this was the big day, were out to see the pilots and crews off, and as he walked by Winchell, one of the squadron's several enlisted pilots who had recently been made warrant officers, made me proud by borrowing my cigarette lighter for luck. The commander of the squadron, Lt. Cdr. E. E. Lindsey, was taped from his waist to his neck following a crash a few days earlier: bad eyesight had caused him to try to land at an odd angle to the flight deck. But he would not give up the battle. When it was suggested that he should stay in sick bay on the day of the attack, he replied, "This is what I have been trained to do," and led his squadron into the greatest sea battle of the century, in which he and most of his men died.

The dive-bombers of Bombing 6 and Scouting 6, thirty-three in all, went off first, the scouts with two one-hundred-pound bright yellow bombs under the wings and a five-hundred-pounder under the fuselage, the bombers with a single yellow one-thousand-pounder. After a long interval during which no other planes got off because of a mix-up on the deck, the bombers were ordered to proceed independently toward target on a course of 231 degrees, distance 142 miles. This plot assumed that Nagumo, the vice-admiral of the Japanese navy, would maintain his course toward Midway, but he turned north to 70 degrees when he recovered his Midway strike, and therefore our bombers flew too far south. The torpedo planes, fourteen TBDs, were on their way next. Each carried two men, the pilot and the radioman-gunner. The mid-seat observer-bombardiers were left behind that day, to save weight and lives, for everyone knew that whatever happened, it was going to be a bad day for the misnamed "Devastators."

We all knew that a new, much improved torpedo plane, the Grumman TBF, was ready for the fleet. One section of the *Hornet* torpedo squadron (VT-8) had already gotten the new planes, and six of them had flown out to Midway, and from there they too attacked the Japanese fleet on June 4, though with no better success than the carrier squadrons. After the torpedo planes, ten fighters went into the air to provide protection from the Japanese fighter planes, the remarkable Zeros, which would be among the lumbering torpedo planes before they came within range of the antiaircraft guns of the Japanese fleet.

Timing and communication were everything in a carrier aircraft strike, but despite years of practice, both broke down from the start. The *Enterprise* squadrons were separated at the outset when the dive bombers went off alone on the wrong course, delaying their arrival at the target until after the torpedo planes had made their run. The torpedo planes took off by themselves to find the Japanese fleet. Low on gas by the time they got to the Japanese carriers after 0900, they started their attack at once, without any dive-bombers or fighters in sight. The fighters, high above, mistakenly identified Torpedo 8 from the *Hornet* as their charge, but didn't help them either. They remained at high altitude where there were no Japanese fighters, as they had all gone down to shoot up the TBDs from sea level; and while VT-6 was dying, the fighters decided that there was no opposition that day and turned around and flew back to the *Enterprise*. Unhindered, the Zeros closed in on the torpedo planes as they began their runs and shot down nine of the fourteen. None of our torpedoes hit, or if they did they did not explode.

The *Enterprise* strike was supposed to take place at the same time that planes from the *Hornet* attacked other Japanese carriers. But things were far worse on the *Hornet* than they were on the *Enterprise*. Cdr. Stanhope Ring, the leader of the *Hornet* air group, led his planes far north of the Japanese fleet, a massive error in navigation that has still not been explained. His bombers returned with their bombs still in their racks, his fighters broke off and ditched when they ran out of gas, his Torpedo 8 squadron, led by Lt. Cdr. John Waldron, broke off early from the group, left the "flight to nowhere," flew directly to the Japanese carriers, attacked, and died, everyone except the famous Ensign Gay.

Only the *Yorktown*, wiser from experience at the Battle of the Coral Sea, sent its planes directly to the Japanese. But the *Yorktown* torpedo squadron, Torpedo 3, had no better luck than the other Devastators, despite being accompanied by both fighters and dive-bombers that attacked simultaneously. Ten of twelve torpedo planes were shot down, again without an explosion on a carrier hull; two made it back to their ship but had to land in the water.

The *Enterprise* dive-bombers eventually found the Japanese carriers and joined with the *Yorktown* Dauntlesses—arriving at the same time by good luck, not planning—to sink three of them, coming at them in classic style, out of the sun. It was over in fifteen minutes, at around 1030. The three Japanese carriers went up like tinder. And in the afternoon the bombers went back and finished off the fourth and last carrier. Four of the six carriers that had carried out the attack on Pearl Harbor —*Kaga*, *Akagi*, *Hiryu*, and *Soryu*—were all burning by evening and would sink before the next morning.

In this famous victory the torpedo planes played an unintended and unforeseen part. The deck-spotting procedures of the Japanese carriers, referred to earlier, required about forty-five minutes to get their bombers and torpedo planes up from the hangar decks and send them out to attack the American fleet. But the torpedo plane attacks forced them to keep their flight decks clear to launch and land fighters, maintaining the maximum number of armed Zeros in the air to deal with the feared torpedo planes. As a result the Japanese could not find time to prepare strikes against the American fleet. Had they been able to do so our losses would surely have been great, for the one strike the Japanese did send out from the carrier that escaped sinking in the first round managed to cripple the *Yorktown*. No one can claim credit for this critical achievement, totally unintended and unheralded for sixty years, except the aircrews whose blazing courage and sense of duty drove them to fly their old planes with their defective torpedoes to a desperate end without flinching.

In the late morning we waited for our planes on the deck of the *Enterprise*, with an eye toward the *Hornet* nearby and the *Yorktown* several miles away to the west. Our fighters came back first, intact, which seemed odd, and then one, two, three, and finally four torpedo planes straggled in separately, and that was it. The last of the planes was so badly shot up that it was deep-sixed immediately after it landed. One pilot, Winchell, and his radioman, Douglas Cossitt, were later picked up out of the water, sixty pounds lighter following seventeen days adrift in a raft. The total losses for our squadron alone were nine out of fourteen crews.

The loss was unimaginable, and even when the survivors, in a condition of shock, told us what kind of a slaughter it had been, it was hard to believe. It came closer to home when one of the surviving torpedo pilots, a bushy-mustached warrant officer named Smith, came out of his cockpit brandishing his .45 automatic and charged up the ladder to the bridge shouting that he was going to kill the lieutenant, James Gray, who had commanded the fighter escort. He was prevented by force from doing it, but the whole scandal was out in an instant that the torpedo planes had attacked alone. The matter has remained an issue in naval aviation to this day, and in 1988 Capt. James Gray rose at a conference on Midway to change his story and declare that he and his fighters had not been able to protect the torpedo planes because the new types of fighters they flew, the F4F-4s, were heavier than the older F4F-3s and guzzled an unexpected amount of gas. But on the *Enterprise* on the morning of June 4, 1942, there was no doubt that the fighters had failed badly, and the torpedo planes had paid the price.

Around noon came the clanging alarm, the bugle call, "All hands man your battle stations," and then a few minutes later, "Bandits at twenty miles and closing, stand by to repel enemy air attack." But we were not the target that day. The *Yorktown*, about ten miles to port, was between us and the Japanese fleet, and it took the full weight of the attack. How glad we secretly were that it was not us. We stood on the deck and watched, as if it were a movie, the flashes and smoke from the antiaircraft guns in the distance. The *Yorktown* heeled over in sharp turns, taking evasive action, while near misses exploded around her. Attacking and defending planes blew up in bright flares. Not all the bombs missed, and when it was over in less than half an hour, the *Yorktown* was down on the port side, dead in the water, and there were holes in her flight deck large enough to make it impossible for her to land her own planes. She was patched up and by 1400 was moving under her own power again, only to be hit by two torpedoes launched in the second and last Japanese strike from the fourth carrier, *Hiryu*, missed in the morning but dispatched soon afterward. Even then she didn't go down until a submarine finished her off on the morning of June 7.

Within a few minutes after the first attack on the *Yorktown*, her dive-bombers and ours began arriving in small clusters and singly. Shot up, some landing in the water, out of gas, some crashing on deck with failing landing gear or no tailhooks and immediately being pushed over the side to make room for the others coming in. But now the mood was triumphant. The bomber pilots could hardly contain themselves. They were shouting and laughing as they jumped out of the cockpits, and the ship that had been so somber a moment before when the torpedo planes returned now became hysterically excited. We were exultant, not just at the revenge for Pearl Harbor, sweet as that was, but at our renewed sense of power and superiority over the Japanese fleet. No one doubted by now that it would be a long war, but to everyone on the ships at Midway it was clear that we would win.

But a lot of faith in our equipment was swept away on June 4. For one, our torpedo planes, the old TBDs, were undeniably death traps, slow, under-armed, and lacking in maneuverability. The Zeros had shot them down at will, not only the *Enterprise* squadron but also the squadrons from the *Yorktown* and *Hornet*. Even the detached group with the new planes, the TBFs and the army B-26s, lost five of the six TBFs and two of the four B-26s flying from Midway. Put it all together and 51 planes had tried to hit the Japanese ships with torpedoes that day. Only 7 landed back at base. This comes to an aircraft loss rate of 86 percent. Out of 124 pilots and crew who were in torpedo planes, 28—including 12 from the army planes— survived; 96 died. VT-8, the *Hornet* squadron, became famous for losing all of its 15 planes and all its men except Ensign Gay, who flew over the carrier he was attacking and crashed on the other side but managed to get out and hide under a cushion in his life jacket. His ashes were spread years later near the point where the torpedo squadrons died so valiantly.

If any of the planes got a hit, they had no effect, for the torpedoes were erratic and either broke up, porpoised, exploded early, or failed to explode. The failure of our torpedoes in planes and submarines during the first three years of the war—which everyone in the fleet knew and talked about—and the refusal of the administrators to acknowledge the problem and fix it, remains one of the scandals of the U.S. Navy. All that reckless heroism with no chance of success even if things had gone well, instead of going about as badly as they could.

Our fighters showed up little better. The Grumman F4F-4s were no match for the Zeros at Midway. Lieutenant Laub, the senior surviving officer of Torpedo 6, remarked sadly that even if our fighters had supported the squadron it would have made no difference because they were inferior to the Zeros. He was

right, for the six fighters from the *Yorktown* that accompanied its torpedo planes, led by the famous Jimmy Thach, were
driven off by the Japanese fighters after losing one plane.

It was the dive-bombers that emerged at Midway as the
primary weapon of naval aviation, and until the end of the
war, dive- or glide-bombing with one type of plane or another
remained our most effective tactic. Thirty-three dive-bombers
in the *Enterprise* group and half that number in the *Yorktown*
group were enough to do what was needed. Even their success, however, turned not on planning so much as on luck and
a piece of rare good judgment by Lt. Cdr. Wade McClusky,
the commander of Air Group 6. Having gone to the point
of no return without sighting the Japanese—who had turned
north when they discovered the American fleet on their flank
—he decided to go on for another ten minutes, during which
time he saw the wake of a Japanese destroyer eighteen thousand feet below going northeast. He chose to follow it, and
over the horizon saw *Kido Butai*, the mighty Japanese attack
fleet, below him, its Combat Air Patrol all down at sea level
shooting up the torpedo planes. When Bombing 5 from the
Yorktown arrived a little later, the bombers went to work together. I have always thought that if there were one single
crucial act in the Pacific war it was Wade McClusky's turn
northeast, and although I never saw him after he landed, I
have often wished him a long and prosperous life.

Battles are well planned, but their outcomes regularly turn
on chance. So it was at Midway, for the Japanese as well as the
Americans. A fatal overconfidence engendered by victories in
the early months of the war no doubt contributed to negli-
gence on their part, but accident also played a crucial role. One
of their scouts from a cruiser was late being launched on the
morning of June 4 and just happened to be the scout assigned
to the sector in which our fleet was located. So, still unaware of
our presence, the Japanese prepared for a second strike against
Midway, thinking that they had all the time in the world. When
they finally learned that we were there they began frantically
rearming for a strike against our carriers. But first they brought
the earlier strike, low on gas, back aboard, intending to send a
full-load strike from all four carriers against us. But it was too
late. The Japanese were brave men, but it is hard not to exult

across fifty years upon reading about the shouts of their lookouts ("Hell Divers!") and their panic as the crews looked up into the sun and saw the dive-bombers there, with the bombs already in the air beneath the planes on their way into the big red rising suns painted on their yellow flight decks. Hard too not to admire the fatalism with which their great pilot and air planner, Cdr. Minoru Genda, met the disaster, with the brief word *Shimatta*, "We goofed."

At the end of the first day of battle the *Enterprise* pilots and those from the *Yorktown* who had landed on the *Enterprise* after sinking the Japanese carriers stood in a long line, waiting to be debriefed, just outside the incinerator where I was back to lighting up for the night's inferno and preparing to duck the slow bullets that hadn't made it to the battle. These were heroes, dressed in their khaki and green nylon flight suits, carrying pistols and knives over their yellow Mae Wests, and describing with quick hands and excited voices how they had gone into their dives, released their bombs, and seen the Japanese flight decks open up in flames just below them. The slaves who rowed the Greek warriors at Salamis or those chained to their benches at Lepanto could not have felt at once prouder or less heroic than I.

The Battle of Midway was fought and won in ninety minutes on the morning of June 4, and it was finished by sunset, when the last of the four Japanese carriers, the *Hiryu*, was gutted. Before withdrawing, the Japanese tried to force a night surface action, but we retreated, and the next day we came back to grapple for their remaining ships. An information officer on the *Enterprise* tried to chalk a map on the huge gray side of the stack so that all on deck could follow the battle—we were fascinated at the new idea of being briefed—but every fifteen minutes the man on the painting scaffold suspended from the top of the stack chalked up a new location and a different size for the fleets. As the information constantly changed and the proximity to the enemy increased or decreased, so did the armaments. Bomb size went from one-thousand-pounders to five-hundreds and back again on the dive-bombers within the space of an hour. This meant endless work for ordnancemen, which at last got me out of the incinerator. I had just been made a petty officer, third class (sixty dollars a month), a certified professional, and I happily ran back and forth trundling bombs and carrying belted ammunition for the machine guns, a part of the ordnance gang again. Aware that this was probably the greatest historical event at which I would ever be present, I looked about for something to fix Midway in my mind forever. I was waiting on the flight deck for a bomb to come up the forward bomb elevator shaft, which was about three feet by four. I looked down the narrow shaft going several hundred feet from the bright sunlight of the day into the depths of the ship, where, close to the keel, the bomb magazines were located. At the very bottom, a bright yellow bomb had just been wheeled on the elevator, so that I was looking down an immensely long tunnel at a bright yellow spot, at once both beautiful and deadly, at the bottom. To this moment I can see it as clearly as if I were still there.

Nothing in the next two days of the battle could match the first, although the excitement remained high and the level of activity feverish. The Japanese fleet proved elusive. We caught only a couple of cruisers and destroyers and hammered them viciously. Our remaining three Devastators were loaded for the last time with torpedoes and sent out on the hunt, but they were not needed and circled the fight without making a run. Without their carriers the Japanese fleet returned home, where news of the battle was suppressed and the crews were kept aboard their ships lest they talk of what had happened. The *Enterprise* returned to Pearl Harbor on the morning of June 13, my nineteenth birthday.

CHAPTER SIX

Sunk

AFTER MIDWAY we were a squadron without pilots or planes. When we returned to Pearl Harbor, the enlisted men of Torpedo 6 were sent to the naval air station at Kaneohe, on the windward side of Oahu, where a new set of pilots with a new type of plane were waiting for us. The few surviving pilots from the old squadron had gone back to the States and, except for a few old hands, the new ones were fresh from flight training and eager to get into the war. Among the old hands was the famous Lt. (jg) John McInerny. He had been a fighter pilot on the *Hornet* at Midway, and on the "flight to nowhere" he had the brass to fly up to his squadron commander, who was calmly proceeding into oblivion, and point to the gas gauge to remind him they had reached the point of no return. Preserving radio silence, the skipper vigorously motioned McInerny back to his place in the formation. But after a few seconds, Mac was back, even more insistent, and the skipper this time ignored him, doubtless thinking something like, "Get your insubordinate Irish ass back where it belongs." But McInerny was a determined realist, and he and his wingman, Johnny Magda, broke away from the fighter formation to return to the ship. After a few moments the rest of the group did the same, and finally the skipper turned back too. They all missed the ship and flew on above an empty ocean until they ran out of gas and ditched. Eight of the ten, Mac among them, were later picked up after several days floating in the ocean. But he was through in fighters and had been sent to fly torpedo planes, a considerable comedown in the aviators' world. He died of cancer in 1986, a great loss to courage and good sense.

The new plane was the Grumman TBF, called the "Avenger," to avenge what had happened to the torpedo planes at Midway. It looked like the latest thing in aviation technology to us. Heavy bodied, with square folding wings, light-blue and white outside, dark green inside, it carried three men, but the radio gunner was now down in a little compartment at the rear of the plane. Above him and slightly forward was the gunner's power turret, containing a single .50-caliber machine gun. Stenciled in bright yellow letters on the armor plate that the gunner pulled up when he was in place were the words "Hard Homo." The meaning was quite a mystery, and a lot of time was wasted trying to figure it out. The most obvious meaning, "hard homogenized steel," was disqualified on the grounds that it was so obvious that there would be no reason to stencil it on the thousands of plates put in the turret to protect the gunner's bottom. Every gunner in the fleet must have spent some time in flight wondering just what the words meant.

The pilot eventually had two fifties in the wings. There was another seat forward of the turret just behind the pilot, designed for an observer. It was, in fact, immediately filled up with new radio gear for which there was no room elsewhere. The engine was much more powerful than the one in the old TBDs, and the plane could turn up 180 knots while carrying a torpedo or full bomb load, stored in a long bomb bay in the belly with folding hydraulic doors. Every one of these features was to become grimly familiar to me at one time or another, but for the moment they seemed only wonders of American engineering and production, ingenious ways of beating the Japanese.

The ground crews studied the manuals that came with the new plane, working long days getting used to its ways. We rode in them frequently to see how all the gear worked, from the smoke-laying equipment, which the navy still considered one of its tactical weapons, to the reel that paid out the cable with the tow target that was used for aircraft and ship's gunnery practice. Both of these pieces of equipment were standard, and both were hated by those of us who installed and worked them. The smoke was toxic and acidic enough to burn a pair of dungarees right off your ass, taking the ass with them if you weren't careful. The tow reel, its gears driven by a fiendish little propeller mounted outside on the fuselage, let kinks develop in the tow wire that could, if you were careless, take a hand off when you tried to free them.

Still, it was a wonderful time. Kaneohe, just across the island and over the high cliffs—Nuuanu Pali—from Honolulu, was all soft breezes, big surf, white beaches, and bright sun every day.

The barracks were concrete, spacious, clean, and cool. Discipline was incredibly lax, and gambling went on all night in the heads, where the lights burned without interruption. For once I made a few dollars and managed to get an overnight liberty in Honolulu. I soon learned why I had no trouble getting a pass. A curfew cleared the streets at 2000; the restaurants had no food and the bars no whiskey. I had a good time, however, renting a room in the posh though empty Alexander Young Hotel downtown, lying in a marble bath smoking a cigar and reading the *Police Gazette*, as naughty a magazine as I could find, but not very naughty.

Promotion was also easy too in an expanding navy. Ratings were now given away with a stroke of a yeoman's typewriter, to the disgust of the old-timers who had laboriously studied manuals and waited years for promotion. There was an argument in the ordnance shack one day about who would go down to the beach and fill some of the practice bombs with sand. No one wanted to go, heavy jobs with shovels being scrupulously avoided in the navy—if you liked that sort of thing there was always the army—and so Murph said that he would make me a petty officer, second class, if I would do it without bellyaching. I thought he was joking, but I did it anyway, and the next week the squadron orders listed my name and the new rating of aviation ordnanceman, second class, paying the munificent sum of seventy-four dollars a month.

At Kaneohe I drifted into a part-time flying arrangement. All regular flight personnel drew additional half-pay, known as "flight skins." The squadron had a few extra sets of skins beyond those needed for the regular pilots and flight crews, and these were passed around among the leading chiefs and various personnel from time to time. Even little fish like me had a chance to get a half or a quarter skin once in a rare while. But you had to put in at least four certified hours a month in the air to qualify. The flight logs were sacred books not to be tampered with, and so actual flight time could not be avoided. Sometimes planes were crammed with ten or twelve persons flying around the island for four hours to get their flight time in.

The new planes had a turret with a .50-caliber machine gun, but there were as yet no specially qualified aerial gunners. It was assumed, however, that any ordnanceman could at least operate the turret and the gun, even if he couldn't hit a barn door. So from time to time, needing to put in a few hours in the air, I became a gunner, complete with a helmet, earphones, a khaki flight suit, and a leather flight jacket with my name and rating stamped in gold on a patch on the breast. Other ord-nancemen remembered the lesson of Midway, and I had little competition for a job of which I was exceedingly proud. Most of the time, though, I worked away on the ground: cleaned guns, bore sighted the fixed guns, loaded bombs and torpe-does, unloaded bombs and torpedoes.

The idyll was over in a month or so, and in late July we packed up and went back to Pearl to go aboard, not the *Enterprise*, which had already sailed for the South Pacific, but the *Hornet*. The old system of keeping air groups and ships together—Air Group 6 went with CV-6, the *Enterprise*; Air Group 5 went with CV-5, the *Yorktown*—around which fierce loyalties were built, was no longer possible: the carriers now took whatever squadrons were trained and available when they sailed. Airedales like us became vagabonds from this time on. Squadrons were seldom again at home on a particular ship, or even in an air group.

Torpedo Squadron 6 was for the moment a part of the *Hornet* Air Group, which was made up of squadrons with various numbers. Because of our loyalty to the *Enterprise* we did not take to the *Hornet*. She was new and had come into the Pacific for the Doolittle Raid, and the paint had never been chipped off her bulkheads, so we now had to turn to on a second ship and spend weeks in the sweaty heat with chipping hammer and wire brush. The *Hornet*'s crew did not take to us either, but it soon ceased to matter, and since the *Enterprise* and *Hornet* were sister ships we could even have the same bunks in the same compartments we had had on the *Enterprise*. Still, it was different and therefore unsettling.

There still remained, it turned out, one part-time general detail I had not been on—everybody went the full round—and now each time a plane landed or took off, I stood at the edge of the flight deck, just aft of the island, dressed in a huge cum-bersome floppy white asbestos suit, complete with boots and a heavy helmet with a glass visor to see through. You carried the helmet since it had no air supply, and you would suffocate in it in a few minutes. In my other hand I had a long chain with a hook at the end. If a plane with a bomb or depth charge aboard crashed and either caught fire or was in danger of catching fire, I put on the helmet, rushed under the plane, and secured the chain around the bomb. At the same time another man, also dressed in an asbestos suit, climbed up the wing of the plane to the cockpit and released the bomb. It then, in theory, fell to the deck, did not explode, and was pulled by my chain, which a number of volunteers had presumably taken hold of, out of the fire and the danger of explosion.

The whole drill had a desperate sound to it, and the asbestos suit had a number of seams and openings that I thought would surely let the fire get to me. My repeated, increasingly insistent questions about this matter got no answers from anyone in charge, and week after week I stood at the aft end of the island, by the mobile crane for clearing wrecks, looking and feeling like a circus clown, hat under arm, getting ready to perform. During the time I was on this detail planes crashed, and I rushed in and hooked the chain on the bomb, but fortunately there was no fire. Never in my time in the service did I see anyone test one of these Daniel suits in a fiery furnace, and I think it just as well.

The ship was hot, but the nights were clear and cool, with a warm light breeze blowing on the flight deck. Everybody off watch congregated on the deck, walking up and down like shadows, stopping here and there to talk. The stars were brilliant, and the sky was crowded with them. The southern heavens were now visible, and the different constellations made it seem as if we had steamed into a world other than that presided over by the North Star and the Big Dipper. After a day at work in the heat, to be on the flight deck at night, cooled by the wind and delighted by the tremendous streams of phosphorescence at the bows of the escort destroyers and cruisers, was more than pleasure. Mostly people on deck at night were silent, but now and then a remarkably free conversation about the meaning of war and life would start with someone you didn't know at all, whose face you couldn't see clearly. Darkness and anonymity were better than daylight for these matters. More open, ironically, and more honest. One day I noticed an unusually earnest member of the squadron, Nelson, lying in his bunk reading *How to Win Friends and Influence People*, the self-improvement book by Dale Carnegie, famous at the time. The foolish title has ensured the book the immortality of true kitsch. I knew it well and saw it again with that sinking feeling that comes from the simultaneous recognition of human need and the futility of trying to satisfy it. My mother, with whom I had had a distant but close relationship, no doubt deeply worried about what was going to happen to a boy with no background and no talent for getting along with people—indeed, almost a genius for the reverse—had made me read it and then quizzed me daily on Dale Carnegie's surefire methods for getting not just along but ahead in the world.

As I walked down the flight deck on some errand a few hours later, Nelson came up alongside me, threw his arm around my shoulder—not done in the navy—and said, "Hey, Al, what's your hometown?" One of Carnegie's basic opening moves. I was thunderstruck. Nelson must surely be an idiot; here in this topsy-turvy world, where death and mutilation were likely to be in every strange sound and sight, what influence could anyone possibly have that would be of any use? Who were these "friends" to be won? Where? I could only stare at him. The gods of war love nothing more than irony, and to be so blind to where and what we were was downright dangerous. Sure enough, a few days later two of our planes, one carrying Nelson, went into a cloud in close formation and never came out. Even the wreckage was never seen. They must have collided, thrown into each other by heavy up- or downdrafts. I used to wonder whether Nelson thought of winning friends and influencing people as the plane suddenly split open and spilled him out into the air, down to the water below, down to the bottom.

The course was south-southwest, across the equator and down to the southwest Pacific—Australia, the New Hebrides, Rabaul, and the Solomon Islands—where the action had shifted after Midway. This was, by late summer 1942, the farthest reach of the Japanese drive, and it was along the line running from the Solomon Islands to New Guinea that the U.S. Navy had elected to defend the shipping lanes to Australia and stop the Japanese expansion. The marines had gone ashore at Guadalcanal in August, and by the end of that same month the carriers had already fought another of the great carrier-to-carrier battles of the Pacific war, the Battle of the Eastern Solomons. The *Hornet*'s long journey from Pearl Harbor ended at the narrow entrance to the reef outside the harbor of Nouméa, the capital of the French territory of New Caledonia. The island was only semitropical, but it seemed romantic from our anchorage out in the windswept bay, with its long mountain chain running down to the beaches and the forests of palms. Ashore, where we went for a brief liberty, Nouméa was a small French colonial town with a square, a cathedral, a cinema, a few stores, and a rickety racetrack that in time would become only too familiar. There wasn't much to it, but the smells and the architecture were genuinely exotic—white plaster and tile roofs. After a few turns around the square, however, and some ice cream made with coconut milk, the sailors crowded back on the dock to catch the next boat back to the ship. The *Hornet* herself was the biggest attraction in the area. Crowds of sailors who were building a base near Nouméa came out in all kinds of craft to tour the carrier. We were happy to serve as guides—it gave us someone different to talk to—and we felt like real heroes compared to these shore-based sailors. When one friendly group told me as they left to be careful not to get sunk, I was quite surprised; the real possibility had never crossed my mind, and I explained quite earnestly to them that a ship this big and powerful could always take care of herself.

At the beginning of September the *Hornet* joined the *Saratoga* and the *Wasp* patrolling below the Solomons to control the air and keep the two Japanese aircraft carriers that had not been at Midway from coming down from Truk and getting at our ships and the marines on Guadalcanal, a name we began to hear for the first time with the dark tones that have never since left it. The area was so filled with Japanese submarines that it was soon called Torpedo Junction, and a short while later the *Saratoga* was hit by a single torpedo and retired for repairs for the second time in the war. A few days later, up to the north and east of Guadalcanal, we were on routine patrol with the *Wasp*. I had been up all night and had worked through the morning as well, and just after lunch I finally found a cool place in the squadron compartment, several decks down below the hangar deck and well aft. The bunks were kept up during the day, but lying on the deck with a duct blowing cool air across me, I went to sleep, only to be awakened almost at once by general quarters.

Few things were taken so seriously as going at once to your battle station when general quarters was sounded, but we had been having alarms and going to quarters night and day for a week with nothing happening. So I decided "to hell with it" for once, pulled a mattress down to conceal me, and went nicely back to sleep, expecting that the drill would be secured in five or at the most ten minutes and that no one would miss me in the ordnance shack, which was where I was supposed to be. The ship remained deadly quiet, however, and suspecting that something was going on, I made my way by a back route through one watertight hatch after another—court-martial offenses—until I got to the hangar deck. There I looked out through one of the open metal curtains and about a half mile away, down on the port side and to the stern, pouring out huge clouds of black smoke, was the *Wasp*, hit hard and going down from several torpedoes from a Japanese submarine.

Everyone was so focused on the burning ship that I was able to sneak quietly, much subdued, into the ordnance shack. Later the question actually did come up of where I had been because without my knowing it I had been put down to fly that day on the antisubmarine patrol that took off when the *Wasp* was hit. It didn't matter—someone else filled in—and I told a story about being slow and getting trapped behind some watertight doors that couldn't be opened. But it was a dramatic lesson, and I never again failed to respond to general quarters, even when the alarm sounded every hour of the day and night for days at a time, which now became the normal way of life, with frequent reports of submarines and sightings of Japanese scout planes.

Unknown new ships, like the battleship *North Carolina* and the antiaircraft cruisers *Juneau* and *San Juan*, began to show up in the task force, proof that American shipyards were hard at work. But no new carriers. We were now down to one, the *Hornet*, in the South Pacific—the *Enterprise* was being repaired —and though the ratio was now three Japanese fleet carriers to one, we raided different Japanese bases and then retired south, once going into Nouméa for supplies. Trying to prevent the Japanese navy from reinforcing and supplying the troops on the Canal and other Solomon islands stretching southeast from New Ireland and the big Japanese base at Rabaul, the U.S. Navy engaged the Japanese in the most ferocious surface battles of the war: cruisers, destroyers, and torpedo boats—even a battleship once in a while—against one another in the dark in the confined waters of "the Slot" between the islands. The Japanese gunnery and tactics were better, especially at night, and we heard of heavy losses, with grim stories of our own cruisers being unprepared for nighttime battles and accidentally firing into one another. "Iron Bottom Bay" became the name of the area between Savo Island and Guadalcanal, where naval gunfire still ruled the ocean—but only at night, when the planes from the "Cactus Air Force" on Henderson Field were grounded.

Tempers grew short and people gave up any attempt to live a normal life. Sandwiches were the standard food, everyone slept where they could with life jackets and helmets nearby, the hatches were dogged down most of the time, the compartments were foul-smelling, and the ship was at general quarters almost constantly. The pilots took to carrying issue sidearms, .45-caliber Colt automatics in a shoulder holster. The heavy guns would weigh them down if they went into the water, but they made them feel more secure should they be shot down and drift ashore on one of the dark little islands that were everywhere on the horizon. I was sent down to the armory one day to draw a case of these antiques from the Spanish-American War—designed to stop Filipino insurrectionists (freedom fighters?) in their tracks—and then sat in the ordnance shack disassembling them, soaking the parts in a solvent to remove the cosmoline in which they had been stored a generation earlier for another enemy, reassembling them, and issuing one gun, plus two clips of ammunition, to any pilot who stopped by to sign for one. If they were sports, they would pay ordnancemen (one of our few cumshaws) to remove the Bakelite handgrips on the butt and put a picture of a girlfriend underneath clear plastic.

The *Enterprise* returned from repairs, running at high speed from Pearl in little more than a week, and on the morning of October 26, 1942, off the Santa Cruz Islands, north and east of the Canal, her search planes found the remaining Japanese fleet carriers, which were coming down from their base at Truk in the Caroline Islands to interfere in the continuing battle between the marines and the Japanese for the possession of the airfield on Guadalcanal. The Japanese fleet was a bit over two hundred miles out, and its scouts found us before we found them.

On the *Hornet*, a few miles from the *Enterprise*, the breeze picked up, as it always did, and the deck vibrated as she turned into the wind and launched the strike group. The planes circled for a time, formed up, and straggled off to the north where a scout plane was broadcasting the location of the enemy fleet, the usual decoy fleet out in front that always seemed to fool our strike groups. The big fleet carriers were about sixty miles behind. A few of our new torpedo planes carried torpedoes but most were now used as glide bombers: "glide" since they couldn't take the steep dive of a dive-bomber but went in at a long medium angle to let their bombs go and then used their speed to get out as fast as possible.

Then both American carriers launched a new CAP, took the morning CAP aboard to be refueled, and immediately sent the planes aloft again to provide a maximum fighter protection against what was surely coming. In the eerie quiet that falls on a carrier after all its planes have gone off on a strike, everyone peered at the horizon. The moments passed as the ship secured from flight quarters and went to general quarters to prepare for the coming attack, sending all bombs and torpedoes to the magazines, emptying the aviation gasoline lines and filling them with CO_2 to prevent fire. Flash burns from explosions had caused many casualties on board ship, and we stuffed our dungarees into our socks, buttoned up our shirt collars and cuffs, put on camphor-impregnated life jackets, smeared any exposed flesh of our hands and faces with a heavy white protective cream, and began to sit and sweat, wearing the old-fashioned World War I helmets, painted navy blue-gray.

Our own strike group and the Japanese sighted each other on their way to their targets, but each passed the other without engaging. I hope they didn't wave, but they may have. By now the hard lesson had been learned by both sides that sinking the enemy carriers was what counted, not shooting down a few planes, so the Americans flew on to find the Japanese ships, the big carriers *Shokaku* and *Zuikaku*—the last two Pearl Harbor carriers—and the Japanese flew on to find the American ships, which they soon did.

A little after 0900, the public address system broke the quiet of the ship with an announcement from the bridge, "Enemy aircraft at fifty miles and closing." In what seemed an unbelievably short time later we heard, "Stand by to repel attack by enemy aircraft," and almost instantly the five-inch guns at the corners of the flight deck began firing—bang-bang-bang—in their heavy slow rhythm, not nearly fast enough it seemed to us. These battles developed speedily, and with the five-inchers still firing, the old navy-built one-point-ones began going off with their much faster but still deliberate rhythm.

In the ordnance shack, just below the flight deck, we could see nothing, only listen, feel the vibrating steel deck, and slide back and forth with the steep turns that came in quick succession. When the new twenty-millimeter guns spaced along the catwalks began their continuous rapid firing, we knew the attack had commenced and that the dive-bombers were coming down and the torpedo planes were making their runs at water level. Some determined warrior had mounted a .30-caliber machine gun in a railing support just to starboard of the island, and when I heard it clattering away, I knew they must be really close. A bomb went off with a great flat bang that shook the ship deep in her bowels, where it had penetrated before the delay fuses fired. Then another big one, and the elevators jumped up in the air and came down, locked, with great bangs.

Then just up the passageway past the dive-bomber ready rooms near the admiral's quarters, there was a huge explosion. A bright red flame came like an express train down the passageway, knocking everything and everybody flat. A Japanese plane had crashed into the signal bridge and then ricocheted into and through the flight deck just forward of the area where we were sitting on the deck with our heads between our knees. Murph was grinning and gripping his cup of moosemilk tightly. The plane's bomb had rolled around and had not gone off, but its gas tanks had exploded.

Pursued by flames, we ran to the aft end of the passageway and up a ladder onto the flight deck at the aft end of the island.

There the one-point-one gun crews were down in a bloody mess. Their magazines had been stacked in a circle behind them, and bullets from a strafing plane had caused them to fire at knee level into the gun tub.

We stood there debating whether to stay on the flight deck or take our chances below. Two great heavy thuds raised and then dropped the entire ship, all twenty thousand tons of it: torpedoes hitting home one after another on the starboard side —the death wounds of the ship, though we didn't know it at the time. The *Hornet*, turning at a sharp angle, shook like a dog shaking off water but immediately began to lose speed and list to starboard, which was terrifying, for you were still alive only so long as the speed was up and the ship was moving. You sense it in the soles of your feet, and it began to feel noticeably different at once, sluggish and dull, the rhythm off, and then another delay-fused bomb went through the flight deck just aft, through the hangar deck, to explode with a sharp sound somewhere deep below, followed by an acrid smell and smoke curling up out of a surprisingly small hole. The rudder was now jammed, and the ship began to turn in circles. The lights went out, and the fire hoses stopped putting water on the fires that now were everywhere.

The flight deck seemed too exposed, so we went down on the hangar deck, already listing sharply to starboard, with the edge of the deck in oily seawater running into the midships elevator pit. Then the forward bulkhead of the hangar deck exploded and the motor and cockpit of a burning Japanese plane crashed into the forward elevator pit. Its bomb also failed to explode, but its gasoline caught fire and the deck around the elevator began to glow. This plane had already done tremendous damage when it crashed into the gun sponsons on the bow of the ship, probably after the pilot was killed; or perhaps he was an early kamikaze, filled with battle will by the sight of the enemy ship so close and with the lust to obliterate it. One of the compartments he hit on his way through the bow was a blanket storage, and his plane had set the blankets afire and scattered them, burning and smoldering, the length of the hangar deck. Fine white blankets with blue bands—these were officers' blankets—and the smell of burning wool mixed with fuel oil remains my dominant sense impression of the day.

The guns stopped firing. The first strike was over, but by now the ship was dead in the water, and you had to be careful, so steep was the angle of the hangar deck, not to slide on the oily steel and out one of the openings and into the water on the starboard side, where the torpedoes had hit below the waterline, flooding the compartments below. The island and bridge hung menacingly out on the starboard side, seeming about to topple over and take the ship with them. There was fire forward where the plane had crashed into the elevator pit, and several bomb holes in the hangar deck were pouring out smoke. Among the burning and smoldering blankets dotted about were bodies, some terribly burned, others dismembered, some appearing unharmed. The burns were the worst, huge blisters oozing fluid, the tight, charred, smelly flesh, the member sometimes projecting as if straining for some final grotesque sexual act. A place not to linger, but there was now all-hands work to be done here. Damage control managed to correct the list somewhat, but power was still out, and firefighting had to go on by hand with buckets and a fire-retardant powder. The cruiser *Northampton* came up to tow the *Hornet*, sending over her steel towing cable to be attached to the anchor chain after the anchor was unshackled. The huge water-filled ship actually moved a bit, until the cable broke on the *Northampton* end and dropped in the water. There was no power on the *Hornet* capstan to haul it in, so it was dropped.

A second attempt was made using a two-inch steel cable that was stowed in the well of the midships elevator pit of the *Hornet*, a dark and slippery place by now, partly underwater. This cable, hundreds of feet long and tremendously heavy, had to be uncoiled and pulled, like some huge, stiff, greasy snake, by hand to the bow of the ship. Everyone in the area was rounded up for the job of getting the cable forward, and we formed a solid line up the hangar deck, slipping and sliding, heaving in rhythm, trying to move the dead weight of this metal boa constrictor. From time to time a single gun would go off, and everyone would drop the cable and take cover. But after a while we did manage to get the cable forward, and a sailor swam to the cruiser with a line to haul the cable across.

No planes would ever land or take off from the *Hornet* again, and the air divisions, my squadron included, provided free hands for the grim task of gathering the dead and wounded. I worked for a time on the flight deck helping to carry the injured crewmen from the gun mounts and the bridge to a corner on the high port side forward where the doctors had set up a hospital and rigged some awnings to protect the wounded from the brilliant sun that shone all day.

As I started back across the flight deck, the guns began firing again as a single dive-bomber made a run on us. I lay flat on the deck, covering as much of my body as possible with my tin hat, trying to work my way into it, and thinking for the first time that I was likely to die, and resenting it, feeling that at nineteen I really hadn't had a chance to do most of the things people do and vowing to do them if I survived. From that moment to this, life has seemed a gift—overtime, in a way—and all the more enjoyable for it. The bomb missed, and I ran to shelter in a compartment in the island where hundreds of other sweating, frightened men huddled behind thin steel bulkheads. By now the ship felt terribly heavy.

All this time the *Enterprise* had remained in the distance while hiding under a squall from the Japanese planes, but about noon she too came under attack. The antiaircraft shells made the sky black, and the ship twisted and turned, but in the end she caught three bombs, one of which killed my friends Whitey and Dallas in the chiefs' galley, but no torpedoes hit, and, patched up, she continued to operate her flight deck. Our strike groups, having heavily damaged but not sunk one of the Japanese carriers, *Shokaku*, were returning. The *Enterprise* would take her own planes aboard and as many of the *Hornet*'s as possible, but the others would have to land in the water, where their crews would be picked up by the destroyers serving as plane guards. The *Enterprise* picked up speed and moved away to the north. On her deck the pilots taking off were shown what became a famous message chalked on a board, "Proceed without *Hornet*." As she became smaller and then went hull down on the horizon, we turned, feeling very lonely, to the business of survival. Three destroyers moved in alongside us on the elevated port side, only a few yards away, with their masts and yards swaying wildly back and forth as they tried to maintain station in the swell while passing hoses over to fight the fires. The *Hornet* did not move at all, but the lighter

destroyers, pitching and rolling, from time to time would crash
against us with a terrible clang. Their rigging would catch in
the catwalk and tear away when they rolled back, their radar
and fire control battered and broken in the process.

Lines were passed across, and we began to pull the wounded
over to a destroyer, some in wire stretchers, others sitting in
a boatswain's chair. Speed was crucial: we expected to be attacked again, and the destroyer would cut loose if that happened. Men stood by the connecting lines with axes. Those
of us on the lines pulling the chairs and stretchers over to the
destroyer ran down the oily hangar deck with the line and then
ran up again, hoping to God that we wouldn't slip and go
crashing into some piece of ragged iron or go skidding out
into the oily water coming in on the starboard side. Fires still
burned forward, bodies lay around the deck, but there was no
time or need to move them now. Below, the work went on
to try to restore some power, but the Japanese aerial torpedoes were real killers, in contrast to our own inept weapons,
and there were no flickering lights indicating that the dynamos
were starting up again. The ship was now the business of the
ship's crew, particularly the engineers and the damage-control
groups, and having nothing to do the Airedales were assembled on that ghoulish hangar deck. I asked an officer if the
smoking lamp was lit. He was naturally annoyed by the foolish
request with the danger of fire everywhere, so he snarled that
surely a sailor could go one day in his life without smoking. I
muttered something about "What if it's the last day?" and got
away with it in the pressure of the moment.

Things did not look good. We were probably going to abandon ship, so it was time to prepare. I could not bear to leave all
those new guns that I had polished so nicely that morning, so
I made my way up to the ordnance shack, picked one out, and
put it in a sack, just in case. Encouraged by my own bravado
and stupidly feeling no fear of the ship rolling over and sinking, I then did one of those foolish and dangerous things that
young men are inclined to do. I made my way down through
several hatches and dark decks to my locker. The water sloshed
ominously on the low side of the compartment, but my locker
was on the high, dry side of the ship. A pillowcase held my
basic gear, including a suit of whites in case we went someplace

where there was liberty, but a diary I had been keeping for some time—contrary to regulations—was reluctantly left behind. In a moment I was back on the hangar deck, the envy of all my friends for having salvaged some clothes, answering muster in preparation for going onto a destroyer.

About 1500 the destroyer USS *Hughes*, DD-410, stretched cargo nets between the two decks. The *Hornet* sat heavy and still, but the *Hughes* rolled and pitched wildly. When she came into the *Hornet* she crushed the net and anything in it between the sides of the two ships. Trial and error taught us the right way to do it. The trick was to jump just as the *Hughes* began to roll out, being careful that your foot landed on one of the tightening ropes, and not in the holes between, for there wasn't time to recover and make your way slowly up a loosening net. If you did it right you landed on the rope, and its stretch would pop you like a trampoline onto the deck of the *Hughes* and into the arms of several of her crew. Carrying my pillowcase filled with my contraband pistol and my liberty whites, I leaped for my life and made it with a great bound of exhilaration. Tricky, but better than going into the oily water where anything could go wrong.

At the best of times in war, a destroyer is a small and crowded ship, and as the wounded and about four hundred additional men squeezed aboard, every space above and below deck was filled to the point where it was difficult to move. Just after I got aboard, another Japanese strike, launched from their last operating carrier, roared in. The *Hughes* cut her lines, pulled away at high speed, and started firing her antiaircraft guns. Looking for a place with some protection, so solid with sailors was the deck that I crawled under the mount of the after five-inch gun, which swung around above me, the bolts holding the gun to the swiveling mount missing me by what seemed no more than a quarter of an inch. The firing directly above and the clang of the hot shell as it came out of the breech was too much for me, and I crawled out thinking what a real mess it was going to be if a plane came in strafing, with the deck absolutely filled with people who couldn't move without going over the side. In a moment one did, and I forced my way into an after deckhouse already crammed with sailors trying to cover up their heads. The enormous power the destroyer was turning up gave a speed of about forty knots and forced the stern deep into the water, forming a huge stern wave that made it impossible to see anything aft except a wall of water. The destroyer was not hit, but it seemed as though we were going to go down because some of the incoming Japanese torpedo planes made their run on the *Hornet* from behind the *Hughes*, zooming along on the wave tops and then juking up and down at the last moment. The carrier took more bombs and one additional torpedo, making her death certain. In the same attack the *Northampton*, trying to avoid a spread of torpedoes aimed at her, dropped the last towing cable, ending that slim hope of saving the *Hornet*.

The destroyer's officers began sorting us out, putting the injured below deck near the sick bay, arranging for each group of survivors on deck to appoint one man to come to the galley to draw food twice a day. The Torpedo 6 ordnance gang, about seven or eight of us, found ourselves aft on the starboard side, sitting on a narrow deck with our backs to the after deckhouse bulkhead and our feet outboard to the rail resting in the scupper. It was an uncomfortably wet place at high speed, but there was a rail welded to the bulkhead just above our heads to which it was possible to tie yourself, even when hanging onto a full pillowcase, which I began to curse but refused to give up. The very long day of October 26, which I always celebrate privately, was drawing toward sunset. We were circling the *Hornet*, but as it became clear that no power could be raised and that the effort to tow was finished, the command was given to abandon ship, and the crew began to go over the side on ropes and to jump into the oily waters. There was no room for any more survivors on the *Hughes*, so as the other ships moved in to pick up the rest of the crew, the *Hughes* turned south and began withdrawing. The Battle of Santa Cruz was over, and sitting on the deck, cold and exhausted, looking at the smoking carrier sitting there at an odd, lumpy angle, I considered for the first time the possibility that we might lose the war. The *Hornet* had been such a big and powerful ship, and yet only a few hits in a brief space of time had been enough to finish it.

But the navy would be back, and even in going down the *Hornet* was tougher than we thought. Later that evening our own destroyers went back to finish her off with their five-inch guns, but after several hundred rounds, they failed to put her down. By then the Japanese surface fleet was getting close—they were still trying to force their famous surface battle—and the American destroyers withdrew, leaving the scene of the battle and the hulk of the *Hornet* to the victors. She was too far gone to be salvaged, though, and a few Japanese long-lance torpedoes blew the bottom out of her during the night, and she went down in more than three miles of water to where she must still be sitting. It seemed the final irony that our torpedoes and guns couldn't even sink our own ship, that we needed the Japanese and their weapons to finally put it down.

CHAPTER SEVEN

Wandering

MURPH MUST have been having ferocious withdrawal symptoms, for he sat all day with his ordnanceman's red-cloth helmet buckled under his chin, his brown, worry-sharpened face with its huge hooked nose looking out to sea like some naval muse of tragedy. It was my turn to go below and get the food for the ordnance gang, still on the deck, and Murphy, in one of his fits of wryness, gave me his chief's hat to wear, which he had carried with him, insisting that with it I could go to the head of the serving line. Since I looked about sixteen years old, in a navy where chiefs were still old and grizzled, it was an obvious joke, but I played my part to the hilt, crashing the line, giving abrupt orders about the corned beef sandwiches and coffee, and never dropping a smile. It must have amused others too because they let me get away with it, even asking admiring questions about how I had made chief at such a young age, to which I responded with tall tales of skill and daring against the enemy.

It took only one night on that exposed passageway on the ship's weather side, splashed all night by waves, to make it absolutely necessary to find some less exposed place on the crowded deck. Getting below was impossible. In the morning we began to scrunch forward to the well deck, where the torpedo tubes were located. A little pushing and shoving, some curses here and there, and we found some room under the inverted vee where the two flues from the boilers came up at an angle and joined about five feet above the deck to form the destroyer's single smokestack. The deck here was hot from the boilers beneath, which was fine for a time, and good for drying out, but it got too hot all too soon. We adapted by laying down cardboard and sleeping on it as long as we could take it, then climbing out to cool off by perching on the torpedo tubes for a time, and then diving back into the heat and sleep. Wherever you were you lashed yourself to something before going to sleep since waves washed over the deck from time to time. We were all pretty numb, which helped, and grateful to be alive under any conditions, which helped even more. But by the end of the fourth day we were just hanging on when the *Hughes* came to the entrance of the New Caledonia reef and took us to the anchorage off Nouméa.

Small craft took us off at once. Trucks met us in the dark, blackout being enforced, and bumped up the island to dump us at a tent camp where we were told to draw a folding army cot and mosquito net and find a place to sleep. Used to the insect-free life aboard ship, I didn't secure the mosquito nets properly, and by morning my feet were so swollen from bites that I couldn't get my shoes on. We were on a beach that backed on a salt marsh and some high, bare mountains. There was an Australian group, wonderfully jolly, camped on one side of us, and a New Zealand regiment, terribly dour, on the other, there to defend the island. Someone had decided that the nearly three thousand men from the *Hornet* would make dandy support troops if the Japanese invaded.

It seemed as if it might come to that one day when two barges were sighted by patrol craft and identified as Japanese carriers leading an invasion force. But fortunately the Japanese never got around to invading New Caledonia, and we passed our time swimming, gambling, and sneaking out over the mountains to pester farmers in isolated farmhouses—"Avez vous vin?" A few bottles of sour wine mixed with juice squeezed from the lemons growing all around us made for a wonderful party. We invited some Australians, and they filled us with stories about what stuffed shirts the New Zealanders were.

The *Hornet* crew was too well trained to be left on the beach for long in a time of shortage of trained personnel, and within a few days the ship's crew was sent off to the States for leave and reassignment. Air squadrons were needed in the ongoing struggle for Guadalcanal, however, and each of the four *Hornet* squadrons was divided in two. One group, made up of those who had been overseas longest, was sent home. The second group was used to form small new squadrons. Having been overseas only a year, I fell into the second group, and we all gathered around Murph, Moyle, Berto, and others to see them off on the trucks and tell them to have one for us in Dago.

The rest of us, a very young group, were reunited with six of our old pilots and given some new planes to form a small squadron to be sent up to the Canal, where the fighting got worse every day. Our flying field was an old colonial French racetrack, with a rickety wooden grandstand for quarters and workshops. It was a pleasant enough place, except that the wind blew dust over everything, including the guns and engines we had just worked on. But life in the grandstand, with its benches for beds and tables, was casual and relaxed, the weather warm and sunny, and we could wander into town whenever there was no work to be done, so long as we weren't out after sundown and curfew. It was nothing like the famous novel by James Michener and musical *South Pacific*, but island life was nice, and an occasional ride in a plane gave a view of a long island stretching out for a hundred miles, mountains down the center, white beaches, and a fine coral reef extending around the entire coast.

It didn't last long, though, and one night after sundown we were told to load the planes with all the spare equipment, pack our gear—there had been an issue of a survivors' kit—and go down to the dock where, at the end of the quiet Nouméan street, hundreds of sailors were lined up in the dark, out to the end of the wharf. The water was full of small squid, and in the kind of weird humor adopted by young men at war, the sailors on the edge of the dock would reach into the water, pick up a squid, and throw it up in the air to let it land on someone's head or face. For the victim, not knowing what the clammy thing was, standing tightly packed in absolute darkness and unable to move, already nervous and uncertain, it was real psychological torture, and the furious reactions came close to breaking out in a riot.

In time, excruciatingly slow time, small craft took us out to the USS *Kittyhawk*, a strange old tub used before the war for hauling boxcars loaded with bananas from Central America. The middle third of the main deck was open so that a crane could lower boxcars onto railroad tracks embedded in a cement deck, where they could then be rolled fore or aft. The *Kittyhawk* was now a plane transport, not a banana transport, and the decks were loaded with planes of all kind, including our own, destined for various islands. The ship was overloaded, and we slept on deck, getting under the upper deck when the rain squalls came, as they often did. Fine, but as we moved in among the planes looking for a place to sleep, dogs started snarling and barking frenziedly.

All along the outer bulkheads were chained German shepherds and Dobermans, the most ferocious bunch of dogs I have ever met. These were war dogs going to Guadalcanal to smell out Japanese soldiers—God help them—in the jungle. Their chains were short enough to keep these excitable creatures from getting at one another, but any human other than their handlers—who seemed to be hiding somewhere—who stumbled into their arc was in big trouble.

By daylight we were beginning to wallow along north between two chains of islands that formed the New Hebrides group, leading up from the south to Guadalcanal. It was rainy and steamy hot, and the islands, low and dark and close, had a look that made you vow not to go near them if you could help it. Food was hard to get in the crowded serving lines, and not worth it when you did, but you could buy candy ("pogey bait") at the ship's store, and a group of us bought a huge bag of small Hershey bars. A new member of the ordnance gang taught three of us to play whist—not bridge but old-fashioned, eighteenth-century whist—and we sat all day long playing, gambling, of course, eating chocolate bars and jumping at the sudden snap of canine teeth whenever the player sitting with his back to the dogs raised his hand and reached back to throw his winning card triumphantly down to take the trick. We agreed that the ace of clubs seemed particularly to excite them. Otherwise, the dogs sat looking at us rather coolly, while we avoided eye contact.

By the next day we were at Espíritu Santo, the largest and northernmost of the New Hebrides. Here we learned that our small torpedo squadron was not going to the Canal but, with a pickup group of fighters, would become the air group of an escort carrier, the USS *Nassau*, anchored off the island. The *Nassau* was one of the many small carriers that had been built in a hurry by adding a flight deck onto the hull of a large freighter, putting in one small elevator aft, rising from the hangar deck to the flight deck, and adding a tiny island about halfway forward on the starboard side for a bridge and air-control. Planes were launched by catapult, the deck not being long enough to fly off and the ship incapable of getting up enough speed to help out very much, twelve or thirteen knots being about tops.

After the great fleet carriers like the *Enterprise* and *Hornet*, the *Nassau* seemed small and dangerous. Our eyes lit at once on the torpedoes, warheads attached, locked in racks running up the side of the hangar deck, the only place aboard ship to put them, probably, but exposed to any accident or explosion. The *Nassau* and her type were not intended for carrier battles, but after the loss of the *Hornet* we were now down to one damaged carrier in the Pacific, the *Enterprise*. If the Japanese made an all-out assault on the Canal anything that could launch planes would be thrown into the battle, and so a few of these small and awkward carriers were backing up the front line. We might be able to surprise a Japanese fleet by coming from some unexpected direction. Once a plane gets in the air it doesn't matter where it came from, super carrier or the deck of a converted cargo ship.

It was a cramped ship, and the squadron was in no mood to make the best of it. We were naval snobs, used to the big ships and the smartness of the prewar navy, and everything about this little tub offended our sense of propriety. We sat around playing cards and bitching endlessly about everything aboard. At anchor the weather was stifling and the humidity overwhelming. We were crammed in a tiny compartment designed for half as many men, and the ship had no ship's store, barbershop, or "gedunk locker" (ice-cream counter). The food was dreadful.

Our planes—TBFs and fighter planes, the F4F Wildcats—were kept ashore on a muddy field where we went daily to work and to gossip with the army, navy, and marine pilots and crewmen who were flying into and out of the Canal daily. Guadalcanal came to have a mythic status as the place of death as stories were told along the flight line of desperate land battles just at the end of the runway mats on Henderson Field; of planes taking off and dropping their bombs almost immediately on Japanese ships coming down the Slot; of nighttime shellings by Japanese battleships; and of our own ships firing into one another in wild confusion during night battles. We ate it up, half longing to go to the mysterious place and half hoping to stay in reserve.

There was only waiting. Christmas and New Year's Day came and went. The natives were happy to climb a coconut tree and throw the nuts down and show us how to open them by putting a sharpened stick in the ground and driving the nut on it, which broke open the husk. But this amusement had its limits. Mail arrived, including Christmas packages sent months before, leaking melted soap and chocolate—everything melted on Espíritu Santo—smelling of after-shave lotion and writing paper. A huge mound of unopened packages belonging to the members of the squadron who had already gone home was piled up in a small compartment where it was raided by anyone in need of a razor or reading matter. Shaving lotion seemed to be in every package, and we were all wondrously fragrant, though we looked like a bunch of pirates.

The intelligence officer of the original squadron had been a notable pain in the ass, and one way of lifting flat spirits was to root through the deteriorating pile of Christmas packages until you found one—there were surprisingly many—addressed to Ensign B. and then to loot it, with many foul jokes about B.'s ancestors, person, and practices. I carried for years an ersatz pigskin toilet kit some loving aunt had sent him, and every time I used it I felt a modest revenge on a foolish but danger-ous man who had threatened to have me shot for falling asleep leaning against a plane one night on the *Hornet* while I was standing guard over the planes on a closed and stifling hangar deck in a temperature over one hundred degrees, after work-ing for more than twenty-four hours. "Ah, ha, Ensign B., you prick," a silent monologue would begin while I washed up in the morning, "you may be arising in some golden place from between the silky loins of your tawny-haired and adoring mis-tress to go have bacon and eggs with the admiral and dictate naval strategy, but I am enjoying the greater pleasure of taking my gear out of your fitted Florentine toilet kit with its watered-silk lining . . ." My feet would be submerged in several inches of soapy water, the sweat running into my eyes to the point where it was hard to shave, the smells of farts and shit from the group of straining men sitting on the open trough clogging my nostrils, some hairy, naked sailor letting loose a string of foul language—but taunting Ensign B. with newly imagined insults kept me happy and smiling.

By the end of January the Japanese assault in the Solomons had lost its sharpest edge, and they largely abandoned their efforts to supply and reinforce their troops, pulling back to Bougainville and to their base at Rabaul. The Japanese advance that had begun at Pearl Harbor had finally been halted. Our anchor came up, and we chugged eastward to a new anchorage off the northern coast of the main island of Fiji, where we were a threat on the flank of any Japanese warships coming down from Truk to the Solomons or the Coral Sea.

There was no port here, and so the ship was anchored, quite alone, offshore, surrounded by a torpedo net that retained the ship's garbage and the sewage from the heads quite efficiently. Uninviting, yes, but as the heat built up, swimming was allowed, and even the most fastidious went booming off the deck, trying to avoid the floating turds in the crystal clear water below. After a while, like many things, it didn't much matter; then the snakes arrived: some kind of white-and-black-striped coral snake that swam upright in the water, moving its tail back and forth in a most sinister fashion. There was debate about whether it was poisonous. No one really seemed to know for sure, but the swimming stopped.

A small group of us were sent ashore to service our planes, located at an army air base. We could eat in the mess hall there, but we seldom did, for it was a long walk—several miles—from where our tents were pitched in a grove of cool trees. There the natives soon found us and brought us sugar cane, coconuts, and pineapples fresh from the fields where they worked. The Fijian natives were noble, intensely black Melanesians, generous and with a fine sense of humor. They were also delighted to see us and to clean out the tents, wash clothes, provide fresh pineapple centers for breakfast, and take us at night to native dances in little one-room schoolhouses, where we sat on mats, joined in the songs, watched the intricate dances by men and women, and drank the local drink, kava, made from some pounded and fermented root. It seemed never to have any effect, but it gave you something to drink and encouraged a spirit of merriment. From time to time military police in jeeps would stop to make sure that no servicemen were mixing with the natives. A whistle from native lookouts would alert us, and we would run out into the fields to hide among the cane or pineapples until the police had left.

Strong loyalties were built up in a short time with the Fijians, involving the exchange of gifts: a woven mat for a pair of shorts or a Zippo cigarette lighter. From time to time we would go to the nearby town of Nandi, inhabited almost entirely by Indians, the descendants of the laborers who had been brought by the British to work in the fields in the late nineteenth century. By this time the Indians had become merchants, who beat silver coins into jewelry and ran small grocery and dry goods shops. The town was dusty and hot, and since we had little money, our pay records having gone down with the ship, we bought nothing with the small emergency pay that was given us. We identified with the Fijians, a carefree warrior people who delighted in filling us with stories about the wicked and unnatural ways of the Indians. We agreed happily, ate more pineapple, drank more kava, and sang endless verses of the Fijian song, "Ise lei, nona nogurawa," or something that I remember that way.

Occasionally, one of us would go back to the ship for a shower and to get cigarettes and candy bars, both of which the Fijians loved. On one of these errands I got caught for shore patrol. In the old days each ship's division took a turn furnishing shore patrolmen to keep order in liberty parties and to see that everyone got back aboard without wrecking anything. The idea was to take care of the men and protect the citizenry from them, not to assert authority. Still, not a popular job, but I was stuck, issued an SP brassard, a nightstick, a pair of canvas leggings, and a .45 automatic in a holster attached to a web belt buckled around the waist. Someone had discovered an old hotel up in the hills, about three miles from the shore up a steep red-dirt road, where cane whiskey was to be had. Worried about the crew going crazy from the heat and the boredom, the executive officer decided to let a liberty party go each day for a couple of hours to see the countryside and have a few drinks.

The day began badly, with a light rain, and worsened as the liberty boat came alongside, an old, battered fifty-foot motor launch ordinarily used for hauling garbage and not cleaned for its new purpose. In the heat, the smell went down into the stomach right away. Mustered on the hangar deck, the liberty party looked fine, as usual—brightly washed, carefully pressed whites; shiny black shoes; clean hats. No neckerchiefs required in this liberty port. Nothing looks more innocent or reassuring about human nature than sailors lined up to go on liberty. Few things look more depraved or less reassuring than when they return, and this liberty party was going to be a monumental demonstration of that truth.

There being no gangway, the sailors scampered smartly down a metal ladder that hung from the quarterdeck down to the motor launch below.

As the launch moved away toward the shore, the rain began to come down and bits of leftover garbage began to slosh around on the deck. There was no dock, so the launch ran aground, and the sailors jumped over the side and frolicked like clean white lambs up the road that was already beginning to turn to oozy red mud and wash into deep gullies. When the rain began to get serious and tropical, the brims of white hats were turned down to shed the downpour.

A large percentage of the old navy was alcoholic, getting blotto whenever they could, and we were driving some world-class sponges toward a long bar in an old wooden resort hotel that sold some of the rawest popskull on the planet. The first real drink after months of imbibing shaving lotion and paint strained through a loaf of bread relaxed them a bit. There was even some good-natured laughter, not the feral, drunken variety, here and there as one group stood under the leaking eaves while the others fought their way to the bar, a dollar a shot, and then new groups elbowed their way through. With the second drink people began to stand on their dignity, ancient quarrels broke forth in new mutinies, and hard words began to be heard. Intentionally, no officers had accompanied this fête, and the SPs had been told to head the gang back down the mountain when things began to get rough. That time arrived with the third drink, as fighting began right down in the mud, with kicks and eye gouging. The Fijian who ran the bar offered the SPs a free drink as we started back, and though it was absolutely against the rules, we knew we were going to need it and took it gratefully.

The sailors had to be forced away from the bar, and straggling, slipping, and falling they made their way cursing down the mountain, stopping from time to time to piss and fight a bit more. In the mud, rain, banana trees, and heavy foliage, discipline began to break down, and some of the squirrellier sailors began to roll in the mud and disappear into the jungle alongside the road. Where they were going, God alone knew. Back to nature, I thought, as, soaking with sweat and rain, I bird-dogged them through the underbrush, trying to keep them moving down the mountain. The SPs were like sheepdogs, fanned out in a semicircle at the rear keeping the flanks in and harrying everyone to keep moving.

In my sector a bitter, drunken black mess attendant started a quarrel with a sailor he cursed as "a dirty Jew." Why the black picked a fight with a quiet Jew rather than a redneck southern WASP, of whom there were many, was beyond me at the time. The old navy was covertly anti-Semitic and openly racist. There were many blacks in the navy, but they were segregated at that time in menial jobs as officers' mess attendants, cooks, and pantrymen. It was a lily-white navy that never gave its racism a thought, and I was about to get a lesson in its strange effects. The black was persistent and, crazed by the cane whiskey and a lot of accumulated frustrations, he kept tackling his victim and wrestling with him in the pouring rain. I separated them time and time again, only to find them once more down in the mud.

At last we got them to the launch, the rain still pouring, and the liberty party—covered with filth and mud, drunk and disorderly—put off from shore to go alongside the *Nassau*. Since there was only a swaying ladder up to the quarterdeck, where the august officer-of-the-deck in his freshly starched whites stood looking pained, getting the drunks to go up was a real problem. There is nothing a drunken sailor likes better than defying authority when returning from liberty. "Quarterdecking" was the standard term for acting a lot drunker and crazier than you were at these times. This particular scene offered lots of opportunities for quarterdecking: dropping off the ladder into the water, to be fished out with a boat hook by the boat crew, or vomiting as close to the officer-of-the-deck as possible.

But my two were the stars. We had separated them in the

launch and kept them that way, sending the mess attendant up the ladder first. But as he got onto the deck, with me following hard after him, instead of turning aft and saluting the flag, with a wild cry he picked up the big wooden box in which liberty cards were deposited and, raising it high over his head, hurled it down the ladder at the Jew who by now was mad as hell himself and cursing down below in the boat. That finished it. The really tough master-at-arms who was on duty on the quarter-deck knocked the mess attendant down and hauled him off in an instant, lest his outstretched body offend the majesty of the navy. Those of us who were SPs that day were only amateur policemen, and we would not have reported the trouble at all, as long as we all got back in one piece, but the masters-at-arms had to be a rough sort, and their ability to keep the peace had been questioned in the full face of authority. I never heard what the punishment was, but I think it must have been awful.

Scuttlebutt began to say that we were going back to the States. The remnants of Air Group 6 were transferred, without planes, to another escort carrier, the *Copahee*. It seemed at first as though it could never happen, but sometime in late February the nets were taken away, the anchor came up, and the ship got under way for San Diego. No room anywhere, so we were given canvas army cots and set them up on the hangar deck. The galley served food all day long and we chowed down at odd hours. Somewhere south of Pago Pago, as we stared longingly at Samoa in the distance, some of the ship's boilers went off line. The already maddeningly slow standard speed of ten knots decreased at once, and the coast of California receded farther into the distance. The USS *Copahee* defined tedium: there on the vast Pacific, sun blazing down, nothing else in sight, the horizon unmoving, proceeding from Fiji to San Diego at six knots, clumping away. Trying to relieve the boredom I got into a poker game over my head, attempted to run a bluff on a card shark, and lost the pay I had finally received and saved for the thirty-day leave we would get in San Diego. Despair and ennui struggled for mastery, but a borrowed fifty cents got me into a penny-ante game made up of those who had lost everything in various bigger games run throughout the ship by the sharks putting together a stake for the fleshpots of America. A run of luck raised my capital to over eighty cents, fifty of which I used to buy a ticket in one of the anchor pools that various entrepreneurs were running.

In an anchor pool there are a set number of chances, each marked with a time. The winner is the owner of the chance marked with the exact time (always officially noted in the ship's log) that the pin is knocked out of the shackle to release the anchor chain, or, if the ship is tying up at a dock, that the monkey fist on the first heaving line strikes the dock. The pool I had bought into had 720 chances, one for each minute in a twelve-hour period—morning or afternoon made no difference—which meant that those who ran the pool had collected three hundred sixty dollars, of which they would give the winner three hundred, keeping a profit of sixty for their efforts. Fair enough, but with only one chance in 720, I forgot about it as the ship at last, in late March, came in sight of the coast, rounded Point Hard On, and worked up to a dock on the western end of North Island. As I looked at the naval training station across the channel, where I had arrived two years before, it seemed a lifetime away. The monkey fist sailed out in the air and landed with a clunk on the dock. The announcement "1024, first line across" came over the loudspeaker. The Airedales were to be transferred to some old buildings in the park at the San Diego Zoo, the other animals having gone somewhere else, and I had started off the ship when it hit me. I scrabbled to find my ticket, and there it was—"1024."

Pure delight! Good old Lady Luck had come through! To get off ship, to go on leave, and to be rich, all at once. Three hundred dollars was a lot of money in those days, but now I had to move fast to make sure that I found the operators of the pool before they left the ship with all the money, or hid out somewhere down in the bilges until I was locked up in the zoo and couldn't get back. These and other dodges had been known, and all my suspicions were aroused, but the sailor who ran this pool was an honest man, hunting all over the ship for me, greeting me with real pleasure, and counting out the money in old, tired tens, fives, twos, and ones, a great wad I couldn't get in my wallet.

A happy, comic ending to a long, grim sixteen months of war, a real lift to the spirit, a feeling that things would work out.

CHAPTER EIGHT

Stateside

THE DESERT sagebrush and mountains that had been so familiar two years before now seemed strange and bleak. The train was crowded, like everything else in the war, and as I looked out the window, I saw the cold March wind blow the snow ahead of it and the drifts lying here and there on the dry brown earth and the hard gray-green of the sage. I had expected my return home to be delightful, but the land seemed hostile after the tropics, and I was cold in my new set of tailor-made blues. My anchor-pool fortune had been partly spent on a Hamilton wristwatch, which I had always wanted—the last of prewar production still in the jewelry store—and a tightly fitted gabardine dress blue uniform: bell bottoms, zipper up the side of the skin-tight blouse, a dragon sewn in gold and green thread on the satin lining inside the front flap of the pants with their thirteen-button flap.

My leave had nearly ended in Union Station in Los Angeles. I had worn my issue dress blues with the loose blouse—we had been issued a full set of uniforms at San Diego—the bottom tied halfway up my chest and folded over to form a roomy pouch in which I had placed the .45 Colt automatic from the *Hornet* I was smuggling home. It was too risky, I thought, to put it in my sea bag, which was searched when I left the base, so along with a hundred rounds of ammunition—some tracer, some ball, some incendiary, the works: all for hunting rabbits! —it went into my blouse, making a grotesque lump. All went well until, in the middle of that huge waiting room, I bent over, and the gun, fully assembled, came sliding out the vee neck of the blouse, hitting the floor with an awful clang and sliding across the slippery surface at high speed. There were shore patrolmen all over the place, and visions of life in the naval prison at Mare Island flashed before my eyes. The SPs in the States at this time were ex-firemen and policemen, law-and-order types, not helpers like I had been in Fiji. Eye contact was enough to get you carded and patted down. I think that others must have seen the gun, but because it was the last thing anyone expected to see on the floor of Union Station, no one recognized it for what it was as, with what seemed nightmarish slowness, step by agonizing step, I ran after it, hunched over to conceal it, and slipped it back in my blouse.

The train pulled into Rawlins in the middle of the night, the temperature below zero, and we drove, my stepfather and I, the forty miles back to Saratoga, with nothing really to say, over the frozen land. By then—the middle of the war—most of the other young men were gone from the town, and I found myself the hero of the moment, invited to speak at the Lions Club on the progress of the war, as if I had any notion of how it was going; but I was flattered to be asked. The father of Bobby Mitwalsky, the marine who had been killed at Wake, broke down in tears and wanted me to explain why we had not gone to his son's rescue. I cried too and explained that we had wanted to, as if the crew had had something to say about it, but that it just hadn't been possible at that time; but we surely would win in the end and avenge old Bobby and his blue fur jacket. Everyone insisted on buying me drinks at the Rustic Bar, where I developed a taste for whiskey sours —it took months to get my stomach deacidified again—and a willingness to tell sea stories and talk naval strategy. All this lionizing was new to me—before the war I had not been one of the up-and-coming young men of even so small a town as Saratoga, Wyoming, population 680—but I took to the new role at once, casting off all restraints of modesty and good sense.

But it was the girls who really surprised me. My appeal to the girls in town had always been rather limited. I never had a regular girlfriend before the war and customarily had gone home after dances swearing never to go again and be humiliated by girls, plain as well as pretty, who found excuses to avoid dancing with me. In later years, my wife always said smugly, implying that she had been good enough to overlook this deficiency, "You looked too young." But in 1943 there were no other men in Saratoga, and the uniform really did, as I had heard rumored overseas, work magic. Girls who would never speak to me before were now willing to dally. Most myths are just that, myths, but the connection between sex and war must have some truth in it, for chastity seemed to have fled the Rocky Mountains to

Alaska or some Arctic place, certainly not to California, for the duration. It was all terribly crude—awkward, drunken fumblings on car seats—but it was hot and full of life, joyously restorative and reassuring, a reminder that, even if clumsily managed, intense pleasure exists in a world that readily offers a lot of dullness and pain. Sex and war initiate us into society, and I began to feel more a part of what was really going on.

I even acquired a regular girlfriend—not very regular since I was in town for only a few days, but still in no time we were "going steady." Her name was Ruth Emery, and I was rather proud of the fact that she was several years older than my nineteen, a schoolteacher in the local grade school, but tongues wagged, and this was not good for her reputation in a small town where schoolteachers were watched by the local hawks for moral conduct. She seemed not to care; she was reckless and jaunty and independent, raised on a ranch near Valley City, North Dakota, with few illusions about life. But she had set her cap at me, and I was flattered. We agreed to be more or less engaged without any formalities and entered into a long, desultory relationship for the remainder of the war.

The past still threatened and could only be faced and then forgotten as much as possible. My mother's grave in the town cemetery on the dry hill overlooking the alkali lake just outside town was already collapsing and pocked with gopher holes. On one side, partly hidden by a rise, were the gray weather-beaten rodeo grounds, where men tried to tame beasts, and on the other was the town dump, spotted here and there with rusting cars from the twenties with unfamiliar names like White, Jordan, and Star. This was right, in the grotesque way life has of explaining what happens, for she was another discard from that era. Her family, Fletchers and Macmillans, lived for a hundred years on land in south Georgia distributed in land lotteries to Revolutionary War soldiers in the early 1800s when the Creeks and the Seminoles were resettled in Oklahoma. Life was rural: small farms, cotton and corn, Primitive Baptist churches, a few slaves until the Civil War, large families. The World War I generation to which she, born in 1900, belonged was the first to leave the land, and with a little education, she married a soldier, moved to town, went to Florida, lost the money from the sale of her father's farm in the land boom, had a child, divorced, and began wandering—Chicago, Memphis, a ranch in Wyoming.

She remarried, became a Catholic, and put a determined face on it all, but she was part of the first generation of really rootless modern Americans, moving restlessly by car about the country, emancipated socially and intellectually to a modest degree, but lost, really, without the supporting ethos and family that had protected people in the years when the continent was being settled. Alienation was the familiar state of my generation of Depression and another world war, but the old people had few defenses against it when it appeared.

People had changed in Saratoga, but not the land. The mountains were still there, as they will be for a long time. Streams of melted snow ran down from them to the Platte River, which ran down to the Missouri, which ran into the Mississippi and then to the Gulf of Mexico. I went up on one sunny day with a neighbor—Vernon Swanson, a crack shot but not drafted because he had lost his trigger finger in a sawmill —to the ranch. The snow was still four feet deep down in the canyon, and we went on snowshoes, exhilarated by clear air and brilliant sun. The snow was melting, and the creek was running rapidly under the ice, giving that tinkle that comes with spring. Beyond the canyon walls the huge peak of Mount Vulcan loomed up above us, heavy and dark green, gradually blocking out the sun as we went farther up the canyon. By the time we reached the cabins of the ranch where I had grown up and my mother had killed herself, the sense of freedom and ease had gone, replaced by the heaviness of the mountains, cold snow, and gloomy pines. Indians avoided these mountains, and I think I know why.

At sea the war and its great battles had seemed more important than mere mountains and rivers, and I thought I had outgrown these pastoral scenes. But now nature reasserted its authority, reminding me of the durability and power that make human affairs, no matter how world-shaking, trivial and passing. The mountain in its unchanging sameness spoke too of nature's complete indifference to human ways of reckoning and feeling. Nature, it said, goes its way, and if humanity wants to tag along, fine, but our schemes and hopes do not affect the flows of nature.

Vernon and I drank whiskey from a clear pint bottle and then threw it up into the air, where it flashed in the light, turning over and over, and broke it with tracers from the salvaged .45. But this bravado only made us feel smaller, and after picking up the broken glass lest it harm some curious animal, we were glad to go down the canyon again, up on the ridge, and out of the shadow, if not the presence, of the mountain.

Thirty days' leave passes like all other time, and the transient barracks at the North Island naval air station was dark and noisy. A Texan in the bunk next to me kept a small rattlesnake that he had found out at the end of one of the runways and amused himself by putting on a glove and making the young snake rattle and strike. Terrified of snakes but ashamed to show how much, I was relieved when I moved to the torpedo squadron of a new Air Group 6 that was forming at North Island. Most of the members of the old squadron had been assigned to shore duty at the Assembly and Repair unit at North Island, but the new squadrons needed a core of veterans and, perhaps because I was younger than most, I was chosen to go back to sea. I was actually glad to join a combat unit again. There was something flat, even degrading, about life ashore: lying about your age to drink in cheap bars, sitting in dull movies, always broke and borrowing a dollar for liberty, shirking work, no sense of unity or purpose with the people you worked with.

Getting back to the squadron was different. Most of the new men were naval reserves who had joined the navy after Pearl Harbor, and they were socially and intellectually upscale from the old hands and the kids like me who had joined at the end of the Depression for lack of a job. There were a few old friends —Moyle was the chief of the ordnance gang. The new pilots and men were excited about going overseas and impressed by those of us who had already been there. McInerny was a hero to these newcomers. New squadrons are busy places, with an enormous amount of preparations for joining the fleet. For the ordnance gang this meant endless loading of practice bombs for mock bombing runs and rigging tow targets for gunnery practice.

One of the new sailors in the squadron was a man who became a close friend, Dick Boone. He later became quite famous as an actor, usually in villainous roles. He was several years older than I and had been educated at Stanford, but we hit it off, and he taught me a lot about the world, books, and art. I remember a small example, for some reason: his correction of my pronunciation of "Eyetalian" to "Italian." I went on several overnight liberties with him, riding the train to Los Angeles and staying with his family in Glendale.

It was the first I had seen of a well-to-do family and home. It was, I learned in time, as troubled as most, but I was overwhelmed by its comfortable ways. The Boones welcomed me warmly, and I soon fell madly in love with their seventeen-year-old daughter, Betty. This they did not welcome so warmly since in every way I was about as bad a prospect as a son-in-law as could be imagined. But their uneasiness never changed their kind attitude toward me. The father was a wealthy lawyer who had laid in a stock of fine whiskey at the beginning of the war. He was generous with it, and I thought it was the height of sophistication to ride the Sunday night train back with Dick from Los Angeles to San Diego at the end of a weekend liberty, drinking scotch—new to my palate—from a dimpled Haig and Haig Pinch bottle. Dick and I went to New York together after the war, sharing an apartment in the Village while I attended Columbia for a term and he went to the Neighborhood Playhouse, a famous method-acting school.

The war was moving on fast—new carriers, new squadrons—and by late May, Air Group 6, later commanded by Lt. Cdr. Edward "Butch" O'Hare, was loaded aboard ship and sent off to finish training on one of the Hawaiian Islands, Maui. O'Hare was a hero of the early war, having been awarded the Congressional Medal of Honor for downing five Japanese planes in one day when flying off the *Lexington* in the Rabaul raid in February 1942. His father had invented the mechanical rabbit chased by the greyhounds at dog races and was the victim of a sensational mob murder ordered, it would seem, by Al Capone. Chicago's O'Hare Airport was named for Butch O'Hare, who died at the end of 1943 in an incident in which I was to be closely involved.

We landed at Pearl Harbor and then, on a bright day with the wind blowing hard, went with all our gear onto a huge cement barge towed by a tug down past the leper colony on Molokai to land at Maui and the navy training field there. Most of Maui was brown and dry, and the field was built below the huge, bare, extinct volcano, Haleakala, that had formed the island. It dominated the landscape, and we often flew down into its dead crater, speckled with greenery. The airfield was rudimentary: short landing strips, earth revetments for the planes, wooden barracks. We were here to learn to work and fly together, and the days were long and busy. The nights, too, since night flying in formation was frequent, but somehow Maui still managed to seem like a tropical resort. The climate was perfect, sun and breeze, the discipline relaxed, and there was a beer garden, only a palm roof over a few rough board tables and benches, but we were allowed two bottles of beer a day, and they tasted like nectar at the end of a long hot day's work. We sat and talked, drinking the cold beer with the late afternoon breeze coming through the sides of the hut. I can remember Dick Boone telling us about life at Stanford, his fraternity doings avidly requested by us, and about his days as a prize-fighter and a painter in Carmel. Best of all he described how after his divorce he had overturned his Ford convertible, which his wife had preempted, when he saw it parked on the street with a big Saint Bernard in the back seat.

As always there was trouble in Paradise. Each of the officers got a bottle of whiskey a week, and one pilot who didn't drink gave a bottle to his radioman, Dutcher, who hoarded it in his locker and refused either to give us any or to drink it himself. This seemed downright inhuman and worthy of the most savage revenge. One night when Dutcher was in the air, we carried his locker out onto the field, where we shot the lock off and, leaving the locker there, took the bottle of whiskey to the empty beer hut and drank it with great satisfaction. Dutcher was extremely unpleasant about the whole business after he returned and found his locker missing, but he gradually came around and ended by saying that he only really minded that we hadn't saved him a drink, the bottle being empty by the time he found us. On another occasion word got around that one of the officers was keeping a kootch, a local whore with a tattoo of a mouse disappearing into her pubic hair, in a cabin down in the bushes, but that she was bored with the officer and wanted to meet virile young enlisted men. With a few beers inside us it seemed a fine idea for a jeepload of us to go down and visit her. She was less overjoyed to see us than we had been led to believe but was persuaded to show us her famous mouse, and in the end she was so pleased by our admiration that she dispensed favors to all, for a price. Whether she really had a relationship with any officer I never learned, but to think so made the experience somehow more satisfactory.

The skipper of the torpedo squadron was a fine man named John Phillips, who had enlisted in the navy back in the late 1920s in order to compete for an appointment to the Naval Academy. He graduated in 1933, getting his wings at Pensacola in 1936, and spent years as an instructor in instrument flying. This skill soon was to be of the utmost importance. One day he announced that he was looking for a new gunner. Moyle, loyal to the survivors of the *Hornet*, recommended me for the job, and after a few trial weeks I settled down to being the lead gunner in the squadron. No one minded, or even brought the matter up, but I had not a bit of training for the job. I knew about machine guns and had a general familiarity with planes, but of aerial gunnery—the deflection angles of two planes closing from different directions and speeds—I knew not a thing except what I had learned from hunting in Wyoming. But I was honored by the job, and it never occurred to me that there were skills in which I was dangerously deficient. But in those days we all picked up what we needed as we went along.

The lead gunner of the second division, flying with McInerny, was the fiercely mustached Buck Varner, former driver of the Los Angeles fire chief's car. I made bets on which division's turret guns would hit the tow-sleeve target most often. One day I persuaded Phillips to move in close to the sleeve and fly parallel with it at exactly the same speed. With this setup you couldn't miss, and the first division blew the target to pieces, leaving huge smears of red—the color of the paint on the tip of our bullets—on the ragged remnant of the target. Phillips stood laughing when we spread the first and second division targets on the tarmac in front of the ready shack. Buck Varner couldn't believe his eyes. For every hit his division had made, marked in black paint, on its target, there were fifty on ours. I played the game out for all it was worth but didn't take his money. Everyone had a beer, and the squadron laughed for days.

Like the old TBD, the TBF was a high-level bomber as well as a torpedo plane, equipped with one of the famous Norden bombsights of which it was always said, wrongly, that they could put a bomb in a pickle barrel from twenty thousand feet. Squadrons of Flying Fortresses had used them at Midway and not gotten a single hit on the Japanese ships. Each TBF gunner was also a bombardier, by virtue of his job, not his training. The radioman who sat down in the tunnel would get up in the turret while the gunner got down on the tunnel seat, opened the bomb-bay doors, turned on the sight in front of him, and looked down through a window in the bay to line up on a target far below. Only the lead plane of the division used the sight, while the other planes released their bombs when they saw the lead plane drop. The whole system, depending on variable winds and temperatures at different levels, was tricky, but I had a certain feel for the sight and great luck combining its functions with a lot of guesswork, raining down practice bombs on target on the bombing range.

The bombers practiced in a hangar, where an automated mobile box, looking something like a metal shoebox with wheels and a target pinned to the top, started from one corner. Riding a framework vehicle, steered by one man while the bomber sat about ten feet above and in front with the sight, you began a run on the slow-moving box. When your simulated bombing plane was directly above the target, you would release a plumb bob, the point of which, after a measured delay, would make a mark in the target. Like everything we did, this exercise was made more interesting by wagering on it. The mark closest to center collected the pool for the day. Boone wept and swore that I cheated, but day after day I walked away with the loot, acquiring a reputation as a master bomber, which I never tested in action since it must have been obvious to the admirals that high-level bombing with torpedo planes was a waste of time. We had the sights only because the army had them and the navy didn't want to be left behind.

The plane's crew's relationship with Lieutenant Commander Phillips was formal. The radioman—a telephone lineman from Reno named Sullivan, short enough to stand upright in the tunnel—and I called him captain, and we asked permission to fire the guns and secure the hatches as if we were on a battleship.

But Phillips was a genial man, given to taking off for the day to have lunch in Honolulu or to fly over the great volcano on the main island of Hawaii, landing at the little Somerset Maugham tropical town of Hilo, where we would wander about while he borrowed a jeep and toured the island. On the way to Honolulu we never missed a chance to fly low over the leper colony on the long spit of land with the cliff at the end on Molokai, and the lepers never failed to come out, either to wave or to shake their fists at us; we never knew which.

There were endless training missions in which the squadron took off, assembled, flew to a target together, bombed it, and then formed up again and flew home. Woe be to the pilot who didn't join the group quickly or fly a tight formation. One poor fellow, known as Dilbert after a cartoon character used in flight training posters who did everything wrong, spent an hour one bright moonlit night trying to find the seventeen other planes of the squadron as we flew back and forth over the great dead volcano. Finally, Phillips had had it and after asking Dilbert for his location, told him to stay right there and we would join up on him. We did, and Ensign Dilbert went back to the pool the next day for further training.

The navy was beginning its drive across the western Pacific.

CHAPTER NINE

Black Panthers

B<small>Y LATE</small> October the idyll was over. The USS *Lexington* (CV-16), a new carrier replacing the old *Lexington* (which was lost in the Coral Sea the previous May), was cruising off the coast, and we flew out to her, practicing from her deck for several days. Returning to Maui, we packed up our gear, stuffed it in the planes, and flew to Ford Island. Pearl Harbor was filled with ships, and as we landed we saw several of the new carriers joining the fleet. The losses of the first year of the war had been made good, and the great drive across the central Pacific that would end in Tokyo Bay less than two years later was beginning. On November 10, Air Group 6 flew out to the *Enterprise* to prepare for an attack on the Japanese bases on the Gilbert Islands at the end of November. After we had landed aboard, the yeoman handed me orders directing me to report to San Francisco for training as a pilot. I had applied in Maui, having always wanted to fly, but had expected nothing to come of the brief physical and written exams I took. Now the orders were there, but there was no way to report until the cruise was over. I would go through the most remarkable events of my life during the next month with the constant thought that if the orders had come one day earlier I would have missed it all.

A huge task force of carriers, cruisers, destroyers, and transports sailed down the central Pacific to the Gilbert Islands, where we were to land troops on Betio (or Tarawa), with its landing field, and, slightly to the north, Butaritari Island in Makin Atoll. The *Enterprise* was assigned to provide air support for the army's Butaritari landing. The marines were to take Tarawa. Both islands were pounded with naval gunfire, and on the morning of November 20 the transports loaded the troops into the assault boats. Carrier planes went in to clean up any targets still standing and provide close support throughout the day.

Makin Atoll was Hollywood perfect: blue water, circular coral reef, white beaches, and coconut palm groves. We in Phillips's plane could see the entire show, flying liaison back and forth not far above the landing and reporting the progress of the assault to the command ship. Tarawa was a bloody mess from the beginning, when the assault boats hung up on the reef, but at Butaritari the attack proceeded like an exercise. The cruisers and destroyers blasted away, squadron after squadron of planes flew in strafing and dropping bombs, a long line of Higgins boats moved up to the southern hammerhead of the island. As the first soldiers rushed up the beach, hundreds of cheering natives rose up out of the recently shelled brush and broken trees and rushed down to greet them with open arms. The Japanese garrison had retreated earlier up the handle of the island, but the natives had stayed behind, eager to see Americans and be rid of the Japanese. It had been assumed that nothing could live through the pounding the assault area had taken, but few of the natives were hurt, and they gave a comic turn to the landing.

Later in the day we circled the island and observed a group of torpedo bombers try to skip bomb a wrecked ship half out of the water near On Chong's Wharf. The wharf, built years ago by a Chinese trader, was a wobbly structure sticking out into the lagoon and was about the only thing with a name on the atoll. A coastal trader that had sunk off it in some long-forgotten storm had been occupied by the Japanese, who were using it as a pillbox from which to fire at our soldiers after they had landed with their supplies on the beach.

Skip bombing was a new and briefly used technique in which you didn't try to hit the target directly but came in on a line with it, about a hundred feet above the water, and dropped the bomb at an angle so that it hit the water and then skipped up in the air and landed on the target. Bang! Utter destruction! Why this was thought a better way of destroying the target than hitting it directly was no more obvious than why two-thousand-pound armor-piercing shells designed for World War I battleships had been converted to skip bombs by installing fins and delay-action fuses. But they had, and they were being used that day on a rusty old wreck that you could kick a hole through. As we circled, eyes fastened on the spectacle, plane after plane came in, dropped its bomb in the sparkling clear water, only to have it hit the shallow sandy bottom, leap up, and skip over the ship to land with a big explosion on the beach side, or skip high up in the air and explode with a flash that threatened the plane that had just dropped it.

It was an exercise in the kind of dangerous futility that wars are made of. As we turned in a wide circle over the island, feeling smugly superior to the skip bombers, there was a ping, only a little one, and a smell of gasoline. It was trickling into the tunnel where Sullivan and an observer, the squadron intelligence officer, were seated. The bomb bay had been filled that day with a huge auxiliary gas tank to allow us to fly liaison all day without having to land to refuel. The auxiliary tank had no self-sealing lining, and when an irritated Japanese gunner took a shot at us, flying slowly, and no doubt infuriatingly, overhead, a lucky hit pierced the tank and the forward bulkhead of the tunnel. The plane filled with fumes that could explode with a single spark. The intelligence officer later wrote himself into the dispatches with a recommendation for a medal for himself—which Phillips did not forward—for saving the plane by pouring coffee from his thermos on the gas, thus, he said, holding down the fumes and preventing an explosion. Fortunately, no one was smoking at the time, and the pilot dropped the big green auxiliary tank on the Japanese lines, hoping that we hit the soldier who had hit us. The gas in the plane evaporated quickly and, nearly out of fuel, we flew back to the *Enterprise* to land, refuel, and take off, without our coffee-pouring intelligence officer, for another afternoon of observing.

There was little resistance on Butaritari, in contrast to the blood being spilled a few miles to the south in the terrible fighting on Tarawa. But the army advanced cautiously, and we flew far ahead of the troops, a few hundred feet above the blue water and the sandy beaches, weaving in and out across the reef and the island, looking for any signs of Japanese support troops or new entrenchments. Mostly we saw only natives, who waved happily. But as we flew back to On Chong's Wharf a Japanese soldier let rip with his machine gun, blowing some pieces off the plane, which then went into a dive that dropped my stomach right out of my belly. "Prepare to crash, prepare to crash," Phillips shouted over the intercom, and then the plane lifted a little. "I think I can hold it with the tabs." The tabs are small inserts in the elevator, controlled separately, that can be rolled up or down to keep the plane in a climb or descent without the pilot having to maintain constant pressure on the elevators. Now they compensated for the down pressure on the loose elevators and kept us in something like steady flight.

A bullet had come through the fuselage in back of the radioman and cut the steel wire elevator control cable that connects the pilot's stick to the elevators. We were okay for the moment, holding flying altitude not far above the water, but the problem had not been solved. Landing on a carrier is tricky business, requiring drumhead-tight control cables for hair-trigger responses. So it looked like a water landing alongside the carrier was the best we could hope for, and such landings, while they often worked, were always highly risky, particularly with faulty controls. Too many things to go wrong: a bump on the head, a jammed hatch, and the plane sinks instantly.

Radioman Sullivan got on the intercom to say that, using his telephone linesman's skills, he thought he could join the two raveled ends of the elevator control cable, which he proceeded to do, standing up in the tunnel below the opening of my gun turret, through which I looked down between my legs with great interest. A lot of time passed, with everyone literally sweating through their khaki flight suits, but finally the splice was made, and though the cable still had a lot of slack, Phillips could make the plane go up and down again using his stick. But that, he explained over the intercom, wasn't good enough for any kind of landing, on the water or the deck. The cable had to be taut and respond more or less instantly to his control. Sullivan, a little over five feet tall and able to walk upright in the tunnel, was a very ingenious and a very courageous fellow, and he said that he thought he could work some cord we were carrying into both sides of the splice and then twist a .50-caliber bullet into the weave and by turning it again and again, as in a tourniquet, take up a lot of the slack. This too worked after a long time, and Phillips finally declared himself willing to try a deck landing on the *Enterprise*.

The crew on the *Enterprise* was less sure. They didn't want the flight deck fouled with a wreck at that point, and though they finally agreed, they made us wait for another eternity, during which time Phillips tried out an idea on Sullivan. "What I am going to need at certain points in the approach and landing is a lot of movement in a hurry, and the patched cable will move the elevator too slowly. On the landing approach, could you stand in the tunnel, holding onto the bullet providing the tension in the cable, and when I say 'NOW' over the intercom, give the cable an instant manual assist in whichever direction it's moving?" Landing on a carrier is rough at the best of times, requiring the crew to be seated and buckled up; but Sullivan agreed to try.

Phillips was a master carrier pilot, and he flew the crippled plane carefully on a lurching approach. Every movement was slow and exaggerated and likely to lead to disaster. Sullivan hung on to the bullet for dear life, locked his feet on whatever he could get for purchase, and in the end, when Phillips said the final "NOW," pulled the cable with all his might to stall the plane out and drop it on deck, getting thrown into his radio as the arresting wire caught the tailhook and the plane stopped short.

November 20 had been an exhaustingly long day, long enough by far, but that night a formation of Japanese bombers flew down from the Marshall Islands to the north to look for our carriers in the darkness. They didn't find us that night, but we were at general quarters, all lights extinguished, for a good part of the time. This was not the only danger. I was sitting on the flight deck, my legs hanging over into the catwalk, when in the complicated maneuvering another carrier cruising with us rushed straight at us, a huge black mass, only to turn at what seemed the last moment and pass by us to port, so close that I could actually call out to the sailors standing helplessly on her deck.

The Japanese had big airfields on the islands in Kwajalein Atoll several hundred miles to the north, out of which they were flying two-engine medium bombers, Bettys, loaded with torpedoes, at the American fleet, hoping to sink a carrier or two. Japanese air losses in the Solomons had been so great in 1943 that they had turned largely to medium-bomber night attacks with torpedoes, flying at wave height to escape radar detection. Our ships were almost helpless in the face of these attacks, for we had as yet no night fighters, and if antiaircraft was fired it would reveal our position. It was decided on the *Enterprise* to do something about the problem, and Adm. Arthur Radford, commanding Task Force 50.2, consulted with Butch O'Hare and Phillips about setting up the first night-fighter operation off carriers, code-named "Black Panther." We had just received our first small airborne radar sets, ASB-1. They were primitive instruments, with a small green screen, about five by seven inches, with a moving arm that briefly lit up bogies as it swept across their location—terribly difficult to read—with a maximum range of about ten miles, and precise only at a much closer range. The operator had to switch from the aerial under one wing to the one under the other to see that side of his circle. Still, we had seen nothing like them before, so they impressed us mightily. Sets had been installed in two of our torpedo planes by a specialist, Lt. (jg) Hazen Rand, who had worked in the development of the airborne naval radar at MIT. After a crash course in operating the rear stinger gun, Rand replaced Sullivan in our tunnel for the Black Panther operation.

The night-fighter plan was straightforward: two radar-equipped TBFs with belly tanks would be launched at dusk to stay up all night. Then, when the bogies appeared later at night, as they usually did, fighters would be launched from the *Enterprise* and join up with the torpedo planes. The ship's fighter director officer (FDO), using the ship's radar and the VHF (Very High Frequency) radio, which the Japanese, it was thought, could not pick up, would vector fighters and a torpedo plane to a point near the bogies. There the more lightly gunned TBF, using its radar, would lead the two heavily armed fighter planes (six wing-mounted .50 calibers each) to where they could see the exhausts of the Japanese planes, which did not have exhaust suppressors at that time, and then break away, leaving the fighters to complete the attack. All could then land at daybreak, avoiding a night landing and the necessity of lighting up the ship, revealing its location to any enemy planes still hunting it.

The plan was modified as time passed, and when bogies appeared in large numbers on the ship's radar screen early on the morning of November 24, two night-fighter groups, each consisting of a torpedo plane—without the belly tanks, thankfully—and two fighters, were catapulted at about 0300. The second TBF was piloted by Lt. John McInerny with Buck Varner in the turret and another radar specialist in the tunnel. It was a confusing flight. We never joined up effectively, and when we did get into a kind of loose formation, the ship's radar couldn't get us in an attack position on the Bettys. Our plane radar found nothing. It was a long night, nearly six hours, of straggling around a dark sky without much sense of where we were and where to go. At about 0500, while we were circling looking for targets, there was a huge flash of light off to the east, like the sun rising, which we later learned was the escort carrier *Liscombe Bay* blowing up after being hit by a Japanese submarine torpedo. She was a small ship with pitifully little protection, and everything in her—gasoline, bombs, torpedoes—blew up all at once. She went down instantly, with the loss of over six hundred men. Our fears about her sister ship, the *Nassau*, when we first saw her at Espíritu Santo had not been exaggerated. Mac's plane developed engine trouble, but he nursed it through the night until he had to land after dawn with only five gallons of gas left in his tanks. The rest of us, disappointed, finally got back aboard about 0830.

The next day, the battle being pretty much over at Makin, we flew down to Tarawa with O'Hare to familiarize ourselves with the field so that we could land there after a Black Panther flight to avoid making the ship illuminate for a landing. A landing on a totally dark deck was still not conceivable. The fight was still going on in the midst of smoldering devastation. The landing field was clear—though it had a lot of holes and no landing lights—but the burned and gutted landing craft were still on the reef far from shore where they had hung up; the marines had gotten out with their weapons and waded ashore in neck-deep water. The bodies still floated in the tide and lay bloated on the sand. All the trees on the island were down in great rubbish heaps.

Early on the night of the 25th the usual flight of Bettys appeared early, but the Black Panthers sat the evening out. If we had launched at that time we would have had to land on Tarawa, and it was clear from the day's inspection that a night landing was out of the question. One snooper passed a few hundred feet over the ship—he may have dropped a torpedo —so close we could see his exhausts, but the *Enterprise* did not open fire so as not to reveal our position. This was all spooky stuff, and the Japanese made it spookier by dropping bright flares and yellow float lights here and there in the darkness, apparently to mark targets and assembly points. With all this going on the crew was nervous and jumpy. One man began shouting at me that it was the duty of the Panthers to be up there in the night defending the ship, which seemed after the past hairy week very unreasonable. Let him go up there and defend the ship is pretty much what I told him, and a brief fight bled off a lot of repressed feelings.

Other Bettys circled from about twenty miles, dropping another string of flares. When they came closer, the battleship *North Carolina* and other escort ships opened up with anti-aircraft guns in a startling explosion and shot down one, possibly two, snoopers. The night went on at general quarters as one or another group of bombers made a move on us and then withdrew to circle about confusedly, dropping more of those ghastly float lights just when you thought they might have gone away. No one got much sleep until the attackers left before dawn, with no hits to show for their effort.

For the night of the 26th another modified night-fighting scheme was designed, using only one section of a torpedo plane and two fighters going out together. One of the fighters was to be flown by Butch O'Hare and the other by his wingman from Fighting Squadron 2 (VF-2), Ens. Warren Skon. Phillips was to fly the torpedo plane with Rand in the tunnel, while I remained, somewhat unsure about all this, in the turret. I often thought that once you got in there and had pulled up the armor plate (wondering what "Hard Homo" meant), you were committed, and whatever happened, there wasn't much you could do about it. Infantry could turn tail at any time, but you were literally and figuratively locked in once you got into the confined space of the turret. This night would prove that theory.

The fighters were to go off the catapult first, followed by the torpedo plane, early in the evening, if the Japanese appeared. Then we would all have to land on the carrier deck in darkness, without lights. The secured landing field at Tarawa had been notified to receive us if we could not get back aboard the carrier, but no one wanted to risk landing on that field in the dark. Once in the air the plan was for the fighters to rendezvous immediately with the torpedo plane and use its radar eye, along with the ship's radar, to get close to the attackers.

Japanese snoopers were already probing the fleet before sunset, and daylight fighters from the *Belleau Wood* shot down one Betty. We Panthers sat in the ready room, wearing red goggles to preserve our night vision. I had no more than the usual worries, but waiting was hard.

About 1800, at dusk, the public address system told us that thirty to forty Bettys closing on the ships had been picked up by radar. A few moments later came that stirring command, "Pilots, man your planes," and the two fighter pilots, Phillips, Rand, and I made our way up to the flight deck and into our planes. Off to starboard three to five miles a string of red flares went off. Why red? I had checked and double-checked all the guns on the torpedo plane: the .30 caliber in the tunnel, the two fifties in the wings, and especially the .50-caliber Browning machine gun in the turret, making sure that the two one-hundred-round cans of ammunition I had —one in the gun, and one secured to the bulkhead below in the tunnel—were fully loaded with perfectly belted ammunition so that there would be no jams at a bad time. The belts for the turret gun were heavy with tracer—one tracer, one armor piercing, one tracer, one incendiary—so that I could see more clearly where the stream of fire was going in the night. A great mistake, it turned out, since too many tracers igniting at the muzzle of the gun blinded me in the darkness. In the turret I checked the intercom, pulled up the armor plate that locked me in with an ominous click, and turned on the hooded gun sight with its lighted orange concentric circles, just behind the bulletproof plateglass in front of me, while the engine turned up and went to full power.

The two fighters went off at 1800, fired from the catapult, and disappeared into the distance, diminishing blue lights visible from their exhaust flares, which could not be suppressed without loss of power. The TBF did have its exhausts covered and so remained invisible until we began firing. The FDO (fighter director officer) seated in the air control on the

Enterprise vectored the fighters out toward the Bettys at once without waiting for the TBF to join them, a change in the plan that would have serious consequences. Torpedo planes always sank below the deck when fired from the catapult, and looking from the backward-facing turret, I could see the huge black deck rise above us and feel the tug of the waves below. But the engine at full power pulled us up and away, and as the wheels and flaps came up we gained altitude and began to move away from the white wakes and bow waves of the task force. The sun set a few minutes later, and the moonless night was completely dark, unlike the moonlit nights we had practiced in at Maui. An overcast began at about 1,500 feet. We expected the fighters to join up with us at once, but they were long gone, and we began a fruitless search for them, feeling annoyed and abandoned since we believed that all our firepower was in the fighters. Although nothing was said I suspected that Butch was looking for glory again.

Though we followed the vectors called out by the FDO trying to bring the planes together, we couldn't catch up with the fighters. I assumed that we had lost them for good and would go back to try to land on the ship. But Phillips was an aggressive pilot, and after a time he decided to see what he could find in the darkness on his own. Rand called out that he had a contact at seven miles and took us in to 4,500 yards before we lost contact. Shortly after 1900 our ships, except for the carriers, opened up with their antiaircraft guns, illuminating the horizon for us in an incredible *son et lumière* show. Still more flares were dropped by the Japanese, lighting up the ships like daylight for a few moments. When the flares burned out all was darkness again, and I found myself in difficulty. The pilot has instruments, particularly an artificial horizon, to tell him whether he is flying level or not, and an altimeter to show whether he is climbing or diving and how far he is above the ocean. The man in the tunnel doesn't care what is going on outside since he is enclosed in a box, oriented by his green radar screen. But in the turret, riding backward, you have no instruments. You stare out into the dark night, and after a time you don't know up from down. The first few turns are okay, but then disorientation begins. A flicker of light could be a star in the sky or a ship on the ocean or another plane coming at you on a fast angle. As long as the changes are not too abrupt and frequent, the seat of your pants gives you a sense of where you are, but a few rapid changes and panic begins to flutter around the edges.

The *Enterprise* radar was still trying to direct both the fighters and the torpedo plane to groups of Bettys, but Phillips was better at the game than O'Hare. He found himself a few miles behind a group of six, and Rand began calling out the range: three miles, two, one, a thousand yards. Then, at two hundred yards, seeing the Bettys' exhausts, Phillips said, "I have them in sight. Attacking." This was unheard of, a lightly armed, clumsy, relatively slow torpedo plane attacking several bombers in a tight, mutually supporting formation, each with five guns—front, rear, top, and two in the waist—but there was no call for a vote, and Phillips swung in behind the rear Betty in the starboard line.

The two .50 calibers in the wings felt like they were tearing the plane apart. As we pulled up and away from the firing run, I could look back and see the surprised enemy opening up with the guns he could bring to bear. Fire flared out at his wing root, where the gas tanks were, and I fired at the flames. He blew up all at once. A long trail of fire went down and down into the blackness of the ocean below, where it kept on burning, a red smear on the black water. The turret .50 caliber, its muzzle less than three feet from my eyes, spewed a flare of burning gases, despite a flash suppressor—all the more for the extra tracer, which in the darkness made it impossible for me to see the illuminated concentric circles of the gun sight. As long as I was seated I was blinded every time I fired. The only thing to do was to unbuckle my safety belt and crouch on my seat, trying to get my eyes high enough to see over the muzzle flare and fire down the line of tracer into the Bettys, illuminated by their firing guns and engine exhausts. It didn't work very well—I still could hardly see—but it worked a little bit, and I remained in that crouched position, my head bent over and forward to fit inside the rounded turret, for the remainder of the flight, except for the trip into the tunnel below.

The Japanese were totally confused. Night fighters from carriers were as unknown to them as they were new to us, and in their excitement the Japanese gunners were firing at one another. As we pulled away from the first kill, the fighter director officer vectored us toward other Bettys, and our own radar once again brought us to within visual range of the dark cigar shapes, their exhaust flares burning blue on both sides. Just as we went into our firing run, O'Hare, who had seen the first plane burning on the water, called us and ordered Phillips to turn on his recognition light so that they could join up: "Turn on your lights, Phil, I'm going to start shooting." The words filled me with terror. The fighters hadn't been able to find anything all night, and now out of the darkness one of the navy's aces was going to start shooting! To tense things up a bit more, Butch added, "I think I got me a Jap." Phillips, cool as ever, replied that he was in a firing run and did not want to alert the enemy but that he would blink a light a few times.

The light told the Betty that something was out there, and it began evasive maneuvers, opening up on us as it did so, but Phillips followed closely, and after a long burst the deadly fire showed again in the gas tanks where the wings joined the fuselage. I poured in some more, and the Betty started down in a controlled dive, making a long water landing, leaving a trail of burning gas about three hundred yards on the water and continuing to burn. I snapped off a burst at another dark cigar shape, and then Rand called out on the intercom, "I'm hit."

"Where?"

"In the foot. My boot has filled with blood. I don't know how bad it is, but I have put a tourniquet above the ankle."

"Are you in pain?"

"Yes."

"Too much to go on working the radar?"

"I don't know. I'll try."

"Kernan, go down and see what you can do."

I unlatched the armor plate below me and crawled down in the bucketing plane to sit on the green aluminum bench beside Rand. His pale thin face looked like a skull in the ghoulish green light of the radar screen. A single bullet had come through the plane just forward of the armor on the floor, where his foot was braced while he peered into the radar scope, and it had torn off the side of his shoe and foot. It wasn't a mortal wound, unless he bled to death, but it looked a painful mess. I put on a bandage and called Phillips on the intercom. "Shall I give him an injection of morphine, Captain?" (We carried Syrettes in the medical kit.) The answer shocked me. "No, we'll need the radar again." The logic was obvious, though I didn't think Rand was going to do much more work that night.

I took the opportunity of being in the tunnel to change the ammunition can for the turret gun, a tough job trying to shove a long heavy can up one minute and pull it down the next while hunched over in close quarters, the plane rising and falling rapidly. Each time I would get it nearly up to where the retaining latch could catch it, the plane would suddenly rise, and the can and I would come down to the deck or be flung against one of the bulkheads, trying all the time not to step on Rand, sitting there with his teeth gritted tight, or to slip in his blood. Finally the ammo can clicked into place, and I jumped back into the turret, glad to get out of the dark and bloody tunnel. We had by this time lost the Japanese planes, but Phillips, true to form, began searching for them again. The radar was our only chance, but now Rand could pick up no blips in any direction. He was making heavy going of it by that time, though trying gamely. We were now circling at some distance from the carrier, and I became disoriented again. The second of the two Bettys that had crashed was burning in a long smear of gasoline on the water, and as we turned in the pitch black, I thought the ocean was the sky and the light from the burning plane another plane turning in a long curve for a run on us. I called out on the intercom that it was attacking and requested permission—this was still the battleship navy—to begin firing. Phillips put me right side up again.

The ship's radar could see both us and the fighters, and the fighter director officer was still trying to maneuver us together. At this point Phillips turned on all our running lights, and the fighters, lit up like Christmas trees, slid menacingly in, coming down across our tail from starboard and above. O'Hare took position on our starboard wing, Skon on the port, bright blue in the flare of their exhausts, six guns jutting out of their wings. Canopy back, goggles up, yellow Mae West, khaki shirt, and helmet, Butch O'Hare sat aggressively forward, looking like the tough navy ace he was, his face sharply illuminated by his canopy light for one last brief instant.

The Japanese 752 Air Group reported losing three planes on the night of November 26, and sinking two carriers and one battleship. They also reported seeing more than three night fighters turn on their lights. This had to be the brief moment when our group, together for the only time that night, was illuminated, and it was at that point that, attracted by our lights, one of the Bettys tried to join up on us. The long black cigar shape came in on the starboard side of the group across the rear of O'Hare, and realizing its fatal mistake, began firing. "Butch, this is Phil. There's a Jap on your tail. Kernan, open fire." I began shooting at the Betty. The air was filled with streams of fire, and a long burst nearly emptied my ammunition can. The Betty, as the tracers arced toward him, continued firing and then abruptly disappeared into the dark to port. I thought I saw O'Hare reappear for a moment, and then he was gone. Something whitish gray appeared in the distance, his parachute or the splash of the plane going in. Skon slid away. I thought that the Jap had shot O'Hare and then disappeared, but I also realized with a sinking feeling that there was a chance I might have hit O'Hare as well in the exchange of fire.

Phillips took us down to drag the surface for a long half hour before we gave up and made our way back to the *Enterprise* at about 2100. Skon landed first without any trouble. But for us the evening was not over. We still had to make a landing on an unlighted carrier deck at night. If it had been done before, it was certainly not standard procedure, and Phillips, despite having a thousand hours as an instrument instructor, had never done it in practice. We homed on the white wake that marked the ship in the water, but there was no light anywhere on deck except the fluorescent wands of the landing signal officer standing on the end of the flight deck. We came in too high, and just as Phillips was about to cut the engine the landing signal officer waved us off. Full throttle, nearly stalling out, wheels, flaps, and hook down, we hung for an eternal moment above the deck, neither rising nor falling. I saw the huge, dark shape of the carrier's island structure just a few feet off our starboard wing, the parked planes on the deck just a few feet below, the men standing there looking up at us. We hung there, then picked up speed and flew away to go around again.

The *Enterprise* captain, Matt Gardner, must have known we would never make it with the cumbersome plane in the dark, so he turned on the shaded lights that marked out the flight deck for the crucial moment. They could only be seen from low and aft by a plane approaching for a landing, so they didn't reveal the ship very much for very long to a submarine or any Bettys still flying about. This time it worked. We dropped heavily on the deck. The corpsmen took Rand away, Phillips disappeared to talk to the admiral, and I made my way to the head just below the flight deck, where I stood and pissed for what seemed like five minutes. On and on it went, emptying all the accumulated fear and tension out with the water that had built up in the longest three hours of my life, before or since.

My first encounter with media arrogance came before I was out of the head. Eugene Burns, an Associated Press correspondent, came charging in and while I was still standing at the urinal trough asked, "What happened? Where were they? How many? Where is O'Hare? How many did you shoot down?" The tone was harshly aggressive, and I didn't feel like talking about it to anyone as abrasive and unpleasant as this guy. He bored right in, though, and began to try to construct the scandal he wanted. "How far away from O'Hare were you when he was hit? Were you shooting too?" And then, there it was: "Did you hit him?"

Really messy firefights don't sort themselves out in the head very clearly, either sooner or later, and heavy feelings of responsibility and guilt lurk around all combat deaths. Without doubt I had fired at the trailing Japanese plane that had tried to join up on us, and he had fired at everything in his range, including O'Hare and us, but had I, blasting away, hit the group commander as well? Had I been trigger-happy as a result of my disorientation and hearing O'Hare saying that he was about to begin shooting? Like the cigar-shaped Betty sliding out of the darkness to our rear, guilt slid across my mind. Letting me know that he was somehow an official who had a right to news and that anything of interest belonged to the public, Burns played on my doubts and shock to try to get me to blurt out some sudden, unconsidered remark that could be turned into sensational fare for his readers. If he had come at me with more sympathy I might have tried to tell him how mixed up it all was, but his bullying got my back up, and I walked off shouting, "Get the hell away from me." He went off muttering about reporting me to the officers, as if I had broken some kind of rule by not telling his newspaper everything, but he never came back. I suppose a public relations officer got hold of him, and in the end he wrote some embarrassingly wild stories, far more fiction than fact, for magazines like the *Saturday Evening Post*, describing O'Hare going down amid a blaze of gunfire while saving a grateful fleet, with bouquets to everyone involved, including me. The official navy version was not so garish, but it downplayed the fatal separation of the fighter planes and the torpedo plane, bringing them together much earlier than they had in fact joined up, and crediting the entire group, not Phillips alone, with two certain, and two possible, kills.

The intelligence officer gave me a cup of his famous coffee and debriefed me. Phillips, unsure of what had happened since he had been facing forward, away from the fight, went down to the sick bay to see Rand before he came to recap the flight with me and to get my view of what had happened. After he had put all the pieces together he accepted Rand's view. Rand, staring hard out of the tunnel window, had a good view of the exchange of fire and later described it with Yankee brevity: "Butch got lost and sought enlightenment by turning on recognition lights in front of a Japanese bomber. The Jap shot up Butch's can and Al Kernan shot the Jap."

Later I sat on the deck in a corner of the ready room for a long time talking to a few friends, Boone and Varner mostly, trying to sort the whole thing out. I tried to sleep, but air-conditioned cold—usually a luxury—made me feel that I was dead. Everyone else was comfortable, snoring away, so it was in my head, but it didn't go away. Shivering, I went over the fight again and again, trying to sort it out and only tangling it up more. I began to brood about bad luck, having had the orders to flight school that would have sent me back to the States rather than sitting here waiting to get killed, if not tonight then tomorrow, when we would be sure to go up again, having had so much success tonight.

Phillips was quite buoyed up by being credited with two enemy kills, unheard of for a torpedo pilot. O'Hare was recommended for another Congressional Medal of Honor, but in the end everyone on the flight received the Navy Cross, which surprised me since enlisted men usually got a lesser medal than the officers. Phillips became the group commander. But we still sat and waited the next two nights for another Black Panther flight, and once we got up to the deck and into the planes. But at the last minute the radar contact faded, and the flight was called off.

By the next night we were gone—Tarawa and Makin having been secured—on our way to attack the Marshall Islands, from which the Bettys had come, with the goal of knocking out the airfields and shipping in preparation for an invasion next month. Death still followed us, and on November 30 one of our planes loaded with depth charges crashed in the water alongside the ship while on antisubmarine patrol. While we watched the crew swimming in the water, the depth charges exploded.

The morning of the attack, December 4, 1943, was cool, the sun just rising as we sat on the hangar deck with the breeze blowing through the open curtains. We were to be the last off and were alone. I stood by the plane looking at the sun, wondering, as many going into battle must have wondered since time began, how I had gotten to that particular place when so many others who had more at stake were not there. Dark thoughts soon passed and fate was accepted in the excitement of taking off and taking the lead of the entire air group on the way to the target. From twenty thousand feet the whole atoll of Kwajalein spread out before us in an enormous boomerang of narrow, white-beached islands, with a big lagoon in the center, dark blue here, light there. The morning was beautiful, visibility unlimited. In the lagoon several Japanese ships were getting under way. Black antiaircraft bursts rocked the plane, and the fighter planes taking off from Roi-Namur far below seemed more interesting than ominous. A Japanese float plane going the other way flew by us, but no one recognized it until after it had passed, and there was no point in firing.

As dive-bombers attacked the ships and the fighters strafed the Japanese planes on the ground, we proceeded in a lordly way southward across the lagoon to the largest island, Kwajalein, at the southern tip, to glide-bomb—a shallower run than dive-bombing—the ground installations and the shipping in the anchorage. Phillips circled and watched, calling attention to targets, and as the last planes finished their runs and left, we went in alone to bomb a merchant ship. We pushed over from twenty thousand feet, and as we neared the bottom of our run through the thick antiaircraft fire, Phillips began firing his guns, which seemed rather odd. As we pulled up and I thought gratefully, "Now I can go to San Francisco," Phillips came on the intercom and admitted wryly that in the dive he had made the mistake of pressing the gun trigger on the front of the stick rather than the bomb release on the top of the stick. Too bad, I thought, but let's get the hell out of here and get me off to flight school. The thought never occurred to him, and around we went for another run, with everything in the area shooting at us. Our bombs seemed to hit the ship, but the painfully learned fact is that it is almost always impossible to tell for certain, even with photographs, and those who make bomb runs are understandably overly optimistic about results.

The return to Pearl Harbor was quiet, and I said goodbye to everyone and flew with Phillips and Sullivan for the last time to Pearl Harbor, from which I went to Ewa, the marine field where those going to flight training out of the fleet were assembled. O'Hare's memory was honored in time by the naming of the largest airport in the United States, O'Hare Field in Chicago, after him. Phillips was killed a few months later at Truk. As air group commander he had shifted from a torpedo plane to a fighter. No one saw what happened, and the plane was never found in the Truk lagoon, which had every kind of wreckage imaginable, but the reasoning was that while he was directing the attack a Japanese fighter came in on him from the rear.

CHAPTER TEN

Solo

ONE OF the advantages the United States had over the Japanese was the ability to replace its losses, including its skilled manpower. At the beginning of the war the Japanese had trained a superior group of naval aviators, but they didn't have a replacement cadre. It was as if they thought the first group so good that they could never die. But the first group died with great bravery in one battle after another, and their places were then taken by recruits with only a few hours of training and no battle experience. The U.S. Navy, however, put an effective pilot-training program into place before the war and continued to produce a steady stream of replacements. By 1943 heavy casualties were expected, and the number of trainees was increased. Enlisted men from the fleet could apply, and this is how I got my chance to be a pilot and an officer at the beginning of 1944.

I went back by ship to San Diego, where I was given a train ticket to San Francisco and told to report to naval headquarters and be assigned to flight training. I stopped to see the Boones, who were, as always, most hospitable. The oldest son of the family, Bill, was an operator who had contacts with everyone, including Frank Sinatra, who was just then extremely popular. Bill took me to one of Sinatra's radio programs and introduced us. The great man was extremely pleasant and invited me to his house, to a party that never seemed to end. I never talked to Sinatra again, but the drinks were free and the girls rather remarkable. Someone asked me if I had any gas coupons, gas being rationed at that time. When I said, "No," he produced a big wad, all counterfeit or stolen, I suppose, but I took them gratefully and used them to drive around when I got leave.

Bill Boone also knew people on the *Los Angeles Times* and arranged for pictures and interviews with me about the death of Butch O'Hare. I was cautious about the media after my brush with Eugene Burns, and it must have showed since the published article styled me "modest little Alvin Kernan." Bill sent a copy to his brother Dick and he, to my chagrin, later sent me a letter addressed to "Modest Little Alvin Kernan."

It was near Christmas when I got to San Francisco, and I expected to get some kind of leave, but since I had had thirty days' leave the previous March, I had used up my quota for that year and was ordered to report to flight training right away. Complaints about it being Christmas and about having missed out on leave in 1942 got me nowhere, but when I produced a fifth of good whiskey the Boones had given me the yeoman delayed my assignment until a later class, thus requiring me to take a thirty-day leave. I took up residence in the elegant Claremont Hotel on the ridge overlooking the bay in Oakland. In a few days I had just enough money left to buy a ticket to Saratoga.

It was bitterly cold in Wyoming, and, having fêted me only nine months earlier, the people had heard my sea stories and were rather unenthused to see me home again so soon. The comings and goings of servicemen, many of whom had been in combat, were getting commonplace. My old friends were all in the service by now, and the girls had all gotten married or had gone out to work in the California aircraft factories, and besides, after my spree in Oakland, I was flat broke. Frank Kernan, my stepfather, couldn't help. He had been elected justice of the peace, which meant that he could fine speeders and hunters and fishermen who were caught with too many deer or fish. He ran a small store in Saratoga, sold insurance, repaired electrical appliances, and kept a line of small gifts and greeting cards. I slept on a spare bed in the back of the store and drove around the county on icy roads with my illegal gas coupons looking for old friends and making dates with girls in Medicine Bow and Rawlins, all of whom, with great good sense, had different things in mind from me.

In the end I was glad to go back to California, realizing somehow that I had left Wyoming for good and that I would never go back to stay. Los Angeles was warm and lively for a few days, but by the time I got to San Luis Obispo in late January, the winter rains had set in and life got difficult. Flight prep school was designed mostly as a way of physically toughening up the V-5 cadets and was run by a bunch of old coaches from high schools and colleges who delighted in putting us

—for our own good of course—through endless exercises, obstacle courses, endurance swims, long-distance runs, speed-agility tests, and so on. The marines among us, yellow from the Atabrine they had taken to prevent malaria, were tough, but most of us sailors were soft from sitting around too much and eating too many beans. Leaping over low walls, climbing ropes, and running cross-country came hard and painfully, but we were young and keen. Better here, it seemed, than back in the Pacific where the great drive across the center of the ocean toward Japan was rolling in high gear. The studies—aeronautics, meteorology, Morse code, navigation—seemed easy enough until I got cocky and failed a major navigational test—carelessly starting the original heading 180 degrees in the wrong direction—and had to attend remedial classes.

Mostly it rained, and we lined up outside our barracks at six in the morning, standing in the pouring rain, day after day. We worked, stood guard, ran to class, exercised, and ate, always damp and cold. Colds were endemic. Midway through the three-month course we were given a thirty-six-hour liberty, from noon on Saturday to midnight on Sunday. San Luis Obispo is about equidistant from Los Angeles and San Francisco, about two hundred miles either way. The entire coast was loaded with military camps, and there must have been a million soldiers, sailors, and marines in that area, many of them trying to get on the few buses and trains for the weekend. The bus depot where I went to catch a ride to Los Angeles looked like the hold of an immigrant ship, and I would never have gotten on the bus except for the help of a friend, a former marine sergeant named Joey Bishop. An Oklahoma Indian, he was short, dark, wiry, and a Guadalcanal veteran. He had helped me get through some of the more difficult parts of the training, like hand-to-hand combat and all-out wrestling, at which he excelled and I did not. He instantly saw that getting aboard the bus in the normal way, through the front door, was hopeless, and without hesitating, he went up the high side of the bus and into one of the open windows, holding out a hand to help me up and through. It was dark by the time we got to Los Angeles, and we immediately headed for the bars.

By noon the next day it was time to try to board another bus to take our dreadful hangovers back to San Luis Obispo.

We got there by midnight, cold and exhausted, and then I stood watch from midnight to 0400, trying desperately to stay awake, while the rain never stopped dripping off the eaves. At the end of the three-month course, there was a ball for the graduating class. With travel and accommodations what they were, it all seemed pretty hopeless, but girls came from all over the country to go to dinner in the mess hall, dance in the local hotel and stay there with chaperones, and walk the next day on Pismo Beach, famous for its clams. No matter what the difficulties, the war was the most exciting show in town, worth any amount of inconvenience. I persuaded Betty Boone to come up for the occasion. Her mother came along, to Betty's chagrin, to make sure that she was safe, and paid for it by spending the dance night in her hotel listening to the drunken soldiery shout obscenities in the street below as they hurled bottles at the wall of the hotel. We three walked up and down Pismo Beach the next day, not knowing what to say, and in the afternoon the Boones departed, gratefully, for Los Angeles.

Flight training school, where we would actually get to fly an airplane, was the next step, and the next day we all went off to various desolate little flying fields in the northwest to learn to fly, first Piper Cubs, and then the yellow open-cockpit biplanes, N2Ss. I went into a school run by a Portland college, Lewis and Clark, out in the desert on the eastern border of Oregon, in a small town called Ontario, near the Snake River. We rode for days on a new kind of short boxcar that had been fitted up with shipboard-type bunks to transport troops, standing at the open doors like hoboes looking out at the countryside. Lewis and Clark, with few students during the war, was keeping alive by running this program and had transformed an old barn into a dormitory, mess hall, and classroom, next to a small macadamized flying field with one modest hangar and two short runways.

We were soon in the cabin of the little Piper Cubs, with the instructor sitting in back, taking off into the pale, sunny Oregon sky. After flying for years in the backseats of warplanes, the light plane with its washing-machine engine sounded a bit risky, but it moved around with agility and it was reassuringly safe, coming out of spins easily and gliding for miles without

power. Turns, climbs, dives, spins, stalls, slips: we practiced for
two hours a day, six days a week. Takeoffs and landings were
the trickiest part, mostly because of strong crosswinds. To land
in a crosswind you had to come in high on the leeward side
of the runway and then slip down to the end of the runway,
just a few feet above ground, pull level, and stall the plane out
into a nice smooth landing. At first there was usually a heavy
bump, and the plane would bounce back into the air and come
down with another bang. Some of these heavy landings ruined
propellers and too many washed you out, as did ground loops
that came from getting caught by the crosswind or applying
too much of the wrong brake while rolling down the field. You
were supposed to solo after six to ten hours of instruction, and
most of us did.

Flying may have been what we were interested in, but there
was still daily physical training. There was a fiendish obstacle
course and other devices that we learned soon to cheat by
running with our heads turned watching the coach. When he
looked away we dived through the lower rungs of contraptions
we were supposed to climb and ran around walls we were supposed to jump over. He knew we were a bunch of slackers and
put great store in the "step test" as a scientific way of demonstrating our lack of fitness. You stepped up on a knee-high
bench and then stepped down, thirty times a minute for five
minutes. Sounds easy, but it was very tiring. Our fitness was
determined by the speed with which the pulse returned to normal. I had low blood pressure to begin with, so my heart rate
didn't have far to go to get back to normal, and on the chart I
always registered as extremely fit. Since the coach had me down
as a goof-off and a miserable athlete, my score infuriated him,
but he seems never to have thought of determining whether we
all began with the same pulse rate. His faith in the uniformity of
nature was as absolute as it was unwarranted.

The town of Ontario was a pleasant little place to which we
could go frequently, there being almost no discipline in the
barracks. Liquor was rationed and sold only in state stores, but
you could keep your weekly bottle in a locker club, and if you
wanted a drink you would give the bartender a key and he
would solemnly open a wooden locker where your whiskey was

stored. For only a modest service charge he would pour out a shot, return the bottle to the locker, give you back the key, and provide ice and whatever else was needed.

As soon as we learned to fly the Cubs we were clamoring to get into the Yellow Perils, and we did so after a month. This was different: more power, an open cockpit, more response on the controls. After a few hours of instruction in these biplanes we began to fly them solo for two hours each day, each plane being sent out to a separate sector somewhere above the Oregon desert, keeping track of your position by watching the Snake River, practicing one maneuver after another. On our own with airplanes, we became adventurous, and there were games like flying under bridges—recklessly dangerous considering how inexperienced we were as pilots. The worst, and therefore the most delightful, stunt was to find a stretch of straight highway without telephone poles and fly along it with the wheels just off the ground. The trick here was to catch a car coming from the opposite direction and fly straight at him and then come back on the stick and jump over the terrified driver. The natives came to loathe us, quite justly, and called in regularly with the plane number to report us. We were real menaces to the life and limbs of others as well as ourselves, and only in wartime would the countryside have put up with us.

Unexpectedly my medal for the night-fighter battle came through. Twenty-five or thirty cadets lined up to hear the station commander read the citation and pin the Navy Cross on me. I wore the medal—one of the few times in my life I ever had a chance to wear it—while we all went into the mess hall and ate the cinnamon buns for which the cook was famous. Then I put it in its box to keep and pass on to my children. It all seemed askew, sitting there munching warm buns in homey surroundings and remembering the wild night for which the medal was awarded. The Navy Cross carried with it a monthly payment of three dollars, which in time I duly got and drew for the remainder of my time in the navy. The circumstances of my award, though strange, were nowhere near as odd as those of Hazen Rand, the radar officer in the Black Panther TBF. He was carried off to sick bay with a Japanese bullet in his foot, nothing serious it was thought, but the wound took years to heal. He also caught some kind of crud in the hospital that was only cured after he got home when he was painted blue all over with fungicide and immersed to the waist in a barrel of gasoline. It took many years for his Navy Cross to catch up with him, and when they decorated him in a stateside hospital they had to borrow one. The medal finally arrived, years later, and the Navy Department sent him two.

The heavy casualties the navy had prepared for in the Pacific had not materialized, and by now there were far too many pilots in training. One way of delaying the problem of what to do with them was to give them leave, and we were, at the end of our three months in Ontario, sent off for fifteen days. I thought that with my new officer's uniform, though without any stripes, I would cut quite a swath in Saratoga. But the town was dead, with all the men my age gone by now, and I hung around for a few days without much to do and then headed out to Los Angeles to see the Boones. Then I went up to Santa Rosa, where the old squadron, Torpedo 6, was re-forming before going to sea again.

The other thing the navy could do to relieve the glut of pilots in training was to extend the already long time of pilots' training by adding more steps along the way. Having been to flight prep and flight training, I now went to preflight school at Saint Mary's College, in Walnut Creek, California, just east of Oakland, where there were no airplanes and we did no flying. We studied more navigation, did endless physical training, and spent hours in the pool. I learned to swim four different strokes and to stay afloat in the pool for six hours with my clothes on, without getting any closer to flying. Like many naval stations by the summer of '44, Saint Mary's fielded numerous athletic teams, largely made up of professional athletes who had enlisted or been drafted—the navy was drafting men by now—and were kept around simply to play various games and add luster to the navy. The football team at Saint Mary's was a rough bunch who had trouble finding someone to practice against. The solution was close at hand. Cadets were issued football uniforms and sent out to provide the team with raw meat as a part of our PT, physical training. We never got the ball; we only lined up for them to block and to run over. But this group of old sailors wasn't having any of it. The coaches exhorted us to stand up like men and threatened us with extra drill and diminished liberty, but each time the center gave the ball to the quarterback on the professional team, we all instantly dropped where we were and covered up our heads with our arms. The backs got some pleasure, I suppose, out of running over us, but we kept our teeth intact and avoided broken bones.

About this time the navy openly admitted for the first time that they had too many pilots in training and that we could expect at the least about another year of training, the length of the full program at the time we began, before we would get our wings. To many it seemed fine. Some risk in training accidents, but better than going out to the fleet again when the war was getting closer to the Japanese homeland. To the kids who joined pilot training direct from civilian life, there really wasn't much alternative since they would be sent to boot camp as apprentice seamen, starting at the bottom of the ladder. For many of us who came from the fleet, however, the extended training was the last straw. V-5 was a dog's life, no freedom at all, constant running here and there being shouted at by a bunch of amateur officers who had never been to sea, studying the same subjects over and over. I decided that I would rather take my chances, get my rating of first-class ordnanceman back, and live a more exciting life. So I resigned from V-5 and got a little paper thanking me for my patriotism and a ticket to Chicago and the Great Lakes naval training station, where all the ex-cadets went to be reassigned.

We were put in a huge wooden hangar filled with double-decker bunks. As our old uniforms were sent to us from home, we began to look like real sailors again, sitting around day after day with nothing to do. Even card playing was out since we had no money, our pay records being in an administrative shuffle somewhere.

There was one diversion—going to parties at night. The people of that area were almost hysterical with hospitality. A serviceman couldn't walk down the street without someone trying to get him to come home for a meal, join in a family party, stay the night. Milwaukee was famous for this kind of generosity, and whenever you felt like a strenuous party you took the Skokie Valley Express, a terrifying train of old trolley cars that rattled seventy miles an hour from Chicago up to

Milwaukee. As you came out of the train people were waiting on the platform to round up servicemen for one kind of a
party or another. Since then, as now, there was entertainment
and there was entertainment, the trick was to spot and join a
group of patriots represented by pretty girls that looked like it
made drinking and dancing part of the fun, rather than going
to a church service or looking at family pictures. If your constitution was robust you would go with one of the many Polish
groups: strong young men, faces red with effort and hernias
threatening to explode, holding beer kegs overhead until everyone filled their mugs. Endless polkas going faster and faster.
I can still hear the stomping of the "Beer Barrel Polka"—"Roll
out the barrel, we'll have a barrel of fun"—louder and louder,
faster and faster. The girls, all of whom had reverted to their
native Polish costumes, were beautiful and devoted to nothing
but dancing, faster and faster, no pause for anything else. Finally, exhausted and beery, you were taken back to the Skokie
Valley Express in the early hours of the morning to rattle—
every rattle inside the head as well as in the wheels—back to
Chicago. After having your morale lifted in an aerie of Polish
Falcons, you were glad to sit around and breathe quietly for a
day or two.

There were again few restrictions on our movements, and
we ought to have enjoyed liberty in a wonderful liberty town,
but we were always broke. I finally moved into Chicago—no
permission needed since there were no roll calls—took a hotel
room, and got a daytime job working in the package section of
the post office, unloading the mail. It was bitterly cold in the
shed and the heavy mailbags stuffed with packages were hard
on the hands, but we were paid at the end of each day. After
a time I moved to a better-paying hourly job in a small defense plant in an old factory, loading with one other sailor four-
hundred-pound iron bars on a tottering dolly and pushing it
onto a rickety elevator, up to another floor, where the bars
were lifted off the dolly to another pile. I never knew what happened to them or what the plant made—possibly nothing at all
—but at five each day the boss would give us cash for whatever
hours we had worked. My hotel demanded payment daily, and
after I had bought a meal and paid the daily rent there was
nothing left over, and so the next day I would go to the factory

again and wrestle with iron bars until it was time to eat and fall into bed exhausted. I stuck with this routine for about a week, calling in each day to be sure that no orders had come for me to report to duty someplace. Then the pointlessness of it began to seep in. I went back to the training station and wangled a week's leave. I decided to let chance decide where to spend the leave, went to the Greyhound bus depot, and asked how far twelve dollars and something, my accumulated savings from work in the defense factory, would take me "riding the Dawg."

It would, it turned out, take me quite a distance: to Bemidji, Minnesota, one of the record cold spots in the country, right up near the Canadian border. I wired Ruth Emery, collect, and she agreed to meet me in Minneapolis. Having worked in Valley City for the last year she was about to set out for a new job teaching in Salem, Oregon. I was taking advantage of her: she paid all the bills, for she cared more for me by a lot than I for her. We were both too tense. She wanted an engagement, even knowing that I was surely one of the last candidates in the world for marriage, by either circumstance or inclination. Pleading the dangers of the war I reluctantly put her on the bus for Salem and took another bus north.

The Lord did provide, for I soon got to talking to another sailor, Curt, going home on leave. He was a reader, as I was, and we talked happily of books. I was reading John Dos Passos's trilogy USA at the time. Curt had had a year of college and praised Thomas Wolfe, Hemingway, Fitzgerald, and other American authors. Asked where I was going, I replied that I had a ticket to Bemidji and hoped to find a place to stay when I got there. He at once invited me to stay at his house, and I did for a couple of days, talking and going fishing for pickerel with him in the nearby lake. His leave was short, and he was off soon. After the war I tried to call Curt to see if he had made it. He had not, but died in an unusual way. Stabbed, his mother said, by a lunatic stranger who came up to him on a Chicago street and put a knife in his heart. Mistaken identity or mindless fury, no one knew.

Two girls who worked for the local dentist arranged for me to stay with the family of one of them, where I was fed and treated like a hero. During the day I would hang around the dental office—the dentist never seemed to be there—sitting in the chair and flirting with the girls. They would clean my teeth from time to time, treat my gums, and provide other dental services. An odd kind of an interlude, but I remember it as a luxuriance associated closely with the mouth and the teeth. In a day or so it was time to go back to Chicago, and the local American Legion provided a rail ticket.

For many, one of the vivid memories of World War II must be sitting up, desperately tired, trying to find some way to sleep in a rattling railroad day coach, with constant movement up and down the aisle, drafts, lights, smells of apples and orange peels. Shifting this way and that, trying to find some way of stretching the legs. After one of those nights, I was back in Chicago, stiff, exhausted, hoping to God there would at last be orders sending me to some kind of regular duty. There were. I had hoped that after two tours of overseas duty I would get to stay stateside for a while. But the orders were for Torpedo Squadron 40, a squadron that had been land-based on Guadalcanal in late 1943 to attack the Japanese bases in the Solomons and Rabaul. Now they had been joined with a fighter squadron to form a small air group to go on an escort carrier.

I was soon off to Los Alamitos, California, a navy field just to the northeast of Long Beach, where VT-40 was in training. Another long train ride back to the California sunshine, but when I got to Los Alamitos in early November, the squadron had transferred to Livermore, about twenty miles to the east of San Francisco Bay. I was given a ticket and sent on my way once more, but I couldn't pass up a chance to see the Boones again, and their hospitality was so warm that I decided to spend a full day sitting around with them. When I did arrive at Livermore I assumed that no one would note the missing day, but the personnel officer did. I had no acceptable explanation, so all I could say was that I had come along as fast as I could, missed trains, and some other mumblings, all as indistinct as possible. This seemed, to my surprise, to challenge him. He was a by-the-book character, and he used to pop up from time to time, hoping to catch me off guard, I think, and ask me why I had been a day late in reporting.

Livermore in November and December was foggy and cold, with no heat in the barracks. We sat around in light clothing, shivering, waiting for the fog to clear so that training flights could go up, but most days we were grounded. Although I was an aerial gunner, there was no crew that needed me. I was not sorry: in all that fog there were many accidents, and I happily worked in the ordnance ground crew. I found no one in the squadron I had known before, but made one of the few close friends I made in the navy. Jim Loughridge, from near Buffalo, was a dapper young man, a lot more culturally sophisticated than I was, and I learned a great deal from him about how to live well in even unpromising circumstances. He shared my growing interest in books, and we sat in bars talking about books like Arthur Koestler's *Darkness at Noon* and James Joyce's *Ulysses*. We went into San Francisco to the opera, or at least the operetta, *Student Prince*; we searched out good restaurants, and on New Year's Eve, for the first time in my life, I drank champagne—wartime champagne, but festive nonetheless. Ruth came down from Salem—this time I paid—but again it was an awkward meeting, lying stiffly in bed side by side and not talking. She laughed at my newfound sophistication, which annoyed me and made me think she was content to go on being a country girl while I had larger aspirations. After a short stay she went back to Oregon, depressed.

Loughridge came down with some mysterious disease and was sent off to a hospital. He had been flying with the commanding officer, Lieutenant Campbell, and I now took over his turret for a few flights. Campbell was as dour as his name, and we didn't get along very well, so we soon parted. But at least the personnel officer stopped asking me about the missing day.

Cigarettes were now in short supply everywhere, and Ceil Boone, who smoked like a chimney, as they used to say, was suffering from nicotine privation. She asked me to send cigarettes, any cigarettes I could find, and I did. We were rationed at the ship's store, and since I smoked heavily myself, I had used up what I could buy that way. There were, however, numerous cigarette machines about the base, and armed with lots of change I went around getting packages of some of the strangest brand names I ever saw and mailing off care packages to Mrs. Boone. Knowing what we know now about smoking, it seems almost criminal that the services supported smoking the way they did with cheap cigarettes. But no one knew at the time the connection with various diseases, and smoking was one of the few pleasures that could be indulged while caught in the endless waiting that war requires. So we all puffed away, and paid the price, as I did with a heart attack, many years later.

I began flying again with Bob Dyer, one of the new ensigns who made up most of the squadron, who was known as "Irish," from Illinois, and with his radioman, Oscar Mullins, a Georgia boy with a dish face, inevitably called "Moon" after the old comic-strip character Moon Mullins. In early February orders came to move the planes and the crews to the Alameda naval air station, adjacent to where the Bay Bridge comes into Oakland. For a few days we were in barracks there, given liberty in San Francisco every night. We longed to stay at the Mark Hopkins Hotel, the setting of a wildly popular novel, *Shore Leave*, by Frederic Wakeman, telling the story of a group of pilots returning from the Pacific after a long cruise who took rooms in the Mark, got fabulously drunk, exchanged brilliant wit, and reeled from one beautiful girl to another. The actuality, however, was going down to the USO and drinking free coffee, hoping to get a chance to dance with one of the few weary girls who were grimly doing their part in the war effort by being friendly with the servicemen. They were nice girls, I thought, but inevitably they ended up having to wrestle with one of the most unwashed of the soldiers and sailors, crying out for help only when they seemed to be in actual danger, as they often were. When the shore patrol hauled off the culprits, usually after banging them on the head with a club for a bit, the girls would look stricken, feeling somehow responsible for the lust they had aroused, however innocently. I had always assumed, like most men, that men had it a lot harder in this life than women, but I learned in that USO how hard it is for young women, and some not so young, to deal with the sex they cannot escape.

Sailors everywhere and at all times know that no matter how hard sea duty, there is always relief in going aboard ship and leaving land behind. So it was again on February 8, 1945, when we picked up our gear and went aboard the USS *Suwanee* (CVE-27), lying at the Alameda dock. Converted from a tanker, she was an awkward, slow, unattractive old waddler with very cramped crew's quarters. But she had been on more invasions than any other navy ship, from North Africa to the Philippines, where her flight deck had been blown off the day the Japanese fleet broke into Leyte Gulf to take the support ships under fire. Go to the carrier museum on board the *Yorktown* in Charleston Harbor and you will find that two escort carriers, the *Suwanee* and the *Liscombe Bay*, suffered more casualties than any other aircraft carrier in the war.

The planes were hoisted aboard, and we were ready to sail, but two of the old hands from Torpedo 40 were still missing as the gangways began to come up. Then a broken-down car came roaring down to the dock, pulling right up to the edge at high speed and screeching to a stop. Both sailors jumped out, running for the last gangway, and then one turned back, opened the driver's door, released the brake, and gave the car a push off the end of the dock into San Francisco Bay. The crew stood on the deck cheering wildly as Cletis Powell leaped across several feet of water to land in the well deck and ask the officer-of-the-deck for permission to come aboard. It was a gallant gesture, but Powell should have missed the ship.

Leaving San Francisco Bay, sailing under the reddish Golden Gate Bridge, picking up the long Pacific swells, and looking back on the white cities on the hills was one of the great experiences of the Pacific war. It was powerful not only in retrospect, as so many events are after the future is known, but at the moment it took place. We were at quarters in undress blue uniforms, lining the flight deck as we went under the bridge, and the ship's horn sounded a salute to the country left behind and got in return blasts from all the other ships in the harbor. It was valedictory, a moving, powerful sensory image of a country united in war and determined to win it. Every man must have wondered whether he would ever come back again— I know I did—and wondered too how many of those standing with him would return. This was my third combat tour, and I knew what would happen. My eyes moved from one face to another of men who are as alive to me now as they were then, but whose bones are washing around the bottom of the sea, tangled in the wreckage of their planes between Okinawa and Taiwan, near islands with such romantic names as Ishigaki, Miyako, and Kerama-retto.

CHAPTER ELEVEN

War's End

BY FEBRUARY 16 we were at Pearl Harbor. We crossed the International Date Line on February 28 and the equator on March 2. The day before I got a ducking when we crashed on a catapult launch. The catapult was a long rail running about fifty feet to the forward edge of the flight deck, with a trolley that ran inside the rail. A plane would be positioned at the rear of the catapult rail, and the trolley was attached to its wheels by two cables leading up to hooks on the inside wheel struts. At the rear the plane would be anchored by a hook attached to the deck by means of a tension ring just strong enough to hold the plane in place when it was turned up to full power. As the plane maneuvered into position, the cables were attached to the struts, and the anchor was hooked up. Then the plane turned up to full power, and after straining at the leash for several seconds, the catapult trolley was fired forward by an explosive charge. The combined power of the engine and the trolley broke the retaining ring at the tail, and the plane jumped forward, down the deck, to be airborne at the edge.

Usually it all went like clockwork, but on March 1, as we sat on the catapult braced for takeoff, when the engine came to full power a defective retaining ring snapped. We began to lumber forward without enough speed to get airborne and toppled over the port side of the ship, down through the catwalk, shearing off metal as we went. Into the water we plunged, went under, and then bobbed up, nose down with the heavy engine. The ship went tearing by high above us. All I saw was Cletis Powell leaning out a porthole in the parachute loft where I had just lost seventy-five dollars to him at blackjack, on credit, yelling, "Al, you don't have to pay. Get out, get out, for God's sake."

No one in the plane was hurt, only disoriented. I made my way out the side of the turret onto the port wing; Mullins came out his tunnel door and got up onto the starboard wing. From opposite sides we opened the life raft stowage compartment, located just forward of the turret, and began pulling. Mullins was smaller and less determined than I, and I nearly pulled him through the stowage tunnel before he let go. I pulled the inflation toggle and the raft filled up satisfactorily, with a big hiss. We stepped in and paddled off with the aluminum oar provided. From the deck of the carrier it had seemed like a light sea, but in the yellow rubber raft we rose and fell ten or fifteen feet. We bobbed over to the plane guard, the destroyer that followed the carrier during landings and takeoffs for just such events, and pulled alongside. It loomed above us, letting lines down from the high bow, leaping up and slamming down in the swell. We swept into the side, the raft overturned and drifted away, and each of us grabbed a line to climb up to the deck. I banged against the side of the ship and was dazed and on the verge of drowning, with a lot of water inside me, until I let loose and drifted back amidships where the deck was much lower and more stable. I came over the side and was soon in a bunk with one of the small bottles of medical whiskey saved for such occasions. Next day the destroyer came alongside the carrier, fired a line over, and delivered us back aboard in a bosun's chair. We were flying again by that afternoon.

The ship had begun to heat up in the living quarters, which, on the *Suwanee*, were grim unpainted crammed cubicles. Bunks were in racks as high as five or six, the lights were always on, lockers were small, the heads were far away, so that going for a shower—always salt water—or to relieve yourself was a long walk, half-naked, through several eating and living compartments. It sounds like nothing now, but it built up pressure day after day, which increased as the temperature went up and we began suffering from heat rashes and raw places where a belt or a trouser leg chafed. It got worse when, on March 4, we anchored in Tulagi Harbor, just across Iron Bottom Bay from Guadalcanal, and there was no longer fresh air coming down the vents to cool the lower decks. The heat rose and the bugs began to make their way from land to feed on what the sea had brought them. We slept in our skivvies—the navy knew no pajamas—and would rise in the morning glad to get out of a "sack" that was damp with perspiration.

After a day or two we went ashore to Henderson Field on Guadalcanal, where a year and a half earlier the Japanese drive south was finally stopped. There had been a tremendous buildup of American forces on Guadalcanal since that time, but now the fighting had shifted away from the southwest Pacific and the island was nearly deserted. We could walk about looking at the muddy jungle swamps and sluggish rivers where so many desperate battles had taken place a short time ago. Elsewhere the Philippines had been retaken; Iwo Jima had recently been stormed by the marines; and the air force, with its B-29s, and the big navy carriers were at work on the mainland of Japan. As the war moved on, the troops had simply moved out of Guadalcanal, leaving, in that careless way of rich Americans, their buildings and a lot of machinery behind them. A library filled several Quonset huts, the books damp and smelling of mold in the rainy climate, and there was only one rule: "If you check a book out, you can't return it." The U.S. Navy Seabees —construction battalions—had left a big ice-making machine running for as long as the fuel in the tank for the engine driving the compressor held out. Beer was plentiful, huge stacks of cardboard cartons of it, with a single guard walking around. We were in a sailors' paradise for a few days—endless beer cooled to low temperatures in big Lister bags filled with ice.

The pilots had gone off on their own parties, and no one bothered us very much, so we lay naked, except for our white hats, in our bunks in one of the numerous empty Quonset huts on the edge of the airfield and drank beer and more beer and still more beer. Something odd began to happen as we drank more and more. It began with just smashing a few bottles on the plywood floor of the Quonset hut as we emptied them. Then, as the floor began to be covered with broken glass, the rule was that anyone wanting to go to the head or get another bottle of beer had to walk barefoot through the ever deepening layer of glass. At first it was possible to work your way around the biggest and sharpest shards of brown glass, but as more and more glass accumulated, the trip became more and more difficult and painful. But this problem was countered by rising drunkenness and its attendant indifference to reality, urged on by the need to piss more often and the desire to drink even more beer.

As each sailor rose from his bunk to try to make the door, cheers and groans accompanied him on his trip. If he winced or turned back he was hooted, if he cut himself and jumped in pain he was laughed at, if he strode bravely through the mess into the dark where the beer was—outside the door and the range of the single bulb burning in the center of the hut— he was cheered and awarded imaginary commendations. Basic anthropology: warriors' drinking and endurance rituals in the longhouse before battle.

In time the game wore itself out as people passed out or simply dropped off to sleep. But it started up again the next day, and anyone visiting the Quonset hut where the aircrew of VT-40 was quartered would have thought he had wandered into some madhouse filled with naked men with badly cut feet and blood all over a litter of broken glass. Then we were all back at sea, with painfully sore feet for a time. We left Tulagi, without nostalgia, on March 14, going north to that remarkable fleet anchorage, Ulithi Atoll, providing antisubmarine patrol for a convoy carrying a Marine Division for the landings on Okinawa on April 1. On the way north a destroyer pulled alongside with mail and transferred my friend Jimmy Loughridge, completely cured of whatever crud had felled him at Livermore, back aboard. Better for him if the crud had kept him in the hospital a bit longer, but no one knows beforehand the turns of fate.

Ulithi is a huge atoll out in the Pacific Ocean, halfway between the Philippines and Guam. The islands that made up the atoll are narrow coral-and-sand strips, only a few yards wide in places, running in a huge circle around an old sunken volcano, with deep blue water in the center. Here the navy had constructed a base for the final attack on Japan, and as we came into the atoll on our little gray escort carrier, the by-now almost unbelievable striking force of the Pacific Fleet was stretched out in front of us. Rows of new battleships, heavy and light cruisers, swarms of destroyers, and the new carrier battle force. The remaining two old carriers were there—the *Enterprise* and the *Saratoga*—and all the old names were there on new ships—*Lexington, Hornet, Yorktown, Wasp*—as well as new old ones like *Essex, Randolph, Franklin, Intrepid,* and on and on. It was the most powerful navy ever assembled and a heart-stirring sight to someone who had seen the burned-out battleship row at Pearl Harbor and had watched the *Enterprise*, the last operating carrier in the fleet, disappear over the horizon at Santa Cruz as the *Hornet* was sinking: "Proceed without *Hornet*."

Among a forest of repair facilities, an airfield, docks (including a huge floating drydock capable of taking any capital ship in the fleet), hospitals, storehouses, and so on, the navy's wisdom had decreed a recreation area for the sailors of the Pacific Fleet. Mog Mog—such was its memorable name—was a tiny islet with a small sand hill at one end and a mangrove swamp at the other. As those fortunate enough to get four hours of liberty, myself among them, came ashore onto the dock, a trail led inland to a fork with a sign that read, "OFFICERS LEFT. ENLISTED PERSONNEL RIGHT." The officers filed off up the sand hill to a club where beer and whiskey were available in small amounts. It was crude but pleasant, I heard from Irish Dyer, with even a beach and swimming.

To the right was a gate in a barbed-wire fence where the shore patrol checked your liberty card and nodded at a chief standing by a huge pile of cases of beer, who then handed you two cans of warm brew. Shiny aluminum cans in hand, you went up over a little rise and saw the swamp, where by now all the foliage had been stripped and most of the trees and bushes pulled down and stamped into a greasy mash of mud covered with sailors in blue dungarees talking and drinking their two cans of beer. Here and there a pipe had been driven into the soaked ground and a funnel inserted into the end to make a crude urinal. These were in constant use. Fights broke out now and again between crews of different ships, and there were even a few drunks who had managed to buy nondrinkers' rations. Mostly, however, even hardened sailors, wild for liberty and drink, blanched at the sight of Mog Mog, and there was —an unheard of thing—a long line of men back at the landings waiting to return to their ships. But having accepted liberty, like mankind getting freedom from God, they could not return it until the appointed hour, when their launch arrived to carry them away from this stygian lake.

Within a week we were at sea again, flying antisubmarine patrols for transports on the way to Okinawa. On March 31 the other carriers of this type, also named after small rural rivers in America—Sangamon, Santee, and Chenango—joined up with the *Suwanee* to form a division to provide close support to the soldiers and marines landing on Okinawa. On Easter Sunday, April 1, the invasion began, and we started flying two and three short strikes a day from about fifty miles offshore to the island, where we circled until the control on the ground at the front called us in to hit a particular target.

The landings were unopposed, the Japanese choosing not to sacrifice troops on the beaches. But the island was honeycombed with elaborate underground bunkers and stone tombs dug into the hills, where the Japanese had holed up and stored supplies. Most often our mission was to fly low up a small valley, come as close as possible to the mouth of a tomb, and then either sling a five-hundred-pound bomb into it or hit it with one or more of the eight five-inch rockets we carried under our wings. Sounds straightforward, but from the air it was nearly impossible, despite smoke signals on the ground, to make out the exact cave we were supposed to go after. And once it was located it was difficult to roar up a steep valley at 200 miles an hour, going close enough to hit the cave but leaving time to pull up and go over the ridge behind. We all worked hard at it and improved with time, but it was always a close thing and sometimes rockets were fired into our own lines when they were too close to the tombs' entrances.

A high cost began to be exacted at once, in the air as well as on the ground. The air group commander, Lieutenant Commander Sampson, was incredibly keen, pressing his attacks hard in his Hellcat to show others the way. He pressed so hard that he was dead in the first week. At the time he seemed to me to be old and grave, but looking back at photos, I see now that he was young, only in his late twenties I would guess, and I am reminded how much the war was the business of young men.

We stayed only a few days at Okinawa until we were sent south on April 8 to take over from a British fleet that had been keeping airfields on the Sakishima Islands, just northeast of Taiwan, unusable. The Japanese were flying whatever planes they had in China to dirt landing fields on two islands in this group—Ishigaki and Miyako—and then loading them with explosives and sending them north as suicide planes, kamikazes, against the invasion fleet and the big carriers. Our job was to continue keeping the fields so full of holes that landings and takeoffs were impossible, work which would go on for months, day after day.

April 13: Roosevelt died. The news was announced over the loudspeaker and brought everyone up short. It is hard to convey the way Roosevelt dominated our world, how he was the only leader we really remembered. He had presided over the terrible later years of the Depression when most of us aboard were growing up, and we remembered him for his "fireside chats" and his reassuring messages about the economy, even as things got worse and worse. He had taken us into the war, wanted it really, but most of us had also considered war against both Japan and Germany inevitable. It was simply in the cards in the late thirties. I had voted, by absentee ballot, for the first time the year before, and just to be different had cast my ballot for Wendell Wilkie rather than Roosevelt, but I had no real reasons for doing so, and now, like everyone else, I was troubled about who would make the decisions. About Truman we knew nothing, but we had no confidence in him for the days ahead, which looked depressingly bleak. We all assumed that there would be landings in Japan by the end of the year, and we feared them as nothing else in the war. After the war I heard a historian say that he had never met a veteran scheduled for the invasion who did not think there was a bullet in Japan that would end directly between his eyes. And he was right.

In the meantime the war went on. The landing signal officer brought a seagull on board, noting that he was "smooth on the controls." We were hurled roughly off the catapults, twice a day, early morning and early afternoon, and then once the next day, at midmorning. It became routine, but the early flights had a particular problem. Reveille was at four, breakfast was almost always beans, and we were launched before five in the dark. There was no time to shit, and as the altitude increased, the gas of the beans expanded and created terrible cramps. I refused to endure it, a veteran grown crusty in my ways at twenty-one, and drove Mullins up into the turret while I squatted on the floor of the tunnel and relieved myself on a piece of red rayon torn from a gunnery target sleeve. The plane had relief tubes that made it possible to urinate in flight, but

the only way to be rid of my load was to tie a knot in the red
rag, open one of the ventilators at the rear of the tunnel, fling
it out, and idly watch out of one of the side ports as this bright
"blivvie" made its way down through the second division flying below and to the rear. There was some protest about red
rags plummeting down through the formation every other day,
but no one ever got hit, and our crew stayed silent.

We lived in a narrow place and a removed time in which
we bombed them and they shot at us. In which we put holes
in their runways and they, with fiendish speed, filled them
up again, and we came back and put more holes in the runways. We made our way back to the ships in a golden-green
haze, with rainstorms and bright shafts of sunlight in a dozen
different places around the horizon. The scene had a magical quality, intensified by the big lift that came from having
survived another run. We feared the islands we bombed, and
with good reason. The intelligence officer told us to avoid
the swamps if we were shot down, so filled were they with
leeches that you could die from loss of blood. We made
our way down to the islands, dived on the rough airfields
in the valleys below, dropped our bombs—usually a string
of hundred-pounders—and fired our rockets. The antiaircraft
fire was intense, and since our job was to bomb the runways
we never attacked the guns directly. The Japanese learned in
time that we never shot at them, so firing at us became an
early form of Nintendo. At the bottom of our runs, when we
were below the ridge lines, the guns were actually firing down
at us, and I could fire furiously back at them.

Inevitably, there were casualties: April 25, Collura, Powell,
to whom I still owed my blackjack losses, and Stewart were
hit in a dive and went in and exploded; April 27, Campbell,
the commanding officer, Jimmy Loughridge, my close friend,
and Zahn were hit and disintegrated in the air. Death was un-
remarkable, but still it was difficult to accept that someone you
knew well and had played cards with in a normal way only a
few hours earlier was now gone forever, not a part of the same
world, or any world for that matter, any longer. I wrote a childish, sentimental letter to Jimmy's widowed mother in James-
town, New York, trying to say that he had lived and died well,
but making a terrible mess of it. Sitting at a table in the mess

compartment I heard that sharp, flat noise that could only be a bomb. I rushed up the ladders to the flight deck, and there was one of our planes, blackened and smoldering, with three bodies alongside.

Our bomb racks were tricky, and sometimes they would not release all the bombs but delay on one or two until you pulled out of the dive and the bomb-bay doors closed. Then the increased gravity would pull an unreleased bomb out of the rack onto the doors. When this happened the arming wire would pull out of the bomb fuse, and its propeller would turn freely in the bomb-bay draft until the bomb was armed. We knew about the problem, and radiomen were under strict orders after a run to look through the glass inset between the tunnel and the bomb bay to make sure that all the bombs were out of there. If they were not, the bomb bay was to be instantly opened with an emergency release in the tunnel and any remaining bombs shaken out by radical maneuvers. But the bomb bay was dark and difficult to see into when closed, and on this day the radioman had missed an armed hundred-pounder lying on the doors because a hydraulic line had been hit by antiaircraft fire and the fluid had obscured the glass window to the bomb bay. When the plane landed, caught the arresting wire, and came to an abrupt stop, the bomb slid forward until it hit the batteries just beneath the pilot, Slingerland, blowing him to kingdom come, and filling the gunner, Joyce, with so many small holes that the serum they poured into him ran right out again. He died that night. The radioman, Dick Morrow, was in a bad way but lived to become a fashionable dance band leader in the Detroit area.

Death was on my mind, for obvious reasons, those days flying to and from Ishigaki staring at "Hard Homo" in yellow letters on a dark green background of armor plate. I had read recently in the overseas edition of *Time*, a great favorite in the fleet, that there were "no atheists in foxholes," but it hadn't worked that way for me. I concluded that war's cruelty and randomness, its indifference to human life, and the speed and ease with which it erases existence are not aberrations but speeded-up versions of how it always is. The evidence is there, I went on to reason, to anyone who will look and see the plain facts his senses, including common sense, offer him—and what else is there to trust, fallible though they may be?—that men and women, like everything else in the world, are, in the poet's words, begotten, born, and die. A young man's raw desire to live made me avoid worrying about the bleakness of total extinction, but we all knew it; it was in our faces, it was the basis of our shared attitude toward one another and life.

There was a Jesuit chaplain aboard who was willing to argue about such questions, and I took advantage of his youthful good nature to play the village atheist. With a swaggering materialism I denounced Catholicism and all religion to the poor red-faced young Irish priest, who could not imagine that a young man brought up in the arms of holy mother the church, once an altar boy, could conceive of a world without a God or any purpose in life other than what we could give it. After a time I ceased tormenting the priest and concentrated on playing bridge, keeping a game going with the same players for weeks at a time, interrupting our playing on the coolness of the well deck only when someone had to fly, and picking up the hands as we had left them when the players returned. A Boston Irishman named Tom McCue, a former worker in a shipyard, was my partner, and we each developed a good sense of how the other bid and played. The waves splashed near us as we played, sitting on top of a big coil of manila rope, but anxious to perfect our skill we played with all the precise rules and formality of some fashionable bridge club in a tournament.

Although we kept the runways on Miyako and Ishigaki torn up, some Japanese planes got through to crash into the fleet. We were all terrorized by the kamikazes, for it is difficult to avoid someone trying to fly into you. The Japanese had always had a feel for the suicidal charge, and when the *Hornet* sank in 1942, two planes had crashed into her and exploded, one only a short distance from where I was sitting. But at the end of the war the "Divine Winds" had become the only effective Japanese weapon, and day after day the young pilots drank their ritual sake, bound up their heads with a silk scarf, and took their samurai swords into the planes with them to fly out and crash into the Yankee ships. Being small carriers, and stationed to the south of the main fleet off Okinawa, we were not attacked in the open sea, but every two weeks or so we had to provision with beans and bombs, literally about all we took aboard, at a little island, Kerama-retto, a supply base near Okinawa. The place had a bad feel. The entrance to what was the flooded center of an old volcano was a long, narrow passage in which there was no room to maneuver. The passage was deep but the sides so narrow that you could nearly reach out and touch the brown rock as the ship slid slowly through. In this situation you were a sitting duck for any kamikaze that came along, and on May 1 one of them took the entire flight deck off our sister ship, the USS *Sangamon*, as she was leaving Kerama-retto. We went there as infrequently as possible and were able to fight off attacks, never getting hit.

May 7: Germany surrendered, and the hope of an end to the war became more real. But there was still the fear of the landings on the Japanese homeland. I can barely remember now what it was like to be always a bit afraid, never to escape that slight sinking feeling in the gut, to awake wet with sweat at night in that unbelievably crowded compartment and hear men here and there crying out in nightmares.

Eventually it came to an end. The battle was won at Okinawa, and land-based planes began to take over the bombing of Ishigaki and Miyako. On June 17 we left for the Philippines and the island of Leyte after eighty-five days at sea, one of the longest cruises of the war, and recognized, with other exploits, by a Presidential Unit Citation for the *Suwanee*, and Distinguished Flying Crosses and Air Medals for the flyers. The Philippines had been retaken but there was little to do in Leyte except walk around in the mud of the marketplace and try to decide whether the cane whiskey the Filipinos sold under names like Freddie Walker, Red and Black, and Three Stooges would blind you as surely as was rumored. We decided it would and returned to the ship muddy but sober.

CHAPTER TWELVE

Peace

B Y JUNE 26, 1945, we were off to Balikpapan to cover the
Australian landings on Borneo. Borneo had been a source
of Japanese oil since the first days of the war, and at one time,
so pure was the product, they were burning it in naval boilers
without refining it. That was dangerous, though, and at the
Battle of the Philippine Sea one of their new carriers, hit by a
submarine torpedo, blew up instantly, so volatile was the unrefined Borneo oil. It still was exciting, passing Celebes and
going down through the Makassar Strait, taking us back to
those first days of the war when the Australian, Dutch, and
American fleets had been overwhelmed off Indonesia. Now
there were no Japanese to be found anywhere, not a plane in
the air to defend the refineries, and we flew back and forth
without dropping our bombs, since the Australians were going
ashore without opposition. It was my last combat mission, if it
can be called that, but I did not know it at the time.

July 7, back to Leyte, where we anchored and took the planes
ashore for several weeks on one of those remarkable coral landing strips the Seabees built across the Pacific. The strips were a
beautiful hard white, made of living coral dredged up from the
nearby bay and kept alive by being watered daily with seawater
from a sprinkler truck. As long as it was watered it continued to
live, and every day the steamrollers crushed it smooth and hard
again. A dazzling light bounced up from that white surface and
gave terrible sunburns to the unwary.

One day we flew to Manila, a hundred miles or so to the
north, to pick up mail. The flight led across the jungles of Samar where, flying a few hundred feet off the ground, we saw
back in the forests high waterfalls and huge flowers, ten or fifteen feet across, and small villages at the end of long dirt trails.
Dyer had business, so Mullins and I hitched a ride into Manila,
which was all ruins. One concrete building alone stood by the
river, painted dark green and offering Red Cross doughnuts,

but everywhere else was deep in mud and sour with the smell of broken timber and crumbled mortar.

The war was clearly winding down, and for the moment the whole vast army and navy that had come to the western Pacific waited for reinforcement from Europe and gathered strength for the fall landings on the southernmost Japanese island, Kyushu. August 3, we went from Leyte to Okinawa, arriving on the 6th and anchoring in the middle of the great fleet assembled there. We flew off the field at Naha from time to time, picking up mail, but mostly we sat at anchor, played bridge, and listened to rumors: that the war was about to end; that Japan would surrender; that the B-29 Superfortresses based on the Marianas were burning entire islands flat; that there was some new secret weapon!

Sometimes we would be organized into baseball teams and sent to a small nearby island to play softball against teams from other ships. The worst players were assigned to the weed-covered outfield, where poisonous snakes sometimes lay concealed, which made for the most cautious outfielders in the world. Any fly ball to the outfield was good for at least a hit, and usually a home run. One day a fielder stumbled over an unexploded five-inch shell and, shouting for us to look, held it in the air and then dropped it into a well, where it exploded with a loud bang. When the dust cleared, the outfielder was standing there looking dazed, blood pouring out of his nose and ears from the concussion.

Returning from our baseball game, we came alongside the ship and began to send sailors up the gangway. At that moment another landing craft came up carrying officers, including the executive officer of the *Suwanee*—a small, dark, mean man—who stood up in the bow, dead drunk, shouting in a loud voice to the officer-of-the-deck, "Get those fucking enlisted men out of there and get us aboard." Protocol was that officers always take precedence in landing, and our boat shoved off immediately, circling while the officers staggered up the gangway after their afternoon of drinking in the officers' club. The gap between enlisted men and officers in the American navy during World War II was medieval. Enlisted men accepted the division as a necessary part of military life, but it never occurred to us that it in any way diminished our status as freeborn citizens who, because of a run of bad luck and some unfortunate circumstances like the Depression, just happened to be down for a brief time. "When we get rich" were still words deep in everybody's psyche. But the exec's words, "those fucking enlisted men," spoke of deep and permanent divisions. He obviously really disliked us, and his words made shockingly clear that he, and maybe the other officers he represented, had no sense that we had shared great dangers and won great victories together. Apparently the exec was not very popular elsewhere, for the captain confined him to quarters for a failure of discipline not long after.

"August 13—they tell us that the war has ended—*Pennsylvania* was torpedoed near us tonight." So reads a note near the end of my flight log. The word crept around the ship during the late afternoon and evening, half-believed, half-not. We had heard several days before that two bombs of a new type had been dropped on Japan, causing tremendous damage. But we agreed after much discussion that bombs were only bombs, no matter how much devastation they caused, and that the Japanese were a tough people, the toughest we had ever seen. It was concluded unlikely that they would surrender, and so the landings were still ahead. Surrender rumors persisted, however, and eventually the captain came on the loudspeaker to tell us that there was a truce, and that the end of the war was likely. There was nothing to do to celebrate, and I felt nothing, absolutely nothing—no exhilaration, no triumph, no anticipation of going home, not even the simple pleasure of having survived. At best there was some symmetry. Having begun the war at Pearl Harbor nearly four years earlier, the wheel had now come full circle, and I was ending it on the last battlefield.

By now it was dark, and around us on ships where the discipline must have been light men began firing guns in the air, creating a sky full of tracers and explosives. It seemed irritating rather than celebratory, an unseemly response somehow to so long and difficult a struggle, an anticlimax in which the end did not live up either to expectations or to what had gone before.

We made our way up the Japanese coast, stopping at one small port after another, where, to our surprise, the people

were quite friendly and seemed to bear us no grudge whatso-
ever. We felt the same way about them. September 15, the last
entry in my flight log, records a flight of three and a half hours
picking up mail from Okinawa and taking it to the ship. I knew
it was most likely my last flight and patted the deck fondly
when we landed.

September 17, anchored in Nagasaki, where the second
atomic bomb had exploded. A long deep inlet to the town that
straggled up the valley and the nearby hill. Aircraft carriers have
a lot of space on the hangar deck when all the planes are parked
on the flight deck, and we were there to provide transport for
thousands of Allied prisoners who were working in the mines
at the head of the valley. Many of them had been there since
the fall of the Dutch empire and the surrender of Singapore.
In the end they did not come aboard but went to hospital
ships that followed us into the harbor. In the stone custom-
house I picked up some Japanese forms and looked out the
door at the devastation of the houses and the factories, among
which people—in the Asian way wearing surgical masks, like
magical protectors from harm—were wandering aimlessly up
and down among the rubble, looking for what had once been
there. Back on the deck of the ship we stood and watched the
people going back and forth all day long. The site was fascinating but not particularly terrible to see. It looked like any other
bombed-out town, and there was no way of comprehending
that one bomb had done it all in an instant. We knew nothing
of U-235, nor of the technology involved, and we cared almost
nothing for the morality of using the bomb, the question that
has so occupied generations since. The issue may have been
raised but only to be disposed of quickly. They had attacked
us, we had finished them with whatever means was at hand.
That is what war is.

Each of us felt, further, that those two bombs had saved
our lives—not life in general, but our own felt, breathing life.
No one who was not there will ever understand how fatalisti-
cally we viewed the invasion of Japan. It had to be done, and
would be, but each of us felt that survival was unlikely. Our
ship was scheduled to provide close inshore support for the
troops landing on the beaches. The Japanese would kamikaze
us with every plane, small and large, that they had left. The

fighting ashore would be ferocious, and if shot down, which was likely on frequent close-support missions, we would have little chance of escape. I had, I felt, lived through a lot, miraculously without a scratch, but my good luck could not continue on into still another year of war. I was now twenty-two, and years had been spent in a great war, mostly at sea in combat conditions. I was not, I realized, ever going to get a chance to live out my late teens and early twenties in the normal way. I wasn't sentimental about it. After all, my whole generation had spent those years in the service, and it was the great adventure of our time; but I did want what was left of life. The bomb gave it to me, and while others do feel otherwise, I remain grateful and unashamed. In after years, when I was on the faculty of liberal universities where it was an unquestioned article of faith that dropping the bombs was a crime against humanity and another instance of American racism, I had to bite my tongue to keep silent, for to have said how grateful I was to the bomb would have marked me as a fascist—the kind I had spent five years fighting!

A few days later we worked our way up the eastern coast of Honshu to the great bay of Tokyo, Mount Fuji visible in the background, and anchored at the Japanese naval base of Yokosuka. There was grim satisfaction in being there, for all around us were the rusty hulls and twisted upper decks of battleships and cruisers that had been sunk at their moorings by naval attacks from our carriers at the end of the war. Ashore, everything as far as the eye could see had been leveled by the fire raids of the B-29 Superfortresses. Here and there a single cement or steel-framed building still stood, only making the rest of the devastation seem more vast and empty. Going ashore one gray day in November, I walked around the abandoned machine shops of the naval base. There were small ships, half-finished, on the way: a midget submarine here, a subchaser there. Inside the sheds the lathes and mechanical hammers stretched out into the gloom. Like most Americans, I had never understood how the Japanese had had the daring to attack a nation so much larger and more powerful than Nippon, and here in this grim place, with ruin all around, the folly of their original attack was manifest.

Despite my age, my promotion to chief petty officer was due, and I decided, since I would be leaving the service shortly, to push for it before discharge. The personnel officer grumbled about the paperwork; he may still have been thinking of that lost day reporting to Livermore. I think too that he thought I looked much too young for the senior enlisted rating in the navy, but regulations required that my case at least be considered, and in due time I was made aviation chief ordnanceman, acting appointment, temporary—about as many qualifications as you can get—which meant that I could hold on to the rating after a year only by signing up for another four years. With flight pay I now earned nearly two hundred dollars a month, which seemed to me like riches, enough to tempt me for a brief time to sign on again and do my twenty before retiring on a pension. I bought some gray trousers and gray shirts and an overseas cap with a chief's insignia in the ship's store of a big nearby tender, and I moved up to the chiefs' quarters. Lots of room, real mattresses, special chow, and a mess room in which to sit and read, listen to the radio, or talk.

There wasn't much talk since most of the old chiefs had already found transport on some ship going home. Release from service was by an elaborate point system built on the number of years of service, size of family, time overseas, decorations, and so on. I had a very high number—more than anyone else in the squadron—but the squadron commander refused to release me on the grounds that I had skills that were still needed. This was foolish, for we didn't even have planes anymore, but he was trying to keep some kind of an organization together, and I was part of his scheme, just as I had been long ago on the beach in New Caledonia. I complained, bitterly, daily, and was finally told that I could go in late November, but on a group of old battleships that were about to depart on an around-the-world voyage—Hong Kong, Singapore, Bombay, Suez, Gibraltar, and Norfolk. I should have leaped at the chance to be a passenger on such a splendid cruise, but I could only think of getting home, and the three months of the trip seemed much too long. So I stayed, waiting in the nearly empty chiefs' quarters for a more direct ship home. A typhoon blew through the bay, and I sat alone in a chair and slid back and forth across the steel deck of the mess room as the ship rolled thirty or more degrees. Not another soul was about.

Then the *Suwanee* got orders to take passengers aboard (they would sleep on cots on the hangar deck) and proceed by way of Pearl Harbor to San Diego to release her crew and be decommissioned. I had decided against making a career of the navy, wanting to go instead to the University of Wyoming. But I had not saved a penny during my years in service. I had allotted my stepfather maybe a thousand dollars from my pay. He eventually returned it all, scrupulously paying interest, when he sold our old ranch, but I had no idea at the time that he would or could ever repay me. Like Jack, the proverbial sailor, I had gambled, drunk, and partied away all my pay—"Jack's a cinch, and every inch a sailor"—and now I was going home nearly broke, with no salable skill. Who needed an aerial gunner? But the government had, in its wisdom, passed the G.I. Bill so that I was miraculously saved from my own folly and guaranteed tuition money for any college I could get into, plus sixty-five dollars a month to live on. I heard later that the G.I. Bill was actually passed to prevent twelve million veterans from flooding the job market, but whatever the reason, it was a gift not to be looked in the mouth, and its unanticipated effects proved as far-reaching for the country as the Homestead Act or the transcontinental railroad.

Upon promotion every chief petty officer was given a clothing allowance of three hundred dollars to buy new uniforms. I had drawn my allowance and had saved the dough to get home and live on. Since I was leaving the navy, no need to buy chief's dress uniforms. But three hundred was nothing; I would spend it in a couple of months buying beer and hamburgers. Better to risk everything.

We had been running a poker game in the squadron compartment for some time, into which all my recent pay had gone. I hesitated, but why not? You had to show a hundred dollars to get a seat, so I sat down and put my hundred in front of me. The game was desultory and low level for a time, and some of the familiar players from the squadron began to drop out. Then, drawn by the game, some hard-eyed gamblers from among our passengers began to drift in—hairy, strangely clothed, armed with knives, hatchets, and other weapons.

The game began to pick up pace a bit. I won a few hands at first, nothing much, but enough to permit me to keep on playing on other people's money. Once the outsiders came in it became the kind of game where you had always to protect yourself. Any sign of weakness and they would use big rolls of bills to force you to throw down a winning hand by running the betting so high that you would drop out. Money was the weapon, and if you were nervous and defensive, worried about losing what you had, you were done for in a short time. So long as you were playing with winnings, however, you could, without being reckless, see bets, even outsized ones, when you knew you had a reasonable chance of winning.

Operating in this way, I began to win steadily. Nothing big in the way of hands. Losing often, but winning just a bit more than I lost. Full houses and fours of a kind were not seen very often in the game that night. A pair of sixes would win a big pot over a pair of fours. Sometimes even a king-high hand would win over a jack-high one. The thing was to stay when it felt right and get out early when it was obvious you had little chance. The evening went on into morning, and the people who wanted to sleep where we were playing, sitting on bunks around a few wooden ammunition boxes with a blanket for cover, went off to find empty bunks elsewhere. But for the most part the watchers were as intense as the players. It was that kind of game. Tense and hostile. There was one other player from the squadron left in the game besides me. A pale, red-headed southerner, he whined a lot about losing the money he had won from us over the past several months to buy a little home for his little family. That money had been stored up in a big roll of pale green U.S. postal money orders, bought at the ship's post office—our only way of stashing money—and now as he lost steadily, the money orders came out, one by one, a hundred dollars at a time, and were endorsed, each one a railing gone from his future porch, a window here, a door there. He couldn't quit until it was all gone, early in the morning, and I suppose I should have felt sorry for him, but all his sanctimony about his family and home built on my money, among others', made each extracted money order pure delight.

By daybreak I knew that I had won a good bit of money, but it is considered a sign of weakness to count your money during a game, showing either fear or greed, probably both. So I just kept stuffing the money in my pocket, changing little bills for big ones when the pot needed change, plugging along. Somewhere in the early morning I began to realize that the gods had once again been very good to me, and that rather than emerging from the navy broke, I was likely, with a little sense, to come out with enough money to make college more than possible.

Winners who leave games like this one abruptly are heartily disliked, and there can be trouble in a game this big. Preparation for departure has to be carefully built up, and so about ten in the morning I began to yawn ostentatiously, talk about work that had to be done that day, and then to say that I could only play six more hands, maybe seven, but no more than eight. This was thought fair since, with warning, the losers—and there were some big ones—were given at least a chance to win back their money. It was all ritual, gambler's manners, but it was important, and to make leaving easier I lost some money in the last hands, quite a lot, unnecessarily. I didn't throw in good hands, but I bet weak ones harder than I ought.

Then, about noon, having used up all my chips so that I didn't have to linger cashing in, I got up, said so long and got the hell out of there. In a deserted corner outside I stopped to count my money. Over three thousand dollars, far more than I had ever had before. Hard to realize now what a fortune it was then. I had played the fool often enough before to know that I had to do something, so I went up to the post office, paid for thirty $100 money orders made out to my stepfather, put them in several envelopes addressed to him, and dropped them down the mail slot. I still had several hundred dollars to live on until I got home, and as the ship got under way for Pearl Harbor and San Diego, I got into my new bunk in the chiefs' quarters, where the bunks were always down—in fact, they couldn't be raised—and slept the dreamless sleep of the fortunate. Good luck substitutes for other virtues!

Pearl Harbor was greatly changed. Liquor, not just beer, was for sale in the bars and by the bottle. The lights were on all over town, and liberty extended to midnight, although no one cared if you were later than that. The navy was clearly falling apart: everyone was going home, all the rules were suspended, and I only hoped the engineers would stay in the boiler room long enough to get the *Suwanee* back to the States. In one bar out near the Royal Hawaiian Hotel I got to drinking with some sailors from the destroyer *Hughes*, which had taken me off the *Hornet* at the Battle of Santa Cruz more than three years before. They all remembered it well, as did I, and I insisted on buying drinks for everyone, until we all went our separate ways, for discharge and for "Uncle Sugar"—the alphabet flags designating Uncle Sam and the United States. No one seemed to be staying in the navy.

CHAPTER THIRTEEN

Uncle Sugar

IN EARLY December we rounded Point Loma, and I reflected on what had happened since I had sailed past it for the first time on the way to Pearl Harbor in November 1941. Now the war was over, and I was a different person. But I wasted few glances backward. All the desires pent up by the long years in service longed for the future. I was eager to get out, meet people, go to college, and begin, so I thought in my innocence, to understand things.

Returning servicemen were gathered in barracks at the head of San Diego Bay and there separated into drafts going to the discharge points nearest to where they had enlisted. Bremerton Navy Yard, opposite Seattle across the always gray and foggy Puget Sound, was where the sailors who came from Wyoming —not too many—went, and in a few days a draft of about twenty from northwestern states was assembled to go by rail to Bremerton. As the senior in the group, I was put in charge. Not an enviable job. There were some real fuck-ups in this draft. I was given tickets and cash for meals for the entire group and told to dole out only so much to each sailor at each meal. Fighting with them about how much money they should get at a time was too much of a problem, and I had had enough of enforcing discipline on people much older and rougher than myself, so I gave each of them their full meal money at one time. The result was predictable. They drank it up at once, and after they sobered up began complaining about being hungry, which impressed me not at all.

In the effort to get millions of servicemen back to their homes, every piece of railway rolling stock in the country was hauled out of the yards and put in service. We were on some old and dusty cars with faded red-plush seats that had been sitting for years on some siding of the Southern Pacific Railroad and were now made up, as was, into a train. They were cold, with no diner or any other facilities. You had to jump off at the frequent stops, rush into a diner, take whatever was

available, and run back to the train, which would then sit
there for another few hours. But no one wanted to risk missing the train.

It wasn't too bad until the second day, when it became obvious that the car was infested with fleas—incredibly hungry,
beady, black fleas. I might have endured the bites except that
I had taken my shoes off to sleep and been bitten all over the
soles of my feet. The itching was unbearable, and as we jerked
our way, stop and go, through Sacramento, I spotted down a
dark street the neon sign of a drugstore, still open late at night.
I didn't want to chance missing the train, but the itch was maddening, so, barefoot, I set off running down the street, burst
into the drugstore, shouted "something for fleabites," paid for
the ointment, and raced back down the street just in time to
catch the last car of the train as it was pulling out.

It took three long nights and days to make our way up
through California and Oregon to northern Washington, but
we made it at last into Seattle and took the ferry across to
Bremerton and the separation center. A physical examination, clearance of all pay due us, a check for the three hundred dollars separation money, a golden lapel button known
as a ruptured duck to show that you had been honorably
discharged, and then the discharge itself. And so after four
years, eight months, and seventeen days I walked out, my
own man again, free to determine how I would spend my
time and my life.

Exactly what to do with this freedom, however, was not
obvious. So I took only a few tentative steps. After buying
and changing into a civilian jacket and some ill-fitting pants,
anxious to get out of uniform, I took the bus to Salem, Oregon, where Ruth was still teaching school. She and I had
corresponded without much feeling off and on over the last
year, and I felt that I ought to see her again; perhaps we ought
to get married. That, after all, was what everyone else did. She
was pretty and excited to see me, but I realized right away
that there was no feeling of love on my side. After a strained
night together I protested that I had to get back to Wyoming, picked up my bag, and walked a long walk with her
down to the bus station. I felt cruel but determined not to
tie myself down at the beginning of my freedom. She was

understandably bitter, and, muttering that someone as cold as I was would have no trouble making his way in the world, she turned her back on the bus and walked away. I went to Wyoming to cash my money orders, buy an old car, drive out to California to see the Boones, and with Dick, now discharged also, set off across country to New York, to see what the future held.

The law seemed the right kind of profession for me, but in my studies at Williams College, where I went after one term at Columbia, I found myself more and more attracted to the kind of literature—Shakespeare's *Hamlet* and Dostoyevsky's *Brothers Karamazov*—that portrayed life in all its fullness, intensity, and immediacy. Other subjects that commanded more of the interest, and the rewards, of the world—biology, economics, political science—seemed too abstract and distant from the experience of being human. Williams gave me a fellowship to go to England to study at Oxford for two years, and afterward I went to graduate school at Yale. By the time I had my doctorate in English literature I was thirty years old and had a wife and two (later four) children. Good fortune gave me a job and in time a chair at Yale, where for twenty years I taught and wrote books on the Renaissance and satire. My special study was the plays of William Shakespeare, which for me were "wisdom literature," a complete world in themselves, like the Bible, that made sense of the actual world. In the late sixties and early seventies I was the associate and then the acting provost at Yale and during those contentious times in the university administration found that all battles are not fought in declared wars.

In 1973 I moved from Yale to Princeton, a greater move than it might seem on the map, to become dean of the Graduate School. After a term at that strenuous job I returned to teaching, research, and writing until I retired from Princeton in 1988, at the age of sixty-five. Retirement gave me an opportunity to write the present book, and, until 2000 and full retirement, to direct a national graduate fellowship program in the humanities for the Andrew W. Mellon Foundation.

In our time veterans of later wars have complained that they were not welcomed when they came home. No parades, no recognition of what they had done by those for whom they had supposedly done it. I think this must be the feeling of all veterans from Caesar's legions to the present. The end of wars is anticlimactic; no one knows what to do or what to say. And once they are over almost everyone used to be willing to forget them. For myself, I never wasted a moment worrying that no one really seemed to know that I had been gone for five years, and the ones who did soon tired of talking about it, very soon. But who cares? What matters is to have survived, to have escaped from the many traps death and war set for us.

BIOGRAPHICAL NOTES

NOTE ON THE TEXTS

NOTES

INDEX

Biographical Notes

Samuel Lynn Hynes (August 29, 1924–October 10, 2019): Born in Chicago, Illinois, the son of Barbara Turner Hynes and Samuel Lynn Hynes, Sr., and the younger brother of Charles Hynes. Family moved to St. Paul, Minnesota, where mother died in 1930. Lived in Julesberg and Fort Collins, Colorado; Philadelphia, Pennsylvania; Fairhope, Alabama; and Moline, Illinois, as father sought work. Family settled in Minneapolis, where father married Nellie Kearny McBride, a widow with three children (William, Rose, and Eileen), in 1934. Graduated high school in 1941. Worked as bank messenger in Minneapolis and as mail carrier for Army in Seattle. Enrolled in University of Minnesota in fall 1942. Volunteered for Navy Flight Program and was called up in March 1943. Trained in Denton, Texas; Athens, Georgia; Memphis, Tennessee; and Pensacola, Florida, where he was commissioned as a second lieutenant in the Marine Corps. Married Elizabeth Ann Igleheart (1924–2008), sister of fellow pilot, in July 1944; they will have two daughters, Miranda (b. 1950) and Joanna (b. 1952). Continued pilot training in Deland, Florida, and at Miramar, Santa Barbara, and El Toro in southern California, where he learned to fly the TBM Avenger bomber. Joined Marine Torpedo Bombing Squadron 232 on Ulithi Atoll in the Caroline Islands in March 1945. Began flying Avengers on antisubmarine patrols and bombing missions. Moved in late April to airfield on Okinawa, where squadron provided air support for ground troops fighting on the island. Flew total of seventy-eight combat missions and was awarded the Distinguished Flying Cross. Used G.I. Bill to return to University of Minnesota, where he studied with Robert Penn Warren and graduated with B.A. in 1947. Earned M.A. in English from Columbia University in 1948 and began teaching at Swarthmore College the following year. As a reserve officer, recalled to active duty during the Korean War and served as instructor at Marine Air Station, Cherry Point, North Carolina, 1952–53. Ended military service with rank of major. Awarded Ph.D. from Columbia in 1956. Moved to Northwestern in 1968 before joining faculty at Princeton in 1976, where he taught until his retirement as Woodrow Wilson Professor of Literature in 1990. For as long as he was able to, followed tradition of celebrating birthday by performing loops and rolls in a biplane. Established reputation as demanding teacher and accomplished lecturer. Areas of expertise included British poetry, especially Thomas Hardy, and war literature. Published *The Patterns of Hardy's Poetry* (1961), *William Golding* (1964), *The Edwardian Turn of Mind* (1968), *Edwardian Occasions* (1972), *The Auden Generation: Literature and Politics in England in the 1930s* (1976), *Flights of Passage: Recollections of a World War II Aviator* (1988), *A War Imagined: The First World War and English Culture* (1990), *The Soldiers' Tale: Bearing Witness to Modern War* (1997), *The Growing Seasons: An American Boyhood Before the War* (2003), *The Unsubstantial Air: American Fliers in the First World War* (2014), and *On War and Writing* (2018). Contributed to *The New Yorker* and *The New York Times*; featured in World War II documentary *The War* (2007), produced by Ken Burns and Lynn Novick. Died of congestive heart failure in Princeton, New Jersey.

Alvin Bernard Kernan (June 13, 1923–May 17, 2018): Born in Manchester, Georgia, the son of Jimmie Katherine Fletcher Peters and Alvin Burbank Peters. Parents were divorced by 1930, and mother married Frank Kernan in 1934. Family moved to ranch in Sierra Madre Mountains in Carbon County, Wyoming. Graduated from Saratoga High School in 1940; ranch failed, and family could not afford to send him to college. In March 1941, at seventeen, borrowed five dollars for bus fare to recruiting center in Cheyenne, where he enlisted in the Navy. Attended boot camp at the U.S. Naval Training Station, San Diego, where he later trained as an aviation ordnanceman. Sailed to Pearl Harbor in November 1941 and was assigned to Torpedo Squadron 6 on board the aircraft carrier USS *Enterprise*. Witnessed aftermath of Japanese attack on Pearl Harbor and launching of Doolittle Raid on Tokyo. Served in Battle of Midway, June 4–7, 1942. Transferred with his squadron to the carrier USS *Hornet* in July. Survived sinking of the *Hornet* in the Battle of Santa Cruz Islands, October 26, 1942. Returned to sea in November 1943 on the *Enterprise*, serving as gunner on TBF Avenger bomber in Torpedo Squadron Six. Awarded Navy Cross for his role in night fighter action off Tarawa, Gilbert Islands, on night of November 26, 1943. Began pilot training at flight school, San Luis Obispo, California, in January 1944. Assigned to Torpedo Squadron 40 as Avenger gunner after the Navy determined it had a surplus of pilot trainees. Returned to sea on the escort carrier USS *Suwannee* in February 1945. Awarded Distinguished Flying Cross for completing twenty combat flights in the Nansei Shoto (Ryukyu Islands), April–May 1945. Discharged with rank of chief petty officer, December 1945. Using G.I. Bill, attended Columbia University for semester before entering Williams College. Graduated with B.A. in 1949. Married Suzanne Scoble (1923–2007) in 1949; they will have four children, Geoffrey, Katherine, Marjorie, and Alvin, Jr. Awarded Moody Fellowship for postgraduate study at Exeter College,

Oxford, where he earned a second B.A. in 1951. Awarded Ph.D. in English literature from Yale University, 1954. Professor of English at Yale, 1954–73; won awards for teaching, served as general editor of the Yale Ben Jonson Series and as acting university provost. Joined faculty at Princeton University in 1973, where graduate students nicknamed him "the Socratic Bulldog" for his question-and-answer technique. Named Avalon Foundation Professor of Humanities in 1982. Retired from Princeton in 1988 and became a director of the Mellon Foundation. An outspoken champion of the humanities, Kernan specialized in English Renaissance drama. Published *The Cankered Muse: Satire of the English Renaissance* (1959), *The Plot of Satire* (1965), *The Playwright as Magician: Shakespeare's Image of the Poet in the English Public Theater* (1979), *The Imaginary Library: An Essay on Literature and Society* (1982), *Samuel Johnson & the Impact of Print* (1987), *The Death of Literature* (1990), *Crossing the Line: A Bluejacket's Odyssey in World War II* (1994, revised edition 2007), *Shakespeare, the King's Playwright: Theater in the Stuart Court, 1603–1613* (1995), an academic memoir, *In Plato's Cave* (2000), *The Fruited Plain: Fables for Postmodern Democracy* (2002), and *The Unknown Battle of Midway: The Destruction of the American Torpedo Squadrons* (2005). Wrote trilogy of short novels about the carrier war in the Pacific, *Love and Glory* (2004), *Attack-Repeat-Attack* (2006), and *Fear in the Dark* (2007), later collected with a new concluding section in *Tumult in the Clouds* (2008). Died in Skillman, New Jersey.

Eugene Bondurant Sledge (November 4, 1923–March 3, 2001) Born in Mobile, Alabama, the son of Mary Frank Sturdivant Sledge and Edward Simmons Sledge, a physician. As a boy, spent much of his time outdoors. Enjoyed birdwatching, hunting, and collecting Civil War relics, interest in which he traced to ancestors' service in the Confederate army. After graduating high school in 1942, enrolled as cadet at Marion Military Institute, junior college with an early commissioning program. Enlisted in the Marine Corps, December 3, 1942. Briefly attended officer training program at Georgia Institute of Technology in the summer of 1943, before beginning basic training at the Marine recruit depot in San Diego. Graduated from boot camp on December 24, 1943, then trained as a mortarman at Camp Elliott outside San Diego. Sailed for the South Pacific on February 28, 1944. After further training in New Caledonia, arrived at Pavuvu in the Solomon Islands, June 3, and was assigned to Company K, 3rd Battalion, 5th Regiment, 1st Marine Division. Acquired nickname "Sledgehammer." Made assault landing at Peleliu, September 15. Endured thirty days of combat before his battalion was relieved. Returned to rest camp on Pavuvu before participating in maneuvers on Guadalcanal. Landed on

Okinawa, April 1, and fought in the southern part of the island from May 1 until the end of the campaign, enduring fifty-two days of combat. Following the Japanese surrender, served in occupying force at Beijing, China, before being honorably discharged in February 1946. Used G.I. Bill to attend Alabama Polytechnic Institute (now Auburn University); graduated with B.S. in Business Administration in 1949. Married Jeanne Arcenaux in 1952; they will have two sons, John (b. 1957) and Henry (b. 1965). Finding postwar readjustment difficult, worked for a time in insurance and real estate before returning to Auburn in 1953, where he earned M.S. in Botany in 1955. Received Ph.D. in Zoology from University of Florida in 1960. Worked in Division of Plant Industries for Florida State Department of Agriculture, 1959–62. Appointed assistant professor of biology at Alabama College (now University of Montevallo), specializing in study of nematodes. Published numerous scholarly articles and became beloved teacher, known for leading birding expeditions; promoted to professor in 1970; retired in 1990. Suffered for years from "ghastly war nightmares"; found strength in scientific inquiry, classical music, poetry, especially that of World War I, and writing. At urging of Jeanne, returned in earnest in the 1970s to memoir he had outlined in 1946, based on notes made in combat in his pocket copy of the New Testament. Wrote memoir, using working title "Into the Abyss," published as *With the Old Breed at Peleliu and Okinawa* in 1981. Died in Montevallo, Alabama, of stomach cancer. A second memoir, *China Marine*, was published posthumously in 2002.

Note on the Texts

This volume collects three memoirs by Americans who served in the armed forces in the Pacific theater during World War II: *With the Old Breed at Peleliu and Okinawa* (1981) by E. B. Sledge, *Flights of Passage: Recollections of a World War II Aviator* (1988) by Samuel Hynes, and *Crossing the Line: A Bluejacket's Odyssey in World War II* (1994, revised 2007) by Alvin Kernan.

Eugene Bondurant Sledge enlisted in the U.S. Marine Corps in 1942 and first saw combat in the invasion of Peleliu in September 1944. During the battle Sledge secretly made penciled notes in the margins of his pocket New Testament. (For security reasons Marines were forbidden to keep personal diaries.) In the fall of 1944, he organized his notes from Peleliu in a memorandum book while in a rest camp on the island of Pavuvu. Sledge continued to make clandestine notes during the Okinawa campaign in the spring of 1945 and drew up a detailed handwritten outline of his wartime experiences when he returned home in 1946. Over the years he collected historical materials and wrote out various episodes while pursuing an education, marrying and starting a family, and teaching biology at the University of Montevallo.

Sledge devoted more time to the project in the 1970s, intending to write a memoir for his family until Jeanne, his wife, encouraged him to seek a publisher. When Sledge sent a portion of the manuscript to John Crown, who had served as a Marine officier on Peleliu, Crown brought it to the attention of Robert W. Smith, the editor of *Marine Corps Gazette*. "Peleliu: A Neglected Battle" appeared in *Marine Corps Gazette* in three parts, November 1979–January 1980. Sledge continued to work on his memoir, using the title "Into the Abyss." On Smith's recommendation, he submitted it to Presidio Press, a publisher specializing in military history. Presidio expressed interest but asked that the 850-page typescript be shortened. Smith suggested cuts and alterations to Sledge, who sent the revised chapters to the press. *With the Old Breed at Peleliu and Okinawa* was published in Novato, California, by Presidio Press on November 15, 1981. Sledge is not known to have made revisions in the work in its later printings, such as the paperbacks published by Bantam (1982) and the New York branch of Oxford University Press (1990). This volume prints the text of the 1981 Presidio Press edition, but corrects a typesetting error in that edition: at 290.36, "Suicide in Trenches" becomes "Suicide in the Trenches."

The maps, photographs, and captions from *With the Old Breed at Peleliu and Okinawa* included in this volume follow those in the 1981 Presidio Press edition, with two exceptions. The map of the Umurbrogol Pocket printed on page 151 in this volume appeared in the 1981 edition without a symbol in the map key for "MANGROVE SWAMP" and without any symbols depicting the location of the mangrove swamps on the map itself. In this volume, the map has been corrected by referring to the map of the Umurbrogol Pocket it is based on, Map 14 in Major Frank O. Hough, *The Assault on Peleliu* (Washington, D.C.: Historical Division, Headquarters U.S. Marine Corps, 1950). In the caption printed at the bottom of the eighth page of the photo insert, "Jap grenade" has been changed to "Japanese grenade" to conform with the usage employed in the other captions.

Samuel Hynes began naval flight training in 1943 and flew seventy-eight combat missions in the Central Pacific as a Marine Corps pilot in 1945. Hynes studied English literature after the war and began teaching at Swarthmore College in 1949 while continuing to fly, first as a Marine reservist and then as a civilian. In the 1950s Hynes began writing in a notebook "things I remembered from my WWII days —anecdotes, dialogues, Marine things. . . . There's a whole page of Marine obscenities, the lyrics to several dirty songs, and an account of being in an electrical thunderstorm at night over the China Sea." He published "A Few Words About Dying," recounting a wartime incident on Okinawa, in the November 1963 number of *Four Quarters*. Hynes continued writing in the notebook and began "putting the notes . . . together, not into a history of the war, but rather a personal account that would make *my* war as real as I could make it." In the early 1970s he sent a draft to his agent, who circulated it among several publishers without success. (Hynes believed the lack of interest was related to the Vietnam War, recalling how a magazine editor told him in 1973 it would not be possible to excerpt a "pro-war book" at that time.)

After setting the manuscript aside for several years, Hynes began rewriting it in the 1980s and published two excerpts in literary journals: "Remembering Okinawa" in the Winter 1985 number of *Tri-Quarterly*, and "The Feeling of Flying" in the Winter 1987 number of *The Sewanee Review*. The memoir was announced for publication under the title *The Unsubstantial Air*, which Hynes would later use for a book about American fliers in World War I. Under the title *Flights of Passage: Recollections of a World War II Aviator*, the memoir was published jointly on March 1, 1988, by Frederic C. Beil, Publisher, in New York, and by the Naval Institute Press in Annapolis, Maryland.

Notes

In the notes below, the reference numbers denote page and line of this volume (the line count includes headings). No note is made for material included in the eleventh edition of *Merriam-Webster's Collegiate Dictionary*. Biblical quotations are keyed to the King James Version. For further biographical background, see E. B. Sledge, *China Marine* (Tuscaloosa: University of Alabama Press, 2002); Samuel Hynes, *The Growing Seasons: An American Boyhood Before the War* (New York: Viking, 2003); and Alvin Kernan, *In Plato's Cave* (New Haven, CT: Yale University Press, 1999). For further historical background and references to other studies, see Samuel Hynes, *The Soldiers' Tale: Bearing Witness to Modern War* (New York: Viking Penguin, 1997); Alvin Kernan, *The Unknown Battle of Midway: The Destruction of the American Torpedo Squadrons* (New Haven, CT: Yale University Press, 2005); Ronald H. Spector, *Eagle Against the Sun: The American War with Japan* (New York: Free Press, 1984); and Richard B. Frank, *Tower of Skulls: A History of the Asia-Pacific War, July 1937–May 1942* (New York: W. W. Norton, 2020).

WITH THE OLD BREED AT PELELIU AND OKINAWA

2.4–5 *The deaths ye . . . were mine*] Rudyard Kipling (1865–1936), "Prelude," *Departmental Ditties and Other Verses* (1886).

3.10 *Fix Bayonets!*] Collection of stories (1926) written and illustrated by John W. Thomason (1893–1944), an officer in the 5th Marine Regiment who had fought in France in 1918.

7.4 New Britain campaign] The 1st Marine Division landed on Cape Gloucester in New Britain on December 26, 1943, and fought on the western part of the island until April 28, 1944, when it was relieved by Army troops. The division lost 310 men killed and 1,083 wounded during the campaign.

17.10 Citadel] A four-year military academy in Charleston, South Carolina, founded in 1843.

18.9 1st Marine Division at Guadalcanal] The division landed on the island on August 7, 1942, and was officially relieved on December 9. During the four-month campaign the division lost 650 men killed, 1,278 wounded, and 31 missing.

22.38 M1] The standard U.S. infantry rifle of World War II, the M-1 was a semi-automatic weapon that fired .30 caliber ammunition, held 8 rounds in its magazine, weighed over 9 pounds, and had an effective range of about 500 yards.

24.27–28 "Three O'Clock in the Morning"] Popular waltz composed in 1919 by Julián Robledo (1887–1940).

29.26 .30 caliber heavy and light machine guns] The M1917A1 heavy machine gun was water-cooled, weighed 40 pounds, was mounted on a tripod weighing 53 pounds, and had a four-man crew; the M1919A4 light machine gun was air-cooled, weighed 31 pounds, was mounted on a 14-pound tripod, and had a two-man crew.

29.27 Browning Automatic Rifle (BAR)] A rifle capable of fully automatic fire that was fed from a 20-round magazine, had an effective range of about 500 yards, and weighed 19 pounds. The M-1 rifle, M1917, M1919, and BAR all used the same .30 caliber ammunition.

34.8 Bougainville . . . Marine raider battalion] The 2nd and 3rd Raider Battalions fought on Bougainville from November 1, 1943, to January 11, 1944. They lost 64 men killed and 204 wounded; overall Marine casualties in the campaign were 423 killed and 1,418 wounded.

36.33 M1 carbine] The M-1 carbine was a semiautomatic weapon that had a 15-round magazine, weighed 6 pounds, and had an effective range of 200 yards. It fired .30 caliber ammunition that was lighter and less powerful than that used in the M-1 rifle.

40.24 Fuzzy Wuzzy] A Sudanese warrior. This term in now considered derogatory.

42.16 Mare Island Naval Prison] The prison was located in the naval shipyard on Mare Island, a peninsula on San Pedro Bay in Vallejo, California.

46.29 history of the 5th Marines] The regiment fought as part of the 1st Marine Division in the invasion of Iraq in 2003 and since then has been deployed several times to Iraq and Afghanistan.

47.6–8 the division . . . Guam] The 3rd Marine Division landed on Guam on July 21, 1944. Organized fighting continued on the island until August 10.

49.23 jungle rot] Skin ulcers caused by bacteria commonly found in the tropics.

51.35 Jerry Colonna] A comedian and trombonist, Colonna (1904–1986) was a regular performer on Bob Hope's radio programs during the 1940s and Hope's USO troupe during World War II.

52.1 Frances Langford, and Patti Thomas] Langford (1913–2005) was a singer, radio performer, and film actress. Patty Thomas (1922–2014) was a tap dancer.

53.15 .45 caliber pistol, and Thompson submachine gun] The M1911A1 semiautomatic pistol had a 7-round magazine, weighed 3 pounds, and had an effective range of 25 yards; the Thompson submachine gun had a 20-round magazine, weighed 12 pounds, and had an effective range of 100 yards. Both weapons used the same .45 caliber ammunition.

56.41 senator from Illinois, Paul Douglas] A graduate of Bowdoin College, Douglas (1892–1976) was a Democratic senator from Illinois, 1949–67.

59.30 *Yamazuki Maru*] The transport was beached on the morning of November 15, 1942, while bringing reinforcements and supplies to the Japanese forces on Guadalcanal.

62.1 *Saipan*] The 2nd and 4th Marine Divisions landed on Saipan on June 15, 1944, and were soon reinforced by the Army's 27th Infantry Division. Organized Japanese resistance continued until July 9, with much of the fighting taking place in rugged mountainous terrain in the center of the island. The campaign cost U.S. forces 3,225 killed, 13,061 wounded, and 326 missing.

63.9–10 Col. Lewis B. ("Chesty") Puller] The commander of the 1st Marine Regiment at Peleliu, Puller (1898–1971) had fought in Haiti and Nicaragua, led a battalion on Guadalcanal, and served as a regimental executive officer on New Britain. During his military career, which included further combat command in Korea, Puller was awarded the Navy Cross five times.

63.11 Maj. Gen. William H. Rupertus] After serving as the assistant commander of the 1st Marine Division on Guadalcanal, Rupertus (1889–1945) led the division on New Britain and Peleliu. He returned to the United States in late 1944 to become commandant of the Marine Corps Schools at Quantico, Virginia, where he died of a heart attack on March 25, 1945.

69.35–39 *Halsey . . . Nimitz*] William F. Halsey (1882–1959) commanded the Third Fleet during the invasion of the Palaus and the subsequent landings in the Philippines. Chester W. Nimitz (1885–1966), Halsey's immediate superior, commanded the Pacific Fleet.

83.2 Sherman tanks] The M4A2 Sherman tank used by the Marines on Peleliu weighed 35 tons, had a five-man crew, a maximum speed of 25 mph, armor ranging in thickness from 25 to 90 mm, and was armed with a 75 mm gun and two .30 caliber machine guns.

84.36 'Flower of the Kwantung Army'] The 14th Infantry Division defending Palau had been transferred to the Pacific in spring 1944 from the Japanese Kwantung Army occupying Manchuria.

85.29 fighting on Corregidor] After four months of aerial and artillery bombardment, the Japanese landed on the island of Corregidor in Manila Bay on May 5, 1942. The American and Filipino garrison surrendered the next day, completing the Japanese conquest of the Philippines.

93.27–30 "The Lord is my . . . comfort me] Psalm 23:1, 4.

111.15–16 "Those Wedding Bells . . . Gang of Mine] Song (1929) composed by Sammy Fain (1902–1989), with lyrics by Irving Kahal (1903–1942) and Willie Raskin (1896–1942).

127.7 F4U Corsair] A single-engine, single-seat fighter, the Corsair had a maximum speed of 415 mph and was armed with six .50 caliber machine guns.

It could carry eight unguided air-to-ground rockets or up to 2,000 pounds of bombs.

129.36 R. V. Burgin] Romus Valton Burgin (1922–2019) recounted his wartime experiences in a memoir, *Islands of the Damned: A Marine at War in the Pacific* (2010), written with Bill Marvel (b. 1938).

138.16–18 Burgin should have . . . the pillbox.] Burgin recalled in *Islands of the Damned* that Sergeant John Marmet later told him that Captain Haldane had intended to recommend him for the Silver Star, but was killed before he was able to write the recommendation.

174.5 *laborers of other oriental extractions*] The laborers included 206 Koreans and 73 Okinawans.

176.18–19 Wilfred Owen's poem "Insensibility"] Owen (1893–1918) wrote the poem in early 1918. It was first published in *Poems* (1920), edited by Siegfried Sassoon.

176.21 Graves, Robert . . . Frank Richards] Graves (1895–1985) wrote an introduction for the 1964 English reprinting of *Old Soldiers Never Die* (1933), a memoir by Frank Richards (1883–1961). Richards and Graves had served together in France in the 2nd Royal Welch Fusiliers, Richards as a private and Graves as a junior officer.

184.39–40 *Men at War* by Ernest Hemingway] *Men at War: The Best War Stories of All Time* (1942), an anthology of fiction and nonfiction pieces introduced by Hemingway and co-edited by Hemingway and the playwright and anthologist William Kozlenko (1907–1984).

188.13 Banana Wars] The 5th Marines fought in Nicaragua, 1927–30, against the rebels led by César Augusto Sandino (1893–1934), who were resisting the U.S. occupation of their country.

188.22 promptly at 0100] This time (i.e., 1 A.M.) is probably the result of a setting error, possibly for 1000 or 1100.

192.20–23 Iwo Jima . . . magnified three times.] Although Iwo Jima was declared secure on March 16, 1945, heavy fighting continued on the island until March 26. American forces lost 6,821 killed and 19,217 wounded in the campaign, with the Marines suffering almost 90 percent of the casualties.

196.19–20 *kunai* grass] Tall grass with sharp-edged leaves, also known as cogon grass.

200.35–36 Japanese suicide planes . . . and *Franklin*] The *Wasp*, *Yorktown*, and *Franklin* were all hit by conventional dive-bombing attacks, not by suicide planes.

200.37–38 loss was 724 killed and 265 wounded] Sledge cites the official Navy figures for casualties on *Franklin*, but more recent research gives figures of 807 killed and 487 wounded.

200.38–39 towed some 12,000 miles to New York] After the fires on the *Franklin* were brought under control, the carrier was towed for sixteen hours until power was restored. *Franklin* then sailed to Ulithi, and later to Pearl Harbor and New York, under its own steam.

209.26 chorus of the "Little Brown Jug"] "Ha, ha, ha, you and me, / Little brown jug, don't I love thee!" is the chorus to the song (1869) by Joseph Eastburn Winner (1837–1918).

210.34 *Lt. Gen. Simon Bolivar Buckner, Jr.*] Buckner (1886–1945) was the son of former Confederate general Simon Bolivar Buckner (1823–1914), who had surrendered Fort Donelson to Ulysses S. Grant in 1862, and Delia Claiborne Buckner (1857–1932), his second wife.

213.1 Zero] A single-engine, single-seat Japanese naval fighter, the highly maneuverable AGM Zero had a maximum speed of 331 mph (increased to 351 mph in later models) and was armed with two 20 mm cannon and two 7.7 mm machine guns.

213.29 "Tommy" (submachine) gun] See note 53.15.

219.11 John Dillinger] Dillinger (1903–1934) led his gang in a series of bank robberies and shoot-outs in several midwestern states from September 1933 until July 22, 1934, when he was fatally shot by FBI agents in Chicago.

260.29 M7s firing 105s] Built on the chassis of the M4 Sherman tank, the M7 self-propelled gun had an open-top hull, and was armed with a 105 mm howitzer and a .50 caliber machine gun.

290.10–16 Sassoon Siegfried . . . and laughter go] Siegfried Sassoon (1886–1967), "Suicide in the Trenches," *Counter-Attack and Other Poems* (1918).

308.26–27 dual-purpose gun] An anti-aircraft gun also used as an anti-tank weapon and as field artillery.

330.6 'thirty' ball] .30 caliber rifle and machine-gun ammunition designed for use against enemy personnel and unarmored targets.

332.38 320mm-spigot-mortar] In a spigot mortar design, the projectile is placed over the firing tube instead of within it.

333.23–26 stone wall . . . Lexington and Concord] Massachusetts militia fired on British troops from behind stone walls as the British withdrew from Concord to Boston on April 19, 1775.

339.20–21 Total American casualties . . . 31,807 wounded] Including losses at sea, U.S. casualties in the Okinawa campaign totaled 12,520 killed and missing and 36,613 wounded.

339.35–36 approximately 42,000 Okinawan civilians] Other estimates of civilian deaths on Okinawa range from 62,000 to more than 100,000.

FLIGHTS OF PASSAGE

348.1   *For John Graves and Les Conner*] John Graves (1920–2013), a former Marine officer who was wounded on Saipan, attended graduate school at Columbia with Samuel Hynes after the war. Graves later became a farmer in his native Texas and published several works of nonfiction, including *Goodbye to a River* (1960), *Hard Scrabble* (1974), and *From a Limestone Ledge* (1980). Lester Conner (1919–2005), an Army veteran of World War II, was a scholar of Irish poetry who taught at Chestnut Hill College in Philadelphia, Swarthmore, and Trinity College, Dublin, and the author of *A Yeats Dictionary: Persons and Places in the Poetry of William Butler Yeats* (1998).

351.9   Rock Island] The Chicago, Rock Island, and Pacific Railroad, also known as the Rock Island Line.

352.17   *G-8 and His Battle Aces*] A series of 110 pulp stories, published 1933–44, by Robert J. Hogan (1897–1963) about the adventures of American fighter ace and spy "G-8" in World War I. Many of the stories incorporated supernatural and science-fiction elements.

352.18   Spads and Nieuports] French single-engine, single-seat biplane fighter aircraft that were also flown by American pilots in World War I.

354.39   Piper Cubs] An American single-engine, two-seat, high-wing monoplane.

359.4   Pi Phi . . . Tri Delt] Phi Beta Phi and Delta Delta Delta, college sororities.

360.4   Lalla Rookh] The heroine of *Lalla Rookh, an Oriental Romance* (1817), a narrative poem by the Irish poet, journalist, and composer Thomas Moore (1779–1852).

362.35   Corsair or an F6F] Corsair, see note 127.7; F6F Hellcat, a single-engine, single-seat naval fighter aircraft developed in response to the Japanese Zero that entered carrier service in September 1943. It had a maximum speed of 376 mph, was armed with six .50 caliber machine guns, and could carry 2,000 pounds of bombs or six 5-inch air-to-ground rockets.

365.29   *Gone With the Wind* . . . two Taras] Tara is the Georgia plantation owned by the O'Hara family in the novel *Gone With the Wind* (1936) by Margaret Mitchell (1900–1949) and its film adaptation (1939).

366.21   Midway or the Coral Sea] U.S. carrier aircraft sank four Japanese carriers and a cruiser in the Battle of Midway, June 3–6, 1942, while the Japanese sank one American carrier and a destroyer. In the Battle of Coral Sea, May 7–8, 1942, U.S. naval forces lost a carrier and two smaller ships while sinking a Japanese light carrier and inflicting damage that prevented two other Japanese carriers from participating in the Midway operation.

367.22–23   armament of the Scharnhorst-class cruiser] The *Scharnhorst* and *Gneisenau* were German battle cruisers armed with nine 280 mm guns.

Launched in 1936, they sank a British aircraft carrier and two destroyers in 1940 and raided Allied merchant shipping in the North Atlantic the following year. *Gneisenau* was seriously damaged by a British bomb in February 1942 and never returned to service; *Scharnhorst* was sunk off Norway by the Royal Navy on December 26, 1943.

367.36–37 hymn . . . peril on the sea] "Eternal Father, Strong to Save" (1860), also known as "The Navy Hymn," was written by William Whiting (1825–1878) and set to music by John Bacchus Dykes (1823–1876).

371.2 *Casablanca*] Film (1942) directed by Michael Curtiz (1886–1962) and written by Julius J. Epstein (1909–2006), Philip G. Epstein (1909–1952), and Howard Koch (1901–1995).

371.5–6 'As Time Goes By'] Song (1931) by Herman Hupfeld (1894–1951).

386.25 brown leg-makeup] Leg makeup was worn in lieu of stockings, which were in short supply due to the demand for nylon and silk in military production.

387.30–31 Andy Hardy movie] Andy Hardy, played by Mickey Rooney (1920–2014), was the hero of sixteen films produced by Metro-Goldwyn-Mayer, 1937–46. The series celebrated a sentimental version of small-town American life.

387.33 'Pistol Packin' Mama'] Song (1942) written by Al Dexter (1905–1984) that was recorded in 1943 by Bing Crosby and the Andrews Sisters.

388.33 'Goodnight, Sweetheart'] Song (1931) by Ray Noble (1903–1978), Jimmy Campbell (1903–1967), and Reg Connelly (1895–1963).

389.32 train in blimps] Blimps were used for anti-submarine patrols and convoy escort duty in the Gulf of Mexico, Caribbean, North and South Atlantic, Mediterranean, and off the California coast.

391.27–29 Montgomery was moving . . . at Stalingrad.] These events occurred in the fall of 1942, before Hynes left Minneapolis to begin his training.

397.22–27 Ted Williams . . . hitter for Boston] Williams (1918–2002) ended the 1941 baseball season with thirty-seven home runs and a .406 batting average. He served as a flight instructor at Pensacola in 1944–45 and flew thirty-nine combat missions in Korea, 1952–53.

397.40 a Zero] See note 213.1.

399.17 CCNY] City College of New York.

400.31 'My Man.'] Originally "Mon Homme" (1920), song with music by Maurice Yvain (1891–1965) and lyrics by Albert Willemetz (1887–1964) and Jacques-Charles (1882–1971). The English lyrics were written by Channing Pollock (1880–1946).

405.32 SNJ's] The SNJ-4 was also used as a training aircraft by the Army Air Forces, where it was designated as the AT-6 Texan.

412.20–22   Tyrone Power . . . multiengined planes] A first lieutenant in the Marine Corps, Power (1914–1958) flew twin-engine transport aircraft in the Pacific in 1945.

415.22   SBD's] The SBD Dauntless was a single-engine scout and dive-bomber with a two-man crew and a maximum speed of 250 mph. It was armed with two .50 caliber and two .30 caliber machine guns and could carry a 1,000-pound bomb.

417.14–15   Indians weren't allowed . . . Federal law] Until 1953 federal law prohibited the sale of liquor to Native Americans throughout the United States.

421.6–8   Benny Goodman Quartet . . . Back Room Boys] The Benny Goodman Quartet recorded "Runnin' Wild" in 1937; singer Nat King Cole (1919–1965) recorded "Sweet Lorraine" in 1940; clarinetist Mezz Mezzrow (1899–1972) and trumpeter Tommy Ladnier (1900–1939) recorded "Comin' On With the Come On" in 1938; Santo "Peck" Pecora (1902–1984) was a New Orleans trombonist.

423.37–38   Virginia Woolf's *Haunted House*] *A Haunted House and Other Short Stories* (1944), posthumous collection by Virginia Woolf (1882–1941).

426.5   H. V. Kaltenborn] Kaltenborn (1878–1965) was a radio news commentator for CBS, 1927–40, and NBC, 1940–55.

430.13–14   Munda . . . Emirau] The Japanese airfield at Munda Point on the island of New Georgia in the western Solomons was captured by Army troops on August 5, 1943, and made into an American air base. Emirau, an island in the Bismarck Archipelago, was occupied without opposition by the Marines in March 1944 and became the site of a U.S. airbase.

431.23–24   TBM's . . . Douglas Devastators] The TBM Avenger had a three-man crew, a maximum speed of 275 mph, and was armed with three .50 caliber and one .30 caliber machine guns. ("TBM" was the designation for an Avenger manufactured by General Motors, "TBF" for one built by Grumman.) The Douglas Devastator had a three-man crew, a maximum speed of 206 mph, and was armed with two .30 caliber machine guns.

432.35   Joe Foss] Flying an F4F Wildcat, Foss (1915–2002) shot down twenty-six Japanese aircraft while serving as executive officer of a Marine fighter squadron based on Guadalcanal, October 1942–January 1943. After being awarded the Medal of Honor, he served a second tour in the South Pacific in 1944 and was then assigned to Marine Air Station Santa Barbara. Foss was later governor of South Dakota, 1955–59, commissioner of the American Football League, 1959–66, and president of the National Rifle Association, 1988–90.

433.11–12   Pappy Boyington] Gregory (Pappy) Boyington (1912–1988) destroyed twenty Japanese aircraft in aerial combat while commanding a Marine Corsair squadron in the Solomon Islands from September 1943 to January 1944, when he was shot down and captured off Rabaul. Awarded the Medal of Honor in March 1944, Boyington remained a prisoner until the end of the war.

433.13–14   fly over a Japanese . . . fight with him] While leading a fighter sweep over Bougainville in October 1943, Boyington repeatedly circled a Japanese air base and taunted the enemy over the radio to come up and fight. When the Japanese responded, the Americans shot down six Zeros while losing one Corsair.

435.4   MacArthur . . . Supreme Commander] General Douglas MacArthur (1880–1964) commanded all land, air, and naval forces in the Southwest Pacific Area, which included Australia, New Guinea and the Bismarck Archipelago, the western Solomons, the Netherlands East Indies (Indonesia), and the Philippines. Admiral Chester Nimitz (1885–1966) was commander-in-chief of land, air, and naval forces in the Pacific Ocean Areas, including Hawaii, the eastern Solomons, the Gilbert, Marshall, Caroline, and Mariana island chains, Iwo Jima, Okinawa, and Formosa (Taiwan).

438.38–39   Illinois Jacquet . . . Howard McGhee] Tenor saxophonist Illinois Jacquet (1922–2004), guitarist Teddy Bunn (1909–1978), and trumpeter Howard McGhee (1918–1987).

441.23   Rita Hayworth] American dancer and film actress Rita Hayworth (1918–1987).

441.30   carbines] See note 36.33.

441.34–35   *For Whom the Bell Tolls*] Film adaptation (1943) of the novel (1940) by Ernest Hemingway (1899–1961), directed by Sam Wood (1883–1949), written by Dudley Nichols (1895–1960), and starring Gary Cooper (1901–1961) and Ingrid Bergman (1915–1982).

442.7   SAE's] Members of the Sigma Alpha Epsilon fraternity.

442.13   *Lady Chatterley's Lover*] Novel (1928) by D. H. Lawrence (1885–1930) that was banned for obscenity in its unexpurgated form in the United States until 1959. A heavily censored version was published by Alfred A. Knopf in 1932, and unexpurgated foreign editions were sometimes smuggled into the U.S.

443.31   Ewa or Santos] The Marine air station at Ewa on Oahu, Hawaii; Espiritu Santo in the New Hebrides.

447.16–18   Dilbert . . . Robert Osborn] "Dilbert Groundloop" was a cartoon character created by Robert Osborn (1904–1994) who appeared on hundreds of posters produced by the Navy's Aviation Training Division.

447.36   *BuAerNews*] A twice-monthly illustrated magazine published by the Navy's Bureau of Aeronautics.

454.27   SB2C's] The SBC2 Helldiver was a single-engine aircraft with a two-man crew and a maximum speed of 295 mph. It was armed with two 20 mm cannon and two .30 caliber machine guns and could carry a 1,000-pound bomb.

457.18   Stan Kenton] Kenton (1904–1994) was a jazz pianist and bandleader.

459.20   the Halls of Montezuma] "From the Halls of Montezuma" is the first line of "The Marines' Hymn," officially adopted in 1929.

460.33   *All Quiet on the Western Front*] Film adaptation (1930) of the novel (1929) by Erich Maria Remarque (1898–1970), directed by Lewis Milestone (1898–1970), screenplay by Maxwell Anderson (1888–1959), George Abbott (1887–1995), and Del Andrews (1894–1942), and starring Lew Ayres (1908–1996).

461.16   the Nicaragua campaign] See note 188.13. The last Marines were withdrawn from Nicaragua in 1933.

462.4–5   *Now, Voyager . . . Have Not*] *Now, Voyager* (1942), film starring Bette Davis (1908–1989) and Paul Henreid (1908–1992), directed by Irving Rapper (1898–1999), screenplay by Casey Robinson (1903–1979), based on the novel (1941) by Olive Higgins Prouty (1882–1974); *Laura* (1944), film starring Gene Tierney (1920–1991), Dana Andrews (1909–1992) and Clifton Webb (1889–1966), directed by Otto Preminger (1905–1986), screenplay by Jay Dratler (1911–1968), Samuel Hoffenstein (1890–1947), and Elizabeth Reinhardt (1909–1954), based on the novel (1943) by Vera Caspary (1899–1987); *To Have and Have Not* (1944), film starring Humphrey Bogart (1899–1957) and Lauren Bacall (1924–2014), directed by Howard Hawks (1896–1977), screenplay by Jules Furthman (1888–1966) and William Faulkner (1897–1962), based on the novel (1937) by Ernest Hemingway.

466.18–20   French 75's . . . First World War] The drink was named after the French 75 mm field gun, which was also used by American troops in World War I.

468.23   Liberty ship] A mass-produced oceangoing transport ship. More than 2,700 Liberty ships were built from 1941 to 1945.

468.30   P–boat] A PBY Catalina twin-engine flying boat.

469.36   *War and Peace*] Novel (1865–69) by Leo Tolstoy (1828–1910).

471.2–3   Dorothy Lamour] A film actress and singer, Lamour (1914–1996) became known as "The Sarong Girl" for her roles in films such as *The Jungle Princess* (1936), *The Hurricane* (1937), and *The Road to Singapore* (1940).

471.16–20   Kwajalein . . . bitterly fought over] U.S. forces captured Kwajalein Atoll, January 31–February 4, 1944, at the cost of 531 killed and 1,462 wounded. American losses in the fighting on Eniwetok Atoll, February 18–23, 1944, were 397 killed and 879 wounded. It is estimated that about 12,000 Japanese were killed on the two atolls.

475.38   defense of Wake Island] The Japanese lost two destroyers when their first attempt to land on Wake Island was repulsed on December 11, 1941. Their second attempt succeeded on December 23, and the 500-man American garrison surrendered.

478.33   Little Orphan Annie] Comic strip character created in 1924 by Harold Gray (1894–1968).

480.8   R5C] Marine Corps designation for the C-46 Commando, a large twin-engine military transport aircraft used by the U.S. Army Air Forces.

484.38   it was February] This may be an error in dating. Cf. 470.10, where Hynes writes about being in Honolulu "on the last day of February in 1945."

485.40–486.1   one crashed into . . . carrier *Franklin*] The carrier hit by the kamikaze at Ulithi on March 11, 1945, was the USS *Randolph*, not the *Franklin*. The attack killed 25 men and wounded 106. Repaired at sea, *Randolph* rejoined the fleet off Okinawa on April 7.

487.35   Tokyo Rose] Generic name for the dozen or so English-speaking women who broadcast propaganda on Japanese radio.

491.22   signs of war] See note 62.1. About 29,000 Japanese military personnel were killed on Saipan, as well as an estimated 22,000 civilians.

494.34   F6F's and F4F's] F6F, see note 362.35. The F6F's predecessor, the F4F Wildcat, a single-engine, single-seat fighter, had a maximum speed of 318 mph and was armed with six .50 caliber machine guns.

499.8   the battle was over] See note 192.20–23. Between 18,000 and 20,000 Japanese soldiers were killed on Iwo Jima.

502.34   Japanese bomber . . . Betty] "Betty" was the American code name for the Japanese G4M bomber, a land-based twin-engine aircraft with a crew of seven. The G4M1 had a maximum speed of 266 mph, was armed with a single 20 mm cannon and four 7.7 mm machine guns, and could carry either a single torpedo or 1,760 pounds of bombs.

508.31–32   Lawrence Tibbett . . . Road to Mandalay] American opera singer Lawrence Tibbett (1896–1960); "On the Road to Mandalay" (1907), song by Oley Sparks (1874–1948) featuring three verses from the poem "Mandalay" (1890) by Rudyard Kipling (1865–1936).

508.37–39   Spencer Tracy . . . a buggy] *Without Love* (1945), directed by Harold S. Bucquet (1891–1946), screenplay by Donald Ogden Stewart (1894–1980) based on the play (1942) by Philip Barry (1896–1949), starring Spencer Tracy (1900–1967) and Katharine Hepburn (1907–2003).

511.20   one night in May] The night of May 24–25, 1945.

514.28–29   odd-shaped, lengthwise paperbacks] Armed Services Editions, published by the Council on Books in Wartime. More than 122 million copies of 1,324 titles were printed for free distribution, 1943–47.

514.31   the *Missouri* . . . shelling] Battleship commissioned in 1944, with main armament of nine 16-inch guns.

518.25   Bandit] Radio code for an enemy aircraft.

518.31–38   Baka bomb . . . enemy ship] Baka, which also means "fool" in Japanese, was the American name for the Ohka (Cherry Blossom) piloted rocket bomb. The Ohka could reach a speed of 580 mph in its final dive and contained a 2,645-pound warhead. Several American destroyers were hit in Ohka attacks during the Okinawa campaign, including the *Mannert L. Abele*, which was sunk on April 12, 1945, with the loss of 84 men.

519.9   Kerama Retto] A small island group about fifteen miles west of Okinawa that was captured by troops of the 77th Infantry Division, March 26–29, 1945.

521.1   Ducks] A six-wheeled amphibious truck equipped with a propeller and rudder that could carry 25 men or 5,000 pounds of cargo.

521.31   Merthiolate] Trade name for thimerosal, an organic mercurial compound used as an antiseptic.

524.26   ASP] Anti-submarine patrol.

524.28   Irving] American name for the J1N1, a twin-engine land-based Japanese night fighter with a two-man crew. It had a maximum speed of 315 mph and was armed with four 20 mm cannon and two 7.7 mm machine guns.

525.4   a Tony] American name for the Ki-61, a single-engine, single-seat land-based Japanese fighter. It had a top speed of 360 mph and was armed with two 20 mm cannon and two 12.7 mm machine guns.

531.2   *Dawn Patrol* and *Wings*] *The Dawn Patrol* (1930), film about British fighter pilots in World War I, directed by Howard Hawks, written by Hawks, Dan Totheroh (1894–1976), and Seton I. Miller (1902–1974), based on a story by John Monk Saunders (1895–1940), starring Richard Barthelmess (1895–1963) and Douglas Fairbanks, Jr. (1909–2000). It was remade under the same title in 1938, directed by Edmund Goulding (1891–1959), written by Totheroh and Miller from the story by Saunders, and starring Errol Flynn (1909–1959), Basil Rathbone (1892–1967), and David Niven (1910–1983). *Wings* (1927), silent film about American fighter pilots in World War I, directed by William A. Wellman (1896–1975), written by John Monk Saunders, Hope Loring (1894–1959), and Louis D. Lighton (1895–1963), and starring Clara Bow (1905–1965), Charles "Buddy" Rogers (1904–1999), and Richard Arlen (1899–1976).

531.28–29   Miyako . . . Amami o Shima] Miyako, island 185 miles southwest of Okinawa; Ishigaki, island 255 miles southwest of Okinawa; Kikai Jima and Amami Oshima, islands about 155 miles north of Okinawa and 235 miles south of Kyushu.

535.15   P-51] The P-51 Mustang was a single-engine, single-seat, land-based fighter. The P-51D had a maximum speed of 440 mph and was armed with six .50 caliber machine guns.

537.20–21 'Green Eyes,' . . . 'Perfidia'] "Green Eyes" (1931) is the English version of "Aquellos Ojos Verdes" (1929), composed by the Cuban American musician Nilo Menéndez (1902–1987). The song became popular in the United States when it was recorded in 1941 by bandleader Jimmy Dorsey (1904–1957). "I'll Never Smile Again" (1940), song by Ruth Lowe (1914–1981). "Perfidia" (1939), song by Mexican composer Alberto Dominguez (1911–1975).

540.15 B-29's] The B-29 Superfortress was a four-engine heavy bomber with a crew of eleven and a cruising speed of 220 mph. It was armed with twelve .50 caliber machine guns and could carry up to 12,000 pounds of bombs.

542.9 Our war ended . . . August 12th] The Japanese government made a conditional offer of surrender on August 10, 1945, but hostilities continued until August 15, when Emperor Hirohito made a radio broadcast announcing Japan's acceptance of the Allied surrender terms.

543.20 PBY's] See note 468.30.

545.25 F7F's] The F7F Tigercat was a twin-engine land-based fighter bomber.

546.30 Billie Holiday singing 'Travellin' Light'] "Trav'lin' Light" (1942), song written by Trummy Young (1912–1984) and Jimmy Mundy (1907–1983) with lyrics by Johnny Mercer (1909–1976), recorded in 1942 by Billie Holiday (1915–1959) and the Paul Whiteman Orchestra.

546.34–37 Joseph Hergesheimer's . . . *The Fountainhead*] *The Three Black Pennys* (1917), novel by Joseph Hergesheimer (1880–1954); *The Fountainhead* (1943), novel by Ayn Rand (1905–1982).

CROSSING THE LINE

558.1 *For my children*] In the 1994 edition of *Crossing the Line*, the dedication page was followed by an epigraph:

> If you would travel farther than all travelers . . . start now on that farthest western way, which does not pause at the Mississippi or the Pacific, nor conduct toward a worn-out China or Japan, but leads on direct, a tangent to this sphere, summer and winter, day and night, sun down, moon down, and at last earth down too.
>
> —Henry David Thoreau, *Walden*

561.1 INTRODUCTION] The introduction by Lawrence Stone first appeared in the 1994 edition.

561.7–10 Seventh Fleet . . . HMS *Chaser*] An American-built escort carrier transferred to the Royal Navy under lend-lease, *Chaser* was part of the British Pacific Fleet, which operated in 1945 as a task force in the Fifth Fleet and then the Third Fleet. (The U.S. Central Pacific fleet alternated commanders in 1944–45. It was known as the Fifth Fleet when under the command of Admiral Raymond A. Spruance and as the Third Fleet when it was led by Admiral

William F. Halsey. Both men reported to Admiral Chester W. Nimitz, the commander of the Pacific Ocean Areas.)

561.23–24 Shotley . . . HMS *Fiji*] Shotley was a Royal Navy training establishment in Suffolk, near Ipswich. *Fiji*, a light cruiser commissioned in May 1940, was sunk by German aircraft off Crete on May 22, 1941, with the loss of 241 of its crew.

563.21 Joseph Heller's *Catch-22*] Novel (1961) by Joseph Heller (1923–1999).

564.8 Lawrence Stone] Stone (1919–1999) was professor of history at Princeton, 1963–90, and the author of several works, including *The Crisis of the Aristocracy, 1558–1641* (1965), *The Causes of the English Revolution, 1529–1642* (1972), and *Family, Sex and Marriage in England 1500–1800* (1977).

565.1 PREFACE . . . YALE EDITION] The 1994 edition of *Crossing the Line* contained the following preface:

> It was once the custom, perhaps still is, when a young man enlisted in the United States Navy for him to be issued a small soft-covered blue book titled *The Bluejackets' Manual*. This book did not come for free. Several dollars were deducted on the first payday for it. It was impossible to manage without this little handbook whose chapters A to N covered such seaman's skills as tying knots—square or turk's head—reading signal flags—Able, Baker, Charley—wearing your hat and when not, saluting correctly, and shipping oars smartly.
>
> Since the chapters stopped at N, recruits used to speculate about what the chapters that came after N covered. Perhaps there were no chapters beyond N, that A to N covered everything known or necessary to be known about naval life. This view was not favored, however, and mysteries grew up around chapters O to Z. These chapters, it was said by some, were for officers only, and covered the duties and pleasures of those strange and distant creatures. They dealt, others said, with special skills such as boilermaking, sheet metal work, torpedo preparation, and quartermasters' responsibilities. With the growing understanding that it was better in the navy never to ask questions, no one I knew ever inquired officially about O to Z, and the content of these remarkable chapters remained a mystery.
>
> It may be, of course, that chapters O through Z exist in numerous copies read every day by someone. But in time I came to feel privately that the navy in its wisdom had reserved O to Z for the sailor's personal experiences: all those things that a young man had to learn about life, as we used to say, the hard way. They couldn't be written down because they were not the same for any two people, and because no one ever believed what someone else told him about these matters. No doubt that is still true—what could have changed it?—but I like to think of my memories of life on the aircraft carriers in what the Japanese call the

Great Pacific War as a "Bluejackets' Manual, Chapters O to Z," which others may find it amusing to compare with their own handbooks to life.

Memory is a tricky thing, and images are far more vivid than dates and sequences. I have consulted histories such as John Toland's *Rising Sun* and John Lundstrom's *The First Team* for the facts, but *Crossing the Line* should be read as a personal memoir, not a history, in which I hope many old friends may recognize themselves and enjoy momentarily reliving shared earlier events.

I take pleasure in mentioning the help given with my manuscript by Dorothy Watson Westgate at the Mellon Foundation, as well as its remarkable president, William G. Bowen, who read a draft and has supported the project with characteristic enthusiasm. At the Naval Institute Press, Anne Collier and Linda O'Doughda have been good friends to this book. I also owe particular thanks to John B. Lundstrom, the most knowledgeable of naval historians about the air war in the early days of World War II in the Pacific. Mr. Lundstrom wrote to me asking for information for a book about Lt. Comdr. Edward H. (Butch) O'Hare he is working on. He was good enough to read the chapter in this book that deals with O'Hare's death and saved me from making a number of errors. He was also generous enough to share some of the materials he had located about the events surrounding O'Hare's death, including the extraordinary find of the reports of the Japanese 752 Air Group described on page 684. Mr. Lundstrom also located the invaluable letter written by Adm. Arthur Radford reporting the formation of the "Black Panther" night-fighting group on the *Enterprise* and subsequent events.

My special thanks are due to Robert Cowley, editor of *MHQ: The Quarterly Journal of Military History*, for his advice at a crucial time, and to my colleague, and friend of many years, the distinguished British historian Lawrence Stone for agreeing to read *Crossing the Line* in manuscript form and to write the foreword. Another friend and colleague, Samuel Hynes, himself a marine aviator in the Pacific in World War II and the author of a remarkable memoir, *Flights of Passage*, urged me to publish what I had mainly intended as a memorial to be left to my children to be read over privately in the years to come.

Alvin Kernan
Princeton, New Jersey

565.16–17 Cincpac . . . ULTRA] Cincpac was an abbreviation for Commander in Chief, Pacific Fleet, used here to refer to Pacific Fleet headquarters. ULTRA was a code word for intelligence obtained by monitoring, intercepting, and decoding enemy radio signals.

569.2 *Snow*] In the 1994 edition this chapter was titled "Home."

575.32–33 the loss . . . Samson] See Judges 16:17–21.

NOTES

577.28–29   comic strip "Peanuts"] Comic strip (1950–2000) written and drawn by Charles M. Schulz (1922–2000).

578.22–24   British-made long Enfields . . . the Springfield] M1917 Enfield rifles were manufactured in the United States, based on a British design. The M1917 Enfield weighed 9.2 pounds; the M1903 Springfield rifle, 8.7 pounds.

579.28–29   Marvin Mudrick] Mudrick (1921–1986) taught English at the University of California–Santa Barbara, from 1949 until his death. His works include *Books Are Not Life, But What Is?* (1979) and *Nobody Here But Us Chickens* (1981).

581.38–40   "Hut sut rawson . . . Yankee dollar."] "The Hut-Sut Song (A Swedish Serenade)" (1941), novelty song by Leo V. Killon (1908–2000), Ted McMichael (1908–2001), and Jack Owens (1912–1982). "Rum and Coca-Cola" (c. 1943), calypso song with words by Lord Invader (Rupert Grant, 1914–1961), set to earlier music (1906) by Lionel Belasco (1881–1967). It was first recorded in 1944 by the Andrews Sisters.

587.13   "Anchors Aweigh"] Unofficial march of the U.S. Navy, originally written in 1906 as a fight song for the U.S. Naval Academy, with music by Charles A. Zimmermann (1861–1916) and lyrics by Alfred Hart Miles (1886–1956). The lyrics were revised in 1926 by George D. Lottman (1899–1942).

591.6   *Intrepid* in New York Harbor] The aircraft carrier *Intrepid* was commissioned in 1943 and served in the Central Pacific, 1944–45. Decommissioned in 1974, *Intrepid* became a floating museum on the Hudson River in New York City in 1982.

593.16   the headspace] An interior dimension in a firearm that determines whether a cartridge is properly seated in the firing chamber.

593.17–21   SBD Douglas "Dauntless" . . . the Zero] For the SBD Dauntless, see note 415.22. The F4F-3 Wildcat had a maximum speed of 331 mph and was armed with four .50 caliber machine guns. It was replaced in early 1942 by the F4F-4, which had folding wings. For the Zero, see note 213.1.

594.32–36   Wake Island . . . or killed] See note 475.38.

595.36–37   how oil embargoes . . . to war] The Japanese government formally decided on July 2, 1941, to occupy southern Indochina and to prepare for war with Britain and the United States. An agreement signed with the Vichy French on July 21 gave Japan military control of southern Indochina, including air and naval bases that could be used to attack Malaya, the Netherlands East Indies, and the Philippines. President Franklin D. Roosevelt responded on July 26 by freezing Japanese assets in the U.S., resulting in an embargo of oil exports to Japan (the U.S. was the source of 80 percent of Japanese oil imports). The Japanese leadership decided on September 6 to go to war with the United States unless the U.S. accepted Japanese domination of China and Southeast Asia. A final decision to begin the war in early December was made in Tokyo on November 5.

595.37 Japanese had invaded China] Fighting broke out near Beijing between Chinese troops and the Japanese legation garrison in July 1937, leading to full-scale war in August.

596.16–17 others had gotten . . . shot down] The Japanese shot down five aircraft from the *Enterprise* on December 7, and another five planes were mistakenly shot down by American anti-aircraft gunners.

597.35–36 off Malaya they sank . . . *Repulse*] The battleship *Prince of Wales* and battle cruiser *Repulse* were sunk on December 10, 1941, with the loss of 837 men.

602.18–19 Nimitz, soon to be . . . Pacific Fleet] Nimitz took command of the Pacific Fleet on December 31, 1941.

607.21 one-point-ones] Anti-aircraft guns firing 1.1-inch shells.

608.5 Bligh] Mutineers seized control of HMS *Bounty* in the South Pacific on April 28, 1789, and set the ship's commander, Lieutenant William Bligh (1754–1817), and eighteen members of the crew adrift in a twenty-foot launch. After sailing more than 3,600 miles, Bligh and his men reached Timor in the Netherlands East Indies on June 14.

608.6–7 *The Raft* . . . ghostwriter] *The Raft* (1942) was written by Robert Trumbull (1912–1992), a correspondent for *The New York Times*, who told the story from the first-person perspective of Harold Dixon (1901–1987).

608.13–16 Tony Pastula . . . Aldrich] Anthony Pastula (1917–1982), the plane's bombardier, and Gene Aldrich (1919–1973), its radio operator and rear gunner.

611.15 *Salt Lake City, Northampton*] The cruiser *Salt Lake City* served until the end of the war and fought in two surface engagements, the Battle of Cape Esperance off Guadalcanal on the night of October 11–12, 1942, and the Battle of the Komandorski Islands in the North Pacific, March 26, 1943. The cruiser *Northampton* served in task forces with the carriers *Enterprise* and *Hornet* before being sunk off Guadalcanal in the Battle of Tassafaronga, November 30, 1942.

611.15 Trafalgar or Jutland] The British won a decisive victory over the combined French-Spanish fleet in the Battle of Trafalgar, fought in the Atlantic off southwest Spain on October 21, 1805. The Battle of Jutland was fought between the British Grand Fleet and German High Seas Fleet in the North Sea off Denmark on May 31–June 1, 1916. Although the British lost more ships and men than the Germans, they retained control of the North Sea.

611.19–20 Bataan had surrendered] The fighting on the Bataan peninsula ended on April 9, 1942, with the surrender of 12,000 American and 63,000 Filipino troops.

616.6 Battle of the Coral Sea] See note 366.21.

616.14   the old *Langley* . . . sunk in Indonesia] The *Langley*, a converted collier, became the first American aircraft carrier in 1922. Reconverted to a seaplane tender in 1937, *Langley* was sunk by Japanese aircraft off Java on February 27, 1942.

619.28–29   the Mackay office] The Mackay Radio and Telegraph Company, founded in 1925.

622.16   Nagumo . . . Japanese navy] Vice Admiral Chuichi Nagumo (1887–1944) commanded the First Air Fleet, the carrier strike force that had attacked Pearl Harbor. He later served as naval commander in the Marianas, where he committed suicide in the final days of the Battle of Saipan.

622.26   Grumman TBF] See note 431.23–24.

623.23   Lt. Cdr. John Waldron] A 1924 graduate of the U.S. Naval Academy, Waldron (1900–1942) assumed command of Torpedo Eight in July 1941. Alvin Kernan dedicated his historical study *The Unknown Battle of Midway* (2005) to Waldron's memory.

625.5   Capt. James Gray] Gray (1914–1998) was credited with shooting down six Japanese aircraft during the war. He retired from the Navy in 1966 with the rank of captain.

625.8   the F4F-4s . . . older F4F-3s] The F4F-4 was equipped with self-sealing fuel tanks and additional armor that made it heavier and slower than the F4F-3.

626.15   army B-26s] A twin-engine aircraft, the B-26 was not designed to be used as a torpedo bomber and very rarely served in that role.

626.22–25   Ensign Gay . . . life jacket.] George Gay (1917–1994) was rescued by a PBY Catalina on June 5.

627.2   famous Jimmy Thach] Lieutenant Commander John (Jimmie) Thach (1905–1981), commander of Fighting Squadron Three at the Coral Sea and Midway, developed an aerial maneuver known as the "Thach Weave" that Wildcat pilots used to successfully counter attacks by Zeros. Thach returned to the United States after Midway to train new pilots and later developed tactics to defend carriers against kamikaze attacks. He retired from the Navy in 1967 with the rank of admiral.

627.18   *Kido Butai*] Japanese: Mobile Force, Strike Force, Striking Force.

628.6–7   great pilot . . . Minoru Genda] The air operations officer of the First Air Fleet, Genda (1904–1989) had played a major role in planning the Pearl Harbor attack.

628.8   *Shimatta*, "We goofed."] Genda reportedly made this remark to Commander Mitsuo Fuchida (1902–1976), the pilot who had led the first attack wave at Pearl Harbor, on the bridge of the *Akagi* shortly after it was hit by an American bomb.

628.20–21   Salamis . . . Lepanto] Battle fought in the Straits of Salamis in 480 B.C.E. in which an alliance of Greek city-states defeated the Persians; battle fought in the Gulf of Patras near Lepanto (Nafpaktos) in western Greece in 1571 in which the Catholic Holy League defeated the Ottomans.

630.13   his squadron commander] Lieutenant Commander Samuel G. Mitchell (1904–1992), commander of Fighting Squadron Eight.

632.10   *Police Gazette*] *The National Police Gazette* was published from 1845 to 1977.

635.2–3   *How to Win* . . . Dale Carnegie] Published in 1936 by Dale Carnegie (1888–1955).

636.3–4   Battle of the Eastern Solomons] On August 24, 1942, U.S. naval aircraft sank the light carrier *Ryujo*, while the *Enterprise* was hit by three bombs and forced to return to Pearl Harbor for extensive repairs.

637.19–20   the *Wasp* . . . Japanese submarine] The *Wasp* was sunk on September 15, 1942.

638.27–28   antiques . . . Spanish-American War] Experience fighting Moro rebels in the southern Philippines, 1901–6, persuaded the U.S. military that in close-range engagements handguns firing .45 caliber ammunition were most effective. In 1911 the Army chose the .45 caliber Colt semi-automatic pistol as its new sidearm, and it was soon adopted by the Navy and Marines as well.

647.8–9   she went down . . . still be sitting] In January 2019 the research vessel *Petrel* discovered the nearly intact wreckage of the *Hornet* resting upright on the ocean floor 17,500 feet below the surface.

650.12–13   famous novel . . . *South Pacific*] *Tales of the South Pacific* (1947), collection of related stories by James Michener (1907–1997), adapted as the musical *South Pacific* (1949), music by Richard Rodgers (1902–1979), with lyrics by Oscar Hammerstein II (1895–1960) and book by Hammerstein and Joshua Logan (1908–1988).

655.19   "Ise lei, nona nogurawa"] Fijian: "Isa Lei, na noqu rarawa." "Oh my! All my sadness!" "Isa Lei" is a Fijian farewell song dating from the early twentieth century.

660.33   naval prison at Mare Island] See note 42.16.

664.39–40   Dick Boone . . . villainous roles] Richard Boone (1917–1981) played villains in Westerns such as *Ten Wanted Men* (1955), *The Tall T* (1957), and *Hombre* (1967) and in the film noir *The Garment Jungle* (1957), but became best known for his role as Paladin, the hero of the television Western *Have Gun—Will Travel* (1957–63).

665.22–23   Neighborhood Playhouse . . . method-acting school] The director of the Playhouse's drama department, Sanford Meisner (1905–1997), rejected the emphasis placed on emotional memory in "the method" taught by Lee Strasberg (1902–1982) and developed his own "Meisner technique."

665.26–31 "Butch" O'Hare . . . February 1942] O'Hare (1914–1943), a 1937 graduate of the U.S. Naval Academy, served under John Thach in Fighting Squadron Three at the beginning of the war. On February 20, 1942, O'Hare found himself the only Wildcat pilot in a position to intercept eight G4M Betty bombers headed toward the *Lexington*. He single-handedly attacked the Japanese formation, shooting down three aircraft and severely damaging another three.

665.31–34 his father . . . by Al Capone] Edward O'Hare (1893–1939) was a lawyer and investor who obtained the patent rights to the mechanical rabbit used at dog tracks. O'Hare entered into a lucrative partnership in the dog racing business with Chicago crime boss Al Capone (1899–1947), then became a valuable informant for the government as it built a case against Capone for tax evasion. After Capone's conviction in 1931, O'Hare continued to do business with underworld figures. He was shot and killed while driving through Chicago on November 8, 1939, a week before Capone's release from federal prison. By then Capone was mentally incapacitated by neurosyphilis, and it is likely that O'Hare's murder was ordered by Frank Nitti (1886–1943), Capone's successor as boss of the Chicago "Outfit."

669.14–15 Dilbert . . . training posters] See note 447.16–18.

671.2 *Black Panthers*] In the 1994 edition this chapter is titled "Night Fighters."

672.10 Higgins boats] New Orleans boat builder Andrew J. Higgins (1886–1952) designed and manufactured the LCVP (Landing Craft, Vehicle and Personnel), which could carry 36 men or a 2.5-ton truck.

673.29–31 resistance on Butaritari . . . fighting on Tarawa] U.S. forces killed 395 Japanese on Makin, November 20–24, 1943, while losing 66 killed and 152 wounded. In the fighting on Tarawa, November 20–23, American losses totaled 1,115 killed and 2,292 wounded, while 4,690 Japanese were killed and 17 were taken prisoner, along with 139 Korean laborers.

675.35 medium bombers, Bettys] See note 503.34.

676.3–4 Adm. Arthur Radford] Radford (1896–1973) later served as chairman of the Joint Chiefs of Staff, 1953–57.

685.15–16 Eugene Burns . . . correspondent] Burns (1906–1958) wrote a story about O'Hare, dated November 29, that appeared in American newspapers on December 11, 1943. It included quotes from Kernan, John Phillips, Warren Skon, Hazen Rand, and Arthur Radford. Burns wrote that the stories told by the airmen "were not in complete agreement," but "the action was swift and in the darkness, with the blinding of tracer fire and the flames from burning planes as the main illumination, so it was natural that none of them would know exactly what happened." After reporting how aerial searches had found no trace of O'Hare or his plane, Burns added, "But forever it will be remembered how Butch saved our task force from the heaviest and longest Japanese torpedo plane night attack."

686.6–8   he wrote some . . . *Saturday Evening Post*] "Butch O'Hare's Last Flight" appeared in *The Saturday Evening Post* on March 11, 1944. After describing how he followed the interception of the Japanese torpedo planes over the radio in the air operations center on the *Enterprise*, Burns wrote: "What seemed the certain, inevitable, deliberate destruction of our ships is gone, and we are saved because Butch waited and waded in at precisely the right moment."

688.25–26   Phillips was killed . . . at Truk] Lieutenant Commander John Phillips (1910–1944), a 1933 graduate of the U.S. Naval Academy, was killed on February 16, 1944.

689.2   *Solo*] In the 1994 edition this chapter was titled "Drifting."

689.32–34   *Los Angeles Times* . . . Butch O'Hare] "Gunner Tells of Last Flight of Dutch O'Hare" appeared in the *Los Angeles Times* on January 2, 1944, accompanied by a photograph of Kernan in uniform. The article quoted him as saying about the Japanese pilots who had turned away on November 26 without launching their torpedoes: "They don't fight like they used to, I think they're yellow. If the positions had been reversed, every one of our planes would have gone in at the carriers, regardless. The Japs used to too, but I think their best pilots are gone."

690.39   V-5] A naval aviation training program.

697.12   "Beer Barrel Polka"] Song with music (1927) by Czech composer Jaromir Vejvoda (1902–1988) and English lyrics (1939) by Lew Brown (1893–1958) and Wladimir Timm (1885–1958).

698.24–25   John Dos Passos's trilogy *USA*] Trilogy by John Dos Passos (1896–1970) comprising the novels *The 42nd Parallel* (1930), *1919* (1932), and *The Big Money* (1936).

700.11–12   Arthur Koestler's . . . *Ulysses*] *Darkness at Noon* (1940), novel by Arthur Koestler (1905–1983); *Ulysses* (1922), novel by James Joyce (1882–1941).

700.13   *Student Prince*] *The Student Prince* (1924), operetta with music by Sigmund Romberg (1887–1951) and lyrics by Dorothy Donnelly (1876–1928), based on *Old Heidelberg* (1901), a play by Wilhelm Meyer-Forster (1862–1934).

700.29–30   Ceil Boone] Cecile Beckerman Boone (1896–1975), mother of Richard Boone.

701.9   Moon Mullins] Central character in *Moon Mullins*, a comic strip created by Frank Willard (1893–1958) in 1923.

701.15   *Shore Leave*] Novel (1944) by Frederic Wakeman (1909–1998).

702.3–4   Leyte Gulf . . . support ships under fire] On the morning of October 25, 1944, one of the three Japanese task forces involved in the Battle of Leyte Gulf attacked an American task unit off Samar that was supporting the landings on Leyte. In the ensuing battle, the Japanese force of four battleships, eight cruisers, and eleven destroyers fought six U.S. escort carriers, three destroyers, and four destroyer escorts. After hours of confused air and surface fighting that included the first kamikaze attack of the war, the Japanese task force abandoned its objective of breaking through to the transport fleet off Leyte and withdrew to the north. U.S. forces sank three Japanese cruisers in the engagement, while losing two escort carriers, two destroyers, a destroyer escort, and 1,583 men killed and missing.

702.6–7   *Suwannee* . . . carrier in the war.] The *Suwannee* lost 107 men killed in kamikaze attacks during the Battle of Leyte Gulf, October 25–26, 1944. The two worst carrier losses in terms of casualties were those of the *Liscome Bay*, torpedoed by a submarine off Makin on November 24, 1943, with 646 men killed, and the escort carrier *Bismarck Sea*, sunk by kamikazes off Iwo Jima on February 21, 1945, with 318 men killed. At least 724 men were killed when the carrier *Franklin* was severely damaged in a dive-bombing attack off Kyushu on March 19, 1945, and the carrier *Bunker Hill* lost 393 dead in a kamikaze attack off Okinawa on May 11, 1945, that badly damaged the ship.

705.2   Guadalcanal . . . a year and a half earlier] The Battle of Guadalcanal ended on February 8, 1943, i.e., two years before the *Suwannee* arrived in March 1945.

705.9   Philippines had been retaken] American troops landed on Luzon on January 9, 1945, and completed the capture of Manila on March 3. The fighting in the Philippines continued on Luzon and Mindanao until the end of the war.

705.23   Lister bags] Large canvas bags used to purify and store water.

708.30–32   he was dead . . . late twenties] Lieutenant Commander Richard Sampson (1915–1945), a 1938 graduate of the U.S. Naval Academy, was killed on April 4, 1945, shortly after turning thirty.

708.39   Ishigaki and Miyako] See note 531.28–29.

709.10–11   "fireside chats"] Name given to the series of thirty evening radio addresses broadcast from the White House by President Franklin D. Roosevelt, 1933–44.

709.16–17   cast my ballot for Wendell Willkie] This read "cast my ballot for Thomas Dewey" in the 1994 edition of *Crossing the Line*. Dewey (1902–1971) was the Republican nominee for president in 1944, while Willkie (1892–1944) was the Republican candidate in 1940.

712.2–3   the poet's words, begotten, born, and die] William Butler Yeats (1865–1939), "Sailing to Byzantium" (1927): "Whatever is begotten, born, and dies."

713.8–9   on May 1 . . . USS *Sangamon*] A kamikaze hit the *Sangamon* on the evening of May 4, 1945, killing 36 men and causing damage that sent the ship back to the United States for repair.

714.8–10   one of their new carriers . . . Borneo oil] The volatility of unrefined Borneo oil may have been a factor in the sinking of the recently commissioned Japanese carrier *Taiho*, which suffered a catastrophic explosion more than six hours after being torpedoed by the USS *Albacore* on June 19, 1944. A second explosion two hours later sank the *Taiho* with the loss of 1,650 men.

716.13–14   war has ended—*Pennsylvania* was torpedoed] For the Japanese surrender offer, see note 542.9. The battleship *Pennsylvania* was hit by a torpedo dropped by a Japanese bomber off Okinawa on the night of August 12.

717.4–6   I knew it was . . . when we landed] In the 1994 edition this appeared as "I knew it was most likely the last flight and patted the deck fondly when we landed, vowing never to fly again; a vow that I held until the late 1960s, when jets made air travel inevitable. I am still startled by the enormous power of the modern jetliners and never fail to compare the huge, smooth surges of energy they ride on to the clattering motors of our planes that had to be nursed along, every foot of altitude squeezed out on the long way to the target, never enough power to get out of trouble if you made a mistake."

717.7–8   Nagasaki . . . second atomic bomb] The second atomic bomb used against Japan was dropped on Nagasaki on August 9, 1945, killing an estimated 40,000 people.

717.14   fall of the Dutch . . . Singapore] The Japanese completed their conquest of the Netherlands East Indies on March 12, 1942; the British garrison in Singapore surrendered on February 15, 1942.

724.2   *Uncle Sugar*] In the 1994 edition the material in this chapter appeared as the conclusion of chapter 12.

726.11–12   Dostoyevsky's *Brothers Karamazov*] Novel (1879–80) by Fyodor Dostoevsky (1821–1881).

727.8   death and war set for us] The 1994 edition of *Crossing the Line* contained the following afterword:

One warm spring day in 1946 I drove down to the fashionable little town on the Main Line outside Philadelphia that Commander Phillips had listed as his home address. I got there in mid-afternoon on a Saturday and went to his house, where I rang the bell and then introduced myself to the woman who came to the door, and to the daughter, about my age, who appeared at once. I told Mrs. Phillips who I was and that I had wanted to tell her what a fine man I thought her husband was. She was graciously polite but flustered and disturbed. Neither my clothes nor my manners were what she was familiar with, and she found it all awkward. They were having a party that afternoon and to have some still living part of her dead husband's life walk through the door in that prosperous little town on that warm spring afternoon when things were getting better could not have been welcome. She bravely asked me to stay for the party but was clearly relieved when I said that I had to get back to New York.

I was slightly hurt but more embarrassed that I had not foreseen how out of place I would be and that I would cause more pain than pleasure. Then too, as I reflected, my own motives were suspect. Was I really trying to be kind or just quarterdecking? But the real lesson that came home to me without thinking about it as I drove back up Route 1 was that there was a barrier between the war and life outside the war that was impossible to cross. Even for those like me who had grown up in the war and survived it, the war could not become a part of life afterwards. It remained a vague and troubling presence in the mind, not easily recalled or talked about, certainly not a part of normal experience woven into the continuing flow of life.

During all these years the war has, though obviously not forgotten, seemed very far away. But it was always there in the background, and in the depths of my mind the war has remained the defining experience of my life, which I came to think might by now be of interest to my children, and perhaps to others.

My great-grandfather William Lott Peters served through the Civil War in Company D of the Fiftieth Georgia Infantry—the fact is proudly registered in brass on his gravestone—which fought, among other great battles, at Gettysburg. I have often longed for his version of the kind of personal memories I have tried to write, but he left no such record. But using the official history of the Civil War, I once traced the movements of his regiment in that battle. It was on the right wing in Longstreet's Corps, and on the second day of the battle, July 2, 1863, went down in the afternoon from the woods on Seminary Ridge, across the Emmitsburg Road, down through the Wheatfield, pushed to the north of Devil's Den, and stopped finally at the narrow stream that runs along the base of Little Round Top (known thereafter as Bloody Run), as the battle petered out in the darkness. I have walked along that route and wondered what William Peters, nineteen years old at the time, ever found again in the seventy-three years of his long and prosperous life on an isolated Georgia farm to match the experience of that day. Still, it must have remained locked up inside him, having nothing to do with the quiet productive life he lived, but making everything else feel somehow slightly unreal.

Index

763

This book is set in 10 point ITC Galliard, a face designed
for digital composition by Matthew Carter and based
on the sixteenth-century face Granjon. The paper is acid-free
lightweight opaque that will not turn yellow or brittle with age.
The binding is sewn, which allows the book to open easily and lie flat.
The binding board is covered in Brillianta, a woven rayon cloth
made by Van Heek–Scholco Textielfabrieken, Holland.
Composition by Dianna Logan, Clearmont, MO.
Printing by Sheridan Grand Rapids, Grand Rapids, MI.
Binding by Dekker Bookbinding, Wyoming, MI.
Designed by Bruce Campbell.

THE LIBRARY OF AMERICA SERIES

Library of America fosters appreciation of America's literary heritage by publishing, and keeping permanently in print, authoritative editions of America's best and most significant writing. An independent nonprofit organization, it was founded in 1979 with seed funding from the National Endowment for the Humanities and the Ford Foundation.

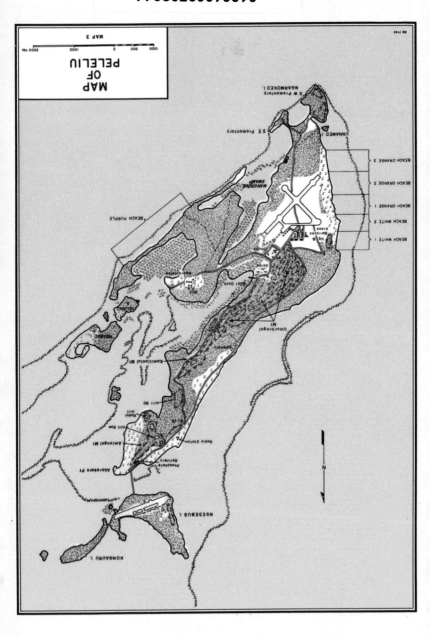

MAP
OF
PELELIU

MAP 3

2000 Yds.   1000   500   0   1000

BEACH ORANGE 3

BEACH ORANGE 2

BEACH ORANGE 1

BEACH WHITE 2

BEACH WHITE 1

S.W. Promontory
NGARMOKED I.

S.E. Promontory

UNNAMED I.

MANGROVE SWAMP

BEACH PURPLE

N